Public Law

CASES, COMMENTARY, AND ANALYSIS

FOURTH EDITION

Craig Forcese
Faculty of Law
University of Ottawa

Richard Haigh
Osgoode Hall Law School
York University

Adam Dodek
Faculty of Law
University of Ottawa

Mary Liston
Peter A Allard School of Law
University of British Columbia

Philip Bryden
Faculty of Law
University of Alberta

Constance MacIntosh
Schulich School of Law
Dalhousie University

emond

Toronto, Canada
2020

Emond Montgomery Publications Limited
1 Eglinton Ave E, Suite 600
Toronto ON M4P 3A1
http://www.emond.ca/lawschool

Printed in Canada.

We acknowledge the financial support of the Government of Canada and the assistance of the Government of Ontario.   Canadä   Ontario

Emond Publishing has no responsibility for the persistence or accuracy of URLs for external or third-party Internet websites referred to in this publication, and does not guarantee that any content on such websites is, or will remain, accurate or appropriate.

Vice president, publishing: Anthony Rezek
Business and product manager: Darren Smith
Director, development and production: Kelly Dickson
Production supervisor: Anna Killen
Production editor: Natalie Berchem
Copy editor: Valerie Adams
Permissions editor: Karen Hunter
Typesetter: S4Carlisle Publishing Services
Proofreader: Darryl Kamo
Printer: Friesens

Library and Archives Canada Cataloguing in Publication

Title: Public law : cases, commentary, and analysis / general editors, Craig Forcese, Adam Dodek, Philip Bryden, Richard Haigh, Mary Liston, Constance MacIntosh.
Other titles: Public law (Toronto, Ont.)
Names: Forcese, Craig, editor. | Dodek, Adam, editor. | Bryden, P., editor. | Haigh, Richard A., 1961- editor. | Liston, Mary, 1965- editor. | MacIntosh, Constance, editor.
Description: Fourth edition.
Identifiers: Canadiana 2020024566X | ISBN 9781772556117 (hardcover)
Subjects: LCSH: Public law—Canada—Textbooks. | LCSH: Public law—Canada—Cases. | LCGFT: Textbooks.
Classification: LCC KE4120 .P82 2020 | DDC 342.71—dc23
ISBN 978-1-77255-611-7

PREFACE TO THE FOURTH EDITION

Almost every law school in Canada, as part of its first-year curriculum, offers a course that focuses on legal processes and legal institutions. Other programs, including those focusing on government studies and public administration, also delve into the world of public law.

Common to these courses is the view that students beginning a career in law or government administration need to understand how the law is made, as well as the nature of and relationships among those institutions that create and apply legal rules and principles. Certainly, in law school, students and law professors might address many of these issues in the conventional, substantive courses of the first-year curriculum; however, introductory public law courses proceed from the premise that these issues are sufficiently foundational to merit separate and in-depth examination. That said, it is also clear that law schools incorporate the study of legal processes and institutions in a wide variety of ways. Some law schools focus on the theoretical aspects of defining law and the law's relationship to social ordering; others may integrate this material more closely with constitutional or procedural questions. Likewise, other, non-law programs may approach public law in different ways, ranging from pure law courses to seminars focusing more on the "machinery of government."

With these observations in mind, our principal objective in assembling these materials was to provide a volume covering essential issues common to the majority of courses addressing legal process and institutional issues. We hope that this book will form the core materials of such courses. We decided that it was better to include less material (and allow individual professors to supplement the volume to best fit their courses) than to risk including material that might be superfluous to some course designs. In other words, we have sought to prepare a volume that can be easily integrated into the variable introductory public law courses offered across the country.

The fourth edition incorporates major changes in Canadian public law since the publication of the third edition in 2015. The past several years have seen some important developments in Canadian public law. Cases like *Vavilov* and *Daniels* have altered the public law terrain in our country.

Since the third edition, Professor Peter Carver has retired as a contributor. We are grateful for his contributions to previous editions, and existing chapters have built on his original work.

In revising the chapters for the fourth edition, we have been very fortunate to receive comments from colleagues who used previous editions, which were very helpful in our preparations, and for which we are extremely grateful. We continue to welcome feedback.

Our contributors have benefited from the assistance of many people in finalizing this volume. All of us extend our thanks to our public law students who, over the years, have taught us even as we have taught them. Their insights have helped us improve this work. Professor Liston would like to thank Spencer Keys, Lauren Marshall, and Nevin Massing for providing excellent research assistance and for giving her the students' perspective on the materials. Professor Dodek would like to thank Professor Ed Ratushny for his foundational work on earlier editions, particularly the chapter on the courts and the judiciary.

Finally, all of us among the contributors would be remiss if we did not thank the diligent editorial team at Emond Publishing for coordinating our efforts and for their editorial and production support.

We hope you enjoy the product of all our labours.

Craig Forcese
Adam Dodek
May 2020

ACKNOWLEDGMENTS

A book of this nature borrows heavily from other published material. We have attempted to request permission from, and to acknowledge in the text, all sources of such material. We wish to make specific references here to the authors, publishers, journals, and institutions that have generously given permission to reproduce in this text works already in print. If we have inadvertently overlooked an acknowledgment or failed to secure a permission, we offer our sincere apologies and undertake to rectify the omission in the next edition.

Aboriginal and Northern Affairs Canada. Statement of Apology to Former Students of Indian Residential Schools (11 June 2008). Reprinted with the permission of Aboriginal Affairs and Northern Development Canada (as it was then).

Canadian Human Rights Tribunal. Canadian Human Rights Tribunal (1989), 10 CHRR D/6094. Reprinted with the permission of the Canadian Human Rights Tribunal.

Canadian Human Rights Tribunal. Canadian Human Rights Tribunal (1989), 10 CHRR D/6097. Reprinted with the permission of the Canadian Human Rights Tribunal.

Canadian Judicial Council. Report to the Canadian Judicial Council by the Inquiry Committee Appointed Under Subsection 63(1) of the Judges Act to Conduct a Public Inquiry into the Conduct of Mr Justice Bienvenue of the Superior Court of Quebec in R v T Théberge (Ottawa: CJC, October 1996). Reprinted with the permission of the Canadian Judicial Council.

Department of Justice Canada. Anne McLellan, *Review of the Roles of the Minister of Justice and Attorney General of Canada* (28 June 2019). Reproduced with the permission of the Department of Justice Canada, 2020.

Department of Justice Canada. "Canada's Court System," online: <http://www.justice.gc.ca/eng/csj-sjc/ccs-acj/pdf/courten.pdf>, pages 3-14. Department of Justice Canada. Reproduced with the permission of the Department of Justice Canada, 2017.

Department of Justice Canada. *Crossing Borders: Law in a Globalized World,* Law Commission of Canada, 2006. Reproduced with the permission of the Department of Justice Canada, 2015.

Elections Canada. The Electoral System of Canada, 3rd ed (Ottawa: Chief Electoral Officer of Canada, 2012). This reproduction is a copy of the version available at <http://elections.ca>. Reproduced with the permission of Elections Canada.

House of Commons. Michel Bedard, Kristen Douglas & Elise-Hurtubise-Loranger, Conflict of Interest at the Federal Level: Legislative Framework (Ottawa: House of Commons, Library of Parliament, 24 November 2010). Reprinted with the permission of the House of Commons.

House of Commons. House of Commons Procedure and Practice, 2nd ed (Ottawa: House of Commons, 2009). Reprinted with the permission of the House of Commons.

House of Commons. Special Committee on the Reform of the House of Commons (Ottawa: Canadian Government Publishing Centre, Supply and Services Canada, 1985). Reprinted with permission of the House of Commons.

Judicial Appointments Commission. "Selection Policy." The following is taken from its website: <https://www.judicialappointments.gov.uk/about-us>. Reprinted with permission.

LexisNexis Canada. Ruth Sullivan, *Sullivan on the Construction of Statutes*, 5th ed (Markham, Ont: Butterworths, 2008). Reproduced with the permission of LexisNexis Canada.

National Inquiry into Missing and Murdered Indigenous Women and Girls. *A Legal Analysis of Genocide: Supplementary Report*, 2019.

Ottawa Citizen. Cristin Schmitz, with files from Lisa Tuominen, Peter O'Neil & Graeme Hamilton, "Federal Judges Often Liberal Donors, Survey Finds," Ottawa Citizen (6 May 2005). Material republished with the express permission of: Ottawa Citizen, a division of Postmedia Network Inc.

Queen's Law Journal. Ann McDonald, "In the Public Interest: Judicial Review of Local Government" (1993) 9 Queen's LJ 62. Reprinted with permission.

Supreme Court of Canada. Remarks of the Right Honourable Beverley McLachlin, PC, presented in Ottawa on 22 November 2004, Respecting Democratic Roles. Reproduced with the permission of the Right Honourable Beverley McLachlin, PC, 2015.

Supreme Court Law Review. Adam M Dodek, "Reforming the Supreme Court Appointment Process, 2004-2014: A 10-Year Democratic Audit" (2014) 67 SCLR (2nd). Reprinted with the permission of Adam M Dodek.

ABOUT THE AUTHORS

Craig Forcese is a full professor at the Faculty of Law (Common Law Section), University of Ottawa, where he also serves as Vice Dean (Graduate Studies). He is also an Adjunct Research Professor and Senior Fellow, Norman Paterson School of International Affairs, Carleton University, and a National Security Crisis Law Fellow, Center on National Security and the Law at Georgetown Law (Washington, DC). Professor Forcese has a BA from McGill University, an MA from the Norman Paterson School of International Affairs, Carleton University, a JD (*summa cum laude*) from the University of Ottawa, and an LLM from Yale University. He is a member in good standing of the bars of Ontario, New York, and the District of Columbia.

Adam Dodek is the Dean and a full professor at the University of Ottawa's Faculty of Law, Common Law Section. He has taught Public Law and Legislation, Constitutional Law, Legal Ethics, and a seminar on the Supreme Court of Canada. He is the author or editor of more than 50 book chapters and journal articles, and he has written or edited eight books. Professor Dodek has received numerous honours, including the Canadian Association of Law Teachers Prize for Academic Excellence (2018), the Mundell Medal for Excellence in Legal Writing (2017), and the Law Society Medal by the Law Society of Ontario (2015). In 2014, *Canadian Lawyer* named Dodek as one of Canada's Most Influential Lawyers.

Philip Bryden, QC is the TC Energy Chair in Administrative and Regulatory Law at the University of Alberta's Faculty of Law. From 2015 to 2019, he was seconded to the Government of Alberta as the Deputy Minister of Justice and Solicitor General and Deputy Attorney General of Alberta. He served as Dean of Law at the University of Alberta from 2009 to 2014, and as Dean of Law at the University of New Brunswick from 2004 to 2009. He was a member of the Faculty of Law at the University of British Columbia from 1985 to 2004. His research and teaching have been primarily in the fields of Canadian administrative law and constitutional law.

Richard Haigh is an assistant professor at Osgoode Hall Law School, director of York's Centre for Public Policy and Law and Co-Director of the Part-Time LLM in Constitutional Law at Osgoode. He has a doctorate from the University of Toronto in the area of freedom of conscience and religion. He has been a senior lecturer at Deakin University in Melbourne, Australia, and a senior advisor at the National Judicial Institute. His recent published works include papers analyzing qualitative effects of interveners at the Supreme Court of Canada, the interpretation of amendments in legislation, the use of metaphor in constitutional adjudication, and division of powers in freedom of expression cases. He is currently working on a large research project assessing quantitative effects of interveners on appellate cases.

Dr Mary Liston (BA Hons [Western], MA [York], LLB [Toronto], PhD [Toronto], Postdoctoral Fellowship in Law and Ethics [Toronto]) is an assistant professor at the Peter A Allard School of Law, University of British Columbia. Her research focuses on advanced and comparative public law, Canadian administrative law, Indigenous administrative law, theories of the rule of law, and law and literature. Professor Liston's work has been cited by the Supreme Court of Canada in several leading cases. She is also a contributor to the casebook *Administrative Law in Context*, 3rd ed (Emond, 2018).

Constance MacIntosh is the Viscount Bennett Professor of Law at the Schulich School of Law, Dalhousie University, and served as the Director of Dalhousie's Health Law Institute for six years. Her research assesses how law and policy engage vulnerable populations, including Indigenous communities and migrant groups, with a particular emphasis on jurisdictional gaps and health policy. She has received numerous teaching awards and is very active in pro bono work. Her recent and forthcoming publications include co-editing a special edition of the Dalhousie Law Journal on current issues in immigration and refugee law, and being a co-author of *Immigration and Refugee Law: Cases, Materials, and Commentary*, 3rd ed (Emond Publishing, 2020).

BRIEF CONTENTS

DETAILED CONTENTS

PART II   THE KEY ACTORS IN PUBLIC LAW

PART III INTERPLAY BETWEEN THE COURTS AND THE POLITICAL BRANCHES OF GOVERNMENT

TABLE OF CASES

A page number in boldface type indicates that the text of the case or a portion thereof is reproduced. A page number in lightface type indicates that the case is merely quoted briefly or discussed. Cases mentioned within excerpts are not listed.

PUBLIC LAW IN CANADA

Public law is complex, fast-moving, politically charged, and utterly fascinating. It involves the study of constitutional fundamentals, rights protection, and the rule of law. It also concerns the separation and balancing of institutional powers, multi-level governance, and democratic accountability. Through the study of legislation, public law introduces you to the importance of statutes and regulations both as forms of law and as political responses to pressing problems in Canadian society. By studying prerogative powers and delegated statutory authority, public law enables you to learn how the executive branch of government exercises its distinctive powers, and how those who exercise these powers may be held accountable to Canadians. And, in examining judicial decisions, you will see how the courts protect rights, but also uphold valid statutes and administrative decisions that serve the public interest. An introduction to the administrative state allows you a glimpse into the multi-faceted nature of the executive branch that administers law and policy through its many actors—ministers, bureaucratic officials, agencies, boards, commissions, and tribunals.

The image of law conveyed in this first paragraph may appear a bit overwhelming. This chapter reduces public law to several building blocks. First, this chapter introduces you to the idea of public law and distinguishes it from private law. It then outlines the basic institutional architecture of public law developed in more detail in subsequent chapters. Lastly, it familiarizes you with several of the basic, recurring tensions that animate this large body of law. Many of your other courses are about the specific "trees" that comprise the legal "forest" in law school. This text provides a bird's-eye view of that forest, allowing you to comprehend public law's size, shape, scope, and contours. Here, we canvass the chief issues addressed in greater detail in chapters to come.

I. BASIC BUILDING BLOCKS

What is public law? Before addressing this question, we must first understand the legal setting in which Canada's laws arise.

A. SOURCES OF LAW

In Part I of this volume, we address a number of preliminary issues, thereby setting the stage for our detailed discussion of public law. We begin with a chapter on legal theory—a treatment, in part, of the question, "What is law?" In the balance of Part I, we then examine in detail how the Canadian legal system reflects the input of many different systems and sources. In this sense, the Canadian legal system is highly pluralist not only in terms of its basic structure, but also in its sources of law.

At the most general level, Canada's legal system comprises: (1) a common law system federally and in most provinces, derived from the English legal system; (2) a civil law system that codifies private law in Quebec, influenced by the French Napoleonic code; (3) international law, to the extent it is "received" into Canadian law by statutes and (with customary international law) as a source of common law; and (4) numerous Indigenous customary legal systems.

Canada is a federation with two different levels of government—federal and provincial/territorial. The Constitution creates a division of powers between the federal and provincial levels. In so doing, it facilitates Canada's legal pluralism by allowing the common law to animate the private law of the provinces and territories other than Quebec, and the civil law to govern private relations in Quebec.

For its part, international law mostly stems from conventions—better known as treaties (and not to be confused with the conventions we mention in discussing unwritten constitutional Canadian law). These are essentially law-making contracts agreed to by states in the international community. It also comes in the form of customary international law—basically, law that is not codified but flows from sufficiently universal practices by states undertaken with a sense of legal obligation. International law enters Canadian law through a sometimes complex process known as reception.

We discuss common, civil, and international law in Chapter 4.

Finally, Canada is currently involved in an ongoing and complex process of recognizing Indigenous and First Nations orders of government, which may take many shapes ranging from the territorial (e.g., Nunavut, created in 1999), to the regional (e.g., Nunatsiavut in Newfoundland and Labrador), to the local (e.g., Tsawwassen First Nation in the lower mainland of British Columbia). We include a comprehensive discussion of the relationship between Indigenous peoples and the law in Chapter 3.

B. ORIGINS OF LAW

Legal pluralism in the Canadian context means more than just law from many different historical origins. It also means law stemming from different institutions.

Law must come from some authoritative source in order for legal subjects to recognize the validity of the laws they are asked to obey. Without an authoritative source, a rule that presents itself as a law will not be recognized as law (see Raymond Wacks, *Law: A Very Short Introduction* (Oxford: Oxford University Press, 2008)). Canadians, for example, need not recognize or obey the laws issued by the Roman Catholic Church or any other religious order (unless, of course, they voluntarily agree to do so, and even then the state will generally not enforce these "laws"). The Canadian public law order is pluralist in its sources of law because it recognizes both written and unwritten sources of law. These sources roughly align with two institutions: legislatures that create written norms, and courts that are the source (or at least the final arbiter) for unwritten norms.

C. WHAT IS PRIVATE LAW?

Canadian law usually distinguishes between public law and private law. The first year of law school embeds this distinction in its very structure. Courses such as contracts, torts, and property make up private law. Courses such as constitutional, criminal, and public law/legislation/ government institutions make up public law. In the upper-year program, public law includes administrative and human rights law, as well as courses involving complex statutes such as tax, securities regulation, immigration, and environmental law. (See also Stephen M Waddams, *Introduction to the Study of Law*, 7th ed (Toronto: Thomson Carswell, 2010).)

Private law is about relationships between legal persons in society. The phrase "legal persons" is used because it includes not just individuals—or "natural persons"—but also corporate bodies (or "artificial" or "juridical" persons). These legal relations establish the rights and duties that exist between these persons in their relations with one another. If, for example, private law establishes that people have a right to bodily integrity, you may owe them a duty of care to ensure that your everyday behaviour does not create harmful risks for them. To take a commonplace example, after a heavy snowfall you may have an obligation (apart from municipal by-laws) to shovel your sidewalk so as not to create risky conditions that may cause a person to have an accidental and very harmful fall on the icy pavement. If you fail to observe that duty, you may be legally required to compensate the injured person for any resulting losses he or she faced because of the accident, such as lost wages from time off work.

Private law rights and obligations can arise from voluntary agreements in contract law, from owning private property in property law, from principles of equity such as unjust enrichment (also known as restitution), and from principles found in tort law, as considered in the example above.

D. WHAT IS PUBLIC LAW?

Public law is different. It is not about the relationships between private persons. Instead, public law structures the legal relationships between individuals and the state and between different institutions within the state. Most students start law school with one particular conception of public law in their minds. Usually, it is criminal law because this is the most widespread depiction of the legal relationship between the individual and the state in Anglo-American popular culture. Constitutional law would be a close second. But neither of these areas exhausts the scope of public law. Public law also structures the legal relationships among and between the three branches of the state: the legislature, the judiciary, and the executive. This relationship is captured in the public law doctrine of the separation of powers. Public law also regulates the partitioning of power between the levels of government in our federal system—a phenomenon known as the division of powers.

Generally speaking, in common law countries, we tend to classify constitutional, administrative, criminal, and other areas of regulatory law (such as environmental or tax law) as public law because these areas of law contain rules that define the scope of governmental authority and the ways it is exercised.

This is not to say that public law and private law are separate universes, completely sealed off from one another. The distinction between public and private law is largely functional, rather than factual. Classifying an area of law as either private or public usefully delineates the activities, participants, and principal concerns that are subject to the rules of that particular area. Certainly, public law is mostly about the state (or at least the state in its relationship with persons). But it is important to recognize that the state can also have private law responsibilities and roles. The world does not divide neatly into "law for the state" and "law for everyone else." For example, when the state breaches a contract or acts negligently, it may be required to pay private law damages to the affected parties in contract or tort law. And in our system, government officials are not generally immunized from criminal culpability if they commit a crime in the course of their official duties.

Likewise, the state may also have a role in relation to the actual implementation of private law relations existing between persons. Thus, statutes promulgated by legislatures may define the substantive rights and duties that individuals owe one another; courts will be responsible for determining those rights; and the executive branch may be called upon to enforce private rights by coercive means.

II. DRILLING DOWN: THE WORKINGS OF PUBLIC LAW

A. PLURALISM IN PUBLIC LAW

With that brief backdrop, we focus now in further detail on some of the ingredients of public law. In this introduction, we begin by returning to the question, "Where does law (and specifically public law) come from?" This is a matter dealt with at length in Chapter 5.

Another way of approaching this question is to ask, "Which comes first: public law or the state?" This is not an easy question to answer, at least in relation to Canada (and its UK inheritance). It is very difficult to disaggregate the emergence of the modern institutions making up the state and the core doctrines of public law that we discuss below. Suffice it to say that public law is deeply organic—a product of history and capricious circumstances more than premeditated design. Put another way, public law is the product of political evolution, and not always (or indeed often) the end product of a rational, master design process. (For an examination of the evolution of public law in the United Kingdom, see Adam Tomkins, *Public Law* (Oxford: Oxford University Press, 2003).)

B. BRANCHES OF THE STATE

In response to the chicken and egg quandary of "which came first, public law or the state," we will begin by describing the basic architecture of the state. In doing so, we anticipate the subjects dealt with in Part II of this book. That section examines the key actors in public law: the legislature (in Chapters 6 and 7); the executive (in Chapter 8); and the judiciary (in Chapter 9).

As the structure of our chapters suggests, the historical evolution of Canada, as in many other liberal democratic states, produced a state that has three key branches (although as we shall see, more nuance can be added to this statement). Thus, the state comprises a legislative branch, an executive branch, and a judiciary. In a federalist state, such as Canada, this tripartite distinction is supplemented (and to a degree replicated) at two levels of government: federal and provincial/territorial.

As we explore in Chapter 8, the executive branch is the most complex branch of the state and is much bigger than simply the prime minister and Cabinet. In Canada, it also encompasses other actors such as the Crown (the Queen and the governor general), the civil service, the military, the police, and many decision-makers in the administrative or regulatory state. In some instances, the executive branch will also include municipal governments and Indigenous band councils. The executive branch in the modern Canadian state also engages in a wide variety of regulatory functions. These regulatory powers are delegated, through statutes, to thousands of administrative and regulatory tribunals at both the federal and provincial levels of government. The state as a regulator affects more individuals and corporations than the Constitution, and decisions made by administrative actors often have significant consequences for affected persons. The removal of a taxi licence, the decision to put a prisoner in segregation, the decision to approve a natural gas pipeline, or the cancellation of a municipal rezoning application are examples of this breadth in administrative decision-making.

But while most of us think of the executive and its functions when we think of government, it is important to recognize that, legally speaking, the executive is a largely subordinate entity in the Canadian state. In Canada, Parliament (and at the provincial level, the legislatures) is sovereign or supreme. Except in the rarest of instances where the executive enjoys some independent legal autonomy, these legislative bodies are the ultimate source of all constitutionally permissible legal powers. While our legislatures may now appear politically weak in connection with the executive and the judiciary, they are in fact legally supreme. We discuss the structure and composition of the legislative branch in Chapter 6 and its functions in Chapter 7.

And, of course, we cannot forget the judiciary, the subject of Chapter 9. Indeed, it is fair to say that first-year law largely focuses on courts and how judges reason. Right at the outset, students of public law should appreciate that courts are unlike the other branches of the state—they are staffed differently and with an eye to quite different considerations than exist for the legislative and executive branches. And, they exercise a very different set of powers. Speaking generally, courts do two things of importance for our purposes: they adjudicate disputes under either private or public law rules, and they review the actions of the other branches of the state to make sure that those branches act lawfully. Along the way, they often need to interpret statutes and regulations or constitutional texts. And for this reason, if no other, you will need to learn about the legislative process, and the role of the courts when they interpret legislative texts.

Public law introduces students to the state as a whole and the functions of its component entities. Because public law is principally concerned with the origins and exercise of governmental authority, public power is a recurring theme and questions about how it is exercised and whether or not it is accountable are recurring concerns. This power is public because it is created and legitimated by legal institutions whose own legitimacy, in turn, is sustained by adherence to the rules governing the exercise of their powers. Public power is intimately related to accountability. The discussion within the chapters that follow illustrates how governmental authority is qualified by legal rules, and how the different legal institutions that are created are made accountable to one another and to the citizenry as a whole. In Part III of this volume we focus special attention on the public law relationship between the judiciary and the other branches, examining the role of judges as interpreters of statutory law (Chapter 10) and as reviewers of both legislative and executive action (Chapter 11).

C. LEGAL BASIS FOR THE STATE

In the balance of this chapter, we will add more detail to our public law discussion above, as a transition to the specialized chapters to come. It may be useful to reread this part as you proceed through the volume, because you will find its observations become clearer the more knowledge you acquire.

We return to the legal basis for the Canadian state structure. In keeping with our nod above to the importance of history, we must underscore that the system, structure, and organization of government in Canada were not created in a vacuum. In some large measure, they are the legacy of a process of colonization and then decolonization. The transition between colonial law and full legal independence took place over a period of almost 200 years. A very brief review of that history helps place the contemporary legal basis for public law in context.

In Chapter 3, we discuss Indigenous legal systems. Our focus here is on the colonial period. As a colony, the territory of what is now Canada had no independent, or autonomous, public law. Its governance was a matter decided by European powers. After the British conquered New France on the Plains of Abraham in 1759 (the Battle of Quebec), France ceded the land it controlled to Great Britain under the *Treaty of Paris, 1763*. The *Royal Proclamation*, 1763, RSC 1985, App II, No 1 provided for the imposition of English law on the new colony, which altered the common law rule that, in the case of conquest, the laws of the conquered state would prevail.

Just over ten years later, the British government recognized that it needed to address growing unrest over the imposition of British rule and laws. In 1774, therefore, the British Parliament enacted, as an imperial statute, the *Quebec Act, 1774*, RSC 1986, App II, No 2 which, among other provisions, restored civil law as the law of Quebec (a wide territory that included much of what is now Ontario), except for the English criminal law, which was retained.

In subsequent decades and after agitation and rebellion in some jurisdictions, the British North American colonies moved gradually toward a system of responsible government. Rather than simply direct rule by Britain through a governor insulated entirely from the local populace, the executive government became more responsive to colonial legislatures competent to pass their own laws. But these local legislatures were still colonial, and imperial statutes continued to reach colonial affairs. As the name suggests, imperial statutes were statutes that applied in the British colonies. Only the British Parliament could make and amend them. The reach of imperial statutes was clarified by the *Colonial Laws Validity Act, 1865* (UK), 28 & 29 Vict c 63. Under this law, an imperial statute, defined as an act of the British Parliament, was deemed to extend to colonies only if the statute expressly or by necessary implication made that clear. The Act was intended to extend the powers of colonial legislatures by clarifying that only those of their laws "repugnant" to an imperial statute applicable to them would be void—all others would be allowed to stand. It also, however, left colonial legislatures unable to alter imperial statutes.

In 1867, the colonies of British North America were joined in Confederation and Canada became a self-ruling dominion. The *British North America Act, 1867* (UK), 30 & 31 Vict, c 3, another imperial statute, created many of the systems of government that exist today (and is still one of Canada's main constitutional documents, renamed in 1982 the *Constitution Act, 1867* (UK), 30 & 31 Vict, c 3, reprinted in RSC 1985, Appendix II, No 5). However, some vestiges of the colonial past remained: in particular, the nature of the *Constitution Act, 1867* as an imperial statute meant that Canada could not amend its own constituting document because s 129 of the *Constitution Act, 1867* maintained the requirement from the *Colonial Laws Validity Act* that imperial statutes applying to Canada could only be altered by Parliament in Westminster. This requirement was subsequently relaxed through the adoption of the *Statute of Westminster, 1931* (UK), c 4, which stated that no law made by the Parliament of the United Kingdom would apply to any of its dominions unless specifically requested and consented to by a dominion. It also repealed the *Colonial Laws Validity Act* and granted to each dominion the power to repeal or amend imperial statutes. One anomaly remained—the *Constitution Act, 1867* was exempt from this provision, mainly in order to ensure that the nature of Canada as a federal system, with coordinate powers granted to the federal Parliament and the provincial legislatures, remained intact. Finally, in 1982, with the "patriation" of the Constitution, through the *Canada Act 1982* (UK), 1982, c 11, and the *Constitution Act, 1982* (being Schedule B to the *Canada Act 1982* (UK), 1982, c 11), Canada's independence became complete. Now, the UK Parliament exercises no jurisdiction over Canadian affairs, and amending Canada's Constitution is the business of the Canadian federal and provincial legislatures. It is also worth noting that until 1949, Canadian judgments could be appealed to the Judicial Committee of the Privy Council, which meant that for many years Canadian judges had to be especially cognizant of Privy Council and House of Lords (the highest UK court of appeal) decisions. This practice was abolished in 1949 by an act of the Canadian Parliament.

As this discussion suggests, the key written sources for modern Canadian public law include the *Constitution Acts, 1867* and *1982*. But there are a number of other written instruments that, when glued together, make up the written constitution. The Constitution itself (in its *Constitution Act, 1982* guise) includes a lengthy annex enumerating the instruments that are part of the written Constitution (many of them imperial instruments inherited from our colonial past). That means that even the modern, written Constitution is not simply a single, self-contained document, but rather a mélange of imperial and Canadian legislative instruments.

But the Constitution does not end here because, in addition to the written texts, Canada's public law order continues to include "unwritten" principles or rules. Accordingly, public law principles come from a number of "unwritten" sources. For instance, "conventions" are the unwritten rules that govern Parliament and the provincial legislatures. Despite being constitutional rules and despite the fact that their existence may be disputed until a court decides the matter, conventions cannot be enforced by the judiciary. Courts can only recognize conventions by declaring that they exist and by articulating the current content of particular conventions. Conventions are only enforced politically and are therefore part of what we call the "political" rather than the "legal" constitution. This means that the way political actors are held accountable is not through the courts, but through the political—and ultimately electoral—systems. Chapters 5 and 6 explore many of the key conventions in our constitutional order.

"Unwritten principles" is an even more opaque term used to describe some unwritten legal norms. Unlike conventions, courts can both create and interpret (courts would probably say "reveal") these principles and enforce them. To interpret principles and give them content, the judiciary usually draws upon Canadian history, morality, and politics. When you read the excerpts from the *Patriation* and *Quebec Secession References* in Chapter 5, look carefully at how these decisions make use of historical facts, Canadian politics, and other narrative frames. These frames are essential to legal argument, and you should think about who gets to frame both the historical debate (if one exists) as well as the competing legal narratives. In public law, unlike private law, more than two sides and multiple arguments are often in play in a particular case. This is another effect of pluralism in public law.

Unwritten principles can be written down for greater clarity and specificity. Modern judicial decisions do just that. But, it is also important to remember that the legislature can shape judicial interpretation of legal principles by articulating the content of relevant principles in a statute. The preamble, purposes, and definitions sections communicate intent about the main legal norms and values that the legislature has embedded in the statute.

This section has briefly explained the transformation of Canada from a colony, then a dominion of the United Kingdom, to a fully independent and sovereign state. But the process of "decolonization" has not ended for Canada. In public law, the legacy of colonization continues to affect Indigenous peoples. In Canadian law, the unwritten constitutional principle of reconciliation—discussed further in Chapter 3—animates and structures the current public law relationship between the Canadian state and Indigenous peoples and is leading to the recognition of different forms of governance for those communities.

D. THE RULE OF LAW, VALIDITY, AND LEGAL AUTHORITY

We wish to pause here and focus special attention on two animating precepts of Canadian public law. Canadian public law contains innumerable unwritten principles, but the two most important are the rule of law and democracy. In the sometimes perplexing Canadian public law tradition, these norms—which are so foundational—are often not expressly mentioned in the written constitutional documents discussed in the section above. The unwritten principle of the rule of law, for example, expressly appears only in the preamble to the *Constitution Act, 1982*: "Whereas Canada is founded upon principles that recognize the supremacy of God and the rule of law."

If you read the written constitutional documents without understanding these important, underlying rules, you will easily obtain the wrong understanding of Canada's system of government. For instance, a read of those documents might lead you to imagine that a powerful Queen rules us, through an exercise of substantial personal authority over our government.

In fact, this is not the case, both because of specific constitutional conventions governing the Queen's relations with executive government and the legislature and because of undergirding concepts like "democracy."

In practice, public power in our system is never truly free and unconstrained as it might be in other political systems that are ruled by authoritarian leaders, dictators, tyrants, or a small number of elites. In our system, governmental authority is sourced and structured by legal rules that ensure that our three branches are made accountable to each another and to the public at large, even if our written constitution does a generally poor job of this task.

As you will see in the following chapters, the unwritten principle of the "rule of law" is foundational for our legal system. The rule of law requires that all state action must comply with the law including, but not limited to, the Constitution. Put another way: no one is above the law, including the state. Historically, the rule of law is associated with several core meanings, as we discuss in Chapter 5. But in its most basic form, it means that public power is to be exercised in keeping with the law, not according to the idiosyncratic likes and dislikes of the people who wield political authority.

In practice, discussion of rule of law often invokes discussions of legal validity and institutional legitimacy. Legal validity is a complex concept that cannot be fully unpacked here; but for lawyers, it means that we are only ruled by laws that other laws declare valid. Put in a somewhat more complex way, it means that certain identifiable and sufficient conditions have been met to permit the label "law" to be attached to a rule of conduct and that this "law" will be considered binding on legal subjects. In a legal sense, valid law can only be produced by an institution with the legal authority to create that law. Once that authority is properly exercised, Canadians have a general obligation to obey this law, unless it is found unconstitutional or otherwise legally defective. Courts clearly play a large role in helping to identify valid law and correct for invalid law on constitutional or other public law grounds.

This legalistic concept of validity stands apart from a second dimension of validity: morality. Legal norms exist alongside other norms that originate from the multiplicity of moralities found in contemporary Canada (i.e., personal, political, ethical, religious, etc.). Many of these moralities do not rise to the level of general acceptance, while others may substantially overlap with each other. In some cases, all or most Canadians may generally share content from these different moralities so that we can see that there may be a larger public morality. One example would be the moral imperative to treat others equally, with respect, and as ends-in-themselves. Historically, this moral imperative informed the legal arguments to end slavery because no one should have a moral or a legal right to own another person as property. It also animated legal requirements to treat women equally with men.

Public law is premised on a separation of law from the moralities that exist in civil society. From a strict legal standpoint, these are considered two completely separate sources of obligations. Our legal system, however, does possess features that invite moral considerations. In public law, statutes often contain imprecise language such as "in the public interest" or "fair and equitable treatment," language that permits decision-makers to include some form of non-legal public morality in their reasoning. Again, courts play a crucial role in overseeing the content and determining the scope of this kind of moral reasoning.

Finally, it is important to acknowledge that historical, customary practices have a bearing on popular discussions of legal validity. Constitutional conventions, discussed above, are an illustration of this kind of constraint. It is because of conventions that the monarch does not rule supreme.

E. DEMOCRACY AND POPULAR AUTHORITY

Democracy means "rule by the people." Ancient Athens provided the original model. There, democracy was a majoritarian and highly participatory model (with several serious flaws such as the exclusion of women and slaves) that cannot be duplicated in modern states. Historical supporters suggested that democracy fundamentally meant a highly participatory and deliberative form of government, while its detractors labelled it "mob rule."

Many contemporary forms of democracy exist. (For an excellent overview of the concept and various models of democracy, see Amy Gutmann, "Democracy" in Robert E Goodin, Philip Pettit & Thomas Pogge, eds, *A Companion to Contemporary Political Philosophy*, 2nd ed, vol 2 (Malden, Mass: Blackwell Publishing, 2007) at 521-31.) Our "Fathers of Confederation" intended our constitution to differ quite radically from the American model. One chief difference was that our Constitution would not be derived from the people. (In the Canadian context, see Alexander Galt, "'Not Derived from the People': Letter from the Fathers of Confederation to the British Colonial Secretary" in Peter Russell et al, eds, *Essential Readings in Canadian Government and Politics* (Toronto: Emond Montgomery, 2010) at 76. For the contrasting American experience, see Bruce Ackerman, *We the People: Foundations* (Cambridge, Mass: Harvard University Press 1993).) Over time, this conception has changed, and we would now characterize our model as a liberal democracy because of the significant influence of liberalism as a political philosophy—that is, a view of society in which individuals enjoy substantial autonomy and that is hostile to an absolute state. Exactly what role the state should have in its relationship with its populace is a question always in flux, and Canadian democracy has therefore undergone significant change since the 18th and 19th centuries and continues to be a work in progress.

The *Quebec Secession Reference* provides essential content for our understanding of the Canadian principle of democracy. In this extraordinary judgment, the Supreme Court of Canada suggested that the principle of democracy has always informed our constitutional design. The Court declared that the principle of democracy includes the right to vote, the right to effective representation, and the right to participate in the political system. The principle of democracy, the Court stated, is also part of the concept of responsible government with its links to ideas of self-government, consent, and a "continuous process of discussion" in the political community (*Reference re Secession of Quebec*, [1998] 2 SCR 217 at para 68). Democracy is related to, but differs from, parliamentary supremacy because the institution of Parliament need not be democratic. And finally, the democratic principle interacts with the principle of the rule of law to provide legitimacy to our public law order.

III. TWO MODES OF ACCOUNTABILITY IN THE EXERCISE OF PUBLIC POWER

As this discussion suggests, public law provides the building blocks of the Canadian state. But it is more than simply a blueprint for the structure of power. In many of its facets (and especially constitutional and administrative law), public law is the law of state accountability. But in approaching this concept of "accountability," students of public law quickly need to come to grips with the pervasive interaction between the worlds of law and politics. This interplay may sometimes produce unsatisfactory results. American legal scholar Sanford Levinson provides a pithy definition of "democratic deficit": "A democratic deficit occurs when ostensibly democratic organizations or institutions in fact fall short of fulfilling what are believed to be the principles of democracy." (See Sanford Levinson, "How the United States Constitution Contributes to the Democratic Deficit in America" (2007) 55 Drake L Rev 859 at 860.)

While much admired around the world, Canada's system of government has several democratic deficits. Depending on to whom you speak, these deficits originate in the first-past-the-post electoral system, the dominance of the executive branch in our system of government, the relative weakness of our legislative branch, and growing citizen apathy, among other problems. Key deficit questions that may occur to you as you work through this volume include:

- How can we strengthen our democracy and especially our legislative branch?
- How can the rule of law enhance the values of accountability, legitimacy, and transparency in government generally and in the executive branch in particular?

- What effective constraints does our judiciary face?
- Should our system be characterized by an institutional dialogue among the three branches?

This book is mostly an introductory text. It is not a normative rethink of Canadian public law. But we can review some themes that you may wish to keep in mind as you proceed, and as you wonder, "Is there a way to build a better system?"

A. POLITICAL ACCOUNTABILITY VERSUS LEGAL ACCOUNTABILITY

State actors exercise public power in a variety of ways: for example, the executive introduces bills in the legislature; following a complex process, the House of Commons debates and potentially passes the bill; the Senate scrutinizes this piece of legislation for flaws and it too debates and potentially passes the bill; the Crown assents to the legislation and enactment is finally procedurally complete and the bill becomes a statute. But the process doesn't really stop there. Administrative actors in agencies, boards, commissions, and tribunals interpret and apply statutes in their day-to-day decision-making. Courts review problems that arise under the statute or in the administrative decision-making that interprets and applies the particular statute. Each of these other state actors and processes needs to be held accountable in a system that is committed to realizing democratic and rule-of-law ideals. Canadian public law provides two routes to realize accountability: political and legal. (For further discussion of achieving accountability in the Canadian state, see Craig Forcese & Adam Freeman, *The Laws of Government: The Legal Foundations of Canadian Democracy* (Toronto: Irwin Law, 2011).)

1. Political Accountability

Canada inherited the Westminster system of parliamentary government from the United Kingdom. Historically, this system operated without a written constitution (or at least a constitution that consolidated its rules in writing in one place). Indeed, to this day, the United Kingdom still does not have a unified written constitution. The lack of a written constitution matters because it means that any law—even one that concerns fundamental rights or foundational principles—can be changed or undone by subsequent laws enacted by a legislature. This is what we mean, in part, by parliamentary supremacy or sovereignty: Parliament may enact any law that it wishes—so long as it was enacted properly—and courts cannot override or strike down this legislation.

This parliamentary sovereignty model contrasts to the other great tradition in the common law world—that of the United States. In contrast to the United Kingdom, the United States embraced in 1789 a model of constitutional supremacy. The American constitution includes a series of amendments that became a Bill of Rights constraining Congress and state legislatures from violating fundamental rights and freedoms such as freedom of speech, due process, and equality rights.

Canada, for its part, drew initial inspiration from the United Kingdom in almost every respect, except federalism. Recall that with the *Constitution Act, 1867* governments became bound by a written text that divided power between the federal and provincial governments (i.e., federalism). Judicial review, at least on federalism grounds, ensured that the judiciary played a prominent role in preventing federal and provincial governments from overstepping their jurisdictions and intruding into the subject matters given to the other level.

In the result, the *Constitution Act, 1867* did not transform parliamentary government. Instead, Canadian public law continued the British traditions of so-called political constitutionalism and responsible government. Political constitutionalism relies on the "capacity of political considerations to prevent or at least dissuade those in authority from using their powers oppressively or abusively." (Catherine Barnard et al, eds, *What About Law?* (Oxford: Hart

Publishing, 2011) at 176.) Elections, for example, represent an indirect method of ensuring accountability when the government of the day must face voter opinion and run on its political record.

We discuss all of this at regular intervals in this book. For our purposes here, it is important to recognize how important a culture of political constitutionalism can be to a successful democratic state. The United Kingdom continues to provide an example of where cultural and political norms and expectations mean that politicians do not regularly interfere with individual rights and freedoms despite the lack of a constitutionalized bill of rights. This is a useful reminder that all branches of the state—not just courts—can and should protect and promote individual rights, and that accountability is not something to be outsourced in full to courts.

2. Legal Accountability and the Constitution

Still, political constitutionalism may provide only imperfect accountability. A government with a majority can control Parliament and weaken that institution's accountability mechanisms (the operation of Question Period, for example). Such a government can also use its power to advantage or disadvantage groups of people in society. This treatment—advantaging or disadvantaging groups—may constitute arbitrary rule or discrimination. This arbitrary treatment may be reflected in the content or effects of legislation. When a minority group is disadvantaged, and the majority of the population agrees with the government in power, the electoral system may not provide either accountability or a political remedy.

The need for a counter-majoritarian check is one chief reason for the entrenchment of a bill of rights in a constitution. Such instruments contribute to the legalization of accountability and are key contributors to the growth of judicial power.

This is, in fact, the road that Canada has travelled in its more recent history. Before 1982, Canada had a statutory bill of rights (enacted in 1960) and a federal human rights (or anti-discrimination) code (enacted in 1977). Canada also had numerous provincial human rights codes (Ontario enacted the first provincial code in 1962). These early human rights documents are regular statutes that can be amended through the regular process or entirely repealed by their respective legislatures. But occasionally you will see lawyers and judges calling them "quasi-constitutional." Be warned: these laws are not, in fact, part of the constitution. But, because they often contain language that gives them priority over other, regular statutes in the event of a conflict, they have a trumping effect that is roughly analogous to what happens when a regular statute and the constitution conflict.

With the patriation of the Constitution in 1982 and the entrenchment of the *Canadian Charter of Rights and Freedoms*, Part I of the *Constitution Act, 1982*, being Schedule B to the *Canada Act 1982* (UK), c 11 (the Charter), the older principle of parliamentary supremacy was severely curtailed, and the "new" principle of constitutional supremacy became paramount in public law. Under the 1982 Constitution, courts were allocated more power to intervene by enabling the judiciary to strike down or invalidate legislation that offended the constitution on grounds much broader than the 1867 concept of federalism. Now the Constitution codified individual and group rights. And, unlike with prior efforts to legislate rights protections, the Charter is not easily amended by Parliament. Any amendment of the Constitution requires adherence to constitutional amendment formulas. Depending on the amendment in question, this process may require substantial (and rare) levels of agreement between the federal and provincial levels of government, discussed in Chapter 5.

And yet, even as in 1982, Canada moved closer to the American model, it still retained features of its earlier public law structure. The Charter, for example, contains two distinctive provisions. The first is s 1. Under s 1, the rights and freedoms guaranteed in the Charter are not absolute. Rather, they are subject to "such reasonable limits prescribed by law as can be demonstrably justified in a free and democratic society." Section 1, therefore, represents an attenuated continuation of the principle of legislative supremacy. Courts will require govern-ments to provide demonstrable justifications under s 1 and, if the government is successful, that legislation may be "saved" because it both furthers a valid objective and affects a right or freedom no more than is necessary.

The second provision, s 33, is the notwithstanding clause. This provision permits Parliament or a provincial legislature to expressly override parts of the Charter by declaring that the par-ticular statute will operate notwithstanding a provision in the Charter concerning fundamental freedoms, or legal or equality rights. Despite the fact that s 33 has rarely been used, Canadian public law scholars remain divided on the desirability and necessity of this clause.

While many viewed these 1982 changes as a great advance in public law, Chapters 5 and 11 discuss how the flexibility inherent in the Westminster model is now lost and con-stitutional change is very difficult given the difficulty of successfully implementing many of the current amending procedures in Canada. In constitutional matters (at least if s 33 is not used for the Charter rights to which it applies), judges effectively now have the final word. In Chapter 11, we conclude this book with an examination of the judicial role in policing the political branches on both constitutional grounds (in the case of both the legislature and executive) and administrative law grounds (in the case of the executive). Here, we end this chapter by posing a recurring question for any public lawyer about the appropriate role of courts in a modern democracy.

B. OTHER FORMS OF LEGAL ACCOUNTABILITY

Judicial review on constitutional grounds is not the only—or even the main—form of the legal oversight of public power. All common law countries share a legal tradition grounded in judicial techniques of statutory interpretation, a concept discussed at length in Chapter 10. Through these various techniques, courts ascertain legislative intent and will in order deter-mine whether or not a statute authorizes particular actions and whether or not errors exist in a statute.

Statutory interpretation brings us back to the separation of powers. The separation of pow-ers entails that each branch of the state is entrusted to perform specific functions. Traditionally understood and much simplified, the legislature makes the law, the judiciary interprets and applies the law, and the executive implements and enforces laws and policies. Chapter 5 more fully elaborates on the separation of powers in Canadian public law and how it is not a set of bright line demarcations. As a constitutional principle, the separation of powers ensures that each branch does not intrude on the powers and responsibilities allocated to the others. The doctrine also aims to prevent the concentration of public power in one branch by permitting each branch to check the others' powers. It is not only an adversarial principle, however, because it also encourages branches to cooperate as constitutional partners in good govern-ance. The necessity of cooperation links the separations of powers to another key constitu-tional principle: the principle of deference. Each branch ought to exhibit deference to others when they are acting appropriately within their functions and constitutional bounds. When it comes to matters of statutory interpretation in judicial review, the principle of deference pos-sesses significant implications for the role of the judiciary.

Statutory interpretation inevitably involves consideration of the institutional interaction among all three branches, sometimes simultaneously. It first implicates the legislature that enacted the statute and crafted a statutory mandate with specific purposes in order to rem-edy a perceived problem in society. Statutory interpretation often involves an executive actor—usually a statutory delegate like an adjudicator, administrative official, police officer, or minister—who advances a particular interpretation of a power or purpose in that statute. And, lastly, the courts become involved when an interpretive dispute arises about the meaning of the legislative text and they are called on to resolve the textual ambiguity.

1. Judicial Interpretation of Statutes

As noted in Part III of this text, we turn to a closer examination of the interrelation between the courts and the political branches of government—the executive and the legislature. In Chapter 10, we consider the role of the courts in applying the statutory law determined by the legislative branch. There, we discuss the doctrines of statutory interpretation, which are designed to inform judicial interpretation of legislative language.

When reviewing statutes, the judiciary engages in one of two approaches. For constitutional interpretation, courts employ the "living tree" approach that ensures that the Constitution is not tied to the dead hand of the past but, instead, evolves to reflect changes in Canadian society. A court's interpretation of a right under this approach considers the historic, linguistic, social, philosophical, and statutory contexts that inform our understanding of that right. A reviewing court also considers the constitutional context in order to interpret the scope of the right or freedom, the apparent conflict with a pressing public purpose, and whether or not any limit on the right may be justified under s 1.

When an interpretive dispute arises regarding a statute, reviewing courts will engage in what is now known as the "modern approach" to statutory interpretation. Judges use this approach to determine legislative intent in order to clarify the words or provision at issue. Most of Chapter 10 is devoted to explaining and exploring the modern approach to statutory interpretation through case law and exercises.

Both of these approaches are dynamic approaches to interpretation. (For an in-depth exploration of the legal and practical issues involved in statutory interpretation, see William N Eskridge Jr, *Dynamic Statutory Interpretation* (Cambridge, Mass: Harvard University Press, 1994).) Static approaches, in contrast, are those approaches that are historically determined or primarily text based. Originalist approaches to constitutional interpretation are examples of static approaches. An originalist approach to interpreting the right to bear arms in the US Constitution would only consider what the "Founding Fathers" intended this right to mean at the time it was entrenched in the Constitution in the 18th century. Among contemporary public law scholars, few can be considered advocates of static approaches to interpretation. In Canadian public law, the Supreme Court of Canada has rejected most static approaches to interpretation.

2. Judicial Oversight of Executive Action

The executive branch is not a single, unified body but, rather, an amalgam of institutions and actors. Despite this reality, we tend to think of the executive branch as "the government," and by "the government," we mean the political executive (usually understood to be the prime minister and Cabinet). Since the Second World War, the executive branch has developed a number of different functions to become the "welfare state." The largest component of the executive branch is the administrative state comprising officials, agencies, boards, commissions, and tribunals. All of these bodies look different and serve different functions. Many work like miniature governments because they combine legislative, executive, and adjudicative functions. Human rights commissions are a good example of this type of fusion. All are independent from the political executive but will vary widely in how much and what type of independence they possess.

The public powers exercised by actors in the administrative state are constrained. Except in rare instances where they exercise something called "prerogative" power, an enabling statute is what gives them their jurisdiction—or scope of power. This statute that provides jurisdiction is also called the "home" statute for that actor and, through it, the legislature delegates a circumscribed set of powers to it. Administrative decision-makers only have the powers that are delegated to them in their enabling or "home" statutes. If these statutory delegates do not conform to the mandate, duties, powers, purposes, and constraints contained in their home statute, their actions will be found *ultra vires* or outside of their jurisdiction by a reviewing court. A reviewing court may determine that these actors exercised their power unfairly, unreasonably, or incorrectly. Public law lawyers and reviewing courts therefore play a fundamental role in supervising executive powers that often lie outside the purview of the regular political mechanisms of accountability and are most certainly largely hidden from the scrutinizing eyes of the general public.

Chapter 11 delves more deeply into these matters. In public law, however, it is important to emphasize again the significance of pluralism and deference. When reviewing administrative decisions, courts often acknowledge the problem of multiple interpretations with the result that no one interpretation may be held to be uniquely right. This is particularly true when the decision under review involves discretionary choices or is heavily fact-based. It may turn out that specialized administrative actors are better equipped than courts to choose between possible, plausible, reasonable interpretations of an ambiguous provision in the home statute. Moreover, the legislature may have intended that the administrative actor should be the primary interpreter, not the courts, and this intention counts as part of the democratic mandate. Courts may therefore be required to show deference to the interpretations made by administrative actors and cannot treat these actors as they would inferior courts. Even if a reviewing court disagrees with an administrative actor's interpretation of its home statute, if that decision constitutes a rationally supported construction of the relevant legislation, judges should not intervene and substitute their own views as they can with an inferior court on a matter of interpretation.

Judicial review in administrative law is an upper-year course, but this textbook introduces you to the common law review of administrative actions and interpretations. The two main grounds of review are for fairness in the procedures used by administrative actors and for reasonableness or correctness in the substance of their decisions. Both grounds of review involve the interpretation of the enabling or home statute and may also involve interpretation of related statutes. The role of the courts in administrative law is twofold: (1) to ensure that the administrative actor acts within the jurisdiction given by the legislature, and (2) to fill statutory gaps by imposing common law constraints on the administrative actor in order to satisfy the demands of the rule of law.

IV. FROM PARLIAMENTARY TO CONSTITUTIONAL SUPREMACY AND BACK?

Recent events provide a plethora of examples of public law crises or democratic deficits: expanding executive power, a dysfunctional Senate, a flawed judicial appointment process, misuse of omnibus and private members' bills in the legislature, controversies over prorogation and the role of the governor general, the perceived irrelevancy of members of Parliament, a pressing need for electoral reform, and a lack of accountability and transparency in government. You will see many instances in this textbook of how public law, and the lack of political will, have contributed to these deficits. The materials that follow constitute an essential foundation for a fuller understanding of Canadian law, Canadian government, and the constitutional basis for Canadian democracy. We also hope that the issues you encounter in public law inspire you to imagine how you can contribute to, or even improve, good governance in Canada.

PART I

SETTING THE STAGE

LEGAL THEORY IN RELATION TO PUBLIC LAW

This first part of the book sets the stage for the deep inquiry into public law that follows in Parts II and III. Here, we include four chapters. Chapters 3 and 4 focus on Canadian "legal pluralism"—that is, the synergy of different legal traditions that animate the modern Canadian legal system. We consider in Chapter 3 the legal relationship between the Canadian state and Indigenous peoples and Indigenous legal traditions. In Chapter 4, we focus on the reception into Canadian law of the common law traditions of the United Kingdom, as well as the influence of the French civil law system on Quebec. We also introduce students to the concept of statutory law and international law. Chapter 5 examines recurring constitutional themes that echo throughout the balance of the book.

But before reaching those matters, this chapter provides theoretical context for all that follows. It provides an overview of several schools of legal theory—positivism, natural law, feminism, critical legal studies, and law and economics—with the intent of showing how competing approaches to understanding the nature of law and its relationship to social and political factors can affect judicial decision-making. It should be stressed that these are a few selected examples from many approaches that could be taken. Those interested in learning more about legal theory will find hundreds of additional resources available in any good law library.

I. INTRODUCTION

Throughout history, those who have thought and written about law have developed a number of diverse theories related to law. At their heart, legal theories have tended to focus on several related questions. First, what is the relationship between law and morality? Is law necessarily derived from universal moral truths? Are morally repugnant laws nevertheless binding? Second, what is the relationship between law and power? Are laws simply rules backed by force? To what degree does law primarily reflect the preferences of powerful societal actors or dominant cultural forces? The answers to these questions not only allow us to differentiate law from non-law, but also shed light on the nature of the multiple sources of law within a society, and the relationship between laws among groups of societies. In considering these questions, we recognize that law is not a discrete set of principles without a context. Legal systems are built around ideas that are historically and culturally specific. Our Anglo-Canadian system of law, based largely on the English common law system, reflects our Canadian values. So too does the Quebec civil law.

In order to situate Canadian public law in relation to some broader social debates, this section looks at public law through the lens of several prominent schools of legal theory: positivism and natural law, feminism, critical legal studies, and law and economics. The study of legal theory is known as "jurisprudence" (the same term is often used inaccurately to refer simply to a body of law, as in "the Supreme Court of Canada's criminal law jurisprudence"). This section is not intended to be a comprehensive survey of jurisprudence, but rather seeks to illustrate how differing conceptualizations of law affect legal outcomes.

II. POSITIVISM AND NATURAL LAW

A principal inquiry in legal theory is the extent to which law should be identified with morality. Positivism and natural law theories, at least in their classical form, treat this fundamental notion very differently. Legal positivism reflects the belief that law is nothing more than the rules and principles that actually govern or regulate a society. Positivism insists on the separation of law and morality, and, as a result, focuses on describing laws without reference to justness or legitimacy. Natural law theory, on the other hand, is aspirational in the sense that laws, properly called, are not simply all those official rules and principles that govern us, but only those that adhere to certain moral truths, most often of a universal and immutable nature.

The basic contours of legal positivism were set out by the philosopher John Austin in the 18th century. He proposed three basic theories about law:

1. that law is a command issued by the "uncommanded commander"—the sovereign;
2. that such commands are backed by threats; and
3. that a sovereign is one who is habitually obeyed.

Although his theory has undergone refinements over the years, the basic idea remains, that law is created by humans.

Natural law, developed through such writers as Aristotle and St Thomas Aquinas, is based on the theory that law arises from "nature" or by beliefs accepted by people; it found some of its greatest proponents within the Catholic Church. In the natural law tradition, for a law to be a true law, it must comport with the values accepted by society. There is little doubt that, at one level, law and morality are linked. Many of our most basic criminal laws, for example, are based on traditional Judeo-Christian conceptions of morality. But law and morality can also part ways: many contract laws, for example, exist to facilitate commercial transactions and do not immediately seem connected to any conception of morality. Moreover, law must address specific and detailed problems and objects, whereas morality is usually framed in general and open-ended concepts. For example, laws related to licensing automobile drivers must spell out specific information on different categories of licence and the age restrictions that might apply. Law is also generally thought to be determinate and certain, while morality can be contingent and relative. Moral disagreements and controversies are issues of great moment that have been debated and argued by philosophers for centuries. Legal disputes and controversies should be capable of resolution by lawyers and judges. In this regard, natural law does not deny the necessity of positive law, but where positive law contravenes natural law, the contravening positive law rules are held by natural law theorists not to be "true" law in the sense that a citizen (or a judge) owes no allegiance to them. Positivists, on the other hand, are not unconcerned with questions of justice, but rather maintain that the issue of what law is, is necessarily separate and distinct from the question of what law ought to be.

The two cases that follow, *Re Drummond Wren* and *Re Noble and Wolf*, arguably represent a natural law and positivist view, respectively, of legal theory. Note how the judge in *Drummond Wren* attempts to appeal to our moral conscience, while the judge in *Noble and Wolf* relies on the supposed certainty of positive law. As an exercise in legal reasoning, however, try to analyze *each* decision on the basis of a natural *and* a positive understanding of law.

Re Drummond Wren
[1945] OR 778, [1945] 4 DLR 674 (H Ct J)

[The Worker's Educational Association (WEA) had purchased a lot in East York (now part of Toronto), intending to build a house on it and then raffle it off for fundraising purposes. The land was restricted by a covenant pronouncing that it was "not to be sold to Jews or persons of objectionable nationality." The WEA applied to have the covenant declared invalid. One of the grounds argued was that the racially restrictive covenant was void as against public policy; another was that it contravened the provisions of the *Racial Discrimination Act*, SO 1944, c 51 passed by the Ontario legislature in 1944. This statute was designed to combat the once prevalent "Whites Only" and "No Jews Allowed" signs that were displayed in store windows, at beaches, and at other public places. Section 1 prohibited the publication or display of representations indicating an intent to discriminate on the basis of race or creed (the contemporary version is s 13 of the Ontario *Human Rights Code*, RSO 1990, c H.19).]

MACKAY J:

The applicant's argument is founded on the legal principle, briefly stated in 7 Hals. (2nd ed.), pp. 153-4, that: "Any agreement which tends to be injurious to the public or against the public good is void as being contrary to public policy." Public policy, in the words of Halsbury, "varies from time to time."

In "The Growth of Law," Mr. Justice Cardozo says:

Existing rules and principles can give us our present location, our bearings, our latitude and longitude. The inn that shelters for the night is not the journey's end. The law, like the traveller, must be ready for the morrow. It must have a principle of growth.

And Mr. Justice Oliver Wendell Holmes, in "The Common Law" says:

The very considerations which judges most rarely mention and always with an apology are the secret root from which the law draws all the juices of life. I mean, of course, what is expedient for the community concerned.

The matter of not creating new heads of public policy has been discussed at some length ... in *Naylor, Benzon & Co. v. Krainische Industrie Gesellschaft*, [1918] 1 KB 331, later affirmed by the Court of Appeal, [1918] 2 KB 486.

There he points out ... that "the Courts have not hesitated in the past to apply the doctrine (of public policy) whenever the facts demanded its application." "The truth of the matter," he says, seems to be that public policy is a variable thing. It must fluctuate with the circumstances of the time. This view is exemplified by the decisions which were discussed by the House of Lords in *Nordenfelt v. Maxim Nordenfelt Guns and Ammunition Co.*, [1894] AC 535. ... The principles of public policy remain the same, though the application of them may be applied in novel ways. The ground does not vary. As it was put by Tindal CJ in *Horner v. Graves* (1831), ... : "Whatever is injurious to the interests of the public is void, on the ground of public policy."

It is a well-recognized rule that courts may look at various Dominion and Provincial Acts and public law as an aid in determining principles relative to public policy ...

First and of profound significance is the recent San Francisco Charter, to which Canada was a signatory, and which the Dominion Parliament has now ratified. The preamble to this Charter reads in part as follows:

> We the peoples of the United Nations determined to save succeeding generations from the scourge of war, which twice in our lifetime has brought untold sorrow to mankind, and to reaffirm faith in fundamental human rights, in the dignity and worth of the human person, in the equal rights of men and women and of nations large and small ... and for these ends to practice tolerance and live together in peace with one another as good neighbors. ...

Under Articles 1 and 55 of this Charter, Canada is pledged to promote "universal respect for, and observance of, human rights and fundamental freedoms for all without distinction as to race, sex, language, or religion."

In the Atlantic Charter to which Canada has subscribed, the principles of freedom from fear and freedom of worship are recognized.

Section 1 of the *Racial Discrimination Act* provides:

> 1. No person shall,
>   (a) publish or display or cause to be published or displayed; or
>   (b) permit to be published or displayed on lands or premises or in a newspaper, through a radio broadcasting station or by means of any other medium which he owns or controls, any notice, sign, symbol, emblem or other representation indicating discrimination or an intention to discriminate against any person or any class of persons for any purpose because of the race or creed of such person or class of persons.

• • •

Proceeding from the general to the particular, the argument of the applicant is that the impugned covenant is void because it is injurious to the public good. This deduction is grounded on the fact that the covenant against sale to Jews or to persons of objectionable nationality prevents the particular piece of land from ever being acquired by the persons against whom the covenant is aimed, and that this prohibition is without regard to whether the land is put to residential, commercial, industrial or other use. How far this is obnoxious to public policy can only be ascertained by projecting the coverage of the covenant with respect both to the classes of persons whom it may adversely affect, and to the lots or subdivisions of land to which it may be attached. So considered, the consequences of judicial approbation of such a covenant are portentous. If sale of a piece of land can be prohibited to Jews, it can equally be prohibited to Protestants, Catholics or other groups or denominations. If the sale of one piece of land can be so prohibited, the sale of other pieces of land can likewise be prohibited. In my opinion, nothing could be more calculated to create or deepen divisions between existing religious and ethnic groups in this Province, or in this country, than the sanction of a method of land transfer which would permit the segregation and confinement of particular groups to particular business or residential areas, or conversely, would exclude particular groups from particular business or residential areas. The unlikelihood of such a policy as a legislative measure is evident from the contrary intention of the recently enacted *Racial Discrimination Act*, and the judicial branch of government must take full cognizance of such factors.

Ontario, and Canada too, may well be termed a Province, and a country, of minorities in regard to the religious and ethnic groups which live therein. It appears to me to be a moral duty, at least, to lend aid to all forces of cohesion, and similarly to repel all fissiparous tendencies which would imperil national unity. The common law courts have, by their actions over the years, obviated the need for rigid constitutional guarantees in our polity by their wise use of the doctrine of public policy as an active agent in the promotion of the public weal. While courts and eminent judges have, in view of the powers of our legislatures, warned against inventing new heads of public policy, I do not conceive that I would be breaking new ground were I to hold the restrictive covenant impugned in this proceeding to be void as against public policy. Rather would I be applying well-recognized principles of public policy to a set of facts requiring their invocation in the interest of the public good.

That the restrictive covenant in this case is directed in the first place against Jews lends poignancy to the matter when one considers that anti-Semitism has been a weapon in the hands of our recently-defeated enemies and the scourge of the world. But this feature of the case does not require innovation in legal principle to strike down the covenant; it merely makes it more appropriate to apply existing principles. If the common law of treason encompasses the stirring up of hatred between different classes of His Majesty's subjects, the common law of public policy is surely adequate to void the restrictive covenant which is here attacked.

My conclusion therefore is that the covenant is void because [it is] offensive to the public policy of this jurisdiction. This conclusion is reinforced, if reinforcement is necessary, by the wide official acceptance of international policies and declarations frowning on the type of discrimination which the covenant would seem to perpetuate.

It may not be inexpedient or improper to refer to a few declarations made by outstanding leaders under circumstances that arrest the attention and demand consideration of mankind. I first quote the late President Roosevelt:

> Citizens, regardless of religious allegiance, will share in the sorrow of our Jewish fellow-citizens over the savagery of the Nazis against their helpless victims. The Nazis will not succeed in exterminating their victims any more than they will succeed in enslaving mankind. The American people not only sympathize with all victims of Nazi crimes but will hold the perpetrators of these crimes to strict accountability in a day of reckoning which will surely come.
>
> I express the confident hope that the Atlantic Charter and the just World Order to be made possible by the triumph of the United Nations will bring the Jews and oppressed people in all lands the four freedoms which Christian and Jewish teachings have largely inspired.

And of the Right Honourable Winston Churchill:

In the day of victory the Jew's sufferings and his part in the struggle will not be forgotten. Once again, at the appointed time, he will see vindicated those principles of righteousness which it was the glory of his fathers to proclaim to the world. Once again it will be shown that, though the mills of God grind slowly, yet they grind exceeding small.

And of General Charles de Gaulle:

Be assured that since we have repudiated everything that has falsely been done in the name of France after June 23rd, the cruel decrees directed against French Jews can and will have no validity in Free France. These measures are not less a blow against the honour of France than they are an injustice against her Jewish citizens.

When we shall have achieved victory, not only will the wrongs done in France itself be righted, but France will once again resume her traditional place as a protagonist of freedom and justice for all men, irrespective of race or religion, in a new Europe.

• • •

I do not deem it necessary for the purpose of this case to deal with [the argument that the covenant violates s 1 of the *Racial Discrimination Act*], except to say that it appears to me to have considerable merit. My opinion as to the public policy applicable to this case in no way depends on the terms of the *Racial Discrimination Act*, save to the extent that such Act constitutes a legislative recognition of the policy which I have applied. ...

An order will therefore go declaring that the restrictive covenant attacked by the applicant is void and of no effect.

Re Noble and Wolf
[1948] OR 579, [1948] 4 DLR 123 (H Ct J)

[Individual cottage lots in the Beach O' Pines subdivision on the shores of Lake Huron contained a covenant that the lands shall not be sold or transferred to any person of the "Jewish, Hebrew, Semitic, Negro or coloured race or blood." Relying on the precedent established in *Re Drummond Wren* three years earlier, Bernard Wolf, an interested purchaser of a cottage lot, applied to have the covenant rendered invalid on grounds of public policy. This time, however, other property owners defended the covenant. The Beach O' Pines Protective Association argued that there was a congenial summer community among its members and cottage value would be lost if any change to its character occurred.]

SCHROEDER J:

Counsel for the vendor cites and relies upon the very able judgment of Mackay J in *Re Drummond Wren*, [1945] 4 DLR 674, rendered on a motion for a declaration that a restrictive covenant that the land was "not to be sold to Jews or persons of objectionable nationality" was void and of no effect. In a carefully considered judgment, Mackay J reached the conclusion, as summarized in the headnote in the Ontario Reports, that the particular covenant was contrary to public policy in that it "tends to create or deepen divisions between religious and ethnic groups, and is in conflict with prevailing public opinion, as exemplified in the *Racial Discrimination Act, 1944*, and other statutes and public documents."

The case cited is a decision of a Court of co-ordinate jurisdiction and I am not necessarily bound by it. Under s. 31 of the *Judicature Act*, RSO 1937, c. 100, I may, if I deem the decision to be wrong and of sufficient importance to be considered in a higher Court, refer this case to the Court of Appeal, but I do not propose to adopt that course. I have given careful consideration and study to the learned judgment of my brother Mackay and regret that I find myself in disagreement with it. It is with the utmost respect that I proceed to state the reasons which have led me to an opposite conclusion.

It may be observed at the outset that Mackay J did not have the benefit of opposing argument on the motion before him. In the case at bar I would have been left in the same position but for the intervention of the persons on whom notice of motion was served pursuant to the order of Mackay J hereinbefore mentioned, because both the vendor and the purchaser were ad idem in their attack upon the validity of the covenant in question. Let it also be stated that in the case before my brother Mackay he was not concerned with a summer colony as in the case under consideration, but with a residential subdivision on O'Connor Drive in the City of Toronto, where the residents sought shelter rather than recreation. Also, the restriction in that case was unlimited in point of duration.

[After describing the sources relied upon by Mackay J, Schroeder J continued:]

Mackay J would seem to have evolved what I regard as an entirely novel head of public policy.

In approaching this aspect of the problem the Court must bear in mind the frequent injunctions of higher tribunals as to the danger of allowing judicial tribunals "to roam unchecked in the field occupied by that unruly horse, public policy." No more enlightening pronouncement can be found, in my opinion, than in the judgment of Lord Atkin in *Fender v. St. John-Mildmay*, [1938] AC 1 ..., from which I quote:

> I propose in the first instance to say something upon the doctrine of public policy generally. My Lords, from time to time judges of the highest reputation have uttered warning notes as to the danger of permitting judicial tribunals to roam unchecked in this field. The "unruly horse" of Hobart CJ is commonplace. I will content myself with two passages both of which have the authority of the approval of Lord Halsbury. In *Jason v. Driefontein Consolidated Mines*, [1902] AC 484, 491, he cites this passage from Marshall on Marine Insurance:
>
>> To avow or insinuate that it might, in any case, be proper for a judge to prevent a party from availing himself of an indisputable principle of law, in a Court of justice, upon the ground of some notion of fancied policy or expedience, is a new doctrine in Westminster Hall, and has a direct tendency to render all law vague and uncertain.

"Public policy," said Parke B in *Egerton v. Brownlow*, ... "is a vague and unsatisfactory term, and calculated to lead to uncertainty and error, when applied to the decision of legal rights; it is capable of being understood in different senses; it may, and does, in its ordinary sense, mean 'political expedience,' or that which is best for the common good of the community; and in that sense there may be every variety of opinion, according to education, habits, talents, and dispositions of each person, who is to decide whether an act is against public policy or not. To allow this to be a ground of judicial decision, would lead to the greatest uncertainty and confusion. It is the province of the statesman, and not the lawyer, to discuss, and of the Legislature to determine, what is best for the public good, and to provide for it by proper enactments. It is the province of the judge to expound the law only; the written from the statutes; the unwritten or common law from the decisions of our predecessors and of our existing Courts, from text writers of acknowledged authority, and upon the principles to be clearly deduced from them by sound reason and just inference; not to speculate upon what is the best, in his opinion, for the advantage of the community. Some of these decisions may have no doubt been founded upon the prevailing and just opinions of the public good; for instance, the illegality of covenants in restraint of marriage or trade. They have become a part of the recognized law, and we are therefore bound by them, but we are not thereby authorized to establish as law everything which we may think for the public good, and prohibit everything which we think otherwise." ...

• • •

To hold on the basis of Canadian treaty obligations and on the basis of the provincial legislation and regulations and other public documents, referred to in the judgment of Mackay J, that there is a public policy in Ontario which prohibits the use of and renders void any covenant such as the one under review, seems to me to involve an arbitrary extension of the rules which say that a given contract is void as being opposed to public policy. It is trite law that common law rights are not to be deemed to be abrogated by statute unless the legislative intent to do so is expressed in very clear language. It follows logically, it seems to me, that for a Court to invent new heads of public policy and found thereon nullification of established rights or obligations—in a sense embarking upon a course of judicial legislation—is a mode of procedure not to be encouraged or approved.

While it may fairly be assumed that the public policy of this country is opposed to the taking of affirmative action by any competent legislative authority which would be inconsistent with the sentiments or ideals expressed in these treaties or enactments, it would, in my view, constitute a radical departure from established principle to deduce therefrom any policy of the law which may be claimed to transcend the paramount public policy that one is not lightly to interfere with the freedom of contract. It is no doubt desirable that freedom of contract should be reconciled with other public interests which are regarded as of not less importance—something which cannot always be accomplished without difficulty; nevertheless, if there is any doubt as to the prevailing public policy or its effect, I should deem it to be the duty of the Court to extend the benefit of the doubt to the contract which the supposed public policy is claimed to supersede. The notion of any danger to public interests involved in the use of restrictive covenants such as the one in question seems to me fanciful and unreal. Whatever view I may entertain, based upon my conception of justice, morality or convenience, I must always have present to my mind the proper conception of the judicial function, namely, to expound and interpret the law and not to create the law based on my individual notion or opinion of what the law ought to be. I cannot conceive of any established principle of law or any principles recognized in the Courts or by the State as part of our public law which enables me to conclude that the covenant under review should be struck down as offending against the policy of the law. Lord Roche, who was one of the dissentient Lords in the case of *Fender v. St. John-Mildmay*, but who did not differ from the majority of the House in the views expressed by them as to the function of the Courts in relation to the matter of public policy, stated ... :

> Now to evolve new heads of public policy or to subtract from existing and recognized heads of public policy if permissible to the Courts at all, which is debatable, would in my judgment certainly only be permissible upon some occasion as to which the legislature was for some reason unable to speak and where there was substantial agreement within the judiciary and where circumstances had fundamentally changed.

In my view it is within the province of the competent legislative bodies to discuss and determine what is best for the public good and to provide for it by the proper enactments. Such matters can with greater propriety and safety be left to the duly elected representatives of the people assembled in Parliament or in the Legislature.

For the reasons set forth, I hold that the said covenant is valid and enforceable and that the vendor has not satisfactorily answered the purchaser's objection thereto.

The motion will, therefore, be dismissed. The vendor shall pay the costs of the third parties who intervened after being served with notice of these proceedings but no costs are awarded to the purchaser who supported the vendor's motion.

An appeal by Wolf to the Ontario Court of Appeal was dismissed—*Noble v Alley*, [1949] OR 503, [1949] 4 DLR 375 (CA). On further appeal to the Supreme Court of Canada, the appeal was allowed and the racially restrictive covenant struck down, but on technical grounds resulting from the application of well-established common law rules—*Noble v Alley*, [1951] SCR 64. There was no discussion on the public policy implications of restrictive covenants.

From the vantage point of the 21st century, discriminatory covenants are obviously unforgivable, and the *Re Noble and Wolf* decision unsatisfactory. But consider this point: after the Ontario Court of Appeal decision in *Re Noble and Wolf*, and before its hearing at the Supreme Court of Canada, the Ontario legislature passed the following provision (now s 22 of the *Conveyancing and Law of Property Act*, RSO 1990, c C.34):

> Every covenant made after the 24th day of March, 1950, that but for this section would be annexed to and run with land and that restricts the sale, ownership, occupation or use of land because of the race, creed, colour, nationality, ancestry or place of origin of any person is void and of no effect.

Similar provisions have been enacted in other provinces in Canada. The legislatures, in other words, acted to correct a deficiency that at least some judges (applying the common law) were unprepared to correct. In our democratic system, how assertive should judges be in applying "public policy" or other grounds to graft new moral positions onto the law? Is that their proper role? Should it matter whether the law in question being applied by the court is a piece of legislation or a common law principle?

As is discussed later in these materials, debates on the proper role of judges in our democratic system are commonplace in Canada, especially following the enactment of the *Canadian Charter of Rights and Freedoms* (Part I of the *Constitution Act, 1982*, being Schedule B to the *Canada Act 1982* (UK), 1982, c 11). It is commonly agreed that, absent a constitutional justification, courts apply (rather than strike down or question) legislation. In so doing, they respond to the "supremacy" of Parliament (or the provincial legislatures) in law-making. But what if the law in question is not a statute, but is instead a common law doctrine—judge-made law? Why should contemporary judges with contemporary moral beliefs defer to the (sometimes quite dated) morality of prior judges? Keep this question in mind when reviewing the next section, which deals with the evolution of law's treatment of women.

Both positivism and natural law are descriptive theories in that they are principally concerned with identifying what law is, as opposed to what law ought to be. (Natural law approaches, while they identify law with reference to normative criteria, are nevertheless engaged in describing law as it exists.) The remaining approaches in this section are normative theories in that they seek to describe how existing laws fail to achieve an external objective, be it gender or class equality or the efficient distribution of scarce societal resources. Feminism, critical legal studies, and law and economics approaches are often critical in their posture and oriented toward reform.

III. FEMINIST PERSPECTIVES ON LAW

A. INTRODUCTION

Feminist perspectives on law look at the extent to which women are disadvantaged by legal rules and institutions that arise in societies that are patriarchal. It is accepted that such societies, to a greater or lesser extent, subordinate the interests of women and fail to account for their experiences in the creation of legal rules. The earliest feminist movements in law, beginning in the late 19th century, centred on gaining the voting franchise for women and the reform of marriage laws. These were largely successful. Once that occurred, the next stage of feminism involved attacks on discriminatory employment practices and criminal laws. It was not until the 1960s, however, that feminism matured into a defined movement and developed more widespread currency.

Much of feminist legal philosophy reflects a critique (and oftentimes a rejection) of liberalism as a political ideology. Laws that existed from the 17th century, even those based on liberal ideals such as individualism and liberty, did not typically respond to the needs of women and more often than not aided in their oppression. So-called liberal laws often contributed to the gross inequality between genders. Despite the ideals of liberalism, many of these laws had existed for centuries (and in some cases still do).

B. EARLY FORMALIST FEMINISM

In its early manifestations, feminism was largely concerned with seeking women's formal equality with men. This required an examination of laws to determine whether there was any express bias against women. The goal was to replace laws that favoured men with more neutral laws. The suffrage movement in the early part of the 20th century (focusing on the vote) followed such an approach.

Prior to 1916, election laws throughout Canada did not allow women to vote. In that year, women in Manitoba, Saskatchewan, and Alberta became enfranchised through political struggle. Laws in those provinces were revised to allow women to vote. Other provinces soon followed suit. In 1918, Parliament passed the *Women's Suffrage Act*, SC 1918, c 20, which gave every female British subject over age 21 the right to vote, as long as she possessed the same qualifications required for men under the provincial franchise.

Despite these political advancements, women remained barred from holding a seat in the Senate; successive federal governments refused to extend women's rights that far. They relied on s 24 of the *British North America Act* of 1867 (now the *Constitution Act, 1867* (UK), 30 & 31 Vict, c 3, reprinted in RSC 1985, Appendix II, No 5), which stated that only "qualified Persons" were eligible to be appointed to the Senate. Governments argued that women would not have been considered to be "qualified persons" at the time the 1867 Act was passed. By 1926, frustrated at continued government inaction, five women—Judge Emily Murphy, Nellie McClung, Louise McKinney, Irene Parlby, and Henrietta Muir Edwards—petitioned to have the government direct the Supreme Court of Canada to rule on the constitutional question whether, based on s 24, women could be considered candidates for the Senate. The Supreme Court of Canada found that "qualified persons" did not include women, basing its judgment on a formulaic and traditional interpretation. An appeal was launched to the Judicial Committee of the Privy Council—the highest level of appeal for Canada at that time. The decision, known as the *"Persons"* case, is excerpted below. The approach the Privy Council took to interpreting the Canadian Constitution, treating constitutions as evolving documents that could respond to changes in society over time, remains an important guide to constitutional interpretation today.

Edwards v AG Canada

[1930] AC 124, 1 DLR 98 (PC) (footnotes omitted)

LORD SANKEY LC:

By s. 24 of the *BNA Act, 1867*, it is provided that, "The Governor General shall from Time to Time, in the Queen's Name, by Instrument under the Great Seal of Canada, summon qualified Persons to the Senate; and, subject to the Provisions of this Act, every Person so summoned shall become and be a Member of the Senate and a Senator."

The question at issue in this appeal is whether the words "qualified persons" in that section include a woman, and consequently whether women are eligible to be summoned to and become members of the Senate of Canada.

Of the appellants, Henrietta Muir Edwards is the Vice-President for the Province of Alberta of the National Council of Women for Canada; Nellie L. McClung and Louise C. McKinney were for several years members of the Legislative Assembly of the said province; Emily F. Murphy is a police magistrate in and for the said province; and Irene Parlby is a member of the Legislative Assembly of the said province and a member of the Executive Council thereof.

[An account of the judgments of the Supreme Court of Canada is omitted.]

Their Lordships are of the opinion that the word "persons" in s. 24 does include women, and that women are eligible to be summoned to and become members of the Senate of Canada.

In coming to a determination as to the meaning of a particular word in a particular Act of Parliament it is permissible to consider two points—namely: (i) The external evidence derived from extraneous circumstances such as previous legislation and decided cases. (ii) The internal evidence derived from the Act itself. As the counsel on both sides have made great researches and invited their Lordships to consider the legal position of women from the earliest times, in justice to their argument they propose to do so and accordingly turn to the first of the above points—namely: (i) The external evidence derived from extraneous circumstances.

The exclusion of women from all public offices is a relic of days more barbarous than ours, but it must be remembered that the necessity of the times often forced on man customs which in later years were not necessary. Such exclusion is probably due to the fact that the deliberative assemblies of the early tribes were attended by men under arms, and women did not bear arms. "*Nihil autem neque publicae neque privatae rei, nisi armati, agunt*": Tac. Germ., c. 13. Yet the tribes did not despise the advice of women. "*Inesse quin etiam sanctum et providum putant, nec aut consilia earum aspernantur aut responsa neglegunt*": Germ., c. 8. The likelihood of attack rendered such a proceeding unavoidable, and after all what is necessary at any period is a question for the times upon which opinion grounded on experience may move one way or another in different circumstances. This exclusion of women found its way into the opinions of the Roman jurists, Ulpian (AD 211) laying it down. "*Feminae ab omnibus officiis civilibus vel publicis remotae sunt*": Dig. 1.16.195. The barbarian tribes who settled in the Roman Empire, and were exposed to constant dangers, naturally preserved and continued the tradition.

In England no woman under the degree of a Queen or a Regent, married or unmarried, could take part in the government of the State. A woman was under a legal incapacity to be elected to serve in Parliament and even if a peeress in her own right she was not, nor is, entitled as an incident of peerage to receive a writ of summons to the House of Lords.

Various authorities are cited in the recent case of Viscountess Rhondda's Claim, where it was held that a woman was not entitled to sit in the House of Lords. Women were, moreover, subject to a legal incapacity to vote at the election of members of Parliament: Coke, 4 Inst., p. 5; *Chorlton v. Lings*; or of town councillor: *Reg. v. Harrald*; or to be elected members of a County Council: *Beresford-Hope v. Sandhurst*. They were excluded by the common law from taking part in the administration of justice either as judges or as jurors, with the single exception of inquiries by a jury of matrons upon a suggestion of pregnancy: Coke, 2 Inst. 119, 3 Bl. Comm. 362. Other instances are referred to in the learned judgment of Willes J in *Chorlton v. Lings*.

No doubt in any code where women were expressly excluded from public office the problem would present no difficulty, but where instead of such exclusion those entitled to be summoned to or placed in public office are described under the word "person" different considerations arise.

The word is ambiguous and in its original meaning would undoubtedly embrace members of either sex. On the other hand, supposing in an Act of Parliament several centuries ago it had been enacted that any person should be entitled to be elected to a particular office it would have been understood that the word only referred to males, but the cause of this was not because the word "person" could not include females but because at Common Law a woman was incapable of serving a public office. The fact that no woman had served or has claimed to serve such an office is not of great weight when it is remembered that custom would have prevented the claim being made, or the point being contested.

Customs are apt to develop into traditions which are stronger than law and remain unchallenged long after the reason for them has disappeared.

The appeal to history therefore in this particular matter is not conclusive.

· · ·

Over and above that, their Lordships do not think it right to apply rigidly to Canada of to-day the decisions and the reasonings therefor which commended themselves, probably rightly, to those who had to apply the law in different circumstances, in different centuries to countries in different stages of development. Referring therefore to the judgment of the Chief Justice and those who agreed with him, their Lordships think that the appeal to Roman Law and to early English decisions is not of itself a secure foundation on which to build the interpretation of the *BNA Act, 1867*. ...

Their Lordships now turn to the second point—namely, (ii) the internal evidence derived from the Act itself.

Before discussing the various sections they think it necessary to refer to the circumstances which led up to the passing of the Act.

The communities included within the Britannic system embrace countries and peoples in every stage of social, political and economic development and undergoing a continuous process of evolution.

His Majesty the King in Council is the final Court of Appeal from all these communities and this Board must take great care therefore not to interpret legislation meant to apply to one community by a rigid adherence to the customs and traditions of another. ...

The *BNA Act* planted in Canada a living tree capable of growth and expansion within its natural limits. The object of the Act was to grant a Constitution to Canada. "Like all written constitutions it has been subject to development through usage and convention": Canadian Constitutional Studies, Sir Robert Borden, (1922), p. 55.

Their Lordships do not conceive it to be the duty of this Board and it is certainly not their desire—to cut down the provisions of the Act by a narrow and technical construction, but rather to give it a large and liberal interpretation so that the Dominion to a great extent, but within certain fixed limits, may be mistress in her own house, as the provinces to a great extent, but within certain fixed limits, are mistresses in theirs. "The Privy Council, indeed, has laid down that Courts of law must treat the provisions of the *British North America Act* by the same methods of construction and exposition which they apply to other statutes. But there are statutes and statutes; and the strict construction deemed proper in the case, for example, of a penal or taxing statute or one passed to regulate the affairs of an English parish, would be often subversive of parliament's real intent if applied to an Act passed to ensure the peace, order and good government of a British colony": Clement's Canadian Constitution, 3rd ed., p. 347.

• • •

It must be remembered, too, that their Lordships are not here considering the question of the legislative competence either of the Dominion or its provinces which arises under ss. 91 and 92 of the Act providing for the distribution of legislative powers and assigning to the Dominion and its provinces their respective spheres of Government. Their Lordships are concerned with the interpretation of an Imperial Act, but an Imperial Act which creates a constitution for a new country. Nor are their Lordships deciding any question as to the rights of women but only a question as to their eligibility for a particular position. No one either male or female has a right to be summoned to the Senate. ...

Such being the general analysis of the Act, their Lordships turn to the special sections dealing with the Senate. [A close textual review of various provisions of the *BNA Act* is omitted.]

• • •

If Parliament had intended to limit the word "persons" in s. 24 to male persons it would surely have manifested such intention by an express limitation as it has done in ss. 41 and 84. The fact that certain qualifications are set out in s. 23 is not an argument in favour of further limiting the class, but is an argument to the contrary because it must be presumed that Parliament has set out in s. 23 all the qualifications deemed necessary for a Senator and it does not state that one of the qualifications is that he must be a member of the male sex. ...

A heavy burden lies on an appellant who seeks to set aside a unanimous judgment of the Supreme Court, and this Board will only set aside such a decision after convincing argument and anxious consideration, but having regard: (1) To the object of the Act—namely, to provide a constitution for Canada, a responsible and developing State; (2) That the word "person" is ambiguous and may include members of either sex; (3) That there are sections in the Act above referred to which show that in some cases the word "person" must include females; (4) That in some sections the words "male persons" is expressly used when it is desired to confine the matter in issue to males, and (5) To the provisions of the *Interpretation Act*; their

Lordships have come to the conclusion that the word "persons" in s. 24 includes members both of the male and female sex and that, therefore, the question propounded by the Governor-General must be answered in the affirmative and that women are eligible to be summoned to and become members of the Senate of Canada, and they will humbly advise His Majesty accordingly.

Appeal allowed.

C. CONTEMPORARY FEMINISM

As feminist analysis became more sophisticated through the 20th century, feminism and feminist legal theory evolved. More theoretical frameworks and disciplines were scrutinized. Areas of law previously thought to be immune to gender discrimination were examined. The disciplines of sociology and criminology were applied to issues such as violence against women. At the same time, the movement also became more fractured. Some strands became radicalized. Others remained more conservative: see Patricia Smith, ed, *Feminist Jurisprudence* (New York: Oxford University Press, 1993).

Today, it is seen as simplistic to argue that there is a monolithic group of "feminist scholars"—like any well-developed philosophy, feminism is now filled with complexity and richness. There are "liberal feminists" who argue that it is possible to have gender equality within a liberal conceptual framework: see Margaret Davies, *Asking the Law Question* (Sydney: Law Book Company Limited, 1994) at 179-90. Other, more radical feminists are not so sure, as divisions between men and women are seen as fundamental and attributable to the very notion of liberal society: see Kate Millet, *Sexual Politics* (New York: Simon & Schuster, 1990). Some would argue that Western law is partial: law's rules and structures are premised on a belief system that prefers men and their view of the world. The legal system is thus paternalistic and male-centred—for example, the idea of "rights" can be seen as a masculine concept. Rights-based cultures create a society where many people care only about their own rights and feel threatened by others who are equally self-absorbed. A male focus on the rights of disconnected individuals ignores the human element of law: see Ngaire Naffine, *Law and the Sexes: Explorations in Feminist Jurisprudence* (Sydney: Allen & Unwin, 1990). Others view law as fostering social practices that are combative and litigation-oriented—where the idea of a dispassionate judge handing down decisions is also cast as male-centric. Vague notions of "policy," "common sense," or "human nature" have also found their way into law, and been used by judges to preserve male privilege: see Catherine McKinnon, "Feminist Discourse, Moral Values and the Law" (1985) 34 Buff L Rev 21.

Regardless of whether one subscribes to a liberal or radical vision of feminism, implicit in many of feminism's central themes is that women, given the ability to reconstruct society, could do better. The subject of abortion provides a good forum to examine how feminist theory may translate this into practice.

Over the past five decades or so, rights surrounding abortion have been one of the most contentious areas of public debate. Prior to that time, many countries had criminalized or restricted most, if not all, forms of abortion. Canada was no different. In 1988, in the case of *R v Morgentaler*, the Supreme Court was asked to determine whether s 251 of the *Criminal Code*—criminalizing the procurement of an abortion unless properly authorized by a physician—was contrary to s 7 of the *Canadian Charter of Rights and Freedoms*, which provides that "Everyone has the right to life, liberty and security of the person and the right not to be deprived thereof except in accordance with the principles of fundamental justice."

The facts are straightforward. Three male doctors, Henry Morgentaler, Leslie Frank Smoling, and Robert Scott, were charged with the offence of procuring a miscarriage contrary to s 251(1). The majority of the Court found the provision to offend the Charter because of the complicated procedures put in place under the law. Justice Bertha Wilson, who agreed with the majority in the end result, rendered a separate opinion. Her decision is an example of a more modern feminist approach to a public law concern—note how her opinion takes a woman's point of view, in finding that a woman should not be required to carry a fetus to term if she does not want to.

R v Morgentaler
[1988] 1 SCR 30, 44 DLR (4th) 385, 62 CR (3d) 1

[Drs Morgentaler, Smoling, and Scott were each charged with conspiracy to pro-cure a miscarriage contrary to ss 251(1) and 423(1)(d) of the *Criminal Code*. They were acquitted at trial, but a Crown appeal against that acquittal was allowed and a new trial ordered. On appeal by the accused to the Supreme Court of Canada it was argued that s 251 of the *Criminal Code* was unconstitutional on the basis that it offended the guarantee to life, liberty, and security of the person found in s 7 of the *Canadian Charter of Rights and Freedoms*. Section 251(1) of the *Criminal Code* prohibits abortions except in circumstances described in s 251(4)—in effect, subsection (4) requires a woman to obtain a certificate from a therapeutic abortion committee and then requires that the abortion be carried out by a physician other than a member of the committee in an accredited or approved hospital. There must be at least three physicians on the committee. Evidence was led at trial as to delays encountered by women attempting to comply with the committee procedure and concerning access to abortion services in many parts of Canada. The majority held that these complicated procedures violated s 7 of the Charter.]

WILSON J:

At the heart of this appeal is the question whether a pregnant woman can, as a constitutional matter, be compelled by law to carry the foetus to term. The legis-lature has proceeded on the basis that she can be so compelled and, indeed, has made it a criminal offence punishable by imprisonment under s. 251 of the *Criminal Code*, RSC 1970, c. C-34, for her or her physician to terminate the pregnancy unless the procedural requirements of the section are complied with.

My colleagues, the Chief Justice and Justice Beetz, have attacked those require-ments in reasons which I have had the privilege of reading. They have found that the requirements do not comport with the principles of fundamental justice in the procedural sense and have concluded that, since they cannot be severed from the provisions creating the substantive offence, the whole of s. 251 must fall.

With all due respect, I think that the Court must tackle the primary issue first. A consideration as to whether or not the procedural requirements for obtaining or performing an abortion comport with fundamental justice is purely academic if such requirements cannot as a constitutional matter be imposed at all. If a pregnant woman cannot, as a constitutional matter, be compelled by law to carry the foetus to term against her will, a review of the procedural requirements by which she may be compelled to do so seems pointless. Moreover, it would, in my opinion, be an exercise in futility for the legislature to expend its time and energy in attempting to remedy the defects in the procedural requirements unless it has some assur-ance that this process will, at the end of the day, result in the creation of a valid criminal offence. I turn, therefore, to what I believe is the central issue that must be addressed.

1. The Right of Access to Abortion

• • •

I agree with the Chief Justice that we are not called upon in this case to delineate the full content of the right to life, liberty and security of the person. This would be an impossible task because we cannot envisage all the contexts in which such a right might be asserted. What we are asked to do, I believe, is define the content of the right in the context of the legislation under attack. Does section 251 of the *Criminal Code* which limits the pregnant woman's access to abortion violate her right to life, liberty and security of the person within the meaning of s. 7?

• • •

The idea of human dignity finds expression in almost every right and freedom guaranteed in the Charter. Individuals are afforded the right to choose their own religion and their own philosophy of life, the right to choose with whom they will associate and how they will express themselves, the right to choose where they will live and what occupation they will pursue. These are all examples of the basic theory underlying the Charter, namely that the state will respect choices made by individuals and, to the greatest extent possible, will avoid subordinating these choices to any one conception of the good life.

Thus, an aspect of the respect for human dignity on which the Charter is founded is the right to make fundamental personal decisions without interference from the state. This right is a critical component of the right to liberty. Liberty ... is a phrase capable of a broad range of meaning. In my view, this right, properly construed, grants the individual a degree of autonomy in making decisions of fundamental personal importance.

This view is consistent with the position I took in the case of *R v. Jones*, [1986] 2 SCR 284. One issue raised in that case was whether the right to liberty in s. 7 of the Charter included a parent's right to bring up his children in accordance with his conscientious beliefs. In concluding that it did I stated at pp. 318-19:

> I believe that the framers of the Constitution in guaranteeing "liberty" as a funda-
> mental value in a free and democratic society had in mind the freedom of the
> individual to develop and realize his potential to the full, to plan his own life to suit
> his own character, to make his own choices for good or ill, to be non-conformist,
> idiosyncratic and even eccentric—to be, in today's parlance, "his own person" and
> accountable as such. John Stuart Mill described it as "pursuing our own good in
> our own way." This, he believed, we should be free to do "so long as we do not
> attempt to deprive others of theirs or impede their efforts to obtain it."

• • •

The question then becomes whether the decision of a woman to terminate her pregnancy falls within this class of protected decisions. I have no doubt that it does. This decision is one that will have profound psychological, economic and social consequences for the pregnant woman. The circumstances giving rise to it can be complex and varied and there may be, and usually are, powerful consider-ations militating in opposite directions. It is a decision that deeply reflects the way the woman thinks about herself and her relationship to others and to society at large. It is not just a medical decision; it is a profound social and ethical one as well. Her response to it will be the response of the whole person.

It is probably impossible for a man to respond, even imaginatively, to such a dilemma not just because it is outside the realm of his personal experience (although this is, of course, the case) but because he can relate to it only by objectifying it, thereby eliminating the subjective elements of the female psyche which are at the heart of the dilemma. As Noreen Burrows, Lecturer in European Law at the University of Glasgow, has pointed out in her essay on "International Law and Human Rights: The Case of Women's Rights," in *Human Rights: From Rhetoric to Reality* (1986), the history of the struggle for human rights from the eighteenth century on has been the history of men struggling to assert their dignity and common humanity against an overbearing state apparatus. The more recent struggle for women's rights has been a struggle to eliminate discrimination, to achieve a place for women in a man's world, to develop a set of legislative reforms in order to place women in the same position as men. It has not been a struggle to define the rights of women in relation to their special place in the societal structure and in relation to the biological distinction between the two sexes. Thus, women's needs and aspirations are only now being translated into protected rights. The right to reproduce or not to reproduce which is in issue in this case is one such right and is properly perceived as an integral part of modern woman's struggle to assert her dignity and worth as a human being.

Given then that the right to liberty guaranteed by s. 7 of the Charter gives a woman the right to decide for herself whether or not to terminate her pregnancy, does s. 251 of the *Criminal Code* violate this right? Clearly it does. The purpose of the section is to take the decision away from the woman and give it to a committee. Furthermore, as the Chief Justice correctly points out ... the committee bases its decision on "criteria entirely unrelated to [the pregnant woman's] priorities and aspirations." The fact that the decision whether a woman will be allowed to terminate her pregnancy is in the hands of a committee is just as great a violation of the woman's right to personal autonomy in decisions of an intimate and private nature as it would be if a committee were established to decide whether a woman should be allowed to continue her pregnancy. Both these arrangements violate the woman's right to liberty by deciding for her something that she has the right to decide for herself.

· · ·

[T]he present legislative scheme for the obtaining of an abortion clearly subjects pregnant women to considerable emotional stress as well as to unnecessary physical risk. I believe, however, that the flaw in the present legislative scheme goes much deeper than that. In essence, what it does is assert that the woman's capacity to reproduce is not to be subject to her own control. It is to be subject to the control of the state. She may not choose whether to exercise her existing capacity or not to exercise it. This is not, in my view, just a matter of interfering with her right to liberty in the sense (already discussed) of her right to personal autonomy in decision-making, it is a direct interference with her physical "person" as well. She is truly being treated as a means—a means to an end which she does not desire but over which she has no control. She is the passive recipient of a decision made by others as to whether her body is to be used to nurture a new life. Can there be anything that comports less with human dignity and self-respect? How can a woman in this position have any sense of security with respect to her person? I believe that s. 251 of the *Criminal Code* deprives the pregnant woman of her right to security of the person as well as her right to liberty.

· · ·

I believe, therefore, that a deprivation of the s. 7 right which has the effect of infringing a right guaranteed elsewhere in the Charter cannot be in accordance with the principles of fundamental justice.

[Wilson J next went on to determine that the *Criminal Code* provisions also offend a woman's freedom of conscience and religion under s 2(a) of the Charter (regardless of whether such conscientiously held beliefs are grounded in religion or a secular morality).]

• • •

Section 251 of the *Criminal Code* takes the decision away from the woman at all stages of her pregnancy. It is a complete denial of the woman's constitutionally protected right under s. 7, not merely a limitation on it. It cannot, in my opinion, meet the proportionality test in *Oakes*. It is not sufficiently tailored to the legislative objective and does not impair the woman's right "as little as possible." It cannot be saved under s. 1. Accordingly, even if the section were to be amended to remedy the purely procedural defects in the legislative scheme referred to by the Chief Justice and Beetz J it would, in my opinion, still not be constitutionally valid.

One final word. I wish to emphasize that in these reasons I have dealt with the existence of the developing foetus merely as a factor to be considered in assessing the importance of the legislative objective under s. 1 of the Charter. I have not dealt with the entirely separate question whether a foetus is covered by the word "everyone" in s. 7 so as to have an independent right to life under that section. The Crown did not argue it and it is not necessary to decide it in order to dispose of the issues on this appeal.

Compared with the other justices in the *Morgentaler* decision, Wilson J looks at the very heart of the matter—whether a pregnant woman can be compelled by law to carry a fetus to term. The judgment is in keeping with her philosophy. Justice Wilson was a Supreme Court of Canada judge during the formative years of the Charter, from 1982 to 1991. She was the first woman appointed to the Supreme Court and participated in many groundbreaking Charter decisions. Feminists, for the most part, heralded her judgments as showing, for the first time, a true understanding of the plight of women in Canadian law: see e.g. Kim Brooks, ed, *Justice Bertha Wilson: One Woman's Difference* (Vancouver: University of British Columbia Press, 2010). Critics saw her as using the Charter to expand the role of a judge beyond principles established by liberal democratic theory and constitutional adjudication. She has been said to be as much a legislator for women's rights as a judge: see Robert E Hawkins & Robert Martin, "Democracy, Judging and Bertha Wilson" (1995) 41 McGill LJ 1.

IV. CRITICAL LEGAL STUDIES

A. INTRODUCTION

Like some forms of feminism, critical legal studies (CLS)—a school of legal theory developed largely during the 1980s in the United States—is a radical alternative to established legal theories. CLS adherents reject that there is any kind of "natural legal order" discoverable by objective means. As described by Alan Thomson:

> While traditional jurisprudence claims to be able to reveal through pure reason a picture of an unchanging and universal unity beneath the manifest changeability and historical variability of laws, legal institutions and practices, and thus to establish a foundation in reason for actual legal systems, critical legal theory not only denies the possibility of discovering a universal foundation for law through pure reason, but sees the whole enterprise of jurisprudence ... as operating to confer a spurious legitimacy on law and legal systems.

(A Thomson, "Critical Approaches to Law: Who Needs Legal Theory?" in I Grigg-Spall & P Ireland, eds, *The Critical Lawyers' Handbook* (London: Pluto Press, 1992) at 2.)

CLS is a direct descendent of legal realism, an approach that rose to prominence in the 1920s and lasted until the 1940s. Legal realism attacked two fundamental axioms of the traditional, formalist understanding of the common law: that common law legal rules were neutral and objective, and that the rules themselves could be determined with sufficient certainty. Realists maintained that all legal rules were indeterminate in the sense that any articulation of a rule was subject to multiple interpretations. As a consequence, when judges decided cases, they were not involved in an objective exercise of discovering the meaning of some pre-existing rule or mechanistically applying a rule to a set of facts (because the indeterminate nature of legal rules conferred discretion on judges to choose from a variety of alternative interpretations), but rather the result would reflect the unstated public policy preferences of the judge. The inconsistent results in the contrasting cases of *Re Drummond Wren* and *Re Noble and Wolf* provide an example of the way in which a judge's predisposition may affect legal outcomes. In essence, legal realism called into question the autonomy of law from broader social and political considerations.

Legal realists also believed in the importance of interdisciplinary approaches to law (given their understanding of law's contingency on social, economic, and political conditions), a view that became even more important to CLS scholars. Because of law's subjectivity, and its connection to other disciplines, the Realists sought to use the law as a tool to change society.

CLS takes this approach further. It is a direct attack on traditional legal theory, scholarship, and education. According to its main precepts, law, far from attempting to symbolize justice, institutionalizes and legitimates the authority and power of particular social groups or classes. The rule of law is not a rational, quasi-scientific ordering of society's norms, but is indeterminate, full of subjective interpretation and a large degree of incoherency.

Much of CLS theory is post-Marxist and usually associated with the left. Three key stages (posited by Trubek) govern the application of CLS ideas to legal thought: "hegemonic consciousness" (a concept derived from the Italian Marxist scholar Antonio Gramsci); "reification" (a Marxist term meaning to convert into something material); and "denial" (the psychoanalytical term as used by Freud). At the first stage, its proponents argue that many, if not most, Western laws are maintained by a system of beliefs that have their foundation in a liberal, market-driven economy. While many see these laws as natural and commonsensical, in fact, they reflect only the transitory, arbitrary interests of a dominant class: see David Trubek, "Where the Action Is: Critical Legal Studies and Empiricism" (1984) 36 Stan L Rev 575.

In the second stage, these beliefs are reified into a material thing: they are presented as essential, necessary, and objective. The laws that prop up this belief system necessarily follow suit, becoming equally incontrovertible.

In the final phase, laws and legal thinking aid in the denial of real truths: they assist in our coping with a vast storehouse of contradictions that would be too painful for us to hold in our consciousness. In other words, for a CLS scholar, the denial occurs between the promise of a certain state of law—such as equality—and the reality—such as the vast amounts of discrimination or racism that can be found so readily in society if only we look.

The liberal belief that law should be certain and neutral is, for CLS scholars, illusory. Law reproduces the oppressive characteristics of contemporary Western societies. Moreover, law is not independent or instrumental—it is simply another form of politics. Lawyers and the legal profession are part of this pretense. But there is nothing special about legal reasoning to distinguish it from other forms of reasoning—nothing about lawyers that should give them a monopoly on reason or justice. In other words, they are neither exceptional nor should they be privileged.

Finally, CLS questions another of law's central assumptions, that the individual is an autonomous agent. While the law assumes that individuals can make decisions based on reason that is detached from political, social, or economic constraints, CLS holds that individuals are tied to, and part of, such things as their communities, socio-economic class, gender, and race, such that they are not truly autonomous actors. Rather, their circumstances determine and therefore limit the choices presented to them.

B. JUDGING WITH CLS: A CASE STUDY

The CLS movement can be very theory-driven and densely philosophical. Along with its post-modernist offshoots, it is still considered radical, avant-garde, and outside most mainstream legal thought. Because of this, the movement was never likely to garner wholesale acceptance outside academia. However, it would be naïve to think that some lawyers and judges who attended law school during the 1970s and 1980s were not influenced by it. In the following excerpt from *R v S (RD)*, compare the judges' approach to questions of race and equality with that of the judges in *Re Drummond Wren* and *Re Noble and Wolf* excerpted above. Consider whether the differing opinions of the judges in *R v S (RD)* arise from different conceptions of the practice of judging itself. Also, examine the differences in approach of the two majority decisions with the approach of the dissent. Which, if any, reflects the insights of CLS scholarship regarding the impossibility of objectivity and the law's lack of autonomy from the social and political context in which law operates?

R v S (RD)
[1997] 3 SCR 484, 151 DLR (4th) 193, 10 CR (5th) 1
(emphasis in original)

[A white police officer arrested a Black 15-year-old youth who had allegedly interfered with the arrest of another youth. The accused was charged with three offences dealing with unlawfully assaulting and unlawfully resisting a police officer. The police officer and the accused were the only witnesses and their accounts of the relevant events differed widely. The Youth Court judge weighed the evidence and determined that the accused should be acquitted. While delivering her oral reasons, the judge remarked in response to a rhetorical question by the Crown, that, although she wasn't saying the specific police officer had misled, police officers had been known to mislead the Court in the past, that they had been known to overreact particularly with non-white groups, and that that would indicate a questionable state of mind. The Crown challenged these comments as raising a reasonable apprehension of bias. The Crown appealed to the Nova Scotia Supreme Court (Trial Division); the appeal was allowed and a new trial was ordered on the basis that the judge's remarks gave rise to a reasonable apprehension of bias. This judgment was upheld by a majority of the Nova Scotia Court of Appeal, and this decision was appealed, in turn, to the Supreme Court of Canada. A majority of the Court favoured Cory J's articulation of the applicable legal standards, although the members of the Court then added separate concurring views, and there were significant differences in the precise application of the legal standard between several concurring and a dissenting decision.]

CORY J:

[61] In this appeal, it must be determined whether a reasonable apprehension of bias arises from comments made by the trial judge in providing her reasons for acquitting the accused.

• • •

B. Ascertaining the Existence of a Reasonable Apprehension of Bias

(i) Fair Trial and the Right to an Unbiased Adjudicator

[91] A system of justice, if it is to have the respect and confidence of its society, must ensure that trials are fair and that they appear to be fair to the informed and reasonable observer. This is a fundamental goal of the justice system in any free and democratic society.

• • •

[95] Canada is not an insular, homogeneous society. It is enriched by the presence and contributions of citizens of many different races, nationalities and ethnic origins. The multicultural nature of Canadian society has been recognized in s. 27 of the Charter. Section 27 provides that the Charter itself is to be interpreted in a manner that is consistent with the preservation and enhancement of the multicultural heritage of Canadians. Yet our judges must be particularly sensitive to the need not only to be fair but also to appear to all reasonable observers to be fair to all Canadians of every race, religion, nationality and ethnic origin. This is a far more difficult task in Canada than it would be in a homogeneous society. Remarks which would pass unnoticed in other societies could well raise a reasonable apprehension of bias in Canada.

• • •

[97] The question which must be answered in this appeal is whether the comments made by Judge Sparks in her reasons give rise to a reasonable apprehension that she was not impartial as between the Crown and the accused. The Crown's position, in essence, is that Judge Sparks did not give the essential and requisite appearance of impartiality because her comments indicated that she prejudged an issue in the case, or to put it another way, she reached her determination on the basis of factors which were not in evidence.

• • •

(iii) What Is Bias?

[103] It may be helpful to begin by articulating what is meant by impartiality. In deciding whether bias arises in a particular case, it is relatively rare for courts to explore the definition of bias. In this appeal, however, this task is essential, if the Crown's allegation against Judge Sparks is to be properly understood and addressed. ...

• • •

[115] ... [I]n the context of the current appeal, it is vital to bear in mind that the test for reasonable apprehension of bias applies equally to all judges, regardless of their background, gender, race, ethnic origin, or any other characteristic. A judge who happens to be black is no more likely to be biased in dealing with black litigants, than a white judge is likely to be biased in favour of white litigants. All judges of every race, colour, religion, or national background are entitled to the same presumption of judicial integrity and the same high threshold for a finding of bias. Similarly, all judges are subject to the same fundamental duties to be and to appear to be impartial.

(v) Judicial Integrity and the Importance of Judicial Impartiality

[116] Often the most significant occasion in the career of a judge is the swearing of the oath of office. It is a moment of pride and joy coupled with a realization of

the onerous responsibility that goes with the office. The taking of the oath is solemn and a defining moment etched forever in the memory of the judge. The oath requires a judge to render justice impartially. To take that oath is the fulfilment of a life's dreams. It is never taken lightly. Throughout their careers, Canadian judges strive to overcome the personal biases that are common to all humanity in order to provide and clearly appear to provide a fair trial for all who come before them. Their rate of success in this difficult endeavour is high.

• • •

[118] It is right and proper that judges be held to the highest standards of impartiality since they will have to determine the most fundamentally important rights of the parties appearing before them. This is true whether the legal dispute arises between citizen and citizen or between the citizen and the state. Every comment that a judge makes from the bench is weighed and evaluated by the community as well as the parties. Judges must be conscious of this constant weighing and make every effort to achieve neutrality and fairness in carrying out their duties. This must be a cardinal rule of judicial conduct.

[119] The requirement for neutrality does not require judges to discount the very life experiences that may so well qualify them to preside over disputes. It has been observed that the duty to be impartial

> does not mean that a judge does not, or cannot bring to the bench many existing sympathies, antipathies or attitudes. There is no human being who is not the product of every social experience, every process of education, and every human contact with those with whom we share the planet. Indeed, even if it were possible, a judge free of this heritage of past experience would probably lack the very qualities of humanity required of a judge. Rather, the wisdom required of a judge is to recognize, consciously allow for, and perhaps to question, all the baggage of past attitudes and sympathies that fellow citizens are free to carry, untested, to the grave.

> True impartiality does not require that the judge have no sympathies or opinions; it requires that the judge nevertheless be free to entertain and act upon different points of view with an open mind. ...

It is obvious that good judges will have a wealth of personal and professional experience, that they will apply with sensitivity and compassion to the cases that they must hear. The sound belief behind the encouragement of greater diversity in judicial appointments was that women and visible minorities would bring an important perspective to the difficult task of judging. ...

[120] Regardless of their background, gender, ethnic origin or race, all judges owe a fundamental duty to the community to render impartial decisions and to appear impartial. It follows that judges must strive to ensure that no word or action during the course of the trial or in delivering judgment might leave the reasonable, informed person with the impression that an issue was predetermined or that a question was decided on the basis of stereotypical assumptions or generalizations.

(vi) Should Judges Refer to Aspects of Social Context in Making Decisions?

[121] It is the submission of the appellant and interveners that judges should be able to refer to social context in making their judgments. It is argued that they should be able to refer to power imbalances between the sexes or between races, as well as to other aspects of social reality. The response to that submission is that each case must be assessed in light of its particular facts and circumstances. Whether or not the use of references to social context is appropriate in the circumstances and

whether a reasonable apprehension of bias arises from particular statements will depend on the facts of the case.

• • •

[123] Certainly judges may, on the basis of expert evidence adduced, refer to relevant social conditions in reasons for judgment. In some circumstances, those references are necessary, so that the law may evolve in a manner which reflects social reality. ...

• • •

(vii) Use of Social Context in Assessing Credibility

• • •

[129] ... [I]t is ... the individualistic nature of a determination of credibility that requires the judge, as trier of fact, to be particularly careful to be and to appear to be neutral. This obligation requires the judge to walk a delicate line. On one hand, the judge is obviously permitted to use common sense and wisdom gained from personal experience in observing and judging the trustworthiness of a particular witness on the basis of factors such as testimony and demeanour. On the other hand, the judge must avoid judging the credibility of the witness on the basis of generalizations or upon matters that were not in evidence.

• • •

[131] At the commencement of their testimony all witnesses should be treated equally without regard to their race, religion, nationality, gender, occupation or other characteristics. It is only after an individual witness has been tested and assessed that findings of credibility can be made. Obviously the evidence of a policeman, or any other category of witness, cannot be automatically preferred to that of accused persons, any more than the testimony of blue eyed witnesses can be preferred to those with gray eyes. That must be the general rule. In particular, any judicial indication that police evidence is always to be preferred to that of a black accused person would lead the reasonable and knowledgeable observer to conclude that there was a reasonable apprehension of bias.

[132] In some circumstances it may be acceptable for a judge to acknowledge that racism in society might be, for example, the motive for the overreaction of a police officer. This may be necessary in order to refute a submission that invites the judge as trier of fact to presume truthfulness or untruthfulness of a category of witnesses, or to adopt some other form of stereotypical thinking. Yet it would not be acceptable for a judge to go further and suggest that all police officers should there-fore not be believed or should be viewed with suspicion where they are dealing with accused persons who are members of a different race. Similarly, it is dangerous for a judge to suggest that a particular person overreacted because of racism unless there is evidence adduced to sustain this finding. It would be equally inappropriate to suggest that female complainants, in sexual assault cases, ought to be believed more readily than male accused persons solely because of the history of sexual vio-lence by men against women.

[133] If there is no evidence linking the generalization to the particular witness, these situations might leave the judge open to allegations of bias on the basis that the credibility of the individual witness was prejudged according to stereotypical generalizations. This does not mean that the particular generalization—that police officers have historically discriminated against visible minorities or that women have historically been abused by men—is not true, or is without foundation. The difficulty is that reasonable and informed people may perceive that the judge has

used this information as a basis for assessing credibility instead of making a genuine evaluation of the evidence of the particular witness' credibility. As a general rule, judges should avoid placing themselves in this position.

[134] To state the general proposition that judges should avoid making comments based on generalizations when assessing the credibility of individual witnesses does not lead automatically to a conclusion that when a judge does so, a reasonable apprehension of bias arises. In some limited circumstances, the comments may be appropriate. Furthermore, no matter how unfortunate individual comments appear in isolation, the comments must be examined in context, through the eyes of the reasonable and informed person who is taken to know all the relevant circumstances of the case, including the presumption of judicial integrity, and the underlying social context.

• • •

C. Application of These Principles to the Facts

[142] Did Judge Sparks' comments give rise to a reasonable apprehension of bias? In order to answer that question, the nature of the Crown's allegation against Judge Sparks must be clearly understood. At the outset, it must be emphasized that it is obviously not appropriate to allege bias against Judge Sparks simply because she is black and raised the prospect of racial discrimination. Further, exactly the same high threshold for demonstrating reasonable apprehension of bias must be applied to Judge Sparks in the same manner it would be to all judges. She benefits from the presumption of judicial integrity that is accorded to all who swear the judicial oath of office. The Crown bears the onus of displacing this presumption with "cogent evidence."

• • •

[149] The history of anti-black racism in Nova Scotia was documented recently by the *Royal Commission on the Donald Marshall Jr. Prosecution* (1989). It suggests that there is a realistic possibility that the actions taken by the police in their relations with visible minorities demonstrate both prejudice and discrimination. I do not propose to review and comment upon the vast body of sociological literature referred to by the parties. It was not in evidence at trial. In the circumstances it will suffice to say that they indicate that racial tension exists at least to some degree between police officers and visible minorities. Further, in some cases, racism may have been exhibited by police officers in arresting young black males.

• • •

[150] However, there was *no* evidence before Judge Sparks that would suggest that anti-black bias influenced *this particular police officer's reactions.*

• • •

[152] [Her] remarks are worrisome and come very close to the line. Yet, however troubling these comments are when read individually, it is vital to note that the comments were not made in isolation. It is necessary to read all of the comments in the context of the whole proceeding, with an awareness of all the circumstances that a reasonable observer would be deemed to know. ...

[153] ... A reasonable and informed person observing the entire trial and hearing the reasons would be aware that Judge Sparks did not conclude that Constable Stienburg misled the court or overreacted on the basis of the racial dynamics of the situation.

• • •

V. Conclusion

[160] In the result the judgments of the Court of Appeal and of Glube CJSC are set aside and the decision of Judge Sparks dismissing the charges against R.D.S. is restored. I must add that since writing these reasons I have had the opportunity of reading those of Major J. It is readily apparent that we are in agreement as to the nature of bias and the test to be applied in order to determine whether the words or actions of a trial judge raise a reasonable apprehension of bias. The differences in our reasons lies in the application of the principles and test we both rely upon to the words of the trial judge in this case. The principles and the test we have both put forward and relied upon are different from and incompatible with those set out by Justices L'Heureux-Dubé and McLachlin.

L'HEUREUX-DUBÉ and McLACHLIN JJ:

I. Introduction

[27] We have read the reasons of our colleague, Justice Cory, and while we agree that this appeal must be allowed, we differ substantially from him in how we reach that outcome. As a result, we find it necessary to write brief concurring reasons.

[28] We endorse Cory J's comments on judging in a multicultural society, the importance of perspective and social context in judicial decision-making, and the presumption of judicial integrity. However, we approach the test for reasonable apprehension of bias and its application to the case at bar somewhat differently from our colleague.

[29] In our view, the test for reasonable apprehension of bias established in the jurisprudence is reflective of the reality that while judges can never be neutral, in the sense of purely objective, they can and must strive for impartiality. It therefore recognizes as inevitable and appropriate that the differing experiences of judges assist them in their decision-making process and will be reflected in their judgments, so long as those experiences are relevant to the cases, are not based on inappropriate stereotypes, and do not prevent a fair and just determination of the cases based on the facts in evidence.

[30] We find that on the basis of these principles, there is no reasonable apprehension of bias in the case at bar. Like Cory J we would, therefore, overturn the findings by the Nova Scotia Supreme Court (Trial Division) and the majority of the Nova Scotia Court of Appeal that a reasonable apprehension of bias arises in this case, and restore the acquittal of R.D.S. This said, we disagree with Cory J's position that the comments of Judge Sparks were unfortunate, unnecessary, or close to the line. Rather, we find them to reflect an entirely appropriate recognition of the facts in evidence in this case and of the context within which this case arose—a context known to Judge Sparks and to any well-informed member of the community.

II. The Test for Reasonable Apprehension of Bias

• • •

A. The Nature of Judging

[38] As discussed above, judges in a bilingual, multiracial and multicultural society will undoubtedly approach the task of judging from their varied perspectives. They will certainly have been shaped by, and have gained insight from, their different experiences, and cannot be expected to divorce themselves from these experiences on the occasion of their appointment to the bench. In fact, such a

transformation would deny society the benefit of the valuable knowledge gained by the judiciary while they were members of the Bar. As well, it would preclude the achievement of a diversity of backgrounds in the judiciary. The reasonable person does not expect that judges will function as neutral ciphers; however, the reasonable person does demand that judges achieve impartiality in their judging.

[39] It is apparent, and a reasonable person would expect, that triers of fact will be properly influenced in their deliberations by their individual perspectives on the world in which the events in dispute in the courtroom took place. Indeed, judges must rely on their background knowledge in fulfilling their adjudicative function. ...

[40] At the same time, where the matter is one of identifying and applying the law to the findings of fact, it must be the law that governs and not a judge's individual beliefs that may conflict with the law. Further, notwithstanding that their own insights into human nature will properly play a role in making findings of credibility or factual determinations, judges must make those determinations only after being equally open to, and considering the views of, all parties before them. The reasonable person, through whose eyes the apprehension of bias is assessed, expects judges to undertake an open-minded, carefully considered, and dispassionately deliberate investigation of the complicated reality of each case before them.

[41] It is axiomatic that all cases litigated before judges are, to a greater or lesser degree, complex. There is more to a case than who did what to whom, and the questions of fact and law to be determined in any given case do not arise in a vacuum. Rather, they are the consequence of numerous factors, influenced by the innumerable forces which impact on them in a particular context. Judges, acting as finders of fact, must inquire into those forces. In short, they must be aware of the context in which the alleged crime occurred.

[42] Judicial inquiry into the factual, social and psychological context within which litigation arises is not unusual. Rather, a conscious, contextual inquiry has become an accepted step towards judicial impartiality. In that regard, Professor Jennifer Nedelsky's "Embodied Diversity and the Challenges to Law" (1997), 42 *McGill LJ* 91, at p. 107, offers the following comment:

> What makes it possible for us to genuinely judge, to move beyond our private idiosyncrasies and preferences, is our capacity to achieve an "enlargement of mind." We do this by taking different perspectives into account. This is the path out of the blindness of our subjective private conditions. The more views we are able to take into account, the less likely we are to be locked into one perspective ... . It is the capacity for "enlargement of mind" that makes autonomous, impartial judgment possible. ...

• • •

IV. Application of the Test to the Facts

• • •

[56] While it seems clear that Judge Sparks *did not in fact* relate the officer's probable overreaction to the race of the appellant R.D.S., it should be noted that if Judge Sparks *had* chosen to attribute the behaviour of Constable Stienburg to the racial dynamics of the situation, she would not necessarily have erred. As a member of the community, it was open to her to take into account the well-known presence of racism in that community and to evaluate the evidence as to what occurred against that background.

[57] That Judge Sparks recognized that police officers sometimes overreact when dealing with non-white groups simply demonstrates that in making her

determination in this case, she was alive to the well-known racial dynamics that may exist in interactions between police officers and visible minorities. ...

• • •

V. Conclusion

[60] In the result, we agree with Cory J as to the disposition of this case. We would allow the appeal, overturn the findings of the Nova Scotia Supreme Court (Trial Division) and the majority of the Nova Scotia Court of Appeal, and restore the acquittal of the appellant R.D.S.

MAJOR J (dissenting):
[1] I have read the reasons of Justices L'Heureux-Dubé and McLachlin and those of Justice Cory and respectfully disagree with the conclusion they reach.

• • •

[3] This appeal should not be decided on questions of racism but instead on how courts should decide cases. In spite of the submissions of the appellant and interveners on his behalf, the case is primarily about the conduct of the trial. A fair trial is one that is based on the law, the outcome of which is determined by the evidence, free of bias, real or apprehended. Did the trial judge here reach her decision on the evidence presented at the trial or did she rely on something else?

• • •

[5] In view of the manner in which this appeal was argued, it is necessary to consider two points. First, we should consider whether the trial judge in her reasons, properly instructed herself on the evidence or was an error of law committed by her. The second, and somewhat intertwined question, is whether her comments above could cause a reasonable observer to apprehend bias. The offending comments in the statement are:

   (i)   "police officers have been known to [mislead the court] in the past";
  (ii)   "police officers do overreact, particularly when they are dealing with non-white groups";
 (iii)   "[t]hat to me indicates a state of mind right there that is questionable";
 (iv)   "[i]t seems to be in keeping with the prevalent attitude of the day"; and,
  (v)   "based upon my comments and based upon all the evidence before the court I have no other choice but to acquit."

[6] The trial judge stated that "police officers have been known to [mislead the court] in the past" and that "police officers do overreact, particularly when they are dealing with non-white groups" and went on to say "[t]hat to me indicates a state of mind right there that is questionable." She in effect was saying, "sometimes police lie and overreact in dealing with non-whites, therefore I have a suspicion that this police officer may have lied and overreacted in dealing with this non-white accused." This was stereotyping all police officers as liars and racists, and applied this stereotype to the police officer in the present case. The trial judge might be perceived as assigning less weight to the police officer's evidence because he is testifying in the prosecution of an accused who is of a different race. Whether racism exists in our society is not the issue. The issue is whether there was evidence before the court upon which to base a finding that this particular police officer's actions were motivated by racism. There was no evidence of this presented at the trial.

[7] Our jurisprudence has repeatedly prohibited the introduction of evidence to show propensity. In the present case had the police officer been charged with

assault the trial judge could not have reasoned that as police officers have been known to mislead the Court in the past that based on that evidence she rejected this police officer's credibility and found him guilty beyond reasonable doubt.

[8] In the same vein, statistics show that young male adults under the age of 25 are responsible for more accidents than older drivers. It would be unacceptable for a court to accept evidence of that fact to find a defendant liable in negligence yet that is the consequence of the trial judge's reasoning in this appeal.

[9] It is possible to read the trial judge's reference to the "prevalent attitude of the day" as meaning her view of the prevalent attitude in society today. If the trial judge used the "prevalent attitude of society" towards non-whites as evidence upon which to draw an inference in this case, she erred, as there were no facts in evidence from which to draw that inference. It would be stereotypical reasoning to conclude that, since society is racist, and, in effect, tells minorities to "shut up," we should infer that this police officer told this appellant minority youth to "shut up." This reasoning is flawed.

[10] Trial judges have to base their findings on the evidence before them. It was open to the appellant to introduce evidence that this police officer was racist and that racism motivated his actions or that he lied. This was not done. For the trial judge to infer that based on her general view of the police or society is an error of law. For this reason there should be a new trial.

• • •

[13] The life experience of this trial judge, as with all trial judges, is an important ingredient in the ability to understand human behaviour, to weigh the evidence, and to determine credibility. It helps in making a myriad of decisions arising during the course of most trials. It is of no value, however, in reaching conclusions for which there is no evidence. The fact that on some other occasions police officers have lied or overreacted is irrelevant. Life experience is not a substitute for evidence. There was no evidence before the trial judge to support the conclusions she reached.

[14] The trial judge could not decide this case based on what some police officers did in the past without deciding that all police officers are the same. As stated, the appellant was entitled to call evidence of the police officer's conduct to show that there was in fact evidence to support either his bias or racism. No such evidence was called. The trial judge presumably called upon her life experience to decide the issue. This she was not entitled to do.

[15] The bedrock of our jurisprudence is the adversary system. Criminal prosecutions are less adversarial because of the Crown's duty to present all the evidence fairly. The system depends on each side's producing facts by way of evidence from which the court decides the issues. Our system, unlike some others, does not permit a judge to become an independent investigator to seek out the facts.

[16] Canadian courts have, in recent years, criticized the stereotyping of people into what is said to be predictable behaviour patterns. If a judge in a sexual assault case instructed the jury or him- or herself that because the complainant was a prostitute he or she probably consented, or that prostitutes are likely to lie about such things as sexual assault, that decision would be reversed. Such presumptions have no place in a system of justice that treats all witnesses equally. Our jurisprudence prohibits tying credibility to something as irrelevant as gender, occupation or perceived group predisposition.

• • •

[18] It can hardly be seen as progress to stereotype police officer witnesses as likely to lie when dealing with non-whites. This would return us to a time in the

history of the Canadian justice system that many thought had past. This reasoning, with respect to police officers, is no more legitimate than the stereotyping of women, children or minorities.

[19] In my opinion the comments of the trial judge fall into stereotyping the police officer. She said, among other things, that police officers have been known to mislead the courts, and that police officers overreact when dealing with non-white groups. She then held, in her evaluation of this particular police officer's evidence, that these factors led her to "a state of mind right there that is questionable." The trial judge erred in law by failing to base her conclusions on evidence.

• • •

[23] I agree with the approach taken by Cory J with respect to the nature of bias and the test to be used to determine if the words or actions of a judge give rise to apprehension of bias. However, I come to a different conclusion in the application of the test to the words of the trial judge in this case. It follows that I disagree with the approach to reasonable apprehension of bias put forward by Justices L'Heureux-Dubé and McLachlin.

[24] The error of law that I attribute to the trial judge's assessment of the evidence or lack of evidence is sufficiently serious that a new trial is ordered.

[25] In the result, I would uphold the disposition of Flinn JA in the Court of Appeal (1995), 145 NSR (2d) 284, and dismiss the appeal.

V. LAW AND ECONOMICS

A. INTRODUCTION

Both positivism and natural law are concerned with concepts of law and justice, even if they diverge as to how the two relate to one another. Both are also based largely on Western, liberal ideas about law and society. In contrast, feminism and critical studies take issue with the liberal basis of law and its relationship to justice; both attempt to establish alternative visions of what justice might be. Law and economics theories look at law from another perspective, grounded less in moral theory and more in ideas about efficiency. As with the other theories, however, law and economics seeks to explain law in operation.

Law and economics scholars have applied economic analysis to explain contract law, crime, torts, family law, property, legislation, abortion, and more: see generally, Ronald Coase, "Economics and Contiguous Disciplines" (1978) 7:2 J Legal Stud 201 and Richard Posner, *The Economic Analysis of Law*, 9th ed (New York: Wolters Kluwer Law & Business, 2014). As in other perspectives on law, there is no single approach to linking law and economics. However, most of the work in this area originated out of the "Chicago School" in the 1970s, which had a strong free-market, neo-liberal, philosophical base.

A traditional law and economics approach applies economics methodology to legal rules in order to assess whether the rules will result in outcomes that are efficient. Efficiency tends to be defined in terms of an ideal where the welfare of each of the relevant parties can no longer be maximized except at the expense of other parties, referred to as a state of "Pareto optimality." In this regard, law and economics is sometimes criticized as ignoring questions respecting distributive justice. Central to all economic analysis is the assumption that human beings are rational actors. Individuals have preferences and act in order to achieve those preferences; they act as if they were rational maximizers of their welfare. This form of analysis was first applied on common law rules developed in private law areas such as torts and contracts. (It is worth noting that behavioural economists have more recently critiqued the very idea of individual rational actors: see e.g. Daniel Kahneman, *Thinking, Fast and Slow* (New York: Farrar, Straus and Giroux, 2011).)

B. PUBLIC LAW AND ECONOMIC THEORY

1. Overview

Like law and justice, however, justice and efficiency are often interrelated. For one, governments have to consider the costs of providing and maintaining the institutions of justice. But more broadly, to the extent that justice involves considerations of utility, efficiency can be seen as a concept concerned with maximizing justice.

An economic approach similar to that employed for private law can therefore be used to understand policy goals in the public realm. The economic theory of regulation, or public choice theory, applies basic economic theory in an attempt to understand public policy. It attempts to explain government intervention as a "corrective" to market failure. The theory seeks to understand why some government programs seem to run counter to the public good, or at least do not maximize the public good. In its pure form the economic theory of public law begins at the same place as the economic theory of private law: policy-makers are assumed to act in order to maximize political support. They are not necessarily attempting to maximize social welfare, therefore, but are motivated largely by self-interest: see J Buchanan & R Tollison, eds, *The Theory of Public Choice—II* (Ann Arbor, Mich: University of Michigan Press, 1984) and Arthur Pigou, *The Economics of Welfare*, 4th ed (London: Macmillan, 1932).

A basic proposition of public choice theory is that diffuse and fragmented groups are less effective than more focused and concentrated groups in achieving success in the political arena and in influencing legislators and regulators: see I McLean, *Public Choice: An Introduction*, 2nd ed (Oxford: Blackwell, 1996) and D Mueller, ed, *Perspectives on Public Choice* (New York: Cambridge University Press, 1997).

If both these expectations are true, one might expect legislation to favour the self-interest of legislators and/or the interests of powerful social groups. There is an echo, therefore, in the public choice critique of the complaints voiced by the CLS and feminist scholars. Ask yourself, as you progress through these materials, whether Canadian public law sufficiently guards against these predicted outcomes.

2. Time Value of Money: An Example

One of the themes in public law is to show how common law has been displaced by policy formulation (in the form of legislation) as the primary means of social regulation: see E Rubin, "Law and Legislation in the Administrative State" (1989) 89 Colum L Rev 369. A number of important questions, therefore, lie at the heart of this analysis: What, in economic terms, is the problem that a legal rule or structure is attempting to resolve? What effect does this rule have on society? Why do we have the laws that we have? Should we have different laws?

Consider how the Supreme Court of Canada relies on some basic economic theory about the value of money and its relationship to contractual breaches in the following decision.

Bank of America Canada v Mutual Trust Co
2002 SCC 43, [2002] 2 SCR 601

[The appellant, Bank of America Canada, had advanced money to a developer, and the respondent, Mutual Trust, had undertaken to advance money to the purchaser of houses being built by the developer in a device called a "Takeout Mortgage Commitment" (TOC). The developer assigned its rights against Mutual Trust to Bank of America Canada. The funds advanced by Mutual Trust under the TOC would have discharged the loan made by Bank of America Canada to the developer. Mutual

Trust backed out of the deal when the real estate market collapsed in the early 1990s. The amount of Bank of America Canada's loss was about $10 million—the difference between what it was owed and what it recovered when it sold the development after Mutual Trust's default.

The trial judge awarded interest on this amount at a compound rate that reflected the interest rate charged in the agreement between the parties. Mutual Trust appealed. The Ontario Court of Appeal allowed its appeal, relying on s 128 of the *Courts of Justice Act* in substituting a simple interest rate for the compound rate allowed by the trial judge. The difference between the two amounts was in the order of $5 million. Bank of America Canada appealed. The Supreme Court upheld the trial court's original approach, contemplating in a part of the judgment the economic concept of the "time-value" of money.]

MAJOR J:

VI. Analysis

A. Jurisdiction

(1) The Time-Value of Money

[21] The value of money decreases with the passage of time. A dollar today is worth more than the same dollar tomorrow. Three factors account for the depreciation of the value of money: (i) opportunity cost (ii) risk, and (iii) inflation.

[22] The first factor, opportunity cost, reflects the uses of the dollar which are foregone while waiting for it. The value of the dollar is reduced because the opportunity to use it is absent. The second factor, risk, reflects the uncertainty inherent in delaying possession. Possession of a dollar today is certain but the expectation of the same dollar in the future involves uncertainty. Perhaps the future dollar will never be paid. The third factor, inflation, reflects the fluctuation in price levels. With inflation, a dollar will not buy as much goods or services tomorrow as it does today ... The time-value of money is common knowledge and is one of the cornerstones of all banking and financial systems.

[23] Simple interest and compound interest each measure the time value of the initial sum of money, the principal. The difference is that compound interest reflects the time-value component to interest payments while simple interest does not. Interest owed today but paid in the future will have decreased in value in the interim just as the dollar example described in paras. 21-22. Compound interest compensates a lender for the decrease in value of all money which is due but as yet unpaid because unpaid interest is treated as unpaid principal.

[24] Simple interest makes an artificial distinction between money owed as principal and money owed as interest. Compound interest treats a dollar as a dollar and is therefore a more precise measure of the value of possessing money for a period of time. Compound interest is the norm in the banking and financial systems in Canada and the western world and is the standard practice of both the appellant and respondent.

(2) Contract Damages

• • •

(b) Restitution Damages

[30] The other side of the coin is to examine the effect of the breach on the defendant. In contract, restitution damages can be invoked when a defendant has,

as a result of his or her own breach, profited in excess of his or her expected profit had the contract been performed but the plaintiff's loss is less than the defendant's gain. So the plaintiff can be fully paid his damages with a surplus left in the hands of the defendant. This occurs with what has been described as an efficient breach of contract. In some but not all cases, the defendant may be required to pay such profits to the plaintiff as restitution damages. ...

[31] Courts generally avoid this measure of damages so as not to discourage efficient breach (i.e., where the plaintiff is fully compensated and the defendant is better off than if he or she had performed the contract) ... Efficient breach is what economists describe as a Pareto optimal outcome where one party may be better off but no one is worse off, or expressed differently, nobody loses. Efficient breach should not be discouraged by the courts. This lack of disapproval emphasizes that a court will usually award money damages for breach of contract equal to the value of the bargain to the plaintiff.

CHAPTER THREE

INDIGENOUS PEOPLES AND PUBLIC LAW

I. INTRODUCTION

We turn now to the first of two chapters on legal pluralism in Canada. Our first subject is the relationship between the Canadian state and Indigenous peoples and their governments, as well as some of the public law consequences of Indigenous legal traditions and rights. A word, first, about terminology. The term "Aboriginal peoples" is used in Canadian law as an umbrella term to refer to three distinct groups of Indigenous people in Canada: First Nations, Inuit, and Métis. However, Indigenous peoples, when using an overarching term, often prefer the term "Indigenous" over "Aboriginal" as the term has international recognition as a collective name for the original peoples. We follow this practice, except where the expression "Aboriginal" (or another expression, such as "Indian") is used as a legal term of art.

Approximately 5 percent of the Canadian population self-identify as Indigenous. As noted by the 1996 Royal Commission on Aboriginal Peoples (RCAP), Indigenous people "often say that they have been here since time immemorial," a claim that is also supported by archeological evidence dating back up to 40,000 years ago (RCAP, Final Report, Volume 1: *Looking Forward, Looking Back* (1996) at 20). Indigenous communities thus successfully governed their communities for thousands of years before the arrival of European settlers, some 150 to 500 years ago, with their own laws and legal processes. (See e.g. Emily Snyder, Val Napoleon & John Borrows, "Gender and Violence: Drawing on Indigenous Legal Traditions" (2015) 48 UBC L Rev 593).

While some early Canadian judges recognized that the assertion of control by the British Crown during the colonial period did not displace Indigenous legal systems, this understanding was largely cast aside through much of the 20th century. Indeed, as part of the colonial strategy to assimilate Indigenous peoples and secure possession of their territories, Indigenous cultural, legal, political, and economic rights were denied or denigrated as inferior by courts as well as government bodies, with devastating effects for Indigenous communities. The following excerpt from a UN report is apposite:

> Much of [Indigenous peoples'] land has been taken away and whatever land is left to them is subject to constant encroachment. Their culture and their social and legal institutions and systems have been constantly under attack at all levels, through the media, the law and the public education systems. It is only natural, therefore, that there should be resistance to further loss of their land and rejection of the distortion or denial of their history and culture and defensive/offensive reaction to the continual linguistic and cultural aggressions and attacks on their way of life, their social and cultural integrity and their very physical existence. They have a right to continue to exist, to defend their lands, to keep and to transmit their culture, their language, their social and legal institutions and systems and their ways of life, which have been illegally and unjustifiably attacked.

(Martinez Cobo, United Nations Special Rapporteur, *Problems of Discrimination Against Indigenous Peoples*, UN Doc E/CN.4/Sub.2/1983/21/add.8 at 49.)

From the early 1900s, to around the 1970s, Canada's provincial and federal governments, and court systems, largely assumed and asserted that Canada's laws, legal institutions, and constitutional arrangements, as commonly understood, came from Europe and that Indigenous peoples did not have a "legal system" prior to European arrival. This line of argument maintained that Indigenous peoples in North America were "pre-legal." It was argued that Indigenous laws, and the rights and interests associated with those laws, were unenforceable, more akin to social values than laws.

Over the past few decades, these views have been successfully challenged in a number of legal forums. The pressing contemporary questions for state actors are not whether Indigenous peoples have laws and legal institutions. Instead the questions focus on clarifying the nature of the laws and legal interests of Indigenous peoples and governments, and understanding the consequences of Indigenous jurisdiction for legitimate decision-making involving state actors.

II. INDIGENOUS PEOPLES AND THE CANADIAN STATE

We begin by describing three views on the constitutional relationship between Indigenous peoples and the Canadian state. These views are not necessarily in conflict. They are offered to illustrate the complexity of the relationship, and some current challenges for determining both what the constitutional relationship is, and what the constitutional relationship should be. The chapter then provides some key contextual information. This includes describing historic relationships between European and Indigenous governments, and explaining shifts in these relationships as Indigenous peoples became less able to assert themselves as polities. Consideration then turns to how the Canadian state and Indigenous peoples have entered a stage of their relationship that is marked by its public law aspects. This renewed relationship is based on striving to legitimately reconcile the Crown's assertion of sovereignty over what is now Canada with the pre-existing and continuing legal and governing rights of Indigenous peoples. This relationship is marked by the recognition and affirmation of Indigenous legal orders as a part of Canada's Constitution. The chapter closes by turning to how human rights violations have become structurally embedded in the state–Indigenous relationship and efforts to unsettle and address this status quo. The chapter draws on litigation, as well as some contemporary treaties and independent reports, to help define the features of the contemporary relationship.

A. THREE VIEWS ON THE CONSTITUTIONAL RELATIONSHIP BETWEEN INDIGENOUS AND NON-INDIGENOUS PEOPLES IN CANADA

Over the last few hundred years, there have been significant shifts in how governance and jurisdictional powers have been shared as between Indigenous and non-Indigenous governments. Some scholars, like Michael Asch, have carefully traced the evolution of this relationship, and raised questions about whether the state's current *de facto* sovereignty over the territory known as "Canada" is legitimate given how some of those powers were obtained. Asch has suggested remedies that rest on identifying Canada's origin—and future—in treaty relationships. Michael Asch, *On Being Here to Stay: Treaties and Aboriginal Rights in Canada* (Toronto: University of Toronto Press, 2014). Key Indigenous legal thinkers are also advancing similar critiques and remedies. See, for example, Hon Harry LaForme & Claire Truesdale, "Section 25 of the Charter; Section 35 of the Constitution Act, 1982: Aboriginal and Treaty Rights—30 Years of Recognition and Affirmation" (2013) 62 SCLR (2nd) 687.

Indigenous scholar John Borrows explores other aspects of the public law relationship between Indigenous peoples and the Canadian state. Like Asch, his emphasis is on how that relationship must evolve. In his scholarship, he considers the role Indigenous law and legal traditions should play as part of the rule of law in Canada. He writes:

> [T]he continent's original inhabitants have never been convinced that the rule of law lies at the heart of their experience with others in this land. In this respect, Canada's legal system is incomplete. Many Indigenous peoples believe their laws provide significant context and detail for judging our relationships with the land, and with one another. Yet Indigenous laws are often ignored, diminished, or denied as being relevant or authoritative in answering these questions. This has led to important queries about the sources of Canada's law, as well as its cultural commitments, institutional receptiveness, and interpretive competency.

(John Borrows, *Canada's Indigenous Constitution* (Toronto: University of Toronto Press, 2010) at 6.)

Finally, the Truth and Reconciliation Commission identifies multiple points of tension in the state–Indigenous relationship, and that a new vision is required that reconciles Indigenous peoples' right to self-determination with the Crown's assertion of sovereignty:

> Aboriginal peoples have always remembered the original relationship they had with early Canadians. That relationship of mutual support, respect, and assistance was confirmed by the Royal Proclamation of 1763 and the Treaties with the Crown that were negotiated in good faith by their leaders. That memory, confirmed by historical analysis and passed down through Indigenous oral histories, has sustained Aboriginal peoples in their long political

struggle to live with dignity as self-determining peoples with their own cultures, laws, and connections to the land.

The destructive impacts of residential schools, the *Indian Act* [RSC 1985, c I-5], and the Crown's failure to keep its Treaty promises have damaged the relationship between Aboriginal and non-Aboriginal peoples. The most significant damage is to the trust that has been broken between the Crown and Aboriginal peoples. That broken trust must be repaired. The vision that led to that breach in trust must be replaced with a new vision for Canada; one that fully embraces Aboriginal peoples' right to self-determination within, and in partnership with, a viable Canadian sovereignty. If Canadians fail to find that vision, then Canada will not resolve long-standing conflicts between the Crown and Aboriginal peoples over Treaty and Aboriginal rights, lands, and resources, or the education, health, and well-being of Aboriginal peoples. Reconciliation will not be achieved, and neither will the hope for reconciliation be sustainable over time. It would not be inconceivable that the unrest we see today among young Aboriginal people could grow to become a challenge to the country's own sense of well-being and its very security.

Reconciliation must become a way of life.

(Truth and Reconciliation Commission, *Honouring the Truth, Reconciling for the Future: Summary of the Final Report of the Truth and Reconciliation Commission of Canada* (2015) at 184).

Consider how the materials in this chapter inform, support, and challenge these positions.

III. INDIGENOUS—STATE RELATIONS PRIOR TO 1982

A. INDIGENOUS GOVERNANCE AND THE EARLY CANADIAN STATE: NATION-TO-NATION RELATIONS

As noted above, various Indigenous peoples have occupied what is now Canada for thousands of years. On their arrival a few hundred years ago, European colonists asserted control as against other European powers. The colonists also had to face the fact that the land was already occupied and governed by Indigenous peoples. Michael Coyle writes that "[w]hen the British won control of New France in 1763, they had no intention of risking war to gain aboriginal lands. Instead ... King George III issued a Royal Proclamation ... " (Michael Coyle, "Addressing Aboriginal Land Rights in Ontario: An Analysis of Past Policies and Options for the Future—Part I" (2005) 31 Queen's LJ 75 at para 11).

The Proclamation forbade settlers from encroaching on Indigenous lands. Citing "great Frauds and Abuses [having] been committed in purchasing Lands of the Indians, to the great prejudice of our Interests, and to the great dissatisfaction of the said Indians," it describes the terms under which land could be acquired:

[I]f at any Time any of the Said Indians should be inclined to dispose of the said Lands, the same shall be Purchased only for Us, in our Name, at some public Meeting or Assembly of the said Indians, to be held for that Purpose. ...

The Proclamation set out the following core principle for how the British settlers and Colonial government were to respect Indigenous land rights:

[I]t is just and reasonable, and essential to our Interest and the Security of our Colonies, that the several Nations or Tribes of Indians with whom We are connected, and who live under our Protection, not be molested or disturbed in the Possession of such parts of Our Dominions and Territories as, not having been ceded to or purchased by Us, are reserved to them ... as their Hunting Grounds.

Colonial governments were also charged with negotiating treaties. These formal agreements were to establish terms with Indigenous governing bodies or representatives for their shared presence on the land. The Royal Proclamation, with its core commitment that the British would not encroach on land that was not ceded or sold, was formally ratified as a Treaty in Niagara in 1764, when representatives from 24 Indigenous communities negotiated and reached agreement with British representatives on its terms. Many of the early treaties, entered into in the 1700s, were similarly of peace and friendship. The core obligations of these treaties were terms such as the Mi'kmaq signatories not entering into military alliances or engaging in trade with the French, and the British preventing their settlers from interfering with the Mi'kmaq. Treaties in the Prairie provinces were entered into much later, and are of a different character. They contain specific terms relating, for example, to acceptable purposes for which land would be used or taken up by the settlers, promises to not interfere with Indigenous hunting practices, and the Europeans providing the Indigenous signatories with certain goods. Many Indigenous peoples did not enter into a historic treaty, especially on the West Coast and in the North. Where treaties were signed, it generally resulted in Europeans being able to establish settlements peacefully. This, in turn, facilitated core colonial projects such as building a railway that would span the country.

The pre-existing Indigenous legal systems sometimes came into direct contact with the settlers' legal system. During the early contact period there were several reported instances of Canadian courts being asked to consider the consequences of a local Indigenous legal system for the colonial legal system.

For example, in *Connolly v Woolrich* (1867), 17 RJRQ 75, a court in Quebec was asked whether a marriage between an Indigenous woman and a non-Indigenous man that was recognized under Cree law was valid for the purposes of colonial inheritance legislation. The practices evidencing the marriage would not be sufficient if the "Common law of England" prevailed. Justice Monk wrote:

> [W]ill it be contended that the territorial rights, political organization, such as it was, or the laws and usages of the Indian tribes were abrogated, that they ceased to exist, when these two European nations began to trade with the aboriginal occupants. In my opinion, it is beyond controversy that they did not, that so far from being abolished, they were left in full force, and were not even modified in the slightest degree, in regard to the civil rights of the natives.

There was thus an explicit recognition of Indigenous and non-Indigenous legal systems operating concurrently in the year that the *British North America Act* ((UK), 30 & 31 Vict, c 3) was enacted. (There are also more recent examples of long-standing Indigenous laws being recognized in Canadian courts, mostly in the areas of marriage and family relations, but with implications for a variety of issues such as interpreting terms regarding beneficiaries in insurance policies. See Borrows, *Canada's Indigenous Constitution* at 52-53.)

B. THE SUPPRESSION OF INDIGENOUS GOVERNANCE AUTHORITY AND PRACTICES

With the influx of settlers, the establishment of sizable British communities, and massive population losses within many Indigenous communities arising from introduced diseases and disruptions to key food sources, Indigenous law and governance systems began to be eroded in many instances. Given this practical shift in power, in the Prairie provinces the "Crown adjusted the treaty process to compel Aboriginal relocation, assimilation, and dispossession of Aboriginal ancestral territory" and pushed communities toward small "reserved" tracts of land. See Jennifer Dalton, "Aboriginal Title and Self-Government in Canada: What Is the True Scope of Comprehensive Land Claims Agreements?" (2006) 22 Windsor Rev Legal Soc Issues 29.

Racist sentiment, cultivated by the eugenic theories of racial superiority that emerged in the late 1800s, informed colonial policy. The Canadian government was determined to assimilate the Indigenous population into the general non-Indigenous population. Eugenic evolutionary theory supported the practice of isolating and thus purportedly "protecting" Indigenous peoples until they were assimilated into "white" culture, with the "protections" also serving the purpose of dispossessing Indigenous peoples from their lands. For a discussion of how evolution theory shaped and continues to shape laws and policies, see C MacIntosh, "From Judging Culture to Taxing 'Indians': Tracing the Legal Discourse of the 'Indian Mode of Life'" (2009) 47 Osgoode Hall LJ 399 at 406.

A federal statute—the *Indian Act*—was drafted to advance these goals of "protection" and assimilation. The Act precluded persons who were not registered as members of the community (or "Band") from living on reserved land, while restricting mobility rights. It also imposed a foreign and limiting governmental regime on reserve-based Indigenous communities, the Band Council system, which both denied women leadership roles and replaced diverse culturally grounded governance models with a singular municipal-style practice. Indigenous land and governance rights, other than the right to reside on reserved land, and to exercise powers authorized by the *Indian Act*, disappeared from the dominant discourse.

In *R v Sparrow*, [1990] 1 SCR 1075, the Supreme Court commented on the sea change (at para 50):

> For many years, the rights of the Indians to their aboriginal lands—certainly as *legal* rights— were virtually ignored. ... For fifty years after the publication of Clement's *The Law of the Canadian Constitution* (3rd ed. 1916), there was a virtual absence of discussion of any kind of Indian rights to land even in academic literature. By the late 1960s, aboriginal claims were not even recognized by the federal government as having any legal status. Thus the *Statement of the Government of Canada on Indian Policy* (1969), although well meaning, contained the assertion (at p. 11) that "aboriginal claims to land ... are so general and undefined that it is not realistic to think of them as specific claims capable of remedy except through a policy and program that will end injustice to the Indians as members of the Canadian community."

Treaty promises also began to have their enforceability questioned. For example, in the 1928 *R v Syliboy* case, the Grand Chief of the Mi'kmaq was charged with having violated provincial hunting legislation. Grand Chief Syliboy argued that a 1752 Treaty of Peace and Friendship prevented provincial legislation from applying to his activities, due to the promise that "the said Tribe of Indians shall not be hindered from but have free liberty to hunt and fish as usual." The judge convicted the Grand Chief, having found that the 1752 agreement "is not a treaty at all" because the Mi'kmaq did not have the status to enter into treaties in the first place. Justice Patterson's words were at striking odds with those spoken by Monk J in *Woolrich*, quoted above, just 61 years earlier. After first asserting that "[t]reaties are unconstrained Acts of independent powers," Patterson J wrote:

> But the Indians were never regarded as an independent power. A civilized nation first discovering a country of uncivilized people or savages held such country as its own until such time as by treaty it was transferred to some other civilized nation. The savages' rights of sovereignty even of ownership were never recognized. Nova Scotia had passed to Great Britain not by gift or purchase from or even by conquest of the Indians but by treaty with France, which had acquired it by priority of discovery and ancient possession; and the Indians passed with it.

• • •

> Having called the agreement a treaty, and having perhaps lulled the Indians into believing it to be a treaty with all the sacredness of a treaty attached to it, it may be the Crown should

not now be heard to say it is not a treaty. With that I have nothing to do. That is a matter for representations to the proper authorities—representations which if there is nothing else in the way of the Indians could hardly fail to be successful.

(*R v Syliboy* (1928), 50 CCC 389 at paras 22 and 26 (NS Co Ct).)

As discussed below, this view has been soundly rejected by more recent court decisions, and historic treaties are constitutionalized and so a part of contemporary constitutional juris- prudence. However, before this shift, Indigenous peoples suffered many indignities. One of these indignities was the forced attendance of Indigenous children at Indian Residential Schools so as to enable assimilation. The Prime Minister of Canada provided a formal apology in 2007, excerpted below.

Aboriginal and Northern Affairs Canada, Statement of Apology—to Former Students of Indian Residential Schools

(11 June 2008), online: *Aboriginal and Northern Affairs Canada*
<https://www.aadnc-aandc.gc.ca/DAM/DAM-INTER-HQ/STAGING/texte
-text/rqpi_apo_pdf_1322167347706_eng.pdf>

For more than a century, Indian Residential Schools separated over 150,000 Aborig- inal children from their families and communities. ... Two primary objectives of the Residential Schools system were to remove and isolate children from the influence of their homes, families, traditions and cultures, and to assimilate them into the dominant culture. These objectives were based on the assumption Aboriginal cul- tures and spiritual beliefs were inferior and unequal. Indeed, some sought, as it was infamously said, "to kill the Indian in the child." Today, we recognize that this policy of assimilation was wrong, has caused great harm, and has no place in our country.

... The Government of Canada built an educational system in which very young children were often forcibly removed from their homes, often taken far from their communities. Many were inadequately fed, clothed and housed. All were deprived of the care and nurturing of their parents, grandparents and communities. First Nations, Inuit and Métis languages and cultural practices were prohibited in these schools. Tragically, some of these children died while attending residential schools and others never returned home.

• • •

To the approximately 80,000 living former students, and all family members and communities, the Government of Canada now recognizes that it was wrong to forc- ibly remove children from their homes and we apologize for having done this. We now recognize that it was wrong to separate children from rich and vibrant cultures and traditions that it created a void in many lives and communities, and we apolo- gize for having done this. ...

The burden of this experience has been on your shoulders for far too long. The burden is properly ours as a Government, and as a country. There is no place in Canada for the attitudes that inspired the Indian Residential Schools system to ever prevail again. You have been working on recovering from this experience for a long time and in a very real sense, we are now joining you on this journey. The Govern- ment of Canada sincerely apologizes and asks the forgiveness of the Aboriginal peoples of this country for failing them so profoundly.

This apology was offered by the federal government as part of the Settlement Agreement. Another key part of the Settlement Agreement was the creation of the Indian Residential Schools Truth and Reconciliation Commission, which supported a variety of truth-telling initiatives while gathering documentation from Indigenous peoples across the country. Its final report, released in 2015, included 94 Calls to Action to enable reconciliation. The Commission offered the following caution:

> The Indian Residential Schools Settlement Agreement, including the creation of the Truth and Reconciliation Commission of Canada, was an attempt to resolve the thousands of lawsuits brought against the government for cases of historical abuse. Its implementation has also been challenging. Canada and the churches have made apologies to Survivors, their families, and communities. Yet, Canadian government actions continue to be unilateral and divisive, and Aboriginal peoples continue to resist such actions. Negotiations on Treaties and land-claims agreements continue with a view to reconciling Aboriginal title and rights with Crown sovereignty. However, many cases remain unresolved. The courts have produced a body of law on reconciliation in relation to Aboriginal rights, which has established some parameters for discussion and negotiations, but there remains no ongoing national process or entity to guide that discussion. What is clear to this Commission is that Aboriginal peoples and the Crown have very different and conflicting views on what reconciliation is and how it is best achieved. The Government of Canada appears to believe that reconciliation entails Aboriginal peoples' acceptance of the reality and validity of Crown sovereignty and parliamentary supremacy, in order to allow the government to get on with business. Aboriginal people, on the other hand, see reconciliation as an opportunity to affirm their own sovereignty and return to the "partnership" ambitions they held after Confederation.

(Truth and Reconciliation Commission, Honouring the Truth, Reconciling for the Future, Summary of the Final Report of the Truth and Reconciliation Commission of Canada (2015) at 187.)

C. THE TURN TO THE JUDICIAL AFFIRMATION OF INDIGENOUS LEGAL RIGHTS

Despite the explicit efforts to suppress and assimilate Indigenous peoples through the period described above, Indigenous peoples persisted in asserting the sanctity of the treaties, and also that the mere arrival of settlers and colonial governments did not displace their laws or right to self-govern. An important decision for treaties was *R v White and Bob*, [1964] 50 DLR (2d) 613 (BCCA). At issue was whether an agreement, signed by colonial representatives and several Indigenous communities in 1854, was a treaty. In a concurring set of reasons, Norris JA wrote the following (at para 104):

> "Treaty" is not a word of art and in my respectful opinion, it embraces all such engagements made by persons in authority as may be brought within the term "the word of the white man" the sanctity of which was, at the time of British exploration and settlement, the most important means of obtaining the goodwill and co-operation of the native tribes and ensuring that the colonists would be protected from death and destruction. On such assurance the Indians relied. ... The unusual (by the standards of legal draftsmen) nature and form of the document ... does not detract from it as being a "Treaty."

The Supreme Court of Canada acknowledged Indigenous people's continuing legal rights in land in 1973. In *Calder v Attorney-General of British Columbia*, [1973] SCR 313 at 328, the Court was asked to consider whether Indigenous interests in land had persisted. They noted: "the fact is that when the settlers came, the Indians were there, organized in societies and occupying the land as their forefathers had done for centuries" and found that this fact had legal consequences. Justice Hall wrote:

Once aboriginal title [or rights in land] is established, it is presumed to continue until the contrary is proven. When the Nishga people came under British sovereignty they were entitled to assert, as a legal right, their Indian title. It being a legal right, it could not thereafter be extinguished except by surrender to the Crown or by competent legislative authority, and then only by specific legislation. There was no surrender by the Nishgas and neither the Colony of British Columbia nor the Province, after Confederation, enacted legislation specifically purporting to extinguish the Indian title nor did the Parliament of Canada.

Justice Hall further found that the Nisga'a's title rights were part of "the guarantee of the Indian rights contained in the [Royal] Proclamation of 1763" and described the Royal Proclamation as having a force in Canada that "is analogous to the status of the Magna Carta." Indigenous legal rights were once again recognized as existing, as a matter of law, by Canadian courts.

IV. SECTION 35 OF THE CONSTITUTION ACT AND THE DOCTRINE OF RECONCILIATION

A. THE CONSTITUTIONALIZATION OF ABORIGINAL AND TREATY RIGHTS

Following an extensive and international advocacy campaign, the rights of Indigenous peoples were entrenched in the *Constitution Act, 1982,* being Schedule B to the *Canada Act 1982* (UK), 1982, c 11. Section 35 "recognizes and affirms the existing aboriginal and treaty rights of the aboriginal peoples of Canada," and defines the "aboriginal" peoples as including Métis, Indian, and Inuit. One effect of these rights having constitutional recognition is that they cannot be extinguished by legislative action. The significance of s 35 for public law is dramatic. As Wayne MacKay observed, the enactment of s 35 meant that "within the written constitutional texts there are now three interacting silos of the Constitution—federalism or division or powers, the Charter of Rights and Aboriginal rights." Wayne MacKay, "Evolving Fundamental Principles and Merging Public Law Silos: The Reshaping of Canada's Constitutional Landscape" (2013) 61 SCLR (2nd) 83 at para 25.

Section 35 has supported the recognition of Indigenous peoples' rights and interests as part of the rule of law in Canada. The Supreme Court of Canada's first decision about this provision was *R v Sparrow.* Musqueam fishers had been charged with violating provincial fishing regulations. They claimed that the constitutionalization of their legal rights in s 35 shielded the fishing practices from provincial law. In the extract below, the Court describes the context for s 35's enactment and also identifies its own expectations for what s 35 will do.

R v Sparrow
[1990] 1 SCR 1075

DICKSON CJ and LA FOREST J:

[53] ... [Section] 35(1) of the *Constitution Act, 1982,* represents the culmination of a long and difficult struggle in both the political forum and the courts for the constitutional recognition of aboriginal rights. The strong representations of native associations and other groups concerned with the welfare of Canada's aboriginal peoples made the adoption of s. 35(1) possible and it is important to note that the provision applies to the Indians, the Inuit and the Métis. Section 35(1), at the least, provides a solid constitutional base upon which subsequent negotiations can take place. It also affords aboriginal peoples constitutional protection against provincial legislative power. ...

[54] In our opinion, the significance of s. 35(1) extends beyond these fundamental effects. Professor Lyon in "An Essay on Constitutional Interpretation" (1988),
26 Osgoode Hall L.J. 95, says the following about s. 35(1), at p. 100:

> ... the context of 1982 is surely enough to tell us that this is not just a codification
> of the case law on aboriginal rights that had accumulated by 1982. Section 35 calls
> for a just settlement for aboriginal peoples. It renounces the old rules of the game
> under which the Crown established courts of law and denied those courts the
> authority to question sovereign claims made by the Crown.

B. ABORIGINAL RIGHTS AND RESTRAINTS ON STATE POWER

In the *Sparrow* decision, the Supreme Court of Canada also considered how the constitutionalization of Aboriginal rights affected the power of the state to enact laws or make decisions that
would otherwise be presumed to be within its discretion given the division of powers within the
Constitution Act, 1867 (UK), 30 & 31 Vict, c 3, reprinted in RSC 1985, Appendix II, No 5.

R v Sparrow
[1990] 1 SCR 1075

[62] There is no explicit language in the provision that authorizes this Court
or any court to assess the legitimacy of any government legislation that restricts
aboriginal rights. Yet, we find that the words "recognition and affirmation" incorporate the fiduciary relationship referred to earlier and so import some restraint
on the exercise of sovereign power. Rights that are recognized and affirmed are
not absolute. Federal legislative powers continue, including, of course, the right to
legislate with respect to Indians pursuant to s. 91(24) of the *Constitution Act, 1867.*
These powers must, however, now be read together with s. 35(1). In other words,
federal power must be reconciled with federal duty and the best way to achieve
that reconciliation is to demand the justification of any government regulation that
infringes upon or denies aboriginal rights.

• • •

[64] ... Implicit in this constitutional scheme is the obligation of the legislature to satisfy the test of justification. The way in which a legislative objective is
to be attained must uphold the honour of the Crown and must be in keeping with
the unique contemporary relationship, grounded in history and policy, between the
Crown and Canada's aboriginal peoples. The extent of legislative or regulatory
impact on an existing aboriginal right may be scrutinized so as to ensure recognition and affirmation.

[65] The constitutional recognition afforded by the provision therefore gives
a measure of control over government conduct and a strong check on legislative
power. While it does not promise immunity from government regulation in a society that, in the twentieth century, is increasingly more complex, interdependent
and sophisticated, and where exhaustible resources need protection and management, it does hold the Crown to a substantive promise. The government is required
to bear the burden of justifying any legislation that has some negative effect on any
aboriginal right protected under s. 35(1).

[The Court then identified what has come to be known as "the *Sparrow* test," which
is used to determine whether a state action is rendered unconstitutional as a result

of unjustifiably infringing on a s 35 right. The first issue is to determine whether, on a *prima facie* basis, the legislation interferes with an existing Aboriginal right. If so, a *prima facie* infringement is made out, and the Crown bears the burden of justifying the infringement. On these matters, the Court wrote:]

[70] To determine whether ... rights have been interfered with such as to consti-tute a *prima facie* infringement of s. 35(1), certain questions must be asked. First, is the limitation unreasonable? Second, does the regulation impose undue hardship? Third, does the regulation deny to the holders of the right their preferred means of exercising that right? The onus of proving a *prima facie* infringement lies on the individual or group challenging the legislation. ...

[71] If a *prima facie* interference is found, the analysis moves to the issue of justification. ... The justification analysis would proceed as follows. First, is there a valid legislative objective? Here the court would inquire into whether the objective of Parliament in authorizing the department to enact regulations ... is valid. The objective of the department in setting out the particular regulations would also be scrutinized. An objective aimed at preserving s. 35(1) rights by conserving and man-aging a natural resource, for example, would be valid. Also valid would be objectives purporting to prevent the exercise of s. 35(1) rights that would cause harm to the general populace or to aboriginal peoples themselves, or other objectives found to be compelling and substantial.

• • •

[75] If a valid legislative objective is found, the analysis proceeds to the second part of the justification issue. Here, we refer back to the guiding interpretive princi-ple [that] ... the honour of the Crown is at stake in dealings with Aboriginal peoples. The special trust relationship and the responsibility of the government vis-à-vis Aboriginals must be the first consideration in determining whether the legislation or action in question can be justified.

• • •

[82] Within the analysis of justification, there are further questions to be addressed, depending on the circumstances of the inquiry. These include the ques-tions of whether there has been as little infringement as possible in order to effect the desired result; whether, in a situation of expropriation, fair compensation is available; and, whether the aboriginal group in question has been consulted with respect to the conservation measures being implemented. ...

As discussed below, this judge-made test for an infringement being justified, and therefore lawful, has been modified where title rights are at issue.

C. THE VAN DER PEET TEST

Aboriginal rights were given further definition in *R v Van der Peet*, [1996] 2 SCR 507, where the Supreme Court of Canada articulated a specific test for identifying whether something constituted an Aboriginal right for the purpose of attracting constitutionalized protection. The court took a purposeful approach, observing that "s. 35(1) did not create the legal doctrine of aboriginal rights; aboriginal rights existed and were recognized under the common law" (para 28), and went on to state:

[31] More specifically, what s. 35(1) does is provide the constitutional framework through which the fact that aboriginals lived on the land in distinctive societies, with their own practices, tradi-tions and cultures, is acknowledged and reconciled with the sovereignty of the Crown.

The substantive rights which fall within the provision must be defined in light of this purpose; the aboriginal rights recognized and affirmed by s. 35(1) must be directed towards the reconciliation of the pre-existence of aboriginal societies with the sovereignty of the Crown.

The Court articulated the following test for identifying Aboriginal rights: "in order to be an aboriginal right an activity must be an element of a practice, custom or tradition integral to the distinctive culture of the aboriginal group claiming the right" (at para 46). The Court stated that the pre-contact period is to be looked to when assessing whether the test is met (at para 60).

The *Van der Peet* test was and remains controversial. Some critiques were acknowledged in *R v Sappier; R v Gray*, below. The case concerned whether Mi'kmaq and Maliseet defendants had an Aboriginal right to cut timber on provincial Crown lands, without provincial authorization.

R v Sappier; R v Gray
2006 SCC 54, [2006] SCR 686

BASTARACHE J:

[20] In order to be an aboriginal right, an activity must be an element of a practice, custom or tradition integral to the distinctive culture of the aboriginal group claiming the right: *R. v. Van der Peet*, [1996] 2 S.C.R. 507, at para. 46. The first step is to identify the precise nature of the applicant's claim of having exercised an aboriginal right: *Van der Peet*, at para. 76. In so doing, a court should consider such factors as the nature of the action which the applicant is claiming was done pursuant to an aboriginal right, the nature of the governmental regulation, statute or action being impugned, and the practice, custom or tradition being relied upon to establish the right: *Van der Peet*, at para. 53. In this case, the respondents were charged with the unlawful cutting and possession of Crown timber. They claimed an aboriginal right to harvest timber for personal use so as a defence to those charges. The statute at issue prohibits the unauthorized cutting, damaging, removing and possession of timber from Crown lands. The respondents rely on the pre-contact practice of harvesting timber in order to establish their aboriginal right.

• • •

[22] ... [I]n order to grasp the importance of a resource to a particular aboriginal people, the Court seeks to understand how that resource was harvested, extracted and utilized. These practices are the necessary "aboriginal" component in aboriginal rights. As Lamer C.J. explained in *Van der Peet*, at para. 20:

> The task of this Court is to define aboriginal rights in a manner which recognizes that aboriginal *rights* are rights but which does so without losing sight of the fact that they are rights held by aboriginal people because they are *aboriginal*. The Court must neither lose sight of the generalized constitutional status of what s. 35(1) protects, nor can it ignore the necessary specificity which comes from granting special constitutional protection to one part of Canadian society. The Court must define the scope of s. 35(1) in a way which captures both the aboriginal and the rights in aboriginal rights. [Emphasis in original.]

Section 35 of the *Constitution Act, 1982* seeks to provide a constitutional framework for the protection of the distinctive cultures of aboriginal peoples, so that their prior occupation of North America can be recognized and reconciled with the sovereignty of the Crown: see, *Van der Peet*, at para. 31. In an oft-quoted passage, Lamer

C.J. acknowledged in *Van der Peet*, at para. 30, that, "the doctrine of aboriginal rights exists, and is recognized and affirmed by s. 35(1), because of one simple fact: when Europeans arrived in North America, aboriginal peoples were already here, living in communities on the land, and participating in distinctive cultures, as they had done for centuries" (emphasis in original deleted). ...

• • •

[40] ... the purpose of this exercise is to understand the way of life of the particular aboriginal society, pre-contact, and to determine how the claimed right relates to it. This is achieved by founding the claim on a pre-contact practice, and determining whether that practice was integral to the distinctive culture of the aboriginal people in question, pre-contact. Section 35 seeks to protect integral elements of the way of life of these aboriginal societies, including their traditional means of survival. ...

• • •

[42] This brings us to the question of what is meant by "distinctive culture." ... Lamer C.J. spoke of the "necessary specificity which comes from granting special constitutional protection to one part of Canadian society" (para. 20). It is that aboriginal specificity which the notion of a "distinctive culture" seeks to capture. However, it is clear that "Aboriginality means more than interesting cultural practices and anthropological curiosities worthy only of a museum" (C.C. Cheng, "Touring the Museum: A Comment on *R. v. Van der Peet*" (1997), 55 U.T. Fac. L. Rev. 419, at para. 34). R.L. Barsh and J. Youngblood Henderson argue that as a result of the *Van der Peet* decision, "culture" has implicitly been taken to mean a fixed inventory of traits or characteristics" ("The Supreme Court's *Van der Peet* Trilogy: Naive Imperialism and Ropes of Sand" (1997), 42 McGill L.J. 993, at p. 1002).

• • •

[45] The aboriginal rights doctrine, which has been constitutionalized by s. 35, arises from the simple fact of prior occupation of the lands now forming Canada. The "integral to a distinctive culture" test must necessarily be understood in this context. As L'Heureux-Dubé J. explained in dissent in Van der Peet, "[t]he 'distinctive aboriginal culture' must be taken to refer to the reality that, despite British sovereignty, aboriginal people were the original organized society occupying and using Canadian lands: *Calder v. Attorney-General of British Columbia, supra*, at p. 328, *per* Judson J., and *Guerin*, [1984] 2 S.C.R. 335, ... at p. 379, per Dickson J. (as he then was)" (para. 159). The focus of the Court should therefore be on the nature of this prior occupation. What is meant by "culture" is really an inquiry into the pre-contact way of life of a particular aboriginal community, including their means of survival, their socialization methods, their legal systems, and, potentially, their trading habits. The use of the word "distinctive" as a qualifier is meant to incorporate an element of Aboriginal specificity. ...

• • •

[48] ... the nature of the right must be determined in light of present day circumstances. As McLachlin C.J. explained in *R. v. Marshall*, [2005] 2 S.C.R. 220, 2005 SCC 43, at para. 25, "[l]ogical evolution means the same sort of activity, carried on in the modern economy by modern means." It is the practice, along with its associated uses, which must be allowed to evolve. The right to harvest wood for the construction of temporary shelters must be allowed to evolve into a right to harvest wood by modern means to be used in the construction of a modern dwelling. Any other conclusion would freeze the right in its pre-contact form.

D. SECTION 35 AND INDIGENOUS LAWS

Some s 35 cases have also discussed the status of Indigenous laws within the Canadian legal order. For example, in *Mitchell v MNR*, 2001 SCC 33, [2001] 1 SCR 911, McLachlin CJ wrote (at para 10):

> European settlement did not terminate the interests of aboriginal peoples arising from their historic occupation and use of the land. To the contrary, aboriginal interests and customary laws were presumed to survive the assertion of sovereignty, and were absorbed into the common law as rights.

McLachlin CJ identified three exceptions to Indigenous interests and laws continuing. These were if: "(1) they were incompatible with the Crown's assertion of sovereignty, (2) they were surrendered voluntarily through the treaty process, or (3) the government extinguished them" prior to the enactment of s 35.

Indigenous scholar John Borrows provides a detailed analysis of *Mitchell* in "Creating an Indigenous Legal Community" (2005) 50 McGill LJ 153. Borrows finds that many Indigenous laws pass Chief Justice McLachlin's test, and so presumptively continue to have force as part of the common law. He writes: "[M]ost Indigenous legal traditions, in my view, are compatible with the Crown's assertion of sovereignty. There is a wide degree of place for interaction and intertwining of indigenous legal values and the values found in the common law and in the civil law" (at para 27). Borrows then goes to state that Indigenous law "is more than just private or Aboriginal community law. Indigenous law is also a part of Canada's constitutional structure. Indigenous legal traditions shape and are embedded within our national legal structure" (at para 28). Borrows provides a series of examples to support his conclusions, including observing how both Indigenous and non-Indigenous peoples have rights under treaties and are recipients of the promises made during the treaty process, and that many of the core treaty rights recognized under treaties are grants of rights from First Nations to the settlers (at para 36).

There is growing research and literature on Indigenous laws regarding how they are part of the contemporary legal and constitutional structure of Canada. For example, the Accessing Justice and Reconciliation Project's goals centre around identifying and articulating the laws of various Indigenous communities. (See e.g. Indigenous Law Research Unit, *Revitalizing Indigenous Law and Changing the Lawscape of Canada* (2014). The project's final report is available online: *Indigenous Bar Association* <http://indigenousbar.ca/indigenouslaw/wp-content/uploads/2013/04/iba_ajr_final_report.pdf>.) There is also a body of work on the practical questions that arise when applying Indigenous law, as well as a literature that asks how state decision-making processes change when informed by Indigenous law. (See e.g. example, Hadley Friedland, "Reflective Frameworks: Methods for Accessing, Understanding and Applying Indigenous Laws" (2013) 11:1 Indigenous LJ 1; Grace Nosek, "Re-Imagining Indigenous People's Role in Natural Resource Development Decision Making: Implementing Free, Prior and Informed Consent in Canada through Indigenous Legal Traditions" (2017) 50 UBC L Rev 90.)

E. SECTION 35 AND MÉTIS RIGHTS

The instances of litigation described above all involved First Nations people. However, s 35 of the *Constitution Act, 1982* also acknowledges and recognizes the Aboriginal rights of Métis people. The Supreme Court of Canada heard its first case on Métis rights in *R v Powley*, 2003

SCC 43, [2003] 2 SCR 207. In this decision, the Court provided the following explanation for the purpose of constitutionalizing the rights of Métis people in s 35 (at para 17):

> [T]he inclusion of the Métis in s. 35 is not traceable to their pre-contact occupation of Canadian territory. The purpose of s. 35 as it relates to the Métis is therefore different from that which relates to the Indians or the Inuit. The constitutionally significant feature of the Métis is their special status as peoples that emerged between first contact and the effective imposition of European control. The inclusion of the Métis in s. 35 represents Canada's commitment to recognize and value the distinctive Métis cultures, which grew up in areas not yet open to colonization, and which the framers of the *Constitution Act, 1982* recognized can only survive if the Métis are protected along with other aboriginal communities.

However, the Court was clear that the "term 'Métis' does not encompass all individuals with mixed Indian and European heritage" (at para 10). The Court explains:

> [I]t refers to distinctive peoples who, in addition to their mixed ancestry, developed their own customs, way of life, and recognizable group identity separate from their Indian or Inuit and European forebears. Métis communities evolved and flourished prior to the entrenchment of European control, when the influence of European settlers and political institutions became pre-eminent.

Based on this assessment, the Court identified a test for determining whether an individual is Métis for the purpose of asserting s 35 rights. The *Powley* test requires the claimant, after identifying the alleged right, to next establish that there was a historic rights-bearing Métis community that was formed after contact but before effective European control in the area, with "shared customs, traditions, and a collective identity" (at para 23) and that this historic community has continuity with a contemporary Métis community. In articulating this element of the test, the Court noted that because of racism and government actions, Métis communities may have gone "underground" and lacked public visibility, but this did not mean that the community ceased to exist (at para 27). Finally, the claimant must show membership in the contemporary community, with membership made out with reference to self-identification, an ancestral connection to the historic community, and acceptance by the modern community as a member. The Court articulated criteria for community acceptance as being "past and ongoing participation in a shared culture, in the customs and traditions that constitute a Métis community's identity" (at para 33).

The *Powley* decision was greeted with excitement by many Métis people. However, in the years following, that excitement diminished. Although many provinces had modified laws and regulations to recognize the rights of First Nations people, Jean Teillet argues that provinces had failed to make such changes for Métis people, and that attempts to negotiate agreements for how s 35 Métis rights would be exercised had not been treated in good faith by provincial governments. See Jean Teillet, "The Métis and Thirty Years of Section 35: How Constitutional Protection for Métis Rights Has Led to the Loss of the Rule of Law" (2012) 58 SCLR (2nd) 333.

Changes to this state of affairs have been prompted by two Supreme Court of Canada decisions, *Manitoba Metis Federation Inc v Canada (AG)*, 2013 SCC 14, [2013] 1 SCR 623 and *Daniels v Canada (Indian Affairs and Northern Development)*, 2016 SCC 12, [2016] 1 SCR 99. These decisions confirmed federal obligations to Métis people, and also identified how the federal Crown had failed in its historic constitutionalized promises to Métis people, such as those made when Manitoba joined Confederation. This has led to flurry of negotiations and agreements. For example, in 2018, the Métis Nation of Alberta concluded a consultation agreement with Canada and in 2019 signed off on a Métis Self-Government Agreement with Canada.

F. TREATY RIGHTS

Section 35 of the *Constitution Act, 1982* recognizes and affirms not just Aboriginal rights, but also treaty rights. The approach that was adopted in *Syliboy* in 1927 has been rejected. A considerable body of jurisprudence has formed on the proper approach to treaties, and their place within the Canadian constitutional order. Some of the core interpretive principles for interpreting treaty terms were described in *R v Badger*, [1996] 1 SCR 771 at 793-94. They include:

> First, it must be remembered that a treaty represents an exchange of solemn promises between the Crown and the various Indian nations. It is an agreement whose nature is sacred. ... Second, the honour of the Crown is always at stake in its dealing with Indian people. ... It is always assumed that the Crown intends to fulfil its promises. No appearance of "sharp dealing" will be sanctioned. ... Third, any ambiguities or doubtful expressions in the wording of the treaty or document must be resolved in favour of the Indians. A corollary to this principle is that any limitations which restrict the rights of Indians under treaties must be narrowly construed. ... Fourth, the onus of proving that a treaty or aboriginal right has been extinguished lies upon the Crown. There must be "strict proof of the fact of extinguishment" and evidence of a clear and plain intention on the part of the government to extinguish treaty rights.

Revisiting these principles in *R v Marshall*, [1999] 3 SCR 456, the Court emphasized that "where a treaty was concluded verbally and afterwards written up by representatives of the Crown, it would be unconscionable for the Crown to ignore the oral terms while relying on the written terms ..." (at para 12). (For a summary list of the principles of treaty interpretation, see *R v Marshall*, above at para 78.) Commenting on these principles, Bradford Morse observes that "the written document merely becomes one more piece of evidence in clarifying the true agreement that was reached among the parties." (Bradford Morse, "Aboriginal and Treaty Rights in Canada" (2013) 62 SCLR (2nd) 569 at para 78.)

In *Mikisew Cree First Nation v Canada (Minister of Canadian Heritage)*, 2005 SCC 69, [2005] 3 SCR 388, Binnie J further elaborated that treaties are to be interpreted in light of treaty negotiations being "an important stage in the long process of reconciliation, but it is only a stage" (at para 54). Thus, in *Grassy Narrows First Nation v Ontario (Natural Resources)*, 2014 SCC 48, [2014] 2 SCR 447 the Court found the exercise of express and contemplated Crown rights under a treaty may require ongoing consultation, and be limited by potential impacts on the Indigenous signatory's treaty rights (at paras 50-52).

G. THE HONOUR OF THE CROWN

Shortly before the *Sappier* decision was released, the Supreme Court of Canada delivered a decision that significantly changed the law of Indigenous–state relations. It focused on some aspects of the justification test that was first articulated in *Sparrow*—in particular, the Court's pronouncement that the "honour of the Crown is always present" in Crown–Indigenous relations, as well as the Court having noted that in assessing whether an infringement is justified, the Court should consider whether the Crown consulted with the Aboriginal people in question (at para 88). In *Haida Nation v British Columbia (Minister of Forests)*, 2004 SCC 73, [2004] 3 SCR 511, the Indigenous claimants argued, successfully, that the honour of the Crown required the Crown to consult with potentially affected Indigenous communities when considering authorizing an action that could affect a known, or likely to be proven, Aboriginal right. That is, the duty arises before rights are proven. The Court wrote (at para 33):

> To limit reconciliation to the post-proof sphere risks treating reconciliation as a distant legalistic goal, devoid of the "meaningful content" mandated by the "solemn commitment" made by the Crown in recognizing and affirming Aboriginal rights and title: *Sparrow, supra*, at p. 1108. It also risks unfortunate consequences when the distant goal of proof is finally

reached, the Aboriginal peoples may find their land and resources changed and denuded. This is not reconciliation. Nor is it honourable.

The scope of the obligation to consult was identified as varying, in response to the strength of the claim that a right is present, and the nature of the potential adverse impact. The *Haida* decision fundamentally altered the analysis of whether Crown behaviour complies with the rule of law, by its focus on how the Crown is to approach decision-making processes if it knows or ought to know that Aboriginal interests may be present and may be affected.

There has been considerable jurisprudence since the *Haida* decision about what sorts of obligations are triggered by the honour of the Crown. One key case is *Manitoba Metis Federation Inc v Canada (AG)*. The Court explains the concept of the honour of the Crown, and how it infuses different aspects of the constitutional and public law relationship between Indigenous people and the Canadian state, in the excerpt below. When reading this extract, consider what it means that in 1996, in *Van der Peet*, the Court referred to "the Crown's sovereignty," while in *Manitoba Metis Federation* (and *Haida Nation*) the Court makes reference to "the Crown's assertion of sovereignty."

Manitoba Metis Federation Inc v Canada (AG)
2013 SCC 14, [2013] 1 SCR 623

McLACHLIN CJ and KARAKATSANIS J (LeBel, Fish, Abella, and Cromwell JJ concurring):

[66] The honour of the Crown arises "from the Crown's assertion of sovereignty over an Aboriginal people and *de facto* control of land and resources that were formerly in the control of that people": *Haida Nation*, at para. 32. In Aboriginal law, the honour of the Crown goes back to the *Royal Proclamation* of 1763, which made reference to "the several Nations or Tribes of Indians with whom We are connected, and who live under our Protection" ... . This "Protection," though, did not arise from a paternalistic desire to protect the Aboriginal peoples; rather, it was a recognition of their strength. Nor is the honour of the Crown a paternalistic concept. The comments of Brian Slattery with respect to fiduciary duty resonate here:

> The sources of the general fiduciary duty do not lie, then, in a paternalistic concern to protect a "weaker" or "primitive" people, as has sometimes been suggested, but rather in the necessity of persuading native peoples, at a time when they still had considerable military capacities, that their rights would be better protected by reliance on the Crown than by self-help.

("Understanding Aboriginal Rights" (1987), 66 Can. Bar Rev. 727, at p. 753)

The ultimate purpose of the honour of the Crown is the reconciliation of preexisting Aboriginal societies with the assertion of Crown sovereignty. As stated in *Taku River Tlingit First Nation v. British Columbia (Project Assessment Director)*, 2004 SCC 74 ... at para. 24:

> The duty of honour derives from the Crown's assertion of sovereignty in the face of prior Aboriginal occupation. It has been enshrined in s. 35(1) of the *Constitution Act, 1982*, which recognizes and affirms existing Aboriginal rights and titles. Section 35(1) has, as one of its purposes, negotiation of just settlement of Aboriginal claims. In all its dealings with Aboriginal peoples, the Crown must act honourably, in accordance with its historical and future relationship with the Aboriginal peoples in question.

[67] The honour of the Crown thus recognizes the impact of the "superimposition of European laws and customs" on pre-existing Aboriginal societies: *R. v. Van der Peet*, [1996] 2 S.C.R. 507, at para. 248, per McLachlin J., dissenting. Aboriginal peoples were here first, and they were never conquered (*Haida Nation*, at para. 25); yet, they became subject to a legal system that they did not share. Historical treaties were framed in that unfamiliar legal system, and negotiated and drafted in a foreign language ... . The honour of the Crown characterizes the "special relationship" that arises out of this colonial practice: *Little Salmon*, at para. 62. As explained by Brian Slattery:

> ... when the Crown claimed sovereignty over Canadian territories and ultimately gained factual control over them, it did so in the face of pre-existing Aboriginal sovereignty and territorial rights. The tension between these conflicting claims gave rise to a special relationship between the Crown and Aboriginal peoples, which requires the Crown to deal honourably with Aboriginal peoples.

[The Court then summarized its jurisprudence on the duties that are triggered by the honour of the Crown. They wrote:]

[73] The honour of the Crown "is not a mere incantation, but rather a core precept that finds its application in concrete practices" and "gives rise to different duties in different circumstances": *Haida Nation*, at paras. 16 and 18. It is not a cause of action itself; rather, it speaks to how obligations that attract it must be fulfilled. Thus far, the honour of the Crown has been applied in at least four situations:

(1) The honour of the Crown gives rise to a fiduciary duty when the Crown assumes discretionary control over a specific Aboriginal interest ... ;

(2) The honour of the Crown informs the purposive interpretation of s. 35 of the *Constitution Act, 1982*, and gives rise to a duty to consult when the Crown contemplates an action that will affect a claimed but as of yet unproven Aboriginal interest ... ;

(3) The honour of the Crown governs treaty-making and implementation ..., leading to requirements such as honourable negotiation and the avoidance of the appearance of sharp dealing ... ; and

(4) The honour of the Crown requires the Crown to act in a way that accomplishes the intended purposes of treaty and statutory grants to Aboriginal peoples ... .

[74] Thus, the duty that flows from the honour of the Crown varies with the situation in which it is engaged. What constitutes honourable conduct will vary with the circumstances.

H. ABORIGINAL TITLE

In 2014, an Indigenous community successfully argued that they possessed pre-existing and continuing rights in land called Aboriginal title. In *Tsilhqot'in Nation v British Columbia*, below, the Court clarified the test for proving Aboriginal title, the rights associated with title, and how federal, provincial, and Indigenous jurisdiction apply in situations of proven and claimed Aboriginal title.

Tsilhqot'in Nation v British Columbia
2014 SCC 44, [2014] 2 SCR 257

McLACHLIN CJ (LeBel, Abella, Rothstein, Cromwell, Moldaver, Karakatsanis, and Wagner JJ concurring):

[50] The claimant group bears the onus of establishing Aboriginal title. The task is to identify how pre-sovereignty rights and interests can properly find expression in modern common law terms. In asking whether Aboriginal title is established, the general requirements are: (1) "sufficient occupation" of the land claimed to establish title at the time of assertion of European sovereignty; (2) continuity of occupation where present occupation is relied on; and (3) exclusive historic occupation. In determining what constitutes sufficient occupation, one looks to the Aboriginal culture and practices, and compares them in a culturally sensitive way with what was required at common law to establish title on the basis of occupation. Occupation sufficient to ground Aboriginal title is not confined to specific sites of settlement but extends to tracts of land that were regularly used for hunting, fishing or otherwise exploiting resources and over which the group exercised effective control at the time of assertion of European sovereignty.

* * *

[Where title is established, the Court determined that the following rights and restrictions on Indigenous governance rights are present:]

[73] Aboriginal title confers ownership rights similar to those associated with fee simple, including: the right to decide how the land will be used; the right of enjoyment and occupancy of the land; the right to possess the land; the right to the economic benefits of the land; and the right to pro-actively use and manage the land.

[74] Aboriginal title, however, comes with an important restriction—it is collective title held not only for the present generation but for all succeeding generations. This means it cannot be alienated except to the Crown or encumbered in ways that would prevent future generations of the group from using and enjoying it. Nor can the land be developed or misused in a way that would substantially deprive future generations of the benefit of the land. Some changes—even permanent changes—to the land may be possible. Whether a particular use is irreconcilable with the ability of succeeding generations to benefit from the land will be a matter to be determined when the issue arises.

[75] The rights and restrictions on Aboriginal title flow from the legal interest Aboriginal title confers, which in turn flows from the fact of Aboriginal occupancy at the time of European sovereignty which attached as a burden on the underlying title asserted by the Crown at sovereignty. Aboriginal title post-sovereignty reflects the fact of Aboriginal occupancy pre-sovereignty, with all the pre-sovereignty incidents of use and enjoyment that were part of the collective title enjoyed by the ancestors of the claimant group—most notably the right to control how the land is used. However, these uses are not confined to the uses and customs of pre-sovereignty times; like other land-owners, Aboriginal title holders of modern times can use their land in modern ways, if that is their choice.

[76] The right to control the land conferred by Aboriginal title means that governments and others seeking to use the land must obtain the consent of the Aboriginal title holders. If the Aboriginal group does not consent to the use, the government's only recourse is to establish that the proposed incursion on the land is justified under s. 35 of the *Constitution Act, 1982*.

[77] To justify overriding the Aboriginal title-holding group's wishes on the basis of the broader public good, the government must show: (1) that it discharged its procedural duty to consult and accommodate, (2) that its actions were backed by a compelling and substantial objective; and (3) that the governmental action is consistent with the Crown's fiduciary obligation to the group: *Sparrow*.

• • •

[81] I agree ... that the compelling and substantial objective of the government must be considered from the Aboriginal perspective as well as from the perspective of the broader public. As stated in *Gladstone*, at para. 72:

> [T]he objectives which can be said to be compelling and substantial will be those directed at either the recognition of the prior occupation of North America by [A]boriginal peoples or—and at the level of justification it is this purpose which may well be most relevant—*at the reconciliation of [A]boriginal prior occupation with the assertion of the sovereignty of the Crown.* [Emphasis added.]

[82] As *Delgamuukw* explains, the process of reconciling Aboriginal interests with the broader interests of society as a whole is the raison d'être of the principle of justification. Aboriginals and non-Aboriginals are "all here to stay" and must of necessity move forward in a process of reconciliation (para. 186). To constitute a compelling and substantial objective, the broader public goal asserted by the government must further the goal of reconciliation, having regard to both the Aboriginal interest and the broader public objective.

[83] What interests are potentially capable of justifying an incursion on Aboriginal title? In *Delgamuukw*, this Court, per Lamer C.J., offered this:

> In the wake of *Gladstone*, the range of legislative objectives that can justify the infringement of [A]boriginal title is fairly broad. Most of these objectives can be traced to the reconciliation of the prior occupation of North America by [A]boriginal peoples with the assertion of Crown sovereignty, which entails the recognition that "distinctive [A]boriginal societies exist within, and are a part of, a broader social, political and economic community" (at para. 73). *In my opinion, the development of agriculture, forestry, mining, and hydroelectric power, the general economic development of the interior of British Columbia, protection of the environment or endangered species, the building of infrastructure and the settlement of foreign populations to support those aims, are the kinds of objectives that are consistent with this purpose and, in principle, can justify the infringement of [A]boriginal title.* Whether a particular measure or government act can be explained by reference to one of those objectives, however, is ultimately a question of fact that will have to be examined on a case-by-case basis. [Emphasis added; emphasis in original deleted; para 165]

[84] If a compelling and substantial public purpose is established, the government must go on to show that the proposed incursion on the Aboriginal right is consistent with the Crown's fiduciary duty towards Aboriginal people.

[85] The Crown's fiduciary duty in the context of justification merits further discussion. The Crown's underlying title in the land is held for the benefit of the Aboriginal group and constrained by the Crown's fiduciary or trust obligation to the group. This impacts the justification process in two ways.

[86] First, the Crown's fiduciary duty means that the government must act in a way that respects the fact that Aboriginal title is a group interest that inheres in present and future generations. The beneficial interest in the land held by the Aboriginal group vests communally in the title-holding group. This means that

incursions on Aboriginal title cannot be justified if they would substantially deprive future generations of the benefit of the land.

[87] Second, the Crown's fiduciary duty infuses an obligation of proportionality into the justification process. Implicit in the Crown's fiduciary duty to the Aboriginal group is the requirement that the incursion is necessary to achieve the government's goal (rational connection); that the government go no further than necessary to achieve it (minimal impairment); and that the benefits that may be expected to flow from that goal are not outweighed by adverse effects on the Aboriginal interest (proportionality of impact). The requirement of proportionality is inherent in the *Delgamuukw* process of reconciliation and was echoed in *Haida*'s insistence that the Crown's duty to consult and accommodate at the claims stage "is proportionate to a preliminary assessment of the strength of the case supporting the existence of the right or title, and to the seriousness of the potentially adverse effect upon the right or title claimed" (para. 39).

There are some internal tensions in this decision. Although Indigenous governance rights over title land include the right to decide how lands are used, the Court nonetheless carves out limited space for the Crown to make decisions that impact those lands without the consent of the Aboriginal title holder, in the name of the public interest. Notably, in weighing the public interest, this test restricts legitimate Crown objectives, tying them to the Crown's fiduciary duties, enabling reconciliation, and ensuring that future enjoyment of the lands by the Aboriginal title-holding people. A different point of tension arises in the Court's finding, not discussed in the extract above, that provincial laws of general application may apply to Aboriginal title lands, as a result of provincial power to regulate land use within the province, as long as any infringement passes the *Sparrow* test as modified above (paras 151-52).

V. MODERN TREATIES AND LAND CLAIMS AGREEMENTS

A. THE ERA OF MODERN TREATIES

Section 35 of the *Constitution Act, 1982* recognizes and affirms treaties. Treaties are defined as including "rights that now exist by way of land claims agreements or may be so acquired" (s 35(3)).

The last "historic" treaty was signed in the 1920s. Following the 1973 decision in *Calder,* the Crown and various Indigenous peoples began again to negotiate treaties. The contemporary treaties, which have the formal name of "comprehensive claims," are complex. Some of the major treaties that have been negotiated include the *James Bay and Northern Quebec Agreement* (1975), the *North-Eastern Quebec Agreement* (1978), the *Western Arctic Inuvialuit Final Agreement* (1984), the *Gwich'in Agreement* (1992), the *Nunavut Land Claims Agreement* (1993), the *Yukon First Nations Land Claim* (1994), the *Sahtu Dene and Métis Agreement* (1994), the *Nisga'a Final Agreement* (2000), the *Tlicho Land Claim* (2003), the *Labrador Inuit Land Claims Agreement* (2003), the *Nunavik Inuit Land Claim Agreement* (2006), the *Tswawassen First Nation Final Agreement* (2009), and the *Maa-nulth First Nations Final Agreement* (2009). For a discussion of comprehensive land claims, see Jennifer Dalton, "Aboriginal Title and Self-Government in Canada: What Is the True Scope of Comprehensive Land Claims Agreements" (2006) 22 Windsor Rev Legal Soc Issues 29.

These modern treaties typically include transfers of land, financial compensation for lost land and other interests, royalty-sharing schemes, fiscal transfer agreements, and determinations of how jurisdiction will be exercised by the federal, provincial/territorial, and Indigenous governments, including how to address conflicting laws. Litigation regarding modern treaties has affirmed that their terms are to be interpreted in light of the precision with which they are drafted, although good faith interpretation and performance on the part of the Crown is implied in the agreement. See *Quebec (AG) v Moses*, 2010 SCC 17, [2010] 1 SCR 557.

Some Indigenous communities see modern treaties as key to enabling their self-governance. Other Indigenous communities reject the treaty process. They see the terms by which the Crown restricts the negotiations as funnelling the process toward outcomes that fail to sufficiently recognize the full scope of their governance and land rights, and so demand unacceptable levels of compromise.

B. MODERN TREATIES AS A "THIRD ORDER OF GOVERNMENT"

Modern treaties have also attracted constitutional controversy. In *Campbell v British Columbia (AG)*, below, a party sought to have a contemporary treaty—the Nisga'a Treaty—declared unconstitutional. The claim was that it granted the Nisga'a Nation legislative jurisdiction that was inconsistent with the division of powers under ss 91 and 92 of the *Constitution Act, 1867.* The excerpt below first describes the governance powers of the Nisga'a pursuant to the treaty. Consider whether these powers constitute self-government. It then describes the constitutional challenge.

Campbell v AG BC/AG Cda & Nisga'a Nation
2000 BCSC 1123

WILLIAMSON J:

[44] ... [T]he plaintiffs do not challenge the transfer to the Nisga'a Nation of fee simple title to the Nisga'a lands, the confirmation of hunting, fishing and trapping rights, or the payment of compensation. They limit their constitutional challenge to what they submit is the establishment of a new order of government ...

Legislative Powers of the Nisga'a Government

[45] The Nisga'a Government has power to make laws in a number of different areas which can be divided generally into two groupings. In the first category, when Nisga'a law conflicts with federal or provincial law, the Nisga'a law will prevail, although in many cases only if it is consistent with comparable standards established by Parliament, the Legislative Assembly, or relevant administrative tribunals.

[46] Generally speaking, the subjects in this category are matters which concern the identity of the Nisga'a people, their education, the preservation of their culture, the use of their land and resources, and the means by which they will make decisions in these areas. ...

[47] Other jurisdictions of the Nisga'a government in this category have specific matters carved out and reserved to the Crown, or to laws generally applicable in the subject area. For example, the right to regulate the use and development of Nisga'a Lands rests with the Nisga'a, but rights of way held or required by the Crown are subject to special provisions. The right to regulate businesses, professions and trades on Nisga'a lands rests with the Nisga'a, but it is subject to provincial laws concerning accreditation, certification and regulation of the conduct of professions and trades.

[48] In the second classification of jurisdiction, when a Nisga'a law conflicts with federal or provincial law, the federal or provincial law will prevail.

[49] The Treaty permits the Nisga'a to establish police services and a police board. Any regimes established pursuant to these provisions require the approval of the provincial cabinet. If the Attorney General of the province is of the opinion that "effective policing in accordance with standards prevailing elsewhere in British Columbia" is not in place, she or he may provide or reorganize policing on the Nisga'a lands, appointing constables or using the provincial police (the R.C.M.P.) as a police force.

[50] The Treaty also provides that the Nisga'a Lisims Government may decide to establish a Nisga'a Court. But again, if that course is followed, its structure and procedures, and the method of selecting judges, must be approved by the provincial cabinet. Further, an appeal from a final decision of the Nisga'a Court lies to the Supreme Court of British Columbia. The Court section of the Treaty includes a number of references to the requirement that any Nisga'a court system must operate in accordance with generally accepted principles. For example, a Nisga'a Court and its judges must comply with "generally recognized principles in respect of judicial fairness, independence and impartiality."

[51] The Nisga'a Government has no authority to make criminal law (that power remains with Parliament). Importantly, a person accused of any offence for which he or she may be imprisoned under Nisga'a law has the right to elect to be tried in the Provincial Court of British Columbia rather than a Nisga'a Court. Any provincial court proceedings would be subject to rights of appeal to the Supreme Court of British Columbia or the Court of Appeal.

• • •

[54] The Nisga'a government may make laws concerning assets the Nisga'a Nation, a Nisga'a village or Nisga'a corporation may hold off Nisga'a lands, but in the event of a conflict between such laws and federal or provincial laws of general application, the latter prevail.

• • •

[56] British Columbia retains the right to licence or approve gambling or gaming facilities on Nisga'a lands, but the Agreement provides that the province will not do so except in accordance with terms established by the Nisga'a government. Such terms, however, must not be inconsistent with federal and provincial laws.

[57] The above paragraphs do not list every jurisdiction and every rule set out in this lengthy and complex agreement about which law will prevail. This review, however, is enough to show that the legislative powers of the Nisga'a Government are significantly limited by the Treaty itself ... .

[58] ... [T]he plaintiffs submit that it is only those portions of the Treaty which allocate legislative power in the Nisga'a Government, and which provide that in the event of a conflict with federal or provincial law Nisga'a law will prevail, which are unconstitutional.

[59] The heart of this argument is that any right to such self-government or legislative power was extinguished at the time of Confederation. Thus, the plaintiffs distinguish aboriginal title and other aboriginal rights, such as the right to hunt or to fish, from the right to govern one's own affairs. They say that in 1867, when the then *British North America Act* (now called the *Constitution Act, 1867*) was enacted, although other aboriginal rights including aboriginal title survived, any right to self-government did not. All legislative power was divided between Parliament and the legislative assemblies. While they concede that Parliament, or the Legislative Assembly, may delegate authority, they say legislative bodies may not give up or abdicate that authority. To do so, they argue, is unconstitutional.

• • •

[64] [Sections 91 and 92] ... lead to at least two related questions. First, when the Parliament of the United Kingdom enacted the *British North America Act* in 1867 was all legislative power distributed through Sections 91 and 92? Second, is the legislative power granted to the Nisga'a Nation a new order of government? I have concluded the answer to both of these questions is "no."

• • •

[71] The plaintiffs argue that all legislative power in Canada is "exhaustively" distributed between Parliament and the legislative assemblies by virtue of the *Constitution Act, 1867.* Consequently, they submit, an amendment to the constitution would be required to allow aboriginal governments, such as the Lisims Government of the Nisga'a Nation established by the Treaty, the power to make laws which prevail over federal or provincial laws. ... the plaintiffs rely principally upon much older decisions from the Privy Council. For example, in *A.G. Ont. v. A.G. Canada*, [1912] A.C. 571 ... [the Privy Council said]:

> Now, there can be no doubt that under this organic instrument the powers distributed between the Dominion on the one hand and the provinces on the other hand cover the whole area of self-government within the whole area of Canada.

[72] This is the heart of the plaintiffs' argument. If the powers granted to Parliament and the legislatures combined "cover the whole area of self-government" within Canada, there can be no legislative power left to aboriginal peoples.

[73] The flaw in this submission, however, becomes evident when one considers what the Privy Council said in the same judgment three pages on at p. 584:

> For whatever belongs to self-government in Canada belongs either to the Dominion or to the provinces, *within the limits* of the British North America Act. [Emphasis added in original.]

[74] What are "the limits of the British North America Act"?

[75] In *R. v. Secretary of State for Foreign and Commonwealth Affairs, ex parte Indian Association of Alberta and others*, [1982] 2 All E.R. 118, [May LJ of] the English Court of Appeal ... quoted with approval the following passage from the decision of Watson J. in *Liquidators of the Maritime Bank of Canada v. Receiver-General of New Brunswick*, [1892] A.C. 437 at 441-2:

> The object of the [*British North America Act*] ... was accomplished by distributing between the Dominion and the provinces, all powers executive and legislative, and all public property and revenues *which had previously belonged to the provinces*; so that the Dominion government should be vested with such of these powers, property, and revenues as were necessary for the due performance of its constitutional functions, and that the remainder should be retained by the provinces for the purposes of provincial government. [Emphasis added in original.]

[76] Thus, what was distributed in ss. 91 and 92 of the *British North America Act* was all of (but no more than) the powers which until June 30, 1867 had belonged to the colonies. Anything outside of the powers enjoyed by the colonies was not encompassed by ss. 91 and 92 and remained outside of the power of Parliament and the legislative assemblies just as it had been beyond the powers of the colonies.

• • •

[81] A consideration of these various observations by the Supreme Court of Canada supports the submission that aboriginal rights, and in particular a right to self-government akin to a legislative power to make laws, survived as one of the unwritten "underlying values" of the Constitution outside of the powers distributed

to Parliament and the legislatures in 1867. The federal-provincial division of powers in 1867 was aimed at a different issue and was a division "internal" to the Crown.

. . .

[83] I now turn to the subject of aboriginal legal systems and law making authority ...[and to] the definition of eminent constitutional scholar Professor Dicey in his *Law of the Constitution*, 10th ed. (London: MacMillan Press, 1959), at page 40, that a law may be defined as "any rule which will be enforced by the courts."

[84] If it need be said, the common law will be enforced by the courts. The common law has long recognized "customs" or rules that have obtained the force of law in a particular locality. Agreements such as treaties negotiated and entered into by exercise of executive prerogative will be enforced by the courts.

[85] History, and a review of the authorities, persuades me that the Aboriginal peoples of Canada, including the Nisga'a, had legal systems prior to the arrival of Europeans on this continent and that these legal systems, although diminished, continued after contact. Aboriginal laws did not emanate from a central print oriented law-making authority similar to a legislative assembly, but took unwritten form. Lord Denning, in *R. v. Secretary of State For Foreign and Commonwealth Affairs* at p. 123 likened aboriginal laws to "custom":

> These customary laws are not written down. They are handed down by tradition from one generation to another. Yet beyond doubt they are well established and have the force of law within the community.

[86] The continued existence of indigenous legal systems in North America after the arrival of Europeans was articulated as early as the 1820s by the Supreme Court of the United States. But the most salient fact, for the purposes of the question of whether a power to make and rely upon aboriginal law survived Canadian Confederation, is that since 1867 courts in Canada have enforced laws made by aboriginal societies. This demonstrates not only that at least a limited right to self-government, or a limited degree of legislative power, remained with aboriginal peoples after the assertion of sovereignty and after Confederation, but also that such rules, whether they result from custom, tradition, agreement, or some other decision making process, are "laws" in the Dicey constitutional sense.

[Thus, the Nisga'a Treaty was found to be consistent with the Canadian Constitution.]

C. MODERN TREATIES AND INDIGENOUS LAW

As noted above, the jurisdiction of Indigenous governments to enact laws is explicitly recognized in the modern treaties. Provisions may also recognize that the unique legal landscape of Indigenous peoples includes historic customary laws and legal principles. The *Labrador Inuit Land Claims Agreement* (2004) provides an example. The Agreement creates an Inuit government for a portion of Labrador, called the Nunatsiavut government. The Agreement states Nunatsiavut shall "maintain a public registry of the Labrador Inuit Constitution, Inuit Laws, including Inuit customary laws," and sets out a process for establishing Inuit law as a matter of fact in judicial or administrative proceedings (s 17.5). The Agreement and the *Labrador Inuit Constitution* contemplate that there may be conflict as among Canadian laws, laws newly passed by the Nunatsiavut government, and Inuit customary laws. In such cases, Inuit customary laws are given priority, unless there is an express extinguishment of the customary law, or the customary law is in conflict with a third core legal Nunatsuivut legal instrument, the *Labrador Inuit Charter of Rights and Responsibilities*. The rights protected under the Inuit

Charter are potentially broader than those that receive protection under the Canadian Charter. It contains provisions relating to

> equality, dignity, security of the person, personal integrity, religious observance, freedom of expression, elections, freedom of movement, private land rights, freedom of trade, fair labour practices, collective bargaining, environment, rights of children, water, health care, social services, education, language, culture, housing, access to information, right to administrative actions and access to courts

(Borrows, *Canada's Indigenous Constitution* at 53).

D. MODERN TREATIES AND THE CONSTITUTIONAL RELATIONSHIP

Despite the complex and specific terms found in modern treaty agreements, the Supreme Court of Canada has confirmed that these treaties do not oust the core legal incidents of the unique relationship between Indigenous peoples and Canada. In *Beckman v Little Salmon/Carmacks First Nation*, 2010 SCC 53, [2010] 3 SCR 103, the question was whether the duty to consult arose despite the modern treaty not identifying a right to consultation about the decision at issue, or if the treaty was a complete code for identifying each party's role in, and jurisdiction over, various decisions. The majority found that the duty to consult was present, by virtue of the rule of law:

> The duty to consult is treated in the jurisprudence as a means (in appropriate circumstances) of upholding the honour of the Crown. Consultation can be shaped by agreement of the parties, but the Crown cannot contract out of its duty of honourable dealing with Aboriginal people ... it is a doctrine that applies independently of the expressed or implied intention of the parties ... .
>
> ... The treaty sets out rights and obligations of the parties, but the treaty is part of a special relationship: "In all its dealings with Aboriginal peoples, from the assertion of sovereignty to the resolution of claims, *and the implementation of treaties*, the Crown must act honourably." [Paragraphs 61-62; emphasis added.]

The majority opened their reasons with a particularly poignant passage that illustrates many of the issues that are discussed in this chapter. They wrote (at para 10):

> The reconciliation of Aboriginal and non-Aboriginal Canadians in a mutually respectful long-term relationship is the grand purpose of s. 35 of the *Constitution Act, 1982*. The modern treaties, including those at issue here, attempt to further the objective of reconciliation not only by addressing grievances over the land claims but by creating the legal basis to foster a positive long-term relationship between Aboriginal and non-Aboriginal communities. Thoughtful administration of the treaty will help manage, even if it fails to eliminate, some of the misunderstandings and grievances that have characterized the past. Still, as the facts of this case show, the treaty will not accomplish its purpose if it is interpreted by territorial officials in an ungenerous manner or as if it were an everyday commercial contract. The treaty is as much about building relationships as it is about the settlement of ancient grievances. The future is more important than the past. A canoeist who hopes to make progress faces forwards, not backwards.

VI. INDIGENOUS PEOPLES AND HUMAN RIGHTS PROTECTIONS

The text above has largely focused on how the constitutionalization of Aboriginal and treaty rights has shaped the public law relationship between Indigenous peoples and the Canadian state, with much of the discussion focusing on lands, resources, and governance rights.

Another key aspect of the public law relationship, which was flagged in our discussion of residential schools above, concerns how Canada has approached the human rights of Indigenous peoples. Recent litigation and an independent inquiry have highlighted other ways that discrimination has become deeply embedded in federal practices concerning Indigenous peoples.

In *First Nations Child and Family Caring Society of Canada v Canada (Minister of Indian Affairs and Northern Development)*, 2016 CHRT 2, the Canadian Human Rights Commission found that Canada had been discriminating against First Nations children because it was persistently and knowingly underfunding essential service delivery for Indigenous children living on First Nation Reserves, including failing to ensure access to health care on the same basis as non-Indigenous children and failing to adequately fund child and family services. This discrimination, in turn, was a significant cause of the extraordinarily high rates of Indigenous children who are apprehended. The Commission ordered Canada to immediately cease discriminating. However, since the decision was released, the Commission has made four remedial non-compliance orders against Canada, the most recent being in 2018 (*First Nations Child & Family Caring Society of Canada v Attorney General of Canada (Minister of Indigenous and Northern Affairs Canada)*, 2018 CHRT 4).

In 2019, the Commission made a further ruling, regarding compensation based on the 2016 findings. The Commission ordered the maximum compensation permitted under the regime. In their reasons they summarize the nature of the human rights violations. One extract reads as follows (at paras 231-35):

> The Panel finds that Canada's conduct was devoid of caution with little to no regard to the consequences of its behavior towards First Nations children and their families both in regard to the child welfare program and Jordan's Principle [which requires that First Nations children receive the same standard of health care as non-Indigenous children]. Canada was aware of the discrimination and of some of its serious consequences on the First Nations children and their families. Canada was made aware by the NPR in 2000 and even more so in 2005 from its participation and knowledge of the WEN DE report. Canada did not take sufficient steps to remedy the discrimination until after the Tribunal's orders. As the Panel already found in previous rulings, Canada focused on financial considerations rather than on the best interest of First Nations children and respecting their human rights.
>
> When looking at the issue of wilful and reckless discriminatory practice, the context of the claim is important. In this case we are in a context of repeated violations of human rights of vulnerable First Nations children over a very long period of time by Canada who has international, constitutional and human rights obligations towards First Nations children and families. Moreover, the Crown must act honourably in all its dealings with Aboriginal Peoples:
>
>> First Nations children and families on reserves are in a fiduciary relationship with AANDC. In the provision of the FNCFS Program, its corresponding funding formulas and the other related provincial/territorial agreements, "the degree of economic, social and proprietary control and discretion asserted by the Crown" leaves First Nations children and families "... vulnerable to the risks of government misconduct or ineptitude" (Wewaykum at para. 80). This fiduciary relationship must form part of the context of the Panel's analysis, along with the corollary principle that in all its dealings with Aboriginal peoples, the honour of the Crown is always at stake. As affirmed by the Supreme Court in Haida Nation, at paragraph 17:
>>
>>> Nothing less is required if we are to achieve "the reconciliation of the pre-existence of aboriginal societies with the sovereignty of the Crown": Delgamuukw, supra, at para. 186, quoting Van der Peet, supra, at para. 31, (see *Decision* 2016 CHRT 2 at, para. 95).
>
> In light of Canada's obligations above mentioned, the fact that the systemic racial discrimination adversely impacts children and causes them harm, pain and suffering is an aggravating factor than cannot be overlooked.

The Panel finds it has sufficient evidence to find that Canada's conduct was wilful and reckless resulting in what we have referred to as a worst-case scenario under our *Act*.

What is more, many federal government representatives of different levels were aware of the adverse impacts that the Federal FNCFS Program had on First Nations children and families and some of those admissions form part of the evidence and were referred to in the Panel's findings.

(*First Nations Child and Family Caring Society of Canada v Attorney General of Canada*, 2019 CHRT 39).

While the actual remedy for compensation has been appealed by the federal government, the factual findings were not. The above extract thus aptly illustrates how fiduciary law, the honour of the Crown, and human rights law merge in this instance.

A National Inquiry investigating murdered and missing Indigenous women and girls has also identified Canada as having engaged in discrimination against Indigenous women and girls. They further found that the systemic and sustained nature of the discrimination constituted genocidal action and discussed Canada's obligations for remedying its breaches of international human rights law. They wrote:

The thousands of stories of violence heard by the National Inquiry over the three intense years of its mandate lifted the veil over the existence of a genocide perpetrated by the Canadian state against Indigenous peoples. This genocide was enabled by colonial structures and policies maintained over centuries until the present day and constitutes a root cause of the violence currently being perpetrated against Indigenous women, girls and 2SLGBTQQIA people.

Legally speaking, this genocide consists of a composite wrongful act that triggers the responsibility of the Canadian state under international law. Canada has breached its international obligations through a series of actions and omissions taken as a whole, and this breach will persist as long as genocidal acts continue to occur and destructive policies are maintained. Under international law, Canada has a duty to redress the harm it caused and to provide restitution, compensation and satisfaction to Indigenous peoples. But first and foremost, Canada's violation of one of the most fundamental rules of international law necessitates an obligation of cessation: Canada must put an end to its perennial pattern of violence against and oppression of Indigenous peoples.

So far, Canada's failure to listen to Indigenous perspectives and to address flagrant violations of their most basic human rights, and in particular those related to violence against Indigenous women, girls, and 2SLGBTQQIA people, has been remarkable. The so-called champion of multiculturalism and fundamental human rights has lamentably and willingly failed to act upon numerous recommendations that have been made over time, through myriad different actors, including the commissions it itself established. However, listening to Indigenous voices is more than a demonstration of good faith: it is a legal requirement. Ending this genocide and providing due reparations require that the government of Canada fully and promptly implement the Calls for Justice made by this National Inquiry. Canada must adopt a decolonizing approach to "resist and undo the forces of colonialism" while acknowledging and dismantling the colonial structures fostering racism, oppression, and other forms of violence perpetrated against Indigenous women, girls, and 2SLGBTQQIA people.

Canada must ensure that "all Indigenous women, girls, and 2SLGBTQQIA people are provided with safe, no-barrier, permanent, and meaningful access to their cultures and languages in order to restore, reclaim, and revitalize their cultures and identities." It must ensure that the rights to health and wellness, human security, justice, culture and equality of Indigenous Peoples are recognized, upheld, and protected on an equitable basis.

Ending the Canadian genocide of Indigenous Peoples requires an honest and active process of decolonization and indigenization of structures, institutions, legislation and policies. The swift implementation of the National Inquiry's Calls for Justice is essential to address the violence against Indigenous women, girls, and 2SLGBTQQIA people. It is also mandated by international law as measures of reparation, a direct consequence of Canada's responsibility for the commission of genocide.

It is time to call it as it is: Canada's past and current colonial policies, actions and inactions towards Indigenous Peoples is genocide. And genocide, as per law binding on Canada, demands accountability. The National Inquiry hopes that its legal analysis and findings will contribute to the necessary discussion on genocide in Canada and trigger further research on this characterization of colonial violence, which is a fundamental root cause of the violence experienced by Indigenous women, girls, and 2SLGBTQQIA people.

(National Inquiry into Missing and Murdered Indigenous Women and Girls, *A Legal Analysis of Genocide: Supplementary Report*, 2019, at 26-27.)

The Inquiry's findings on genocide did indeed provoke national discussion. In public and academic forums, there have been heated exchanges concerning whether "genocide" is a legally accurate term to characterize the systemic character of the violence that Indigenous women and girls have experienced and continue to experience. Some commentators have expressed frustration with this controversy, as causing a distraction away from a focus on the needed actions, while others—on both sides—remain steadfastly committed to debating whether the term has been properly applied. While the debate continues in legal academic circles, the federal government has accepted that genocide occurred and committed to addressing the Inquiry's Calls to Action. There has also been international attention, which has dovetailed with the call for further research. In particular, Amnesty International has indicated that the findings on genocide may require an investigation, and the United Nations Human Rights Office has urged Canada itself to undertake an in-depth investigation into the facts and findings that led to the conclusion of genocide.

Thus, courts and inquires continue to reveal troubling aspects of the public law relationship between Indigenous peoples and Canada. In doing so, they provoke public and political dialogue about how to reform that relationship while also proposing their own fact-specific mechanisms and strategies for reform.

CHAPTER FOUR

SOURCES OF CANADIAN LAW

Despite renewed recognition of Indigenous interests in Canadian law, it is still a fact that almost all of Canadian law stems from its European inheritance. Indeed, note how in the discussion on Indigenous rights in Chapter 3, the recent revival of Indigenous rights in modern Canada is characterized as a "common law" creation, or a product of constitutional changes by Canada's political bodies.

This observation raises a question: how were Canada's dominant common (and in Quebec, civil) law traditions "received" from their European origins? Not surprisingly, given the ultimate success of Britain in claiming sovereignty over northern North America, British concepts of "reception" determine the response to this question. This chapter focuses on this question.

We then introduce readers to the concept of "statutory law"—that is, law promulgated by legislative bodies—and its relationship with the "common law." Finally, we shift focus to examine a final area of law increasingly important in Canadian practice: international law.

I. THE COMMON AND CIVIL LAW TRADITIONS

A. RECEPTION OF EUROPEAN LAW

Instructors of public law are sometimes asked how European law came to dominate the law of Canada. The short answer is "because Canada was a colony." The more complex answer has to do with the rules on the movement of law from the British colonial power to its colonies. We think it worthwhile for readers to have some sense of these doctrines.

William Blackstone, in his *Commentaries on the Laws of England*, best summarized how colonial laws were to apply in the New World. The laws in force depended on whether colonies were simply settled, were conquered, or were ceded by Indigenous peoples. In the case of conquest or cession, pre-existing laws of the Indigenous sovereign should remain in force, subject to modification or replacement by the Crown or Parliament where necessary to operate government. The English common law was to have little or no authority. In the case of settlement, by comparison, a legal vacuum existed that must be filled; some form of law was required to govern new colonies. In the case of British settlements, this was a mixture of common and statutory law: see "Introduction," sec IV, in *Blackstone's Commentaries*, vol 1 (London: Cavendish, 2001).

The decision of the Judicial Committee of the Privy Council (known generally as "the Privy Council") in *Cooper v Stuart* highlights the basic principles surrounding the rules of reception. Lord Watson provides a general overview of how British colonies adopted English law. The case focused on the application of the common law "rule against perpetuities" (a property law rule designed to limit the duration of a condition imposed as part of the transfer of land) in the New South Wales colony, now part of Australia.

Cooper v Stuart
(1889), 14 App Cas 286 (PC)

LORD WATSON:

In support of the second objection, it was maintained for the appellant, in the first place, that the English rule against perpetuities, as now settled, applied in all its entirety to the Colony of New South Wales in the year 1823; and, in the second place, that the rule, as established in the law of England, applies to reservations made by the Crown in the interests of the public.

• • •

It does not appear to their Lordships to be necessary, for the purposes of the present case, to decide whether the Crown, in attaching such reservations to grants of land in England, would be affected by the rule against perpetuities. In order to succeed in this appeal, it is not enough for the appellant to establish that the Crown would be within the rule here; he must also shew [sic] that the rule, in so far as it affects the Crown, was operative in the Colony of New South Wales at the time when his land was originally granted to William Hutchinson; and that, in the opinion of their Lordships, he has failed to do.

The extent to which English law is introduced into a British Colony, and the manner of its introduction, must necessarily vary according to circumstances. There is a great difference between the case of a Colony acquired by conquest or cession, in which there is an established system of law, and that of a Colony which consisted of a tract of territory practically unoccupied, without settled inhabitants or settled law, at the time when it was peacefully annexed to the British dominions. The Colony of New South Wales belongs to the latter class. In the case of such a Colony the Crown may by ordinance, and the Imperial Parliament, or its own legislature when it comes to possess one, may by statute declare what parts of the common and statute law of England shall have effect within its limits. But, when that is not done, the law of England must (subject to well-established exceptions) become from the outset the law of the Colony, and be administered by its tribunals. In so far as it is reasonably applicable to the circumstances of the Colony, the law of England must prevail, until it is abrogated or modified, either by ordinance or statute. The often-quoted observations of Sir William Blackstone (1 Comm. 107) appear to their Lordships to have a direct bearing upon the present case. ...

Blackstone, in that passage, was setting right an opinion attributed to Lord Holt, that all laws in force in England must apply to an infant Colony of that kind. If the learned author had written at a later date he would probably have added that, as the population, wealth, and commerce of the Colony increase, many rules and principles of English law, which were unsuitable to its infancy, will gradually be attracted to it; and that the power of remodelling its laws belongs also to the colonial legislature.

Their Lordships have not been referred to any Act or Ordinance declaring that the laws of England, or any portion of them, are applicable to New South Wales. There was no land law or tenure existing in the Colony at the time of its annexation to the Crown; and, in that condition of matters, the conclusion appears to their Lordships to be inevitable that, as soon as colonial land became the subject of settlement and commerce, all transactions in relation to it were governed by English law, in so far as that law could be justly and conveniently applied to them. ...

Their Lordships have recently had occasion to consider, in *Jex v. McKinney and Others*, the authorities bearing upon the question of the suitability of English law to colonial circumstances. That case differed from the present in this respect, that there the law of England was introduced into the Colony by statute, and not by the silent operation of constitutional principles; but its introduction was qualified by words which excluded the application of laws prevailing here which were unsuitable in their nature to the needs of the Colony.

The rule against perpetuities, as applied to persons and gifts of a private character, though not finally settled in all its details, until a comparatively recent date, is, in its principle, an important feature of the common law of England. To that extent it appears to be founded upon plain considerations of policy, and, in some shape or other, finds a place in most, if not in all, complete systems of jurisprudence. Their Lordships see no reason to suppose that the rule, so limited, is not required in New South Wales by the same considerations which have led to its introduction here, or that its operation in that colony would be less beneficial than in England. The learned judges of the Supreme Court of the colony, in deciding this case, proceeded on the assumption that the rule applies there as between subject and subject; and their Lordships are of opinion that the assumption is well founded.

Assuming next (but for the purposes of this argument only) that the rule has, in England, been extended to the Crown, its suitability, when so applied, to the necessities of a young Colony raises a very different question. The object of the Government, in giving off public lands to settlers, is not so much to dispose of the land to pecuniary profit as to attract other colonists. It is simply impossible to foresee what land will be required for public uses before the immigrants arrive who are to constitute the public. Their prospective wants can only be provided for in two ways, either by reserving from settlement portions of land, which may prove to be useless for the purpose for which they are reserved, or by making grants of land in settlement, retaining the right to resume such parts as may be found necessary for the uses of an increased population. To adopt the first of these methods might tend to defeat the very objects which it is the duty of a colonial governor to promote; and a rule which rests on considerations of public policy cannot be said to be reasonably applied when its application may probably lead to that result.

Their Lordships have, accordingly, come to the conclusion that, assuming the Crown to be affected by the rule against perpetuities in England, it was nevertheless inapplicable, in the year 1823, to Crown grants of land in the Colony of New South Wales, or to reservations or defeasances in such grants to take effect on some contingency more or less remote, and only when necessary for the public good.

As this discussion suggests, the applicable rules of reception varied between conquered and settled colonies. In North America, the problem of determining which of these rules of reception would apply was compounded by two facts: (1) Indigenous peoples were already present, so true "settlement" in Blackstone's definition could not apply; and (2) France also had an interest in much of British North America, and claimed much of its territory. Indeed, much of modern-day Ontario and Quebec were originally part of New France, which was then conquered by the English in 1759 and ceded by France in the *Treaty of Paris, 1763*.

In practice, the rule of conquest was applied to central Canada, and the rule on settlement everywhere else. Although this did not immediately occur—English law was initially imposed on the new colony of Quebec—the *Quebec Act, 1774* ((UK) 14 Geo III, c 83) correctly restored the pre-conquest French civil law as the law of Quebec. Subsequently, the *Constitutional Act, 1791* ((UK) 31 Geo III, c 31) divided Quebec into two provinces: English-speaking Upper Canada and French-speaking Lower Canada. After a short time, Upper Canada enacted legislation receiving the common law of England as the applicable legal code. In Lower Canada, except for criminal matters, the "Laws of Canada" applied in relation to "Property and Civil Rights"—that is, private law matters. The "Laws of Canada" meant the civil law of New France, which consisted mainly of the *Coutume de Paris* supplemented by Roman law, legislation, and canon laws. These various sources were codified in 1866 by the *Civil Code of Lower Canada*.

Meanwhile, the Maritimes and (when established) the western provinces were largely governed by the British common law. These regions were regarded as "settled" (as opposed to conquered) territories (an approach that ignored the Indigenous presence). As Peter Hogg notes:

> The settled classification entailed the automatic reception of English, not French law, a result that was congenial to the English population. In the case of the three maritime provinces, which as a matter of historical fact were acquired by cession from France, the possibility of the survival of French law seems never to have been seriously considered. The reception of English law into these provinces has often been explained on the patently false belief that they were "settled" colonies.

(*Constitutional Law of Canada*, student ed (Toronto: Carswell, 2017) sec 2.1 at 2-2 to 2-3.)

The rules of reception dictated that the entire body of English law, both statutory and common, was imported into the settled colony. Local exceptions and variances were allowed where the received laws would be unsuitable to the circumstances of the colony. In the case of statute law, the date of reception was important because it was used to determine which English statutory law applied: all statutes passed prior to such date were automatically "received" (unless clearly unsuitable) and remained in force. Those passed after such date did not apply unless, expressly or by clear implication, they were intended to apply. Even a statute that was repealed in England after the reception date would still be in force in the colonies unless it was clearly intended to be repealed in a colony.

In Canada, the dates of reception of some provinces are not clearly marked because there was no obvious statutory source providing for the administration of a province or colony. For example, Ontario, British Columbia, and Alberta received the common law on September 17, 1792, November 19, 1858, and July 15, 1870, respectively; whereas Manitoba "received" the common law through the grant of "Rupert's Land" to the Hudson Bay Company on May 2, 1670, but subsequently adopted a statute fixing July 15, 1870 as the date of reception. Thus, the courts became the arbiters of settlement dates for some provinces and determined the date of statutory reception to be "the date of the institution of a local legislature in a colony": see *Young v Blaikie* (1822), 1 Nfld LR 277 at 283 (SC).

The date of reception for the common law was much less important. As discussed further below, common law decisions simply declared what had always been the law from time immemorial. Therefore, common law decisions operated retrospectively and applied to all colonies equally. Common law, as Blackstone also noted, is a universal, uniform set of principles and precepts. That the Privy Council was the final court of appeal throughout the British Empire, and could ensure some measure of uniformity over the common law, aided this notion. Once a decision was made by either the Privy Council or the House of Lords (the United Kingdom's highest court, now known as the UK Supreme Court) on a common law principle, all common law jurisdictions, at least in the formative years, would accept that decision as binding.

B. NATURE OF THE COMMON AND CIVIL LAW

As this discussion implies, the common law is an English invention. It is judge-made law, developed through the common law courts (as opposed to the Court of Chancery—see below). In its beginning, the common law did not consist of any written "laws" as we would understand them today, but was simply a collection of court decisions, not always written down. Two fundamental ideas permeate traditional common law theory: (1) judges do not make the law but merely declare it; and (2) all relevant past decisions are considered as evidence of the law, and judges infer from these precedents what is the true law in a given instance. In strict terms, therefore, the common law is the law constructed out of a series of cases. Blackstone described it in this way:

> [I]t is an established rule to abide by former precedents, where the same points come again in litigation: as well to keep the scale of justice even and steady, and not liable to waver with every new judge's opinion; as also because the law in that case being solemnly declared and determined, what before was uncertain, and perhaps indifferent, is now become a permanent rule, which it is not in the breast of any subsequent judge to alter or vary from, according to his private sentiments: he being sworn to determine, not according to his private judgment, but according to the known laws and customs of the land; not delegated to pronounce a new law, but to maintain and expound the old one.

(Blackstone, "Introduction," sec III, in *Commentaries on the Laws of England*, vol 1 (London: Cavendish, 2001) at 51.)

Under this 18th-century view, the common law is perceived as a set of fixed rules, unearthed by judges from cases through deductive legal reasoning, analogy, and application of precedent. Case law is then reported in volumes, approved and vetted by judges, which contain, in theory, all the given law up to that date.

Contemporary understanding of the common law has changed (as was shown in some of the legal theories discussed in Chapter 2). But some of the elegance and simplicity of it has remained. Although common law jurisdictions such as Canada no longer rely exclusively on case law—as this book makes plain in later chapters, statutory sources of law are ubiquitous in all provinces—it is largely true that cases remain a key source of law, while statutes are (at least traditionally) seen as incursions into the common law. This underlying methodology has shaped and continues to shape the thinking of common law lawyers and jurists.

Quebec, on the other hand, inherited the vastly different legal tradition of the civil law. This following discussion on the "civilian" tradition is necessarily brief. For a more elaborate discussion on the civilian system in Quebec (and one on which the present discussion relies), see Julie Bedard, "Transsystemic Teaching of Law at McGill: Radical Changes, Old and New Hats" (2001) 27 Queen's LJ 237.

France, before the Revolution, was divided into provinces, each of which had its law-making parliament. Provinces of northern and central France were governed by customary laws, while the south of France was governed by written law, derived from the laws of old Rome.

From 1608 to 1664, the first colonists of New France followed the customary law that was in effect from their own province of origin in France. In 1664, the King of France decreed that the colony would be subject to the customary law of Paris, which ended the existing patchwork of laws. "Paris Custom" would serve as the main source of law throughout New France. Later, authorities went on to add French law to the customary law, which included royal decrees and ordinances, canon law relating to marriages, and Roman law relating to obligations.

Despite its origin as customary law, the Custom of Paris was a codified system of law. It was first enacted in 1510, and revised in 1580. In its revised form, as first adopted in Quebec, it was divided into 12 titles, comprising nearly 300 sections. These existed in Quebec until the defeat of the French in 1759; when the British passed the *Quebec Act, 1774*, the provisions were reintroduced.

In 1866 the laws were codified into the *Civil Code of Lower Canada*. The Code's provisions were derived primarily from the judicial interpretations of the law that had been in force to that date in Lower Canada, although it was also inspired by some of the modernizations found in the 1804 Napoleonic Code and the Louisiana Civil Code. At Confederation, the *Civil Code of Lower Canada* replaced most of the laws inherited from the Custom of Paris, but incorporated some elements of English law as it had been applied in Lower Canada, such as the English law of trusts.

What makes a civilian legal system different from a common law system? Unlike the English common law, civil law arises out of the Roman law of Justinian's *Corpus Juris Civilis*. The civil law is based not on cases but established laws, generally written as broad legal principles. It also includes doctrinal writings and interpretations written by learned scholars. This contrasts to the common law's judge-centred application of facts to uncovered legal rules.

Many civilian jurisdictions rely on civil codes; however, the difference between civil and common law lies more in their different methodological approaches as opposed to codification per se. In civil law countries, legislation is seen as the primary source of law. Judgments normally rely on the provisions of codes and statutes, from which solutions in particular cases are derived. Judicial reasoning is based extensively on the general principles of the rule or code. On the other hand, common law methodology, even where statutory sources of law are present, employs analogical reasoning from statutory provisions to fill gaps.

This "bijuralism" remains largely intact today. As a result, Canada is a mixed-law jurisdiction. This means that the British common law is the basis of private law in all provinces except Quebec. Canadian federal law, which applies in all provinces, also derives from the common law. Private law in Quebec, on the other hand, is based on the French civil law tradition. But as a result of the overwhelming influence of the common law, the Quebec legal system has many aspects of a common law jurisdiction.

Quebec's private law derives from its current manifestation of the *Civil Code*, its provincial statutes, and from federal private law. The *Civil Code of Quebec* reflects the bijural nature of Canada's legal systems: it relies on civil law jurisdictions such as France and Germany to preserve its civilian integrity, but marries that with common law rules to ensure better harmonization with the rest of Canada and the United States. Civilian law methodology therefore evolves within a larger common law institutional framework.

As examples, Quebec's legislative, judicial, executive, and administrative institutions and processes belong to the English tradition, while the content of many of its private laws are civilian-based. The Quebec National Assembly is a law-making body that follows closely the parliamentary style of the English system. Quebec judges are not graduates of a school for the judiciary, as are their counterparts in most civilian jurisdictions, but are drawn from among practising lawyers as common law judges are. Quebec Superior Courts are responsible for the administration of all laws, provincial and federal; whereas most civilian court systems are separated jurisdictionally into public and private disputes. Judges behave and perform in a common law style, as Bedard, above, notes at 246:

> Judicial decisions in Quebec are reported in the English rather than the French mode. Judges give individual opinions, and dissenting opinions are not only permitted but frequent. This is inconsistent with the civil law theory that there can only be one answer to a

legal question as the logical outcome of deductive reasoning. The style of judgments is also much closer to that of English or American cases than of French cases. Although *stare decisis* [defined below] is not part of Quebec law, court decisions are given considerable weight in judicial analysis.

All of this occurs within a context of an adversarial regime and procedural rules that would be familiar to any common law lawyer in the rest of Canada. For a brief history of Canada and its dual legal systems, see GP Browne, ed, *Documents on the Confederation of British North America* (Toronto: McClelland & Stewart, 1969), and Peter Hogg, *Constitutional Law of Canada*, above.

C. THE OPERATION OF COMMON LAW AND PRECEDENT

How does the common law work in practice? The law must have some stability and certainty. The genius of the common law is that it makes adherence to legal principles established on past cases a foundational principle that inevitably leads to a more or less stable and certain legal structure. Reliance on past cases is called the principle of *stare decisis* (let the decision stand) and is related to the doctrine of precedent. In common law systems, precedents are usually made up of principles from previous cases; the principles, however, may arise from the interpretation of a statute or constitutional provision, or through the common law reasoning employed by a previous judge or judges. *Stare decisis* is the formal term to describe how the common law relies on precedent. The value of a precedent is connected to the level of court from which it originates.

In common law systems, lawyers must pay careful attention to the rank of a court in the judicial hierarchy for two reasons: first, because a higher-ranking court is not bound to follow the decision of a lower court, and second, because some courts do not apply the rule of *stare decisis* with respect to their own prior decisions. In Chapter 9, we provide a more thorough overview of the contemporary structure of the Canadian court system. For our purposes here, however, there are lower courts, intermediate appeal courts, and the highest appeal court.

The outward simplicity of the question of a court's ranking is made more complicated because the hierarchy and the attitude of various courts have changed from time to time. For example, appeals from Canadian courts to the Judicial Committee of the Privy Council were abolished in stages, starting with criminal appeals in 1933, and ending with all appeals in 1949. This means that decisions of the Privy Council during this period are binding on Canadian courts, but not after. In Ontario, from 1895 to 1931, there was a section of the *Judicature Act*, RSO 19180, c 223 obliging a judge of the High Court not "to disregard or depart from a prior known decision of any other judge of co-ordinate authority on any question of law or practice without his concurrence" (see e.g. RSO 1927, c 88, s 31(2)). Moreover, the Supreme Court of Canada is now not bound by its own decisions or those of the Privy Council, although it was in the past (see *Reference re Agricultural Products Marketing*, [1978] 2 SCR 1198 at 1257). In sum, the current position for most courts in Canada is as follows:

- All Canadian courts, except the Supreme Court of Canada, are bound to follow a precedent of the Supreme Court of Canada and any pre-1949 decision of the Privy Council that has not been overruled by the Supreme Court of Canada. A minority opinion of the Supreme Court of Canada is, however, not binding.
- Provincial courts of appeal are not bound to follow a decision of the appellate court of another province.
- Provincial courts of appeal will generally be bound by their own prior decisions (in Ontario, if the liberty of the subject is involved or the prior decision was given *per incuriam*—inadvertently, without consideration of an applicable authority or statutory provision—then this rule may be relaxed: see *R v Govedarov, Popovic and Askov* (1974), 3 OR (2d) 23 (CA); appellate courts in certain other provinces, however, have allowed

themselves greater freedom in overruling their own prior decisions (see Gerald L Gall, *The Canadian Legal System*, 2nd ed (Toronto: Carswell, 1983) at 220 and 226, and authorities cited therein).

- Provincial courts lower than the highest appellate court are bound to follow a decision of that province's appellate court.
- Provincial courts at any level are not bound by the decisions of the appellate courts of other provinces or by decisions of the Federal Court of Appeal.
- A decision of a court of coordinate jurisdiction (in practice, courts of the same level in the appeal hierarchy) is not binding; however, it is highly persuasive. This is because Canada's court system is unified under the Supreme Court of Canada and the presence of judicial comity, which is the respect that one court holds for the decisions of another.

(Adapted from Paul Perell, "Stare Decisis and Techniques of Legal Reasoning and Legal Argument" in *Best Guide to Canadian Legal Research*, (1987) 2 *Legal Research Update* 11.)

Precedent in law helps in categorization. Precedent economizes on information and minimizes idiosyncratic conclusions. It thus serves a variety of purposes: it aids in the stability and coherence of the law, making it more predictable; it provides fairness in decision-making; it promotes efficiency and eliminates sources of error, such as judicial bias; and it fulfills a symbolic role by recognizing the relationship between courts and the legislature. It therefore has independent value.

The difficulty for lawyers is often determining which parts of a precedent are binding in subsequent cases. As Stephen Waddams notes:

> Not everything a judge says in the course of deciding a case can be binding on her successors, or the common law would have perished long before now from a surfeit of precedents. What is said to be binding is the "decision," but this is an ambiguous concept. The actual facts of the case never arise again in identical form. ... A general rule is given that explains the result in the instant case and will apply to at least some other cases. It is this rule, called the *ratio decidendi* (reason of deciding) that is said to constitute the binding rule for purposes of precedent. Everything else that is said by the judge is called *obiter dicta* (things said by the way). In theory the *ratio decidendi* is binding on lower courts, but the *obiter dicta* are not.

(Stephen Waddams, *Introduction to the Study of Law*, 7th ed (Toronto: Carswell, 2010) at 79.)

The *ratio decidendi* literally means "the rule decided." It is not self-defining. As Waddams further states (at 81):

> [T]here is no "true" *ratio decidendi* of a decision. The *ratio decidendi* of a case is only as wide as a subsequent court will concede it to be. This is not to say that the doctrine of *stare decisis* is meaningless. Sometimes a judge will find herself unable to distinguish a former case on any rationally acceptable ground. But the doctrine is a good deal less rigid than it might at first appear.

Every case has to be looked at from two points of view: (1) that of the narrowest rule that a subsequent unkind court will concede has been laid down, and (2) the widest rule that a later friendly court could use to support a more novel position: see Karl Llewellyn, *The Bramble Bush: On Our Law and Its Study* (Dobbs Ferry, NY: Oceana Publications, 1960) at 68.

An example illustrates these issues. In the Supreme Court of Canada case of *Seneca College v Bhadauria*, [1981] 2 SCR 181 (a case concerned with whether the human rights regime set out in the Ontario *Human Rights Code* covers the entire field of anti-discrimination law, including common law actions for damages arising from discriminatory behaviour), Laskin CJ stated:

> For the foregoing reasons, I would hold that not only does the Code foreclose any civil action based directly upon a breach thereof but it also excludes any common law action based on an invocation of the public policy expressed in the [Ontario *Human Rights Code*]. The Code itself has laid out the procedures for vindication of that public policy, procedures which the plaintiff respondent did not see fit to use.

On a wide reading of Laskin CJ's reasoning, no claim based on a breach of the Ontario *Human Rights Code*, or the public policy found within it, is available to any future litigant (unless the Supreme Court of Canada decides to overrule itself) because the Code is an exhaustive expression of all matters related to human rights.

Yet consider the following excerpt from *Canada Trust Co v Ontario Human Rights Commission*. In it, Tarnopolsky JA applies a much narrower reading of *Bhadauria*—"distinguishing" that case and constraining it to its facts—in order to allow the claim for discrimination in the context of a trust claim. Notice how he quotes the exact paragraph from Laskin CJ above but then goes on to narrow its application. Do you find his reasoning satisfactory?

Canada Trust Co v Ontario Human Rights Commission
(1990), 74 OR (2d) 481 (CA)

[This case was concerned with whether the terms of a scholarship trust established in 1923 are contrary to public policy. If they are, the question then is whether the cy-près doctrine can be applied to preserve the trust. The terms of the trust restricted the scholarship funds to white Christians of British nationality or British parentage.]

TARNOPOLSKY JA (concurring in result):
All these submissions can be summarized into three main issues:

1. Did McKeown J have jurisdiction to determine this matter or should he have deferred to the jurisdiction of the Ontario Human Rights Commission?

• • •

Since 1971, the Ontario Human Rights Commission and its equivalents in the Provinces of Alberta and British Columbia, together with other bodies, have expressed concerns over conditions of eligibility to officials of the trustee. There are universities which, in the last ten years, have also complained or expressed concern to officers of the Foundation regarding eligibility requirements. Notwithstanding instances of this kind, the Foundation receives approximately 230 new and renewal applications annually.

Evidence was submitted to McKeown J to show that there exist in Ontario and elsewhere in Canada numerous educational scholarships which contain eligibility restrictions based on race, ancestry, place of origin, ethnic origin, citizenship, creed, sex, age, marital status, family status and handicap.

III. The Jurisprudence

(1) Jurisdiction—Human Rights Commission or Court?

The Ontario Human Rights Commission submitted that McKeown J should have deferred to the Commission to exercise its jurisdiction under the Human Rights Code, 1981 with respect to the complaint against the trustee that the Leonard Trust contravenes the Code. In considering this submission one must start with the following fundamental proposition offered by Dubin ACJO in *Blainey v. Ontario Hockey Assn.* (1986), 54 OR (2d) 513, at pp. 532-33:

> ... [T]he Human Rights Code provides a comprehensive scheme for the investigation and adjudication of complaints of discrimination. There is a very broad right of appeal to the Court from the ultimate determination of a board of inquiry constituted under the Human Rights Code. The procedure provided for in the Human

Rights Code must first be pursued before resort can be made to the Court. This was so held in *Board of Governors of Seneca College v. Bhadauria*, [1981] 2 SCR 181, 124 DLR (3d) 193. ... Chief Justice Laskin, speaking for the Court, stated at p. 183 SCR, pp. 194-5 DLR:

> In my opinion, the attempt of the respondent to hold the judgment in her favour on the ground that a right of action springs directly from a breach of The Ontario Human Rights Code cannot succeed. The reason lies in the comprehensiveness of the Code in its administrative and adjudicative features, the latter including a wide right of appeal to the Courts on both fact and law.

And at pp. 194-5 SCR, p. 203 DLR:

> The view taken by the Ontario Court of Appeal is a bold one and may be commended as an attempt to advance the common law. In my opinion, however, this is foreclosed by the legislative initiative which overtook the existing common law in Ontario and established a different regime which does not exclude the courts but rather makes them part of the enforcement machinery under the Code.
>
> For the foregoing reasons, I would hold that not only does the Code foreclose any civil action based directly upon a breach thereof but it also excludes any common law action based on an invocation of the public policy expressed in the Code. The Code itself has laid out the procedures for vindication of that public policy, procedures which the plaintiff respondent did not see fit to use.

Nevertheless, although this may be taken as a starting proposition, I agree with McKeown J that in this case several factors militate towards the High Court, as the superior court of inherent jurisdiction in this province, assuming jurisdiction despite a complaint being filed with the Human Rights Commission with respect to the same subject-matter.

In the first place, the state of the law dealt with by this court and the Supreme Court of Canada in *Seneca College of Applied Arts and Technology v. Bhadauria*, [1981] 2 SCR 181 is in contrast with the situation in this case. In *Bhadauria* this court had attempted "to advance the common law" in filling a void by creating a new tort of discrimination. The Supreme Court held that not to be necessary because of the comprehensive scheme of the Ontario Human Rights Code, RSO 1970, c. 318 [later RSO 1980, c 340]. Here, however, we are concerned with the administration of a trust, over which superior courts have had inherent jurisdiction for centuries and, in particular, with respect to charitable or public trusts. As noted at the beginning of this judgment, the trustee in this case applied to the High Court for advice and direction pursuant to the trust instrument itself as well as s. 60 of the *Trustee Act*.

Second, we are not concerned here with a typical proceeding under the Human Rights Code, 1981 in which an allegation of discrimination is brought against a respondent. The Commission's first mandate is to effect a settlement. However, the trustee has no authority, absent authorization of the trust deed or legislation or a court order, to enter into a settlement which would be contrary to the terms of the trust. Even if no settlement could be effected and a board of inquiry were to be appointed, there is serious question as to whether the board could grant an adequate remedy. Its remedial authority is governed by s. 40(1) of the Code. If a Code infringement is found, the board may, by order,

    (a)   direct the party to do anything that, in the opinion of the board, the party ought to do to achieve compliance with this Act, both in respect of the complaint and in respect of future practices; and

(b)   direct the party to make restitution, including monetary compensation, for loss arising out of the infringement, and, where the infringement has been engaged in wilfully or recklessly, monetary compensation may include an award, not exceeding $10,000, for mental anguish.

These remedial powers do not appear to give the board of inquiry the power to alter the terms of the trust or declare it void. In any case, resort to a court would have to be made to determine authoritatively whether such power exists.

Finally, I agree with McKeown J that this is not a case where the fact-finding role of the Commission and a board of inquiry would be required. Even in *Bell v. Ontario Human Rights Commission*, [1971] SCR 756, 18 DLR (3d) 1, where some further fact-finding and, particularly, fact-verification might have been useful, Martland J, on behalf of the majority on the Supreme Court of Canada, quoted Lord Goddard in *R v. Tottenham and District Rent Tribunal; Ex parte Northfield (Highgate) Ltd.*, [1957] 1 QB 103, at p. 108, to the effect that:

> ... [W]here there is a clear question of law not depending upon particular facts—because there is no fact in dispute in this case—there is no reason why the applicants should not come direct to this court for prohibition. ...

Similarly, here, I agree with McKeown J that we are concerned with a question of law; there are no facts in dispute. The trustee is entitled to come to the superior court pursuant to s. 60 of the *Trustee Act* to seek advice and direction.

[Tarnopolsky JA invoked the cy-près doctrine to bring the trust into accord with public policy by removing all offensive restrictions, thus permitting it to remain a fund for academic scholarships.]

D. COMMON LAW AND EQUITY

We have already examined our legal inheritances such as the British common law, the French civil law, and Indigenous systems of law. The term "common law" in those discussions was used in the wide sense to distinguish it from the civilian law systems. It was used to mean a system of law based primarily on judicial decisions. But "common law" has a variety of other "internal" meanings according to context. For instance, common law must sometimes be distinguished from the body of law produced from the Chancery Court and known as equity.

Equity is formally defined as the body of law developed by the Court of Chancery prior to that court's dismantling—in most common law countries this was shortly after 1873. Courts of Chancery were originally separate from the common law courts. Thus, equity developed in tandem with the common law. Its original function was to provide a corrective to the perceived harshness of the common law. The equitable jurisdiction began as a fluid, pragmatic, conscience-based system of law, profoundly anti-formal and anti-establishment. Cases were decided according to the rules of equity and good conscience; there was no abstract, formal methodology and no strict doctrine of precedent.

This is not as strange an idea as it might seem. Some form of equity is probably necessary in any modern legal system. Law as a body of rules and principles is by its nature concerned with generalities—groups or classes of persons and events, rather than individuals and discrete happenings. Because of this, law sometimes fails to achieve adequate justice in the particular case. Equity is a supplementary system that allows for the exigencies of the special case. In its ideal form, its principles are more clearly tied to considerations of conscience, morality, and the conduct of particular persons than those of the law.

In Canada, equity has provided some of the more progressive decisions in the area of private law. Typically, matters falling within the equitable jurisdiction of Chancery courts included disputes relating to:

- property (trusts; married women's property; equitable rules related to transfer);
- contracts (remedies such as specific performance and injunctions; undue influence, mistake, and misrepresentation);
- procedure (set-off and account);
- guardianship; and
- commercial matters (fiduciary duties; subrogation and contribution).

In 1873, the administration of the equitable and common law systems was fused in the United Kingdom through the adoption of the judicature acts (copied shortly thereafter in Canadian jurisdictions). These acts ended the existence of the separate Chancery Court. Since then, equitable principles have continued to develop alongside common law principles: the rules of common law and equity are now applied concurrently in all superior courts, with equity prevailing in cases of conflict.

The modern view of the equitable jurisdiction is that of a body of rules, principles, maxims, and doctrines that originated in the Court of Chancery but that has continued to evolve and develop since Chancery was abolished. It is now simply part of our law. Equitable doctrines continue to exist, but they are referred to as equitable only because of historical accident, not because they are substantially different from common law doctrines. Nevertheless, these doctrines are important components of Canadian law in the 21st century and reflect a continuing commitment to conscience and moral-based decision-making. Furthermore, despite the fact that the bulk of equity jurisprudence arose in the private law realm, equitable principles are slowly making inroads into public law.

DeLaurier v Jackson is an early example of a case in which the equitable doctrine of fiduciary was invoked to protect the religious upbringing of a child. Note how the court relies on equitable principles to interpret a statutory provision.

DeLaurier v Jackson
[1934] SCR 149, 1 DLR 790

[Appellants applied in the Supreme Court of Ontario for the custody of their infant child Thelma, who, for about ten years from early infancy, had been in the care of the respondents. The appellants were Roman Catholics. The respondents were Protestants, and the child had become identified with the respondents' church. The application was dismissed, an appeal to the Court of Appeal for Ontario was dismissed, and an appeal was brought to the Supreme Court of Canada.]

HUGHES J:

The appellants rely strongly on section 24 of the *Infants Act*, RSO, 1927, chapter 186, which reads as follows:

Nothing in this Act shall change the law as to the authority of the father in respect of the religious faith in which his child is to be educated.

Section 21 of the *Judicature Act*, RSO, 1927, chapter 88, provides as follows:

In questions relating to the custody and education of infants, and generally in all matters in which there is any conflict or variance between the rules of equity and the rules of the common law with reference to the same matter, the rules of equity shall prevail.

In equity a principle was early established that the court might control or ignore the parental right but in so doing it should act cautiously, and should act in opposition to the parent only when judicially satisfied that the welfare of the child required that the parental right should be suspended or superseded.

In the present case, Mr. Justice Kerwin interviewed the infant and then dismissed the application of the appellants, and Mr. Justice McEvoy had some time before [he] dismissed a similar application after seeing the parties and hearing their evidence. The Court of Appeal affirmed these dismissals, and, as the orders of dismissal were in the nature of discretionary orders, I do not know on what principle this Court can now interfere. The appeal, therefore, should be dismissed with costs, against which should be set off the costs of the motion to quash the appeal fixed at $75.

CROCKET J: ... One thing the evidence clearly shews—that Thelma has been completely out of touch with her natural parents for a period of now over ten years and that her mother has had no contact with her since a few weeks or at most a few months after her birth.

After a careful examination of the evidence and the learned trial judge's (Kerwin J) conclusion thereupon and the reasons he gives for his decision, we are satisfied that he in no manner disregarded the provisions of s. 24 of the Ontario *Infants Act*, upon which the appellants much rely. The effect of this section, no doubt, is that none of the provisions of that statute shall be deemed to alter whatever authority the father may otherwise by law possess as to the religious faith in which his child is to be educated. This authority, however wide it may have been at common law, must now be measured by the rules of equity, which in virtue of the express provisions of the *Judicature Act* prevail in Ontario as they do in England, and, in cases of this kind, recognize the welfare of the child as the predominant consideration. If the general welfare of the child requires that the father's rights in respect of the religious faith in which his offspring is to be reared, should be suspended or superseded, the courts in the exercise of their equitable jurisdiction have undoubted power to override them, as they have power to override all other parental rights, though in doing so they must act cautiously. ...

Due consideration is, of course, to be given in all cases to the father's wishes but if the court is satisfied in any case upon a consideration of all the facts and circumstances, as shewn by the evidence, that the father's wishes conflict with the child's own best interests, viewed from all angles—material, physical, moral, emotional and intellectual as well as religious—then the father's wishes must yield to the welfare of the child.

In recent years, equitable principles have been adapted to public law circumstances. The equitable fiduciary obligation, long thought to apply only to private matters, has evolved into the public realm. In certain circumstances, as the next three excerpts show, the Crown may be under a fiduciary obligation to particular individuals or groups.

Guerin v The Queen
[1984] 2 SCR 335, 13 DLR (4th) 321, 59 BCLR 301

DICKSON J (Beetz, Chouinard, and Lamer JJ concurring):

The question is whether the appellants, the Chief and Councillors of the Musqueam Indian Band, suing on their own behalf and on behalf of all other members of the Band, are entitled to recover damages from the federal Crown in respect of the leasing to a golf club of land on the Musqueam Indian Reserve. Collier J, of the Trial Division of the Federal Court, declared that the Crown was in breach of trust. He assessed damages at $10,000,000. The Federal Court of Appeal allowed a Crown appeal, set aside the judgment of the Trial Division and dismissed the action.

Before adverting to the facts, reference should be made to several of the relevant sections of the *Indian Act*, RSC 1952, c. 149, as amended. Section 18(1) provides in part that reserves shall be held by Her Majesty for the use of the respective Indian Bands for which they were set apart. Generally, lands in a reserve shall not be sold, alienated, leased or otherwise disposed of until they have been surrendered to Her Majesty by the Band for whose use and benefit in common the reserve was set apart (s. 37). A surrender may be absolute or qualified, conditional or unconditional (s. 38(2)). To be valid, a surrender must be made to Her Majesty, assented to by a majority of the electors of the Band, and accepted by the Governor in Council (s. 39(1)).

• • •

IV. Fiduciary Relationship

The issue of the Crown's liability was dealt with in the courts below on the basis of the existence or non-existence of a trust. In dealing with the different consequences of a "true" trust, as opposed to a "political" trust, Le Dain J noted that the Crown could be liable only if it were subject to an "equitable obligation enforceable in a court of law." I have some doubt as to the cogency of the terminology of "higher" and "lower" trusts, but I do agree that the existence of an equitable obligation is the *sine qua non* for liability. Such an obligation is not, however, limited to relationships which can be strictly defined as "trusts." As will presently appear, it is my view that the Crown's obligations vis-à-vis the Indians cannot be defined as a trust. That does not, however, mean that the Crown owes no enforceable duty to the Indians in the way in which it deals with Indian land.

In my view, the nature of Indian title and the framework of the statutory scheme established for disposing of Indian land places upon the Crown an equitable obligation, enforceable by the courts, to deal with the land for the benefit of the Indians. This obligation does not amount to a trust in the private law sense. It is rather a fiduciary duty. If however, the Crown breaches this fiduciary duty it will be liable to the Indians in the same way and to the same extent as if such a trust were in effect.

The fiduciary relationship between the Crown and the Indians has its roots in the concept of aboriginal, native or Indian title. The fact that Indian Bands have a certain interest in lands does not, however, in itself give rise to a fiduciary relationship between the Indians and the Crown. The conclusion that the Crown is a fiduciary depends upon the further proposition that the Indian interest in the land is inalienable except upon surrender to the Crown.

An Indian Band is prohibited from directly transferring its interest to a third party. Any sale or lease of land can only be carried out after a surrender has taken place, with the Crown then acting on the Band's behalf. The Crown first took this responsibility upon itself in the Royal Proclamation of 1763. It is still recognized in the surrender provisions of the *Indian Act*. The surrender requirement, and the responsibility it entails, are the source of a distinct fiduciary obligation owed by the Crown to the Indians. In order to explore the character of this obligation, however, it is first necessary to consider the basis of aboriginal title and the nature of the interest in land which it represents.

• • •

In [the political trust cases] the party claiming to be beneficiary under a trust depended entirely on statute, ordinance or treaty as the basis for its claim to an interest in the funds in question. The situation of the Indians is entirely different. Their interest in their lands is a pre-existing legal right not created by Royal Proclamation, by s. 18(1) of the *Indian Act*, or by any other executive order or legislative provision.

• • •

Indians have a legal right to occupy and possess certain lands, the ultimate title to which is in the Crown. While their interest does not, strictly speaking, amount to beneficial ownership, neither is its nature completely exhausted by the concept of a personal right. It is true that the *sui generis* interest which the Indians have in the land is personal in the sense that it cannot be transferred to a grantee, but it is also true, as will presently appear, that the interest gives rise upon surrender to a distinctive fiduciary obligation on the part of the Crown to deal with the land for the benefit of the surrendering Indians. These two aspects of Indian title go together, since the Crown's original purpose in declaring the Indians' interest to be inalienable otherwise than to the Crown was to facilitate the Crown's ability to represent the Indians in dealings with third parties. The nature of the Indians' interest is therefore best characterized by its general inalienability, coupled with the fact that the Crown is under an obligation to deal with the land on the Indians' behalf when the interest is surrendered. Any description of Indian title which goes beyond these two features is both unnecessary and potentially misleading.

(c) The Crown's Fiduciary Obligation

The concept of fiduciary obligation originated long ago in the notion of breach of confidence, one of the original heads of jurisdiction in Chancery. In the present appeal its relevance is based on the requirement of a "surrender" before Indian land can be alienated.

The Royal Proclamation of 1763 provided that no private person could purchase from the Indians any lands that the Proclamation had reserved to them, and provided further that all purchases had to be by and in the name of the Crown, in a public assembly of the Indians held by the governor or commander-in-chief of the colony in which the lands in question lay. As Lord Watson pointed out in *St. Catherine's Milling [and Lumber Co v The Queen* (1888), 14 App Cas 46], at p. 54, this policy with respect to the sale or transfer of the Indians' interest in land has been continuously maintained by the British Crown, by the governments of the colonies when they became responsible for the administration of Indian affairs, and, after 1867, by the federal government of Canada. Successive federal statutes, predecessors to the present *Indian Act*, have all provided for the general inalienability of Indian reserve land except upon surrender to the Crown, the relevant provisions in the present Act being ss. 37-41.

The purpose of this surrender requirement is clearly to interpose the Crown between the Indians and prospective purchasers or lessees of their land, so as to prevent the Indians from being exploited. This is made clear in the Royal Proclamation itself, which prefaces the provision making the Crown an intermediary with a declaration that "great Frauds and Abuses have been committed in purchasing Lands of the Indians, to the great Prejudice of our Interests, and to the great Dissatisfaction of the said Indians ... ." Through the confirmation in the *Indian Act* of the historic responsibility which the Crown has undertaken, to act on behalf of the Indians so as to protect their interests in transactions with third parties, Parliament has conferred upon the Crown a discretion to decide for itself where the Indians' best interests really lie. This is the effect of s. 18(1) of the Act.

This discretion on the part of the Crown, far from ousting, as the Crown contends, the jurisdiction of the courts to regulate the relationship between the Crown and the Indians, has the effect of transforming the Crown's obligation into a fiduciary one. Professor Ernest Weinrib maintains in his article "The Fiduciary Obligation" (1975), 25 UTLJ 1, at p. 7, that "the hallmark of a fiduciary relation is that the relative legal positions are such that one party is at the mercy of the other's discretion." ...

... [W]here by statute, agreement, or perhaps by unilateral undertaking, one party has an obligation to act for the benefit of another, and that obligation carries with it a discretionary power, the party thus empowered becomes a fiduciary. Equity will then supervise the relationship by holding him to the fiduciary's strict standard of conduct.

It is sometimes said that the nature of fiduciary relationships is both established and exhausted by the standard categories of agent, trustee, partner, director, and the like. I do not agree. It is the nature of the relationship, not the specific category of actor involved that gives rise to the fiduciary duty. The categories of fiduciary, like those of negligence, should not be considered closed. See, e.g. *Laskin v. Bache & Co. Inc.* (1971), 23 DLR (3d) 385 (Ont. CA), at p. 392; *Goldex Mines Ltd. v. Revill* (1974), 7 OR 216 (Ont. CA), at p. 224.

It should be noted that fiduciary duties generally arise only with regard to obligations originating in a private law context. Public law duties, the performance of which requires the exercise of discretion, do not typically give rise to a fiduciary relationship. As the "political trust" cases indicate, the Crown is not normally viewed as a fiduciary in the exercise of its legislative or administrative function. The mere fact, however, that it is the Crown which is obligated to act on the Indians' behalf does not of itself remove the Crown's obligation from the scope of the fiduciary principle. As was pointed out earlier, the Indians' interest in land is an independent legal interest. It is not a creation of either the legislative or executive branches of government. The Crown's obligation to the Indians with respect to that interest is therefore not a public law duty. While it is not a private law duty in the strict sense either, it is nonetheless in the nature of a private law duty. Therefore, in this *sui generis* relationship, it is not improper to regard the Crown as a fiduciary.

KLB v British Columbia
2003 SCC 51, [2003] 2 SCR 403

[The appellants suffered abuse in two successive foster homes. In the second home, the appellants were also exposed to inappropriate sexual behaviour by the older adopted sons. On one occasion, K was sexually assaulted by one of these young men. The trial judge found that the government had failed to exercise reasonable care in arranging suitable placements for the children and in monitoring and supervising these placements. She also found that the children had suffered lasting damage as a result of their stays in the two homes. She rejected the defence that the tort actions were barred by the BC *Limitation Act*. The Court of Appeal allowed the Crown's appeal. All three judges found that the appellants' claims were statute-barred, with the exception of K's claim for sexual assault. In addition, all three judges overturned the ruling that the government had breached its fiduciary duty to the children. The majority, however, upheld the trial judge's conclusion that the government was vicariously liable and in breach of a non-delegable duty of care in the placement and supervision of the children. The appellants appealed to the Supreme Court of Canada.]

McLACHLIN CJ:

[1] This appeal raises the question of whether, and on what grounds, the government can be held liable for the tortious conduct of foster parents toward children whom the government has placed under their care. The appeal was heard together with *M.B. v. British Columbia*, [2003] 2 SCR 477, 2003 SCC 53, and *E.D.G. v. Hammer*, [2003] 2 SCR 459, 2003 SCC 52, which raise many of the same issues.

• • •

III. Analysis

A. Is There Any Legal Basis on Which the Government Could Be Held Liable for the Harm That the Appellants Suffered in Foster Care?

[11] Three grounds of government liability were canvassed by the trial judge, and a fourth added by the Court of Appeal: (1) direct negligence by the government; (2) vicarious liability of the government for the tortious conduct of the foster parents; (3) breach of non-delegable duty by the government; and (4) breach of fiduciary duty by the government.

• • •

4. Liability for Breach of Fiduciary Duty

[38] The parties to this case do not dispute that the relationship between the government and foster children is fiduciary in nature. This Court has held that parents owe a fiduciary duty to children in their care: *M. (K.) v. M. (H.)*, [1992] 3 SCR 6. Similarly, the British Columbia Court of Appeal has held that guardians owe a fiduciary duty to their wards: *B. (P.A.) v. Curry* (1997), 30 BCLR (3d) 1. The government, through the Superintendent of Child Welfare, is the legal guardian of children in foster care, with power to direct and supervise their placement. The children are doubly vulnerable, first as children and second because of their difficult pasts and the trauma of being removed from their birth families. The parties agree that, standing in the parents' stead, the Superintendent has considerable power over vulnerable children, and that his placement decisions and monitoring may affect their lives and well-being in fundamental ways.

[39] Where the parties disagree is over the content of the duty that this fiduciary relationship imposes on the government—over what actions and inactions amount to a breach of this duty. The appellants argue that the duty is simply to act in the best interests of foster children. The government, on the other hand, argues for a more narrowly defined duty—a duty to avoid certain harmful actions that constitute a betrayal of trust, of loyalty and of disinterest. For the reasons that follow, I conclude that the government's view must prevail.

[40] First a procedural point. Fiduciary duties arise in a number of different contexts, including express trusts, relationships marked by discretionary power and trust, and the special responsibilities of the Crown in dealing with aboriginal interests. Although the parties' view seemed to be that the Superintendent's fiduciary duty was a private law duty arising from the relationship between the Superintendent and the children, they also suggested at times that it arose from the public law responsibilities imposed on the Superintendent by the *Protection of Children Act*. On the latter view, the Superintendent's fiduciary obligations would be closer to the fiduciary obligations of the Crown toward aboriginal peoples, which have been held to include a requirement of using due diligence in advancing particular interests of aboriginal peoples: *Wewaykum Indian Band v. Canada*, [2002] 4 SCR 245, 2002 SCC 79; *Blueberry River Indian Band v. Canada (Department of Indian Affairs and Northern Development)*, [1995] 4 SCR 344; *Guerin v. The Queen*, [1984] 2 SCR 335. In my opinion, this latter view of the Superintendent's fiduciary obligation cannot succeed. A fiduciary obligation to promote the best interests of foster children while in foster care cannot be implied from the statute, because the statute evinces a clear intent that these children be nurtured in a private home environment; and, as discussed above, this effectively eliminates the government's capacity to exercise close supervision in relation to the foster parents' day-to-day conduct. The statute could not, therefore, consistently imply that the Superintendent stands under a fiduciary duty to exercise due diligence in ensuring on a day-to-day basis that the foster children's best interests are promoted.

[41] What, however, might the content of the fiduciary duty be if it is understood, instead, as a private law duty arising simply from the relationship of discretionary power and trust between the Superintendent and the foster children? In *Lac Minerals Ltd. v. International Corona Resources Ltd.*, [1989] 2 SCR 574, at pp. 646-47, La Forest J noted that there are certain common threads running through fiduciary duties that arise from relationships marked by discretionary power and trust, such as loyalty and "the avoidance of a conflict of duty and interest and a duty not to profit at the expense of the beneficiary." However, he also noted that "[t]he obligation imposed may vary in its specific substance depending on the relationship" (p. 646). Because such obligations will vary in their content depending on the nature of the relationship involved, we should determine the content of the obligation owed by the government to foster children by focussing on analogous cases. This suggests that in determining the content of the fiduciary obligation here at issue, we should focus generally on cases dealing with the relationship of children to caregivers, and more particularly on the relationship between parents (in whose stead the Superintendent stands) and their children.

• • •

[50] Returning to the facts of this case, there is no evidence that the government put its own interests ahead of those of the children or committed acts that harmed the children in a way that amounted to betrayal of trust or disloyalty. The worst that can be said of the Superintendent is that he, along with the social workers, failed properly to assess whether the children's needs and problems could be met in the designated foster homes; failed to discuss the limits of acceptable discipline with the foster parents; and failed to conduct frequent visits to the homes given that they were overplaced and had a documented history of risk (trial judgment, at para. 74). The essence of the Superintendent's misconduct was negligence, not disloyalty or breach of trust. There is no suggestion that he was serving anyone's interest but that of the children. His fault was not disloyalty, but failure to take sufficient care.

[51] I would therefore uphold the Court of Appeal's conclusion that the government did not breach its fiduciary duty to the appellants.

Subsequent cases involving the Crown's treatment toward Indigenous peoples have cemented the finding of a fiduciary relationship outlined in *Guerin* but also added to its scope by including other equitable-like obligations. For instance, in *Manitoba Metis Federation v Canada (AG)*, the Supreme Court of Canada considered the historical role of the Crown in its relationship with the Métis of Manitoba. We discussed this case in Chapter 3, but it is useful to reproduce a portion of it here as illustrative of the sort of factual circumstances in which fiduciary duties arise in relation to Indigenous peoples.

Manitoba Metis Federation Inc v Canada (AG)
2013 SCC 14, [2013] 1 SCR 623

McLACHLIN CJ and KARAKATSANIS J (LeBel, Fish, Abella, and Cromwell JJ concurring):

[1] Canada is a young nation with ancient roots. The country was born in 1867, by the consensual union of three colonies—United Canada (now Ontario and Quebec), Nova Scotia and New Brunswick. Left unsettled was whether the new nation would be expanded to include the vast territories to the west, stretching from modern Manitoba to British Columbia. The Canadian government, led by Prime Minister John A. Macdonald, embarked on a policy aimed at bringing the western territories within the boundaries of Canada, and opening them up to settlement.

[2] This meant dealing with the indigenous peoples who were living in the western territories. On the prairies, these consisted mainly of two groups—the First Nations, and the descendants of unions between white traders and explorers and Aboriginal women, now known as Métis.

[3] The government policy regarding the First Nations was to enter into treaties with the various bands, whereby they agreed to settlement of their lands in exchange for reservations of land and other promises.

[4] The government policy with respect to the Métis population—which, in 1870, comprised 85 percent of the population of what is now Manitoba—was less clear. Settlers began pouring into the region, displacing the Métis' social and political control. This led to resistance and conflict. To resolve the conflict and assure peaceful annexation of the territory, the Canadian government entered into negotiations with representatives of the Métis-led provisional government of the territory. The result was the *Manitoba Act, 1870*, S.C. 1870, c. 3 ("*Manitoba Act*"), which made Manitoba a province of Canada. [See Chapter 11.]

In other areas of public law, there is still some uncertainty regarding the Crown's equitable obligations. The outer limits of Crown fiduciary responsibility—or other quasi-equitable doctrines—remain untested. See, for example, *Authorson v Canada (AG)*, 2003 SCC 39, [2003] 2 SCR 40.

II. STATUTORY LAW

A. INTRODUCTION

As noted in the previous section, much of early English law developed through the accumulation of case law and the interpretation of judges, as opposed to being set out in legislation. In essence, this is the definition of the common law. Whole areas of law, particularly those studied in the first year of law school, such as contracts, torts, and property, have developed largely from common law rules. There has been little in the way of statutory law to effect changes in these areas.

Parliament and provincial legislatures are free, however, to enact new statutes to displace the common law. They are also free to develop policy in entirely new directions, not by replacing or modifying the common law, but by enacting statutes in undeveloped areas. In modern states, many areas of law are almost wholly controlled by statutory enactments. Later chapters of this book focus on statutes and the rules that govern them. In this introduction, we simply make a few key points about the relationship between statutes and the common law.

B. STATUTES AND THE COMMON LAW: A COMPLEX MIX

One basic principle of common law interpretation is that a statutory rule will supersede a judge-made rule. This is relatively easy to apply in many situations. For example, where a court interprets a rule banning "vehicles" from a public park so as not to include baby carriages, and a legislature then passes a new provision defining "vehicles" expressly to include baby carriages, the prior court decision is no longer valid. But the theory may be more difficult to apply where the statutory scheme does not expressly overturn a common law rule, or where the common law ventures into new territories.

The interplay among common law, statutory law, and constitutional law can be complex. Consider the issue of same-sex marriage, a subject of debate around the world. As a result of the decision by the Supreme Court of Canada in the *Reference re Same-Sex Marriage*, 2004 SCC 79, [2004] 3 SCR 698, and the ensuing legislation, the *Civil Marriage Act*, SC 2005, c 33, it is now legal everywhere in Canada for persons to marry someone of the same sex.

This recent shift in policy overcomes a century or more of common and civil law tradition—the definition of marriage as the union of one man and one woman was a common law rule that applied in all the common law provinces; in Quebec, the heterosexual definition was implicit in the 1866 *Civil Code of Lower Canada* and became explicit when new civil code provisions were confirmed by federal legislation as recently as 2001.

The impetus for the modern changes allowing same-sex marriage arose piecemeal, through a series of constitutional cases that began by establishing equal benefits for gay and lesbian couples. See, for example, *M v H*, [1999] 2 SCR 3, and *Egan v Canada*, [1995] 2 SCR 513. Then, in the early part of the 2000s, a trilogy of cases in British Columbia, Ontario, and Quebec challenged the heterosexual definition of marriage itself as a breach of the *Canadian Charter of Rights and Freedoms*: *EGALE Canada Inc v Canada (AG)*, 2001 BCSC 1365, 95 BCLR (3d) 122; *Halpern v Canada (AG)* (2003), 65 OR (3d) 161 (CA); *Catholic Civil Rights League v Hendricks* (2004), 238 DLR (4th) 577 (Qc CA), aff'g [2002] RDF 1022 (Qc SC). The following excerpt from *Halpern v Canada (AG)* gives a brief glimpse into the intricate relationship among custom, common law, civil law, and constitutional law that exists in contemporary Canada.

Halpern v Canada (AG)
(2003), 65 OR (3d) 161, 172 OAC 276, 225 DLR (4th) 529 (CA)

BY THE COURT (McMurtry CJO, MacPherson and Gillese JJA):

A. Introduction

[1] The definition of marriage in Canada, for all of the nation's 136 years, has been based on the classic formulation of Lord Penzance in *Hyde v. Hyde and Woodmansee* (1866), LR 1 P & D 130, [1861-73] All ER Rep. 175 at p. 177 All ER, p. 133

P & D: "I conceive that marriage, as understood in Christendom, may for this purpose be defined as the voluntary union for life of one man and one woman, to the exclusion of all others." The central question in this appeal is whether the exclusion of same-sex couples from this common law definition of marriage breaches ss. 2(a) or 15(1) of the *Canadian Charter of Rights and Freedoms* (the "Charter") in a manner that is not justified in a free and democratic society under s. 1 of the Charter.

[2] This appeal raises significant constitutional issues that require serious legal analysis. That said, this case is ultimately about the recognition and protection of human dignity and equality in the context of the social structures available to conjugal couples in Canada.

[3] In *Law v. Canada (Minister of Employment and Immigration)*, [1999] 1 SCR 497, 170 DLR (4th) 1, at p. 530 SCR, Iacobucci J, writing for a unanimous court, described the importance of human dignity:

Human dignity means that an individual or group feels self-respect and self-worth. It is concerned with physical and psychological integrity and empowerment. Human dignity is harmed by unfair treatment premised upon personal traits or circumstances which do not relate to individual needs, capacities, or merits. It is enhanced by laws which are sensitive to the needs, capacities, and merits of different individuals, taking into account the context underlying their differences. Human dignity is harmed when individuals and groups are marginalized, ignored, or devalued, and is enhanced when laws recognize the full place of all individuals and groups within Canadian society.

[4] The *Ontario Human Rights Code*, RSO 1990, c. H.19, also recognizes the importance of protecting the dignity of all persons. The preamble affirms that "the inherent dignity and the equal and inalienable rights of all members of the human family is the foundation of freedom, justice and peace in the world." It states:

[I]t is public policy in Ontario to recognize the dignity and worth of every person and to provide for equal rights and opportunities without discrimination that is contrary to law, and having as its aim the creation of a climate of understanding and mutual respect for the dignity and worth of each person so that each person feels a part of the community and able to contribute fully to the development and well-being of the community and the Province[.]

[5] Marriage is, without dispute, one of the most significant forms of personal relationships. For centuries, marriage has been a basic element of social organization in societies around the world. Through the institution of marriage, individuals can publicly express their love and commitment to each other. Through this institution, society publicly recognizes expressions of love and commitment between individuals, granting them respect and legitimacy as a couple. This public recognition and sanction of marital relationships reflect society's approbation of the personal hopes, desires and aspirations that underlie loving, committed conjugal relationships. This can only enhance an individual's sense of self-worth and dignity.

[6] The ability to marry, and to thereby participate in this fundamental societal institution, is something that most Canadians take for granted. Same-sex couples do not; they are denied access to this institution simply on the basis of their sexual orientation.

[7] Sexual orientation is an analogous ground that comes under the umbrella of protection in s. 15(1) of the Charter: see *Egan v. Canada*, [1995] 2 SCR 513, 124 DLR

(4th) 609, and *M. v. H.*, [1999] 2 SCR 3, 171 DLR (4th) 577. As explained by Cory J in *M. v. H.* at pp. 52-53 SCR:

> In *Egan* ... this Court unanimously affirmed that sexual orientation is an analogous ground to those enumerated in s. 15(1). Sexual orientation is "a deeply personal char-acteristic that is either unchangeable or changeable only at unacceptable personal costs" (para. 5). In addition, a majority of this Court explicitly recognized that gays, lesbians and bisexuals, "whether as individuals or couples, form an identifiable minority who have suffered and continue to suffer serious social, political and eco-nomic disadvantage" (para. 175, per Cory J; see also para. 89, per L'Heureux-Dubé J).

[8] Historically, same-sex equality litigation has focused on achieving equality in some of the most basic elements of civic life, such as bereavement leave, health care benefits, pensions benefits, spousal support, name changes and adoption. The question at the heart of this appeal is whether excluding same-sex couples from another of the most basic elements of civic life—marriage—infringes human dig-nity and violates the Canadian Constitution.

B. Facts

(1) The Parties and the Events

[9] Seven gay and lesbian couples (the "Couples") want to celebrate their love and commitment to each other by getting married in civil ceremonies. In this respect, they share the same goal as countless other Canadian couples. Their reasons for wanting to engage in a formal civil ceremony of marriage are the same as the rea-sons of heterosexual couples. By way of illustration, we cite the affidavits of three of the persons who seek to be married:

[Affidavits omitted.]

[10] The Couples applied for civil marriage licences from the Clerk of the City of Toronto. The Clerk did not deny the licences but, instead, indicated that she would apply to the court for directions, and hold the licences in abeyance in the interim. The Couples commenced their own application. By order dated August 22, 2000, Lang J transferred the Couples' application to the Divisional Court. The Clerk's application was stayed on consent.

[11] In roughly the same time frame, the Metropolitan Community Church of Toronto ("MCCT"), a Christian church that solemnizes marriages for its heterosexual congregants, decided to conduct marriages for its homosexual members. Previ-ously, MCCT had felt constrained from performing marriages for same-sex couples because it understood that the municipal authorities in Toronto would not issue a marriage licence to same-sex couples. However, MCCT learned that the ancient Christian tradition of publishing the banns of marriage was a lawful alternative under the laws of Ontario to a marriage licence issued by municipal authorities: see *Marriage Act*, RSO 1990, c. M.3, s. 5(1).

• • •

[14] In compliance with the laws of Ontario, MCCT submitted the requisite documentation for the two marriages to the Office of the Registrar General: see *Vital Statistics Act*, RSO 1990, c. V.4, s. 19(1) and the Regulations under the *Marriage Act*, RRO 1990, Reg. 738, s. 2(3). The Registrar refused to accept the documents for registration, citing an alleged federal prohibition against same-sex marriages. As a result, MCCT launched its application to the Divisional Court.

• • •

C. Issues

[25] We frame the issues as follows:

(1) What is the common law definition of marriage? Does it prohibit same-sex marriages? (2) Is a constitutional amendment required to change the common law definition of marriage, or can a reformulation be accomplished by Parliament or the courts? (3) Does the common law definition of marriage infringe MCCT's rights under ss. 2(a) and 15(1) of the Charter? (4) Does the common law definition of marriage infringe the Couples' equality rights under s. 15(1) of the Charter? (5) If the answer to question 3 or 4 is "Yes," is the infringement saved by s. 1 of the Charter? (6) If the common law definition of marriage is unconstitutional, what is the appropriate remedy and should it be suspended for any period of time?

D. Analysis

[26] Before turning to the issues raised by the appeal, we make four preliminary observations.

[27] First, the definition of marriage is found at common law. The only statutory reference to a definition of marriage is found in s. 1.1 of the *Modernization of Benefits and Obligations Act*, SC 2000, c. 12, which provides:

> 1.1 For greater certainty, the amendments made by this Act do not affect the meaning of the word "marriage," that is, the lawful union of one man and one woman to the exclusion of all others.

[28] The *Modernization of Benefits and Obligations Act* is the federal government's response to the Supreme Court of Canada's decision in *M. v. H.* The Act extends federal benefits and obligations to all unmarried couples that have cohabited in a conjugal relationship for at least one year, regardless of sexual orientation. As recognized by the parties, s. 1.1 does not purport to be a federal statutory definition of marriage. Rather, s. 1.1 simply affirms that the Act does not change the common law definition of marriage.

[29] Second, it is clear and all parties accept that, the common law is subject to Charter scrutiny where government action or inaction is based on a common law rule. Accordingly, there is no dispute that the AGC was the proper respondent in the applications brought by the Couples and MCCT, and that the common law definition of marriage is subject to Charter scrutiny.

• • •

(1) The Common Law Rule Regarding Marriage

[35] The preliminary argument on this appeal advanced by the Couples is that there is no common law bar to same-sex marriages. The intervener Egale Canada Inc. ("Egale") supported this argument and expanded on the Couples' submissions.

[36] As previously mentioned, the classic formulation of marriage is found in the English decision of *Hyde v. Hyde and Woodmansee*, "the voluntary union for life of one man and one woman, to the exclusion of all others." Egale argues that *Hyde* and *Corbett v. Corbett*, [1970] 2 All ER 33 (PDA), the other English case cited as authority for the common law restriction against same-sex marriage, have a weak jurisprudential foundation and ought not to be followed. Egale points out that *Hyde* dealt with the validity of a potentially polygamous marriage, and argues that the comments in *Hyde* about marriage being between opposite-sex persons are obiter. With respect to Corbett, Egale argues that it is based on outdated, narrow notions of

sexual relationships between women and men. The Couples adopt Egale's submissions, and further argue that *M. v. H.* overruled, by implication, any common law restriction against same-sex marriages.

[37] In our view, the Divisional Court was correct in concluding that there is a common law rule that excludes same-sex marriages. This court in *Iantsis v. Papatheodorou*, [1971] 1 OR 245 at p. 248, 15 DLR (3d) 53, adopted the *Hyde* formulation of marriage as the union between a man and a woman. This understanding of the common law definition of "marriage" is reflected in s. 1.1 of the *Modernization of Benefits and Obligations Act*, which refers to the definition of "marriage" as "the lawful union of one man and one woman to the exclusion of all others." Further, there is no merit to the submission that *M. v. H.* overruled, by implication, the common law definition of "marriage." In *M. v. H.*, Iacobucci J stated, at p. 83:

> This appeal does not challenge traditional conceptions of marriage, as s. 29 of the [*Family Law Act*, RSO 1990, c F.3] expressly applies to unmarried opposite-sex couples. That being said, I do not wish to be understood as making any comment on marriage or indeed on related issues.

(2) Constitutional Amendment

[38] The *Constitution Act, 1867* divides legislative powers relating to marriage between the federal and provincial governments. The federal government has exclusive jurisdiction over "Marriage and Divorce": s. 91(26). The provinces have exclusive jurisdiction over the solemnization of marriage: s. 92(12).

[39] The intervenor, The Association for Marriage and the Family in Ontario (the "Association"), takes the position that the word "marriage," as used in the *Constitution Act, 1867*, is a constitutionally entrenched term that refers to the legal definition of marriage that existed at Confederation. The Association argues that the legal definition of marriage at Confederation was the "union of one man and one woman." As a constitutionally entrenched term, this definition of marriage can be amended only through the formal constitutional amendment procedures. As a consequence, neither the courts nor Parliament have jurisdiction to reformulate the meaning of marriage.

• • •

[41] In our view, the Association's constitutional amendment argument is without merit for two reasons. First, whether same-sex couples can marry is a matter of capacity. There can be no issue, nor was the contrary argued before us, that Parliament has authority to make laws regarding the capacity to marry. Such authority is found in s. 91(26) of the *Constitution Act, 1867*.

[42] Second, to freeze the definition of marriage to whatever meaning it had in 1867 is contrary to this country's jurisprudence of progressive constitutional interpretation. This jurisprudence is rooted in Lord Sankey's words in *Edwards v. AG Canada*, [1930] AC 124, [1929] All ER Rep. 571 (PC) at p. 136 AC: "The *British North America Act* planted in Canada a living tree capable of growth and expansion within its natural limits." Dickson J reiterated the correctness of this approach to constitutional interpretation in *Hunter v. Southam Inc.*, [1984] 2 SCR 145, 11 DLR (4th) 641, at p. 155 SCR:

> The task of expounding a constitution is crucially different from that of construing a statute. A statute defines present rights and obligations. It is easily enacted and as easily repealed. A constitution, by contrast, is drafted with an eye to the future. Its function is to provide a continuing framework for the legitimate exercise of

governmental power and, when joined by a Bill or a Charter of Rights, for the unremitting protection of individual rights and liberties. Once enacted, its provisions cannot easily be repealed or amended. It must, therefore, be capable of growth and development over time to meet new social, political and historical realities often unimagined by its framers. The judiciary is the guardian of the constitution and must, in interpreting its provisions, bear these considerations in mind.

[43] In *Constitutional Law of Canada*, looseleaf (Scarborough: Carswell, 1997) at 15-43 to 15-44, Professor Peter W. Hogg explained that Canada has changed a great deal since Confederation, and "[t]he doctrine of progressive interpretation is one of the means by which the *Constitution Act, 1867* has been able to adapt to the changes in Canadian society."

• • •

[46] In our view, "marriage" does not have a constitutionally fixed meaning. Rather, like the term "banking" in s. 91(15) and the phrase "criminal law" in s. 91(27), the term "marriage" as used in s. 91(26) of the *Constitution Act, 1867* has the constitutional flexibility necessary to meet changing realities of Canadian society without the need for recourse to constitutional amendment procedures.

[The Court found that the common law definition of "marriage" infringed the claimants' rights under s 15(1) of the Charter and this definition was not saved by s 1 of the Charter.]

• • •

[156] To remedy the infringement of these constitutional rights, we:

(1) declare the existing common law definition of marriage to be invalid to the extent that it refers to "one man and one woman";
(2) reformulate the common law definition of marriage as "the voluntary union for life of two persons to the exclusion of all others";
(3) order the declaration of invalidity in (1) and the reformulated definition in (2) to have immediate effect;
(4) order the Clerk of the City of Toronto to issue marriage licences to the Couples; and
(5) order the Registrar General of the Province of Ontario to accept for registration the marriage certificates of Kevin Bourassa and Joe Varnell and of Elaine and Anne Vautour.

In the aftermath of *Halpern*, the federal government decided to accept the result reached by the Ontario Court of Appeal and thus did not seek leave to appeal to the Supreme Court of Canada. Two intervenors, the Association for Marriage and the Family in Ontario and the Interfaith Coalition on Marriage and the Family, tried to have the Supreme Court hear an appeal; however, their motion for leave to appeal was quashed by the Court on October 10, 2003.

In July 2003 the federal government produced a draft bill that would redefine marriage. Before proceeding with the introduction of the bill in Parliament, the government decided to refer four questions regarding its validity to the Supreme Court of Canada. The Court handed down its decision in *Reference re Same-Sex Marriage*, 2004 SCC 79, [2004] 3 SCR 698, upholding the bill and effectively allowing same-sex marriages in all provinces. The bill was passed into law and is known as the *Civil Marriage Act*. The Act allows for same-sex marriage while ensuring religious freedom by allowing officials of religious groups to refuse to perform any marriage if doing so would be contrary to their religious beliefs.

III. INTERNATIONAL LAW

Discussions of Canadian law often ignore international law. This is an unfortunate oversight, given the increasing importance of international law in shaping Canadian domestic law. Consider the Law Commission's brief overview below of international law and its reception into Canadian domestic law.

Law Commission of Canada, Crossing Borders: Law in a Globalized World
(Ottawa: Government of Canada, 2006)

I. The Separate Species of Law

In the modern legal system, two different (and at times separate) species of law exist: international and domestic.

A. Domestic Law

Domestic law is the body of principle most people encounter most of the time. In Canada, domestic law exists as legislation enacted by the legislatures or made as regulations by the executives. Outside Québec, domestic law also comes in the form of the common law, an amorphous body of principle developed by common law courts through the application of precedent, and persisting most vigorously in the private law areas of torts, contracts and property. At the pinnacle of domestic law is constitutional law. In Canada, constitutional law comes in both written and unwritten forms. Written constitutional law is essentially entrenched legislation, incapable of amendment without special procedures, and given pre-eminence over conflicting statutory law. Unwritten constitutional law also has this primacy, but is the product of judicial decision-making.

B. International Law

International law also comes in different flavours. The two most significant sources of international law are treaties and "customary international law." Put simply, treaties are law-making contracts between states. When the treaty binds two states, it is known as a "bilateral" treaty. When it binds a larger number of states, it is called a "multilateral" treaty. There is no magic to the term "treaty." Treaties go by a variety of alternate names, including treaty, convention, covenant, protocol, agreement, charter, and statute. While there are historical reasons for the use of these terms, the international legal effect of a treaty does not vary according to the word used to describe it.

There are literally thousands of treaties, webbing the world together in a complicated pattern of bilateral and multilateral international legal obligations. Some constitute an exchange of promises between states as to how they will act on the international plane. They affect a state's foreign policy without necessitating changes to domestic law. Others require states to change their internal policies, practices and often laws in order to meet obligations set out in the treaty.

Customary international law is a very different concept. Treaties are binding on the states that are parties to them, and generally on no others. Customary international law binds all states, excepting only those that have been sufficiently persistent in rejecting it prior to its emergence as a binding norm. The content of a treaty is discerned from its text. Customary international law is much more amorphous. It is formed by general and universal state practice, undertaken by states with a sense of legal obligation (called *opinio juris*). When these two ingredients—state practice and the *opinio juris*—become sufficiently widespread among the states of the world (a threshold not clearly defined by international law), the practice in question is said to become legally binding as customary international law.

A commonly cited example is the *Universal Declaration of Human Rights*. Originally introduced as a resolution of the UN General Assembly in 1948, the Declaration was intended as a purely aspirational document, without legal force. It was, in other words, "soft" law, a concept discussed in greater detail below. Over time, however, a combination of state practice and an emerging view on the legally obligatory nature of the rights found in the document have prompted many to consider the Declaration customary international law, in whole or at least in part. In 1995, a Canadian minister reported that: "Canada regards the principles of the Universal Declaration of Human Rights as entrenched in customary international law binding on all governments." [Government of Canada, "Notes for an Address by the Honourable Christine Stewart, Secretary of State (Latin America and Africa) at the 10th Annual Consultation Between Non-Governmental Organizations and the Department of Foreign Affairs and International Trade" (Ottawa, January 17, 1995).]

• • •

III. International Law as Part of Canadian Law

[F]or the most part, the executive branch of the federal government negotiates treaties and other international instruments on behalf of Canada. Once a treaty is signed and ratified, Canada is bound and must comply with it or risk being found in contravention. The government must ensure that domestic law does not run counter to international law. How does international law interact with domestic law? The answer depends on the source of the international law: does it come from treaties or from customary law?

A. Receiving Treaties into Domestic Law and Questions of Legitimacy

1. "Dualism" and the Separate Solitudes of Domestic and International Law

Canada traditionally considers domestic law and treaty law as two distinct universes. By approaching these two spheres of law as separate solitudes, Canada is a "dualist" jurisdiction. An international treaty may require Canada, as a matter of international law, to change its domestic law. But in the dualist tradition, that treaty has no direct effect in domestic law until domestic legislation is passed to "transform" or "implement" it into Canadian law.

2. Dualism as a Rational Reaction to Democratic Legitimacy Questions in International Law-Making

At one level, dualism is a sensible philosophy. It seems a necessary response to the Canadian system, where Parliament and the provincial legislatures are supposed to make laws but where the federal executive branch dominates treaty-making. If treaties entered into by the federal executive had immediate and direct effect as the laws of Canada, the government's treaty-making power could enable the executive to do an end-run around Parliament's federal law-making monopoly. By concluding an international treaty requiring, for instance, extended patent protection, the executive would essentially legislate a matter otherwise governed by an Act of Parliament, in this case the *Patent Act*. In this way, the executive would short-circuit Parliament's supremacy in law-making.

Moreover, if treaties had immediate effect as laws, the federal executive could also bypass the division of powers in the *Constitution Act, 1867* by employing its treaty-signing powers to legislate in areas of provincial jurisdiction.

To avoid these problems, Canadian law insists that treaties be transformed into domestic federal law by an Act of Parliament. In constitutional law, when a treaty deals with provincial matters, it is the provincial legislatures who must legislate the treaty into domestic law. Put another way, dualism responds to concerns about the democratic legitimacy of the treaty-making process by factoring elected legislatures back into the equation.

3. The Dualist Dilemma

Dualism may be driven by legitimate concerns. It does, however, create real problems. When Parliament fails to implement treaty law into domestic law the result is an unfortunate legal quandary: Canada is bound by the treaty as a matter of international law, and yet its policy-makers need not abide by the treaty under the terms of domestic law. This problem is remedied if the federal government delays ratification until Parliament and the provincial legislatures revise laws to bring them into compliance with the anticipated international obligation. There are, however, instances where Canada's domestic laws remain unmodified, even as new treaties are ratified.

Subsequently, when legislators become sensitive to allegations of non-compliance with Canada's international obligations, they will enact legislation transforming treaty obligations into domestic law. But in so doing, federal and provincial legislators must curb their discretion and implement an agreement ratified only by the federal executive branch. Little practical room remains for a legislator intent on observing Canada's international obligations to query, amend or reject a bill implementing an international obligation.

In summary, when the federal government exercises its power to conclude an international treaty, Parliament and provincial legislatures may face a dilemma in cases where the law is not consistent with the treaty. They may choose to disregard that international obligation, preserving their supreme law-making role in Canadian democracy at the potential cost of Canada's adherence to an international rule of law. Alternatively, they may implement these international requirements into domestic law, but with their role limited to stamping "approved" onto a treaty concluded exclusively by the federal executive branch. As globalization increases, this dilemma will become progressively more acute.

• • •

B. Customary International Law Reception and Legitimacy

1. The Incorporation of Customary International Law

Canada's approach to customary international law is very different from its "dualist" treaty reception doctrines. Once a rule becomes recognized as customary law, it is *automatically* part of the Canadian common law. With customary international law, in other words, Canada is a "monist" rather than a "dualist" jurisdiction.

But, like the rest of the common law, directly-incorporated customary international law can always be displaced or overturned by a statute that is inconsistent with it. The Ontario Court of Appeal recently summarized the rule this way: "customary rules of international law are directly incorporated into Canadian domestic law unless explicitly ousted by contrary legislation. So far as possible, domestic legislation should be interpreted consistently with those obligations." [*Bouzari v Iran* (2004), 71 OR (3d) 675 at paras 65-66 (CA). See also *Jose Pereira E Hijos SA v Canada (AG)*, [1997] 2 FC 84 at para 20 (TD).]

2. Issues Raised by the Incorporation of Customary International Law

Several obvious issues are raised by this approach. First, when a legislature *does* legislate in a manner that displaces customary international law, Canada may be subsequently in violation of its international obligations.

Second, if customary international law is part of the *common law* of Canada, its existence as domestic law is a matter determined by the courts exclusively. This customary international law is itself created by the international system in an organic rather than negotiated fashion. If customary international law is subsequently incorporated directly into Canadian law by the courts, there may never be any clear and direct input by political branches of government into the rules by which law in Canada is made binding.

On a third, related point, since the content of customary international law is sometimes uncertain (and disputed), courts asked to apply it as the domestic law of Canada rely on expert testimony (often competing) from international lawyers and academics, raising further questions of legitimacy.

But how offensive these last two phenomena are to Canada's democratic order may be debated. Certainly, the common law tradition in Canada accepts that courts should have a law-making role, applying a domestic law developed by judges and not legislators. Is this tradition suddenly illegitimate when judges rely on outside experts to guide their deliberations?

CHAPTER FIVE

RECURRING CONSTITUTIONAL PRINCIPLES IN CANADIAN PUBLIC LAW

As we explained briefly in Chapter 1, public law concerns the relationship between the state and civil society. By contrast, private law (e.g., property, torts, and contract) concerns legal relationships between private persons, and rests on the principle that private persons can create legal rights and duties between each other solely based on consent. The state, on the other hand, may impose obligations on private persons without their individual consent. It does so as the holder of all authoritative power in society. That the state holds all legitimate power is a form of guarantee that individuals and corporate persons cannot exercise arbitrary power over one another. Nevertheless, in a society governed by the rule of law, the state itself may not act arbitrarily. To be legitimate, the state must act in accordance with law established by democratic institutions. The starting point in assessing the legitimacy of state action—and its adherence to "the rule of law"—is the Constitution. The purpose of this chapter is to show how the Constitution of Canada plays this crucial role.

This chapter embodies one central idea: the best way to understand the meaning and significance of public law is to come to grips with a few foundational principles that underlie the structure of public law. These principles derive both from the text of Canada's Constitution and from the logic of its design. The useful thing about these foundational principles is that they can be consistently relied on: once we define them and establish their boundaries in relation to each other, we can count on them to point us in the right direction to answering real-world legal problems. They are the closest thing we have to touchstones in the seemingly ever-shifting world of legal interpretation and argument. In the Canadian legal system, one will not hear a court saying things such as "here we have an exception to the principle of the rule of law," or "constitutional supremacy does not apply in these circumstances." The principles apply, and they help to solve legal problems.

The discussion proceeds in the following fashion. Section I seeks to answer the basic question of what we understand the "Constitution of Canada" to mean and to comprise. This is important to understanding the relationship between the "written Constitution," or text of the Constitution, and the "unwritten" aspects of the Constitution. This relationship is one of the central issues addressed by the Supreme Court of Canada in *Reference re Secession of Quebec*, [1998] 2 SCR 217 (*Quebec Secession Reference*), a case in which the Court provided a mini-treatise on the nature of Canadian constitutionalism in the context of the most fundamental question any political community can face: whether and how the community can be broken up. The *Quebec Secession Reference* touches on several of the themes discussed in this chapter. For that reason, we set it out in a lengthy edited excerpt at the end of Section I and make repeated references to it thereafter.

Section II examines nine foundational principles that structure public law in Canada. These principles, along with brief summary definitions, are the following:

1. Rule of law—All exercises of legitimate public power must have a source in law, and every state actor is subject to constraint of the law.
2. Constitutional supremacy—The Constitution is the supreme law of the society, and any ordinary law that is inconsistent with the Constitution is of no force or effect.
3. Parliamentary supremacy—Subject to the Constitution, the legislative branch of the state is the holder of all legitimate public power and may enact any ordinary statute law and (generally) delegate any of its power as it deems fit.
4. Federalism—Parliamentary supremacy in Canada is subject to the division of law-making powers or jurisdictions between a national Parliament and the legislatures of the provinces, as set out in the Constitution.
5. Separation of powers—Public power is exercised through three institutional branches at the federal and provincial levels—the legislature, the executive, and the judiciary—and each branch has distinct constitutional functions.
6. Judicial independence—The judicial branch of the state must have a sufficient degree of institutional independence from the legislative and executive branches of the state in order to perform its constitutional functions.

7. Democracy—The notion of majority rule and consent by the governed to be governed, manifest in the existence of freely elected legislative bodies at the provincial level and in the federal House of Commons (although not the Senate, making the federal legislature only partially democratic).

8. Protection of minorities—The protection of minorities tempers the notion of majority rule, especially in relation to language, religion, and education rights, but also through more general rights and liberties.

9. Indigenous rights—As discussed in Chapter 3, Canadian public law cannot be understood without an appreciation of the status of Indigenous peoples, the question of self-governance, and the rights of Indigenous people in Canadian society and law.

The discussion of each principle is followed by excerpts from judgments of the Supreme Court of Canada that illustrate how the principle in question is understood in Canadian law.

The chapter concludes in Section III with an examination of how the Constitution of Canada can be amended. While a constitution serves a crucial purpose by providing a stable grounding for relationships between the state and civil society and between state institutions (the two kinds of relationships that together constitute the major concerns of public law), it must also be capable of adapting to the changing nature and conditions of the society it purports to govern. The question of how the Constitution of Canada can be amended has long been one of the most troubled areas of Canadian law and politics. It lay at the heart of the *Quebec Secession Reference*, and also served as the subject of two important decisions rendered by the Supreme Court of Canada in 2014, both of which are discussed in Section III: *Reference re Supreme Court Act, ss 5 and 6*, 2014 SCC 21, [2014] SCR 433 [*Supreme Court Act Reference*] and *Reference re Senate Reform*, 2014 SCC 32, [2014] 1 SCR 704 [*Senate Reform Reference*].

I. THE CONSTITUTION OF CANADA

This chapter addresses eight of the principles that underpin public law in Canada (the Indigenous rights, the ninth principle mentioned above, are addressed in Chapter 3). From where are these principles derived? The short answer is the Canadian Constitution. However, with two or three exceptions, we would be hard pressed to point to specific textual provisions in the Constitution where the principles are clearly set out, much less defined. In an important sense, then, the principles derive from unwritten constitutional sources as much as written sources. The idea that the Constitution has both written and unwritten components has been confirmed by the Supreme Court of Canada on several occasions—most famously in the *Quebec Secession Reference*. Nevertheless, it deserves explanation because we commonly think of Canada as having a written constitution.

A. TEXT OF THE CONSTITUTION

The phrases "text of the Constitution" and "constitutional text" refer to those components of the Constitution reduced to writing by political actors, or "framers." Canada's written constitution is largely embodied in two documents produced at distinct historical moments: the *Constitution Act, 1867* (UK), 30 & 31 Vict, c 3, reprinted in RSC 1985, Appendix II, No 5 and the *Constitution Act, 1982*, being Schedule B to the *Canada Act 1982* (UK), 1982, c 11. The former document set out the terms of a federal system of government through the division of legislative powers between a national Parliament and the provincial legislatures. The latter document encompasses the *Canadian Charter of Rights and Freedoms* (the Charter), which guarantees a set of individual and minority rights, as well as provisions dealing with Aboriginal rights, equalization, and a process for constitutional amendment.

The *Constitution Act, 1982* provides a definition of the Constitution of Canada:

52(1) The Constitution of Canada is the supreme law of Canada, and any law that is inconsistent with the provisions of the Constitution is, to the extent of the inconsistency, of no force or effect.

(2) The Constitution of Canada includes

(a) the *Canada Act 1982*, including this Act;

(b) the Acts and orders referred to in the schedule; and

(c) any amendment to any Act or order referred to in paragraph (a) or (b).

All of the listed instruments are written documents. However, by using the word "includes," s 52(2) implies that the Constitution comprises elements in addition to those listed, and this has been understood to contemplate the presence of *unwritten* components of the Constitution.

The Supreme Court of Canada has recognized two principal sources of unwritten constitutional norms—"constitutional conventions" and "unwritten principles of the Constitution." While sharing several qualities, these two concepts differ in important respects, including the purposes they serve, their legal status, and how they are derived or recognized.

B. CONVENTIONS OF THE CONSTITUTION

The British Constitution, while considered an unwritten construct (apart from several disparate statutes dealing with aspects of governance in the United Kingdom), has long been understood to include certain accepted understandings that govern the workings and interaction of the branches of the state. In stating in the preamble to the *Constitution Act, 1867* that Canada was to have "a Constitution similar in Principle to that of the United Kingdom," the framers of Canada's Constitution signalled their intention to adopt those same conventions, and indeed the very concept of conventions, from British theory and practice.

The Supreme Court of Canada's clearest and most influential statement on the nature of conventions in Canada's constitutional framework is found in *Re: Resolution to Amend the Constitution* ("the *Patriation Reference*"), a case decided in the midst of a constitutional crisis. The text of the Constitution adopted in 1867 contained no amending formula defining the degree of agreement needed between Canada's governments to alter their powers or make other major changes. After failing to reach agreement with the provinces on a series of changes, the federal government of Prime Minister Pierre Trudeau decided in 1980 to pursue amendment and "patriation" of the Constitution on the basis of agreement with only two of ten provinces, Ontario and New Brunswick. The other eight provinces (the so-called "Gang of Eight") went to court to argue that the federal action breached a convention of the Constitution that required provincial agreement before any amendment could be made that affected their powers. A majority of six justices of the Supreme Court agreed. In doing so, the majority made the following findings about the nature and effect of conventions of the Constitution:

1. Conventions come into existence based on three factors:
    a. a practice or agreement developed by political actors;
    b. a recognition by political actors that they are bound to follow the convention; and
    c. the existence of a normative reason—that is, a purpose—for the convention. (In the *Patriation Reference* itself, the majority located a normative reason for a convention of "substantial provincial agreement" in the federal nature of Canadian democracy.)
2. Although part of the Constitution, conventions are not "law," and as such cannot be enforced by the courts. They acquire and retain their binding force by agreement, and ultimately in the realm of politics. However, courts may recognize a convention exists, and declare whether proposed government action is or is not in accordance with convention.

Re: Resolution to Amend the Constitution
[1981] 1 SCR 753

MARTLAND, RITCHIE, DICKSON, BEETZ, CHOUINARD, and LAMER JJ:

The Nature of Constitutional Conventions

A substantial part of the rules of the Canadian constitution are written. They are contained not in a single document called a constitution but in a great variety of statutes some of which have been enacted by the Parliament at Westminster, such as the *British North America Act, 1867* [now the *Constitution Act, 1867*] ...

• • •

But many Canadians would perhaps be surprised to learn that important parts of the constitution of Canada, with which they are the most familiar because they are directly involved when they exercise their right to vote at federal and provincial elections, are nowhere to be found in the law of the constitution. For instance it is a fundamental requirement of the constitution that if the opposition obtains the majority at the polls, the government must tender its resignation forthwith. But fundamental as it is, this requirement of the constitution does not form part of the law of the constitution.

It is also a constitutional requirement that the person who is appointed prime minister or premier by the Crown and who is the effective head of the government should have the support of the elected branch of the legislature; in practice this means in most cases the leader of the political party which has won a majority of seats at a general election. Other ministers are appointed by the Crown on the advice of the prime minister or premier when he forms or reshuffles his cabinet. Ministers must continuously have the confidence of the elected branch of the legislature, individually and collectively. Should they lose it, they must either resign or ask the Crown for a dissolution of the legislature and the holding of a general election. Most of the powers of the Crown under the prerogative are exercised only upon the advice of the prime minister of the cabinet which means that they are effectively exercised by the latter, together with the innumerable statutory powers delegated to the Crown in council.

Yet none of these essential rules of the constitution can be said to be a law of the constitution. It was apparently Dicey who, in the first edition of his *Law of the Constitution*, in 1885, called them the "conventions of the constitution," an expression which quickly became current. What Dicey described under these terms are the principles and rules of responsible government, several of which are stated above and which regulate the relations between the Crown, the prime minister, the cabinet and the two Houses of Parliament. These rules developed in Great Britain by way of custom and precedent during the nineteenth century and were exported to such British colonies as were granted self-government.

• • •

A federal constitution provides for the distribution of powers between various legislatures and governments and may also constitute a fertile ground for the growth of constitutional conventions between those legislatures and governments. It is conceivable for instance that usage and practice might give birth to conventions in Canada relating to the holding of federal-provincial conferences, the appointment of lieutenant governors, the reservation and disallowance of provincial legislation. It was to this possibility that Duff CJ alluded when he referred to "constitutional usage or constitutional practice" in *Reference re Disallowance and Reservation of Provincial Legislation* [[1938] SCR 71], at p. 78. ...

The main purpose of constitutional conventions is to ensure that the legal framework of the constitution will be operated in accordance with the prevailing constitutional values or principles of the period. For example, the constitutional value which is the pivot of the conventions stated above and relating to responsible government is the democratic principle: the powers of the state must be exercised in accordance with the wishes of the electorate; and the constitutional value or principle which anchors the conventions regulating the relationship between the members of the Commonwealth is the independence of the former British colonies.

Being based on custom and precedent, constitutional conventions are usually unwritten rules. Some of them, however, may be reduced to writing and expressed in the proceedings and documents of imperial conferences, or in the preamble of statutes such as the *Statute of Westminster, 1931*, or in the proceedings and documents of federal–provincial conferences. They are often referred to and recognized in statements made by members of governments.

The conventional rules of the constitution present one striking peculiarity. In contradistinction to the laws of the constitution, they are not enforced by the courts. One reason for this situation is that, unlike common law rules, conventions are not judge-made rules. They are not based on judicial precedents but on precedents established by the institutions of government themselves. Nor are they in the nature of statutory commands which it is the function and duty of the courts to obey and enforce. Furthermore, to enforce them would mean to administer some formal sanction when they are breached. But the legal system from which they are distinct does not contemplate formal sanctions for their breach.

Perhaps the main reason why conventional rules cannot be enforced by the courts is that they are generally in conflict with the legal rules which they postulate and the courts are bound to enforce the legal rules. The conflict is not of a type which would entail the commission of any illegality. It results from the fact that legal rules create wide powers, discretions and rights which conventions prescribe should be exercised only in a certain limited manner, if at all.

• • •

Requirements for Establishing a Convention

The requirements for establishing a convention bear some resemblance with those which apply to customary law. Precedents and usage are necessary but do not suffice. They must be normative. We adopt the following passage of Sir W. Ivor Jennings, *The Law and the Constitution* (5th ed., 1959), at p. 136:

> We have to ask ourselves three questions: first, what are the precedents; secondly, did the actors in the precedents believe that they were bound by a rule; and thirdly, is there a reason for the rule? A single precedent with a good reason may be enough to establish the rule. A whole string of precedents without such a reason will be of no avail, unless it is perfectly certain that the persons concerned regarded them as bound by it.

[The six justices went on to apply the three-part test set out by Professor Jennings. On question (i), they found that in terms of precedent, in all 22 instances of amendments to the Canadian Constitution prior to 1981, there had been approval by affected provinces. The justices concluded that "no amendment changing provincial legislative powers has been made since Confederation when agreement of a province whose legislative powers would have been changed was withheld." On question (ii), the justices found that although the record was imprecise, the prime ministers and premiers on those 22 earlier occasions appeared to have acted on the basis that provincial agreement was necessary. The justices went on to deal with question (iii).]

A Reason for the Rule

The reason for the rule is the federal principle. Canada is a federal union. The preamble of the BNA Act states that

> ... the Provinces of Canada, Nova Scotia, and New Brunswick have expressed their Desire to be federally united ... .

The federal character of the Canadian Constitution was recognized in innumerable judicial pronouncements. We will quote only one, that of Lord Watson in *Liquidators of the Maritime Bank of Canada v. Receiver-General of New Brunswick* [[1892] AC 437 (PC)], at pp. 441-42:

> The object of the Act was neither to weld the provinces into one, nor to subordinate provincial governments to a central authority, but to create a federal government in which they should all be represented, entrusted with the exclusive administration of affairs in which they had a common interest, each province retaining its independence and autonomy.

The federal principle cannot be reconciled with a state of affairs where the modification of provincial legislative powers could be obtained by the unilateral action of the federal authorities. It would indeed offend the federal principle that "a radical change to ... [the] constitution [be] taken at the request of a bare majority of the members of the Canadian House of Commons and Senate" (*Report of Dominion Provincial Conference, 1931*, at p. 3).

• • •

The purpose of this conventional rule is to protect the federal character of the Canadian Constitution and prevent the anomaly that the House of Commons and Senate could obtain by simple resolutions what they could not validly accomplish by statute.

• • •

Conclusion

We have reached the conclusion that the agreement of the provinces of Canada, no views being expressed as to its quantification, is constitutionally required for the passing of the "Proposed Resolution for a Joint Address to Her Majesty the Queen respecting the Constitution of Canada" and that the passing of this Resolution without such agreement would be unconstitutional in the conventional sense.

From the perspective of public law, it is important to note that conventions mostly deal with the relationships between state institutions and officials, and not between government and citizens. While serving to limit the conflict between institutions of governance, conventions have little to say about the limits on state power as a whole.

In the *Patriation Reference*, the Supreme Court of Canada decided that unilateral patriation and amendment of the Constitution by the federal government would be "unconstitutional in the conventional sense." It also decided, however, that conventions do not have the force of law and cannot be enforced by courts. In fact, a majority of the Court concluded that it was lawful for the federal government to proceed with its unilateral project to amend the Constitution. Nevertheless, the decision as a whole caused all 11 governments of Canada to make one further attempt to negotiate an agreement on constitutional reform, which resulted in the *Constitution Act, 1982*. Sixteen years later, the Supreme Court of Canada was again called on to make a ruling on the shape of the Constitution in the context of a constitutional crisis, resulting in the *Quebec Secession Reference*.

C. UNWRITTEN PRINCIPLES OF THE CONSTITUTION

In the *Quebec Secession Reference*, the Supreme Court of Canada developed a new understanding of the unwritten aspects of the Constitution. The Court said that in addition to conventions, the Constitution also contained several "unwritten principles." In fact, the Court based its ruling on the law governing the secession of a province from Canada on four unwritten principles: (1) federalism; (2) democracy; (3) constitutionalism and the rule of law; and (4) protection of minority rights. Unlike conventions, the Court said that unwritten principles of the Constitution are legally binding. While, in practice, the Court has since shown little inclination to apply and enforce these doctrines in disputes that have come before it, unwritten principles are crucial to understanding the legal constraints under which public power is exercised by the Canadian state. This chapter does not strictly track the Court's discussion of those four principles. The principles discussed in Section II of this chapter are those that are particularly helpful to understanding the shape and operation of public law in Canada. The inspiration for this discussion is nevertheless largely drawn from the *Quebec Secession Reference*. There, the Court described the principles as forming the "architecture" of the Constitution, or in other words, as being derived from its underlying logic. It is interesting to note that in its two 2014 decisions on the constitutional roles of the Supreme Court and the Senate, respectively (the *Supreme Court Act Reference* and the *Senate Reform Reference*, discussed in Section III, below), the Court returned to and emphasized this "architecture" metaphor. That is essentially the sense in which the eight principles discussed in this chapter should be understood.

The *Quebec Secession Reference* arose from circumstances following the holding of a referendum on the sovereignty of Quebec by the government of Quebec in October 1995. In that referendum, the vote in favour of Quebec's secession fell just below the figure of 50 percent. The federal government of Prime Minister Jean Chrétien decided that for future purposes, the country should know whether Quebec (or any other province) could effect lawful secession from Canada by virtue merely of a majority vote in a referendum. It referred three questions related to this issue to the Supreme Court of Canada.

The federal government took the position before the Court that secession of a province required an amendment to the Constitution pursuant to the amending formula adopted in the *Constitution Act, 1982*, and further, that secession should come within s 41, which requires unanimous agreement of Parliament and the legislatures of every province. Needless to say, this would make secession exceedingly difficult to achieve. It should be noted that "secession" of a province is not expressly mentioned anywhere in the Constitution, including the amending formula. The government of Quebec objected to the very idea of referring what it believed to be the "political" question of secession to the Supreme Court and refused to participate in the Court's proceedings. The Court, however, appointed a Quebec law firm as "friend of the court," or *amicus curiae*, to make the argument that secession could be effected simply by majority vote in a referendum. Following argument, the Court rendered a unanimous decision that differed from the positions advanced by both Canada and the *amicus* counsel. While the Court agreed with Canada that secession could be achieved only by constitutional amendment, it went on to say that a "clear majority" voting "yes" to a "clear question" in a referendum on sovereignty would give rise to a legal duty to negotiate on secession by all Canadian governments. The Court came to this decision based on its analysis of the four unwritten principles mentioned above.

With respect to the role and nature of constitutional principles, note in particular the Court's discussion at paras 49 to 54 dealing with the relationship between the unwritten principles and the text of the Constitution. The discussion has an internal momentum. It starts by describing unwritten constitutional principles as part of the structure or "architecture" of the Constitution, a form of background to the text or wording of the Constitution, with the text retaining primacy. The Court then states that the principles may be helpful to a proper interpretation of the text. In its final and most striking statement, the Court describes unwritten principles as having the force of law and imposing substantive limits on the powers of government.

There seems little doubt that with its reasoning in the *Quebec Secession Reference*, the Supreme Court effectively expanded judicial authority in the constitutional sphere. The text of the Constitution is written by political representatives at the federal and provincial levels. Unwritten principles can be identified and elucidated only by courts. It is important to note, however, that in recognizing the primacy of the text of the Constitution, the Court implicitly stated that unwritten principles cannot be viewed as overriding the text of the Constitution.

Reference re Secession of Quebec
[1998] 2 SCR 217

THE COURT:

I. Introduction

[1] This Reference requires us to consider momentous questions that go to the heart of our system of constitutional government. The observation we made more than a decade ago in *Reference re Manitoba Language Rights*, [1985] 1 SCR 721 (*Manitoba Language Rights Reference*), at p. 728, applies with equal force here: as in that case, the present one "combines legal and constitutional questions of the utmost subtlety and complexity with political questions of great sensitivity." In our view, it is not possible to answer the questions that have been put to us without a consideration of a number of underlying principles. An exploration of the meaning and nature of these underlying principles is not merely of academic interest. On the contrary, such an exploration is of immense practical utility. Only once those underlying principles have been examined and delineated may a considered response to the questions we are required to answer emerge.

[2] The questions posed by the Governor in Council by way of Order in Council PC 1996-1497, dated September 30, 1996, read as follows:

1. Under the Constitution of Canada, can the National Assembly, legislature or government of Quebec effect the secession of Quebec from Canada unilaterally?

2. Does international law give the National Assembly, legislature or government of Quebec the right to effect the secession of Quebec from Canada unilaterally? In this regard, is there a right to self-determination under international law that would give the National Assembly, legislature or government of Quebec the right to effect the secession of Quebec from Canada unilaterally?

3. In the event of a conflict between domestic and international law on the right of the National Assembly, legislature or government of Quebec to effect the secession of Quebec from Canada unilaterally, which would take precedence in Canada?

. . .

III. Reference Questions

. . .

[32] As we confirmed in *Reference re Objection by Quebec to a Resolution to amend the Constitution*, [1982] 2 SCR 793, at p. 806, "The *Constitution Act, 1982* is now in force. Its legality is neither challenged nor assailable." The "Constitution of Canada" certainly includes the constitutional texts enumerated in s. 52(2) of the *Constitution Act, 1982*. Although these texts have a primary place in determining constitutional rules, they are not exhaustive. The Constitution also "embraces unwritten, as well as written rules," as we recently observed in the *Provincial Judges Reference* [*Ref re Remuneration of Judges of the Prov Court of PEI*, [1997] 3 SCR 3], at para. 92. Finally, as was said in the *Patriation Reference* [*Re: Resolution to amend the Constitution*, [1981] 1 SCR 753], at p. 874, the Constitution of Canada includes

the global system of rules and principles which govern the exercise of constitutional authority in the whole and in every part of the Canadian state.

These supporting principles and rules, which include constitutional conventions and the workings of Parliament, are a necessary part of our Constitution because problems or situations may arise which are not expressly dealt with by the text of the Constitution. In order to endure over time, a constitution must contain a comprehensive set of rules and principles which are capable of providing an exhaustive legal framework for our system of government. Such principles and rules emerge from an understanding of the constitutional text itself, the historical context, and previous judicial interpretations of constitutional meaning. In our view, there are four fundamental and organizing principles of the Constitution which are relevant to addressing the question before us (although this enumeration is by no means exhaustive): federalism; democracy; constitutionalism and the rule of law; and respect for minorities. The foundation and substance of these principles are addressed in the following paragraphs. We will then turn to their specific application to the first reference question before us.

. . .

[49] What are those underlying principles? Our Constitution is primarily a written one, the product of 131 years of evolution. Behind the written word is an historical lineage stretching back through the ages, which aids in the consideration of the underlying constitutional principles. These principles inform and sustain the constitutional text: they are the vital unstated assumptions upon which the text is based. The following discussion addresses the four foundational constitutional principles that are most germane for resolution of this Reference: federalism, democracy, constitutionalism and the rule of law, and respect for minority rights. These defining principles function in symbiosis. No single principle can be defined in isolation from the others, nor does any one principle trump or exclude the operation of any other.

[50] Our Constitution has an internal architecture, or what the majority of this Court in *OPSEU v. Ontario (Attorney General)*, [1987] 2 SCR 2, at p. 57, called a "basic constitutional structure." The individual elements of the Constitution are linked to the others, and must be interpreted by reference to the structure of the Constitution

as a whole. As we recently emphasized in the *Provincial Judges Reference*, certain underlying principles infuse our Constitution and breathe life into it. Speaking of the rule of law principle in the *Manitoba Language Rights Reference, supra*, at p. 750, we held that "the principle is clearly implicit in the very nature of a Constitution." The same may be said of the other three constitutional principles we underscore today.

[51] Although these underlying principles are not explicitly made part of the Constitution by any written provision, other than in some respects by the oblique reference in the preamble to the *Constitution Act, 1867*, it would be impossible to conceive of our constitutional structure without them. The principles dictate major elements of the architecture of the Constitution itself and are as such its lifeblood.

[52] The principles assist in the interpretation of the text and the delineation of spheres of jurisdiction, the scope of rights and obligations, and the role of our political institutions. Equally important, observance of and respect for these principles is essential to the ongoing process of constitutional development and evolution of our Constitution as a "living tree," to invoke the famous description in *Edwards v. Attorney-General for Canada*, [1930] AC 124 (PC), at p. 136. As this Court indicated in *New Brunswick Broadcasting Co. v. Nova Scotia (Speaker of the House of Assembly)*, [1993] 1 SCR 319, Canadians have long recognized the existence and importance of unwritten constitutional principles in our system of government.

[53] Given the existence of these underlying constitutional principles, what use may the Court make of them? In the *Provincial Judges Reference, supra*, at paras. 93 and 104, we cautioned that the recognition of these constitutional principles (the majority opinion referred to them as "organizing principles" and described one of them, judicial independence, as an "unwritten norm") could not be taken as an invitation to dispense with the written text of the Constitution. On the contrary, we confirmed that there are compelling reasons to insist upon the primacy of our written constitution. A written constitution promotes legal certainty and predictability, and it provides a foundation and a touchstone for the exercise of constitutional judicial review. However, we also observed in the *Provincial Judges Reference* that the effect of the preamble to the *Constitution Act, 1867* was to incorporate certain constitutional principles by reference, a point made earlier in *Fraser v. Public Service Staff Relations Board*, [1985] 2 SCR 455, at pp. 462-63. In the *Provincial Judges Reference*, at para. 104, we determined that the preamble "invites the courts to turn those principles into the premises of a constitutional argument that culminates in the filling of gaps in the express terms of the constitutional text."

[54] Underlying constitutional principles may in certain circumstances give rise to substantive legal obligations (have "full legal force," as we described it in the *Patriation Reference, supra*, at p. 845), which constitute substantive limitations upon government action. These principles may give rise to very abstract and general obligations, or they may be more specific and precise in nature. The principles are not merely descriptive, but are also invested with a powerful normative force, and are binding upon both courts and governments. "In other words," as this Court confirmed in the *Manitoba Language Rights Reference, supra*, at p. 752, "in the process of Constitutional adjudication, the Court may have regard to unwritten postulates which form the very foundation of the Constitution of Canada." It is to a discussion of those underlying constitutional principles that we now turn.

Federalism

[55] It is undisputed that Canada is a federal state. Yet many commentators have observed that, according to the precise terms of the *Constitution Act, 1867*, the

federal system was only partial. See, e.g., K.C. Wheare, *Federal Government* (4th ed. 1963), at pp. 18-20. This was so because, on paper, the federal government retained sweeping powers which threatened to undermine the autonomy of the provinces. Here again, however, a review of the written provisions of the Constitution does not provide the entire picture. Our political and constitutional practice has adhered to an underlying principle of federalism, and has interpreted the written provisions of the Constitution in this light. For example, although the federal power of disallowance [of provincial statutes] was included in the *Constitution Act, 1867,* the underlying principle of federalism triumphed early. Many constitutional scholars contend that the federal power of disallowance has been abandoned (e.g., P.W. Hogg, *Constitutional Law of Canada* (4th ed. 1997), at p. 120).

[56] In a federal system of government such as ours, political power is shared by two orders of government: the federal government on the one hand, and the provinces on the other. Each is assigned respective spheres of jurisdiction by the *Constitution Act, 1867.* ... In interpreting our Constitution, the courts have always been concerned with the federalism principle, inherent in the structure of our constitutional arrangements, which has from the beginning been the lodestar by which the courts have been guided.

[57] This underlying principle of federalism, then, has exercised a role of considerable importance in the interpretation of the written provisions of our Constitution. In the *Patriation Reference* ... , at pp. 905-9, we confirmed that the principle of federalism runs through the political and legal systems of Canada. Indeed, Martland and Ritchie JJ, dissenting in the *Patriation Reference*, at p. 821, considered federalism to be "the dominant principle of Canadian constitutional law." With the enactment of the Charter, that proposition may have less force than it once did, but there can be little doubt that the principle of federalism remains a central organizational theme of our Constitution. Less obviously, perhaps, but certainly of equal importance, federalism is a political and legal response to underlying social and political realities.

[58] The principle of federalism recognizes the diversity of the component parts of Confederation, and the autonomy of provincial governments to develop their societies within their respective spheres of jurisdiction. The federal structure of our country also facilitates democratic participation by distributing power to the government thought to be most suited to achieving the particular societal objective having regard to this diversity. The scheme of the *Constitution Act, 1867,* it was said in *Re the Initiative and Referendum Act,* [1919] AC 935 (PC), at p. 942, was

> not to weld the Provinces into one, nor to subordinate Provincial Governments to a central authority, but to establish a central government in which these Provinces should be represented, entrusted with exclusive authority only in affairs in which they had a common interest. Subject to this each Province was to retain its independence and autonomy and to be directly under the Crown as its head.

More recently, in *Haig v. Canada,* [1993] 2 SCR 995, at p. 1047, the majority of this Court held that differences between provinces "are a rational part of the political reality in the federal process." It was referring to the differential application of federal law in individual provinces, but the point applies more generally. A unanimous Court expressed similar views in *R v. S. (S.),* [1990] 2 SCR 254, at pp. 287-88.

[59] The principle of federalism facilitates the pursuit of collective goals by cultural and linguistic minorities which form the majority within a particular province. This is the case in Quebec, where the majority of the population is French-speaking, and which possesses a distinct culture. This is not merely the result of chance. The social

and demographic reality of Quebec explains the existence of the province of Quebec as a political unit and indeed, was one of the essential reasons for establishing a federal structure for the Canadian union in 1867. The experience of both Canada East and Canada West under the *Union Act, 1840* (UK), 3-4 Vict., c. 35, had not been satisfactory. The federal structure adopted at Confederation enabled French-speaking Canadians to form a numerical majority in the province of Quebec, and so exercise the considerable provincial powers conferred by the *Constitution Act, 1867* in such a way as to promote their language and culture. It also made provision for certain guaranteed representation within the federal Parliament itself.

[60] Federalism was also welcomed by Nova Scotia and New Brunswick, both of which also affirmed their will to protect their individual cultures and their autonomy over local matters. All new provinces joining the federation sought to achieve similar objectives, which are no less vigorously pursued by the provinces and territories as we approach the new millennium.

Democracy

[61] Democracy is a fundamental value in our constitutional law and political culture. While it has both an institutional and an individual aspect, the democratic principle was also argued before us in the sense of the supremacy of the sovereign will of a people, in this case potentially to be expressed by Quebecers in support of unilateral secession. It is useful to explore in a summary way these different aspects of the democratic principle.

[62] The principle of democracy has always informed the design of our constitutional structure, and continues to act as an essential interpretive consideration to this day. A majority of this Court in *OPSEU v. Ontario*, ... confirmed that "the basic structure of our Constitution, as established by the *Constitution Act, 1867*, contemplates the existence of certain political institutions, including freely elected legislative bodies at the federal and provincial levels." As is apparent from an earlier line of decisions emanating from this Court, including *Switzman v. Elbling*, [1957] S.C.R. 285, *Saumur v. City of Quebec*, [1953] 2 S.C.R. 299, *Boucher v. The King*, [1951] S.C.R. 265, and *Reference re Alberta Statutes*, [1938] S.C.R. 100, the democracy principle can best be understood as a sort of baseline against which the framers of our Constitution, and subsequently, our elected representatives under it, have always operated. It is perhaps for this reason that the principle was not explicitly identified in the text of the *Constitution Act, 1867* itself. To have done so might have appeared redundant, even silly, to the framers. As explained in the *Provincial Judges Reference, supra*, at para. 100, it is evident that our Constitution contemplates that Canada shall be a constitutional democracy. Yet this merely demonstrates the importance of underlying constitutional principles that are nowhere explicitly described in our constitutional texts. The representative and democratic nature of our political institutions was simply assumed.

[63] Democracy is commonly understood as being a political system of majority rule. It is essential to be clear what this means. The evolution of our democratic tradition can be traced back to the *Magna Carta* (1215) and before, through the long struggle for Parliamentary supremacy which culminated in the English *Bill of Rights* of 1689, the emergence of representative political institutions in the colonial era, the development of responsible government in the 19th century, and eventually, the achievement of Confederation itself in 1867. "[T]he Canadian tradition," the majority of this Court held in *Reference re Provincial Electoral Boundaries (Sask.)*, [1991] 2 S.C.R. 158, at p. 186, is "one of evolutionary democracy moving in uneven steps toward the goal of universal suffrage and more effective representation." Since

Confederation, efforts to extend the franchise to those unjustly excluded from participation in our political system—such as women, minorities, and aboriginal peoples—have continued, with some success, to the present day.

[64] Democracy is not simply concerned with the process of government. On the contrary, as suggested in *Switzman v. Elbling, supra*, at p. 306, democracy is fundamentally connected to substantive goals, most importantly, the promotion of self-government. Democracy accommodates cultural and group identities: *Reference re Provincial Electoral Boundaries*, at p. 188. Put another way, a sovereign people exercises its right to self-government through the democratic process. In considering the scope and purpose of the *Charter*, the Court in *R. v. Oakes*, [1986] 1 S.C.R. 103, articulated some of the values inherent in the notion of democracy (at p. 136):

> The Court must be guided by the values and principles essential to a free and democratic society which I believe to embody, to name but a few, respect for the inherent dignity of the human person, commitment to social justice and equality, accommodation of a wide variety of beliefs, respect for cultural and group identity, and faith in social and political institutions which enhance the participation of individuals and groups in society.

[65] In institutional terms, democracy means that each of the provincial legislatures and the federal Parliament is elected by popular franchise. These legislatures, we have said, are "at the core of the system of representative government": *New Brunswick Broadcasting, supra*, at p. 387. In individual terms, the right to vote in elections to the House of Commons and the provincial legislatures, and to be candidates in those elections, is guaranteed to "Every citizen of Canada" by virtue of s. 3 of the *Charter*. Historically, this Court has interpreted democracy to mean the process of representative and responsible government and the right of citizens to participate in the political process as voters (*Reference re Provincial Electoral Boundaries, supra*) and as candidates (*Harvey v. New Brunswick (Attorney General)*, [1996] 2 S.C.R. 876). In addition, the effect of s. 4 of the *Charter* is to oblige the House of Commons and the provincial legislatures to hold regular elections and to permit citizens to elect representatives to their political institutions. The democratic principle is affirmed with particular clarity in that s. 4 is not subject to the notwithstanding power contained in s. 33.

[66] It is, of course, true that democracy expresses the sovereign will of the people. Yet this expression, too, must be taken in the context of the other institutional values we have identified as pertinent to this Reference. The relationship between democracy and federalism means, for example, that in Canada there may be different and equally legitimate majorities in different provinces and territories and at the federal level. No one majority is more or less "legitimate" than the others as an expression of democratic opinion, although, of course, the consequences will vary with the subject matter. A federal system of government enables different provinces to pursue policies responsive to the particular concerns and interests of people in that province. At the same time, Canada as a whole is also a democratic community in which citizens construct and achieve goals on a national scale through a federal government acting within the limits of its jurisdiction. The function of federalism is to enable citizens to participate concurrently in different collectivities and to pursue goals at both a provincial and a federal level.

[67] The consent of the governed is a value that is basic to our understanding of a free and democratic society. Yet democracy in any real sense of the word cannot exist without the rule of law. It is the law that creates the framework within which

the "sovereign will" is to be ascertained and implemented. To be accorded legitimacy, democratic institutions must rest, ultimately, on a legal foundation. That is, they must allow for the participation of, and accountability to, the people, through public institutions created under the Constitution. Equally, however, a system of government cannot survive through adherence to the law alone. A political system must also possess legitimacy, and in our political culture, that requires an interaction between the rule of law and the democratic principle. The system must be capable of reflecting the aspirations of the people. But there is more. Our law's claim to legitimacy also rests on an appeal to moral values, many of which are imbedded in our constitutional structure. It would be a grave mistake to equate legitimacy with the "sovereign will" or majority rule alone, to the exclusion of other constitutional values.

[68] Finally, we highlight that a functioning democracy requires a continuous process of discussion. The Constitution mandates government by democratic legislatures, and an executive accountable to them, "resting ultimately on public opinion reached by discussion and the interplay of ideas" (*Saumur v. City of Quebec*, *supra*, at p. 330). At both the federal and provincial level, by its very nature, the need to build majorities necessitates compromise, negotiation, and deliberation. No one has a monopoly on truth, and our system is predicated on the faith that in the marketplace of ideas, the best solutions to public problems will rise to the top. Inevitably, there will be dissenting voices. A democratic system of government is committed to considering those dissenting voices, and seeking to acknowledge and address those voices in the laws by which all in the community must live.

[69] The *Constitution Act, 1982* gives expression to this principle, by conferring a right to initiate constitutional change on each participant in Confederation. In our view, the existence of this right imposes a corresponding duty on the participants in Confederation to engage in constitutional discussions in order to acknowledge and address democratic expressions of a desire for change in other provinces. This duty is inherent in the democratic principle which is a fundamental predicate of our system of governance.

Constitutionalism and the Rule of Law

[70] The principles of constitutionalism and the rule of law lie at the root of our system of government. The rule of law, as observed in *Roncarelli v. Duplessis*, [1959] SCR 121, at p. 142, is "a fundamental postulate of our constitutional structure." As we noted in the *Patriation Reference* ... , at pp. 805-6, "[t]he 'rule of law' is a highly textured expression, importing many things which are beyond the need of these reasons to explore but conveying, for example, a sense of orderliness, of subjection to known legal rules and of executive accountability to legal authority." At its most basic level, the rule of law vouchsafes to the citizens and residents of the country a stable, predictable and ordered society in which to conduct their affairs. It provides a shield for individuals from arbitrary state action.

[71] In the *Manitoba Language Rights Reference* ... , at pp. 747-52, this Court outlined the elements of the rule of law. We emphasized, first, that the rule of law provides that the law is supreme over the acts of both government and private persons. There is, in short, one law for all. Second, we explained, at p. 749, that "the rule of law requires the creation and maintenance of an actual order of positive laws which preserves and embodies the more general principle of normative order." It was this second aspect of the rule of law that was primarily at issue in the *Manitoba Language Rights Reference* itself. A third aspect of the rule of law is, as recently confirmed in the *Provincial Judges Reference* ... , at para. 10, that "the exercise of

all public power must find its ultimate source in a legal rule." Put another way, the relationship between the state and the individual must be regulated by law. Taken together, these three considerations make up a principle of profound constitutional and political significance.

[72] The constitutionalism principle bears considerable similarity to the rule of law, although they are not identical. The essence of constitutionalism in Canada is embodied in s. 52(1) of the *Constitution Act, 1982*, which provides that "[t]he Constitution of Canada is the supreme law of Canada, and any law that is inconsistent with the provisions of the Constitution is, to the extent of the inconsistency, of no force or effect." Simply put, the constitutionalism principle requires that all government action comply with the Constitution. The rule of law principle requires that all government action must comply with the law, including the Constitution. This Court has noted on several occasions that with the adoption of the Charter, the Canadian system of government was transformed to a significant extent from a system of Parliamentary supremacy to one of constitutional supremacy. The Constitution binds all governments, both federal and provincial, including the executive branch (*Operation Dismantle Inc. v. The Queen*, [1985] 1 SCR 441, at p. 455). They may not transgress its provisions: indeed, their sole claim to exercise lawful authority rests in the powers allocated to them under the Constitution, and can come from no other source.

[73] An understanding of the scope and importance of the principles of the rule of law and constitutionalism is aided by acknowledging explicitly why a constitution is entrenched beyond the reach of simple majority rule. There are three overlapping reasons.

[74] First, a constitution may provide an added safeguard for fundamental human rights and individual freedoms which might otherwise be susceptible to government interference. Although democratic government is generally solicitous of those rights, there are occasions when the majority will be tempted to ignore fundamental rights in order to accomplish collective goals more easily or effectively. Constitutional entrenchment ensures that those rights will be given due regard and protection. Second, a constitution may seek to ensure that vulnerable minority groups are endowed with the institutions and rights necessary to maintain and promote their identities against the assimilative pressures of the majority. And third, a constitution may provide for a division of political power that allocates political power amongst different levels of government. That purpose would be defeated if one of those democratically elected levels of government could usurp the powers of the other simply by exercising its legislative power to allocate additional political power to itself unilaterally.

[75] The argument that the Constitution may be legitimately circumvented by resort to a majority vote in a province-wide referendum is superficially persuasive, in large measure because it seems to appeal to some of the same principles that underlie the legitimacy of the Constitution itself, namely, democracy and self-government. In short, it is suggested that as the notion of popular sovereignty underlies the legitimacy of our existing constitutional arrangements, so the same popular sovereignty that originally led to the present Constitution must (it is argued) also permit "the people" in their exercise of popular sovereignty to secede by majority vote alone. However, closer analysis reveals that this argument is unsound, because it misunderstands the meaning of popular sovereignty and the essence of a constitutional democracy.

[76] Canadians have never accepted that ours is a system of simple majority rule. Our principle of democracy, taken in conjunction with the other constitutional principles discussed here, is richer. Constitutional government is necessarily

predicated on the idea that the political representatives of the people of a province have the capacity and the power to commit the province to be bound into the future by the constitutional rules being adopted. These rules are "binding" not in the sense of frustrating the will of a majority of a province, but as defining the majority which must be consulted in order to alter the fundamental balances of political power (including the spheres of autonomy guaranteed by the principle of federalism), individual rights, and minority rights in our society. Of course, those constitutional rules are themselves amenable to amendment, but only through a process of nego-tiation which ensures that there is an opportunity for the constitutionally defined rights of all the parties to be respected and reconciled.

[77] In this way, our belief in democracy may be harmonized with our belief in constitutionalism. Constitutional amendment often requires some form of sub-stantial consensus precisely because the content of the underlying principles of our Constitution demand it. By requiring broad support in the form of an "enhanced majority" to achieve constitutional change, the Constitution ensures that minority interests must be addressed before proposed changes which would affect them may be enacted.

[78] It might be objected, then, that constitutionalism is therefore incompatible with democratic government. This would be an erroneous view. Constitutional-ism facilitates—indeed, makes possible—a democratic political system by creating an orderly framework within which people may make political decisions. Viewed correctly, constitutionalism and the rule of law are not in conflict with democracy; rather, they are essential to it. Without that relationship, the political will upon which democratic decisions are taken would itself be undermined.

Protection of Minorities

[79] The fourth underlying constitutional principle we address here concerns the protection of minorities. There are a number of specific constitutional provi-sions protecting minority language, religion and education rights. Some of those provisions are, as we have recognized on a number of occasions, the product of historical compromises. As this Court observed in *Reference re Bill 30, An Act to amend the Education Act (Ont.)*, [1987] 1 S.C.R. 1148, at p. 1173, and in *Reference re Education Act (Que.)*, [1993] 2 S.C.R. 511, at pp. 529-30, the protection of minority religious education rights was a central consideration in the negotiations leading to Confederation. In the absence of such protection, it was felt that the minorities in what was then Canada East and Canada West would be submerged and assimilated. See also *Greater Montreal Protestant School Board v. Quebec (Attorney General)*, [1989] 1 S.C.R. 377, at pp. 401-2, and *Adler v. Ontario*, [1996] 3 S.C.R. 609. Similar concerns animated the provisions protecting minority language rights, as noted in *Société des Acadiens du Nouveau-Brunswick Inc. v. Association of Parents for Fairness in Education*, [1986] 1 S.C.R. 549, at p. 564.

[80] However, we highlight that even though those provisions were the product of negotiation and political compromise, that does not render them unprincipled. Rather, such a concern reflects a broader principle related to the protection of min-ority rights. Undoubtedly, the three other constitutional principles inform the scope and operation of the specific provisions that protect the rights of minorities. We emphasize that the protection of minority rights is itself an independent principle underlying our constitutional order. The principle is clearly reflected in the Char-ter's provisions for the protection of minority rights. See, e.g., *Reference re Public Schools Act (Man.), s. 79(3), (4) and (7)*, [1993] 1 S.C.R. 839, and *Mahe v. Alberta*, [1990] 1 S.C.R. 342.

[81] The concern of our courts and governments to protect minorities has been prominent in recent years, particularly following the enactment of the Charter. Undoubtedly, one of the key considerations motivating the enactment of the Charter, and the process of constitutional judicial review that it entails, is the protection of minorities. However, it should not be forgotten that the protection of minority rights had a long history before the enactment of the Charter. Indeed, the protection of minority rights was clearly an essential consideration in the design of our constitutional structure even at the time of Confederation: *Senate Reference*, ... Although Canada's record of upholding the rights of minorities is not a spotless one, that goal is one towards which Canadians have been striving since Confederation, and the process has not been without successes. The principle of protecting minority rights continues to exercise influence in the operation and interpretation of our Constitution.

[82] Consistent with this long tradition of respect for minorities, which is at least as old as Canada itself, the framers of the *Constitution Act, 1982* included in s. 35 explicit protection for existing aboriginal and treaty rights, and in s. 25, a non-derogation clause in favour of the rights of aboriginal peoples. The "promise" of s. 35, as it was termed in *R. v. Sparrow*, [1990] 1 S.C.R. 1075, at p. 1083, recognized not only the ancient occupation of land by aboriginal peoples, but their contribution to the building of Canada, and the special commitments made to them by successive governments. The protection of these rights, so recently and arduously achieved, whether looked at in their own right or as part of the larger concern with minorities, reflects an important underlying constitutional value.

The Operation of the Constitutional Principles in the Secession Context

[83] Secession is the effort of a group or section of a state to withdraw itself from the political and constitutional authority of that state, with a view to achieving statehood for a new territorial unit on the international plane. In a federal state, secession typically takes the form of a territorial unit seeking to withdraw from the federation. Secession is a legal act as much as a political one. By the terms of Question 1 of this Reference, we are asked to rule on the legality of unilateral secession "[u]nder the Constitution of Canada." This is an appropriate question, as the legality of unilateral secession must be evaluated, at least in the first instance, from the perspective of the domestic legal order of the state from which the unit seeks to withdraw. As we shall see below, it is also argued that international law is a relevant standard by which the legality of a purported act of secession may be measured.

[84] The secession of a province from Canada must be considered, in legal terms, to require an amendment to the Constitution, which perforce requires negotiation. The amendments necessary to achieve a secession could be radical and extensive. Some commentators have suggested that secession could be a change of such a magnitude that it could not be considered to be merely an amendment to the Constitution. We are not persuaded by this contention. It is of course true that the Constitution is silent as to the ability of a province to secede from Confederation but, although the Constitution neither expressly authorizes nor prohibits secession, an act of secession would purport to alter the governance of Canadian territory in a manner which undoubtedly is inconsistent with our current constitutional arrangements. The fact that those changes would be profound, or that they would purport to have a significance with respect to international law, does not negate their nature as amendments to the Constitution of Canada.

[85] The Constitution is the expression of the sovereignty of the people of Canada. It lies within the power of the people of Canada, acting through their

various governments duly elected and recognized under the Constitution, to effect whatever constitutional arrangements are desired within Canadian territory, including, should it be so desired, the secession of Quebec from Canada. As this Court held in the *Manitoba Language Rights Reference* ... , at p. 745, "[t]he Constitution of a country is a statement of the will of the people to be governed in accordance with certain principles held as fundamental and certain prescriptions restrictive of the powers of the legislature and government." The manner in which such a political will could be formed and mobilized is a somewhat speculative exercise, though we are asked to assume the existence of such a political will for the purpose of answering the question before us. By the terms of this Reference, we have been asked to consider whether it would be constitutional in such a circumstance for the National Assembly, legislature or government of Quebec to effect the secession of Quebec from Canada *unilaterally*.

[86] The "unilateral" nature of the act is of cardinal importance and we must be clear as to what is understood by this term. In one sense, any step towards a constitutional amendment initiated by a single actor on the constitutional stage is "unilateral." We do not believe that this is the meaning contemplated by Question 1, nor is this the sense in which the term has been used in argument before us. Rather, what is claimed by a right to secede "unilaterally" is the right to effectuate secession without prior negotiations with the other provinces and the federal government. At issue is not the legality of the first step but the legality of the final act of purported unilateral secession. The supposed juridical basis for such an act is said to be a clear expression of democratic will in a referendum in the province of Quebec. This claim requires us to examine the possible juridical impact, if any, of such a referendum on the functioning of our Constitution, and on the claimed legality of a unilateral act of secession.

[87] Although the Constitution does not itself address the use of a referendum procedure, and the results of a referendum have no direct role or legal effect in our constitutional scheme, a referendum undoubtedly may provide a democratic method of ascertaining the views of the electorate on important political questions on a particular occasion. The democratic principle identified above would demand that considerable weight be given to a clear expression by the people of Quebec of their will to secede from Canada, even though a referendum, in itself and without more, has no direct legal effect, and could not in itself bring about unilateral secession. Our political institutions are premised on the democratic principle, and so an expression of the democratic will of the people of a province carries weight, in that it would confer legitimacy on the efforts of the government of Quebec to initiate the Constitution's amendment process in order to secede by constitutional means. In this context, we refer to a "clear" majority as a qualitative evaluation. The referendum result, if it is to be taken as an expression of the democratic will, must be free of ambiguity both in terms of the question asked and in terms of the support it achieves.

[88] The federalism principle, in conjunction with the democratic principle, dictates that the clear repudiation of the existing constitutional order and the clear expression of the desire to pursue secession by the population of a province would give rise to a reciprocal obligation on all parties to Confederation to negotiate constitutional changes to respond to that desire. The amendment of the Constitution begins with a political process undertaken pursuant to the Constitution itself. In Canada, the initiative for constitutional amendment is the responsibility of democratically elected representatives of the participants in Confederation. Those representatives may, of course, take their cue from a referendum, but in legal terms, constitution-making in Canada, as in many countries, is undertaken by the

democratically elected representatives of the people. The corollary of a legitimate attempt by one participant in Confederation to seek an amendment to the Constitution is an obligation on all parties to come to the negotiating table. The clear repudiation by the people of Quebec of the existing constitutional order would confer legitimacy on demands for secession, and place an obligation on the other provinces and the federal government to acknowledge and respect that expression of democratic will by entering into negotiations and conducting them in accordance with the underlying constitutional principles already discussed.

[89] What is the content of this obligation to negotiate? At this juncture, we confront the difficult inter-relationship between substantive obligations flowing from the Constitution and questions of judicial competence and restraint in supervising or enforcing those obligations. This is mirrored by the distinction between the legality and the legitimacy of actions taken under the Constitution. We propose to focus first on the substantive obligations flowing from this obligation to negotiate; once the nature of those obligations has been described, it is easier to assess the appropriate means of enforcement of those obligations, and to comment on the distinction between legality and legitimacy.

[90] The conduct of the parties in such negotiations would be governed by the same constitutional principles which give rise to the duty to negotiate: federalism, democracy, constitutionalism and the rule of law, and the protection of minorities. Those principles lead us to reject two absolutist propositions. One of those propositions is that there would be a legal obligation on the other provinces and federal government to accede to the secession of a province, subject only to negotiation of the logistical details of secession. This proposition is attributed either to the supposed implications of the democratic principle of the Constitution, or to the international law principle of self-determination of peoples.

[91] For both theoretical and practical reasons, we cannot accept this view. We hold that Quebec could not purport to invoke a right of self-determination such as to dictate the terms of a proposed secession to the other parties: that would not be a negotiation at all. As well, it would be naive to expect that the substantive goal of secession could readily be distinguished from the practical details of secession. The devil would be in the details. The democracy principle, as we have emphasized, cannot be invoked to trump the principles of federalism and rule of law, the rights of individuals and minorities, or the operation of democracy in the other provinces or in Canada as a whole. No negotiations could be effective if their ultimate outcome, secession, is cast as an absolute legal entitlement based upon an obligation to give effect to that act of secession in the Constitution. Such a foregone conclusion would actually undermine the obligation to negotiate and render it hollow.

[92] However, we are equally unable to accept the reverse proposition, that a clear expression of self-determination by the people of Quebec would impose *no* obligations upon the other provinces or the federal government. The continued existence and operation of the Canadian constitutional order cannot remain indifferent to the clear expression of a clear majority of Quebecers that they no longer wish to remain in Canada. This would amount to the assertion that other constitutionally recognized principles necessarily trump the clearly expressed democratic will of the people of Quebec. Such a proposition fails to give sufficient weight to the underlying constitutional principles that must inform the amendment process, including the principles of democracy and federalism. The rights of other provinces and the federal government cannot deny the right of the government of Quebec to pursue secession, should a clear majority of the people of Quebec choose that goal, so long as in doing so, Quebec respects the rights of others. Negotiations would be necessary to address the interests of the federal government, of Quebec and the

other provinces, and other participants, as well as the rights of all Canadians both within and outside Quebec.

[93] Is the rejection of both of these propositions reconcilable? Yes, once it is realized that none of the rights or principles under discussion is absolute to the exclusion of the others. This observation suggests that other parties cannot exercise their rights in such a way as to amount to an absolute denial of Quebec's rights, and similarly, that so long as Quebec exercises its rights while respecting the rights of others, it may propose secession and seek to achieve it through negotiation. The negotiation process precipitated by a decision of a clear majority of the population of Quebec on a clear question to pursue secession would require the reconciliation of various rights and obligations by the representatives of two legitimate majorities, namely, the clear majority of the population of Quebec, and the clear majority of Canada as a whole, whatever that may be. There can be no suggestion that either of these majorities "trumps" the other. A political majority that does not act in accordance with the underlying constitutional principles we have identified puts at risk the legitimacy of the exercise of its rights.

[94] In such circumstances, the conduct of the parties assumes primary constitutional significance. The negotiation process must be conducted with an eye to the constitutional principles we have outlined, which must inform the actions of *all* the participants in the negotiation process.

[95] Refusal of a party to conduct negotiations in a manner consistent with constitutional principles and values would seriously put at risk the legitimacy of that party's assertion of its rights, and perhaps the negotiation process as a whole. Those who quite legitimately insist upon the importance of upholding the rule of law cannot at the same time be oblivious to the need to act in conformity with constitutional principles and values, and so do their part to contribute to the maintenance and promotion of an environment in which the rule of law may flourish.

[96] No one can predict the course that such negotiations might take. The possibility that they might not lead to an agreement amongst the parties must be recognized. Negotiations following a referendum vote in favour of seeking secession would inevitably address a wide range of issues, many of great import. After 131 years of Confederation, there exists, inevitably, a high level of integration in economic, political and social institutions across Canada. The vision of those who brought about Confederation was to create a unified country, not a loose alliance of autonomous provinces. Accordingly, while there are regional economic interests, which sometimes coincide with provincial boundaries, there are also national interests and enterprises (both public and private) that would face potential dismemberment. There is a national economy and a national debt. Arguments were raised before us regarding boundary issues. There are linguistic and cultural minorities, including aboriginal peoples, unevenly distributed across the country who look to the Constitution of Canada for the protection of their rights. Of course, secession would give rise to many issues of great complexity and difficulty. These would have to be resolved within the overall framework of the rule of law, thereby assuring Canadians resident in Quebec and elsewhere a measure of stability in what would likely be a period of considerable upheaval and uncertainty. Nobody seriously suggests that our national existence, seamless in so many aspects, could be effortlessly separated along what are now the provincial boundaries of Quebec. As the Attorney General of Saskatchewan put it in his oral submission:

> A nation is built when the communities that comprise it make commitments to it, when they forego choices and opportunities on behalf of a nation, ... when the communities that comprise it make compromises, when they offer each other

guarantees, when they make transfers and perhaps most pointedly, when they receive from others the benefits of national solidarity. The threads of a thousand acts of accommodation are the fabric of a nation. ...

[97] In the circumstances, negotiations following such a referendum would undoubtedly be difficult. While the negotiators would have to contemplate the possibility of secession, there would be no absolute legal entitlement to it and no assumption that an agreement reconciling all relevant rights and obligations would actually be reached. It is foreseeable that even negotiations carried out in conformity with the underlying constitutional principles could reach an impasse. We need not speculate here as to what would then transpire. Under the Constitution, secession requires that an amendment be negotiated.

[98] The respective roles of the courts and political actors in discharging the constitutional obligations we have identified follows ineluctably from the foregoing observations. In the *Patriation Reference*, a distinction was drawn between the law of the Constitution, which, generally speaking, will be enforced by the courts, and other constitutional rules, such as the conventions of the Constitution, which carry only political sanctions. It is also the case, however, that judicial intervention, even in relation to the *law* of the Constitution, is subject to the Court's appreciation of its proper role in the constitutional scheme.

[99] The notion of justiciability is, as we earlier pointed out in dealing with the preliminary objection, linked to the notion of appropriate judicial restraint. We earlier made reference to the discussion of justiciability in *Reference re Canada Assistance Plan* ... , at p. 545:

> In exercising its discretion whether to determine a matter that is alleged to be non-justiciable, the Court's primary concern is to retain its proper role within the constitutional framework of our democratic form of government.

In *Operation Dismantle* ... , at p. 459, it was pointed out that justiciability is a "doctrine ... founded upon a concern with the appropriate role of the courts as the forum for the resolution of different types of disputes." An analogous doctrine of judicial restraint operates here. Also, as observed in *Canada (Auditor General) v. Canada (Minister of Energy, Mines and Resources)*, [1989] 2 SCR 49 (the Auditor General's case), at p. 91:

> There is an array of issues which calls for the exercise of judicial judgment on whether the questions are properly cognizable by the courts. Ultimately, such judgment depends on the appreciation by the judiciary of its own position in the constitutional scheme.

[100] The role of the Court in this Reference is limited to the identification of the relevant aspects of the Constitution in their broadest sense. We have interpreted the questions as relating to the constitutional framework within which political decisions may ultimately be made. Within that framework, the workings of the political process are complex and can only be resolved by means of political judgments and evaluations. The Court has no supervisory role over the political aspects of constitutional negotiations. Equally, the initial impetus for negotiation, namely a clear majority on a clear question in favour of secession, is subject only to political evaluation, and properly so. A right and a corresponding duty to negotiate secession cannot be built on an alleged expression of democratic will if the expression of democratic will is itself fraught with ambiguities. Only the political actors would have the information and expertise to make the appropriate judgment as to the point at which, and the circumstances in which, those ambiguities are resolved one way or the other.

[101] If the circumstances giving rise to the duty to negotiate were to arise, the distinction between the strong defence of legitimate interests and the taking of positions which, in fact, ignore the legitimate interests of others is one that also defies legal analysis. The Court would not have access to all of the information available to the political actors, and the methods appropriate for the search for truth in a court of law are ill-suited to getting to the bottom of constitutional negotiations. To the extent that the questions are political in nature, it is not the role of the judiciary to interpose its own views on the different negotiating positions of the parties, even were it invited to do so. Rather, it is the obligation of the elected representatives to give concrete form to the discharge of their constitutional obligations which only they and their electors can ultimately assess. The reconciliation of the various legitimate constitutional interests outlined above is necessarily committed to the political rather than the judicial realm, precisely because that reconciliation can only be achieved through the give and take of the negotiation process. Having established the legal framework, it would be for the democratically elected leadership of the various participants to resolve their differences.

[102] The non-justiciability of political issues that lack a legal component does not deprive the surrounding constitutional framework of its binding status, nor does this mean that constitutional obligations could be breached without incurring serious legal repercussions. Where there are legal rights there are remedies, but as we explained in the *Auditor General's* case, supra, at p. 90, and *New Brunswick Broadcasting* ... , the appropriate recourse in some circumstances lies through the workings of the political process rather than the courts.

[103] To the extent that a breach of the constitutional duty to negotiate in accordance with the principles described above undermines the legitimacy of a party's actions, it may have important ramifications at the international level. Thus, a failure of the duty to undertake negotiations and pursue them according to constitutional principles may undermine that government's claim to legitimacy which is generally a precondition for recognition by the international community. Conversely, violations of those principles by the federal or other provincial governments responding to the request for secession may undermine their legitimacy. Thus, a Quebec that had negotiated in conformity with constitutional principles and values in the face of unreasonable intransigence on the part of other participants at the federal or provincial level would be more likely to be recognized than a Quebec which did not itself act according to constitutional principles in the negotiation process. Both the legality of the acts of the parties to the negotiation process under Canadian law, and the perceived legitimacy of such action, would be important considerations in the recognition process. In this way, the adherence of the parties to the obligation to negotiate would be evaluated in an indirect manner on the international plane.

[104] Accordingly, the secession of Quebec from Canada cannot be accomplished by the National Assembly, the legislature or government of Quebec unilaterally, that is to say, without principled negotiations, and be considered a lawful act. Any attempt to effect the secession of a province from Canada must be undertaken pursuant to the Constitution of Canada, or else violate the Canadian legal order. However, the continued existence and operation of the Canadian constitutional order cannot remain unaffected by the unambiguous expression of a clear majority of Quebecers that they no longer wish to remain in Canada. The primary means by which that expression is given effect is the constitutional duty to negotiate in accordance with the constitutional principles that we have described herein. In the event secession negotiations are initiated, our Constitution, no less than our history, would call on the participants to work to reconcile the rights, obligations and

legitimate aspirations of all Canadians within a framework that emphasizes constitutional responsibilities as much as it does constitutional rights.

[105] It will be noted that Question 1 does not ask how secession could be achieved in a constitutional manner, but addresses one form of secession only, namely unilateral secession. Although the applicability of various procedures to achieve lawful secession was raised in argument, each option would require us to assume the existence of facts that at this stage are unknown. In accordance with the usual rule of prudence in constitutional cases, we refrain from pronouncing on the applicability of any particular constitutional procedure to effect secession unless and until sufficiently clear facts exist to squarely raise an issue for judicial determination.

II. PRINCIPLES UNDERPINNING PUBLIC LAW

The object of public law is to bring the actions of the state, and of state officials, under the control of law. To put it another way, the purpose of public law is to remove arbitrariness from state action, meaning the arbitrary rule of individuals—that is, leaders and their officials—over civil society. Although this idea can be stated simply, it is not simple. The state comprises individual people who make authoritative decisions over the lives and interests of other individuals. In what sense can the (potentially arbitrary) rule of individuals be supplanted by the rule of an abstraction like law? This question can lead to profound philosophical speculation and debate. For our purposes, however, it is sufficient to show how the Canadian answer to that question proceeds through a series of principles. While all seven principles discussed in this section interact with each other (and with the Indigenous rights discussed in Chapter 3), we think it possible to see how they form a linked series of concepts, each one building on the ones preceding it. We start by considering the principle of "rule of law."

A. THE PRINCIPLE OF THE RULE OF LAW

The preamble to the *Constitution Act, 1982* reads, "Whereas Canada is founded upon principles that recognize the supremacy of God and the rule of law." The phrase "rule of law" is frequently cited and can mean a number of things. In *Re Manitoba Language Rights*, [1985] 1 SCR 721, a unanimous Supreme Court of Canada said (at paras 59-60):

> The rule of law, a fundamental principle of our Constitution, must mean at least two things. First, that the law is supreme over officials of the government as well as private individuals, and thereby preclusive of the influence of arbitrary power ... .
>
> Second, the rule of law requires the creation and maintenance of an actual order of positive laws which preserves and embodies the more general principle of normative order. Law and order are indispensable elements of civilized life.

We are concerned with the first of these two statements—the idea that government and government officials are all subject to the law. This idea is commonly said to mean that "government officials must be subject to the same law as everyone else in society." That understanding, however, is slightly misleading. Government and government officials have powers—powers to make decisions binding on society as a whole—that individual citizens do not have. Therefore, making officials subject to the rule of law requires that they be subject to legal obligations going *beyond* the obligations owed by private citizens. This extra layer of legal obligation is public law. Public law has two principal components known to the law school curriculum: constitutional law and administrative law.

Constitutional law places limits on the *law-making* activities of the state and state actors. Canada, like many contemporary societies, has answered the question of how to make law the governing principle in society when that law is made by human beings, by having a constitution that represents, as some have called it, "a law to make law," a set of ground rules for law-making. This idea creates a distinction between "constitutional law" and "ordinary," or non-constitutional law, with the former being supreme over the latter.

The concept of the rule of law speaks to the supremacy of both constitutional law and ordinary law over the actions of state officials. With respect to their *executive activities*, the rule of law states that officials only have power to act in society to the degree that they have been granted that power by ordinary law—almost always that means by statutes. Administrative law is the law that ensures that state officials act within the authority granted by statutes. This has two quite practical implications. First, government actors may always be questioned about the legal source of their actions—and must always be able to give an answer; and second, the exercise of government authority is always subject to review by the judiciary with respect to whether it falls within and is consistent with a statutory grant.

In the *Quebec Secession Reference*, the Supreme Court of Canada referred in a similar way to the principles of "rule of law" and "constitutionalism" as being closely connected, but distinguishable (at para 72):

> The constitutionalism principle bears considerable similarity to the rule of law, although they are not identical. The essence of constitutionalism in Canada is embodied in s. 52(1) of the *Constitution Act, 1982*, which provides that "[t]he Constitution of Canada is the supreme law of Canada, and any law that is inconsistent with the provisions of the Constitution is, to the extent of the inconsistency, of no force or effect." Simply put, the constitutionalism principle requires that all government action comply with the Constitution. The rule of law principle requires that all government action must comply with the law, including the Constitution.

In this usage, the rule of law is broader than constitutionalism, and indeed its necessary prerequisite. Much could be said about the relationship between these two concepts. The next two subsections deal with issues going to the scope of the rule of law principle in limiting state action. The first issue speaks to the potential for the principle to impose limits on substantive law-making authority, a potential increased by a ruling by the court striking down court hearing fees found to interfere with citizens' "access to justice." The second goes to the idea that the rule of law principle bars state officials from using statutory authority to act in an arbitrary fashion.

1. Substantive Limits on Legislation

As this discussion suggests (and as we discuss further below), the Constitution is supreme over other law—including that enacted by Parliament or the legislatures as statute law. Section 52(1) of the *Constitution Act, 1982*, cited above, makes this clear. While the written Constitution has only included this clarity since 1982, the principle of constitutional supremacy was accepted long before that—indeed, the written federalism principles in the *Constitution Act, 1867* have always constrained and trumped inconsistent legislation.

But does this mean that every aspect of the Constitution—written or unwritten—has this trumping effect? One issue that the Supreme Court's discussion of unwritten constitutional principles in the *Quebec Secession Reference* left unanswered was whether the principles identified by the Court could serve as the basis for constitutional challenges to ordinary laws, even where the text of the Constitution did not do so. That is, do unwritten principles have substantive content that places limits on what legislatures can enact in statutes? With respect to the rule of law principle, this could include the idea that ordinary law must meet certain qualitative standards—including not being retrospective, or not being directed at a small class of persons—in order to be constitutional, quite apart from any limits expressly stated in the Constitution. This idea was examined in *British Columbia v Imperial Tobacco Canada Ltd* [*Imperial Tobacco*].

In 2000, the BC legislature enacted the *Tobacco Damages and Health Care Costs Recovery Act*, SBC 2000, c 30, creating a civil cause of action for the BC government against tobacco manufacturers with respect to health care costs incurred by the government for tobacco-related illnesses resulting from tortious or other misconduct by the manufacturers. The legislation facilitated the making of aggregate claims for expenses incurred for whole populations of affected individuals, created evidentiary presumptions in favour of the government, and expressly stated that it operated retrospectively. Pursuant to the legislation, the government commenced legal actions against several large tobacco manufacturers. The defendant companies challenged the constitutionality of the legislation.

The manufacturers argued that the impugned legislation breached the unwritten constitutional principles of judicial independence and the rule of law. With respect to the latter, the defendants argued that several features of the statute—including its retrospective effect, its particularity in creating a cause of action between a single plaintiff and a small group of defendants, and certain presumptions favouring the plaintiff—violated substantive norms of the rule of law principle. Justice Major wrote the Court's unanimous decision.

British Columbia v Imperial Tobacco Canada Ltd
2005 SCC 49, [2005] 2 SCR 473

MAJOR J:

[1] The *Tobacco Damages and Health Care Costs Recovery Act*, SBC 2000, c. 30 (the "Act"), authorizes an action by the government of British Columbia against a manufacturer of tobacco products for the recovery of health care expenditures incurred by the government in treating individuals exposed to those products. Liability hinges on those individuals having been exposed to tobacco products because of the manufacturer's breach of a duty owed to persons in British Columbia, and on the government of British Columbia having incurred health care expenditures in treating disease in those individuals caused by such exposure.

[2] These appeals question the constitutional validity of the Act. The appellants, each of which was sued by the government of British Columbia pursuant to the Act, challenge its constitutional validity on the basis that it violates (1) territorial limits on provincial legislative jurisdiction; (2) the principle of judicial independence; and (3) the principle of the rule of law.

• • •

I. Background

A. The Legislation

[4] The Act, in its entirety, is reproduced in the Appendix. Its essential aspects are summarized below.

[5] Section 2(1) is the keystone of the Act. It reads:

> The government has a direct and distinct action against a manufacturer to recover the cost of health care benefits caused or contributed to by a tobacco related wrong.

• • •

[7] Viewed in this light, s. 2(1) creates a cause of action by which the government of British Columbia may recover from a tobacco manufacturer money spent treating disease in British Columbians, where such disease was caused by exposure to a tobacco product (whether entirely in British Columbia or not), and such exposure was caused by that manufacturer's tort in British Columbia, or breach of a duty owed to persons in British Columbia.

[8] The cause of action created by s. 2(1), besides being "direct and distinct," is not a subrogated claim: s. 2(2). Nor is it barred by the *Limitation Act*, RSBC 1996, c. 266, s. 6(1). Crucially, it can be pursued on an aggregate basis—i.e. in respect of a population of persons for whom the government has made or can reasonably be expected to make expenditures: s. 2(4)(b).

[9] Where the government's claim is made on an aggregate basis, it may use statistical, epidemiological and sociological evidence to prove its case: s. 5(b). It need not identify, prove the cause of disease or prove the expenditures made in respect of any individual member of the population on which it bases its claim: s. 2(5)(a). Furthermore, health care records and related information in respect of individual members of that population are not compellable, except if relied upon by an expert witness: ss. 2(5)(b) and (c). However, the court is free to order the discovery of a "statistically meaningful sample" of the health care records of individual members of that population, stripped of personal identifiers: ss. 2(5)(d) and (e).

[10] Pursuant to ss. 3(1) and (2), the government enjoys a reversed burden of proof in respect of certain elements of an aggregate claim. Where the aggregate claim is, like the one brought against each of the appellants, to recover expenditures in respect of disease caused by exposure to cigarettes, the reversed burden of proof operates as follows. ...

[11] In this way, it falls on a defendant manufacturer to show that its breach of duty did not give rise to exposure, or that exposure resulting from its breach of duty did not give rise to the disease in respect of which the government claims for its expenditures. The reversed burden of proof on the manufacturer is a balance of probabilities: s. 3(4).

[12] Where the aforementioned presumptions apply, the court must determine the portion of the government's expenditures after the date of the manufacturer's breach that resulted from exposure to cigarettes: s. 3(3)(a). The manufacturer is liable for such expenditures in proportion to its share of the market for cigarettes in British Columbia, calculated over the period of time between its first breach of duty and trial: ss. 3(3)(b) and 1(6).

[13] In an action by the government, a manufacturer will be jointly and severally liable for expenditures arising from a joint breach of duty (i.e. for expenditures caused by disease, which disease was caused by exposure, which exposure was caused by a joint breach of duty to which the manufacturer was a party): s. 4(1).

[14] Pursuant to s. 10, all provisions of the Act operate retroactively.

• • •

III. Issues

[25] McLachlin CJ stated the following constitutional questions:

• • •

3. Is the *Tobacco Damages and Health Care Costs Recovery Act*, SBC 2000, c. 30, constitutionally invalid, in whole or in part, as offending the rule of law?

IV. Analysis

• • •

C. Rule of Law

[57] The rule of law is "a fundamental postulate of our constitutional structure" (*Roncarelli v. Duplessis*, [1959] SCR 121, at p. 142) that lies "at the root of our system of government" (*Reference re Secession of Quebec*, [1998] 2 SCR 217, at para. 70). It is expressly acknowledged by the preamble to the *Constitution Act, 1982*, and implicitly recognized in the preamble to the *Constitution Act, 1867*: see *Reference re Manitoba Language Rights*, [1985] 1 SCR 721, at p. 750.

[58] This Court has described the rule of law as embracing three principles. The first recognizes that "the law is supreme over officials of the government as well as private individuals, and thereby preclusive of the influence of arbitrary power": *Reference re Manitoba Language Rights*, at p. 748. The second "requires the creation and maintenance of an actual order of positive laws which preserves and embodies the more general principle of normative order": *Reference re Manitoba Language Rights*, at p. 749. The third requires that "the relationship between the state and the individual ... be regulated by law": *Reference re Secession of Quebec*, at para. 71.

[59] So understood, it is difficult to conceive of how the rule of law could be used as a basis for invalidating legislation such as the Act based on its content. That is because none of the principles that the rule of law embraces speak directly to the terms of legislation. The first principle requires that legislation be applied to all those, including government officials, to whom it, by its terms, applies. The second principle means that legislation must exist. And the third principle, which overlaps somewhat with the first and second, requires that state officials' actions be legally founded. See R. Elliot, "References, Structural Argumentation and the Organizing Principles of Canada's Constitution" (2001), 80 *Can. Bar Rev.* 67, at pp. 114-15.

[60] This does not mean that the rule of law as described by this Court has no normative force. As McLachlin CJ stated in Babcock, at para. 54, "unwritten constitutional principles," including the rule of law, "are capable of limiting government actions." See also *Reference re Secession of Quebec*, at para. 54. But the government action constrained by the rule of law as understood in *Reference re Manitoba Language Rights* and *Reference re Secession of Quebec* is, by definition, usually that of the executive and judicial branches. Actions of the legislative branch are constrained too, but only in the sense that they must comply with legislated requirements as to manner and form (i.e. the procedures by which legislation is to be enacted, amended and repealed).

[61] Nonetheless, considerable debate surrounds the question of what additional principles, if any, the rule of law might embrace, and the extent to which they might mandate the invalidation of legislation based on its content. P.W. Hogg and C.F. Zwibel write in "The Rule of Law in the Supreme Court of Canada" (2005), 55 UTLJ 715, at pp. 717-18:

> Many authors have tried to define the rule of law and explain its significance, or lack thereof. Their views spread across a wide spectrum. ... T.R.S. Allan, for example, claims that laws that fail to respect the equality and human dignity of individuals are contrary to the rule of law. Luc Tremblay asserts that the rule of law includes the liberal principle, the democratic principle, the constitutional principle, and the federal principle. For Allan and Tremblay, the rule of law demands not merely that positive law be obeyed but that it embody a particular vision of social justice. Another

strong version comes from David Beatty, who argues that the "ultimate rule of law" is a principle of "proportionality" to which all laws must conform on pain of invalidity (enforced by judicial review). In the middle of the spectrum are those who, like Joseph Raz, accept that the rule of law is an ideal of constitutional legality, involving open, stable, clear, and general rules, even-handed enforcement of those laws, the independence of the judiciary, and judicial review of administrative action. Raz acknowledges that conformity to the rule of law is often a matter of degree, and that breaches of the rule of law do not lead to invalidity.

See also W.J. Newman, "The Principles of the Rule of Law and Parliamentary Sovereignty in Constitutional Theory and Litigation" (2005), 16 NJCL 175, at pp. 177-80.

[62] This debate underlies Strayer JA's apt observation in *Singh v. Canada (Attorney General)*, [2000] 3 FC 185 (CA), at para. 33, that "[a]dvocates tend to read into the principle of the rule of law anything which supports their particular view of what the law should be."

[63] The appellants' conceptions of the rule of law can fairly be said to fall at one extreme of the spectrum of possible conceptions and to support Strayer JA's thesis. They submit that the rule of law requires that legislation (1) be prospective; (2) be general in character; (3) not confer special privileges on the government, except where necessary for effective governance; and (4) ensure a fair civil trial. And they argue that the Act breaches each of these requirements, rendering it invalid.

[64] A brief review of this Court's jurisprudence will reveal that none of these requirements enjoy constitutional protection in Canada. But before embarking on that review, it should be said that acknowledging the constitutional force of anything resembling the appellants' conceptions of the rule of law would seriously undermine the legitimacy of judicial review of legislation for constitutionality. That is so for two separate but interrelated reasons.

[65] First, many of the requirements of the rule of law proposed by the appellants are simply broader versions of rights contained in the Charter. For example, the appellants' proposed fair trial requirement is essentially a broader version of s. 11(d) of the Charter, which provides that "[a]ny person charged with an offence has the right ... to ... a fair and public hearing." But the framers of the Charter enshrined that fair trial right only for those "charged with an offence." If the rule of law constitutionally required that all legislation provide for a fair trial, s. 11(d) and its relatively limited scope (not to mention its qualification by s. 1) would be largely irrelevant because everyone would have the unwritten, but constitutional, right to a "fair ... hearing." (Though, as explained in para. 76, infra, the Act provides for a fair trial in any event.) Thus, the appellants' conception of the unwritten constitutional principle of the rule of law would render many of our written constitutional rights redundant and, in doing so, undermine the delimitation of those rights chosen by our constitutional framers. That is specifically what this Court cautioned against in *Reference re Secession of Quebec*, at para. 53:

> Given the existence of these underlying constitutional principles, what use may the Court make of them? In [*Ref re Remuneration of Judges of the Provincial Court of PEI*], at paras. 93 and 104, we cautioned that *the recognition of these constitutional principles ... could not be taken as an invitation to dispense with the written text of the Constitution. On the contrary, we confirmed that there are compelling reasons to insist upon the primacy of our written constitution.* A written constitution promotes legal certainty and predictability, and it provides a foundation and a touchstone for the exercise of constitutional judicial review. [Emphasis added.]

[66] Second, the appellants' arguments overlook the fact that several constitutional principles other than the rule of law that have been recognized by this Court—most notably democracy and constitutionalism—very strongly favour upholding the validity of legislation that conforms to the express terms of the Constitution (and to the requirements, such as judicial independence, that flow by necessary implication from those terms). Put differently, the appellants' arguments fail to recognize that in a constitutional democracy such as ours, protection from legislation that some might view as unjust or unfair properly lies not in the amorphous underlying principles of our Constitution, but in its text and the ballot box. See *Bacon v. Saskatchewan Crop Insurance Corp.* (1999), 180 Sask. R 20 (CA), at para. 30, Elliot, at pp. 141-42, Hogg and Zwibel, at p. 718, and Newman, at p. 187.

[67] The rule of law is not an invitation to trivialize or supplant the Constitution's written terms. Nor is it a tool by which to avoid legislative initiatives of which one is not in favour. On the contrary, it requires that courts give effect to the Constitution's text, and apply, by whatever its terms, legislation that conforms to that text.

[68] A review of the cases showing that each of the appellants' proposed requirements of the rule of law has, as a matter of precedent and policy, no constitutional protection is conclusive of the appellants' rule of law arguments.

(1) Prospectivity in the Law

[69] Except for criminal law, the retrospectivity and retroactivity of which is limited by s. 11(g) of the Charter, there is no requirement of legislative prospectivity embodied in the rule of law or in any provision of our Constitution. Professor P.W. Hogg sets out the state of the law accurately (in *Constitutional Law of Canada* (loose-leaf ed.), vol. 1, at p. 48-29):

> Apart from s. 11(g), Canadian constitutional law contains no prohibition of retroactive (or ex post facto laws). There is a presumption of statutory interpretation that a statute should not be given retroactive effect, but, if the retroactive effect is clearly expressed, then there is no room for interpretation and the statute is effective according to its terms. Retroactive statutes are in fact common.

[70] Hence, in *Air Canada v. British Columbia*, [1989] 1 SCR 1161, at p. 1192, La Forest J, writing for a majority of this Court, characterized a retroactive tax as "not constitutionally barred." And in *Cusson v. Robidoux*, [1977] 1 SCR 650, at p. 655, Pigeon J, for a unanimous Court, said that it would be "untenable" to suggest that legislation reviving actions earlier held by this Court (in *Notre-Dame Hospital v. Patry*, [1975] 2 SCR 388) to be time-barred was unconstitutional.

[71] The absence of a general requirement of legislative prospectivity exists despite the fact that retrospective and retroactive legislation can overturn settled expectations and is sometimes perceived as unjust: see E. Edinger, "Retrospectivity in Law" (1995), 29 UBC L Rev. 5, at p. 13. Those who perceive it as such can perhaps take comfort in the rules of statutory interpretation that require the legislature to indicate clearly any desired retroactive or retrospective effects. Such rules ensure that the legislature has turned its mind to such effects and "determined that the benefits of retroactivity [or retrospectivity] outweigh the potential for disruption or unfairness": *Landgraf v. USI Film Products*, 511 US 244 (1994), at p. 268.

[72] It might also be observed that developments in the common law have always had retroactive and retrospective effect. Lord Nicholls of Birkenhead recently explained this point in *In re Spectrum Plus Ltd.*, [2005] 3 WLR 58, [2005] UKHL 41, at para. 7:

A court ruling which changes the law from what it was previously thought to be operates retrospectively as well as prospectively. The ruling will have a retrospective effect so far as the parties to the particular dispute are concerned, as occurred with the manufacturer of the ginger beer in *Donoghue v. Stevenson*, [1932] AC 562. When Mr Stevenson manufactured and bottled and sold his ginger beer the law on manufacturers' liability as generally understood may have been as stated by the majority of the Second Division of the Court of Session and the minority of their Lordships in that case. But in the claim Mrs Donoghue brought against Mr Stevenson his legal obligations fell to be decided in accordance with Lord Atkin's famous statements. Further, because of the doctrine of precedent the same would be true of everyone else whose case thereafter came before a court. Their rights and obligations would be decided according to the law as enunciated by the majority of the House of Lords in that case even though the relevant events occurred before that decision was given.

This observation adds further weight, if needed, to the view that retrospectivity and retroactivity do not generally engage constitutional concerns.

(2) Generality in the Law, Ordinary Law for the Government, and Fair Civil Trials

[73] Two decisions of this Court defeat the appellants' submission that the Constitution, through the rule of law, requires that legislation be general in character and devoid of special advantages for the government (except where necessary for effective governance), as well as that it ensure a fair civil trial.

[74] The first is *Air Canada*. In it, a majority of this Court affirmed the constitutionality of 1981 amendments to the *Gasoline Tax Act, 1948*, RSBC 1960, c. 162, that retroactively taxed certain companies in the airline industry. The amendments were meant strictly to defeat three companies' claims, brought in 1980, for reimbursement of gasoline taxes paid between 1974 and 1976, the collection of which was *ultra vires* the legislature of British Columbia. The legislative amendments, in addition to being retroactive, were for the benefit of the Crown, aimed at a particular industry with readily identifiable members and totally destructive of that industry's ability to pursue successfully their claims filed a year earlier. Nonetheless, the constitutionality of those amendments was affirmed by a majority of this Court.

[75] The second is *Authorson v. Canada (Attorney General)*, [2003] 2 SCR 40, 2003 SCC 39, in which this Court unanimously upheld a provision of the *Department of Veterans Affairs Act*, RSC 1985, c. V-1, aimed specifically at defeating certain disabled veterans' claims, the merits of which were undisputed, against the federal government. The claims concerned interest owed by the government on the veterans' benefit accounts administered by it, which interest it had not properly credited for decades. Though the appeal was pursued on the basis of the *Canadian Bill of Rights*, SC 1960, c. 44, the decision confirmed that it was well within Parliament's power to enact the provision at issue—despite the fact that it was directed at a known class of vulnerable veterans, conferred benefits on the Crown for "undisclosed reasons" (para. 62) and routed those veterans' ability to have any trial—fair or unfair—of their claims. See para. 15:

> The *Department of Veterans Affairs Act*, s. 5.1(4) takes a property claim from a vulnerable group, in disregard of the Crown's fiduciary duty to disabled veterans. However, that taking is within the power of Parliament. The appeal has to be allowed.

[76] Additionally, the appellants' conception of a "fair" civil trial seems in part to be of one governed by customary rules of civil procedure and evidence. As should be evident from the analysis concerning judicial independence, there is no constitutional right to have one's civil trial governed by such rules. Moreover, new rules are not necessarily unfair. Indeed, tobacco manufacturers sued pursuant to the Act will receive a fair civil trial, in the sense that the concept is traditionally understood: they are entitled to a public hearing, before an independent and impartial court, in which they may contest the claims of the plaintiff and adduce evidence in their defence. The court will determine their liability only following that hearing, based solely on its understanding of the law as applied to its findings of fact. The fact that defendants might regard that law (i.e. the Act) as unjust, or the procedural rules it prescribes as unprecedented, does not render their trial unfair.

[77] The Act does not implicate the rule of law in the sense that the Constitution comprehends that term. It follows that the Act is not unconstitutional by reason of interference with it.

The Supreme Court of Canada had a further opportunity to consider an argument going to substantive content of the rule of law principle in *British Columbia (AG) v Christie*, 2007 SCC 21, [2007] 1 SCR 873. There, the Court rejected the idea that the rule of law incorporates a right of access to legal counsel in all judicial proceedings, a right that the plaintiff claimed was violated by a provincial tax on lawyers' services. Together with *Imperial Tobacco*, *Christie* appeared to close the door to arguments that the rule of law principle gives rise to substantive rights capable of serving as a basis for challenging the constitutionality of statutes. This position appears to have changed, however, with the majority judgment of the Court in *Trial Lawyers Association of British Columbia v British Columbia (AG)*, 2014 SCC 59, [2014] 3 SCR 31, decided in late 2014.

In the *Trial Lawyers* case, the association challenged a regulation that imposed a court hearing fee on plaintiffs to civil litigation, except for those found to be "impoverished." In the case giving rise to the challenge, the plaintiff in a family law dispute had been charged $3,600 for a ten-day court hearing. The association argued that such a fee imposed a significant barrier to access to justice for many middle-class litigants. This breached a constitutional right of "access to justice" located in s 96 of the *Constitution Act, 1867* (understood to protect the "core jurisdiction" of superior courts in Canada) and the principle of the rule of law. A majority of the Court agreed. Justice Rothstein wrote a sharp dissent, in which he attacked what he termed the majority's broad reading of the rule of law principle for undermining the primacy of the Constitution's text. Having been reopened by *Trial Lawyers*, this debate is likely to continue.

Trial Lawyers Association of British Columbia v British Columbia (AG)
2014 SCC 59, [2014] 3 SCR 31

McLACHLIN CJ (LeBel, Abella, Moldaver, and Karakatsanis JJ concurring):

[1] The issue in this case is whether court hearing fees imposed by the Province of British Columbia that deny some people access to the courts are constitutional. The trial judge, upheld on appeal, held that the legislation imposing the fees was unconstitutional. I agree.

• • •

II. Facts

[3] This case began as a family action (2009 BCSC 434 (CanLII)). Ms. Vilardell and Mr. Dunham began a relationship in England and came to British Columbia, Canada, with their daughter. The relationship foundered, and the question arose—who should have custody of the child? Ms. Vilardell wanted to return with the child to Spain, her country of origin. Mr. Dunham wanted to keep the child in British Columbia. Ms. Vilardell also claimed an interest in Mr. Dunham's house.

[4] Ms. Vilardell went to court to have these issues resolved. In order to get a trial date, she had to undertake in advance to pay a court hearing fee. At the outset of the trial, Ms. Vilardell asked the judge to relieve her from paying the hearing fee. The judge reserved his decision on this request until the end of the trial, so he could address the question of ability to pay after hearing evidence respecting the parties' means, circumstances, and entitlement to property.

[5] The parties were not represented by lawyers, and the hearing took 10 days. The hearing fee amounted to some $3,600.00—almost the net monthly income of the family (2012 BCSC 748, 260 C.R.R. (2d) 1, at para. 396). Ms. Vilardell is not an "impoverished" person in the ordinary sense of the word. She is qualified as a veterinary surgeon in Europe. She was unemployed in the year leading up to the trial; the "family" income appears to have come mainly from her partner. She had some assets, including about $10,000 in savings in a Canadian bank account, $10,000 in a Barclays Investment Savings Account in the United Kingdom, and $4,500 in a registered retirement account in Spain. However, after legal fees had depleted her savings, she could not afford the hearing fee.

• • •

[16] The Province argues that the hearing fee scheme is a valid exercise of the provincial power over the administration of justice under s. 92(14) of the *Constitution Act, 1867*.

[17] The question arises: What, if any, are the limits of the scope of provincial authority over the administration of justice under s. 92(14)? The authority is a wide one, but it must be exercised harmoniously with the core jurisdiction of provincial superior courts protected by s. 96. The issue in this case comes down to whether s. 96 is infringed by legislation that imposes hearing fees that deny some people access to the courts.

V. Analysis

A. The Province Has the Power to Impose Hearing Fees

[18] The Province has the power to legislate with respect to the administration of justice under s. 92(14) of the *Constitution Act, 1867*. This includes the power to charge fees for court services.

[19] Section 92(14) of the *Constitution Act, 1867* provides:

> 92. In each Province the Legislature may exclusively make Laws in relation to ...
>
> > 14. The Administration of Justice in the Province, including the Constitution, Maintenance, and Organization of the Provincial Courts, both of Civil and of Criminal Jurisdiction, and including Procedure in Civil matters in those Courts.

[20] In *British Columbia (Attorney General) v. Christie*, 2007 SCC 21, [2007] 1 S.C.R. 873, this Court said:

> The legislature has the power to pass laws in relation to the administration of justice in the province under s. 92(14) of the Constitution Act, 1867. *This implies the power of the province to impose at least some conditions on how and when people have a right to access the courts.* Therefore, *B.C.G.E.U.* cannot stand for the proposition that every limit on access to the courts is automatically unconstitutional. [Emphasis added; para 17.]

[21] Hearing fees fall squarely within the "administration of justice" and may be used to defray some of the cost of administering the justice system, to encourage the efficient use of court resources, and to discourage frivolous or inappropriate use of the courts.

• • •

B. The Provinces' Power to Impose Hearing Fees Is Not Unlimited

[24] On its face, s. 92(14) does not limit the powers of the provinces to impose hearing fees. However, that does not mean that the province can impose hearing fees in any fashion it chooses. Its power to impose hearing fees must be consistent with s. 96 of the *Constitution Act, 1867* and the requirements that flow by necessary implication from s. 96.

• • •

[31] It is not suggested that legislating hearing fees that prevent people from accessing the courts would abolish or destroy the existence of the courts. The question is rather whether legislating hearing fees that prevent people from accessing the courts infringes on the core jurisdiction of the superior courts.

[32] The historic task of the superior courts is to resolve disputes between individuals and decide questions of private and public law. Measures that prevent people from coming to the courts to have those issues resolved are at odds with this basic judicial function. The resolution of these disputes and resulting determination of issues of private and public law, viewed in the institutional context of the Canadian justice system, are central to what the superior courts do. Indeed, it is their very book of business. To prevent this business being done strikes at the core of the jurisdiction of the superior courts protected by s. 96 of the *Constitution Act, 1867.* As a result, hearing fees that deny people access to the courts infringe the core jurisdiction of the superior courts.

• • •

[37] This is consistent with the approach adopted by Major J. in *Imperial Tobacco*. The legislation here at issue—the imposition of hearing fees—must conform not only to the express terms of the Constitution, but to the "requirements ... that flow by necessary implication from the express terms of the Constitution." The right of Canadians to access the superior courts flows by necessary implication from the express terms of s. 96 of the Constitution, as we have seen. It follows that the province does not have the power under s. 92(14) to enact legislation that prevents people from accessing the courts.

[38] While this suffices to resolve the fundamental issue of principle in this appeal, the connection between s. 96 and access to justice is further supported by considerations relating to the rule of law. This Court affirmed that access to the courts is essential to the rule of law in *B.C.G.E.U. v. British Columbia (Attorney General)*, [1988] 2 S.C.R. 214. As Dickson C.J. put it, "[t]here cannot be a rule of law

without access, otherwise the rule of law is replaced by a rule of men and women who decide who shall and who shall not have access to justice" ... .

• • •

[41] This Court's decision in *Christie* does not undermine the proposition that access to the courts is fundamental to our constitutional arrangements. The Court in Christie—a case concerning a 7 percent surcharge on legal services—proceeded on the premise of a fundamental right to access the courts, but held that not "every limit on access to the courts is automatically unconstitutional" (para. 17). In the present case, the hearing fee requirement has the potential to bar litigants with legitimate claims from the courts. The tax at issue in *Christie*, on the evidence and arguments adduced, was not shown to have a similar impact.

[42] Nor does the argument that legislatures generally have the right to determine the cost of government services undermine the proposition that laws cannot prevent citizens from accessing the superior courts. (Indeed, the Attorney General does not assert such a proposition.) The right of the province to impose hearing fees is limited by constitutional constraints. In defining those constraints, the Court does not impermissibly venture into territory that is the exclusive turf of the legislature. Rather, the Court is ensuring that the Constitution is respected.

[43] I conclude that s. 92(14), read in the context of the Constitution as a whole, does not give the provinces the power to administer justice in a way that denies the right of Canadians to access courts of superior jurisdiction. Any attempt to do so will run afoul of the constitutional protection for the superior courts found in s. 96.

• • •

[49] To recap, provinces may impose hearing fees as part of the administration of justice. However, this power does not extend to hearing fees that effectively prevent litigants from accessing the courts because they cannot afford the fees.

[50] On the findings of the trial judge, the hearing fee scheme at issue in this case places an undue hardship on litigants and impedes the right of British Columbians to bring legitimate cases to court.

• • •

[64] I conclude that the hearing fee scheme prevents access to the courts in a manner inconsistent with s. 96 of the Constitution and the underlying principle of the rule of law. It therefore falls outside the Province's jurisdiction under s. 92(14) to administer justice.

• • •

ROTHSTEIN J (dissenting):

[80] Courts do not have free range to micromanage the policy choices of governments acting within the sphere of their constitutional powers. This appeal concerns the constitutionality of a hearing fee scheme contained in the British Columbia *Supreme Court Civil Rules*, B.C. Reg. 168/2009, to encourage the efficient use of courtroom time in civil courts and to recoup some of the costs for the provision of such time. The appellants submit that the imposition of hearing fees is unconstitutional. The majority finds that the hearing fees do fall within the powers of a province to make laws in relation to the administration of justice in the province but that they are nevertheless unconstitutional when they cause undue hardship to some litigants and effectively prevent their access to courts. In the majority's view, s. 96 of the *Constitution Act, 1867*, supported by the rule of law, provides a general right to access the courts. They find that this right is undermined by hearing fees that Canadians cannot afford.

[81] In my respectful view, the British Columbia hearing fee scheme does not offend any constitutional right. The majority must base its finding on an overly broad reading of s. 96, with support from the unwritten constitutional principle of the rule of law, because there is no express constitutional right to access the civil courts without hearing fees.

• • •

The Rule of Law

[91] The majority reads the unwritten principle of the rule of law as supporting the striking down of legislation otherwise properly within provincial jurisdiction. It is true that this Court has, on occasion, turned to unwritten principles to fill in "gaps in the express terms of the constitutional text" (*Reference re Remuneration of Judges of the Provincial Court of Prince Edward Island*, [1997] 3 S.C.R. 3, at para. 104). But there are no such gaps in the text of s. 92(14). With respect, gaps do not exist simply because the courts believe that the text should say something that it does not. This Court, in *Reference re Secession of Quebec*, [1998] 2 S.C.R. 217, reiterated its earlier insistence on the primacy of the written constitutional text, stating that unwritten principles "could not be taken as an invitation to dispense with the written text of the Constitution" (para. 53, affirming *Re: Remuneration of Judges*, at paras. 93 and 104). The written constitutional provisions guide government action and provide the touchstone for judicial review, anchoring the authority of courts to invalidate noncompliant laws enacted by democratically elected governments.

[92] There is no express right of general access to superior courts for civil disputes in the text of the Constitution. Rather, the Constitution specifies the particular instances in which access to courts is guaranteed. Section 24(1) of the Charter provides that persons whose Charter rights have been infringed or denied may apply to the courts for a remedy. It is in this sense that this Court, in *B.C.G.E.U. v. British Columbia (Attorney General)*, [1988] 2 S.C.R. 214, held that access to courts for the purpose of vindicating Charter rights is protected (pp. 228-29). Section 11(d) of the Charter guarantees persons charged with an offence the right "to be presumed innocent until proven guilty according to law in a fair and public hearing by an independent and impartial tribunal."

[93] But the majority uses the rule of law to support reading a general constitutional right to access the superior courts into s. 96. This provision of the *Constitution Act, 1867* requires that the existence and core jurisdiction of superior courts be preserved, but this does not, for the reasons herein, necessarily imply the general right of access to superior courts described by the majority. So long as the courts maintain their character as judicial bodies and exercise the core functions of courts, the demands of the Constitution are satisfied. In using an unwritten principle to support expanding the ambit of s. 96 to such an extent, the majority subverts the structure of the Constitution and jeopardizes the primacy of the written text.

• • •

[96] The majority proposes to invalidate those provincial laws relating to the administration of justice that, in their view, are contrary to the rule of law. The unwritten principle of the rule of law, as defined by this Court, consists of three elements:

(1) "[T]he law is supreme over officials of the government as well as private individuals, and thereby preclusive of the influence of arbitrary power" (*Reference re Manitoba Language Rights*, [1985] 1 S.C.R. 721, at p. 748);

(2) The rule of law "requires the creation and maintenance of an actual order of positive laws which preserves and embodies the more general principle of normative order" (ibid., at p. 749); and

(3) "[T]he exercise of all public power must find its ultimate source in a legal rule" (*Reference re Secession of Quebec*, at para. 71, quoting *Re: Remuneration of Judges*, at para. 10).

As this Court found in *British Columbia v. Imperial Tobacco Canada Ltd.*, 2005 SCC 49, [2005] 2 S.C.R. 473, "none of the principles that the rule of law embraces speak directly to the terms of legislation" (para. 59).

[97] This Court has clearly and persuasively cautioned against using the rule of law to strike down legislation:

So understood, *it is difficult to conceive of how the rule of law could be used as a basis for invalidating legislation* such as the Act based on its content. ...

(*Imperial Tobacco*, at paras. 59-60)

[98] To circumvent this caution against using the rule of law as a basis for striking down legislation, the majority characterizes the rule of law as a limitation on the jurisdiction of provinces under s. 92(14) of the *Constitution Act, 1867*. The majority acknowledges that imposing hearing fees is a permissible exercise of the province's jurisdiction according to the written constitutional text—that is, s. 92(14) (para. 23). But they ultimately conclude that the hearing fees fall outside the province's jurisdiction in part because the fees are inconsistent with the unwritten principle of the rule of law (paras. 38-40). Dressing the rule of law in division-of-powers clothing does not disguise the fact that the rule of law, an unwritten principle, cannot be used to support striking down the hearing fee scheme.

[99] In using the rule of law to support the striking down of legislation that is indisputably within the scope of s. 92(14) of the *Constitution Act, 1867*, without attention to this Court's entrenched understanding of the rule of law, the majority ignores this Court's caution in *Imperial Tobacco*:

The rule of law is not an invitation to trivialize or supplant the Constitution's written terms. Nor is it a tool by which to avoid legislative initiatives of which one is not in favour. On the contrary, *it requires that courts give effect to the Constitution's text, and apply, by whatever its terms, legislation that conforms to that text.* [Emphasis added; para. 67.]

With respect, the rule of law does not demand that this Court invalidate the hearing fee scheme—if anything, it demands that we uphold it.

[100] The unwritten principles of our Constitution often work at cross purposes. Even if we were to accept that the rule of law favours striking down the hearing fees, the unwritten principle of democracy favours upholding legislation passed by democratically elected representatives which conforms to the express terms of the Constitution. As the Court stated in *Imperial Tobacco*, "in a constitutional democracy such as ours, protection from legislation that some might view as unjust or unfair properly lies not in the amorphous underlying principles of our Constitution, but in its text and the ballot box" (para. 66).

[101] *Imperial Tobacco* offers yet another caution against reading the unwritten principle of the rule of law too broadly: it would "render many of our written constitutional rights redundant and, in doing so, undermine the delimitation of those rights chosen by our constitutional framers" (para. 65). As noted above, s. 11(d) of the Charter specifically includes a right of access to the courts for a person charged with an offence and s. 24(1) gives this right to those vindicating their Charter rights.

These provisions would be unnecessary if the Constitution already contained a more general right to access superior courts.

[102] In any event, the rule of law is a vague and fundamentally disputed concept. In *Imperial Tobacco*, this Court endorsed the observation of Strayer J.A. that "[a]dvocates tend to read into the principle of the rule of law anything which supports their particular view of what the law should be" (para. 62, citing *Singh v. Canada (Attorney General)*, [2000] 3 F.C. 185 (C.A.), at para. 33). To rely on this nebulous principle to invalidate legislation based on its content introduces uncertainty into constitutional law and undermines our system of positive law.

• • •

[117] For the reasons above:

(a) I would answer the constitutional question stated in this appeal as follows:

Are the hearing fees set out in paragraph 14 of Appendix C, Schedule 1 (B.C. Reg. 10/96, as amended) and the hearing fees set out in paragraphs 9 and 10 of Appendix C, Schedule 1 (B.C. Reg. 168/2009, as amended), unconstitutional on the basis that they infringe a right of access to justice and thereby offend the rule of law?

No.

2. Arbitrary Exercises of Statutory Power

The idea that all state officials are subject to the legal order, and to the same legal obligations as are individual citizens, was most famously affirmed by a majority of the Supreme Court in *Roncarelli v Duplessis*. The case arose in 1959, prior to the adoption of the Charter and its protections of freedom of religion and expression. In the absence of those constitutional arguments, the Supreme Court of Canada relied on a basic understanding of the rule of law to condemn a questionable use of statutory power. The director of the province's liquor commission, acting under the express direction of Premier Maurice Duplessis, revoked the licence of a Montreal restaurateur who had posted bail for several hundred members of the Jehovah's Witnesses, a group that had attracted the particular animus of the Premier. The director purported to be acting under the commission's unqualified statutory power to cancel permits "at its discretion." The Court rejected the idea that any statute could delegate such untrammelled power to a government official, or that the Premier could manipulate his own powers to pursue a personal vendetta. Statutory powers must be limited to the express or implied purposes for which they were granted, a principle enforceable by the judiciary. The most bold and well-known statement of the principles appeared in the opinion of Justice Ivan Rand:

Roncarelli v Duplessis
[1959] SCR 121

RAND J (Judson J concurring):

It is then wholly as a private citizen, an adherent of a religious group, holding a liquor licence and furnishing bail to arrested persons for no other purpose than to enable them to be released from detention pending the determination of the charges against them, and with no other relevant considerations to be taken into account, that he is involved in the issues of this controversy.

The complementary state of things is equally free from doubt. From the evidence of Mr. Duplessis and Mr. Archambault alone, it appears that the action taken by the latter as the general manager and sole member of the Commission was dictated by Mr. Duplessis as Attorney-General and Prime Minister of the province; that that step was taken as a means of bringing to a halt the activities of the Witnesses, to punish the appellant for the part he had played not only by revoking the existing licence but in declaring him barred from one "forever," and to warn others that they similarly would be stripped of provincial "privileges" if they persisted in any activity directly or indirectly related to the Witnesses and to the objectionable campaign. The respondent felt that action to be his duty, something which his conscience demanded of him; and as representing the provincial government his decision became automatically that of Mr. Archambault and the Commission. ...

In these circumstances, when the *de facto* power of the Executive over its appointees at will to such a statutory public function is exercised deliberately and intentionally to destroy the vital business interests of a citizen, is there legal redress by him against the person so acting? This calls for an examination of the statutory provisions governing the issue, renewal and revocation of liquor licences and the scope of authority entrusted by law to the Attorney-General and the government in relation to the administration of the Act.

The liquor law is contained in RSQ 1941, c. 255, entitled *An Act Respecting Alcoholic Liquor*. A Commission is created as a corporation, the only member of which is the general manager ... . Dealing with cancellation, the section [s 35 of the Act] provides that the "Commission may cancel any permit at its discretion." ... The provisions of the statute, which may be supplemented by detailed regulations, furnish a code for the complete administration of the sale and distribution of alcoholic liquors directed by the Commission as a public service, for all legitimate purposes of the populace. It recognizes the association of wines and liquors as embellishments of food and its ritual and as an interest of the public. As put in Macbeth, the "sauce to meat is ceremony," and so we have restaurants, cafés, hotels and other places of serving food, specifically provided for in that association. ...

The field of licensed occupations and businesses of this nature is steadily becoming of greater concern to citizens generally. It is a matter of vital importance that a public administration that can refuse to allow a person to enter or continue a calling which, in the absence of regulation, would be free and legitimate, should be conducted with complete impartiality and integrity; and that the grounds for refusing or cancelling a permit should unquestionably be such and such only as are incompatible with the purposes envisaged by the statute: the duty of a Commission is to serve those purposes and those only. A decision to deny or cancel such a privilege lies within the "discretion" of the Commission; but that means that decision is to be based upon a weighing of considerations pertinent to the object of the administration.

In public regulation of this sort there is no such thing as absolute and untrammelled "discretion," that is that action can be taken on any ground or for any reason that can be suggested to the mind of the administrator; no legislative Act can, without express language, be taken to contemplate an unlimited arbitrary power exercisable for any purpose, however capricious or irrelevant, regardless of the nature or purpose of the statute. Fraud and corruption in the Commission may not be mentioned in such statutes but they are always implied as exceptions. "Discretion" necessarily implies good faith in discharging public duty; there is always a perspective within which a statute is intended to operate; and any clear departure from its lines or objects is just as objectionable as fraud or corruption. Could an applicant be refused a permit because he had been born in another province, or because of the colour of his hair? The legislature cannot be so distorted.

To deny or revoke a permit because a citizen exercises an unchallengeable right totally irrelevant to the sale of liquor in a restaurant is equally beyond the scope of the discretion conferred. There was here not only revocation of the existing permit but a declaration of a future, definitive disqualification of the appellant to obtain one: it was to be "forever." This purports to divest his citizenship status of its incident of membership in the class of those of the public to whom such a privilege could be extended. Under the statutory language here, that is not competent to the Commission and *a fortiori* to the government or the respondent. ...

It may be difficult if not impossible in cases generally to demonstrate a breach of this public duty in the illegal purpose served; there may be no means, even if proceedings against the Commission were permitted by the Attorney-General, as here they were refused, of compelling the Commission to justify a refusal or revocation or to give reasons for its action; on these questions I make no observation; but in the case before us that difficulty is not present: the reasons are openly avowed.

The act of the respondent through the instrumentality of the Commission brought about a breach of an implied public statutory duty toward the appellant; it was a gross abuse of legal power expressly intended to punish him for an act wholly irrelevant to the statute, a punishment which inflicted on him, as it was intended to do, the destruction of his economic life as a restaurant keeper within the province. Whatever may be the immunity of the Commission or its member from an action for damages, there is none in the respondent. He was under no duty in relation to the appellant and his act was an intrusion upon the functions of a statutory body. The injury done by him was a fault engaging liability ... . That, in the presence of expanding administrative regulation of economic activities, such a step and its consequences are to be suffered by the victim without recourse or remedy, that an administration according to law is to be superseded by action dictated by and according to the arbitrary likes, dislikes and irrelevant purposes of public officers acting beyond their duty, would signalize the beginning of disintegration of the rule of law as a fundamental postulate of our constitutional structure. An administration of licences on the highest level of fair and impartial treatment to all may be forced to follow the practice of "first come, first served," which makes the strictest observance of equal responsibility to all of even greater importance; at this stage of developing government it would be a danger of high consequence to tolerate such a departure from good faith in executing the legislative purpose. ...

"Good faith" in this context, applicable both to the respondent and the general manager, means carrying out the statute according to its intent and for its purpose; it means good faith in acting with a rational appreciation of that intent and purpose and not with an improper intent and for an alien purpose; it does not mean for the purposes of punishing a person for exercising an unchallengeable right; it does not mean arbitrarily and illegally attempting to divest a citizen of an incident of his civil status.

B. THE PRINCIPLE OF CONSTITUTIONAL SUPREMACY

If the rule of law principle holds that "all exercises of legitimate public power must have a source in law, and every state official or agency is subject to constraint of the law," a logical next question would be, "What is that source of law in Canada and by what law is every state actor bound?" The answer to that question is found in the principle of constitutional supremacy—that is, the Constitution is the source of powers to make law, and all (ordinary) laws so made must be consistent with the terms of the Constitution, or else be found invalid and of no force or effect. After 1867, the principle of constitutional supremacy had operated in Canada in the sense that laws could be ruled to be invalid on the basis that they conflicted with the division of powers between the federal and provincial levels of government. However, the Supreme Court of Canada confirmed in the *Quebec Secession Reference* that only in 1982 did Canada complete a transformation from a system based "largely" on the principle of parliamentary supremacy, to one of constitutional supremacy. The transformation was completed by the adoption in 1982 of the *Canadian Charter of Rights and Freedoms*—written constitutional rights that placed limits in the interests of individuals on the substantive laws that could be enacted by Canada's sovereign legislatures—and, of course, by the express statement of constitutional supremacy in s 52 of the *Constitution Act, 1982*. Recall that s 52(1) reads, "The Constitution of Canada is the supreme law of Canada, and any law that is inconsistent with the provisions of the Constitution is, to the extent of the inconsistency, of no force or effect."

The principle of constitutional supremacy implies certain sub-principles concerning public law that help to understand its nature. These sub-principles include the following.

1. A Hierarchy in Law

To state that the Constitution is Canada's "supreme law" implies that there is a hierarchy in law between constitutional law and non-constitutional law, or "ordinary law." In the Canadian legal tradition, "ordinary law" comprises statute law (written laws enacted by legislators) and common law (private law principles developed over time by judicial precedent). Just as the principle of constitutional supremacy means that constitutional law overrides ordinary law where the two are in conflict, so too the principle of parliamentary supremacy, discussed below, means that express statements of law found in statutes override the common law rules established by judicial precedent.

The hierarchical relationship among common law, statute law, and constitutional law is a reliable feature of Canadian law (outside the civil law tradition of Quebec, which eschews the notion of a common law) that knows of no exceptions. Nevertheless, there are two conceptual difficulties that deserve attention in this account. First, a significant proportion of Canadian law takes the form of "subordinate" or "secondary" legislation—that is, law written by government officials, not legislators, pursuant to authority given them in statutes. Well-known examples of subordinate legislation include regulations and municipal by-laws. Where do these rules and regulations fit into the hierarchy of Canadian law? As the term "subordinate legislation" suggests, regulations are subordinate to the law of their parent statute, and so any inconsistency between the statute and a regulation is decided in favour of the former. To the extent a regulation is properly and expressly authorized by statute, the regulation will override a common law rule.

Second, the relationship between the Constitution and common law in the Charter era has been subject to some complexity. The Supreme Court of Canada made early statements to the effect that the Charter should not be applied directly to the common law so as to invalidate rules of the common law—see *RWDSU v Dolphin Delivery*, [1986] 2 SCR 573. The Court was concerned that direct application of the Charter to the common law would have the undesirable consequence of making all private legal relations subject to the Charter. More recent statements, however, have expanded the reach of Charter law to influence the development of common law rules. See, for example, *RWDSU, Local 558 v Pepsi-Cola Canada Beverages (West) Ltd*, 2002 SCC 8, [2002] 1 SCR 156 (freedom of expression requires that the common law allow for secondary picketing in labour disputes); and *Grant v Torstar Corp*, 2009 SCC 61, [2009] 3 SCR 640 (freedom of expression requires introducing a defence of "responsible journalism" into the common law of defamation). In these latter cases, the Court has confirmed that the principle of constitutional supremacy means that the common law should, in the incremental case-by-case fashion by which it evolves, be brought into conformity with Charter values.

2. The Need for Constitutional Adjudication

To effect constitutional supremacy requires a mechanism for adjudicating alleged inconsistencies between the Constitution and ordinary law, including the power to declare ordinary laws to be inconsistent and therefore invalid. Constitutional provisions can never be so detailed as to be "self-enforcing" in the sense that everyone agrees with how they apply in all circumstances. The Constitution must be interpreted in order to be applied to the complex and ever-variable conditions within Canadian society.

The logic of constitutional supremacy means that the task of interpreting and enforcing the Constitution ought not to be performed by the same body that enacts the ordinary law subject to constitutional scrutiny—that is, the legislature. Legislators would rarely if ever declare the laws they had passed to be unconstitutional. This does not mean that legislatures cannot play a significant role in developing understandings of constitutional text, or in making persuasive arguments about why particular legislation is consistent with that text. However, it does mean that the legislature cannot be the authoritative voice on the Constitution's interpretation.

In the ordinary course, our system requires that a judiciary with the authority to interpret and apply the Constitution will check the legislature. This judicial function speaks in turn to the need for a robust principle of judicial independence, protecting the interpreters of the Constitution from political interference in their decision-making. The logic of constitutional supremacy does not define the name or particular composition of the body playing this adjudicative function. In the United States, the US Supreme Court expressly confirmed this role for itself in a famous decision by John Marshall CJ, *Marbury v Madison*, 5 US (Cranch 1) 137 (1803), excerpted in Chapter 11. Canada's courts and the Judicial Committee of the Privy Council assumed this jurisdiction with respect to the division of powers from the earliest days of Confederation, without feeling the need to discuss the source of their authority to do so. Section 52 of the *Constitution Act, 1982* now provides that source. In Canada, the role has been assigned to the same courts and judges that decide all legal disputes in this society. Other countries—such as Germany and South Africa—have developed special adjudicative bodies or constitutional courts whose sole jurisdiction lies in that domain. The point is that a system of constitutional supremacy requires an independent body with interpretive powers.

There has been debate in Canada over whether administrative tribunals—that is, adjudicative bodies established by the legislature as part of the executive branch of government such as labour relations boards and human rights tribunals—should be entitled to interpret and apply the Constitution to invalidate legislation. Earlier doubts in this regard appear now to have been resolved. In *Nova Scotia (Workers' Compensation Board) v Martin; Nova Scotia (Workers' Compensation Board) v Laseur*, 2003 SCC 54, [2003] 2 SCR 504, Gonthier J writing for the Court observed (at para 34) that the question should be

> answered by applying a presumption, based on the principle of constitutional supremacy ... that all legal decisions will take into account the supreme law of the land. Thus, as a rule, "an administrative tribunal which has been conferred the power to interpret law holds a concomitant power to determine whether that law is constitutionally valid."

The *Martin* approach was upheld by the Supreme Court in *R v Conway*, 2010 SCC 22, [2010] 1 SCR 765, a case dealing with the constitutional jurisdiction of Ontario's forensic psychiatric review board.

The notion that administrative tribunals, which are non-judicial bodies with varying degrees of independence from executive government, are empowered to apply the Constitution and the Charter may seem inconsistent with the notion of constitutional interpretation by an independent judiciary. However, as a matter of constitutional principle, Canadian law guarantees a right to any person affected by a tribunal decision to have that decision "judicially reviewed." Ultimately, therefore, independent courts have the final adjudicative word. This is discussed further in Chapter 11.

3. The Democracy Principle and Constitutional Amendments Requiring a Super-Majority

The Supreme Court emphasized an unwritten "democracy principle" in the *Quebec Secession Reference*, but what does it mean? The simplest idea is that of the will of a majority. To a greater or lesser degree depending on the nature and quality of a particular electoral system, legislatures express the preferences of a voting majority in a democratic society (but note that the voting majority may not necessarily be a numerical majority). These preferences may change over time, and at any one time there may be a great many "majorities" represented in Parliament going to a whole host of different policy issues. Moreover, as discussed in Chapters 6 and 7, the *Constitution Act, 1867*, the Charter, and electoral law statutes (read together) create legislatures whose membership is determined through voting by citizens (the exception being the Senate at the federal level).

This idea that the legislature expresses the preferences of a majority is considered important in several different ways that matter for public law. Majority will, for example, underscores the importance we accord the institution of Parliament as well as the election of provincial legislatures by popular franchise. As discussed in Section II.C below, the parliamentary principle was considered supreme in our Westminster system until Canada transformed itself into a system of constitutional supremacy. Nevertheless, we cannot forget that such supremacy finds one historical source in the "supremacy of the sovereign will of the people" since we are also a constitutional democracy (*Quebec Secession Reference* at paras 61-62). We can trace this idea back to the ancient Greeks, who in the 5th century created this system of government (*demokratia*, or "rule by the people"). It is important to keep in mind that, while the principle of democracy is therefore related to the principles of parliamentary supremacy and federalism, and overlap exists in their respective content, we should be mindful to keep some of the content of the principle of democracy distinct from its "cousin" principles. This is because, on their own, federal levels and legislatures do not have to be democratic in nature.

In addition to the sovereign will of the people just discussed, recollect how the Supreme Court in the *Quebec Secession Reference* further described the principle of democracy as linked to the process of making representative and responsible government (*Quebec Secession Reference* at para 65). The right to vote and the electoral process provide one way to participate in the political process and are the very means we use to choose *who* will represent us in federal and provincial legislatures. Underscoring the importance of these processes, both the Charter's s 3 right to vote and s 4 obligation to hold general elections are not subject to the s 33 override. This textbook discusses a number of elections—cases forming what many call the "law of democracy"—but one that more deeply delves into this idea of democratic representation is *Shell Canada Products Ltd v Vancouver (City)*, [1994] 1 SCR 231, a case concerning municipal government (see Chapter 8).

A third essential feature of democracy, according to the Supreme Court in the *Quebec Secession Reference*, is that it is connected to the self-government of a sovereign people (such as the Canadian nation or Indigenous peoples), as well as respect for cultural and group identity (such as Quebec's distinct society and the many distinctive Indigenous cultures in Canada). This is a different sense of representative government than what we discussed above. Our electoral system imperfectly assists in ensuring that our representatives reflect a diverse society. It is flawed, but Canadian democracy is also an "evolutionary democracy moving in uneven steps toward the goal of universal suffrage and more effecting representation" (*Reference re Provincial Electoral Boundaries (Sask)*, [1991] 2 SCR 158, cited in *Quebec Secession Reference* at para 63). Such a conception has supported the extension of the franchise to men without property, women, minorities such as Chinese Canadians, and Indigenous peoples. In *Sauvé v Canada (Chief Electoral Officer)*, 2002 SCC 68, [2002] 3 SCR 519, the Supreme Court highlighted this aspect of the principle when it controversially struck down s 51(e) of the *Canada Elections Act*, SC 2000, c 9, which denied the right to vote to penitentiary inmates serving a sentence of two years or more. The majority of the Court held that the s 3 right to vote contained in the Charter is so fundamental for a well-functioning democracy that the government would have to provide a compelling justification under s 1 to deny it. The Court disagreed with the government that the denial of such a fundamental right could legitimately advance democratic values such as inclusiveness, equality, and citizen participation. Moreover, the Court rejected disenfranchisement as a valid form of state punishment partly because disenfranchisement had a deleterious effect on Indigenous peoples, who are disproportionately incarcerated in Canadian penitentiaries, but also because of the connection with Canada's colonial history and the historical denial of the right to vote for Indigenous peoples. The case is also notable for a robust dissent that would have upheld the provision.

Fourth, democracy is often understood narrowly. We can consider it as simple majority rule. We can also see it as another accountability mechanism. In this sense it can be seen as a complementary partner to the rule of law principle as a means to minimize the abuse of political power by having the executive branch be more accountable to the legislative branch. But there are more complex ways of understanding democracy too. In the *Quebec Secession Reference*, the Supreme Court alludes to these more complex conceptions when it talks about the consent of the governed (at para 67), the importance of participation in public institutions (at para 67), and the need to have a "continuous process of discussion" (at para 68) in our political culture generally and specifically when we build majorities that hear and include the voices of minorities. In addition to majoritarian, populist, and liberal democracy, then, the Supreme Court may also be alluding to participatory democracy, social democracy, and deliberative democracy in its judgment. Future case law may add more substantive content to this basic conception of democracy found in the *Quebec Secession Reference*.

Following from this idea of a continuous process of discussion, democracy possesses an "inescapable disharmony," as political philosopher Amy Gutmann puts it (Amy Gutmann, "Democracy," in Robert E Goodin, Philip Pettit & Thomas W Pogge, *A Companion to Contemporary Political Philosophy*, 2nd ed (Oxford: Blackwell Publishing) at 522). Even the best and most inclusive form of democracy cannot result in universal agreement among individual citizens about politically and morally controversial issues. On this account, what we can best do is ensure that good public deliberation occurs without acrimony and violence, that we seek the best information we can, and that we listen and respect various perspectives before we come to a conclusion on what (in our opinion) the best resolution may be. In this way, the principle of democracy can also be deeply connected to the protection of minorities and counter-majoritarianism. Such a democracy is sometimes called a "liberal democracy"—a democracy in which majorities cannot run roughshod over minority rights. (Of course, not every democracy is a liberal democracy: at the time of writing, we are witnessing the emergence of populist "illiberal democracies" in parts of world, where majority will is mobilized to polarize majorities against minorities.)

The majoritarian nature of democracy creates recurring dynamics in public law. One dynamic is to limit legislatures and legislation to protect minority interests—that is, to put the "liberal" in "liberal democracy." This concept is discussed below as "counter-majoritarianism." Another dynamic, however, concerns recognizing the legitimacy of the choices that legislatures make in enacting legislation. When reviewing legislation, judges may disagree with the choices that the legislature has made and embedded in legislation. It may be the judges' view that these choices result in "bad" law. But, unless these choices are unconstitutional, judges are obliged to show judicial restraint in the face of such "bad" law (e.g., a statute that repeals a carbon tax in the face of a growing climate crisis). This issue is more fully addressed later in Chapter 7 when we consider parliamentary law-making. The ability of legislatures to pass legislation that is of inferior quality also poses a problem for judges in judicial review as they are not empowered to correct for flaws in the legislative process or in legislative form (such as omnibus bills).

Finally, a fundamental relationship also exists between democracy and the ways we can change our written constitution. Constitutional supremacy implies that a constitution cannot be amended in the same way that ordinary legislation is enacted. If the same Parliament that passes ordinary legislation is also able to amend the Constitution itself, it is not effectively bound by the Constitution because it can merely alter its terms whenever it encounters a constitutional difficulty. The process for amending a constitution must involve a "super-majority," which brings in more elements of society than comprise a legislative majority. The particular super-majority required will speak to a nation's understanding of itself and what is most important to its ongoing existence. The amending formula adopted in part V of the *Constitution Act, 1982* (discussed in Section III, below) turns largely on federalism. Most amendments require the agreement of Parliament together with most of the provincial legislatures, and some call for the unanimous agreement of Parliament and *all* provincial legislatures. In the case of Aboriginal and treaty rights guaranteed in s 35(1) of the *Constitution Act, 1982*, amendments can be made only following a conference of the federal and provincial governments to which "representatives of the aboriginal peoples of Canada" have been invited. The word "entrenched" is a familiar term in Canadian constitutionalism. For a right to be "entrenched" in the Constitution means that the right has the degree of permanence accorded by constitutional status, such that it can be amended or removed only by operation of the applicable super-majority.

Read *Shell Canada Products Ltd v Vancouver (City)*, [1994] 1 SCR 231, in Chapter 8. How does the principle of democracy inform both the majority and the dissent's decisions?

For a recent, controversial, and spirited use of the unwritten principle of democracy, see *City of Toronto v Ontario (AG)*, 2018 ONSC 5151, a case concerning judicial review of the *Better Local Government Act, 2018*, SO 2018, c 11. This statute radically redrew the City of Toronto's electoral districts in the middle of the City's elections. Justice Belobaba of the Ontario Court of Justice took a novel approach to interpreting the democracy principle, while the Ontario Court of Appeal took a more measured approached. See *Toronto (City) v Ontario (AG)*, 2019 ONCA 732.

For further discussion of the potential for new democracy-enhancing limits on the principle of parliamentary sovereignty, see Vincent Kazmierski, "Draconian but Not Despotic: The Unwritten Limits of Parliamentary Sovereignty in Canada" (2010) 41:2 Ottawa L Rev 245 and Adam M Dodek, "Omnibus Bills: Constitutional Constraints and Legislative Liberations" (2017) 48:1 Ottawa L Rev 5.

4. Protection of Minorities and a Counter-Majoritarian Purpose

Constitutional supremacy, however, also represents a check on majoritarian democracy. The Constitution does guard rights and liberties for individuals and some minorities—especially (although not exclusively) in the Charter and in the Aboriginal rights protected in s 35 of the *Constitution Act, 1982*. Any limits the Constitution places on what can be enacted as substantive law are limits placed on majority preferences. The limits may serve to protect the interests of individuals, minority groups, or regional populations. The point is that the very nature of a supreme constitution is to rein in the power of legislative majorities. The adjudicative body that interprets and enforces the Constitution must therefore be recognized as having the legitimate function of ruling against majority preferences. This is not to say that judicial rulings on constitutional issues must always or necessarily run counter to majority views as expressed by legislatures, or that legislatures always accurately express views of a majority. It is to say that in a system of constitutional supremacy, the power to interpret and enforce the Constitution against majority preferences must be present.

The particular checks on majoritarianism embodied in a constitution have a historical dimension. That is, the framers of a constitution anticipate for the future what values deserve protection from majority preferences. Present majorities may well find themselves subject to constitutional limits created by people with very different views, in a very different society. For this reason, the need for ways to amend a constitution is recognized in all known political communities.

C. THE PRINCIPLE OF PARLIAMENTARY SUPREMACY

In the *Quebec Secession Reference*, the Supreme Court stated the following (at para 73):

> This Court has noted on several occasions that with the adoption of the Charter, the Canadian system of government was transformed to a significant extent from a system of Parliamentary supremacy to one of constitutional supremacy.

What does "parliamentary supremacy" (or "sovereignty") mean? How does it relate to "constitutional supremacy"? If the Canadian system of government has been "transformed to a significant extent" from one to the other, what remains of parliamentary supremacy and how important is it to our public law?

The principle of parliamentary supremacy is the basic principle of British constitutional law that Canada's founders adopted in 1867. That they intended to do so is made clear in the preamble to the *Constitution Act, 1867*, which states that it is the desire of the federating provinces to adopt "a Constitution similar in Principle to that of the United Kingdom."

British constitutional history is the story of a long and often bloody struggle to bring the monarchy and executive government under the authority of Parliament as the body representing the people of the country. The evolution of Parliament into a representative body elected by universal adult franchise is itself a dramatic and somewhat later developing story, unfinished for those concerned about a continued legislative role for the unelected House of Lords in the United Kingdom and the Senate in Canada. Nevertheless, to the degree elected legislatures embody democratic values, the idea of parliamentary or legislative supremacy is itself a profoundly democratic idea.

The simplicity of parliamentary supremacy as a constitutional principle explains why it does not require a written embodiment. Indeed, the British Constitution is famously unwritten. If the framers of Canada's Constitution truly wished to adopt the British principle, why did they do so in a written document, the *Constitution Act, 1867*? The short answer is federalism. Canada was founded on the basis of dividing legislative power between a national legislature— Parliament—and regional or provincial legislatures. As with a contract of any complexity intended to bind wary parties not sure how far each can be trusted, this could only be done in writing. The division of powers between the federal and provincial legislatures became the distinctive Canadian answer to the question of "who" has law-making authority.

If the existence of a written constitution that placed limits on which jurisdiction could pass what laws is all that is required to have "constitutional supremacy," then Canada has operated on this basis since 1867. That is not, however, how the Canadian system was understood. Rather, the principle of parliamentary supremacy remained predominant, qualified only by federalism. That is, Canada's federal and provincial legislatures were understood to be the sole sovereign holders of state authority, subject to authority being divided between them along the lines largely set out in ss 91 and 92 of the *Constitution Act, 1867*. With the limited exception of denominational school rights in s 93 and official language protections in s 133, Canada's legislatures remained able between them to enact any law they so chose. The doctrine of exhaustion of state power meant that if one level of legislature was unable to enact a law for jurisdictional reasons, then the law could be passed by the other level.

With the *Constitution Act, 1982*, Canada adopted both a *Charter of Rights and Freedoms* and an express declaration of constitutional supremacy. These two developments were hardly coincidental. The Charter imposed significant new limits on the substantive laws that could be passed by either level of legislature—that is, it provided a new and significantly different answer to the question of "what" laws can be enacted. With these limits, the concept of parliamentary supremacy was modified beyond a point at which it could reasonably continue to character-ize the constitutional system. The limits placed on substantive law-making by the Charter, together with the existing limits on who can pass which laws set out in ss 91 and 92 of the 1867 Act, virtually required a recognition of the written Constitution as being the supreme source of law-making authority in Canada.

The framers of the *Canadian Charter of Rights and Freedoms* were sensitive to the impact that entrenched individual rights would have on the principle of parliamentary supremacy, Certain provincial governments strenuously defended this principle. They reached a compro-mise with the federal government and the other provinces by agreeing to include an override or "notwithstanding" provision, s 33, in the Charter. The override allows either Parliament or a provincial legislature to enact legislation in contravention of certain Charter rights if the legis-lation contains an explicit declaration pursuant to s 33. The effect of s 33 of the Charter was to reinforce the principle of parliamentary supremacy, albeit in an attenuated form.

For this and other reasons, parliamentary sovereignty retains considerable utility and explanatory power with respect to Canadian law. In particular, it remains important for under-standing the relationship between legislative and executive power in Canada. While constitu-tional supremacy ensures that Parliament and the provincial legislatures must comply with the Constitution, the principle of parliamentary supremacy ensures that executive government must comply with the directives established for it by the legislature. In this way, executive gov-ernment is made subject to the Constitution—that is, executive action must comply with the provisions of the Constitution because it can be authorized only by statutes that themselves are consistent with the Constitution.

Babcock v Canada, below, provides an example of how the Supreme Court has approached parliamentary sovereignty as a principle in Canadian constitutional law. In *Babcock*, the gov-ernment of Canada sought to rely on a statutory right of non-disclosure of Cabinet docu-ments, despite the documents having already been disclosed in the course of litigation. The applicants sought to invoke unwritten principles such as the rule of law to support an argu-ment that disclosure should be required despite the clear statutory statement to the contrary. The Court found that parliamentary sovereignty decided the issue.

Babcock v Canada (AG)
2002 SCC 57, [2002] 3 SCR 3

McLACHLIN CJ (Gonthier, Iacobucci, Major, Bastarache, Binnie, Arbour, and LeBel JJ concurring):

[1] This case raises the issue of when, if ever, Cabinet confidences must be dis-closed in litigation between the government and private citizens.

[2] On June 6, 1990, the Treasury Board of Canada set the pay of Department of Justice lawyers working in the Toronto Regional Office at a higher rate than that of lawyers working elsewhere. Vancouver staff lawyers brought an action in the Supreme Court of British Columbia, contending that by failing to pay them the same salaries as Toronto lawyers the government breached their contracts of employment and the fiduciary duty toward them.

[3] The action proceeded, and the parties exchanged lists of relevant documents in December 1996, as required by the BC Supreme Court Rules. A supplemental list of documents was delivered by the government in June 1997. The government listed a number of documents as producible.

· · ·

[5] ... The government, nearly two years after it delivered the first list of documents, changed its position on disclosure of documents. It delivered a certificate of the Clerk of the Privy Council pursuant to s. 39(1) of the *Canada Evidence Act*, RSC 1985, c. C-5, objecting to the disclosure of 51 documents and any examination thereon, on the ground that they contain "information constituting confidences of the Queen's Privy Council for Canada." The certificate claimed protection for 12 government documents previously listed as producible (some of which had already been disclosed), for five documents in the control or possession of the plaintiffs, and for 34 government documents and information previously listed as not producible.

[6] The plaintiffs (respondents) brought an application to compel production of the documents for which the government claimed protection. The chambers judge, Edwards J, ruled against them, holding that s. 39 of the *Canada Evidence Act* was constitutional and clear. If the Clerk of the Privy Council filed a certificate, that was the end of the matter, and the courts had no power to set the certificate aside. A majority of the Court of Appeal reversed this decision and ordered production of the documents on the ground that the government had waived its right to claim confidentiality by listing some of the documents as producible and by disclosing selective information in the McCoy affidavit. The government appeals this decision to this Court.

• • •

III. Issues

[14] 1. What is the nature of Cabinet confidentiality and the processes by which it may be claimed and relinquished? 2. Is s. 39 of the *Canada Evidence Act* constitutional?

IV. Discussion

A. The Principles

[15] Cabinet confidentiality is essential to good government. The right to pursue justice in the courts is also of primary importance in our society, as is the rule of law, accountability of the executive, and the principle that official actions must flow from statutory authority clearly granted and properly exercised. Yet sometimes these fundamental principles conflict. How are such conflicts to be resolved? That is the question posed by this appeal.

• • •

[21] Section 39 of the *Canada Evidence Act* is Canada's response to the need to provide a mechanism for the responsible exercise of the power to claim Cabinet confidentiality in the context of judicial and quasi-judicial proceedings. It sets up a process for bringing information within the protection of the Act. Certification by the Clerk of the Privy Council or by a minister of the Crown, is the trigger by which information becomes protected. The Clerk must certify that the "information constitutes a confidence of the Queen's Privy Council for Canada." For more particularity, s. 39(2) sets out categories of information that falls within its scope.

[22] Section 39(1) permits the Clerk to certify information as confidential. It does not restrain voluntary disclosure of confidential information. ...

[23] If the Clerk or minister *chooses* to certify a confidence, it gains the protection of s. 39. Once certified, information gains greater protection than at common

law. If s. 39 is engaged, the "court, person or body with jurisdiction" hearing the matter *must* refuse disclosure; "disclosure of the information shall be refused." Moreover, this must be done "without examination or hearing of the information by the court, person or body." This absolute language goes beyond the common law approach of balancing the public interest in protecting confidentiality and disclosure on judicial review. Once information has been validly certified, the common law no longer applies to that information.

• • •

C. The Constitutionality of Section 39

[53] Because s. 39 applies to the undisclosed documents, it is necessary to consider the constitutional questions in this case. The respondents argue that s. 39 of the *Canada Evidence Act* is of no force or effect by reason of one or both of the preamble to the *Constitution Act, 1867* and s. 96 of the *Constitution Act, 1867.*

(1) The Preamble to the Constitution Act, 1867

[54] The respondents in this case challenge the constitutionality of s. 39 and argue that the provision is *ultra vires* Parliament because of the unwritten principles of the Canadian Constitution: the rule of law, the independence of the judiciary, and the separation of powers. Although the unwritten constitutional principles are capable of limiting government actions, I find that they do not do so in this case.

[55] The unwritten principles must be balanced against the principle of Parliamentary sovereignty. In *Commission des droits de la personne v. Attorney General of Canada*, [1982] 1 SCR 215, this Court upheld as constitutional s. 41(2) of the *Federal Court Act*, the predecessor to s. 39, which permitted the government to claim absolute privilege over a broader class of confidences.

[56] Recently, the Federal Court of Appeal considered the constitutional validity of s. 39 of the *Canada Evidence Act* in *Singh* [*Singh v Canada (Attorney General)*, 2000 CanLII 17100 (FCA), [2003] 3 FC 185]. On the basis of a thorough and compelling review of the principle of parliamentary sovereignty in the context of unwritten constitutional principles, Strayer JA held that federal Crown privilege is part of valid federal law over which Parliament had the power to legislate. Strayer JA concluded at para. 36:

> ... [T]he rule of law cannot be taken to invalidate a statute which has the effect of allowing representatives of the Crown to identify certain documents as beyond disclosure: that is, the rule of law does not preclude a special law with a special result dealing with a special class of documents which, for long standing reasons based on constitutional principles such as responsible government, have been treated differently from private documents in a commercial law suit.

[57] I share the view of the Federal Court of Appeal that s. 39 does not offend the rule of law or the doctrines of separation of powers and the independence of the judiciary. It is well within the power of the legislature to enact laws, even laws which some would consider draconian, as long as it does not fundamentally alter or interfere with the relationship between the courts and the other branches of government.

[Justice L'Heureux-Dubé concurred in separate reasons.]

D. THE PRINCIPLE OF FEDERALISM

The basis for Confederation in 1867 was the agreement by the political leaders of the separate British colonies of Canada, New Brunswick, and Nova Scotia to divide sovereign legislative power between a federal government and regional or provincial governments, and to separate Canada into the provinces of Ontario and Quebec. As the Supreme Court stated in *Quebec Secession Reference*, the recognition of provincial legislatures with extensive areas of jurisdiction, principally over all private legal relationships under the rubric of "property and civil rights within the province," was the *sine qua non* of Confederation for the leaders and people of Quebec and the maritime provinces. The Court identified "federalism" as an unwritten principle of the Constitution, describing it as the means of recognizing regional cultural diversity at the founding of Canada, particularly with respect to the distinct nature of Quebec as a predominantly French-speaking society. The discussion of federalism between paras 55 and 60 of the *Quebec Secession Reference* provides a rich historical context for understanding the principle.

The principal textual source of this division of powers is found in ss 91 and 92 of the *Constitution Act, 1867*, which set out lists of enumerated federal and provincial powers, respectively. Ever since the Privy Council decision of *Hodge v The Queen* in 1883, the national and provincial legislatures have been understood as "coordinate" authorities, with equal sovereign status derived from the Constitution.

Sections 91 and 92 set out "subject matters," or areas of regulatory or legislative concern, that fall within the exclusive jurisdiction of the respective legislative bodies. Matters within federal jurisdiction include criminal law in s 91(27), trade and commerce in s 91(2), and banking in s 91(15). Matters within provincial jurisdiction include hospitals (other than marine hospitals) in s 92(7) and municipalities in s 92(8). The most important provincial jurisdiction is that over "property and civil rights" in s 92(13). This phrase, used in the *Quebec Act, 1774*, 14 Geo III c 83 to refer to all private law matters (which by that statute reverted to the local French civil law tradition developed in New France before its cession to Britain in 1763), encompasses all matters of civil obligation, including contract, tort, and family law. For this reason, provinces have the more extensive jurisdiction over regulation of economic matters in Canada, other than those relating to international and interprovincial trade and commerce, which are understood to fall within s 91(2). Section 93 of the *Constitution Act, 1867* confers jurisdiction over education to the provinces, while s 95 grants a paramount authority to Parliament with respect to immigration.

The opening paragraph of s 91 grants a residual law-making power to Parliament under the phrase "peace, order and good government of Canada" (colloquially known as POGG). The existence of a residual power for all matters not expressly covered in the text of the Constitution means that there is an exhaustive distribution of legislative powers between the two levels of legislature: prior to 1982, it was frequently said that there was no law that could not be enacted by either Parliament or the provincial legislatures. This could no longer be said after 1982 because of the adoption of the Charter, which places limits (the same limits) on both legislative levels.

For the first 115 years of Confederation, Canadian constitutional law largely concerned the elaboration by the judiciary of the boundaries and interrelationships between the federal and provincial jurisdictions established by these general terms. A significant part of the judicial discussion concerned the understanding of the relationship between the POGG power and the enumerated heads of power in s 92, especially property and civil rights. Until 1949, the final court of appeal for Canadian law was the Judicial Committee of the Privy Council (JCPC), a subdivision of the British House of Lords responsible for appeals from the former colonies. The JCPC played a major role in the evolution of Canadian federalism. It became noted as an exponent of strong provincial powers and, in particular, for limiting POGG as a source of federal jurisdiction to circumstances of national crisis and emergency, such as occurred in wartime. For much of the period subsequent to 1949, the Supreme Court of Canada has modified this understanding and incrementally expanded the scope for federal authority and overlapping powers between the two levels of government. Given that the federal government appoints Supreme Court of Canada justices, this has on occasion caused discontent among provinces and led to calls for constitutional amendment to the appointment process for the Court.

E. THE PRINCIPLE OF THE SEPARATION OF POWERS

The separation of powers doctrine refers to the division of governmental functions between the legislative, executive, and judicial branches of the state. Each branch is defined by its relationship to law: the making of law (legislature), the implementing of law (executive), and the interpreting and applying of law (judiciary). The framers of the American Constitution adopted a model of strict separation between the three branches for the purpose of balancing them against each other and reducing the possibility of concentrating public power in any one person or institution.

The parliamentary tradition adopted by Canada's founders does not rely on a similarly strict separation of legislative, executive, and judicial powers. It gives pre-eminence to the legislative branch, to which the executive is made subordinate. Furthermore, the parliamentary system contemplates an overlapping of personnel between the legislature and the executive. The prime minister and members of his or her Cabinet, who comprise the executive council "advising" the head of state (the Queen), are elected members of the legislature. This is not the case in the United States. There, the president as chief executive has constitutional powers independent of Congress, is elected separately from Congress, and appoints Cabinet members from outside Congress.

The absence of a strict separation of powers doctrine has led some to question the utility of the concept for Canadian constitutional law. Take, for example, Dickson CJ's comments in *Re Residential Tenancies Act*, [1981] 1 SCR 714:

> [T]here is no general "separation of powers" in the *British North America Act, 1867*. Our Constitution does not separate the legislative, executive, and judicial functions and insist that each branch of government exercise only its own function.

Nevertheless, the distinction between the legislature, executive, and judiciary is important to Canadian public law. It serves two principal purposes: (1) a functional purpose of identifying the institutional homes of each of the three major forms of public power, and (2) a normative purpose of providing general boundaries for the operation of each institution.

1. Functional Role of the Separation of Powers: The Relationships Among the Legislative, Executive, and Judicial Branches of the Canadian State

On the functional side, the *Constitution Act, 1867* expressly divides public power among the three branches of the state. Part III of the Act describes "executive power" at the federal level (ss 9 to 16); Part IV deals with federal "legislative power" (ss 17 to 57); and part V, with provincial "executive power" (ss 58 to 68) and provincial "legislative power" (ss 69 to 90). Part VII deals with the "judicature" (ss 96 to 101).

Each of the three branches of the Canadian state represents and exercises its own unique form of authoritative decision-making. Legislative decision-making is prospective (oriented to the future), broad in impact (oriented to the public interest, or the interests of large groups), and open-ended in range of outcomes. Judicial decision-making is retrospective (oriented to past events), localized in impact (oriented to individual disputes), and narrow in outcome (oriented to the application of principles to facts to produce the "right" outcome). Executive or administrative decision-making shares features of both legislative and judicial decision-making, and is the most difficult to define.

A few words, then, about the executive branch and its relationships to the legislative and judicial branches of the state in Canada seem in order. The executive branch replicates the duality created by federalism, with executives at the federal and provincial levels. Identifying the full and proper extent of the "executive" in Canada is not always straightforward. The executive includes all ministries of government and their employees—the civil service. It also includes the armed forces and Crown corporations. It may include statutorily created bodies that carry out largely "governmental" functions. At some point, however, where the control of an entity is derived more from private sources, such as the membership of a registered society or corporation, than from ministerial sources, we are no longer dealing with the executive, but with an entity belonging to civil society. This line is not always easy to draw—institutions that lie at the margins may include universities and other post-secondary institutions, hospitals, and professional regulatory bodies. We discuss the composition of the executive in greater detail in Chapter 8.

Commentators often argue that the executive branch dominates Canada's system of government, that the prime minister and premiers exercise an authority over their parties and over the legislatures that is unusual among Western democracies. (See e.g. Jeffrey Simpson, *The Friendly Dictatorship: Reflections on Canadian Democracy* (Toronto: McClelland & Stewart, 2001).) To the extent this may be true, it is largely a product of politics, not law.

In law, the executive branch is subordinate to the legislature. The relationship between the legislative and executive branches in Canada has two important features. First, subject to the relatively minor sources of power found in the "royal prerogative" and the Constitution, the executive branch derives any power it has solely from the laws or statutes passed by the legislature. That is, the executive must locate any authority it has to act in Canadian society from a statutory source. By way of statutes, legislators delegate elements of their sovereign power to executive actors, be that the federal or provincial Cabinet, a particular minister of the Crown, or a local public health official. The delegation is made on the terms of the statute, and can always be revoked by the legislature by amendment or repeal. And indeed, the "royal prerogative"—effectively the common law powers of the Crown—may also be displaced by statute. In this sense, the executive in Canada (unlike that in the United States, where the president has many independent powers derived from the Constitution) is almost wholly dependent on and subordinate to the legislative branch for its authority to act.

The second feature of the relationship between the legislative and executive branches in Canada is that by constitutional convention, the executive is responsible to the legislature. This is the essential meaning of "responsible government" in the parliamentary tradition. Convention requires that the prime minister and his or her ministry command the support (or "confidence") of a majority of elected legislators. (As discussed in Chapter 7, should the prime minister and his or her government lose the confidence of the legislature, the prime minister must either resign and a new government be formed from the existing membership of the House of Commons or seek a dissolution of Parliament and the holding of new elections.)

With respect to the relationship between the executive and the judiciary in Canada, the key area of concern is that of administrative law. If constitutional law is the area of law that concerns the adjudication by courts of whether a legislature has acted within the boundaries of its constitutional authority, then administrative law can be understood as that area concerned with whether the executive has acted within the boundaries of its *statutory* authority.

In Canada, superior courts exercise a supervisory jurisdiction over the exercise of executive government authority. This is the subject matter of administrative law. Because executive government derives all its authority to act from statutes (save and except for those few matters where authority is derived from royal prerogative), that authority is limited to the jurisdiction granted by statutory delegation from the legislature. Superior courts in the Anglo-Canadian tradition have historically assumed the role of ensuring that executive government acts within its delegated statutory authority. In practice, this role is performed by allowing all persons adversely affected by government action to petition the superior courts seeking "judicial review" of executive decision-making. This administrative law or judicial review jurisdiction is understood to be a matter of common law development, and therefore not itself dependent on being granted by legislatures.

The significance of this common law supervisory jurisdiction has been underlined by the Supreme Court of Canada's identification of judicial review of executive action as having constitutional status. In *Crevier v AG (Québec)*, [1981] 2 SCR 220, the Court stated that judicial review of executive powers is a "hallmark" of superior court jurisdiction, and so cannot be withdrawn from those courts by provincial legislatures. In *MacMillan-Bloedel Ltd v Simpson*, [1995] 4 SCR 725, the Court confirmed that Parliament is also constitutionally barred from infringing this "core jurisdiction" of superior courts.

We return to these topics in Chapters 8 and 11.

2. Normative Role of the Separation of Powers: Preventing Overstepping of Institutional Roles

The principle of the separation of powers has occasionally assumed the role of an argument for limiting the ability of one branch of the state to intrude on the activity of another—most frequently, to limit the ability of courts themselves to act in a legislative or executive capacity. This has been illustrated by Supreme Court judgments dealing with the power of the judiciary to order remedies for breaches of Charter rights under s 24(1) of the *Charter of Rights and Freedoms*, which reads:

> 24(1) Anyone whose rights or freedoms, as guaranteed by this Charter, have been infringed or denied may apply to a court of competent jurisdiction to obtain such remedy as the court considers appropriate and just in the circumstances.

In *Doucet-Boudreau v Nova Scotia (Minister of Education)*, 2003 SCC 62, [2003] 3 SCR 3, the Court dealt with a challenge by the province of Nova Scotia to the constitutionality of a s 24(1) order by a superior court judge that not only obliged the Ministry of Education to complete construction of new schools for minority French-language instruction, but also to report periodically to the judge on its compliance with the order. The province argued that a "structural injunction" of this kind improperly placed the Court in the role of an administrator and usurped the functions of executive government. Justices LeBel and Deschamps, in dissent, agreed with Nova Scotia. The Court majority upheld the trial judge's order, but made the following comments (at paras 33 and 34) about the need to maintain a boundary between judicial and executive functions in the remedial area (see Chapter 11 for a longer excerpt):

> This tradition of compliance [with court orders] takes on a particular significance in the constitutional law context, where courts must ensure that government behaviour conforms with constitutional norms but in doing so must also be sensitive to the separation of function among the legislative, judicial and executive branches. While our Constitution does not expressly provide for the separation of powers ... , the functional separation among the executive, legislative and judicial branches of governance has frequently been noted. ... In *New Brunswick Broadcasting Co. v. Nova Scotia (Speaker of the House of Assembly)*, [1993] 1 SCR 319, McLachlin J (as she then was) stated, at p. 389:

> > Our democratic government consists of several branches: the Crown, as represented by the Governor General and the provincial counterparts of that office; the legislative body; the executive; and the courts. It is fundamental to the working of government as a whole that all these parts play their proper role. It is equally fundamental that no one of them overstep its bounds, that each show proper deference for the legitimate sphere of activity of the other.

In other words, in the context of constitutional remedies, courts must be sensitive to their role as judicial arbiters and not fashion remedies which usurp the role of the other branches of governance by taking on tasks to which other persons or bodies are better suited. Concern for the limits of the judicial role is interwoven throughout the law. The development of the doctrines of justiciability, and to a great extent mootness, standing, and ripeness resulted from concerns about the courts overstepping the bounds of the judicial function and their role vis-à-vis other branches of government.

In *Ontario v Criminal Lawyers' Association of Ontario*, below, the Supreme Court dealt with the question of whether judges have the inherent power to order the attorney general of a province to pay a specified amount to an *amicus curiae* (a lawyer appointed by a court to act as a "friend of the court" where the court deems this necessary). A 5:4 majority of the justices based their negative answer to the question on the separation of powers doctrine.

Ontario v Criminal Lawyers' Association of Ontario
2013 SCC 43, [2013] 3 SCR 3

KARAKATSANIS J (McLachlin CJ and Rothstein, Moldaver, and Wagner JJ concurring):

• • •

(2) Separation of Powers

[27] This Court has long recognized that our constitutional framework prescribes different roles for the executive, legislative and judicial branches ... . The content of these various constitutional roles has been shaped by the history and evolution of our constitutional order ... .

[28] Over several centuries of transformation and conflict, the English system evolved from one in which power was centralized in the Crown to one in which the powers of the state were exercised by way of distinct organs with separate functions. The development of separate executive, legislative and judicial functions has allowed for the evolution of certain core competencies in the various institutions vested with these functions. The legislative branch makes policy choices, adopts laws and holds the purse strings of government, as only it can authorize the spending of public funds. The executive implements and administers those policy choices and laws with the assistance of a professional public service. The judiciary maintains the rule of law, by interpreting and applying these laws through the independent and impartial adjudication of references and disputes, and protects the fundamental liberties and freedoms guaranteed under the Charter.

[29] All three branches have distinct institutional capacities and play critical and complementary roles in our constitutional democracy. However, each branch will be unable to fulfill its role if it is unduly interfered with by the others. In *New Brunswick Broadcasting Co. v. Nova Scotia (Speaker of the House of Assembly)*, 1993 CanLII 153 (SCC) ... , McLachlin J. affirmed the importance of respecting the separate roles and institutional capacities of Canada's branches of government for our constitutional order, holding that "[i]t is fundamental to the working of government as a whole that all these parts play their proper role. It is equally fundamental that no one of them overstep its bounds, that each show proper deference for the legitimate sphere of activity of the other" ... .

[30] Accordingly, the limits of the court's inherent jurisdiction must be responsive to the proper function of the separate branches of government, lest it upset the balance of roles, responsibilities and capacities that has evolved in our system of governance over the course of centuries.

[31] Indeed, even where courts have the jurisdiction to address matters that fall within the constitutional role of the other branches of government, they must give sufficient weight to the constitutional responsibilities of the legislative and executive branches, as in certain cases the other branch will be "better placed to make such decisions within a range of constitutional options" (*Canada (Prime Minister) v. Khadr*, 2010 SCC 3, ... at para. 37).

· · ·

[81] Allowing superior and statutory court judges to direct an Attorney General as to how to expend funds on the administration of justice, in the absence of a constitutional challenge or statutory authority, is incompatible with the different roles, responsibilities and institutional capacities assigned to trial judges, legislators and the executive in our parliamentary democracy.

· · ·

[83] While the rule of law requires an effective justice system with independent and impartial decision makers, it does not exist independently of financial constraints and the financial choices of the executive and legislature. Furthermore, in our system of parliamentary democracy, an inherent and inalienable right to fix a trial participant's compensation oversteps the responsibilities of the judiciary and blurs the roles and public accountability of the three separate branches of government. In my view, such a state of affairs would imperil the judicial process; judicial orders fixing the expenditures of public funds put public confidence in the judiciary at risk.

The *Khadr* case mentioned by the Court in para 31 of the *Criminal Lawyers' Association* decision concerns Omar Khadr, a Canadian citizen who had been detained by American authorities at the prison facility in Guantanamo, Cuba, on charges that at age 15 he had killed a US soldier in Afghanistan. While deciding that the Canadian government had indeed breached Khadr's Charter s 7 rights to liberty and security of person by participating in his harsh interrogation in Guantanamo, the Court nevertheless declined to order that the government make a formal request to the US government for his repatriation to Canada, viewing such an order as an intrusion on the executive's royal prerogative power to conduct diplomacy with foreign countries as it sees fit.

Canada (Prime Minister) v Khadr
2010 SCC 3, [2010] 1 SCR 44

THE COURT (McLachlin CJ and Binnie, LeBel, Deschamps, Fish, Abella, Charron, Rothstein, and Cromwell JJ):

[33] Second, is the remedy sought precluded by the fact that it touches on the Crown prerogative over foreign affairs? A connection between the remedy and the breach is not the only consideration. As stated in *Doucet-Boudreau*, an appropriate and just remedy is also one that "must employ means that are legitimate within

the framework of our constitutional democracy" (para. 56) and must be a "judicial one which vindicates the right while invoking the function and powers of a court" (para. 57). The government argues that courts have no power under the Constitution of Canada to require the executive branch of government to do anything in the area of foreign policy. It submits that the decision not to request the repatriation of Mr. Khadr falls directly within the prerogative powers of the Crown to conduct foreign relations, including the right to speak freely with a foreign state on all such matters: P.W. Hogg, *Constitutional Law of Canada* (5th ed. Supp.), at p. 1-19.

[34] The prerogative power is the "residue of discretionary or arbitrary authority, which at any given time is legally left in the hands of the Crown": *Reference as to the Effect of the Exercise of Royal Prerogative of Mercy upon Deportation Proceedings*, [1933] SCR 269, at p. 272, *per* Duff CJ, quoting A.V. Dicey, *Introduction to the Study of the Law of the Constitution* (8th ed. 1915), at p. 420. It is a limited source of non-statutory administrative power accorded by the common law to the Crown: Hogg, at p. 1-17.

[35] The prerogative power over foreign affairs has not been displaced by s. 10 of the *Department of Foreign Affairs and International Trade Act*, RSC 1985, c. E-22, and continues to be exercised by the federal government. The Crown prerogative in foreign affairs includes the making of representations to a foreign government: *Black v. Canada (Prime Minister)* (2001), 199 DLR (4th) 228 (Ont. CA). We therefore agree with O'Reilly J's implicit finding (paras. 39, 40 and 49) that the decision not to request Mr. Khadr's repatriation was made in the exercise of the prerogative over foreign relations.

[36] In exercising its common law powers under the royal prerogative, the executive is not exempt from constitutional scrutiny: *Operation Dismantle v. The Queen*, [1985] 1 SCR 441. It is for the executive and not the courts to decide whether and how to exercise its powers, but the courts clearly have the jurisdiction and the duty to determine whether a prerogative power asserted by the Crown does in fact exist and, if so, whether its exercise infringes the *Charter* (*Operation Dismantle*) or other constitutional norms (*Air Canada v. British Columbia (Attorney General)*, [1986] 2 SCR 539).

[37] The limited power of the courts to review exercises of the prerogative power for constitutionality reflects the fact that in a constitutional democracy, all government power must be exercised in accordance with the Constitution. This said, judicial review of the exercise of the prerogative power for constitutionality remains sensitive to the fact that the executive branch of government is responsible for decisions under this power, and that the executive is better placed to make such decisions within a range of constitutional options. The government must have flexibility in deciding how its duties under the power are to be discharged: see, e.g., *Reference re Secession of Quebec*, [1998] 2 SCR 217, at paras. 101-2. But it is for the courts to determine the legal and constitutional limits within which such decisions are to be taken. It follows that in the case of refusal by a government to abide by constitutional constraints, courts are empowered to make orders ensuring that the government's foreign affairs prerogative is exercised in accordance with the constitution: *United States v. Burns*, 2001 SCC 7, [2001] 1 SCR 283.

[38] Having concluded that the courts possess a narrow power to review and intervene on matters of foreign affairs to ensure the constitutionality of executive action, the final question is whether O'Reilly J misdirected himself in exercising that power in the circumstances of this case (*R v. Bjelland*, 2009 SCC 38, [2009] 2 SCR 651, at para. 15; *R v. Regan*, 2002 SCC 12, [2002] 1 SCR 297, at paras. 117-18). (In fairness to the trial judge, we note that the government proposed no alternative (trial judge's reasons, at para. 78).) If the record and legal principle support his

decision, deference requires we not interfere. However, in our view that is not the case.

[39] Our first concern is that the remedy ordered below gives too little weight to the constitutional responsibility of the executive to make decisions on matters of foreign affairs in the context of complex and ever-changing circumstances, taking into account Canada's broader national interests. For the following reasons, we conclude that the appropriate remedy is to declare that, on the record before the Court, Canada infringed Mr. Khadr's s. 7 rights, and to leave it to the government to decide how best to respond to this judgment in light of current information, its responsibility for foreign affairs, and in conformity with the *Charter*.

[40] As discussed, the conduct of foreign affairs lies with the executive branch of government. The courts, however, are charged with adjudicating the claims of individuals who claim that their *Charter* rights have been or will be violated by the exercise of the government's discretionary powers: *Operation Dismantle*.

[41] In some situations, courts may give specific directions to the executive branch of the government on matters touching foreign policy. For example, in *Burns*, the Court held that it would offend s. 7 to extradite a fugitive from Canada without seeking and obtaining assurances from the requesting state that the death penalty would not be imposed. The Court gave due weight to the fact that seeking and obtaining those assurances were matters of Canadian foreign relations. Nevertheless, it ordered that the government seek them.

[42] The specific facts in *Burns* justified a more specific remedy. The fugitives were under the control of Canadian officials. It was clear that assurances would provide effective protection against the prospective *Charter* breaches: it was entirely within Canada's power to protect the fugitives against possible execution. Moreover, the Court noted that no public purpose would be served by extradition without assurances that would not be substantially served by extradition with assurances, and that there was nothing to suggest that seeking such assurances would undermine Canada's good relations with other states: *Burns*, at paras. 125 and 136.

[43] The present case differs from *Burns*. Mr. Khadr is not under the control of the Canadian government; the likelihood that the proposed remedy will be effective is unclear; and the impact on Canadian foreign relations of a repatriation request cannot be properly assessed by the Court.

F. THE PRINCIPLE OF JUDICIAL INDEPENDENCE

Judicial independence is a constitutional doctrine closely tied to the separation of powers. The Supreme Court has described judicial independence as the "lifeblood of constitutionalism in democratic societies": see *The Queen v Beauregard*, [1986] 2 SCR 56 at 70. It is "essential to the achievement and proper functioning of a free, just and democratic society based on the principles of constitutionalism and the rule of law": see *Mackin v New Brunswick (Minister of Finance); Rice v New Brunswick*, 2002 SCC 13 at para 34, [2002] 1 SCR 405.

Before returning to a discussion of the independence principle, it may be useful to review the relationship of the judiciary and judicial role in Canada to the other principles reviewed in this section. We have seen that the judicial role is central to the rule of law and to constitutional supremacy in Canada. In the preceding section, we covered the role of the judiciary in maintaining the separation of powers in the Canadian state, including in ensuring that executive authority is exercised within boundaries set by the sovereign legislatures. With respect to the principle of federalism, the courts both adjudicate the division of powers between the provincial and federal legislative levels, and are themselves subject to a structure of a federal nature. And protection of minorities may depend on courts enforcing provisions of the Constitution offering that protection, in a manner that may be counter-majoritarian and therefore at odds with an uncritical vision of democracy.

The *Constitution Act, 1867* contains provisions on the "Judicature" in ss 96 to 101. Section 96 provides that the federal executive shall appoint the justices of the country's superior courts. The superior courts in Canada are often referred to as "section 96 courts." Superior courts are understood to exercise the inherent jurisdiction of the monarch's courts, as understood in the British legal tradition. Although the power to appoint judges to superior courts is assigned by the Constitution to the federal government, it is the provinces, exercising their authority over the "administration of justice" in s 92(14) of the *Constitution Act, 1867,* that establish these courts in their respective jurisdiction. Each province also has a system of non–s 96 courts, to which the province has the authority to appoint judges.

Under s 101, Parliament is accorded the authority to create courts for the "better administration of the laws of Canada"—understood to mean laws passed by Parliament itself. Using this authority, Parliament has enacted the *Federal Courts Act*, RSC 1985, c F-7, which establishes the trial-level Federal Court of Canada and the Federal Court of Appeal. The Federal Courts' jurisdiction and power are statutory, not inherent, but they otherwise play a role similar to that of the provincial superior courts. Administrative law jurisdiction in Canada has been divided between the Federal Courts and the provincial superior courts, roughly on the basis of whether the executive actor in question is empowered under a federal or provincial statute.

Section 101 also authorizes Parliament to create a "general court of appeal" for Canada. In 1875, Parliament enacted the *Supreme Court Act*, RSC 1985, c S-26, creating the Supreme Court of Canada to play this role. This ordinary federal statute, with amendments, remains the source of the Supreme Court's existence and role. The *Constitution Act, 1982* appears to have entrenched changes to the Court's composition and the process for appointing its justices. The degree to which this does, or does not, entrench the Supreme Court itself formed the subtext of the *Supreme Court Act Reference*, discussed in Section III below.

The seemingly slender foundation in the text of the Constitution for the judicial system in Canada has not prevented the courts themselves from carving out an indispensable and essentially unassailable position in Canada's constitutional system. This position goes to what the Supreme Court of Canada has identified as the "core jurisdiction" of superior courts, which encompasses two crucial public law powers: (1) the jurisdiction to rule on the constitutional validity of all ordinary laws in Canada, and (2) the jurisdiction to supervise the activities of executive government and other statutorily delegated actors to ensure that they act within their statutory authority. The former role represents the superior courts' "constitutional law" jurisdiction; the latter role represents its "administrative law" jurisdiction.

The principle of judicial independence flows from these two roles. If the judiciary is to perform its constitutional and administrative law roles meaningfully, then judges must act independently of the legislative and executive branches of the state. Judicial independence ensures that "judges, as the arbiters of disputes, are at complete liberty to decide individual cases on their merits without interference": see *Ell v Alberta*, 2003 SCC 35 at para 21, [2003] 1 SCR 857. It insulates judges from retaliation from other branches of government for their decisions and guarantees that "the power of the state is exercised in accordance with the rule of law and the provisions of our Constitution. In this capacity, courts act as a shield against unwarranted deprivations by the state of the rights and freedoms of individuals": see *Ell*, at para 22.

Judicial independence also preserves the separation of powers between the three branches of our democracy by "depoliticizing" the relationship between the judiciary and the other two branches: "the legislature and executive cannot, and cannot appear to, exert political pressure on the judiciary, and conversely ... members of the judiciary should exercise reserve in speaking out publicly on issues of general public policy that are or have the potential to come before the courts, that are the subject of political debate, and which do not relate to the proper administration of justice": see *Ref re Remuneration of Judges of the Prov Court of PEI; Ref re Independence and Impartiality of Judges of the Prov Court of PEI* (the "*Provincial Judges*

Reference"), [1997] 3 SCR 3 at para 140. In this respect, the concept of judicial independence is counter-majoritarian, and one in relation to which the democracy principle does not hold full sway.

The actual content of judicial independence is discussed in detail in Chapter 9.

III. CONSTITUTIONAL AMENDMENT

A constitution embodies legal stability, but it must also account and allow for change. The balance between the need to make a constitution difficult to amend, while still allowing it to evolve to meet the changing needs of the society it governs, is one of the great challenges of constitutional law. It has certainly been one of the great challenges of Canada's constitutional history.

A. THE AMENDING FORMULA IN PART V OF THE CONSTITUTION ACT, 1982

The Canadian Constitution lacked any formal amending process until 1982. The framers of the *Constitution Act, 1867* did not include in the document any provisions addressing how the people or governments of the dominion could make amendments to the Constitution. This reflected their understanding of Canada as a colony of the United Kingdom. Just as the *Constitution Act, 1867* was a statute of the Imperial Parliament in London, so too its amendment was left to British parliamentarians. In effect, the "super-majority" required of Canadians with respect to amending their own constitution was the need to request that this be undertaken in London.

The project of patriating the Constitution and thereby accomplishing the last stage of national independence and sovereignty foundered for decades precisely over the failure to achieve agreement on a new, domestic amending formula. This was hardly surprising given that a debate over a constitutional amending process is a debate over political power. For many years, Quebec sought a veto over any constitutional change that would affect the powers of its government or touch on issues of language and culture. Other provinces either opposed Quebec's veto, or sought their own veto. After years of failing to achieve agreement, the federal government of Prime Minister Pierre Trudeau moved forward in 1980-81 with a unilateral proposal to patriate the Constitution with a domestic amending formula of its own design. This resulted in a constitutional crisis. In the *Patriation Reference* in 1981, the Supreme Court ruled that federal unilateralism, though lawful, breached a convention of the Constitution requiring "substantial" agreement of the provinces.

Representatives of the federal and provincial governments met in a constitutional conference in November 1981 and agreed on the terms of the *Constitution Act, 1982*, including the amending formula in part V of the Act. The formula did not include a veto for any single province. The government of Quebec, alone of all provinces, did not agree to the new Constitution, a position that has remained true for all succeeding governments of Quebec since that time. Nevertheless, in the *Quebec Veto Reference* (*Re: Objection by Quebec to a Resolution to Amend the Constitution*, [1982] 2 SCR 793), the Supreme Court ruled that Quebec's agreement was not needed for purposes of meeting the "substantial agreement" standard, and the *Constitution Act, 1982* came into force and effect with respect to the entire country, Quebec included.

The process for amending the Constitution of Canada is set out in part V of the *Constitution Act, 1982*, which actually sets out five distinct amending formulas applying to different circumstances:

1. the general formula for all amendments not falling within formulas (2) through (5), which requires the agreement of Parliament and the legislatures of at least two-thirds of the provinces having at least 50 percent of the population of Canada (s 38);

2.   unanimity of Parliament and all provincial legislatures (s 41);
3.   Parliament, and the legislatures of just those provinces affected by an amendment (s 43);
4.   Parliament alone, with respect to its own institutions (s 44); and
5.   a provincial legislature alone, with respect to the provincial constitution (s 45).

The general amending formula turns on federalism, in that the parties to any amendment are the federal and provincial legislatures. Similarly, amendment works through representative institutions. There is no role in the formula for popular initiatives, referenda, or constitutional conferences.

The adoption of a domestic amending formula in the Constitution after 115 years of Confederation left an important question unanswered: would the amending formula prove workable? Almost 40 years have passed since 1982 and events have not provided a definitive answer to that question, because Canadians and their governments have not succeeded in making any major constitutional amendments despite strenuous efforts to do so. In 1987, the federal government and the governments of all ten provinces agreed to a set of amendments known as the Meech Lake Accord, whose principal purpose was to reconcile the province of Quebec with the Constitution of Canada. Included in the Accord were proposed amendments to the Constitution that would recognize Quebec as a "distinct society" within Canada and limit the federal government's power to spend in areas of provincial jurisdiction. Public opposition to the Accord developed in several areas of the country, leading to a full-blown constitutional crisis. The three-year period set out in s 39(2) of the *Constitution Act, 1982* expired before all legislatures passed resolutions endorsing the Accord, and it failed. This failure led to a renewed two-year effort to negotiate a new agreement on a wider package of amendments, including proposals for Aboriginal self-government and an elected Senate. The Charlottetown Accord, as it was called, was put to a national referendum in October 1992. The Constitution does not contemplate referendums as part of the amending process, so the 1992 referendum was understood to be advisory in nature. Nevertheless, when majorities in Quebec and the western provinces rejected the Accord, the federal and provincial governments declined to proceed with the changes it proposed. Thus, five years of intense, often wrenching public debate had achieved nothing with respect to what were viewed as the major issues in Canada's constitutional life. The fallout from these events included the referendum on secession in Quebec in 1995, the *Quebec Secession Reference* in 1998, and decisions by successive federal governments to avoid talk of constitutional reform whenever possible.

This dynamic changed somewhat in 2012 when the federal government of Prime Minister Stephen Harper proposed to make reforms to the Senate of Canada. In particular, the government proposed to introduce term limits on the appointments of senators (from appointments to the age of 75, to appointments of nine years), and to oblige future prime ministers to "consider" for appointment those persons who won Senate elections in any province that agreed to hold elections under federally mandated rules. The government took the position that it could make these changes through passage of an ordinary federal statute, as they did not involve amendments requiring provincial agreement under part V of the *Constitution Act, 1982*. When the province of Quebec raised objections, to which several other provinces agreed, the matter was referred to the Supreme Court of Canada. Before the Court could decide that matter, it was called on to decide a different case dealing with constitutional amendment, a case surprisingly involving an appointment to the Supreme Court of Canada.

1. Amendment of the Supreme Court of Canada: The Supreme Court Act Reference

In the *Supreme Court Act Reference*, the Supreme Court dealt with a challenge to the lawfulness of Prime Minister Stephen Harper's proposed appointment of Justice Marc Nadon of the

Federal Court of Appeal to the Supreme Court of Canada. When the government announced its intention to appoint Nadon J to the country's highest court, Ontario lawyer Rocco Galati filed a petition to block the appointment on the basis that Nadon J, as a member of the Federal Court of Appeal, did not come within the eligibility criteria for appointment to one of the three Quebec seats on the Supreme Court of Canada set out in s 6 of the *Supreme Court Act*:

> 6. At least three of the judges shall be appointed from among the judges of the Court of Appeal or of the Superior Court of the Province of Quebec or from among the advocates of that Province.

Galati, soon followed by the Government of Quebec, took the position that a sitting member of the Federal Court of Appeal was neither a judge of the Quebec courts nor a *current* advocate (lawyer) in that province. In order to have the matter resolved quickly, the government of Canada referred the question of Nadon J's eligibility to the Supreme Court itself.

At first blush, the *Reference* appeared to raise a question of statutory interpretation, and a narrow one at that. However, to buttress Canada's position that Federal Court judges who had *formerly* been registered members of the Bar of Quebec met the requirements of s 6, Parliament added a "declaratory" provision to the *Supreme Court Act* intended to clarify the meaning of s 6:

> 6.1 For greater certainty, for the purpose of section 6, a judge is from among the advocates of the Province of Quebec if, at any time, they were an advocate of at least 10 years standing at the bar of that Province.

This amendment effectively raised the stakes in the *Reference*. When a 6:1 majority of the Court ruled that on a proper reading, s 6 of the *Supreme Court Act* (which dated back to the Act's origin in 1875) did *not* include former members of the Quebec bar like Nadon J, it then became necessary to say whether s 6.1 applied. This raised a question of its constitutionality. Section 41(d) of the *Constitution Act, 1982* reads:

> 41. An amendment to the Constitution of Canada in relation to the following matters may be made by proclamation issued by the Governor General under the Great Seal of Canada only where authorized by resolutions of the Senate and House of Commons and of the legislative assembly of each province: ...
>
> (d) the composition of the Supreme Court of Canada ... .

Opponents of the Nadon appointment argued that s 6.1 purported to change the "composition" of the Court, and so could not be enacted by Parliament unilaterally, but only by unanimous agreement of the federal government and all ten provinces. The six-justice majority of the Supreme Court of Canada agreed. In effect, the Court's judgment meant that important aspects of the Court's structure, which were put in place by "ordinary" federal legislation in the 19th century, had been "constitutionalized" by the arrangements of 1982. In fact, the Court concluded, this constitutionalizing of the Court occurred much earlier than 1982, when the Supreme Court of Canada replaced the Judicial Committee of the Privy Council as Canada's highest court in 1949 or soon thereafter. When that happened, the Supreme Court became a fundamental institution of Canadian governance and federalism—so fundamental that Parliament acting on its own could no longer alter it. This idea, that certain institutions are so fundamental to the country's political and legal structure that they can only be reformed on the basis of substantial, if not unanimous, agreement of all of Canada's governments, had clear implications for the *Senate Reform Reference*. Indeed, the Court decided that case along similar lines within two months of the *Supreme Court Act Reference*.

The *Supreme Court Act Reference* is reproduced in Chapter 10 on statutory interpretation.

2. Amendment and the Senate of Canada: The Senate Reform Reference

In mid-2013, the Conservative government of Prime Minister Stephen Harper put before Parliament a bill to effect several changes to the composition and functioning of the Canadian Senate. Specifically, Bill C-7 proposed two significant changes: (1) the introduction of a non-renewable term limit of nine years for Senate appointees, to replace the provision in s 29 of the *Constitution Act, 1867* imposing mandatory retirement for senators at age 75; and (2) the creation of a framework by which provinces that wished to do so could hold periodic "consultative elections" for nominees to the Senate from the province, the results of which elections "must be considered" by the prime minister in exercising his or her power under the Constitution to provide names of appointees to the governor general. The stated purpose of Bill C-7 was to move forward with democratizing the Senate in ways that were within the sole authority of Parliament and did not require the agreement of any or all provinces. In so saying, the government of Canada admitted its pessimism about obtaining provincial agreement to any more significant Senate reform.

The Government of Quebec opposed this unilateral effort by the government of Canada to alter the Senate in the ways described. Quebec maintained its long-held position that significant amendments to the role and status of the Senate require substantial agreement by the provinces. Quebec referred the question of the constitutionality of Bill C-7 to the Quebec Court of Appeal. The government of Canada responded by issuing its own reference to the Supreme Court of Canada. The government asked the Court to answer three main questions:

1. Does the introduction of a framework of consultative elections for senators require an amendment to the Constitution subject to part V of the *Constitution Act, 1982*?
2. Does a change to the term limits for senators fall within Parliament's unilateral power to amend the Constitution set out in s 41 of the *Constitution Act, 1982*?
3. Under what formula in part V does abolition of the Senate fall—unanimous agreement of the federal government and the governments of all provinces in s 44, or the "general formula" of Canada together with two-thirds of the provinces having at least 50 percent of the population (the 7 + 50 formula)?

This third question was not raised by Bill C-7 itself, but the government of Canada asked the Court to answer it for future purposes.

In a unanimous judgment, the Court answered each question in terms that rejected the position put forward by the government of Canada. The Court decided that introducing a framework for consultative election of senators required amending the Constitution under the general formula; that imposing term limits for senators of something less than "the rest of a person's working life" could not be done unilaterally by Parliament; and that abolition of the Senate would require unanimous agreement of all Canada's governments and legislatures.

The immediate political and legal impact of the Court's opinion in the *Senate Reform Reference* is significant. On the political side, the Court made it clear that Senate reform will only be able to be achieved on the basis of a substantial degree of consensus among the governments of Canada. Such a consensus is difficult to achieve at the best of times, but it is all the more elusive when it comes to regional power shifts, as Senate reform almost surely would represent. On the legal side, the judgment in the *Senate Reform Reference* provides extensive direction on how to interpret the intricate provisions in part V of the *Constitution Act, 1982*. The Court clarified, for instance, that the "default" provision is the 7 + 50 formula set out in s 38, which applies to all amendments to the Constitution unless the circumstances clearly demonstrate that one of s 41, 43, or 44—viewed as exceptional provisions—applies.

For our purpose of understanding how the Constitution operates to structure the exercise of public authority in Canada, there are two principal things to note from the case. First, the Supreme Court relied heavily on the idea that the Constitution has an underlying "architecture," and that understanding the architecture is important to interpreting the wording or text of the Constitution. Second, the Court rejected what it considered to be "narrow textual" readings of the Constitution, which can or will lead to results that are inconsistent with a full understanding of the history and purposes of Canada's constitutional arrangements.

The *Senate Reform Reference* is reproduced in Chapter 6 on the composition of Parliament.

B. JUDICIAL INTERPRETATION AND THE "LIVING TREE"

The difficulty Canada has experienced in making formal amendments to the Constitution since 1982 should not be taken to mean that the Constitution is a static entity, unresponsive to changes in the society it purports to govern. This subsection and the next explore two recognized ways in which constitutional evolution occurs in Canada even in the absence of formal amendments to the text of the Constitution. The first of these involves an approach to interpretation that permits the judiciary to read constitutional text in light of changes in society and contemporary uses of language. While this "living tree" approach is well accepted in Canadian jurisprudence, it is not uncontroversial.

Former US Chief Justice Charles Evans Hughes stated: "The Constitution is what the Judges say it is." This sounds at first like a declaration of unbridled judicial power. In another sense, it is merely a truism. The general language in which constitutions are written does not apply itself. It must be interpreted in order to be applied. As stated above, the very idea of constitutional supremacy calls for an adjudicative institution—a judiciary that has the authority to interpret and apply constitutional text to real-world circumstances.

There are many different tools and techniques for textual interpretation, and few judges or lawyers employ only one. Nevertheless, in the field of constitutional interpretation, two general approaches are commonly conceived as the leading, and competing, schools. The first is known as the historical or originalist approach. At the risk of greatly oversimplifying this approach, proponents of originalism believe that constitutional text should be understood as having a single, unchanging meaning—the meaning intended by those who wrote and ratified the text. This provides the Constitution with needed stability. Should the meaning of the text cease to speak to the needs of contemporary society, then this problem should be addressed by amending the text. So long as formal amendment processes require the operation of democratic processes, the community will assume responsibility for constitutional evolution in the appropriate arena of political life.

The second approach is known under various names—sometimes the "progressive" or "living tree" approach. This is the alternative favoured by the Supreme Court of Canada. This approach conceives of the text of the Constitution as not being frozen in meaning to one time and place—partly because much of the text may never have had a single agreed-on meaning. Rather, it seeks to give a reasoned reading of the text that makes sense of it at the time it is being interpreted. This approach was first stated to be appropriate to Canadian constitutionalism by the Judicial Committee of the Privy Council in the *"Persons"* case in 1930 (*Edwards v AG Canada*, [1930] AC 124, excerpted in Chapter 2). In this case, the Judicial Committee of the Privy Council reversed the Supreme Court of Canada's decision that because the word "persons" in 1867 was intended to refer only to men, women could not be "qualified persons" for the purpose of being appointed to the Senate. The lords stated that the open-textured language of a constitution should be viewed as a "living tree" that is capable of growth and evolution. In this way, the judiciary assumes a modest role in keeping a constitution in tune with the times and making it less necessary for text to be amended.

The Supreme Court of Canada has used the living-tree metaphor on a number of occasions, including in the *Reference re Same-Sex Marriage*, 2004 SCC 79, [2004] 3 SCR 698. The Court ruled unanimously that Parliament had the power to enact legislation defining marriage for civil purposes as a relationship between "two persons," thereby allowing for same-sex marriage and rejecting an originalist argument that the word "marriage" in s 91(26) of the

Constitution Act, 1867 must be understood as solely referring to a relationship between persons of the opposite sex.

The progressive or living-tree approach may on occasion remove the necessity (or rather, relieve the political pressure) for constitutional amendment. It does not replace it. Nor does it take away from the significance of amending procedures as being the locus of fundamental issues of political power in society.

C. UNWRITTEN PRINCIPLES OF THE CONSTITUTION

Part V of the *Constitution Act, 1982* appears to provide a complete code for the process of constitutional amendment by Canada's governments. The federal government sought to rely on this understanding when it initiated a reference to the Supreme Court on the issue of whether Quebec (or, presumably, any other province) has the power under the Constitution to secede unilaterally from Canada. In 1995, the Parti Québécois (PQ) government of Quebec had come within 50,000 votes of winning a referendum on sovereignty. It appeared that the PQ government's assumption had been that a majority vote for sovereignty in a referendum would form the legal basis for secession without agreement of the rest of Canada. The reference by the federal government challenged this assumption. The government argued to the Court that secession of a province necessarily involves amendment of the Constitution, and that this can only be effected through the processes set out in part V. It cannot be lawfully accomplished, the government argued, solely through a vote in a referendum. Referendums, after all, are not mentioned in part V and have no status other than as an informal means for governments to consult with their constituents.

The Supreme Court's subtle judgment in the *Quebec Secession Reference* managed to affirm much of this position, while at the same time establishing that the Constitution has a depth beyond the text and comprehends legal obligations not found in its text. As we have seen, the Court identified four unwritten principles that are part of the "architecture" of the Constitution—the principles of democracy, federalism, constitutionalism and the rule of law, and protection of minority rights. The justices rejected the idea, advanced by counsel acting as *amicus curiae* on behalf of the sovereignist position, that the principle of democracy alone could justify basing a lawful secession on a referendum vote. The Court found that democracy must be qualified by each of the other principles, which together meant that secession could be achieved only in accordance with part V. However, the Court added, a vote representing a "clear majority" on a "clear question" in favour of secession would be sufficient to create a legal duty to negotiate on the part of the other parties to the federation. The Court described this as a duty to negotiate the terms of secession in good faith, but not a duty to reach agreement on any particular terms, or at all. In this way, the Court recognized a constitutional role for a referendum that nowhere appears in part V.

PART II

THE KEY ACTORS IN PUBLIC LAW

PARLIAMENT AND ITS COMPONENTS

Having set the stage of Canadian public law, it is now time to examine in greater detail the key public law "actors": the legislature, the executive, and the judiciary. In this first chapter on this theme, we focus on legislatures and legislators. The most important law-making institutions in this country are, of course, the federal Parliament and provincial legislatures. Our focus here is on Parliament, although much of our discussion of this federal body applies equally to its provincial counterparts.

This chapter sets the stage by describing the separate institutions that make up Parliament: the monarch and her delegate, the governor general; the Senate; and the House of Commons. The focus here is on how Canadian public law determines who gets to hold these offices. The chapter that follows describes how Parliament is called into session, prorogued, and dissolved and examines the role of several of the key actors in Parliament, including political parties, the speakers, and parliamentary committees. It also then discusses "parliamentary law": the rules and procedures that guide Parliament's functioning. Finally, it sets out the very important procedure by which parliamentary bills become statutes.

What is Parliament and how does it function? Section 17 of the *Constitution Act, 1867* (UK), 30 & 31 Vict, c 3, reprinted in RSC 1985, Appendix II, No 5 creates the "Parliament of Canada" consisting of "the Queen, an Upper House styled the Senate, and the House of Commons." In this first section we describe how the membership of these three components of Canada's Parliament is determined.

I. THE MONARCH AND GOVERNOR GENERAL

The monarch—currently Queen Elizabeth II—plays a double role in the Canadian constitutional framework. Not only is the monarch part of the Parliament, the *Constitution Act, 1867* also vests the "Executive Government" in the Queen, a matter discussed further in Chapter 8. The Queen is, in other words, Canada's official head of state. In practice, however, many of the

Queen's powers are to be exercised by the governor general. Section 10 of the *Constitution Act, 1867* provides:

> The Provisions of this Act referring to the Governor General extend and apply to the Governor General for the Time being of Canada, or other the Chief Executive Officer or Administrator for the Time being carrying on the Government of Canada *on behalf and in the Name of the Queen*, by whatever Title he is designated. [Emphasis added.]

Meanwhile, by letters patent issued by George VI in 1947, the governor general is "to exercise all powers and authorities lawfully belonging to Us in respect of Canada."

In contrast to many republican systems, the Canadian head of state is not elected. His or her identity depends, in the case of the monarch, on birth, and in the case of the governor general, on appointment.

A. SELECTING THE MONARCH

The identity of the monarch—and thus of Canada's titular head of state—is determined in the United Kingdom according to rules of heredity and antiquated laws of succession, most notably the famous *Act of Settlement*, 1701, 12 & 13 Will III, c. 2. This venerable statute bars Catholics from assuming the Crown, and even precludes the monarch from marrying a Roman Catholic. Furthermore, the monarch must be in communion with the Church of England. The Act's dictates are clearly discriminatory, viewed from the optic of modern human rights law. It has, therefore, been challenged in Canadian courts as a violation of the *Canadian Charter of Rights and Freedoms*. Consider the following case, one that provides important insight into the constitutional status of the monarchy in Canada.

O'Donohue v Canada
(2003), 109 CRR (2d) 1 (Ont Sup Ct J), aff'd [2005] OJ No 965 (QL) (CA)

ROULEAU J:

[1] The applicant, Tony O'Donohue, has brought the present application for a declaration that certain provisions of the *Act of Settlement, 1701*, are of no force or effect as they discriminate against Roman Catholics in violation of the equality provisions of the *Canadian Charter of Rights and Freedoms*. ... [O]nly the issues of standing and justiciability are to be dealt with at this point. Should I grant the applicant standing and find justiciability the matter will proceed to be heard on the merits; if not, the application will be struck.

• • •

[2] Mr. O'Donohue is a Canadian citizen and a Roman Catholic. He believes that certain provisions of the *Act of Settlement* are clearly discriminatory against Roman Catholic people and offensive to the Roman Catholic faith. For many years he has tried, through various political means, to have the *Act of Settlement* changed. He has had no success.

[3] The *Act of Settlement* is an imperial statute adopted by the United Kingdom in 1701. By its terms it provides that it is an act "established and declared" in the "Kingdoms of England, France and Ireland, and the dominions thereunto belonging." As a result it became and remains part of the laws of Canada.

[4] The *Act of Settlement* contains several provisions but one in particular addresses the difficult succession issues that led to civil war in England in the latter

part of the 17th century. This provision in effect provides that Roman Catholics cannot accede to the Crown of England, nor be married to someone who holds the Crown. ...

[5] Mr. O'Donohue brings the present application to have those parts of the *Act of Settlement*, insofar as they refer to Roman Catholics and limit their rights, declared to be in breach of s. 15(1) of the *Canadian Charter of Rights and Freedoms* and of no force or effect. ...

• • •

[13] ... [T]he determination of whether a matter is justiciable "is, first and foremost, a normative enquiry into the appropriateness as a matter of constitutional judicial policy of the courts deciding a given issue or, instead, deferring to other decision-making institutions of the polity." ... "[T]here is an array of issues which calls for the exercise of judicial judgment on whether the questions are properly cognizable by the courts. Ultimately, such judgment depends on the appreciation by the judiciary of its own position in the constitutional scheme."

[14] The constitutional scheme of our democratic government consists of four branches: the Crown, the legislative body, the executive and the courts. As set out in *New Brunswick Broadcasting Co. v. Nova Scotia (Speaker of the House of Assembly)*, ... "it is fundamental to the working of government as a whole that all these parts play their proper role. It is equally fundamental that no one of them overstep its bounds, that each show proper deference for the legitimate sphere of activity of the other."

[15] In the present case all parties acknowledge that if the impugned portions of the *Act of Settlement* have constitutional status then the matter is not justiciable. It is well settled that the Charter cannot be used to amend or trump another part of our constitution. ...

[16] The respondents maintain that even if the impugned provisions of the *Act of Settlement* are not part of the Constitution, they clearly are part of the Rules of Succession. They argue that a finding that the Rules of Succession are justiciable would run contrary to the intent of Parliament and constitutional convention among the Commonwealth nations, and would be beyond the proper role of the courts within our constitutional framework.

[17] The impugned portions of the *Act of Settlement* are a key element of the rules governing succession to the British Crown. They were enacted following a long period of civil and religious strife. They confirmed that only the Protestant heirs of Princess Sophia, the Electoress of Hanover, are entitled to assume the throne. The Act of Settlement together with other statutes establish the legitimate heir to the British Crown. ...

[18] Canada was established as a constitutional monarchy. This fundamental aspect of our constitutional structure is both recognized and maintained by the *Constitution Act, 1982*, being Schedule B to the *Canada Act 1982* (UK), 1982, c. 11. It is found, among other places, in the preamble to the Constitution.

[19] It is well recognized that the preamble to the Constitution identifies the organizing principles of our Constitution and can be used to fill in gaps in the express terms of the constitutional text ... .

[20] The preamble to the *Constitution Act, 1867* ... provides as follows:

Whereas the Provinces of Canada, Nova Scotia, and New Brunswick have expressed their Desire to be federally united into One Dominion under the Crown of the United Kingdom of Great Britain and Ireland, with a Constitution similar in Principle to that of the United Kingdom. ...

[21] This portion of the preamble confirms not only that Canada is a constitutional monarchy, but also that Canada is united under the Crown of the United Kingdom of Great Britain. A constitutional monarchy, where the monarch is shared with the United Kingdom and other Commonwealth countries, is, in my view, at the root of our constitutional structure.

[22] The role of the Queen is provided for in s. 9 of the *Constitution Act, 1867,* which reads as follows:

> The Executive Government and Authority of and over Canada is hereby declared to continue and be vested in the Queen.

[23] The office of the Queen is such a fundamental part of our constitutional structure that amendments to the Constitution in respect of that office require the unanimous consent of the federal and provincial governments (see s. 41(a) of the *Constitution Act, 1982*).

• • •

[24] Since the Queen occupies such a central place in the Canadian Constitution, the respondents submit that the rules governing the succession to the throne are themselves essential to the proper functioning of this branch of our constitutional scheme. In the result, these rules are by necessity incorporated into the Constitution of Canada.

• • •

[27] ... [I]t is clear that Canada's structure as a constitutional monarchy and the principle of sharing the British monarch are fundamental to our constitutional framework. In light of the preamble's clear statement that we are to share the Crown with the United Kingdom, it is axiomatic that the rules of succession for the monarchy must be shared and be in symmetry with those of the United Kingdom and other Commonwealth countries. One cannot accept the monarch but reject the legitimacy or legality of the rules by which this monarch is selected.

• • •

[29] If the courts were free to review and declare inoperative certain parts of the rules of succession, Canada could break symmetry with Great Britain, and could conceivably recognize a different monarch than does Great Britain. In fact, Canada could arguably reanimate the debate regarding the heir to the throne, an argument that was resolved by the *Act of Settlement*. This would clearly be contrary to settled intention, as demonstrated by our written Constitution, and would see the courts changing rather than protecting our fundamental constitutional structure.

[30] The fact that the rules of succession are part of our constitutional fabric is further supported by an analysis of the way in which these rules of succession have functioned within the Commonwealth.

[31] By the *Statute of Westminster, 1931* (UK) ... the United Kingdom agreed that it would no longer impose British statutes on the various dominions without their accord. It also provided that the British monarch would continue to be the monarch of various Commonwealth countries including Canada. In order to recognize that the United Kingdom would no longer impose British statutes on the dominions, but also to ensure that the rules of succession which had previously been imposed by the United Kingdom on those Commonwealth countries continued to be consistent, the British Parliament set out in the preamble to the *Statute of Westminster* the following:

> And whereas it is meet and proper to set out by way of preamble to this Act that, inasmuch as the Crown is the symbol of the free association of the members of the

British Commonwealth of Nations, and as they are united by a common allegiance to the Crown, it would be in accord with the established constitutional position of all the members of the Commonwealth in relation to one another that any alteration in the law touching the Succession to the Throne or the Royal Style and Titles shall hereafter require the assent as well as of the Parliaments of all the Dominions as of the Parliament of the United Kingdom:

[32] The *Statute of Westminster* is a part of the Constitution of Canada by virtue of it being listed in the schedule to the Constitution (*Constitution Act, 1982*, s. 52(2)(b)).

[33] As a result of the *Statute of Westminster* it was recognized that any alterations in the rules of succession would no longer be imposed by Great Britain and, if symmetry among commonwealth countries were to be maintained, any changes to the rules of succession would have to be agreed to by all members of the Commonwealth. This arrangement can be compared to a treaty among the Commonwealth countries to share the monarchy under the existing rules and not to change the rules without the agreement of all signatories. While Canada as a sovereign nation is free to withdraw from the arrangement and no longer be united through common allegiance to the Crown, it cannot unilaterally change the rules of succession for all Commonwealth countries. Unilateral changes by Canada to the rules of succession, whether imposed by the court or otherwise, would be contrary to the commitment given in the *Statute of Westminster*, would break symmetry and breach the principle of union under the British Crown set out in the preamble to the *Constitution Act, 1867*. Such changes would, for all intents and purposes, bring about a fundamental change in the office of the Queen without securing the authorizations required pursuant to s. 41 of the *Constitution Act, 1982*.

• • •

[36] The impugned positions of the *Act of Settlement* are an integral part of the rules of succession that govern the selection of the monarch of Great Britain. By virtue of our constitutional structure whereby Canada is united under the Crown of Great Britain, the same rules of succession must apply for the selection of the King or Queen of Canada and the King or Queen of Great Britain. As stated by Prime Minister St. Laurent to the House of Commons during the debate on the bill altering the royal title:

> Her Majesty is now Queen of Canada but she is the Queen of Canada because she is Queen of the United Kingdom. ... It is not a separate office ... it is the sovereign who is recognized as the sovereign of the United Kingdom who is our Sovereign ... .

[37] These rules of succession, and the requirement that they be the same as those of Great Britain, are necessary to the proper functioning of our constitutional monarchy and, therefore, the rules are not subject to Charter scrutiny.

[38] In the present case the court is being asked to apply the Charter not to rule on the validity of acts or decisions of the Crown, one of the branches of our government, but rather to disrupt the core of how the monarchy functions, namely the rules by which succession is determined. To do this would make the constitutional principle of Union under the British Crown together with other Commonwealth countries unworkable, would defeat a manifest intention expressed in the preamble of our Constitution, and would have the courts overstep their role in our democratic structure.

[39] In conclusion, the *lis* raised in the present application is not justiciable and there is no serious issue to be tried. ... The application is dismissed.

The question of royal succession has since been revisited. Consider the following decision from the Ontario Court of Appeal.

Teskey v Canada (AG)
2014 ONCA 612

BLAIR, PEPALL, AND HOURIGAN JJA:

[1] Mr. Teskey is a Roman Catholic. He objects to Canada's participation in the development of a Commonwealth consensus assenting to changes proposed by the Government of the United Kingdom in the royal succession rules.

[2] The consensus was forged at a meeting of the First Ministers of 16 Commonwealth countries that recognize the Queen as their head of state in Perth, Australia in 2011 (the Perth Agreement). The United Kingdom Government introduced a Bill to effect the changes and Canada formally provided its assent in the form of legislation that has been passed but not yet proclaimed in force.

[3] The changes to the succession rules abolish the system of male preference primogeniture and remove the provision that anyone who marries a Roman Catholic is ineligible to succeed to the monarchy. However, they do not go far enough, in Mr. Teskey's view, because they continue to preclude any person who is a Roman Catholic from succeeding to the throne. This prohibition is discriminatory and contravenes his rights and the rights of other Canadian Roman Catholics, under s. 15 of the *Canadian Charter of Rights and Freedoms*, he submits.

[4] Mr. Teskey therefore commenced an application seeking various declaratory relief, including:

  (a)   that *The Canada Act*, 1982, prevents Canada from consenting to the application in Canada of legislation passed by the Parliament of the United Kingdom;

  (b)   that changes to the succession to the Crown of Canada require substantive Canadian legislation;

  (c)   that the Government of Canada lacked the legal capacity of consent to the Perth Agreement;

  (d)   that all legislative provisions or rules which prohibit Catholics from ascending to the Crown of Canada are of no force and effect; and

  (e)   that the United Kingdom's *Succession to the Crown Bill* violates s. 15 of the *Charter*.

[5] On August 9, 2013, Regional Senior Justice Hackland dismissed the application ... . He did so on two grounds: (1) that the application did not raise a justiciable issue; and (2) that the appellant did not have standing to bring the application. He relied heavily on the decision of Rouleau J. (as he then was) in *O'Donohue v. Canada* ... which was affirmed by this Court. ... In *O'Donohue*, the same succession rule was challenged on the basis that it was discriminatory and therefore violated s. 15. The application there was dismissed on the same two bases, namely, justiciability and standing.

[6] We agree with Hackland R.S.J. that Mr. Teskey's application does not raise justiciable issues and that Mr. Teskey lacked standing to bring the application. The rules of succession are a part of the fabric of the constitution of Canada and incorporated into it and therefore cannot be trumped or amended by the *Charter*, and Mr. Teskey does not have any personal interest in the issue raised (other than being a member of the Roman Catholic faith) and does not meet the test for public interest standing.

Canada implemented the Perth Agreement through the *Succession to the Throne Act*, SC 2013, c 6. That Act provided, simply, "The alteration in the law touching the Succession to the Throne set out in the bill laid before the Parliament of the United Kingdom and entitled *A Bill to Make succession to the Crown not depend on gender; to make provision about Royal Marriages; and for connected purposes* is assented to" (s 2). The result was to change succession to the throne—without using the constitutional amendment process set out in part V (and specifically s 41) of the *Constitution Act, 1982*, being Schedule B to the Canada Act 1982 (UK), 1982, c 11. Section 41 specifies that any change to the "office of the Queen" requires resolutions for the House of Commons, the Senate, and every provincial legislature.

Two Quebec law professors sued, claiming that the succession change was unconstitutional. That lawsuit was dismissed in 2019 by the Quebec Court of Appeal, whose judgment is summarized in English by the Société québécoise d'information juridique as follows:

Motard c Procureur Général du Canada
2019 QCCA 1826

KASIRER, C. GAGNON, RANCOURT:

Appeal from a judgment of the Superior Court dismissing an application for a declaration of constitutional invalidity of the Succession to the Throne Act, 2013 ... Dismissed.

The Perth Agreement, signed on October 28, 2011, called for the repeal of the rule of male primogeniture such that the eldest child of the sovereign, without regard to the child's sex, would be first in the line of succession. It also called for the repeal of the rule prohibiting anyone who marries a Roman Catholic from succeeding to the throne.

Before enacting the Succession to the Crown Act 2013 (U.K.), (2013, c. 20), the Parliament of the United Kingdom complied with the constitutional convention referred to in the Preamble to the Statute of Westminster 1931 (U.K.), ... and requested Canada's assent to the amendment of the rules of succession to the throne.

The appellants were wrong to challenge the principle of symmetry accepted by the trial judge, whereby the King or Queen of the United Kingdom is also the King or Queen of Canada. The judge committed no reviewable error in finding that the British rules of succession are not integrated *ex proprio vigore* [of its own force] in Canada. There was therefore no need to resort to the amendment procedure in Part V of the Constitution Act, 1982 ... to give assent to the amendment in British law to the British rules of succession. The enactment of a statute of assent by the Canadian Parliament such as the one passed in 2013 was sufficient.

• • •

The appellant's arguments that the British rules of royal succession fall under the "office of the Queen" protected by s. 41(a) of the Constitution Act, 1982 and that the statute is invalid because it was not enacted according to the procedure set out in that provision are rejected. That provision protects the institution of the monarchy, but not the procedural rules that allow a person to accede to the throne. The Canadian statute makes no change to the powers, status or constitutional role vested in the Queen and therefore does not affect the "office of the Queen."

The Ontario Court of Appeal has also considered the role of the monarch in the modern Canadian Constitution, in a case challenging (unsuccessfully) the oath of loyalty sworn to the Queen by naturalized Canadian citizens. Consider its views on the evolution of the Queen's relations with the Canadian state.

McAteer v Canada (AG)
2014 ONCA 578

WEILER JA:

[33] The appellants argue that the Queen is a symbol of hereditary privilege that connotes British ethnic dominance in Canada and is antithetical to minorities' rights.

[34] The application judge observed that the appellants' objections to the oath are borne out of their insistence on a "plain-meaning" interpretation that is divorced from Canada's history and evolution as a nation. I agree. The history of the Crown and its role in Canada, outlined below, supports the application judge's conclusion.

[35] British rule was cemented on September 8, 1760, when Governor Vaudreuil surrendered New France to a British invasion force by the Articles of Capitulation. Until a definitive treaty was signed, New France was under military occupation and rule. The definitive treaty, the Treaty of Paris, was signed three years later in 1763 between England, France and Spain.

[36] Steps towards democratization soon began. The Royal Proclamation of 1763 gave the colonies the power to summon a General Assembly and gave the representatives of the people the power to make laws for the public peace, welfare and good government of the colony. In the meantime, all persons inhabiting the colonies were governed by the laws of England. The laws of England at the time required persons not born in Great Britain to swear an oath of allegiance to the King that contained specific provisions rejecting the Catholic faith. The oath was required before these individuals could obtain the privileges of British subjects, such as the right to vote and to hold office.

[37] An imperial statute, the *Quebec Act, 1774*, 14 Geo. III, c. 83, replaced the oath of allegiance with one that no longer made reference to the Protestant faith. Thus, the oath in the *Quebec Act* was a compromise that recognized the religious freedom of French Canadians.

[38] A few decades later, the "loyalists" came to Canada out of a desire to remain loyal to the Crown after the American Revolution. However, their loyalty should not be confused with blind allegiance to authority. As the application judge noted, at para. 75, "the loyalists shared with their counterparts to the south the ethos of dissent against authority—albeit democratic rather than revolutionary dissent." These loyalists brought with them the "important idea of lawful opposition," that is, the concept that one can remain loyal to the Crown while still expressing dissent: Constance MacRae-Buchanan, "American Influence on Canadian Constitutionalism," in J. Ajzenstat, ed, *Canadian Constitutionalism: 1791-1991* (Canadian Study of Parliament Group: 1991), at pp. 153-54. They brought with them to Canada the idea that factions, partisanship and dissent help strengthen the nation and that allegiance to the Queen does not preclude opposing views: MacRae-Buchanan, at p. 154. Shortly thereafter, the *Constitutional Act, 1791*, 31 Geo. III, c. 31, divided Quebec into two provinces, Upper Canada and Lower Canada, which were separated by the present-day boundary between Ontario and Quebec. The *Constitutional Act* repealed portions of the *Quebec Act* dealing with the powers and composition of the council, and it made provision for an elected assembly. Other portions of the *Quebec Act*, such as that respecting the oath, were not repealed.

[39] Conflict between the elected assembly on the one hand and the Governor and the appointed council on the other led to rebellion in Upper and Lower Canada in 1837. After it had been put down, Lord Durham recommended the institution of responsible government. He also recommended the union of the two Canadas.

These recommendations were implemented by the *Union Act*, 1840, 3 & 4 Vict., c. 35. The two provinces were known as the Province of Canada.

[40] At that time, the Parliament of Westminster functioned as a Parliament for the United Kingdom and as an Imperial Parliament, that is, as the legislative body for the overseas territories of the British Empire. However, the colonies were given the power to pass their own laws pertaining to naturalization, subject to the usual confirmation by the Crown: *An Act for the Naturalization of Aliens*, 1847, 10 & 11 Vict., c. 83. Statutes pertaining to the Province of Canada, Nova Scotia and New Brunswick all contained an oath of allegiance as a requirement for naturalization: *Report of the Royal Commissioners for Inquiring into the Laws of Naturalization and Allegiance* (London: George Edward Eyre & William Spottiswoode for Her Majesty's Stationary Office, 1869), at Appendix, pp. 10-12.

[41] With Confederation the *Constitution Act, 1867*, was passed. The preamble to the *Constitution Act, 1867*, gave Canada: "a Constitution similar Principle to that of the United Kingdom."

[42] Some pertinent provisions of the structure of the government of Canada set out in the *Constitution Act, 1867* are:

> 9. The Executive Government and Authority of and over Canada is hereby declared to continue and be vested in the Queen.

> 17. There shall be One Parliament for Canada, consisting of the Queen, an Upper House styled the Senate, and the House of Commons.

[43] Each member of the Senate or House of Commons of Canada is required by s. 128 of the *Constitution Act, 1867* to take the oath contained in Schedule 5 of that Act before taking his or her seat. The oath prescribed in Schedule 5 of the *Constitution Act, 1867*, which is clearly constitutional, is remarkably similar to the oath of allegiance to which the appellants object. The wording of that oath is as follows:

> I A.B. do swear, That I will be faithful and bear true Allegiance to Her Majesty Queen Victoria.

> Note. The Name of the King or Queen of the United Kingdom of Great Britain and Ireland for the Time being is to be substituted from Time to Time, with proper Terms of Reference thereto.

[44] The power to legislate respecting "naturalization and aliens" was granted to the federal parliament in s. 91(25). The Dominion of Canada continued to have the power to repeal or alter naturalization legislation: *Constitution Act, 1867*, s. 129. However, pursuant to the *Colonial Laws Validity Act*, 1865, 28 & 29 Vict., c. 63, that legislation could not be inconsistent with the laws of Great Britain.

[45] The restriction on repealing or amending pre-Confederation imperial statutes was removed by the *Statute of Westminster*, 1931, 22 Geo. V, c. 4. It enabled Canada to pass laws that were previously precluded by the *Colonial Laws Validity Act*. Thus, the *Statute of Westminster* was a significant development for Canadian sovereignty, in that it permitted Canada to pass laws that were inconsistent with certain British laws for the first time.

[46] Canadians are no longer British citizens: see *Citizenship Act*, s. 32(2).

[47] The *Constitution Act, 1982* completed the "Canadianization" of the Crown. As the Supreme Court has explained, "the proclamation of the *Constitution Act, 1982* removed the last vestige of British authority over the Canadian Constitution": *Reference re Secession of Quebec*, [1998] 2 S.C.R. 217, at para. 46.

[48] The evolution of Canada from a British colony into an independent nation and democratic constitutional monarchy must inform the interpretation of the reference to the Queen in the citizenship oath. As Canada has evolved, the symbolic meaning of the Queen in the oath has evolved. The Federal Court of Appeal in *Roach* read the reference to the Queen as a reference not to the person but to the institution of state that she represents. MacGuigan J.A., for the majority, indicated at p. 416 that the oath, properly understood, required a citizenship applicant to simply "express agreement with the fundamental structure of our country as it is."

[49] The application judge noted, at para. 60, that "Her Majesty the Queen in Right of Canada (or Her Majesty the Queen in Right of Ontario or the other provinces), as a governing institution, has long been distinguished from Elizabeth R. and her predecessors as individual people."

[50] I agree with the application judge's comments. Viewing the oath to the Queen as an oath to an individual is disconnected from the reality of the Queen's role in Canada today. During the heyday of the Empire, British constitutional theory saw the Crown as indivisible. At that time, there was no need to distinguish between the sovereign's role as an individual and as the head of the executive; nor was there any need in unitary Great Britain to differentiate between the roles that the Crown plays: see The Hon. Bora Laskin, *The British Tradition In Canadian Law* (London: Stevens & Sons, 1969), at pp. 117-119.

[51] However, as Canada developed as an independent federalist state, the conception of the Queen (commonly referred to as the Crown) evolved. Unlike the unitary role of the Crown at the height of the British Empire, its role in Canada is divided into three distinct roles. First, the Queen of Canada plays a legislative role in assenting to refusing assent to, or reserving bills of the provincial legislature or Parliament—a role that is performed through the Governor General and the Lieutenant Governors. Second, the Queen of Canada is the head of executive authority pursuant to sections 9 and 12 of the *Constitution Act, 1867.* Third, the Queen of Canada is the personification of the State, i.e., with respect to Crown prerogatives and privileges: Laskin, at pp. 119-20. "The law and learning of Crown privileges and immunities came to the colonies as received or imposed English law, and through section 129 of the *British North America Act* [which continues the laws in force in Canada, Nova Scotia, or New Brunswick at the date of Union] they were absorbed in the Canadian federation." Laskin, at 120. Thus, English constitutional law, which had gradually subjected nearly all royal prerogative power to parliamentary sovereignty, made its way into Canada. Moreover, the Crown may for some purposes fall within provincial power under s. 92 of the *Constitution Act, 1867,* and for other purposes fall within federal power under s. 91. For the purposes of Canadian federalism, the Crown therefore cannot be viewed as a single indivisible entity: Laskin, at p. 119. The Crown is "separate and divisible for each self-governing dominion or province or territory": *R. v. Secretary of State for Foreign and Commonwealth Affairs, ex parte Indian Association of Alberta*, [1982] Q.B. 892, at 917 (Eng. C.A.), per Lord Denning.

[52] As the application judge noted, the Queen of Canada fulfils these varying roles figuratively, not literally. The Hon. Bora Laskin explains, at pp. 118-19, that "Her Majesty has no personal physical presence in Canada ... . [O]nly the legal connotation, the abstraction that Her Majesty or the Crown represents, need be considered for purposes of Canadian federalism. The fact that Interpretation Acts whether the federal Act or provincial Acts, give the term "Her Majesty" or the Crown" a personal meaning, is [an] anachronism." The oath to the Queen of Canada is an oath to our form of government, as symbolized by the Queen as the apex of our Canadian parliamentary system of constitutional monarchy.

• • •

[54] Although the Queen is a person, in swearing allegiance to the Queen of Canada, the would-be citizen is swearing allegiance to a symbol of our form of government in Canada. This fact is reinforced by the oath's reference to "the Queen of Canada," instead of "the Queen." It is not an oath to a foreign sovereign. Similarly, in today's context, the reference in the oath to the Queen of Canada's "heirs and successors" is a reference to the continuity of our form of government extending into the future.

B. SELECTING THE GOVERNOR GENERAL

The governor general is selected closer to home. In practice, the monarch appoints the governor general. However, by Canadian constitutional convention, the Queen follows the Canadian prime minister's recommendation in appointing the governor general. Thus, while she is customarily consulted in advance, the Queen takes her direction from what is known as an "instrument of advice"—essentially a personal letter from the prime minister. There are no legal criteria constraining the prime minister's choice for governor general. Convention probably dictates that only Canadians may now be appointed, and Canadian practice strongly favours alternating anglophone and francophone representatives. At its base, however, the prime minister's selection is a political decision.

The first Canadian governors general were former diplomats or at least diplomat/politicians. Between 1979 and 1999, Canada's four governors general were former politicians. In three instances, these former members of Parliament were from the party in power at the time of the appointment, prompting some critics to suggest that the governor general's position had tumbled from diplomatic symbol to political patronage plum. Two recent appointments—Prime Minister Jean Chrétien's selection of apparently non-partisan Adrienne Clarkson and Prime Minister Paul Martin's naming of Michaëlle Jean—followed yet another pattern: appointment of non-political figures from the arts and media community representing Canada's burgeoning multicultural fabric. The last governor general, David Johnston, was a prominent academic prior to his appointment by Prime Minister Stephen Harper. The current governor general, Julie Payette, is a scientist and former astronaut. There is no fixed term of office for governors general, but they tend to serve for approximately five years.

II. SENATE

Unusually for a modern democracy, Canada has an *unelected* upper chamber of the federal legislature. Section 24 of the *Constitution Act, 1867* expressly anticipates the *appointment* of senators by the governor general:

> The Governor General shall from Time to Time, in the Queen's Name, by Instrument under the Great Seal of Canada, summon qualified Persons to the Senate; and, subject to the Provisions of this Act, every Person so summoned shall become and be a Member of the Senate and a Senator.

In exercising this power, the governor general follows the advice of the prime minister, as required by constitutional convention.

In the past, there was legal controversy over whether the reference to "persons" in s 24 included women. This doubt—so peculiar to modern eyes—was resolved with a "yes" in the famous *"Persons"* case, decided by the Judicial Committee on the Privy Council as *Edwards v AG of Canada*, [1930] AC 124 in 1929, reproduced in Chapter 2. In that decision, Lord Sankey wrote:

> The exclusion of women from all public offices is a relic of days more barbarous than ours, but it must be remembered that the necessity of the times often forced on man customs which in later years were not necessary. ...

Customs are apt to develop into traditions which are stronger than law and remain unchallenged long after the reason for them has disappeared.

The appeal to history therefore in this particular matter is not conclusive.

The law lords then observed later in the decision:

The *British North America Act* planted in Canada a living tree capable of growth and expansion within its natural limits. The object of the Act was to grant a Constitution to Canada. Like all written constitutions it has been subject to development through usage and convention. ...

Their Lordships do not conceive it to be the duty of this Board—it is certainly not their desire—to cut down the provisions of the Act by a narrow and technical construction, but rather to give it a large and liberal interpretation so that the Dominion to a great extent, but within certain fixed limits, may be mistress in her own house, as the provinces to a great extent, but within certain fixed limits, are mistresses in theirs.

While gender discrimination is no longer part of the Canadian Constitution, the appointments process continues to fuel substantial controversy—it has too often been treated as a means for the party in power to reward friends and supporters. Many proposals exist for senate reform, although none has been successful. Given this deadlock, provincial governments have occasionally attempted to assert control over appointments. Most notably, Alberta enacted the *Senatorial Selection Act*, RSA 2000, c S-5, providing for the direct election of senatorial candidates. Once selected by election, the provincial government is to submit the nominees' names to the federal government, identifying these individuals as persons who may be summoned to the Senate for the purpose of filling vacancies relating to Alberta.

This law has had only a modest impact on senator selections. Alberta has had four elections, in 1989, 1999, 2004, and 2012. Stan Waters was elected in 1989, and in fact, was appointed to the Senate in 1990 by Prime Minister Brian Mulroney, then trying to elicit provincial support for the Meech Lake Accord. However, Prime Minister Jean Chrétien declined to appoint the two so-called senators-in-waiting elected in 1999—Bert Brown and Ted Morton. In response, Brown sued in the Alberta courts seeking a declaration that the senatorial appointment provisions of the 1867 Act were contrary to democratic principles, as set out by the Supreme Court in the *Quebec Secession Reference* (*Reference Re Secession of Quebec*, [1998] 2 SCR 217), discussed at length in Chapter 5. See *Brown v Alberta* (1999), 177 DLR (4th) 349 (Alta CA). In a second case, brought in the Federal Court, the Reform Party of Canada sought an interlocutory injunction to restrain the governor general from appointing a senator from Alberta, unless that person has been elected pursuant to the provisions of the *Senatorial Selection Act*. See *Samson v Canada (AG)* (1998), 165 DLR (4th) 342 (FCTD). Both cases were unsuccessful, mostly because the courts considered the appointment issue a political and not a legal matter.

Following the 2006 election, Prime Minister Stephen Harper promised to rethink the manner in which senators are selected. The Harper government repeatedly tabled bills that would amend the *Constitution Act, 1867* to impose term limits on new senators, restricting their tenure to eight years. (The current Constitution allows senators to remain in office until age 75.) Additional legislation was proposed that, in its final form, would steer the prime minister to honour provincial senatorial selection laws in the recommendations on Senate appointments made to the governor general, opening the door to a Senate with an elected composition. These law projects died repeatedly in Parliament for several reasons, and the whole reform process came to a halt after the government referred the ideas to the Supreme Court to assess their constitutionality. The Court's response, reproduced below, brought an end to the Harper government's strategy of pragmatic Senate micro-reform.

Reference re Senate Reform
2014 SCC 32, [2014] 1 SCR 704

THE COURT:

I. Introduction

[1] The Senate is one of Canada's foundational political institutions. It lies at the heart of the agreements that gave birth to the Canadian federation. Yet from its first sittings, voices have called for reform of the Senate and even, on occasion, for its outright abolition.

[2] The Government of Canada now asks this Court, under s. 53 of the *Supreme Court Act*, R.S.C. 1985, c. S-26, to answer essentially four questions: (1) Can Parliament unilaterally implement a framework for consultative elections for appointments to the Senate? (2) Can Parliament unilaterally set fixed terms for Senators? ... and (4) What degree of provincial consent is required to abolish the Senate?

[3] We conclude that Parliament cannot unilaterally achieve most of the proposed changes to the Senate, which require the consent of at least seven provinces representing, in the aggregate, at least half of the population of all the provinces. We further conclude that abolition of the Senate requires the consent of all of the provinces. Abolition of the Senate would fundamentally change Canada's constitutional structure, including its procedures for amending the Constitution, and can only be done with unanimous federal–provincial consensus.

• • •

III. The Senate

[13] It is appropriate to briefly introduce the institution at the heart of this Reference.

[14] The framers of the *Constitution Act, 1867* sought to adapt the British form of government to a new country, in order to have a "Constitution similar in Principle to that of the United Kingdom": preamble. They wanted to preserve the British structure of a lower legislative chamber composed of elected representatives, an upper legislative chamber made up of elites appointed by the Crown, and the Crown as head of state.

[15] The upper legislative chamber, which the framers named the Senate, was modeled on the British House of Lords, but adapted to Canadian realities. As in the United Kingdom, it was intended to provide "sober second thought" on the legislation adopted by the popular representatives in the House of Commons: John A. Macdonald, Province of Canada, Legislative Assembly, *Parliamentary Debates on the Subject of the Confederation of the British North American Provinces*, 3rd Sess., 8th Prov. Parl. (the *"1865 Debates"*), February 6, 1865, at p. 35. However, it played the additional role of providing a distinct form of representation for the regions that had joined Confederation and ceded a significant portion of their legislative powers to the new federal Parliament: *Figueroa v. Canada (AG)*, 2003 SCC 37, [2003] 1 S.C.R. 912, at paras. 164-66, *per* LeBel J. While representation in the House of Commons was proportional to the population of the new Canadian provinces, each region was provided equal representation in the Senate irrespective of population. This was intended to assure the regions that their voices would continue to be heard in the legislative process even though they might become minorities within the overall population of Canada: George Brown, *1865 Debates*, February 8, 1865, at p. 88; D. Pinard, "The Canadian Senate: An Upper House Criticized Yet Condemned

to Survive Unchanged?," in J. Luther, P. Passaglia and R. Tarchi, eds., *A World of Second Chambers: Handbook for Constitutional Studies on Bicameralism* (2006), 459, at p. 462.

[16] Over time, the Senate also came to represent various groups that were under-represented in the House of Commons. It served as a forum for ethnic, gender, religious, linguistic, and Aboriginal groups that did not always have a meaningful opportunity to present their views through the popular democratic process: B. Pelletier, "Réponses suggérées aux questions soulevées par le renvoi à la Cour suprême du Canada concernant la réforme du Sénat" (2013), 43 *R.G.D.* 445 ("Réponses suggérées"), at pp. 485-86.

[17] Although the product of consensus, the Senate rapidly attracted criticism and reform proposals. Some felt that it failed to provide "sober second thought" and reflected the same partisan spirit as the House of Commons. Others criticized it for failing to provide meaningful representation of the interests of the provinces as originally intended, and contended that it lacked democratic legitimacy.

• • •

IV. The Part V Amending Procedures

[21] The statute that created the Senate—the *Constitution Act, 1867*—forms part of the Constitution of Canada and can only be amended in accordance with the Constitution's procedures for amendment: s. 52(2) and (3), *Constitution Act, 1982*. Consequently, we must determine whether the changes contemplated in the Reference amend the Constitution and, if so, which amendment procedures are applicable.

[22] Before answering these questions, we discuss constitutional amendment in Canada generally. We examine in turn the nature and content of the Constitution of Canada, the concept of constitutional amendment, and the Constitution's procedures for amendment.

A. The Constitution of Canada

[23] The Constitution of Canada is "a comprehensive set of rules and principles" that provides "an exhaustive legal framework for our system of government": *Reference re Secession of Quebec*, [1998] 2 S.C.R. 217 ("*Secession Reference*"), at para. 32. It defines the powers of the constituent elements of Canada's system of government—the executive, the legislatures, and the courts—as well as the division of powers between the federal and provincial governments: *Reference re Remuneration of Judges of the Provincial Court of Prince Edward Island*, [1997] 3 S.C.R. 3 ("*Provincial Court Judges Reference*"), at para. 108. And it governs the state's relationship with the individual. Governmental power cannot lawfully be exercised, unless it conforms to the Constitution: s. 52(1), *Constitution Act, 1982*; *Secession Reference*, at paras. 70-78; *Reference re Supreme Court Act, ss. 5 and 6*, 2014 SCC 21, [2014] 1 S.C.R. 433 ("*Supreme Court Act Reference*"), at para. 89.

[24] The Constitution of Canada is defined in s. 52(2) of the *Constitution Act, 1982* as follows:

> 52. ...
>
> (2) The Constitution of Canada includes
>
>   (a) the *Canada Act 1982*, including this Act;
>
>   (b) the Acts and orders referred to in the schedule; and
>
>   (c) any amendment to any Act or order referred to in paragraph (a) or (b).

The documents listed in the Schedule to the *Constitution Act, 1982* as forming part of the Constitution include the *Constitution Act, 1867.* Section 52 does not provide an exhaustive definition of the content of the Constitution of Canada: *Supreme Court Act Reference*, at paras. 97-100; *Secession Reference*, at para. 32.

[25] The Constitution implements a structure of government and must be understood by reference to "the constitutional text itself, the historical context, and previous judicial interpretations of constitutional meaning": *Secession Reference*, at para. 32; see, generally, H. Cyr, "L'absurdité du critère scriptural pour qualifier la constitution" (2012), 6 *J.P.P.L.* 293. The rules of constitutional interpretation require that constitutional documents be interpreted in a broad and purposive manner and placed in their proper linguistic, philosophic, and historical contexts: *Hunter v. Southam Inc.*, [1984] 2 S.C.R. 145, at pp. 155-56; *Edwards v. Attorney-General for Canada*, [1930] A.C. 124 (P.C.), at p. 136; *R. v. Big M Drug Mart Ltd.*, [1985] 1 S.C.R. 295, at p. 344; *Supreme Court Act Reference*, at para. 19. Generally, constitutional interpretation must be informed by the foundational principles of the Constitution, which include principles such as federalism, democracy, the protection of minorities, as well as constitutionalism and the rule of law: *Secession Reference*; *Provincial Court Judges Reference*; *New Brunswick Broadcasting Co. v. Nova Scotia (Speaker of the House of Assembly)*, [1993] 1 S.C.R. 319; *Reference re Manitoba Language Rights*, [1985] 1 S.C.R. 721.

[26] These rules and principles of interpretation have led this Court to conclude that the Constitution should be viewed as having an "internal architecture," or "basic constitutional structure": *Secession Reference*, at para. 50; *OPSEU v. Ontario (AG)*, [1987] 2 S.C.R. 2, at p. 57; see also *Supreme Court Act Reference*, at para. 82. The notion of architecture expresses the principle that "[t]he individual elements of the Constitution are linked to the others, and must be interpreted by reference to the structure of the Constitution as a whole": *Secession Reference*, at para. 50; see also the discussion on this Court's approach to constitutional interpretation in M.D. Walters, "Written Constitutions and Unwritten Constitutionalism," in G. Huscroft, ed., *Expounding the Constitution: Essays in Constitutional Theory* (2008), 245, at pp. 264-65. In other words, the Constitution must be interpreted with a view to discerning the structure of government that it seeks to implement. The assumptions that underlie the text and the manner in which the constitutional provisions are intended to interact with one another must inform our interpretation, understanding, and application of the text.

B. Amendments to the Constitution of Canada

[27] The concept of an "amendment to the Constitution of Canada," within the meaning of Part V of the *Constitution Act, 1982*, is informed by the nature of the Constitution and its rules of interpretation. As discussed, the Constitution should not be viewed as a mere collection of discrete textual provisions. It has an architecture, a basic structure. By extension, amendments to the Constitution are not confined to textual changes. They include changes to the Constitution's architecture.

C. The Part V Amending Procedures

[28] Part V of the *Constitution Act, 1982* provides the blueprint for how to amend the Constitution of Canada (see Appendix). It tells us what changes Parliament and the provincial legislatures can make unilaterally, what changes require substantial federal and provincial consent, and what changes require unanimous agreement.

(1) History

[29] The Part V amending formula reflects the principle that constitutional change that engages provincial interests requires both the consent of Parliament and a significant degree of provincial consent. ...

• • •

(2) The Amending Procedures

[32] Part V contains four categories of amending procedures. The first is the general amending procedure (s. 38, complemented by s. 42), which requires a substantial degree of consensus between Parliament and the provincial legislatures. The second is the unanimous consent procedure (s. 41), which applies to certain changes deemed fundamental by the framers of the *Constitution Act, 1982*. The third is the special arrangements procedure (s. 43), which applies to amendments in relation to provisions of the Constitution that apply to some, but not all, of the provinces. The fourth is made up of the unilateral federal and provincial procedures, which allow unilateral amendment of aspects of government institutions that engage purely federal or provincial interests (ss. 44 and 45).

(a) The General Amending Procedure

[33] Section 38 of the *Constitution Act, 1982* provides:

38.(1) An amendment to the Constitution of Canada may be made by proclamation issued by the Governor General under the Great Seal of Canada where so authorized by

(a) resolutions of the Senate and House of Commons; and

(b) resolutions of the legislative assemblies of at least two-thirds of the provinces that have, in the aggregate, according to the then latest general census, at least fifty per cent of the population of all the provinces.

(2) An amendment made under subsection (1) that derogates from the legislative powers, the proprietary rights or any other rights or privileges of the legislature or government of a province shall require a resolution supported by a majority of the members of each of the Senate, the House of Commons and the legislative assemblies required under subsection (1).

(3) An amendment referred to in subsection (2) shall not have effect in a province the legislative assembly of which has expressed its dissent thereto by resolution supported by a majority of its members prior to the issue of the proclamation to which the amendment relates unless that legislative assembly, subsequently, by resolution supported by a majority of its members, revokes its dissent and authorizes the amendment.

(4) A resolution of dissent made for the purposes of subsection (3) may be revoked at any time before or after the issue of the proclamation to which it relates.

[34] The process set out in s. 38 is the general rule for amendments to the Constitution of Canada. It reflects the principle that substantial provincial consent must be obtained for constitutional change that engages provincial interests. Section 38 codifies what is colloquially referred to as the "7/50" procedure—amendments to the Constitution of Canada must be authorized by resolutions of the Senate, the House of Commons, and legislative assemblies of at least seven provinces whose population represents, in the aggregate, at least half of the current population of all the provinces. Additionally, it grants to the provinces the right to "opt out" of constitutional

amendments that "derogat[e] from the legislative powers, the proprietary rights or any other rights or privileges of the legislature or government of a province."

[35] By requiring significant provincial consensus while stopping short of unanimity, s. 38 "achieves a compromise between the demands of legitimacy and flexibility": J. Cameron, "To Amend the Process of Amendment," in G.-A. Beaudoin et al., *Federalism for the Future: Essential Reforms* (1998), 315, at p. 324. Its "underlying purpose ... is to protect the provinces from having their rights or privileges negatively affected without their consent": Monahan and Shaw, at p. 192.

[36] The s. 38 procedure represents the balance deemed appropriate by the framers of the *Constitution Act, 1982* for most constitutional amendments, apart from those contemplated in one of the other provisions in Part V. Section 38 is thus the procedure of general application for amendments to the Constitution of Canada. As a result, the other procedures in Part V should be construed as exceptions to the general rule.

[37] Section 42 complements s. 38 by expressly identifying certain categories of amendments to which the 7/50 procedure in s. 38(1) applies:

> 42.(1) An amendment to the Constitution of Canada in relation to the following matters may be made only in accordance with subsection 38(1):
> (a) the principle of proportionate representation of the provinces in the House of Commons prescribed by the Constitution of Canada;
> (b) the powers of the Senate and the method of selecting Senators;
> (c) the number of members by which a province is entitled to be represented in the Senate and the residence qualifications of Senators;
> (d) subject to paragraph 41(d), the Supreme Court of Canada;
> (e) the extension of existing provinces into the territories; and
> (f) notwithstanding any other law or practice, the establishment of new provinces.
> (2) Subsections 38(2) to (4) do not apply in respect of amendments in relation to matters referred to in subsection (1).

[38] This provision serves two purposes. First, the express inclusion of certain matters in s. 42 provided the framers of the *Constitution Act, 1982* with greater certainty that the 7/50 procedure would apply to amendments in relation to those matters: J.D. Whyte, "Senate Reform: What Does the Constitution Say?," in J. Smith, ed., *The Democratic Dilemma: Reforming the Canadian Senate* (2009), 97, at p. 102. Second, the provincial right to "opt out" of certain amendments contemplated in s. 38(2) to (4) does not apply to the categories of amendments in s. 42. This ensures that amendments made under s. 42 will apply consistently to all the provinces and allows the changes contemplated in the provision to be implemented in a coherent manner throughout Canada.

[39] Section 42(1)(b) of the *Constitution Act, 1982* expressly makes the general amendment procedure applicable to amendments in relation to "the powers of the Senate and the method of selecting Senators." We discuss below the meaning of this statutory language and its bearing on the questions before us.

(b) The Unanimous Consent Procedure

[40] Section 41 of the *Constitution Act, 1982* sets out an amending procedure requiring unanimous consent in relation to certain matters:

> 41. An amendment to the Constitution of Canada in relation to the following matters may be made by proclamation issued by the Governor General under the

Great Seal of Canada only where authorized by resolutions of the Senate and House of Commons and of the legislative assembly of each province:

(a) the office of the Queen, the Governor General and the Lieutenant Governor of a province;

(b) the right of a province to a number of members in the House of Commons not less than the number of Senators by which the province is entitled to be represented at the time this Part comes into force;

(c) subject to section 43, the use of the English or the French language;

(d) the composition of the Supreme Court of Canada; and

(e) an amendment to this Part.

[41] Section 41 requires the unanimous consent of the Senate, the House of Commons, and all the provincial legislative assemblies for the categories of amendments enumerated in the provision. It "accords the highest level of constitutional protection and entrenchment" to the enumerated matters: W.J. Newman, "Living with the Amending Procedures: Prospects for Future Constitutional Reform in Canada" (2007), 37 *S.C.L.R.* (2d) 383, at p. 388. It is an exception to the general amending procedure. It creates an exacting amending procedure that is designed to apply to certain fundamental changes to the Constitution of Canada. Professor Pelletier aptly describes the rationale for requiring unanimity for the enumerated categories of amendments:

[TRANSLATION] ... the unanimity rule provided for in section 41 of the 1982 Act is justified by the need ... to give each of the partners of Canada's federal compromise a veto on those topics that are considered the most essential to the survival of the state.

(B. Pelletier, La modification constitutionnelle au Canada (1996), at p. 208)

• • •

V. How Can the Senate Changes Contemplated in the Reference Be Achieved?

[49] The Reference questions ask whether Parliament, acting alone, can reform the Senate by creating consultative elections to select senatorial nominees endorsed by the populations of the various provinces and territories, by limiting senatorial tenure to fixed terms, and by removing the personal wealth and real property requirements for Senators. We will address each of these issues in turn.

A. Consultative Elections

[50] The text of the *Constitution Act, 1867* provides for the formal appointment of Senators by the Governor General:

24. The Governor General shall from Time to Time, in the Queen's Name, by Instrument under the Great Seal of Canada, summon qualified Persons to the Senate; and, subject to the Provisions of this Act, every Person so summoned shall become and be a Member of the Senate and a Senator.

32. When a Vacancy happens in the Senate by Resignation, Death, or otherwise, the Governor General shall by Summons to a fit and qualified Person fill the Vacancy.

In practice, constitutional convention requires the Governor General to follow the recommendations of the Prime Minister of Canada when filling Senate vacancies.

[51] The Attorney General of Canada (supported by the attorneys general of Saskatchewan and Alberta as well as one of the *amici curiae*) submits that implementing consultative elections for Senators does not constitute an amendment to the Constitution of Canada. He argues that this reform would not change the text of the *Constitution Act, 1867*, nor the means of selecting Senators. He points out that the formal mechanism for appointing Senators—summons by the Governor General acting on the advice of the Prime Minister—would remain untouched. Alternatively, he submits that if introducing consultative elections constitutes an amendment to the Constitution, then it can be achieved unilaterally by Parliament under s. 44 of the *Constitution Act, 1982*.

[52] In our view, the argument that introducing consultative elections does not constitute an amendment to the Constitution privileges form over substance. It reduces the notion of constitutional amendment to a matter of whether or not the letter of the constitutional text is modified. This narrow approach is inconsistent with the broad and purposive manner in which the Constitution is understood and interpreted, as discussed above. While the provisions regarding the appointment of Senators would remain textually untouched, the Senate's fundamental nature and role as a complementary legislative body of sober second thought would be significantly altered.

[53] We conclude that each of the proposed consultative elections would constitute an amendment to the Constitution of Canada and require substantial provincial consent under the general amending procedure, without the provincial right to "opt out" of the amendment (s. 42). We reach this conclusion for three reasons: (1) the proposed consultative elections would fundamentally alter the architecture of the Constitution; (2) the text of Part V expressly makes the general amending procedure applicable to a change of this nature; and (3) the proposed change is beyond the scope of the unilateral federal amending procedure (s. 44).

(1) Consultative Elections Would Fundamentally Alter the Architecture of the Constitution

[54] The implementation of consultative elections would amend the Constitution of Canada by fundamentally altering its architecture. It would modify the Senate's role within our constitutional structure as a complementary legislative body of sober second thought.

[55] The *Constitution Act, 1867* contemplates a specific structure for the federal Parliament, "similar in Principle to that of the United Kingdom": preamble. The Act creates both a lower *elected* and an upper *appointed* legislative chamber: s. 17. It expressly provides that the members of the lower chamber—the House of Commons—"shall be elected" by the population of the various provinces: s. 37. By contrast, it provides that Senators shall be "summoned" (i.e. appointed) by the Governor General: ss. 24 and 32.

[56] The contrast between election for members of the House of Commons and executive appointment for Senators is not an accident of history. The framers of the *Constitution Act, 1867* deliberately chose executive appointment of Senators in order to allow the Senate to play the specific role of a complementary legislative body of "sober second thought."

[57] As this Court wrote in the *Upper House Reference*, "[i]n creating the Senate in the manner provided in the Act, it is clear that the intention was to make the Senate a thoroughly independent body which could *canvass dispassionately the measures of the House of Commons*": p. 77 (emphasis added). The framers sought to endow the Senate with independence from the electoral process to which members

of the House of Commons were subject, in order to remove Senators from a partisan political arena that required unremitting consideration of short-term political objectives.

[58] Correlatively, the choice of executive appointment for Senators was also intended to ensure that the Senate would be a *complementary* legislative body, rather than a perennial rival of the House of Commons in the legislative process. Appointed Senators would not have a popular mandate—they would not have the expectations and legitimacy that stem from popular election. This would ensure that they would confine themselves to their role as a body mainly conducting legislative review, rather than as a coequal of the House of Commons. As John A. Macdonald put it during the Parliamentary debates regarding Confederation, "[t] here is ... a greater danger of an irreconcilable difference of opinion between the two branches of the legislature, if the upper be elective, than if it holds its commission from the Crown": *1865 Debates*, February 6, 1865, at p. 37. An appointed Senate would be a body "calmly considering the legislation initiated by the popular branch, and preventing any hasty or ill considered legislation which may come from that body, *but it will never set itself in opposition against the deliberate and understood wishes of the people*": *ibid.*, at p. 36 (emphasis added).

[59] The appointed status of Senators, with its attendant assumption that appointment would prevent Senators from overstepping their role as a complementary legislative body, shapes the architecture of the *Constitution Act, 1867*. It explains why the framers did not deem it necessary to textually specify how the powers of the Senate relate to those of the House of Commons or how to resolve a deadlock between the two chambers. Indeed, on its face the *Constitution Act, 1867* grants as much legislative power to the Senate as to the House of Commons, with the exception that the House of Commons has the exclusive power to originate appropriation and tax bills (s. 53). As Professor Smith aptly summarizes:

> [The framers'] original answer to the clash that would inevitably occur between elected chambers was to make the Senate appointed. This assured that a government enjoying the confidence of the House of Commons would normally be able to have its legislation adopted by Parliament, but gave the Senate the ability to act as a check in those rare instances when it was absolutely necessary.

(D.E. Smith, *The Canadian Senate in Bicameral Perspective* (2003), at p. 169; see also A. Heard, "Constitutional Doubts about Bill C-20 and Senatorial Elections," in Smith, *The Democratic Dilemma*, 81, at p. 95.)

[60] The proposed consultative elections would fundamentally modify the constitutional architecture we have just described and, by extension, would constitute an amendment to the Constitution. They would weaken the Senate's role of sober second thought and would give it the democratic legitimacy to systematically block the House of Commons, contrary to its constitutional design.

[61] Federal legislation providing for the consultative election of Senators would have the practical effect of subjecting Senators to the political pressures of the electoral process and of endowing them with a popular mandate. Senators selected from among the listed nominees would become popular representatives. They would have won a "true electoral contest" (*Quebec Senate Reference*, at para. 71), during which they would presumably have laid out a campaign platform and made electoral promises: Pelletier, "Réponses suggérées," at pp. 470-71. They would join the Senate after acquiring the mandate and legitimacy that flow from popular election.

[62] The Attorney General of Canada counters that this broad structural change would not occur because the Prime Minister would retain the ability to ignore the

results of the consultative elections and to name whomever he or she wishes to the Senate. We cannot accept this argument. Bills C-20 and C-7 are designed to result in the appointment to the Senate of nominees selected by the population of the provinces and territories. Bill C-7 is the more explicit of the two bills, as it provides that the Prime Minister "must" consider the names on the lists of elected candidates. It is true that, in theory, prime ministers could ignore the election results and rarely, or indeed never, recommend to the Governor General the winners of the consultative elections. However, the purpose of the bills is clear: to bring about a Senate with a popular mandate. We cannot assume that future prime ministers will defeat this purpose by ignoring the results of costly and hard-fought consultative elections: see for example the discussion in M.D. Walters, "The Constitutional Form and Reform of the Senate: Thoughts on the Constitutionality of Bill C-7" (2013), 7 *J.P.P.L.* 37, at pp. 47-48. A legal analysis of the constitutional nature and effects of proposed legislation cannot be premised on the assumption that the legislation will fail to bring about the changes it seeks to achieve.

[63] In summary, the consultative election proposals set out in the Reference questions would amend the Constitution of Canada by changing the Senate's role within our constitutional structure from a complementary legislative body of sober second thought to a legislative body endowed with a popular mandate and democratic legitimacy.

(2) The Wording of Part V Indicates That the Proposal for Consultative Elections Attracts the General Amending Procedure

[64] Our view that the consultative election proposals would amend the Constitution of Canada is supported by the language of Part V. The words employed in Part V are guides to identifying the aspects of our system of government that form part of the protected content of the Constitution. Section 42(1)(b) of the *Constitution Act, 1982* provides that the general amending procedure (s. 38(1)) applies to constitutional amendments in relation to "the method of selecting Senators" ("*le mode de sélection des sénateurs*"). This broad wording covers the implementation of consultative elections, indicating that a constitutional amendment is required and making that amendment subject to the general procedure: H. Brun, G. Tremblay and E. Brouillet, *Droit constitutionnel* (5th ed. 2008), at p. 343; Whyte, at p. 106; see also C.-E. Côté, "L'inconstitutionnalité du projet d'élections fédérales sénatoriales" (2010), 3 *R.Q.D.C.* 81, at p. 83, cited in the *Quebec Senate Reference*, at para. 50; Walters, "The Constitutional Form and Reform of the Senate," at p. 52.

[65] The words "the method of selecting Senators" include more than the formal appointment of Senators by the Governor General. "[S]ection 42(b) refers to the method of *selecting* persons for appointment, not the means of appointment": Whyte, at p. 106 (emphasis in original). By employing this language, the framers of the *Constitution Act, 1982* extended the constitutional protection provided by the general amending procedure to the entire process by which Senators are "selected." The proposed consultative elections would produce lists of candidates, from which prime ministers would be expected to choose when making appointments to the Senate. The compilation of these lists through national or provincial and territorial elections and the Prime Minister's consideration of them prior to making recommendations to the Governor General would form part of the "method of selecting Senators." Consequently, the implementation of consultative elections falls within the scope of s. 42(1)(b) and is subject to the general amending procedure, without the provincial right to "opt out."

· · ·

(4) Conclusion on How Consultative Elections Can Be Achieved

[70] We conclude that introducing a process of consultative elections for the nomination of Senators would change our Constitution's architecture, by endowing Senators with a popular mandate which is inconsistent with the Senate's role as a complementary legislative chamber of sober second thought. This would constitute an amendment to the Constitution of Canada in relation to the method of selecting Senators. It thus attracts the general amending procedure, without the provincial right to "opt out": s. 42(1)(b), *Constitution Act, 1982*.

B. Senatorial Tenure

[71] It is not disputed that a change in the duration of senatorial terms would amend the Constitution of Canada, by requiring a modification to the text of s. 29 of the *Constitution Act, 1867.* Section 29(2) provides:

> (2) A Senator who is summoned to the Senate ... shall ... hold his place in the Senate until he attains the age of seventy-five years.

The question before us is which Part V procedure applies to amend this provision.

[72] The Attorney General of Canada argues that changes to senatorial tenure fall residually within the unilateral federal power of amendment in s. 44, since they are not expressly captured by the language of s. 42. He also contends that the imposition of the fixed terms contemplated in the Reference would constitute a minor change that does not engage the interests of the provinces, because those terms are equivalent in duration to the average length of the terms historically served by Senators.

[73] In essence, the Attorney General of Canada proposes a narrow textual approach to this issue. Section 44 of the *Constitution Act, 1982* provides: "Subject to sections 41 and 42, Parliament may exclusively make laws amending the Constitution of Canada in relation to ... the Senate ... ." Neither s. 41 nor s. 42 expressly applies to amendments in relation to senatorial tenure. It follows, in his view, that the proposed changes to senatorial tenure are captured by the otherwise unlimited power in s. 44 to make amendments in relation to the Senate.

[74] We agree that the language of s. 42 does not encompass changes to the duration of senatorial terms. However, it does not follow that all changes to the Senate that fall outside of s. 42 come within the scope of the unilateral federal amending procedure in s. 44: see Whyte, at pp. 102-3.

[75] We are unable to agree with the Attorney General of Canada's interpretation of the scope of s. 44. As discussed, the unilateral federal amendment procedure is limited. It is not a broad procedure that encompasses all constitutional changes to the Senate which are not expressly included within another procedure in Part V. The history, language, and structure of Part V indicate that s. 38, rather than s. 44, is the general procedure for constitutional amendment. Changes that engage the interests of the provinces in the Senate as an institution forming an integral part of the federal system can only be achieved under the general amending procedure. Section 44, as an exception to the general procedure, encompasses measures that maintain or change the Senate without altering its fundamental nature and role.

[76] When discussing the scope of the unilateral federal procedure in the federal government's 1980 proposal for an amending formula, the then–Minister of Justice Jean Chrétien made statements to the effect that it would allow Parliament to make constitutional amendments for the Senate's continued maintenance and proper functioning, such as, for example, a modification of the Senate's quorum

requirement at s. 35 of the *Constitution Act, 1867: Minutes of Proceedings and Evidence of the Special Joint Committee of the Senate and of the House of Commons on the Constitution of Canada*, No. 53, February 4, 1981, at p. 50. He made clear, however, that significant Senate reform which engages the interests of the provinces could only be achieved with their consent: *ibid.*, at pp. 67-68.

[77] In our view, this understanding of the unilateral federal procedure applies to Part V. The Senate is a core component of the Canadian federal structure of government. As such, changes that affect its fundamental nature and role engage the interests of the stakeholders in our constitutional design—i.e. the federal government and the provinces—and cannot be achieved by Parliament acting alone.

[78] The question is thus whether the imposition of fixed terms for Senators engages the interests of the provinces by changing the fundamental nature or role of the Senate. If so, the imposition of fixed terms can only be achieved under the general amending procedure. In our view, this question must be answered in the affirmative.

[79] As discussed above, the Senate's fundamental nature and role is that of a complementary legislative body of sober second thought. The current duration of senatorial terms is directly linked to this conception of the Senate. Senators are appointed roughly for the duration of their active professional lives. This security of tenure is intended to allow Senators to function with independence in conducting legislative review. This Court stated in the *Upper House Reference* that, "[a]t some point, a reduction of the term of office might impair the functioning of the Senate in providing what Sir John A. Macdonald described as 'the sober second thought in legislation'": p. 76. A significant change to senatorial tenure would thus affect the Senate's fundamental nature and role. It could only be achieved under the general amending procedure and falls outside the scope of the unilateral federal amending procedure.

• • •

VI. Senate Abolition: How Can It Be Achieved?

[95] Finally, the Reference asks which of two possible procedures applies to abolition of the Senate: the general amending procedure or the unanimous consent procedure?

[96] The Attorney General of Canada argues that the general amending procedure applies because abolition of the Senate falls under matters which Part V expressly says attract that procedure—amendments in relation to "the powers of the Senate" and "the number of members by which a province is entitled to be represented in the Senate" (s. 42(1)(b) and (c)). Abolition, it is argued, is simply a matter of "powers" and "members": it literally takes away all of the Senate's powers and all of its members. Alternatively, the Attorney General of Canada argues that since abolition of the Senate is not expressly mentioned anywhere in Part V, it falls residually under the general amending procedure.

[97] We cannot accept the Attorney General's arguments. Abolition of the Senate is not merely a matter of "powers" or "members" under s. 42(1)(b) and (c) of the *Constitution Act, 1982*. Rather, abolition of the Senate would fundamentally alter our constitutional architecture—by removing the bicameral form of government that gives shape to the *Constitution Act, 1867*—and would amend Part V, which requires the unanimous consent of Parliament and the provinces (s. 41(e), *Constitution Act, 1982*).

• • •

[102] To interpret s. 42 as embracing Senate abolition would depart from the ordinary meaning of its language and is not supported by the historical record. The mention of amendments in relation to the powers of the Senate and the number of Senators for each province presupposes the continuing existence of a Senate and makes no room for an indirect abolition of the Senate. Within the scope of s. 42, it is possible to make significant changes to the powers of the Senate and the number of Senators. But it is outside the scope of s. 42 to altogether strip the Senate of its powers and reduce the number of Senators to zero.

· · ·

VII. Conclusion

[111] The majority of the changes to the Senate which are contemplated in the Reference can only be achieved through amendments to the Constitution, with substantial federal–provincial consensus. The implementation of consultative elections and senatorial term limits requires consent of the Senate, the House of Commons, and the legislative assemblies of at least seven provinces representing, in the aggregate, half of the population of all the provinces: s. 38 and s. 42(1)(b), *Constitution Act, 1982*. ... As for Senate abolition, it requires the unanimous consent of the Senate, the House of Commons, and the legislative assemblies of all Canadian provinces: s. 41(e), *Constitution Act, 1982*.

In the future, formal senate reform will require consent of both the federal and most of the provincial legislatures, a political scenario that makes further progress on this matter very difficult. Since 2015, however, the Trudeau government has reshaped the Senate by appointing only "independent" senators, as opposed to senators who caucus with a political party in the Senate. As described on the relevant government website, prospective senators apply (or may be nominated) "through an open application process based on transparent, merit-based criteria and requirements under the Constitution." An independent advisory board for Senate appointments then assesses candidates and provides "non-binding, merit-based recommendations to the Prime Minister." The result is a Senate in which most members do not identify formally with the two traditional parties represented in the Senate—the Conservatives or the Liberals. Sitting as "independent" groupings, these senators are not "whipped" (that is, compelled or at least strongly encouraged) by political parties to support or oppose legislation. This change greatly affects (and complicates) the political (although not the legal) process by which legislation passes through the Senate, and opinion is divided among observers about how positive the move to "independent" senators has been.

The Senate is also controversial in the degree to which it fails to reflect the notion of representation by population. Section 22 of the *Constitution Act, 1867* partitions Canada into four "divisions," entitled to equal representation in the Senate. These divisions are Ontario, Quebec, the maritime provinces, and the western provinces. Each province within these last two divisions, as well as the Northwest Territories and the Yukon, is to be represented by a specified number of senators. Pursuant to the *Constitution Act, 1999 (Nunavut)* 46-47 Elizabeth II, 1997-98, c 15, one senator represents Nunavut. The resulting Senate representation by province, when contrasted to the population of each province, produces striking imbalances. For instance, Nova Scotia senators comprise 9.52 percent of the Senate, while by the end of the last decade, Nova Scotia had 2.58 percent of the Canadian population. This pattern recurs for all of the Atlantic provinces. In comparison, Ontario—with almost 39 percent of the population—had representation that amounts to just under 23 percent of the Senate. Alberta and British Columbia were also underrepresented by nearly 6 and 8 percent, respectively.

Correcting this problem would require an amendment to the *Constitution Act, 1867* that, under the applicable constitutional amendment formula, would require approval by the federal Parliament and at least seven provinces that collectively have at least 50 percent of the Canadian population.

III. HOUSE OF COMMONS

Unlike senators, members of the House of Commons are elected, a requirement anticipated by s 37 of the *Constitution Act, 1867*. Elections to the House of Commons are run according to a rich blend of constitutional and statutory law. Section 3 of the Charter says, for example, that "[e]very citizen of Canada has the right to vote in an election of members of the House of Commons or of a legislative assembly and to be qualified for membership therein." The precise manner in which members of Parliament are elected is governed by the *Canada Elections Act*, SC 2000, c 9, a very detailed statute designed to guarantee fair electoral contests.

Consider the following overview of elections of members of Parliament to the House of Commons.

Elections Canada, The Electoral System of Canada, 3rd ed
(Ottawa: Chief Electoral Officer of Canada, 2012)

Representation in the House of Commons is based on geographical divisions called electoral districts, also known as ridings. At the federal level, the number of electoral districts is established through rules (the "representation formula") set out in the *Constitution Act, 1867*. There are currently 308 electoral districts [this number rose to 338 for the 2015 federal election], each with a corresponding seat in the House of Commons. ...

Since 1964, independent commissions have been entrusted with adjusting electoral district boundaries based on population changes identified in every 10-year census. According to the *Electoral Boundaries Readjustment Act*, the commissions (one for each province) must also consider communities of interest or of identity, historical patterns and the geographic size of electoral districts. The process of readjusting the boundaries is commonly called redistribution.

The three-member electoral boundaries commissions are usually chaired by a judge, chosen by the chief justice of the province. The two other members are appointed by the Speaker of the House of Commons. Commissions are not required for Yukon, the Northwest Territories or Nunavut since each territory is a single electoral district.

Elections Canada provides the commissions with technical, administrative and financial support to help them carry out their responsibilities. Each commission publishes its proposal, holds hearings where members of the public and parliamentarians can provide their input, then issues a report to the House of Commons. If members of the House of Commons file objections to the report, the commission may opt to make adjustments. All final decisions about the new electoral boundaries are made by the commissions and published in the Canada Gazette as a representation order.

The redistribution process can take about two years to complete. The new boundaries and names are used at the first general election called at least seven months after the representation order is proclaimed.

In 2011, Parliament adopted the *Fair Representation Act*. On top of shortening the time frame for the redistribution process, its primary effect was to change the representation formula. Provinces that had become under-represented relative to their share of the population would gain seats in the 2013 redistribution. As a result, Ontario gained 15 seats, British Columbia and Alberta each received six more, while Quebec grew by three seats. The total number of electoral districts and corresponding seats [were] 338 for the general election ... in 2015.

Despite the *"Fair Representation Act"* of 2011, do not assume that there is absolute voter parity between the ridings from which MPs are elected. Not every Canadian's vote is "worth" the same amount and, generally speaking, a vote is worth more in the less densely populated rural ridings than in the crowded urban electoral districts. Is such unevenness in a voter's capacity to influence elections consistent with s 3 of the Charter? Consider the following case, which concerns provincial electoral districts in Saskatchewan.

Reference re Prov Electoral Boundaries (Sask)
[1991] 2 SCR 158

McLACHLIN J:

This appeal involves a constitutional challenge to provincial electoral distribution in the province of Saskatchewan. My conclusion is that the electoral boundaries created by *The Representation Act, 1989*, SS 1989-90, c. R-20.2, do not violate the right to vote enshrined in s. 3 of the *Canadian Charter of Rights and Freedoms*.

I reach this conclusion through consideration of a number of subsidiary issues:

    I   The Question to Be Answered

• • •

   III Defining the Right to Vote
   IV Is the Right to Vote Violated by the Saskatchewan Boundaries?
   V   Section l and Justification

I The Question to Be Answered

This case comes to us as an appeal from a reference to the Saskatchewan Court of Appeal (1991), 90 Sask. R 174. The reference requested that court's opinion on the following questions:

In respect of the constituencies defined in the *Representation Act, 1989*:

   (a) Does the variance in the size of voter populations among those constituencies, as contemplated by s. 20 of *The Electoral Boundaries Commission Act*, ... and recommended in the Saskatchewan *Electoral Boundaries Commission 1988 Final Report*, infringe or deny rights or freedoms guaranteed by the *Canadian Charter of Rights and Freedoms*? If so, in what particulars? Is any such limitation or denial of rights or freedoms justified by s. 1 of the *Canadian Charter of Rights and Freedoms*?

   (b) Does the distribution of those constituencies among urban, rural and northern areas, as contemplated by s. 14 of *The Electoral Boundaries Commission Act*, ... and recommended in the Saskatchewan *Electoral Boundaries Commission 1988 Final Report*, infringe or deny rights or freedoms guaranteed by the *Canadian Charter of Rights and Freedoms*? If so, in what particulars? Is any such limitation or denial of rights or freedoms justified by s. 1 of the *Canadian Charter of Rights and Freedoms*?

Different views have been expressed as to what issues these questions raise. The appellant asserts that what is at issue is the constitutional validity of *The Representation Act, 1989*. The respondent contends that the question is not whether the Act was unconstitutional, but whether the electoral boundaries created pursuant to the Act violate the Charter.

I am of the view that it is the boundaries themselves which are at issue on this appeal. The questions focus, not on the Act, but on the constitutionality of "the variance in the size of voter populations among [the] constituencies" and "the distribution of those constituencies among urban, rural and northern areas." In so far as *The Representation Act, 1989* defines the constituencies, the validity of that Act is indirectly called into question. And in so far as *The Electoral Boundaries Commission Act* provides the criteria by which the boundaries are to be fixed, that Act may affect the answers given to the questions posed. But the basic question put to this Court is whether the variances and distribution reflected in the constituencies themselves violate the Charter guarantee of the right to vote.

• • •

III Defining the Right to Vote

Section 3 of the *Canadian Charter of Rights and Freedoms* reads as follows:

> 3. Every citizen of Canada has the right to vote in an election of members of the House of Commons or of a legislative assembly and to be qualified for membership therein.

The question is simply stated: What is meant by "the right to vote" in s. 3? Before addressing this question it is necessary to address the way the Court should go about determining the content of the right.

A. General Principles Applicable to Defining the Right

The content of a *Charter* right is to be determined in a broad and purposive way, having regard to historical and social context. As Dickson J (as he then was) said in *R v. Big M Drug Mart Ltd.*, [1985] 1 SCR 295, at p. 344:

> In my view this analysis is to be undertaken, and the purpose of the right or freedom in question is to be sought by reference to the character and the larger objects of the *Charter* itself, to the language chosen to articulate the specific right or freedom, to the historical origins of the concepts enshrined, and where applicable, to the meaning and purpose of the other specific rights and freedoms with which it is associated within the text of the *Charter*. The interpretation should be, as the judgment in *Southam* emphasizes, a generous rather than a legalistic one, aimed at fulfilling the purpose of the guarantee and securing for individuals the full benefit of the *Charter*'s protection. At the same time it is important not to overshoot the actual purpose of the right or freedom in question, but to recall that the *Charter* was not enacted in a vacuum, and must therefore, as this Court's decision in *Law Society of Upper Canada v. Skapinker* ... illustrates, be placed in its proper linguistic, philosophic and historical contexts.

From this general statement of principle I turn to more particular considerations which bear relevance to this appeal.

The first of these is the doctrine that the *Charter* is engrafted onto the living tree that is the Canadian constitution ... . Thus, to borrow the words of Lord Sankey in *Edwards v. Attorney-General for Canada*, ... it must be viewed as "a living tree capable of growth and expansion within its natural limits."

The doctrine of the constitution as a living tree mandates that narrow technical approaches are to be eschewed ... . It also suggests that the past plays a critical but non-exclusive role in determining the content of the rights and freedoms granted by the *Charter*. The tree is rooted in past and present institutions, but must be capable of growth to meet the future. As Dickson J stated in *R v. Big M Drug Mart Ltd.* ... :

> ... the *Charter* is intended to set a standard upon which *present as well as future* legislation is to be tested. Therefore the meaning of the concept of freedom of conscience and religion is not to be determined solely by the degree to which that right was enjoyed by Canadians prior to the proclamation of the *Charter*. [Emphasis in original.]

This admonition is as apt in defining the right to vote as it is in defining freedom of religion. The right to vote, while rooted in and hence to some extent defined by historical and existing practices, cannot be viewed as frozen by particular historical anomalies. What must be sought is the broader philosophy underlying the historical development of the right to vote—a philosophy which is capable of explaining the past and animating the future.

This appeal also engages the general principle that practical considerations must be borne in mind in constitutional interpretation ... . Courts must be sensitive to what Frankfurter J (*McGowan v. Maryland*, 366 US 420 (1961)) calls "the practical living facts" to which a legislature must respond ... . This is nowhere more true than in considering the right to vote, where practical considerations such as social and physical geography may impact on the value of the citizen's right to vote.

Of final and critical importance to this appeal is the canon that in interpreting the individual rights conferred by the *Charter* the Court must be guided by the ideal of a "free and democratic society" upon which the *Charter* is founded. As Dickson CJ stated in *R v. Oakes* ... :

> The Court must be guided by the values and principles essential to a free and democratic society which I believe embody, to name but a few, respect for the inherent dignity of the human person, commitment to social justice and equality, accommodation of a wide variety of beliefs, respect for cultural and group identity, and faith in social and political institutions which enhance the participation of individuals and groups in society.

The first task on an appeal such as this is to define the scope of the right to vote under s. 3 of the *Charter*. The second is to evaluate the existing electoral boundaries in the light of that definition to determine if they violate s. 3 of the *Charter*. If a violation is found, a third task arises—determining whether the limitation on the right is "demonstrably justified in a free and democratic society" and hence saved under s. 1 of the *Charter*. The general principles to which I have referred, while bearing particularly on the task of defining the ambit of the right, also animate the second and third steps of the analysis.

B. The Focus of the Debate

The question for resolution on this appeal can be summed up in one sentence: to what extent, if at all, does the right to vote enshrined in the *Charter* permit deviation from the "one person–one vote" rule? The answer to this question turns on what one sees as the purpose of s. 3. Those who start from the premise that the purpose of the section is to guarantee equality of voting power support the view that only minimal deviation from that ideal is possible. Those who start from the premise that the purpose of s. 3 is to guarantee effective representation see the right to vote as comprising many factors, of which equality is but one. The contest, as I see it, is most fundamentally between these two views, although the submissions before us vary in the emphasis they place on different factors and hence on where they would draw the line.

The Saskatchewan Court of Appeal, as I read its reasons, fell into the camp of those who see the purpose of s. 3 as guaranteeing equality of voting power *per se*. It suggested that the only deviation permissible from the ideal of equality under s. 3 is that required by the practical problems of ensuring that the number of voters in each constituency is mathematically equal on the day of voting .... On the basis of this definition, it found that the electoral boundaries in Saskatchewan violated s. 3 of the *Charter*. Other considerations, such as geography, historical boundaries and community interests, fell to be considered under s. 1. The court found that the boundaries were not justified under s. 1, except for the two northern ridings where population is extremely sparse.

In this Court, the respondent, supporting the judgment of the Court of Appeal, urged that the goal of s. 3 is equality of voting power, as nearly as may possibly be achieved. The appellant, while not going so far as to deny the importance of equality in a meaningful right to vote, urged that equality was but one of many factors relevant to the right to vote enshrined in s. 3 and that the fundamental purpose of s. 3 was not to ensure equality of voting power, but effective and fair representation conducive to good government. The interveners tended to ally themselves with one of these two positions, stressing their own particular perspectives. For example, Equal Justice for All urged no deviation from equality, except as might be justified in aid of disadvantaged groups, while the Attorney General for Alberta went so far as to deny equality's place as a "core" or "fundamental" value in assessing the right to vote.

C. The Meaning of the Right to Vote

It is my conclusion that the purpose of the right to vote enshrined in s. 3 of the *Charter* is not equality of voting power *per se*, but the right to "effective representation." Ours is a representative democracy. Each citizen is entitled to be *represented* in government. Representation comprehends the idea of having a voice in the deliberations of government as well as the idea of the right to bring one's grievances and concerns to the attention of one's government representative; as noted in *Dixon v. B.C. (A.G.)*, [1989] 4 WWR 393, at p. 413, elected representatives function in two roles—legislative and what has been termed the "ombudsman role."

What are the conditions of effective representation? The first is relative parity of voting power. A system which dilutes one citizen's vote unduly as compared with another citizen's vote runs the risk of providing inadequate representation to the citizen whose vote is diluted. The legislative power of the citizen whose vote is diluted will be reduced, as may be access to and assistance from his or her representative. The result will be uneven and unfair representation.

But parity of voting power, though of prime importance, is not the only factor to be taken into account in ensuring effective representation. Sir John A. Macdonald in introducing the *Act to re-adjust the Representation in the House of Commons*, SC 1872, c. 13, recognized this fundamental fact (House of Commons Debates, Vol. III, 4th Sess., p. 926 (June 1, 1872)):

> ... it will be found that, ... while the principle of population was considered to a very great extent, other considerations were also held to have weight; so that different interests, classes and localities should be fairly represented, that the principle of numbers should not be the only one.

Notwithstanding the fact that the value of a citizen's vote should not be unduly diluted, it is a practical fact that effective representation often cannot be achieved without taking into account countervailing factors.

First, absolute parity is impossible. It is impossible to draw boundary lines which guarantee exactly the same number of voters in each district. Voters die, voters move. Even with the aid of frequent censuses, voter parity is impossible.

Secondly, such relative parity as may be possible of achievement may prove undesirable because it has the effect of detracting from the primary goal of effective representation. Factors like geography, community history, community interests and minority representation may need to be taken into account to ensure that our legislative assemblies effectively represent the diversity of our social mosaic. These are but examples of considerations which may justify departure from absolute voter parity in the pursuit of more effective representation; the list is not closed.

It emerges therefore that deviations from absolute voter parity may be justified on the grounds of practical impossibility or the provision of more effective representation. Beyond this, dilution of one citizen's vote as compared with another's should not be countenanced. I adhere to the proposition asserted in *Dixon, supra*, at p. 414, that "only those deviations should be admitted which can be justified on the ground that they contribute to better government of the populace as a whole, giving due weight to regional issues within the populace and geographic factors within the territory governed."

This view of the meaning of the right to vote in s. 3 of the *Charter* conforms with the general principles of interpretation discussed at the outset.

The first and most important rule is that the right must be interpreted in accordance with its purpose. As will be seen, there is little in the history or philosophy of Canadian democracy that suggests that the framers of the *Charter* in enacting s. 3 had as their ultimate goal the attainment of voter parity. That purpose would have represented a rejection of the existing system of electoral representation in this country. The circumstances leading to the adoption of the *Charter* negate any intention to reject existing democratic institutions. As noted in *Dixon, supra*, at p. 412: "There is no record of such fundamental institutional reform having been mentioned at the conferences that preceded the adoption of the [proposed] *Charter.*" Nor was the issue raised by any of the plethora of interest groups making submissions in respect of voting rights during the prolonged Joint Senate and House of Commons Committee Hearings on the proposed *Charter*. The framers of the *Charter* had two distinct electoral models before them—the "one person–one vote" model espoused by the United States Supreme Court ..., and the less radical, more pragmatic approach which had developed in England and in this country through the centuries and which was actually in place. In the absence of any supportive evidence to the contrary (as may be found in the United States in the speeches of the founding fathers), it would be wrong to infer that in enshrining the right to vote in our written constitution the intention was to adopt the American model. On the contrary, we should assume that the goal was to recognize the right affirmed in this country since the time of our first Prime Minister, Sir John A. Macdonald, to effective representation in a system which gives due weight to voter parity but admits other considerations where necessary.

I turn next to the history of our right to vote. As already noted, the history of our right to vote and the context in which it existed at the time the *Charter* was adopted support the conclusion that the purpose of the guarantee of the right to vote is not to effect perfect voter equality, in so far as that can be done, but the broader goal of guaranteeing effective representation. As I noted in *Dixon, supra*, at p. 409, democracy in Canada is rooted in a different history than in the United States:

Its origins lie not in the debates of the founding fathers, but in the less absolute recesses of the British tradition. Our forefathers did not rebel against the English tradition of democratic government as did the Americans; on the contrary, they embraced it and changed it to suit their own perceptions and needs.

I went on to describe the Canadian tradition as one of evolutionary democracy moving in uneven steps toward the goal of universal suffrage and more effective representation, which even in its advanced stages tolerates deviation from voter parity in the interests of better representation:

What is that tradition? It was a tradition of evolutionary democracy, of increasing widening of representation through the centuries. But it was also a tradition which, even in its more modern phases, accommodates significant deviation from the ideals of equal representation. Pragmatism, rather than conformity to a philosophical ideal, has been its watchword.

Other Commonwealth countries have affirmed the same tradition. Thus the Australian High Court rejected a "one person – one vote" approach in favour of an approach which permitted consideration of countervailing factors: *Attorney-General (Aus.); Ex rel. McKinlay v. Commonwealth* (1975), 135 CLR 1. Stephen J wrote, at p. 57:

It is, then, quite apparent that representative democracy is descriptive of a whole spectrum of political institutions, each differing in countless respects yet answering to that generic description ... .

To contend that the presence of what is described as "as near as practicable equality of numbers" within electoral divisions is essential to representative democracy, to a legislature "chosen by the people," is to deny proper meaning to language and to ignore long chapters in the evolution of democratic institutions both in this country and overseas, in which, representative democracy having been attained, its details have undergone frequent changes in response to community pressures but have failed to possess this feature of equality of numbers on which the plaintiffs now insist.

To return to the metaphor of the living tree, our system is rooted in the tradition of effective representation and not in the tradition of absolute or near absolute voter parity. It is this tradition that defines the general ambit of the right to vote. This is not to suggest, however, that inequities in our voting system are to be accepted merely because they have historical precedent. History is important in so far as it suggests that the philosophy underlying the development of the right to vote in this country is the broad goal of effective representation. It has nothing to do with the specious argument that historical anomalies and abuses can be used to justify continued anomalies and abuses, or to suggest that the right to vote should not be interpreted broadly and remedially as befits *Charter* rights. Departures from the Canadian ideal of effective representation may exist. Where they do, they will be found to violate s. 3 of the *Charter*.

I turn finally to the admonition that courts must be sensitive to practical considerations in interpreting *Charter* rights. The "practical living fact," to borrow Frankfurter J's phrase, is that effective representation and good government in this country compel those charged with setting electoral boundaries sometimes to take into account factors other than voter parity, such as geography and community interests. The problems of representing vast, sparsely populated territories, for example, may dictate somewhat lower voter populations in these districts; to insist on voter parity might deprive citizens with distinct interests of an effective voice in the legislative process as well as of effective assistance from their representatives in their "ombudsman" role.

This is only one of a number of factors which may necessitate deviation from the "one person–one vote" rule in the interests of effective representation.

In the final analysis, the values and principles animating a free and democratic society are arguably best served by a definition that places effective representation at the heart of the right to vote. The concerns which Dickson CJ in *Oakes* associated with a free and democratic society—respect for the inherent dignity of the human person, commitment to social justice and equality, respect for cultural and group identity, and faith in social and political institutions which enhance the participation of individuals in society—are better met by an electoral system that focuses on effective representation than by one that focuses on mathematical parity. Respect for individual dignity and social equality mandate that citizen's votes not be unduly debased or diluted. But the need to recognize cultural and group identity and to enhance the participation of individuals in the electoral process and society requires that other concerns also be accommodated.

In summary, I am satisfied that the precepts which govern the interpretation of *Charter* rights support the conclusion that the right to vote should be defined as guaranteeing the right to effective representation. The concept of absolute voter parity does not accord with the development of the right to vote in the Canadian context and does not permit of sufficient flexibility to meet the practical difficulties inherent in representative government in a country such as Canada. In the end, it is the broader concept of effective representation which best serves the interests of a free and democratic society.

IV Do the Saskatchewan Boundaries Violate the Right to Vote?

• • •

I turn then to the contention that the distribution of seats itself violates s. 3 of the *Charter*. As already noted, variances between southern seats fall within plus or minus 25 percent of the provincial quotient. Moreover, the distribution between urban and rural seats closely approximates the actual split between urban and rural population. It remains, however, to consider whether unjustifiable deviations exist with respect to particular ridings in the southern half of the province.

Before examining the electoral boundaries to determine if they are justified, it may be useful to mention some of the factors other than equality of voting power which figure in the analysis. One of the most important is the fact that it is more difficult to represent rural ridings than urban. The material before us suggests that not only are rural ridings harder to serve because of difficulty in transport and communications, but that rural voters make greater demands on their elected representatives, whether because of the absence of alternative resources to be found in urban centres or for other reasons. Thus the goal of effective representation may justify somewhat lower voter populations in rural areas. Another factor which figured prominently in the argument before us is geographic boundaries; rivers and municipal boundaries form natural community dividing lines and hence natural electoral boundaries. Yet another factor is growth projections. Given that the boundaries will govern for a number of years—the boundaries set in 1989, for example, may be in place until 1996 projected population changes within that period may justify a deviation from strict equality at the time the boundaries are drawn.

Against this background, I turn to the boundaries themselves.

• • •

In summary, the evidence supplied by the province is sufficient to justify the existing electoral boundaries. In general, the discrepancies between urban and rural ridings is small, no more than one might expect given the greater difficulties associated with representing rural ridings. And discrepancies between particular ridings appear to be justified on the basis of factors such as geography, community interests and population growth patterns. It was not seriously suggested that the northern boundaries are inappropriate, given the sparse population and the difficulty of communication in the area. I conclude that a violation of s. 3 of the *Charter* has not been established.

In these circumstances, it is unnecessary to consider s. 1.

V Conclusion

I would allow the appeal and answer both Reference Questions in the negative.

As every observer of Canadian politics knows, elections are contested by political parties. A political party is a defined entity in s 2 of the *Canada Elections Act*: a political party is "an organization one of whose fundamental purposes is to participate in public affairs by endorsing one or more of its members as candidates and supporting their election." Consider the following discussion of political parties by Canada's election administrator.

Elections Canada, The Electoral System of Canada, 3rd ed
(Ottawa: Chief Electoral Officer of Canada, 2012)

First Past the Post

How Are Candidates Elected to Parliament?

Canada's electoral system is referred to as a "single-member plurality" system (also commonly called a "first-past-the-post" system). In every electoral district, the candidate with the highest number of votes wins a seat in the House of Commons and represents that electoral district as its member of Parliament. An absolute majority (more than 50 percent of the votes in the electoral district) is not required for a candidate to be elected.

Any number of candidates can run for election in an electoral district, but a candidate can run in only one riding, either independently or under the banner of a registered political party. Similarly, each party can endorse only one candidate in an electoral district. ...

Candidates who are endorsed by a registered political party can have the name of that party appear under their name on the ballot. Those who run for election without a party affiliation can choose to have either "Independent" or no affiliation appear under their name on the ballot. In the most recent election, less than four percent of candidates ran without a party affiliation.

The *Canada Elections Act* defines a political party as an organization that has as one of its fundamental purposes participating in public affairs by endorsing one or more of its members as candidates and supporting their election to the House of Commons. Political parties that meet this definition can register with the Chief Electoral Officer to gain official status and become eligible to obtain certain monetary and other benefits under the Act. The financial benefits of registration are outlined in the chapter on political financing. There are non-financial advantages as well—for example, political parties that successfully apply for registration at least 60 days before the issue of the election writs can have their name appear on the ballot under the names of the candidates they endorse.

Until the early 2000s, the *Canada Elections Act* required a registered party to run candidates in at least 50 electoral districts. The Supreme Court struck down this rule in 2003 in *Figueroa v Canada (AG)*, below. Consider the reasoning applied by the Court and its vision of electoral democracy, and the role of political parties in it.

Figueroa v Canada (AG)
2003 SCC 37, [2003] 1 SCR 912

IACOBUCCI J (McLachlin CJ and Major, Bastarache, Binnie, and Arbour JJ concurring):

I. Introduction

[1] This appeal raises fundamental questions in respect of the democratic process in our country. More specifically, this appeal focuses on the purpose and meaning to be given to s. 3 of the *Canadian Charter of Rights and Freedoms*, which confers on each citizen the right to vote in the election of members of the House of Commons and the provincial legislative assemblies and to be qualified for membership therein. The issue is whether federal legislation that restricts access to certain benefits to political parties that have nominated candidates in at least 50 electoral districts violates s. 3. I conclude that it does and would therefore allow the appeal.

• • •

IV. Issues

[16] The question to be determined in this appeal is whether ss. 24(2), 24(3) and 28(2) of the *Elections Act* infringe s. 3 of the *Charter* by withholding from candidates nominated by political parties that have failed to satisfy the 50-candidate threshold the right to issue tax receipts for donations received outside the election period, the right to transfer unspent election funds to the party, and the right to list their party affiliation on the ballot papers—and, if so, whether that infringement is reasonable and demonstrably justified under s. 1 of the *Charter*.

• • •

V. Analysis

A. Does the 50-Candidate Threshold Violate Section 3 of the Charter?

[18] The first question to be determined in this appeal is whether the restriction on the right of candidates to issue tax receipts for donations received outside the election period, to transfer unspent election funds to the party, and to list their party affiliation on the ballot papers infringes s. 3 of the *Charter*. This requires the Court to perform two tasks. The first is to define the purpose of s. 3 of the *Charter*. The second is to evaluate the 50-candidate threshold in light of that definition in order to determine whether it violates s. 3 of the *Charter*.

(1) Section 3 of the Charter

[19] Under s. 3 of the *Charter*, "[e]very citizen of Canada has the right to vote in an election of members of the House of Commons or of a legislative assembly and

to be qualified for membership therein." On its face, the scope of s. 3 is relatively narrow: it grants to each citizen no more than the bare right to vote and to run for office in the election of representatives of the federal and provincial legislative assemblies. But *Charter* analysis requires courts to look beyond the words of the section. In the words of McLachlin CJBCSC (as she then was), "[m]ore is intended [in the right to vote] than the bare right to place a ballot in a box": *Dixon v. British Columbia (AG)*, [1989] 4 WWR 393, at p. 403.

[20] In order to determine the scope of s. 3, the Court must first ascertain its purpose. ... In interpreting the scope of a *Charter* right, courts must adopt a broad and purposive approach that seeks to ensure that duly enacted legislation is in harmony with the purposes of the *Charter*.

[21] This Court first considered the purpose of s. 3 in *Reference re Provincial Electoral Boundaries (Sask.)*, [1991] 2 SCR 158 ("*Saskatchewan Reference*"). In determining that s. 3 does not require absolute equality of voting power, McLachlin J held that the purpose of s. 3 is "effective representation" (p. 183). This Court has subsequently confirmed, on numerous occasions, that the purpose of s. 3 is effective representation. ...

• • •

[25] But the right to effective representation contemplates more than the right to an effective representative in Parliament or a legislative assembly. ... [T]he purpose of s. 3 includes not only the right of each citizen to have and to vote for an elected representative in Parliament or a legislative assembly, but also to the right of each citizen to play a meaningful role in the electoral process. This, in my view, is a more complete statement of the purpose of s. 3 of the *Charter*.

[26] Support for the proposition that s. 3 should be understood with reference to the right of each citizen to play a meaningful role in the electoral process, rather than the election of a particular form of government, is found in the fact that the rights of s. 3 are participatory in nature. Section 3 does not advert to the composition of Parliament subsequent to an election, but only to the right of each citizen to a certain level of participation in the electoral process. On its very face, then, the central focus of s. 3 is the right of each citizen to participate in the electoral process. This signifies that the right of each citizen to participate in the political life of the country is one that is of fundamental importance in a free and democratic society and suggests that s. 3 should be interpreted in a manner that ensures that this right of participation embraces a content commensurate with the importance of individual participation in the selection of elected representatives in a free and democratic state. Defining the purpose of s. 3 with reference to the right of each citizen to play a meaningful role in the electoral process, rather than the composition of Parliament subsequent to an election, better ensures that the right of participation that s. 3 explicitly protects is not construed too narrowly.

• • •

[28] As this Court frequently has acknowledged, the free flow of diverse opinions and ideas is of fundamental importance in a free and democratic society. ... Put simply, full political debate ensures that ours is an open society with the benefit of a broad range of ideas and opinions. ... This, in turn, ensures not only that policy makers are aware of a broad range of options, but also that the determination of social policy is sensitive to the needs and interests of a broad range of citizens.

[29] It thus follows that participation in the electoral process has an intrinsic value independent of its impact upon the actual outcome of elections. To be certain, the electoral process is the means by which elected representatives are selected and governments formed, but it is also the primary means by which the average citizen

participates in the open debate that animates the determination of social policy. The right to run for office provides each citizen with the opportunity to present certain ideas and opinions to the electorate as a viable policy option; the right to vote provides each citizen with the opportunity to express support for the ideas and opinions that a particular candidate endorses. In each instance, the democratic rights entrenched in s. 3 ensure that each citizen has an opportunity to express an opinion about the formation of social policy and the functioning of public institutions through participation in the electoral process.

[30] ... Democracy, of course, is a form of government in which sovereign power resides in the people as a whole. In our system of democracy, this means that each citizen must have a genuine opportunity to take part in the governance of the country through participation in the selection of elected representatives. The fundamental purpose of s. 3, in my view, is to promote and protect the right of each citizen to play a meaningful role in the political life of the country. Absent such a right, ours would not be a true democracy.

• • •

(2) Does the 50-Candidate Threshold Violate Section 3?

[38] Consequently, the essential question to be determined is whether the 50-candidate threshold interferes with the capacity of individual citizens to play a meaningful role in the electoral process. In order to answer this question, the Court must answer two prior questions. First, do the members and supporters of political parties that nominate fewer than 50 candidates play a meaningful role in the electoral process? And if so, does the restriction on the right to issue tax receipts for donations received outside the election period, to transfer unspent election funds to the party and to list their party affiliation on the ballot papers interfere with the capacity of the members and supporters of political parties that nominate fewer than 50 candidates to play a meaningful role in the electoral process?

(a) The Role of Political Parties That Nominate Candidates in Fewer Than 50 Electoral Districts

[39] ... It is my conclusion that the ability of a political party to make a valuable contribution to the electoral process is not dependent upon its capacity to offer the electorate a genuine "government option." Rather, political parties enhance the meaningfulness of individual participation in the electoral process for reasons that transcend their capacity (or lack thereof) to participate in the governance of the country subsequent to an election. Irrespective of their capacity to influence the outcome of an election, political parties act as both a vehicle and outlet for the meaningful participation of individual citizens in the electoral process.

[40] With respect to the ability of a political party to act as an effective vehicle for the meaningful participation of individual citizens in the electoral process, it is important to note that political parties have a much greater capacity than any one citizen to participate in the open debate that the electoral process engenders. By doing so in a representative capacity, on behalf of their members and supporters, political parties act as a vehicle for the participation of individual citizens in the political life of the country. Political parties ensure that the ideas and opinions of their members and supporters are effectively represented in the open debate occasioned by the electoral process and presented to the electorate as a viable option. If those ideas and opinions are not subsequently adopted by the government of the day, it is not because they have not been considered, but, rather, because they have received insufficient public support.

[41] Importantly, it is not only large political parties that are able to fulfil this function. It likely is true that a large party will be able to play a larger role in the open discourse of the electoral process, but it does not thereby follow that the capacity of a political party to represent the ideas and opinions of its members and supporters in the electoral process is dependent upon its capacity to offer the electorate a "government option." Large or small, all political parties are capable of introducing unique interests and concerns into the political discourse. Consequently, all political parties, whether large or small, are capable of acting as a vehicle for the participation of individual citizens in the public discourse that animates the determination of social policy.

[42] For example, marginal or regional parties tend to dissent from mainstream thinking and to bring to the attention of the general public issues and concerns that have not been adopted by national parties. They might exert less influence than the national parties, but still can be a most effective vehicle for the participation of individual citizens whose preferences have not been incorporated into the political platforms of national parties. It is better that an individual citizen have his or her ideas and concerns introduced into the open debate of the electoral process by a political party with a limited geographical base of support than not to have his or her ideas and concerns introduced into that debate by any political party at all.

[43] In respect of their ability to act as an effective outlet for the meaningful participation of individual citizens in the electoral process, the participation of political parties in the electoral process also provides individuals with the opportunity to express an opinion on governmental policy and the proper functioning of public institutions. A vote for a candidate nominated by a particular party is an expression of support for the platform or policy perspectives that the party endorses. The participation of political parties thereby enhances the capacity of individual citizens to express an opinion as to the type of country that they would like Canada to be through the exercise of the right to vote.

[44] Once again, the capacity of a political party to provide individual citizens with an opportunity to express an opinion on governmental policy and the proper functioning of public institutions is not dependent upon its capacity to participate in the governance of the country subsequent to an election. As the preceding paragraph suggests, participation as a voter is not only about the selection of elected representatives. Irrespective of its effect on the outcome of an election, a vote for a particular candidate is an expression of support for a particular approach or platform. Whether that vote contributes to the election of a candidate or not, each vote in support of that approach or platform increases the likelihood that the issues and concerns underlying that platform will be taken into account by those who ultimately implement policy, if not now then perhaps at some point in the future.

[45] As a consequence, there is no reason to think that political parties that have not satisfied the 50-candidate threshold do not act as an effective outlet for the meaningful participation of individual citizens in the electoral process. There is no correlation between the capacity of a political party to offer the electorate a government option and the capacity of a political party to formulate a unique policy platform for presentation to the general public. In each election, a significant number of citizens vote for candidates nominated by registered parties in full awareness that the candidate has no realistic chance of winning a seat in Parliament—or that the party of which she or he is a member has no realistic chance of winning a majority of seats in the House of Commons. Just as these votes are not "wasted votes," votes for a political party that has not satisfied the 50-candidate threshold are not wasted votes either. As a public expression of individual support for certain perspectives and opinions, such votes are an integral component of a vital and dynamic democracy.

[46] It is thus my conclusion that the members and supporters of political parties that nominate candidates in fewer than 50 electoral districts do play a meaningful role in the electoral process. They are both a vehicle for the participation of individual citizens in the open debate occasioned by the electoral process and an outlet for the expression of support for political platforms that are different from those adopted by political parties with a broad base of support. The question that thus arises is whether the 50-candidate threshold interferes with the right of such citizens to play a meaningful role in the electoral process.

(b) The Impact of the 50-Candidate Threshold

[47] As outlined earlier, the effect of the 50-candidate threshold is to extend the benefits of registration only to those parties that have nominated candidates in 50 electoral districts. At issue in this appeal are the rights of candidates to issue tax receipts for donations received outside the election period, to transfer unspent election funds to the party and to include their party affiliation on the ballot papers. The question to be determined is whether withholding these benefits from candidates of parties who have not met the 50-candidate threshold undermines the right of each citizen to meaningful participation in the electoral process. In each instance, it is my opinion that the threshold does, in fact, have this effect.

• • •

[58] For these reasons, I conclude that the 50-candidate threshold does infringe s. 3 of the *Charter*. It undermines both the capacity of individual citizens to influence policy by introducing ideas and opinions into the public discourse and debate through participation in the electoral process, and the capacity of individual citizens to exercise their right to vote in a manner that accurately reflects their preferences. In each instance, the threshold requirement is inconsistent with the purpose of s. 3 of the *Charter*: the preservation of the right of each citizen to play a meaningful role in the electoral process.

B. Is the Infringement Saved by Section 1 of the Charter?

[59] In order to justify the infringement of a *Charter* right under s. 1, the government must demonstrate that the limitation is reasonable and demonstrably justifiable in a free and democratic society. This involves a two-step analysis, pursuant to *Oakes* ... and related cases. ... Throughout this process the burden rests on the government. The government first must demonstrate that the objective of the legislation is sufficiently pressing and substantial to warrant violating a *Charter* right. The objectives must be neither "trivial" nor "discordant with the principles integral to a free and democratic society." ... Once this has been established, the government must then demonstrate that the infringement is proportionate, namely, that the legislation is rationally connected to the objective, that it minimally impairs the *Charter* right in question, and that the salutary benefits of the legislation outweigh the deleterious effects.

• • •

[61] In his factum, the Attorney General of Canada submits that the objective of the 50-candidate threshold is "to enhance the effectiveness of Canadian elections, in both their process *and* outcome" (emphasis in original). More specifically, the Attorney General submits that the 50-candidate threshold advances three separate goals: (i) to improve the effectiveness of the electoral process; (ii) to protect the

integrity of the electoral financing regime; and (iii) to ensure that the process is able to deliver a viable outcome for our form of responsible government. To provide a more complete analysis of the federal government's arguments under s. 1, I deal with each objective advanced separately. Consequently, in the analysis below, I consider each of the proposed objectives in turn to determine first whether the government has demonstrated that any of the specific objectives is of pressing and substantial importance and, second, that the violation of s. 3 is proportionate.

[The majority concluded that the 50-candidate minimum was not saved by s 1. As summarized in the official headnote:

> While the objective of ensuring the cost-efficiency of the tax credit scheme is pressing and substantial, the 50-candidate threshold does not meet the proportionality branch of the *Oakes* test. There is no connection whatsoever between the objective and the threshold requirement with respect to transfers of unspent election funds or listing party affiliations on ballot papers. Nor is the restriction on the right of political parties to issue tax receipts for donations received outside the election period rationally connected to the objective. The connection between legislation that has no impact upon either the number of citizens allowed to claim the tax credit or the size of the credit and the objective is tenuous at best. Moreover, the government has provided no evidence that the threshold actually improves the cost-efficiency of the tax credit scheme. The legislation also fails the minimal impairment test because cost savings can be achieved without violating s. 3. Further, any benefits associated with the reduced costs of the tax credit scheme do not outweigh the deleterious effects of this legislation.

> While preserving the integrity of the electoral process is a pressing and substantial concern in a free and democratic state, this objective provides no justification for the restriction on the right of candidates to list their party affiliation on the ballot papers. The same is true of the restriction on the right to issue tax credits and the right to transfer unspent election funds to the party. Furthermore, even if the restrictions on the right to issue the tax credit and the right to retain unspent election funds prevent the misuse of the electoral financing regime, the legislation fails the minimal impairment test. In each instance, the government has failed to demonstrate that it could not achieve the same results without violating s. 3 of the *Charter*.

> Lastly, articulating the objective as ensuring a viable outcome for responsible government in the form of majority governments is problematic. In any event, the 50-candidate threshold fails the rational connection test and its salutary benefits have not been shown to outweigh its deleterious effects.]

• • •

[90] In the final analysis, I conclude both that the 50-candidate threshold is inconsistent with the right of each citizen to play a meaningful role in the electoral process, and that the government has failed to justify this violation.

In recent years, substantial public attention in Canada has focused on fair elections, and especially controversy over practices that may distort electoral outcomes. Consider the following decision from the Supreme Court of Canada in a case in which an election result was contested for irregularities. Note how the Court's majority uses principles of statutory interpretation in trying to understand the scope of the *Canada Elections Act*. Statutory interpretation is a subject dealt with in detail on Chapter 10.

Opitz v Wrzesnewskyj
2012 SCC 55, [2012] 3 SCR 76

ROTHSTEIN and MOLDAVER JJ (Deschamps and Abella JJ concurring):

I. Introduction

[1] A candidate who lost in a close federal election attempts to set aside the result of that election. We are asked to disqualify the votes of several Canadian citizens based on administrative mistakes, notwithstanding evidence that those citizens were in fact entitled to vote. We decline the invitation to do so. The *Canadian Charter of Rights and Freedoms* and the *Canada Elections Act*, S.C. 2000, c. 9 ("Act"), have the clear and historic purposes of enfranchising Canadian citizens, such that they may express their democratic preference, and of protecting the integrity of our electoral process. Following these objectives and the wording of the Act, we reject the candidate's attempt to disenfranchise entitled voters and so undermine public confidence in the electoral process.

[2] At issue in this appeal are the principles to be applied when a federal election is challenged on the basis of "irregularities." We are dealing here with a challenge based on administrative errors. There is no allegation of any fraud, corruption or illegal practices. Nor is there any suggestion of wrongdoing by any candidate or political party. Given the complexity of administering a federal election, the tens of thousands of election workers involved, many of whom have no on-the-job experience, and the short time frame for hiring and training them, it is inevitable that administrative mistakes will be made. If elections can be easily annulled on the basis of administrative errors, public confidence in the finality and legitimacy of election results will be eroded. Only irregularities that affect the result of the election and thereby undermine the integrity of the electoral process are grounds for overturning an election.

[3] The 41st Canadian federal election took place on May 2, 2011. In the electoral district (or "riding") of Etobicoke Centre, 52,794 votes were cast. After a judicial recount, Ted Opitz was the successful candidate with a plurality of 26 votes. Borys Wrzesnewskyj was the runner-up.

[4] Mr. Wrzesnewskyj applied under s. 524(1)(b) of the Act, to have the election annulled, on the basis that there were "irregularities ... that affected the result of the election." ...

• • •

III. Analysis

A. The Canada Elections Act

[10] The right of every citizen to vote, guaranteed by s. 3 of the Charter, lies at the heart of Canadian democracy. The franchise has gradually broadened in Canada over the course of history from male property owners 21 years of age and older to the present universal suffrage of citizens aged 18 and over. Universal suffrage is reflected in s. 3 of the Act, which provides that a person is "qualified" to vote if he or she is a Canadian citizen and is 18 years of age or older.

[11] Canada is divided into "electoral districts" (commonly known as "ridings"): Charter, s. 3, and *Constitution Act, 1867*, ss. 40, 51 and 51A. Etobicoke Centre is an electoral district. Section 6 of the Act requires that a qualified elector be ordinarily resident in one of the polling divisions within the electoral district. Persons who are

qualified as electors are entitled to vote for a member of Parliament for the electoral district in which the elector is ordinarily resident.

[12] The [*Canada Elections Act*] also sets out detailed procedures for voting that turn the constitutional right of citizens to vote into a reality on election day. What follows is a brief description of the procedural provisions that give rise to the issues in this appeal.

[13] Electoral districts in Canada are subdivided into polling divisions, each of which contains at least 250 electors (s. 538 of the Act). For each polling division, a returning officer establishes one or more polling stations (s. 120(1)). Each polling division considered in this judgment had only one polling station. Each station is overseen by a deputy returning officer ("DRO") and a poll clerk (s. 32). Sometimes several polling divisions may have polling stations in the same building, at separate tables. Certain polling divisions cover only residents of two or more institutions, often senior citizens' residences. In such cases, the returning officer can establish "mobile" polling stations to be located in each of the institutions (ss. 125 and 538(5)). The Chief Electoral Officer ("CEO") is required to maintain a national register of electors ("NROE") containing the name, sex, date of birth and address of electors (s. 44). Between elections, the CEO updates the NROE using data from various government sources. Shortly after an election is called, the CEO prepares a preliminary list of electors ("PLE") for each polling division, based on the NROE (s. 93). A process of revision of the PLE is then undertaken (ss. 96 ff.). Before polling day, official lists of electors ("OLEs") are prepared for use at each polling station (s. 106).

[14] Many electors will be on the OLE of their assigned polling division, by "enumeration." Since age and citizenship are prerequisites for inclusion on the OLE, those listed do not have to establish their age and citizenship when they come to vote. To vote, these electors must prove their identity and residence by one of three means: (a) providing government-issued identification with photo and address (s. 143(2)(a)); (b) providing two pieces of authorized identification, at least one of which establishes their address (s. 143(2)(b)); or (c) taking a prescribed oath and being vouched for by someone on the OLE in the same polling division (s. 143(3)). Once identity and residence are established, the voter is given a ballot.

[15] Electors who are not on the OLE can have their names added on election day by the process of "registration" (s. 161(1)). To register, the elector must provide proof of identity and residence. Where the elector satisfies these requirements, the DRO will complete a registration certificate and the elector will sign it (s. 161(4)). Electors who register must also establish their age and citizenship. This is accomplished by signing a declaration to that effect, which appears on the registration certificate.

[16] Section 161(5) of the Act provides that, where a registration certificate is completed, the OLE is deemed to have been modified in accordance with the certificate. After polling day, the returning officer uses the registration certificates to update the OLE, and the CEO creates a final list of electors ("FLE") for each electoral district (s. 109). The FLE is an updated list containing the names of those electors who were enumerated on the OLE as well as those who voted by registration.

[17] Vouching is a procedure designed to enable persons to vote who lack appropriate identification. An elector may prove his or her identity by being vouched for by a person whose name appears on the list of electors for the same polling division. A voucher can only vouch once. A person who has been vouched for cannot vouch for someone else in the same election (s. 161(1)(b), (6) and (7)).

[18] The Act also establishes requirements for record-keeping by election officials. After the issue of the writ to call an election, a returning officer appoints one DRO and one poll clerk for each polling station in the electoral district for which he or she is responsible (s. 32). Once the DRO is satisfied that an elector's identity

and residence have been proven, the name of the elector is crossed off the OLE and the elector is allowed to vote (s. 143(4)). Once the elector has voted, the poll clerk is required to indicate on the list that the vote was cast by placing a check mark in a box set aside for that purpose (s. 162(b)). The poll clerk is also required to make entries in a "poll book." The required entries include various matters, such as whether an elector has taken an oath, the type of oath he or she has taken and the fact that the elector has voted using a registration certificate (s. 162(f) and (j)).

B. Interpreting the Relevant Statutory Provision

(1) Part 20 of the Act

[19] Part 20 of the Act deals with contested elections. Section 524(1) provides:

> 524.(1) Any elector who was eligible to vote in an electoral district, and any candidate in an electoral district, may, by application to a competent court, contest the election in that electoral district on the grounds that
>> (a) under section 65 the elected candidate was not eligible to be a candidate;
> or
>> (b) *there were irregularities, fraud or corrupt or illegal practices that affected the result of the election*. [Emphasis in original.]

[20] The remedy the court may provide is in s. 531(2):

> (2) After hearing the application, the court may dismiss it if the grounds referred to in paragraph 524(1)(a) or (b), as the case may be, are not established and, where they are established, shall declare the election null and void or may annul the election, respectively.

The use of the word "respectively" means that where the grounds in s. 524(1)(a) are established, a court must declare the election null and void; where the grounds in s. 524(1)(b) are established, a court may annul the election. Conversely, a court may not annul an election unless the grounds in s. 524(1)(b) are established.

· · ·

[23] In deciding whether to annul an election, an important consideration is whether the number of impugned votes is sufficient to cast doubt on the true winner of the election or whether the irregularities are such as to call into question the integrity of the electoral process. Since voting is conducted by secret ballot in Canada, this assessment cannot involve an investigation into voters' actual choices. If a court is satisfied that, because of the rejection of certain votes, the winner is in doubt, it would be unreasonable for the court not to annul the election.

(2) Meaning of "Irregularities ... That Affected the Result of the Election"

[24] This case involves interpreting the phrase "irregularities ... that affected the result of the election." The phrase is composed of two elements: "irregularities" and "affected the result." As we shall explain, "irregularities" are serious administrative errors that are capable of undermining the electoral process—the type of mistakes that are tied to and have a direct bearing on a person's right to vote.

[25] "Affected the result" asks whether someone not entitled to vote, voted. Manifestly, if a vote is found to be invalid, it must be discounted, thereby altering the vote count, and in that sense, affecting the election's result. "Affected the result" could also include a situation where a person entitled to vote was improperly prevented from doing so, due to an irregularity on the part of an election official. That is not the case here and we need not address it.

[26] In construing the meaning of "irregularities ... that affected the result," we have taken into account a number of aides to statutory interpretation, among them: (1) the constitutional right to vote and the objectives of the Act; (2) the text and context of s. 524; and (3) the competing democratic values engaged.

(a) The Constitutional Right to Vote and the Objectives of the Act

[27] Canadian democracy is founded upon the right to vote. Section 3 of the Charter provides:

> 3. Every citizen of Canada has the right to vote in an election of members of the House of Commons or of a legislative assembly and to be qualified for membership therein.

• • •

[29] The constitutional guarantee of the right to vote in s. 3 of the Charter is a fundamental provision, not subject to constitutional override under s. 33 of the Charter. Section 3 provides that citizens have the right to vote *"in an election of members of the House of Commons or of a legislative assembly."* [Emphasis in original.] The right to vote in the election of "members of the House of Commons" reflects Canada's constitutional character as a parliamentary form of government. Citizens have the right to vote in a specific electoral district, choosing among various candidates who wish to be the Member of Parliament for that district ... .

[30] Section 6 of the Act recognizes that all persons meeting the three requirements of age, citizenship and residence are "entitled" to vote. It reads:

> 6. Subject to this Act, every person who is qualified as an elector is entitled to have his or her name included in the list of electors for the polling division in which he or she is ordinarily resident and to vote at the polling station for that polling division.

Section 6 uses the term "polling division." Polling divisions exist within electoral districts for administrative simplicity and voter convenience on election day (J.P. Boyer, *Election Law in Canada: The Law and Procedure of Federal, Provincial and Territorial Elections* (1987), vol. I, at p. 101). The Charter right to vote is for the Member of Parliament for the electoral district in which the voter resides.

[31] On a plain reading of s. 6, qualification and residence in a polling division give an individual the entitlement or right to be included on the list of electors for that polling division, and to vote. Section 6 *does not* provide that inclusion on the list of electors is a prerequisite to the right to vote. [Emphasis in original.] Such a reading reverses the effect of the provision. Entitlement to be on the list and entitlement to vote are consequences of being a citizen, being of age, and being resident in the polling division.

[32] In this regard, it should be noted that s. 6 is a complete definition of "entitlement" in the Act. The definition is not altered by any other provision. "Entitlement" consists only of the fundamental requirements of age, citizenship, and residence.

[33] In so concluding, we recognize that the opening words of s. 6 are "[s]ubject to this Act." However, a distinction must be made between the requirements of "entitlement" in s. 6 itself, which appears in Part 1 of the Act under the heading "Electoral Rights," and the procedural mechanisms applicable on election day which appear in Part 9 of the Act under the heading "Voting." The Act establishes procedures to allow those citizens who have the right to vote to do so on election day. For example, ss. 148.1 and 149, which appear in Part 9, require procedures to be followed in establishing identity and residence, and in registering, before voting. These are procedural provisions designed to satisfy election officials that voters have the

attributes that entitle them to vote. The purpose of procedural provisions in the Act is to enfranchise those persons having a right to vote under s. 6, and to prevent persons without the right to vote, from voting.

[34] The procedural safeguards in the Act are important; however, they should not be treated as ends in themselves. Rather, they should be treated as a means of ensuring that only those who have the right to vote may do so. It is that end that must always be kept in sight.

[35] It is well accepted in the contested election jurisprudence that the purpose of the Act is to enfranchise all persons entitled to vote and to allow them to express their democratic preferences. Courts considering a denial of voting rights have applied a stringent justification standard ... .

[36] The words of an Act are to be read in their "entire context and in their grammatical and ordinary sense harmoniously with the scheme of the Act, the object of the Act, and the intention of Parliament" ... . The constitutional right to vote and the enfranchising purpose of the Act are of central importance in construing the words "irregularities ... that affected the result."

[37] It is well recognized in the jurisprudence that where electoral legislation is found to be ambiguous, it should be interpreted in a way that is enfranchising ... .

[38] While enfranchisement is one of the cornerstones of the Act, it is not freestanding. Protecting the integrity of the democratic process is also a central purpose of the Act. The same procedures that enable entitled voters to cast their ballots also serve the purpose of preventing those not entitled from casting ballots. These safeguards address the potential for fraud, corruption and illegal practices, and the public's perception of the integrity of the electoral process. (See *Henry* ..., at paras. 305-6.) Fair and consistent observance of the statutory safeguards serves to enhance the public's faith and confidence in fair elections and in the government itself, both of which are essential to an effective democracy ... .

(b) The Text and Context of Section 524

[39] Just as the enfranchising purpose of the Act informs the interpretation of the phrase "irregularities ... that affected the result" in s. 524, so too does the text of the provision itself. Parliament's use of the word "irregularities" in s. 524 of the Act is significant. A different phrase, "any non-compliance with the provisions of the Act," could have been used. Moreover, if Parliament had intended that any deviation from the statutory procedure be a basis on which to annul an election, it would have spoken in terms of "non-compliance." Instead, it used "irregularities," suggesting that Parliament intended to restrict the scope of administrative errors that give rise to overturning an election.

[40] How is the meaning of "irregularities" restricted? The well-known "associated words" or *"noscitur a sociis"* rule of interpretation assists in this regard. The rule states that a term or an expression should not be interpreted without taking the surrounding terms into account. "The meaning of a term is revealed by its association with other terms: it is known by its associates" ... .

[41] Professor Sullivan defines the "associated words" rule as follows:

> The associated words rule is properly invoked when two or more terms linked by "and" or "or" serve an analogous grammatical and logical function within a provision. This parallelism invites the reader to look for a common feature among the terms. This feature is then relied on to resolve ambiguity or limit the scope of the terms. Often the terms are restricted to the scope of their broadest common denominator.

(Sullivan on the Construction of Statutes (5th ed. 2008), at p. 227)

[42] The word "irregularities" appears as part of the following phrase: "irregularities, fraud or corrupt or illegal practices." These are words that speak to serious misconduct. To interpret "irregularity" as meaning any administrative error would mean reading it without regard to the related words.

[43] The common thread between the words "irregularities, fraud or corrupt or illegal practices" is the seriousness of the conduct and its impact on the integrity of the electoral process. Fraud, corruption and illegal practices are serious. Where they occur, the electoral process will be corroded. In associating the word "irregularity" with those words, Parliament must have contemplated mistakes and administrative errors that are serious and capable of undermining the integrity of the electoral process. ...

(c) Competing Democratic Values

[44] Central to the issue before us is how willing a court should be to reject a vote because of statutory non-compliance. Although there are safeguards in place to prevent abuse, the Act accepts some uncertainty in the conduct of elections, since in theory, more onerous and accurate methods of identification and record-keeping could be adopted. The balance struck by the Act reflects the fact that our electoral system must balance several interrelated and sometimes conflicting values. Those values include certainty, accuracy, fairness, accessibility, voter anonymity, promptness, finality, legitimacy, efficiency and cost. But the central value is the Charter-protected right to vote.

[45] Our system strives to treat candidates and voters fairly, both in the conduct of elections and in the resolution of election failures. As we have discussed, the Act seeks to enfranchise all entitled persons, including those without paper documentation, and to encourage them to come forward to vote on election day, regardless of prior enumeration. The system strives to achieve accessibility for all voters, making special provision for those without identification to vote by vouching. Election officials are unable to determine with absolute accuracy who is entitled to vote. Poll clerks do not take fingerprints to establish identity. A voter can establish Canadian citizenship verbally, by oath. The goal of accessibility can only be achieved if we are prepared to accept some degree of uncertainty that all who voted were entitled to do so.

[46] The practical realities of election administration are such that imperfections in the conduct of elections are inevitable. As recognized in *Camsell v. Rabesca*, [1987] N.W.T.R. 186 (S.C.), it is clear that "in every election, a fortiori those in urban ridings, with large numbers of polls, irregularities will virtually always occur in one form or another" (p. 198). A federal election is only possible with the work of tens of thousands of Canadians who are hired across the country for a period of a few days or, in many cases, a single 14-hour day. These workers perform many detailed tasks under difficult conditions. They are required to apply multiple rules in a setting that is unfamiliar. Because elections are not everyday occurrences, it is difficult to see how workers could get practical, on-the-job experience.

[47] The provision for contesting elections in Part 20 of the Act serves to restore accuracy and reliability where it has been compromised. However, tension exists between allowing an application to contest an election on the basis of irregularities and the need for a prompt, final resolution of election outcomes. The Act provides, in s. 525(3):

> (3) An application shall be dealt with without delay and in a summary way.

[48] It should be remembered that annulling an election would disenfranchise not only those persons whose votes were disqualified, but every elector who voted in the riding. That voters will have the opportunity to vote in a by-election is not a perfect answer, as Professor Steven F. Huefner writes:

> ... a new election can never be run on a clean slate, but will always be colored by the perceived outcome of the election it superseded. New elections may also be an inconvenience for the voters, and almost certainly will mean that a different set of voters, with different information, will be deciding the election. Moreover, there can be no guarantee that the new election will itself be free from additional problems, including fraud. In the long term, rerunning elections might lead to disillusionment or apathy, even if in the short term they excite interest in the particular contest. Frequent new elections also would undercut democratic stability by calling into question the security and efficiency of the voting mechanics.

("Remedying Election Wrongs" (2007), 44 *Harv. J. on Legis.* 265, at pp. 295-96)

[49] Permitting elections to be lightly overturned would also increase the "margin of litigation." The phrase "margin of litigation" describes an election outcome close enough to draw post-election legal action: Huefner, at pp. 266-67.

[50] The current system of election administration in Canada is not designed to achieve perfection, but to come as close to the ideal of enfranchising all entitled voters as possible. Since the system and the Act are not designed for certainty alone, courts cannot demand perfect certainty. Rather, courts must be concerned with the integrity of the electoral system. This overarching concern informs our interpretation of the phrase "irregularities ... that affected the result."

(d) Conclusion: The Meaning of "Irregularities ... That Affected the Result"

[51] Having regard to the centrality of the constitutional right to vote, the enfranchising purpose of the Act, the language of s. 524, and the numerous democratic values engaged, we conclude that an "irregularit[y] ... that affected the result" of an election is a breach of statutory procedure that has resulted in an individual voting who was not entitled to vote. Such breaches are serious because they are capable of undermining the integrity of the electoral process.

(3) When Is an "Irregularit[y] ... That Affected the Result" Established?

• • •

[74] The following approach should be followed in determining whether there were "irregularities ... that affected the result of the election": An applicant must prove that a procedural safeguard designed to establish an elector's entitlement to vote was not respected. This is an "irregularity." An applicant must then demonstrate that the irregularity "affected the result" of the election because an individual voted who was not entitled to do so. In determining whether the result was affected, an application judge may consider any evidence in the record capable of establishing that the person was in fact entitled to vote despite the irregularity, or that the person was not in fact entitled to vote.

[75] If it is established that there were "irregularities ... that affected the result of the election," a court may annul the election. In exercising this discretion, if a court is satisfied that, because of the rejection of certain votes, the winner is in doubt, it

would be unreasonable for the court not to annul the election. For the purposes of this application, the "magic number" test will be used to make that determination.

[On this test, the election should be annulled when the number of rejected votes is equal to or greater than the successful candidate's margin of victory.]

The Court's majority then applied these principles to the votes contested in the case. The following text from the official summary outlines the majority's conclusions, and resulted in the challenge being dismissed:

Applying these principles to this appeal, at least 59 of the 79 votes disqualified by the application judge should be restored. The remaining 20 votes are less than O's plurality of 26. Although the remaining 20 votes are not discussed, there is no reason to believe that any of the 20 voters were not in fact entitled to vote. Because W has failed to establish that at least 26 votes should be disqualified, his application to annul the election should be dismissed.

The application judge made two errors of law. With respect to polls 31 and 426, he misstated the onus of proof five times, in the context of making crucial findings of fact, and it cannot be confidently said that he did not reverse the onus of proof. For polls 174 and 89, he failed to consider material evidence in reaching his findings. In light of these two errors of law, the application judge's findings at these polls are not entitled to deference. Because the evidence is exclusively documentary and the Act requires a contested election application to proceed without delay, it is incumbent on this Court to reach its own conclusion on the validity of the votes in these polling divisions rather than remit the case to the application judge for redetermination.

At polls 31 and 426, a total of 41 required registration certificates were missing. If the certificates were never completed this would amount to an "irregularity," satisfying the first step of the test. Here, however, there was evidence that indicates the certificates were completed but were misplaced after the election. Considering the whole of the evidence, W failed to establish, on a balance of probabilities, that there was an "irregularity." For 13 of these voters at poll 31, there was positive proof that they were entitled to vote. They were on the list of electors at poll 31 or at other polls in the riding. This evidence confirms the decision to restore these votes. Although the minority also restores these votes, their explanation for doing so is contrary to their position that a voter must establish his entitlement before receiving and casting a ballot.

At poll 174, eight individuals who were vouched for are identified in the poll book by their relationship to the person who vouched for them, rather than by their full name. There was, however, evidence in the list of electors from which it could be inferred that the vouching was properly conducted. W failed to establish an "irregularity."

At poll 89, 10 registration certificates were not signed by the voters, but were instead signed only by the election official. With respect to these votes, W established that there was an "irregularity." W failed, however, to show that the irregularity "affected the result" of the election. There was evidence from which it could reasonably be inferred that the 10 voters were entitled to vote and that the misplaced signatures were simply a clerical mistake.

The minority, for its part, counted up the disqualified votes differently, and concluded that enough of these votes contained irregularities that the election should be annulled.

Electoral irregularities are one thing. Consider now the following decision of the Federal Court, examining the infamous "robocalling" events of the 2011 federal election. Here, the Court was dealing with the much more serious problem of outright electoral fraud.

McEwing v Canada (AG)
2013 FC 525

MOSLEY J:

I. Introduction

[1] In his remarks to the Standing Committee on Procedure and House Affairs of the House of Commons on March 29, 2012, Mr. Marc Mayrand, Chief Electoral Officer of Canada, made the following comments about the allegations that are at the heart of these applications:

> These are very serious matters that strike at the integrity of our democratic process. If they are not addressed and responded to, they risk undermining an essential ingredient of a healthy democracy, namely the trust that electors have in the electoral process.

[2] The applicants, eight Canadian citizen voters residing in six electoral districts, brought these proceedings to annul the results of the 2011 General Election in their ridings because of efforts to suppress votes that occurred during that election. Those efforts involved telephone calls purporting to be from Elections Canada. In the calls, voters were told that the locations of polling stations in their districts had been moved from the places specified in the printed information provided by Elections Canada prior to the day of the vote. The information was false and Elections Canada neither made nor authorized those calls.

[3] The calls struck at the integrity of the electoral process by attempting to dissuade voters from casting ballots for their preferred candidates. This form of "voter suppression," was, until the 41st General Election, largely unknown in this country.

[4] The evidence presented in these applications points to a concerted campaign by persons who had access to a database of voter information maintained by a political party. It was not alleged that any of the candidates of that party, including those who were successful in the six ridings at issue, were responsible for this campaign but that others took it upon themselves to attempt to influence the election results in their favour.

[5] As a result of these actions, the applicants seek to set aside the 2011 Election results in the six ridings under Part 20 of the *Canada Elections Act*, SC 2000, c 9 [the Act].

[6] The central issue to be determined in these proceedings was the effect the calls had, if any, on the election results in the six subject ridings. If satisfied that the calls affected the result in one or more of the ridings or called into question the integrity of the electoral process, the Court may annul the outcome in that riding or ridings. For the reasons that follow, I find that electoral fraud occurred during the 41st General Election but I am not satisfied that it has been established that the fraud affected the outcomes in the subject ridings and I decline to exercise my discretion to annul the results in those districts.

II. Background

[7] These applications were brought ten months after the election. Complaints about misleading and harassing calls had been made to Elections Canada both before and during the election day on May 2, 2011 but the matter did not attract much public attention until, in late February 2012, journalists found in an Edmonton court file an "Information to Obtain a Production Order Pursuant to Section

487.012 of the Criminal Code" ("ITO") sworn by Allan Mathews, an Elections Canada investigator. The Mathews ITO became a public document after a return was made to the court on the execution of the production order. The media then began to report widely that Elections Canada officials were actively investigating complaints made during and after the election.

[8] The Mathews ITO was filed to obtain records from an Edmonton-based company called RackNine Inc., in relation to complaints by voters that there had been efforts to suppress votes in the electoral district of Guelph, Ontario. Mr. Mathews described the nature of the complaints as follows:

> Individual electors have described to me receiving telephone calls around 10:00 hours of the morning of May 2, 2011. The caller was usually described as a recorded female voice giving a bilingual message, who claimed to be calling on behalf of Elections Canada.

The English message received by electors is as follows:

> This is an automated message from Elections Canada. Due to the projected increase in poll turnout your voting location has been changed. Your new voting location is at... Once again your new poll location is at... If you have any questions please call our hotline at 1-800-434-4456. We apologize for any inconvenience that this may cause.

[9] Mr. Mathews further deposed that Elections Canada does not telephone individual electors and did not make the calls in question. The assertion that the polling stations had been changed was untrue. The making of these calls by a person or persons unknown, in Mr. Mathews' belief, wilfully prevented or endeavoured to prevent an elector from voting contrary to paragraph 281(g) of the Act. As a result, he alleged, offences had been committed contrary to s 491(3)(d) and s 482(b) of the Act.

[10] Media accounts subsequent to the publication of the Mathews ITO reported that similar illicit telephone calls had been reported in other ridings. On March 15, 2012 the Chief Electoral Officer, Marc Mayrand, issued a statement: "Chief Electoral Officer of Canada Addresses Allegations of Wrongdoing During the 41st General Election." Mr Mayrand's statement indicated that Elections Canada had, as of that date, received over 700 complaints from Canadians describing specific circumstances where they believed that wrongdoing had occurred during the 41st General Election. As of the date of Mr. Mayrand's appearance before the Standing Committee on Procedure and House Affairs two weeks later, on March 29, 2012, close to 40,000 Canadians had contacted Elections Canada to express their concerns in response to the media reports.

[11] This was the context in which these applications were filed with the Court. They contest the results of the election in the six electoral districts of Elmwood-Transcona, Nipissing-Timiskaming, Saskatoon-Rosetown-Biggar, Vancouver Island North, Winnipeg South Centre and Yukon.

• • •

III. The Statutory and Jurisprudential Framework

A. The Canada Elections Act

[30] As noted at the outset, these proceedings were brought by applications under the *Canada Elections Act*. The present version of this statute was enacted by Parliament in 2000 to implement the recommendations of a series of reports, including that of a Royal Commission on Electoral Reform and Party Financing

tabled in 1992, five reports produced by a Special Committee of the House of Commons during 1992 and 1993 and others submitted to Parliament by the Chief Electoral Officer, notably that following the 36th General Election in 1997.

[31] These reports called for the repeal of the existing legislation, the former *Canada Elections Act* dating from 1970, the *Dominion Controverted Elections Act*, RSC 1985, c C-39, the *Disenfranchising Act*, RSC 1985, c D-3, originally enacted in 1894, and the *Corrupt Practices Inquiries Act*, RSC 1985, c C-45, adopted in 1876. They also called for consolidation of the administrative framework for federal elections, the offences and penalties for violations and the procedures for contesting or controverting electoral results into one comprehensive code.

[32] One of the effects of the adoption of these recommendations in the 2000 Act is that the jurisprudence under the former legislation may be of limited value in interpreting the new enactments.

[33] In considering the relevant provisions of the 2000 Act, I have had the benefit of the views expressed by Justice Lederer in *Wrzesnewskyj*, above, and those of the majority and minority opinions of the Supreme Court of Canada on appeal from that decision in *Opitz v Wrzesnewskyj*, 2012 SCC 55 [*Opitz*].

[34] As stated by the majority in *Opitz* at paragraph 1, section 3 of the *Canadian Charter of Rights and Freedoms*, Part I of the *Constitution Act, 1982*, being Schedule B to the *Canada Act 1982* (UK), 1982, c 11 [Charter], and the provisions of the *Canada Elections Act* have the clear and historic purposes of enfranchising Canadian citizens and of protecting the integrity of our electoral process.

[35] Canadian citizens are guaranteed the right to vote for the candidate of their choice to serve as the Member of Parliament for the electoral district in which the citizen resides. Section 3 of the Charter provides:

> 3. Every citizen of Canada has the right to vote in an election of members of the House of Commons or of a legislative assembly and to be qualified for membership therein.

[36] Section 6 of the Canada Elections Act gives practical effect to that guarantee by providing that persons who are qualified as electors are entitled to have their names included in the list of electors for the electoral division in which they are ordinarily resident and to vote at the polling station for that electoral division at federal elections.

[37] The procedure for determining the lists of electors for each polling division is set out in Part 7 of the Act. Preparation for the vote is governed by Part 8. It is the responsibility of the returning officer to establish one polling station for each polling division (s 120(1)). Additional stations may be established if justified by the number of electors in the district, with the prior approval of the Chief Electoral Officer (s 120(2)). Additional provisions in Part 8 specify the nature of the locations that may serve as polling stations, with regard to such considerations as accessibility and privacy, and the appointment of officials to manage and secure the premises. Part 9 contains the method for setting the voting hours.

[38] The selection of the location of each polling station is among the responsibilities of the returning officers for each district with the approval of the Chief Electoral Officer. That would include any relocation of a polling station. The scheme of the legislation suggests that any notification to electors of such a change would also be the responsibility of the returning officers and Chief Electoral Officer.

[39] Section 281 prohibits anyone from interfering with an elector when marking a ballot, from making false statements or from preventing an elector from voting. Interference with an elector would include the type of conduct complained of

in this proceeding; that is, deliberately providing false information about a change in the location of a polling station.

[40] Part 19 of the Act, containing sections 479-521.1, deals with enforcement issues. Section 480 creates a general offence of obstructing the electoral process. Other specific offences are set out in sections 481 to 499. These include the offence of electoral fraud under s 482(b) (inducing a person to refrain from voting or refrain from voting for a particular candidate "by any pretence or contrivance") and that set out in paragraph 491(3)(d) (wilfully preventing or endeavouring to prevent an elector from voting at an election). These are the offences, according to the ITOs, which are being investigated by the Commissioner of Canada Elections in regard to the 2011 elections.

[41] Section 500 contains the general punishment provisions for the offences created by the preceding sections. The maximum penalties range from a fine of not more than $1,000 or three months' imprisonment, or both, in most cases and a fine of $25,000 in one case, on summary conviction, to a fine of $5,000 or five years' imprisonment on conviction by indictment. Corrupt and illegal practices by candidates and their official agents are dealt with in s 502, which carries a five year maximum penalty and proscription from holding electoral or appointed office for up to seven years from the date of conviction.

[42] The office of Commissioner of Canada Elections is provided for in sections 509 to 515 of Part 19. The Commissioner is appointed by the Chief Electoral Officer and is responsible for ensuring that the Act is complied with and enforced. The Chief Electoral Officer can direct the Commissioner to conduct an inquiry and the Commissioner can initiate an inquiry and receive complaints. Section 511 authorizes the Commissioner to refer a matter to the Director of Public Prosecutions if he or she believes on reasonable grounds that an offence has been committed. The Director of Public Prosecutions shall decide whether to initiate a prosecution (s 511(1)).

• • •

[48] Part 20 of the Act now provides for civil applications to overturn an election. It is a complete code for the validity of an election to be challenged by a candidate or an elector and the result will touch upon the election outcome, not provide sanctions against individuals. ...

• • •

[75] In *Opitz*, the Supreme Court used the "magic number" test to determine whether the application judge should have annulled the result. ...

[76] The majority acknowledged, at para 73, ... "that another, more realistic method for assessing contested election applications might be adopted by a court in a future case." The Supreme Court thus left open the question of whether irregularities could be such as to call into question the integrity of the electoral process. That conclusion may be reached more easily, I expect, where the ground cited for annulment is not irregularities at the ballot box but electoral fraud, corruption or illegality.

• • •

[83] In summary, there are three steps required to annul under the Act in the context of the vote suppression allegations before the Court. The applicants must first demonstrate one of the four circumstances in s 524(1)(b): irregularities, fraud, corrupt practices, or illegal practices. Once the first step has been achieved, if even a single vote is shown to not have been cast due to one of the four above circumstances in a subject riding, the Court acquires the discretionary power to annul the results in that district under 531(2). The third step is for the Court to consider either the "magic

number" test (explained in *Opitz* at paras 71-72) or another appropriate test (envisaged by *Opitz* at para 73) and decide whether to exercise its discretionary power.

• • •

C. Did the Fraud Call into Question the Integrity of the Elections?

[252] This case was problematic from the outset, as the applicants acknowledged, because of the challenges they faced in collecting evidence to support what they rightly identified as a widespread attempt at voter suppression. The evidence of fraud was most clearly demonstrated in the Guelph investigation. As the investigations continued, the Commissioner's officers uncovered evidence that the Guelph experience was not unique and that similar attempts were made across the country including in the six subject ridings. The applicants' own experience on Election Day supports those findings.

[253] Canadians have confidence in the integrity of our electoral procedures. The sanctity of the poll and the ballot box in this country is reflected in the frequent invitations Canada receives to provide independent observers to supervise foreign elections. There may have been isolated instances of electoral misbehaviour in the past but, as noted above, incidents of voter suppression of the nature discussed in these reasons have not been known in this country prior to the 41st General Election. For that reason, I don't doubt that the confidence rightfully held by Canadians has been shaken by the disclosures of widespread fraudulent activities that have resulted from the Commissioner's investigations and the complaints to Elections Canada.

[254] Had I found that any of the successful electoral candidates or their agents were implicated in any way in the fraudulent activity, I would not have hesitated to exercise my discretion to annul the result even if the reverse magic number had not been shown to have been reached in the riding in question. No such evidence was led.

[255] The scale of the fraud has to be kept in perspective. According to the Report of the Chief Electoral Officer of Canada on the 41st general election of May 2, 2011, found on the website of Elections Canada, a total of 66,146 polls at which 14,823,408 electors cast their ballots were set up and operated across Canada on polling day. The number and location of the complaints received by Elections Canada from across Canada indicates that the voter suppression effort was geographically widespread but, apart from Guelph, thinly scattered.

[256] While they appear to have been targetted towards voters who had previously expressed a preference for an opposition party (or anyone other than the government party), the evidence in this proceeding does not support the conclusion that the voter suppression efforts had a major impact on the credibility of the vote.

[257] Elections Canada has responded to the complaints received and they continue to be actively investigated. At the time of writing, the press reported that the Director of Public Prosecutions had authorized the Commissioner to commence a prosecution under Part 19 of the Act. These institutions and the Courts have the capacity to address this effort to strike at the integrity of our democratic process.

D. Should the Court Exercise Its Discretion to Annul the Elections?

[258] Having considered the matter very carefully and with a full appreciation for the concerns about the integrity of the electoral process that have motivated these applications, I am unable to conclude that I should exercise my discretion to annul the 2011 election results in any of the subject ridings because of the fraud that occurred.

CHAPTER SEVEN

THE FUNCTIONS
OF PARLIAMENT

Now that you understand the actors who populate Parliament, it is time to examine how they come together and perform their functions. This chapter describes how Parliament is called into session, prorogued, and dissolved and examines the role of several of the key actors in Parliament, including political parties, the speakers, and parliamentary committees. It also then discusses "parliamentary law": the rules and procedures that guide Parliament's functioning. Finally, it sets out the very important procedure by which parliamentary bills become statutes.

I. BRINGING THE CONSTITUENT ELEMENTS
OF PARLIAMENT TOGETHER

A Parliament is not a permanent feature, meeting indefinitely. Canada has had 42 Parliaments since 1867, and at the time of this writing, was in the midst of its 43rd. Thus, federal Parliaments have been summoned 43 times and dissolved on 42 occasions. Elections to the House of Commons take place in the period after the dissolution of the old Parliament and the summoning of a new Parliament. During the life of a Parliament itself, most Parliaments (although not the 42nd) have been "prorogued" between different "sessions" of that Parliament. In this section, we discuss the process of summoning, proroguing, and dissolving a Parliament.

A. SUMMONING

Section 38 of the *Constitution Act, 1867* (UK), 30 & 31 Vict, c 3, reprinted in RSC 1985, Appendix II, No 5 empowers the governor general "from Time to Time, in the Queen's Name, by Instrument under the Great Seal of Canada, [to] summon and call together the House of Commons." However, this apparent discretion to determine the timing of Parliaments is greatly constrained by constitutional convention, and now the Charter rule requiring annual sittings of Parliament.

By constitutional convention, the governor general calls Parliament to session on the advice of the prime minister. This convention is codified in the Writ of Election, enacted as Schedule 1 in the *Canada Elections Act*, SC 2000, c 9. This writ empowers the monarch (and thus the governor general) to set the date for a new Parliament "by and with the advice" of the prime minister.

Consider the events that follow soon after the summoning of a new Parliament.

House of Commons, House of Commons Procedure and Practice
2nd ed (Ottawa: House of Commons, 2009) (footnotes omitted)

Proceedings on Opening Day of a Parliament

The opening of a Parliament is also the opening of the first session of that Parliament. Two procedures distinguish it from the opening of subsequent sessions. These are the taking and subscribing of the oath of allegiance by Members and the election of a Speaker.

Members Sworn In

Following a general election, the Clerk of the House receives from the Chief Electoral Officer certificates of election for Members of the House as they become available. In order for the elected Members to take their seats in the House, it is required by the *Constitution Act, 1867* that they first subscribe to an oath of allegiance. As an alternative to swearing the oath, the Members may make a solemn affirmation. ...

Election of the Speaker

Section 44 of the *Constitution Act, 1867* provides for the election of a Speaker as the first item of business when Members assemble following a general election. The Standing Orders provide for the manner in which the Speaker is elected. On the day appointed by proclamation for the meeting of a new Parliament, the Members are summoned by the division bells to assemble in the Chamber, where they receive the Usher of the Black Rod, who reads a message requesting the immediate attendance of the House in the Senate Chamber.

In a procession led by the Clerk of the House, the Members go to the Senate. There, a Deputy of the Governor General is seated at the foot of the Throne, and the Speaker of the Senate addresses the Members on the Deputy's behalf, informing them that "... His (Her) Excellency the Governor General does not see fit to declare the causes of his (her) summoning the present Parliament of Canada, until a Speaker of the House of Commons shall have been chosen, according to law ... ."

This means that the Speech from the Throne will not be read until a Speaker has been elected. The Members then return to the House and proceed to elect a presiding officer.

Presentation of the Speaker to the Governor General

Following the election of the Speaker, at the time fixed for the purpose of appearing for the formal opening of Parliament with a Speech from the Throne, the House again receives the Usher of the Black Rod, who conveys the message of the Governor General requesting the presence of the House in the Senate. The procession is led by the Usher of the Black Rod, followed by the Sergeant-at-Arms (bearing the Mace), the Speaker, the Clerk and the Members. At the Bar of the Senate, the newly-elected Speaker stands on a small platform, removes his or her hat and receives an acknowledgement from the Governor General, who is seated on the Throne. The Speaker addresses the Governor General by an established formula. ...

The Speaker of the Senate, on behalf of the Governor General, makes the traditional reply ... .

Opening of a Session

As previously noted, the swearing-in of Members and the election of a Speaker are the distinguishing features of the summoning of a new Parliament for the opening of its first session; in subsequent sessions, there are no such preliminary proceedings in the House. The opening of a session—whether it is the first or a subsequent session—is marked by the reading of the Speech from the Throne. On each opening of a session, the House assembles with the Speaker in the Chair, receives the Usher of the Black Rod and proceeds in due course to the Senate for the reading of the Speech from the Throne.

• • •

Speech from the Throne and Subsequent Proceedings in the House

The Speech from the Throne imparts the causes of summoning Parliament, prior to which neither House can embark on any public business. It marks the first occasion, after a general election, or a prorogation, that Parliament meets in an assembly of its three constituent parts: the House of Commons, the Senate and the Sovereign, or the Sovereign's representative.

The Speech from the Throne usually sets forth in some detail the government's view of the condition of the country and provides an indication of what legislation it intends to bring forward. After hearing the Speech, the Speaker and Members return to the House. If the session is the first of a new Parliament, the newly-elected Speaker will have made the traditional statement claiming for the House all its "undoubted rights and privileges." This is reported by the Speaker to the House on returning from the Senate. The business for the day's sitting then proceeds.

The routine items typically dealt with by the House on the first day of a session [include:]

Pro forma bill: Before proceeding to the consideration of the Speech from the Throne, the House gives first reading to the *pro forma* Bill C–1, *An Act respecting the Administration of Oaths of Office*. Typically, the Bill is introduced by the Prime Minister; it receives first reading but is not proceeded with any further during the session. Its purpose is to assert the independence of the House of Commons and its right to choose its own business and to deliberate without reference to the causes of summons as expressed in the Speech from the Throne.

Report of Speech from the Throne: The Speaker reports to the House on the Speech from the Throne, informing the House that "to prevent mistakes" a copy of the Speech has been obtained; its text is published in the *Debates*. A motion is then moved, usually by the Prime Minister, for the Speech from the Throne to be considered either "later this day" or on a future day ... .

The Throne Speech is followed by debate on a motion for an "Address in Reply to the Speech from the Throne." This address is essentially a *pro forma* thanks to the Queen or governor general. However, amendments and sub-amendments to the address made by the opposition parties may be introduced and debated. A failure by the government to defeat these opposition amendments and carry an unamended address in reply is generally a confidence matter. We discuss the concept of "confidence" below.

B. PROROGATION

Once summoned, a given Parliament is generally divided into several sessions, separated by a prorogation. A prorogation is again the prerogative of the governor general, acting on the advice of the prime minister. A prorogation (or, for that matter, a dissolution of Parliament, pending an election) may not endure indefinitely, however. Section 5 of the Charter provides that "[t]here shall be a sitting of Parliament and of each legislature at least once every twelve months." Put another way, Parliament cannot be entirely sidelined. Consider the implications of prorogation.

House of Commons, House of Commons Procedure and Practice

2nd ed (Ottawa: House of Commons, 2009) (footnotes omitted)

Prorogation of a Parliament, a prerogative act of the Crown taken on the advice of the Prime Minister, results in the termination of a session. ... Both the House of Commons and the Senate then stand prorogued until the opening of the next session. ...

Effects of Prorogation

Prorogation of a session brings to an end all proceedings before Parliament. With certain exceptions, unfinished business "dies" on the *Order Paper* and must be started anew in a subsequent session.

Bills which have not received Royal Assent before prorogation are "entirely terminated" and, in order to be proceeded with in the new session, must be reintroduced as if they had never existed. On occasion, however, bills have been reinstated at the start of a new session at the same stage they had reached at the end of the previous session. This has been accomplished either with the unanimous consent of the House or through the adoption of a motion to that effect, after notice and debate. The House has also adopted provisional amendments to the Standing Orders to carry over legislation to the next session, following a prorogation.

Since 2003, prorogation has had almost no practical effect on Private Members' Business. ... If consideration of an item at a certain stage had begun but had not been completed, the item is restored at the beginning of that stage, as if no debate had yet occurred. Private Members' bills that were referred to a committee in the previous session are deemed referred back to the same committee. Private Members' bills which have been read a third time and passed are sent again to the Senate.

Committees, including special and legislative committees, cease to exist and all orders of reference lapse. Committee memberships, except the membership of the Standing Committee on Procedure and House Affairs, are terminated and all Chairs and Vice-Chairs cease to hold office. The Panel of Chairs for legislative committees also ceases to exist.

In addition, when the House is prorogued, no documents may be tabled until the first day of the new session. ...

In general, during a prorogation Members are released from their parliamentary duties until, in the new session, the House and its committees resume activities. ...

Whether a governor general has the power to refuse a prorogation requested by the prime minister was a matter of some importance in 2008, during what might be labelled the "prorogation crisis." In a nutshell, the opposition political parties were galvanized in late 2008 by (depending on whom you believe) the Conservative government's apparent indifference to an emerging global economic crisis or its proposal to eliminate part of the political party subsidies (the most significant effect of which would have been felt by the relatively cash-poor opposition parties and not the Conservatives). The opposition parties proposed something of an ad hoc coalition and combined to table a motion of non-confidence in the government. As discussed below, if a non-confidence motion is carried in the Commons, the government falls. In the 40th minority Parliament, the opposition parties together controlled a majority of votes in the Commons and, voting in a block, they would have been sure to succeed in the non-confidence motion. Because Parliament had only recently been summoned after the fall 2008 election, they obviously anticipated that, should the government fall, the coalition would first be invited to form a new government before the governor general opted to dissolve Parliament and return to the polls.

To stave off a vote on the non-confidence motion, Prime Minister Stephen Harper postponed voting on the measure for a week and then subsequently asked the governor general to prorogue Parliament, a highly unorthodox request in such a young Parliament. Because the move was so clearly designed to prevent (or at least delay) a planned non-confidence vote, a difficult question arose as to whether a government could escape the judgment of Parliament by forcing its closure during the period of prorogation. The opposition parties urged that the governor general not grant the prorogation—and collectively signalled to the governor general that all three parties had lost confidence in the government and that the Liberals and NDP had agreed to form a new government, with the support of the Bloc Québécois, if the Conservatives fell. In the end, however, the governor general agreed to prorogue Parliament and, by the time Parliament returned nearly eight weeks later, the opposition coalition had collapsed, removing the immediate threat to the Conservative government.

These actions prompted a debate both in academia and more generally on whether the governor general had acted properly in granting the prorogation request, with some observers concluding that she had not, while others suggested that she had. See, for example, the collection of essays compiled in Peter H Russell & Lorne Sossin, eds, *Parliamentary Democracy in Crisis* (Toronto: University of Toronto Press, 2009) and the discussion and works cited in Craig Forcese & Aaron Freeman, *The Laws of Government: The Legal Foundations of Canadian Democracy*, 2nd ed (Toronto: Irwin Law, 2011) ch 5. The question of whether a decision by the prime minister to seek prorogation may be reviewed in court is something we address in Chapter 11.

C. DISSOLUTION

Both the *Constitution Act, 1867* (s 50) and the Charter (s 4(1)) limit the duration of a Commons to five years (except in times of war or insurrection). These provisions mean that (without such a war or insurrection) Parliament must be dissolved, and elections must happen at least every five years. Almost always, however, Parliaments do not last five years, and the governor general acts at a time of the prime minister's choosing in dissolving a Parliament. This dissolution prompts a new electoral cycle, governed by the *Canada Elections Act*. The obvious concern with such a system is that it allows—and often has allowed—a prime minister to time dissolutions and elections for partisan advantage. Nothing has changed constitutionally, although in the federal Parliament, there are now provisions (s 56.1) in the *Canada Election Act* fixing election dates every four years. This new law does not change the powers of the governor general. The governor general retains his or her constitutional power to dissolve Parliament before these fixed dates, something that usually would happen at the request of the prime minister (as occurred in 2008). This exact issue arose in 2008.

On September 7, 2008, Prime Minister Stephen Harper advised the governor general to dissolve Parliament and set an election date of October 14, 2008, contrary to s 56.1 of the recently amended *Canada Elections Act*. The governor general agreed. The subsequent election resulted in a second minority government for Prime Minister Stephen Harper's Conservative Party. Democracy Watch (a national non-profit, non-partisan citizen's organization advocating democratic reform, government accountability, and corporate responsibility) launched a legal challenge based on the Prime Minister's advice to the governor general to call the election, arguing that it violated his statutory obligations in the *Canada Elections Act* not to call a "snap election." One of the principles on which Democracy Watch based its legal argument was that a prime minister should not be able to time a general election to his or her own partisan advantage. Fixed-term dates, therefore, represent an appropriate constitutional constraint on a prime minister's apparently unlimited executive discretion. It lost at both the Federal Court and Federal Court of Appeal, and the Supreme Court of Canada denied leave to appeal. In its reasons (*Conacher v Canada (Prime Minister)*, 2010 FCA 131), the Federal Court of Appeal noted:

> [6] The appellants forcefully argued that this interpretation leaves section 56.1 with no meaning. We disagree. Subsection 56.1(2) is a clear expression of the will of Parliament, a will that, on the express terms of subsection 56.1(1), in no way binds the Governor General. But under our constitutional framework and as a matter of law, the Governor General may consider a wide variety of factors in deciding whether to dissolve Parliament and call an election. In this particular case, this may include any matters of constitutional law, any conventions that, in the Governor General's opinion, may bear upon or determine the matter, Parliament's will as expressed in subsection 56.1(2), advice from the Prime Minister, and any other appropriate matters.
>
> [7] If the section were interpreted in the manner suggested by the appellants, the Prime Minister would be prohibited from advising the Governor General that an election should be held because of dire need or an event of grave importance. We do not accept that section 56.1 has that result. Such a drastic result would require the clearest of statutory wording. This is a further indication that section 56.1, as drafted, does not affect the Prime Minister's ability to give advice to the Governor General.

There are, however, instances where a prime minister might be *forced* by constitutional convention to seek a dissolution from the governor general at a time not of his or her choosing. Constitutional convention requires a prime minister to resign his or her government *or* seek parliamentary dissolution after a "no confidence" vote by the House. Without a no confidence vote in the House, it seems unlikely that the governor general has the power to dissolve Parliament when opposed by the prime minister.

Nevertheless, it is not always clear where a vote in the House of Commons is one of no confidence. Consider the views of the 1985 "McGrath committee."

Special Committee on the Reform of the House of Commons, Report
(Ottawa: Canadian Government Publishing Centre, Supply and Services Canada, June 1985)

The confidence of the House of Commons in the governing party lies at the heart of what we have come to know as responsible government. This form of government requires that the cabinet be responsible for its actions to an elected legislature. It implies necessarily that there be a policy-making body of ministers bound to provide unanimous advice to the Sovereign; that the public service be under the control of political leaders responsible to the legislature; and that both the executive and the legislature be responsible to the people.

Ministerial responsibility, along with the fusion of the executive and legislative branches, are distinguishing features of responsible government. The rules relating to these features are not set down in the Constitution. They are governed by convention, precedent and common sense. There is no single definition of ministerial responsibility; there are, in fact, three parts to the doctrine.

First there is the responsibility of a minister to the Queen or the Governor General; this is often overlooked, but it is basic to our constitutional order. Governments are not elected but appointed, and ministers serve not for a term, but until they die, resign or are dismissed.

Second, there is the individual responsibility of a minister to the House. This revolves around the questions of when a minister should offer his or her resignation and when should it be accepted or asked for. The answers seem to turn on the personal and political relationship between the minister and the prime minister. The principle is accepted, however, that where there is personal culpability on the part of a minister, in the form of private or public conduct regarded as unbecoming and unworthy of a minister of the Crown, the minister should resign.

The third responsibility is that of the ministry collectively to the House. If the confidence of the House is lost, it spells the end for the ministry unless the government is granted a dissolution and is sustained by the electorate.

Confidence from an Historical Perspective

The standing of a government in the House and the passage of its legislative program have come to be regarded as essential parts of responsible government. This was not always the case. In the nineteenth century political parties gained importance. This led to significant changes in the United Kingdom and in Canada as the parties, and particularly the leaders, appealed for votes in an enlarged and increasingly pluralistic electorate. The task of the House of Commons was reduced to voting on the legislation and estimates presented to it by the government.

The rarity of defeats of government measures in Great Britain (except in the minority situation in 1924) led rapidly to the development of a constitutional myth that every vote was a test of confidence. Any dissenting or cross-voting members on the government side were seen to be placing the government in jeopardy or risking dissolution of the House. In recent years, there has been more and more cross-party voting. In the seven-year period between April 1972 and April 1979, there were sixty-five defeats of government measures in the British House. This was not the end of responsible government. The government did not cease to govern. It was simply forced to modify or abandon some of its policies in deference to the House. Even with the large government majorities in recent years, there has not been a return to the inflexibility of the executive that marked earlier administrations. This kind of flexibility is not unlike what existed in early Canadian parliaments in the time of Sir John A. Macdonald when government measures were defeated a number of times without the government falling.

Recent British experience makes it clear that at present losing a vote, even on a financial measure, is not automatically a matter of non-confidence entailing either resignation of the government or a dissolution of the Commons. The government can decide how it will treat its loss. Whatever a government may say or imply in order to intimidate its own parliamentary supporters, a lost vote in itself does not involve resignation or dissolution.

The same phenomenon of lost votes that took place in Great Britain in the 1970s was also evident in Canada during that same period and, to a lesser extent, even earlier. At the start of the first session of the twenty-ninth parliament Prime Minister Trudeau said, "Some things for us will be questions of confidence. Some things would mean the demise of the government. ... But I hasten to add that other questions, if they go against us, will not be interpreted by the government as a defeat of the government. We shall accept amendments."

The minority government of Pierre Trudeau lost eight of eighty-one recorded votes between 1972 and 1974. Setting aside the vote of May 8, 1974, which brought down the government, four of the lost votes were on government bills, two were on motions pertaining to parliamentary committees, and one was on a supply item, specifically on a supplementary estimate of $19,000 for Information Canada.

The minority governments of Lester Pearson lost three votes. Two were on appeals of a ruling made by the Speaker. The third came February 19, 1968. A vote ended with the defeat on third reading of Bill C-193 respecting income tax. This vote was regarded as sufficiently serious to require the government to introduce a motion to the effect that the House did not consider its vote of February 19 as a vote of non-confidence in the government. The motion was passed, after debate, on February 28.

It is clear from both British and Canadian experience that a government that has lost a vote in the House on a matter of confidence faces the choice of resigning or asking for dissolution. A government that has lost a vote on some other matter may remain in office and may choose to ask for a vote of confidence.

Since every vote in the House is not a matter of confidence, it is not true that a government that loses a vote in the House can simply have the House dissolved. As a rule, the Governor General accepts the advice of the prime minister. In certain cases, however, the Governor General is justified in refusing an immediate request for dissolution. ...

Precedent shows that responsible government does not break down and government does not become unworkable when the executive bows to the wishes of the House on a wide variety of matters in a wide variety of circumstances. It is useful by way of summary to place government defeats into three categories, noting that each one invites a different response from the government.

A government defeated on a vote of confidence is expected to resign or seek a dissolution. Three types of votes can be termed confidence votes. First, there are explicitly worded votes of confidence. These state expressly that the House has or has not confidence in the government. Next are motions made votes of confidence by a declaration of the government. The government may declare that if defeated on a particular motion before the House, even one that is not an explicitly worded vote of confidence, it will resign or seek a dissolution. Then there are implicit votes of confidence. Traditionally, certain matters have been deemed to involve confidence, even though not declared to be so by the prior statement of the government. Falling within this category is the granting of supply. Failure to grant supply is regarded as the established means by which the House can demonstrate its lack of confidence in the ministry. However, it should be noted that a single defeat on a specific estimate would not in itself constitute a vote of non-confidence. In fact, because of the multiplicity of votes on all the aspects of supply, this is largely a category that has fallen into disuse. One could argue that this type of defeat actually belongs in the category of defeats that are not votes of confidence.

The second category is lost votes on items central to government policy but not made matters of confidence prior to the vote. The government in this case can either seek an explicit vote of confidence from the House or resign or request a dissolution. If the government opted for resignation or asked for dissolution, this would make the lost vote one of confidence retrospectively. There should normally be few votes that fall into this category.

The last group is votes on items not at the heart of government policy; these are obviously the most numerous during any parliament. Although a lost vote on second reading of a major bill might fall within the second category mentioned above, a loss on one or more of the many divisions during the committee and report stages would usually fall within this third classification. ...

In conclusion, we offer several observations. Although they can have no legal effect in our system of government, they should serve as an indication of the direction in which this committee believes the House of Commons should develop.

- A government should be careful before it declares or designates a vote as one of confidence. It should confine such declarations to measures central to its administration.
- While a defeat on supply is a serious matter, elimination or reduction of an estimate can be accepted. If a government wishes, it can designate a succeeding vote as a test of confidence or move a direct vote of confidence.
- Defeats on matters not essential to the government's program do not require it to arrange a vote of confidence, whether directly or on some procedural or collateral motion.
- Temporary loss of control of the business of the House does not call for any response from the government whether by resignation or by asking for a vote of confidence.

Note one of the McGrath committee observations: "As a rule, the Governor General accepts the advice of the prime minister. In certain cases, however, the Governor General is justified in refusing an immediate request for dissolution." In 1926, Governor General Julian Byng called upon Conservative leader Arthur Meighen to form a government when Prime Minister William Lyon Mackenzie King resigned after being refused dissolution. King had sought this dissolution to pre-empt a lost confidence vote for his minority Liberal government, held together in a precarious coalition with the Progressives in a Parliament produced via an election held only eight months before (and in session for an even briefer period of six months). When Meighen's government quickly collapsed and Parliament was dissolved, King campaigned on Lord Byng's failure to respond to his original dissolution request, soundly defeating the Conservatives.

It seems almost certain, however, that Byng acted in keeping with constitutional convention: a governor general may refuse a dissolution in the wake of the resignation of (at least a minority) government, where another prime-minister-apparent is able to command the confidence of the Commons, whether this person comes from the opposition or from within the governing party. Indeed, the governor general may have a constitutional duty to exercise this power of refusal.

The exercise of this "reserve" power is likely most legitimate where a government seeks a dissolution soon after an election. In comparison, use of the reserve power to refuse dissolution is less appropriate if exercised several years into a Parliament, at a time near its natural expiry. In those circumstances, it is better for the question of government leadership to be decided by the people in an election. For a discussion of reserve powers, see Andrew Heard, *Canadian Constitutional Conventions* (Toronto: Oxford University Press, 1991) at 23-24; Eugene A Forsey & GC Eglington, *The Question of Confidence in Responsible Government* (Ottawa: Special Committee on the Reform of the House of Commons, 1985) at 152ff.

II. KEY ACTORS IN PARLIAMENT

While in session, parliamentary procedures implicate several key actors, including political parties, the Speaker, and parliamentary committees. We discuss each of these players in turn.

A. POLITICAL PARTIES

As noted in Chapter 6, political parties are a recognized entity in Canadian election law. Politically, parties act to marshal collective resources in the hope of achieving electoral success. Parties are also, however, the partial product of two *legal* aspects of parliamentary democracy.

First, decision-making in Parliament depends on swaying a majority of votes in each chamber. For example, the Commons makes decisions through the device of motions, basically a question put to the House by the Speaker in response to a proposition made by a member. There are several different species of motion, each governed by its own procedural niceties. Eventually, however, all motions are debated, amended, superseded, adopted, negatived, or withdrawn. (A "superseded" motion is one replaced by another motion.) The success of a motion is determined by whether it attracts a majority of votes.

There is a constitutional reason for this. Consider s 49 of the *Constitution Act, 1867*: "Questions arising in the House of Commons shall be decided by a *Majority* of Voices other than that of the Speaker, and when the Voices are equal, but not otherwise, the Speaker shall have a Vote" (emphasis added). Note also s 36: "Questions arising in the Senate shall be decided by a *Majority* of Voices, and the Speaker shall in all Cases have a Vote, and when the Voices are equal the Decision shall be deemed to be in the Negative" (emphasis added). These rules encourage parliamentarians to organize as political parties: entities that command the loyalty of their members and, if those members are elected in sufficient numbers, allow control of a majority of the Commons.

A second constitutional motivation for parties stems from the confidence convention: by constitutional convention, the individual commanding the confidence of the Commons (that is, its majority) is appointed prime minister. Thus, party control of a majority of the House brings with it executive power.

Both legal considerations ensure that Westminster parliamentary systems are preoccupied (and sometimes obsessed) with maintaining "party discipline"—the *en bloc* votes of party members (or at least a coalition of different party members) sufficient to constitute a majority. In this environment, individual members of Parliament are not always (or, in some Parliaments, even usually) able to vote their conscience. Instead, they may be obliged to toe the party line. Indeed, party backbench members of Parliament are sometimes described derisively as little more than voting machines. Prime Minister Pierre Trudeau famously observed that members of Parliament were "nobodies" 50 yards from the Commons. Other commentators have referred to backbenchers in the governing party as "trained seals." See, for example, editorial, "MPs No Longer Trained Seals," *Halifax Daily News* (14 October 2002) 11; Charles Gordon, "At Last, Backbench Liberals Who Don't Want to Be Trained Seals," *Ottawa Citizen* (1 March 2003) B6.

In the result, there has been substantial discussion of a so-called democratic deficit in federal politics—that Parliaments (or at least Parliaments in which a single party controls a majority of seats in the House of Commons) play a paltry, secondary role in Canadian governance because of party discipline. Assembled in 2003, parliamentarians reviewing the question of parliamentary reform complained that

> the House of Commons and the Senate are no longer places in which meaningful debate occurs. The impetus to get the government's business through and the strongly enforced party discipline have combined to limit the number of voices heard in Parliament. In most matters of public debate, Canadians have many different points of view, while only a limited number of views are expressed within the walls of Parliament—largely as a result of party discipline. Parliament must put the richness of opinion that exists in the Canadian public to the service of the Canadian public by allowing for those multiple voices to be heard in Parliament.

(*The Parliament We Want: Parliamentarians' Views on Parliamentary Reform* (Ottawa: Library of Parliament, 2003), online: *Government of Canada* <http://publications.gc.ca/collections/Collection/YM41-3-2003E.pdf>)

Put another way, Parliament has become a place for ramming through government policy, not querying its merits. In the early 2000s, there seemed to be some support for the idea of more "free votes" in Parliament—circumstances in which MPs voted their conscience, not just as the party leader dictated. However, in the words of a 2007 report of the Library of Parliament, "the cycle of procedural reform that began in 2004 appears to have stalled, at least while current minority government conditions persist" (J Stilborn, *Parliamentary Reform and the House of Commons*, PRB 07-43E (Ottawa: Library of Parliament, 2007) at 4). Thirteen years after this report, nothing has happened that would change this conclusion. For example, the 2015 Liberal election platform promised free votes, but subject to important exceptions (for example, votes implementing the Liberal electoral platform). In the 42nd Parliament that followed, Bill C-14, which implemented medical assistance in dying, was a free vote for all parties (although Liberal Cabinet ministers were required to vote with their government).

The political affiliation of a given parliamentarian is a matter of politics, not law. There is no requirement that a parliamentarian be a member of a party, or that a party have a certain number of members. However, so-called "official" party status is reserved for parties possessing a minimum number of members in the Commons. Thus, once a party claims the allegiance of at least 12 members, certain benefits flow to it. Within the chamber of the Commons, these include membership on the Commons Board of Internal Economy and additional allowances for the party leader, whip, and house leader sitting in the Commons. Furthermore, recognized parties can tap into caucus research funds authorized by that Commons Board.

In Commons proceedings themselves, once the 12-MP threshold is reached, party members are then entitled to sit together, have their party affiliation noted with their name in the official records and on television broadcasts of proceedings, and are allowed a larger number of questions during question period.

B. THE SPEAKER

Further key players in Parliament are the Speakers of the two houses of Parliament. In the Commons, the Speaker is a member of Parliament elected to the Speaker's position by other MPs. The manner of his or her selection, and many of his or her powers, are set out in the "standing orders" of the House of Commons. These standing orders are internal procedural rules established by the Commons pursuant to its parliamentary "privileges" and discussed further below. Consider the following discussion of the Speaker's selection and function.

House of Commons, House of Commons Procedure and Practice

2nd ed (Ottawa: House of Commons, 2009) (footnotes omitted)

The Speaker of the House of Commons holds a position which is one not only of historical significance but also of great responsibility. The holder of the office performs functions falling into three main categories. First, the Speaker presides over debate in the House and is responsible for enforcing and interpreting all rules and practices and for the preservation of order and decorum in the proceedings of the House. Second, the Speaker is the chief administrative officer of the House of Commons. Third, the Speaker is the representative or spokesperson for the House in its relations with authorities or persons outside Parliament.

• • •

Guardian of Rights and Privileges

It is the responsibility of the Speaker to act as the guardian of the rights and privileges of Members and of the House as an institution. At the opening of each Parliament, the House is summoned to the Senate Chamber where the newly-elected Speaker addresses the Crown or its representative and claims for the Commons all of its accustomed rights and privileges. The claim holds good for the life of the Parliament and is not repeated in the event of the election of a new Speaker during the course of a Parliament. Freedom of speech may be the most important of the privileges accorded to Members of Parliament; it has been described as:

> ... a fundamental right without which they would be hampered in the performance of their duties. It permits them to speak in the House without inhibition, to refer to any matter or express any opinion as they see fit, to say what they feel needs to be said in the furtherance of the national interest and the aspirations of their constituents.

The right to freedom of speech is not, however, absolute; there are restrictions imposed by the House on its Members, derived from practice, convention, and the rules agreed to by the House. For example, the Standing Orders provide for time limits on speeches, and according to the *sub judice* convention, Members refrain from discussion of many matters which are currently under consideration by a court. The duty of the Speaker is to ensure that the right of Members to free speech is protected and exercised to the fullest possible extent; this is accomplished in part by ensuring that the rules and practices of the House are applied and that order and decorum are maintained. Whenever a Member brings to the attention of the House a possible breach of a right or privilege, the responsibility of the Speaker is to determine whether or not *prima facie* a breach of privilege has occurred. In practice the Speaker, in hearing an alleged question of privilege, may intervene to remind Members of the Speaker's role and to request that the Member's remarks be directed to providing facts to establish the existence of a *prima facie* case. At the Speaker's discretion, other Members may be permitted to participate. Only when the Speaker has ruled the matter to be a *prima facie* question of privilege can a motion be brought formally before the House for its consideration.

Order and Decorum

As the arbiter of House proceedings, the Speaker's duty is to preserve order and decorum in the House and to decide any matters of procedure that may arise.

This duty carries with it a wide-ranging authority extending to matters as diverse as the behaviour and attire of Members, the conduct of proceedings, the rules of debate and disruptions on the floor of the Chamber and in its galleries. When a decision on a matter of procedure or a question of order is reached, the Standing Orders require that the Speaker identify which Standing Order or other authority is being applied to the case.

Sometimes, a ruling is delivered quickly and with a minimum of explanation. At other times, circumstances do not permit an immediate ruling. The Speaker may allow discussion of the point of order before he or she comes to a decision. The Speaker might also reserve his or her decision on a matter, returning to the House at a later time to deliver the ruling. Once the Speaker has ruled, the matter is no longer open to debate or discussion. On some occasions, the Speaker has, however, chosen to amend or clarify a previous ruling.

In addition to ruling on procedural issues, Speakers may make statements with a view to providing information, clarification or direction to the House.

There are a number of ways in which the Speaker may act to ensure that order and decorum are preserved:

- The rules governing the conduct of debate empower the Speaker to call a Member to order if the Member persists in repeating an argument already made in the course of debate, or in addressing a subject which is not relevant to the question before the House. ...
- If the Speaker has found it necessary to intervene in order to call a Member to order, he or she may then choose to recognize another Member, thus declining to give the floor back to the offending Member. ...
- The most severe sanction available to the Speaker for maintaining order in the House is "naming," a disciplinary measure reserved for Members who persistently disregard the authority of the Chair. If a Member refuses to heed the Speaker's requests to bring his or her behaviour into line with the rules and practices of the House, the Speaker has the authority to name that Member (i.e., to address the Member by name rather than by constituency or title, as is the usual practice) and, without putting the question to the House, to order his or her withdrawal from the Chamber for the remainder of the sitting day. ...
- Another means of preserving order in the Chamber is the Speaker's discretionary power to order the withdrawal of strangers: that is, anyone who is not a Member or an official of the House of Commons (e.g., Senators, diplomats, government officials, journalists or members of the general public). This measure has been used to clear the galleries of individuals whose presence has been a cause of disruption. ...

• • •

Casting Vote

The Speaker does not participate in debate and votes only in cases of an equality of voices; in such an eventuality, the Speaker is responsible for breaking the tie by casting a vote.

In theory, the Speaker has the same freedom as any other Member to vote in accordance with his or her conscience; however, the exercise of this responsibility could involve the Speaker in partisan debate, which would adversely affect the confidence of the House in his or her impartiality. Therefore, certain conventions have developed as a guide to Speakers (and Chairs in a Committee of the Whole) in the infrequent exercise of the casting vote. Concisely put, the Speaker normally votes to maintain the *status quo*. This entails voting in the following fashion:

- whenever possible, leaving the matter open for future consideration and allowing for further discussion by the House;
- whenever no further discussion is possible, preserving the possibility that the matter might somehow be brought back in the future and be decided by a majority of the House; and
- leaving a bill in its existing form rather than causing it to be amended.

C. PARLIAMENTARY COMMITTEES

Parliamentary committees are subsets of Parliament tasked with much of the detailed work in Parliament. Consider the following description of committee functions and membership.

House of Commons, House of Commons Procedure and Practice
2nd ed (Ottawa: House of Commons, 2009)

The House of Commons has an extensive committee system. There are various types of committees: standing, standing joint, legislative, special, special joint and subcommittees. They differ in their membership, the terms of reference they are given by the House, and their longevity.

Standing Committees

Standing committees form a majority of the committees established by the House of Commons. Their authority flows from their large number (24) and the variety of studies entrusted to them, but also from the fact that they return session after session as their existence is entrenched in the Standing Orders. Composed of 11 or 12 Members representing all recognized parties in the House, they play a crucial role in the improvement of legislation and the oversight of government activities.

[T]heir titles and mandates cover every main area of federal government activity, but for a few exceptions. However, they do not match its administrative structure exactly. Standing committees fall into three broad categories: (1) those overseeing one or more federal departments or organizations, (2) those responsible for matters of House and committee administration and procedure, and (3) those with transverse responsibilities that deal with issues affecting the entire government apparatus. The latter are likely to work with other committees in discharging their mandates.

General Mandate

The Standing Orders set out a general mandate for all standing and standing joint committees, with a few exceptions. They are empowered to study and report to the House on all matters relating to the mandate, management, organization and operation of the departments assigned to them. More specifically, they can review:

- the statute law relating to the departments assigned to them;
- the program and policy objectives of those departments, and the effectiveness of their implementation thereof;

- the immediate, medium and long-term expenditure plans of those departments and the effectiveness of the implementation thereof; and
- an analysis of the relative success of those departments in meeting their objectives.

In addition to this general mandate, other matters are routinely referred by the House to its standing committees: bills, estimates, Order-in-Council appointments, documents tabled in the House pursuant to statute, and specific matters which the House wishes to have studied. In each case, the House chooses the most appropriate committee on the basis of its mandate.

Specific Mandates

The Standing Orders set out specific mandates for some standing committees, on the basis of which they are to study and report to the House:

- The **Standing Committee on Procedure and House Affairs** deals with, among other matters, the election of Members; the administration of the House and the provision of services and facilities to Members; the effectiveness, management and operations of all operations which are under the joint administration and control of the two Houses, except with regard to the Library of Parliament; the review of the Standing Orders, procedure and practice in the House and its committees; the consideration of business related to private bills; the review of the radio and television broadcasting of the proceedings of the House and its committees; the *Conflict of Interest Code for Members of the House of Commons*; and the review of the annual report of the Conflict of Interest and Ethics Commissioner with respect to his or her responsibilities under the *Parliament of Canada Act*. The Committee also acts as a striking committee, recommending the list of members of all standing and legislative committees, and the Members who represent the House on standing joint committees. It also establishes priority of use of committee rooms, and is involved in designating the items of Private Members' Business as votable or non-votable.
- The **Standing Committee on Citizenship and Immigration**, among other matters, monitors the implementation of the principles of the federal multiculturalism policy throughout the Government of Canada.
- The **Standing Committee on Government Operations and Estimates** has a very broad mandate that includes, among other matters, the review of the effectiveness, management and operation, together with the operational and expenditures plans of the central departments and agencies; the review of estimates for programs delivered by more than one department or agency; the review of the effectiveness, management and operation of activities related to the use of new and emerging information and communication technologies by the government; and the review of the process for consideration of estimates and supply by parliamentary committees.
- The **Standing Committee on Human Resources, Skills and Social Development and the Status of Persons with Disabilities** is responsible for, among other matters, proposing, promoting, monitoring and assessing initiatives aimed at the social integration and equality of disabled persons.
- The **Standing Committee on Justice and Human Rights** is responsible for, among other matters, the review of reports of the Canadian Human Rights Commission.
- The **Standing Committee on Official Languages** deals with, among other matters, official languages policies and programs, including reports of the

Commissioner of Official Languages. The Committee's mandate is derived from a legislative provision requiring that a committee of either House or both Houses be specifically charged with review of the administration of the *Official Languages Act* and the implementation of certain reports presented pursuant to this statute.

- The **Standing Committee on Public Accounts** deals with, among other matters, the review of the Public Accounts of Canada and all reports of the Auditor General of Canada.

- The **Standing Committee on Access to Information, Privacy and Ethics** reviews, among other matters, the effectiveness, management and operation together with the operational and expenditure plans relating to three Officers of Parliament: the Information Commissioner, the Privacy Commissioner and the Conflict of Interest and Ethics Commissioner. It also reviews their reports, although in the case of the Conflict of Interest and Ethics Commissioner, the reports concerned relate to his or her responsibilities under the *Parliament of Canada Act* regarding public office holders and reports tabled pursuant to the *Lobbyists Registration Act*. In cooperation with other standing committees, the Committee also reviews any bill, federal regulation or Standing Order which impacts upon its main areas of responsibility: access to information, privacy and the ethical standards of public office holders. It may also propose initiatives in these areas and promote, monitor and assess such initiatives.

- The **Standing Committee on Finance** is empowered to review proposals relating to the government's budgetary policy.

Standing Joint Committees

In addition to the standing committees, there are two standing joint committees: one on the Library of Parliament and one on the Scrutiny of Regulations. These are described as "joint" because their membership consists of Members of the House of Commons and Senators. In contrast to standing committees, moreover, the number of members can vary. Struck for each session of Parliament, their status is formalized by statute and confirmed by the Standing Orders of the House of Commons and the Rules of the Senate.

• • •

Legislative Committees

Legislative committees are created on an *ad hoc* basis by the House solely to draft or review proposed legislation. They therefore do not return from one session to the next, as standing and standing joint committees do. They are established as needed when the House adopts a motion making a referral, and cease to exist upon presentation of their report on the draft legislation to the House. They consist of a maximum of 15 Members drawn from all recognized political parties, plus the Chair.

Their mandate is restricted to examining and inquiring into the bill referred to them by the House, and presenting a report on it with or without amendments. They are not empowered to consider matters outside the provisions of the bill, nor can they submit comments or recommendations in a substantive report to the House. However, if the House has instructed a committee to prepare a bill, it is empowered under the Standing Orders to recommend in its report the principles, scope and general provisions of the bill and may include recommendations regarding legislative wording.

Special Committees

As in the case of legislative committees, special committees are *ad hoc* bodies created as needed by the House. Unlike legislative committees, however, they are not usually charged with the study of a bill, but rather with inquiring into a matter to which the House attaches particular importance. Every special committee is established by an order of reference of the House. The motion usually defines its mandate and may include other provisions covering its powers, membership—the number of members varies—and the deadline for presentation of its final report to the House. The content of the motion varies with the specific task entrusted to the committee. Special committees cease to exist upon presentation of their final report.

Special Joint Committees

Special joint committees are created for the same purposes as special committees: to study matters of great importance. However, they are composed of Members of the House of Commons and Senators. They are established by order of reference from the House, and another from the Senate.

The House that wishes to initiate a special joint committee first adopts a motion to establish it and includes a provision inviting the other Chamber to participate in the proposed committee's work. The motion also includes any instruction to the committee, and sets out the powers delegated to it. It may also designate the members of the committee, or specify how they are to be selected.

Decisions of one House concerning the membership, mandate and powers of a proposed joint committee are communicated to the other House by message. Both Houses must be in agreement about the mandate and powers of the committee in order for it to be able to undertake its work. Once a request to participate in a joint committee is received, the other House, if it so desires, adopts a motion to establish such a committee and includes a provision to be returned to the originating House, stating that it agrees to the request. Once the originating House has been informed of the agreement of the other Chamber, the committee can be organized. A special joint committee ceases to exist when it has presented its final report to both Houses.

The mandate of a special joint committee is set out in the order of reference by which it is established. In the past, special joint committees have been set up to inquire into such matters as child custody, defence, foreign policy, a code of conduct for Members and Senators and Senate reform. Constitutional issues have often been referred to special joint committees. From time to time, they have also been charged with review of legislation, either by being empowered to prepare a bill or by the referral of a bill to the committee after second reading.

Subcommittees

Subcommittees are working groups that report to existing committees. They are normally created by an order of reference adopted by the committee in question. They may also be created directly by the House, but this is less common. The establishment of subcommittees may also be provided for in the Standing Orders.

The establishment of subcommittees is usually designed to relieve parliamentary committees of planning and administrative tasks, or to address important issues relating to their mandate. A subcommittee is able to devote all the necessary attention to the mandate it is given, whereas the committee it reports to is likely to be dealing with a heavy agenda and conflicting priorities. Subcommittees generally have a lower level of activity than the committees they report to, but in some cases they may be just as busy. Apart from the cases in which they are created by the House or required pursuant to the Standing Orders, a parliamentary committee is under no obligation to strike subcommittees, the decision rests entirely with its members.

Unless provision has already been made in the Standing Orders, it is up to the committee—or the House, as the case may be—that creates a subcommittee to establish its mandate in an order of reference, specifying its membership (the number of members varies), powers and any other conditions that are to govern its deliberations. Depending on the circumstances and the type of mandate it is assigned, a subcommittee will exist as long as the main committee does, or will cease to exist when its task is completed.

Not every type of committee can create subcommittees. Under the Standing Orders, standing committees (including, where the House is concerned, standing joint committees) may do so. In practice, most of them create a subcommittee on agenda and procedure, commonly referred to as a "steering committee," to help them plan their work. A steering committee is the only type of subcommittee a legislative committee is empowered to create under the Standing Orders. Special committees may create subcommittees only if empowered to do so by the House (and by the Senate, in the case of a special joint committee).

Once established, subcommittees carry out their own work within the mandate entrusted to them. They are free to adopt rules to govern their activities, provided these are consistent with the framework established by the main committee. Subcommittees report to their main committee with respect to resolutions, motions or reports they wish the main committee to concur in. Proposals by a steering committee as to how the main committee's work is to be organized must be approved by the committee itself. In every case, this is achieved by having the subcommittee adopt a report for presentation to the main committee. Unless the House or the committees decide otherwise, main committees may amend the reports of their subcommittees before concurring in them.

As this extract suggests, committees are potentially quite powerful actors, and indeed where witnesses before them are uncooperative, may draw on Parliament's contempt powers. The latter are part of Parliament's parliamentary privilege, a concept described below. As described by Joseph Maingot, this means that

[a]ny act or omission that obstructs or impedes either House of Parliament in the performance of its functions, or that obstructs or impedes any Member or officer of such House in the discharge of his duty, or that has a tendency, directly or indirectly, to produce such results may be treated as contempt even though there is no precedent of the offence.

(Joseph P Maingot, *Parliamentary Privilege in Canada*, 2nd ed (Montreal: McGill-Queen's University Press, 1997) at 193.)

In April 2008, the House of Commons agreed to a motion holding a then-RCMP deputy commissioner

in contempt of Parliament for providing false and misleading testimony to the House of Commons Standing Committee on Public Accounts on February 21, 2007; and that the House of Commons take no further action as this finding of contempt is, in and of itself, a very serious sanction

(House of Commons, *Journals*, No 76, 39th Parl, 2nd Sess (10 April 2008)).

The move followed a Commons public account committee probe into the mismanagement of the RCMP's pension and insurance plans, and criticism by that committee of the officer's apparently contradictory (and, in the eyes of parliamentarians, "misleading" or perhaps "untruthful") evidence on the issue (House of Commons Standing Committee on Public Accounts, Third Report, 39th Parl, 1st Sess (February 2008) at 10). The event had significant implications for the officer's reputation. She retired from the RCMP only months later ("RCMP Officer Retires After Contempt Citation," *Globe and Mail* (8 November 2008) A13).

The contempt citation ultimately issued by the Commons was controversial, with critics raising serious concerns about the level of due process accorded by parliamentarians to the RCMP officer. (See e.g. Kathryn May, "Mountie Found in Contempt," *Montreal Gazette* (11 April 2008) A10; Kathryn May, "Parliamentary Privilege Used as a 'Sword' Against Citizens, Political Experts Warn," *Ottawa Citizen* (24 April 2008) A1.) The lawyer for the officer asserted that "[t]his process is fundamentally flawed. ... There's no due process in it. We have what are, in effect, amateur fact-finders operating in an environment where there is no due process for the witness" (Steve Rennie, "Find Mountie in Contempt, Panel Advises," *Winnipeg Free Press* (13 February 2008) A7). The parliamentary law counsel contested this view, arguing that "the process was fair, even when measured by legal standards that don't apply, and as fair as it ought to have been in view of the nature of the proceedings" (Rob Walsh, "Fairness in Committees" (Summer 2008) Can Parliamentary Rev 23 at 26). In the wake of more considered investigations suggesting the committee was wrong, some parliamentarians clearly now regret their treatment of the officer. See Colin Freeze, "Former Mountie Wants Her Apology After Being Found in Contempt," *Globe and Mail* (2 November 2012).

III. PARLIAMENTARY PROCEDURE

How does Parliament perform its law-making functions? In this section, we begin by examining the sources of law governing the parliamentary law-making function, before reviewing the actual procedure followed in converting a bill (a law project) into a statute (a binding piece of legislation).

"Parliamentary law"—the body of rules determining parliamentary procedure—flows from an array of sources: the Constitution; assorted statutes such as the *Parliament of Canada Act*, RSC 1985, c P-1; the standing orders; and assorted usages, customs, and precedents, as assessed by the Speaker. In the sections that follow, we highlight some of this parliamentary law.

A. CONSTITUTIONAL AND LEGISLATIVE BASIS: PARLIAMENTARY PRIVILEGE

The starting point for understanding "parliamentary law" is the Constitution. The Canadian Constitution incorporates British parliamentary traditions via the preamble to the *Constitution Act, 1867*. This Act endows Canada with "a Constitution similar in Principle to that of the United Kingdom" (preamble). The 1867 Act also speaks of Parliament possessing parliamentary "privileges," as does the *Parliament of Canada Act*.

"Parliamentary privileges" are those rights "necessary to ensure that legislatures can perform their functions, free from interference by the Crown and the courts": *Provincial Judges Reference*, [1997] 3 SCR 3 at para 10. "Privilege," in this context, often means "the legal exemption from some duty, burden, attendance or liability to which others are subject": see *New Brunswick Broadcasting Co v Nova Scotia*, [1993] 1 SCR 319 at para 117, per McLachlin J. Consider the Supreme Court of Canada's most recent analysis of "parliamentary privilege," its scope, and the role of the courts in deciding its existence.

Canada (House of Commons) v Vaid
2005 SCC 30, [2005] 1 SCR 667

BINNIE J:

[1] The former Speaker of the House of Commons, the Honourable Gilbert Parent, is accused of constructively dismissing his chauffeur, Mr. Satnam Vaid,

for reasons that amount to workplace discrimination and harassment under the *Canadian Human Rights Act*. ... The issue on this appeal is whether it is open to the Canadian Human Rights Tribunal to investigate Mr. Vaid's complaint.

[2] The former Speaker denies any impropriety, but he joins the House of Commons in a preliminary objection that the hiring and firing of House employees are "internal affairs" which may not be questioned or reviewed by any tribunal or court outside the House itself. This immunity, the appellants say, emerged from the struggle for independence by the House of Commons from the prerogatives of the King, the authority of the Royal courts of law, and the special rights of the House of Lords reaching back in part to the time of the Tudor Kings and Queens in the 16th century. The appellants contend that these hard-won powers and immunities, collectively referred to as the privileges of Parliament, permit the Senate and the House to conduct their employee relations free from interference from the Canadian Human Rights Commission or any other body outside Parliament itself.

[3] The respondent Canadian Human Rights Commission, which seeks to investigate Mr. Vaid's allegations, says it is unthinkable that Parliament would seek to deny its employees the benefit of labour and human rights protections which Parliament itself has imposed on every other federal employer.

[4] There are few issues as important to our constitutional equilibrium as the relationship between the legislature and the other branches of the State on which the Constitution has conferred powers, namely the executive and the courts. The resolution of this issue is especially important when the action of the Speaker sought to be immunized from outside scrutiny is directed against a stranger to the House (i.e., not a Member or official) who is remote from the legislative functions that parliamentary privilege was originally designed to protect. ... The purpose of privilege is to recognize Parliament's *exclusive* jurisdiction to deal with complaints within its privileged sphere of activity. The proper focus, in my view, is not the grounds on which a particular privilege is exercised, but the prior question of the existence and scope of the privilege asserted by Parliament in the first place.

[5] Focusing, then, on the scope of the claimed privilege, the respondents argue that the duties of the Speaker's chauffeur appear too remote from the legislative function of the House and that the respondent Vaid's dismissal is not immunized from external review by virtue of parliamentary privilege. ...

· · ·

[20] It is a wise principle that the courts and Parliament strive to respect each other's role in the conduct of public affairs. Parliament, for its part, refrains from commenting on matters before the courts under the *sub judice* rule. The courts, for their part, are careful not to interfere with the workings of Parliament. None of the parties to this proceeding questions the pre-eminent importance of the House of Commons as "the grand inquest of the nation." Nor is doubt thrown by any party on the need for its legislative activities to proceed unimpeded by any external body or institution, including the courts. It would be intolerable, for example, if a member of the House of Commons who was overlooked by the Speaker at question period could invoke the investigatory powers of the Canadian Human Rights Commission with a complaint that the Speaker's choice of another member of the House discriminated on some ground prohibited by the *Canadian Human Rights Act*, or to seek a ruling from the ordinary courts that the Speaker's choice violated the member's guarantee of free speech under the Charter. These are truly matters "internal to the House" to be resolved by its own procedures. Quite apart from the potential interference by outsiders in the direction of the House, such external intervention would inevitably create delays, disruption, uncertainties and costs which would

hold up the nation's business and on that account would be unacceptable even if, in the end, the Speaker's rulings were vindicated as entirely proper.

[21] Parliamentary privilege, therefore, is one of the ways in which the fundamental constitutional separation of powers is respected. In Canada, the principle has its roots in the preamble to our *Constitution Act, 1867* which calls for "a Constitution similar in Principle to that of the United Kingdom." Each of the branches of the State is vouchsafed a measure of autonomy from the others. Parliamentary privilege was partially codified in art. 9 of the UK *Bill of Rights* of 1689. ... Parliamentary privilege is a principle common to all countries based on the Westminster system, and has a loose counterpart in the Speech or Debate Clause of the United States Constitution, art. 1, §6, cl. 1.

[22] The respondent Vaid does not quarrel either with the existence or the importance of parliamentary privilege. His argument is that the Speaker's attempt to treat his dismissal from his job as chauffeur as an expression of such lofty doctrine is to overreach, if not trivialize, its true role and function. Even if the employment arrangements of some employees closely connected to the legislative process are covered by privilege, the respondents argue that the Speaker goes too far in attempting to throw the mantle of this ancient doctrine over the dealings of the House with such support staff as chauffeurs, picture framers, locksmiths, car park administrators, catering staff and others who play comparable supporting roles on Parliament Hill.

[23] Over the years, the assertion of parliamentary privilege has varied in its scope and extent. ...

[24] It is evident that there have been variations in the extent of privilege asserted by Parliament over the years, as well as a difference on occasion between the scope of a privilege asserted by Parliamentarians and the scope of a privilege the courts have recognized as justified. ... In resolving such conflicts it is important that both Parliament and the courts respect "the legitimate sphere of activity of the other":

> Our democratic government consists of several branches: the Crown, as represented by the Governor General and the provincial counterparts of that office; the legislative body; the executive; and the courts. It is fundamental to the working of government as a whole that all these parts play their proper role. It is equally fundamental that no one of them overstep its bounds, that each show proper deference for the legitimate sphere of activity of the other. (*New Brunswick Broadcasting Co. v. Nova Scotia (Speaker of the House of Assembly)*, [1993] 1 SCR 319, *per* McLachlin J, at p. 389)

• • •

[29] While there are some significant differences between privilege at the federal level, for which specific provision is made in s. 18 of the *Constitution Act, 1867*, and privilege at the provincial level, which has a different constitutional underpinning, many of the relevant issues concerning privilege were resolved in *New Brunswick Broadcasting* and earlier cases, and there is no need to repeat the analysis here. For present purposes, it is sufficient to state a number of propositions that are now accepted both by the courts and by the parliamentary experts.

1. Legislative bodies created by the *Constitution Act, 1867* do not constitute enclaves shielded from the ordinary law of the land. "The tradition of curial deference does not extend to everything a legislative assembly might do, but is firmly attached to certain specific activities of legislative assemblies, i.e., the so-called privileges of such bodies." ... Privilege "does not embrace

and protect activities of *individuals,* whether members or non-members, simply because they take place within the precincts of Parliament." ...

2. Parliamentary privilege in the Canadian context is the sum of the privileges, immunities and powers enjoyed by the Senate, the House of Commons and provincial legislative assemblies, and by each member individually, without which they could not discharge their functions. ...

3. Parliamentary privilege does not create a gap in the general public law of Canada but is an important part of it, inherited from the Parliament at Westminster by virtue of the preamble to the *Constitution Act, 1867* and in the case of the Canadian Parliament, through s. 18 of the same Act. ...

4. Parliamentary privilege includes "the *necessary immunity* that the law provides for Members of Parliament, and for Members of the legislatures of each of the ten provinces ... *in order for these legislators to do their legislative work.*" ... The idea of necessity is thus linked to the autonomy required by legislative assemblies and their members to do their job.

5. The historical foundation of every privilege of Parliament is necessity. If a sphere of the legislative body's activity could be left to be dealt with under the ordinary law of the land without interfering with the assembly's ability to fulfill its constitutional functions, then immunity would be unnecessary and the claimed privilege would not exist. ...

6. When the existence of a category (or sphere of activity) for which inherent privilege is claimed (at least at the provincial level) is put in issue, the court must not only look at the historical roots of the claim but also to determine whether the category of inherent privilege *continues* to be necessary to the functioning of the legislative body today. Parliamentary history, while highly relevant, is not conclusive. ...

7. "Necessity" in this context is to be read broadly. The time-honoured test, derived from the law and custom of Parliament at Westminster, is what "the dignity and efficiency of the House" require: "If a matter falls within this necessary sphere of matters without which the *dignity and efficiency of the House* cannot be upheld, courts will not inquire into questions concerning such privilege. All such questions will instead fall to the exclusive jurisdiction of the legislative body." ...

8. Proof of necessity may rest in part in "shewing that it has been long exercised and acquiesced in" (*Stockdale v. Hansard,* at p. 1189). The party who seeks to rely on the immunity provided by parliamentary privilege has the onus of establishing its existence. ...

9. Proof of necessity is required only to establish the existence and scope of a *category* of privilege. Once the category (or sphere of activity) is established, it is for Parliament, not the courts, to determine whether in a particular case the *exercise* of the privilege is necessary or appropriate. In other words, within categories of privilege, Parliament is the judge of the occasion and manner of its exercise and such exercise is not reviewable by the courts: "Each specific instance of *the exercise* of a privilege need not be shown to be necessary." ...

10. "Categories" include freedom of speech ... ; control by the Houses of Parliament over "debates or proceedings in Parliament" (as guaranteed by the *Bill of Rights* of 1689) including day-to-day procedure in the House ... ; the power to exclude strangers from proceedings ... ; disciplinary authority over members ... ; and non-members who interfere with the discharge of parliamentary duties ..., including immunity of members from subpoenas

during a parliamentary session. ... Such general categories have historically been considered to be justified by the exigencies of parliamentary work.

11. The role of the courts is to ensure that a claim of privilege does not immunize from the ordinary law the consequences of conduct by Parliament or its officers and employees that exceeds the necessary scope of the category of privilege. ...

12. Courts are apt to look more closely at cases in which claims to privilege have an impact on persons outside the legislative assembly than at those which involve matters entirely internal to the legislature. ...

• • •

[41] Parliamentary privilege is *defined* by the degree of autonomy necessary to perform Parliament's constitutional function. ...

• • •

[43] While much latitude is left to each House of Parliament, such a purposive approach to the definition of privilege implies important limits. There is general recognition, for example, that privilege attaches to "proceedings in Parliament." Nevertheless, ... not "*everything that is said or done within the Chamber during the transaction of business forms part of proceedings in Parliament*. Particular words or acts may be entirely unrelated to any business which is in course of transaction, or is in a more general sense before the House as having been ordered to come before it in due course." ... "Particular words or acts may be entirely unrelated to any business being transacted or ordered to come before the House in due course."

• • •

[45] Parliament's sovereignty when engaged in the performance of its legislative duties is undoubted ... .

[46] All of these sources point in the direction of a similar conclusion. In order to sustain a claim of parliamentary privilege, the assembly or member seeking its immunity must show that the sphere of activity for which privilege is claimed is so closely and directly connected with the fulfillment by the assembly or its members of their functions as a legislative and deliberative body, including the assembly's work in holding the government to account, that outside interference would undermine the level of autonomy required to enable the assembly and its members to do their work with dignity and efficiency.

• • •

[52] I therefore turn to the appellants' contention that "the power of the Speaker of the House of Commons to hire, manage and dismiss House employees is among the constitutionally entrenched parliamentary privileges over which the House has exclusive jurisdiction. This exclusive jurisdiction extends to the investigation and adjudication of workplace discrimination claims" ... .

• • •

[70] [Having also reviewed Canadian authority and found it silent on the issue,] I conclude that British authority does not establish that the House of Commons at Westminster is immunized by privilege in the conduct of *all* labour relations with *all* employees irrespective of whether those categories of employees have any connection (or nexus) with its legislative or deliberative functions, or its role in holding the government accountable.

• • •

[72] [Turning to the "necessity test,"] [t]he employment roster of the House of Commons in 2005 is very different from that of 1867. In the early period, the House of Commons had only 66 permanent staff and 67 sessional employees. At present,

according to the Human Resources Section of the House of Commons, there are 2377 employees. These include many departments and services unknown in 1867. The Library of Parliament alone employs 298 people, more than twice the total number of House employees in 1867. The Information Services for the House now has 573 employees. Not all of these greatly expanded services relate directly to the House's function as a legislative and deliberative body. Parliamentary Precinct Services employs over 800 staff including a locksmith, an interior designer, various curators, five carpenters, a massage therapist, two picture framers, a chief of parking operations and two traffic constables. Parliamentary Corporate Services includes several kitchen chefs, lesser cooks and helpers, three dishwashers/potwashers and other catering support staff. There is no doubt that the House of Commons regards *all* of its employees as helpful but the question is whether that definition of the scope of the privilege it asserts is too broad. Is the management of *all* employees ... "so closely and directly connected with proceedings in Parliament that intervention by the courts would be inconsistent with Parliament's sovereignty as a legislative and deliberative assembly"? ... In other words, can it be said that immunity from outside scrutiny in the management of *all* service employees is such that without it ... the House and its members "could not discharge their functions"? ...

• • •

[75] I have no doubt that privilege attaches to the House's relations with *some* of its employees, but the appellants have insisted on the broadest possible coverage without leading any evidence to justify such a sweeping immunity, or a lesser immunity, or indeed any evidence of necessity at all. We are required to make a pragmatic assessment but we have been given no evidence on which a privilege of more modest scope could be delineated. ...

[76] The appellants having failed to establish the privilege in the broad and all-inclusive terms asserted, the respondents are entitled to have the appeal disposed of according to the ordinary employment and human rights law that Parliament has enacted with respect to employees within federal legislative jurisdiction.

B. STANDING ORDERS

In *Vaid*, the Supreme Court grappled with privilege as a source of potential immunity of parliamentarians from human rights law. (Note: do not assume from this discussion that parliamentarians are themselves immunized by privilege for, for example, their criminal conduct. There is no such immunity in Canada.) As the discussion in that case suggests, however, parliamentary privilege is a broad concept that extends beyond these immunity issues. It includes Parliament's power "to establish rules of procedure for itself and to enforce them," without external interference (House of Commons, *Beauchesne's Rules and Forms of the House of Commons of Canada*, 6th ed (Toronto: Carswell, 1989) at 14). Courts have specifically held that Canada's legislatures have the power to administer that part of the statute law relating to their internal procedure, as well as to determine the content of such things as Standing Orders on Procedure, without any intervention from the courts. See *Carter v Alberta*, 2002 ABCA 303 at 48, 222 DLR (4th) 40, citing Maingot, *Parliamentary Privilege in Canada*, 2nd ed (Montreal: McGill-Queen's University Press, 1997) at 183-87; *Ontario (Speaker of the Legislative Assembly) v Ontario (Human Rights Commission)* (2001), 54 OR (3d) 595 at para 48 (CA).

Parliament has exercised this internal governance right. Both houses of the federal Parliament have promulgated their own rules of procedure. We focus on the standing orders of the House of Commons, but broadly speaking, these Commons rules are replicated in the Senate's own procedural code.

The standing orders are rules of procedure adopted by at least a simple majority vote of the members of the Commons. They constitute a fairly comprehensive code of Commons operations, including in relation to Commons law-making. The orders, however, do not anticipate every circumstance, and their meaning often requires interpretation. For this reason, order 1 of the standing orders provides that where the orders are silent, "procedural questions shall be decided by the Speaker or Chair, whose decisions shall be based on the usages, forms, customs, and precedents of the House of Commons of Canada and on parliamentary tradition in Canada and other jurisdictions, so far as they may be applicable to the House."

We turn now to examining how these standing orders and other legal standards govern law-making in Parliament.

IV. PARLIAMENTARY LAW-MAKING

Our discussion of parliamentary law-making focuses on both substance and procedure. Substantively, what is the scope of Parliament's law-making jurisdiction? Procedurally, what process does Parliament follow?

A. THE SCOPE OF PARLIAMENT'S LAW-MAKING JURISDICTION

Parliamentary supremacy, discussed in Chapter 5, means that Parliament and its provincial counterparts are the only truly sovereign body in Canadian constitutional law. In its classic form, supremacy means that Parliament is the source of all power, and Parliament has the jurisdiction "to make or unmake any law whatever": see Albert Venn Dicey, *Introduction to the Study of the Law of the Constitution*, 10th ed (Toronto: Macmillan, 1961) at 39.

Of course, in Canada, there is no full federal parliamentary supremacy. Parliament is subordinated to other constraints in the Constitution, most notably the division of powers between the federal and provincial governments in the *Constitution Act, 1867* and (subject to s 33 or the prospect of a s 1 justification) constitutionally protected individual rights and liberties found in the Charter. But so long as it falls within these constitutional bounds, Parliament may make any law on any topic it wishes, as an exercise of its parliamentary supremacy. See the discussion in *Babcock v Canada (AG)*, 2002 SCC 57, [2002] 3 SCR 3, excerpted in Chapter 5.

1. The Power to Pass Bad Laws

Does this parliamentary supremacy also mean that Parliament or provincial legislatures are free to pass careless, unwise, or ill-motivated statutes, so long as these flaws do not also constitute constitutional violations? The answer is "yes." Consider the following cases.

Bacon v Saskatchewan Crop Insurance Corp
(1999), 180 Sask R 20 (CA)

WAKELING JA (for the court):

[1] This appeal calls into question the legality of the Gross Revenue Insurance Program (GRIP) as it was applied in 1992 by the Saskatchewan Crop Insurance Corporation (SCIC). The appellants are Wayne Bacon and Gary Svenkeson who sued as representatives of three hundred and eighty six farmers who were registered under GRIP 91 and took exception to the manner in which GRIP 92 had been legislatively imposed upon them by virtue of the passage of amendments to *The Agricultural*

Safety Net Act, SS 1990-91 c. A-14.2 as amended SS 1992, c. 51. The appellants brought this action against SCIC and the Government of Saskatchewan (Government) to set aside the legislation establishing GRIP 92 and seeking damages.

• • •

[3] ... [T]he government felt it was necessary to change the concept of GRIP 91 and structure a new program referred to as GRIP 92 intended for the next year. ... [T]he government [also] felt compelled to pass *The Farm Income Insurance Legislation Amendment Act*, 1992, SS 1992 c. 51. The purpose of this legislation was to establish the changed terms of the GRIP 1991 contract for the year 1992 and to extinguish any claims for breach of contract that might otherwise arise as a result of this change. This Amendment Act was assented to on August 24, 1992 but was effective January 1, 1991.

[4] At trial, the appellants contended the Government had no authority to pass this legislation as governments, like everyone else, are subject to the law. The rule of law is a concept or principle so fundamental that even governments are not exempt from its application. This meant the laws of the land, including those relating to contractual obligations, are as binding upon the government as upon the public. As a consequence, the Government had no legal authority to pass legislation imposing a new contract and extinguishing the right to sue for the breach of the earlier contract.

• • •

[7] The argument advanced by the appellants can be best understood by a reference to the following opening paragraphs of their factum:

> It should be established clearly at the outset what this case is not about. This case is not about the *Canadian Charter of Rights and Freedoms*. ...
>
> Secondly, this case is not about the division of powers in the Constitution between the federal and provincial governments. It is acknowledged that this case involves property and civil rights within the province. It is further acknowledged that this is within the jurisdiction of the Government of Saskatchewan in the context as this case as presented, and there will be no argument advanced by the Plaintiffs that the facts of this case suggest that in somehow the legislation challenged is contrary to the aspect of the division of powers within the Constitution.
>
> This case is about the Rule of Law in the democratic society. The concept of the Rule of Law, will be submitted as something far more basic to the interaction of state and individual than either the Charter of Rights, or the division of federal and provincial powers.
>
> The Rule of Law was a legal concept that pre-dates the notion of a formal written Constitution, and which provides the basis for the common law control over the state in its interaction with individuals.

• • •

[11] The Government ... contends the role of Parliament (which is a word I use to include legislatures) is supreme when acting within its constitutional limits, as was the case in this instance. For this reason, the question of whether the passage of the legislation was an arbitrary use of power need not be asked.

• • •

[15] The appellants found their case on the contention that a new and more enlightened approach to the concept of the supremacy of Parliament has now emerged based on a greater respect for the rule of law. The freshness of this new approach was acknowledged in this fashion in their factum:

The phrase "rule of law" has been developed and expanded as the concept of democracy continues to change to suit the continuing needs and aspirations of the public.

[16] The start of this evolutionary process is said to have its foundation in the Magna Carta which contained the statement "the King is under no man save God and the Law." This may, indeed, be a cornerstone for the concept of the rule of law, but fails to be of great assistance to the appellant since it does nothing to restrict the supremacy of Parliament as being the principal source of the law.

[17] The appellants then turn to the comments of the Supreme Court justices in *Roncarelli v. Duplessis* ... as being a more recent application of the doctrine of the rule of law. In this case, the actions of Duplessis (who was at the time both the Premier and Attorney General of Quebec) were set aside as being arbitrary and without lawful authority.

[18] This is an example of where the courts have acted to prevent the arbitrary use of power by a public official which was unsupported by legislative authority, even though that official was of the highest rank. The appellants contend this judgment is the modern cornerstone for the development of the emerging concept of the importance of the rule of law. I am unable to see it in this light. The judgment issued nearly 40 years ago as an instance where an abuse of power by an official was found to be contrary to the concept of the rule of law and to date it has never been applied as anything more than an illustration of the application of the rule of law to prevent officials from acting arbitrarily without the support of lawful authority.

• • •

[23] The appellants [also rely on] the most recent pronouncements of the Supreme Court as contained in the *Reference re Secession of Quebec* which did not bring into question the extent of the supremacy of Parliament but did require a consideration of the nature of federalism as it exists in Canada. ...

• • •

[25] ... They interpret the statement "the law is supreme over the acts of both government and private persons" [found in the case] as being an unequivocal indication the government has no more right to avoid its contractual obligations then does a private person.

[26] This is not what I take from this statement. It is nothing more than an acceptance that the law as it exists is applicable to both government and private persons. It is a fundamental statement of the obligation of governments which is not challenged by any of the parties to this appeal. However, the law, including the common law, is subject to change by legislation and when changed it is this changed law which is the "one law for all." The law, which is applicable to us all, cannot be taken as static and unchangeable. It is forever evolving and Parliament plays a major role in its development. There is no statement in the *Secession* case which would suggest otherwise.

• • •

[30] The protection we treasure as a democratic country with the rule of law as "a fundamental postulate" of our constitution is twofold. Protection is provided by our courts against arbitrary and unlawful actions by officials while protection against arbitrary legislation is provided by the democratic process of calling our legislators into regular periods of accountability through the ballot box. This concept of the rule of law is not in any way restricted by the Supreme Court's statement that nobody including governments is beyond the law. That statement is a reference to the law as it exists from time to time and does not create a restriction on

Parliament's right to make laws, but is only a recognition that when they are made they are then applicable to all, including governments.

• • •

[36] ... [T]he public's protection from the arbitrary use of power by officials is provided by the Courts in situations such as was dealt with in *Roncarelli v. Duplessis*, but the public's protection from the arbitrary use of power by the elected legislators is the ballot box. We place our confidence in the Courts to the extent they will recognize and deal with arbitrary actions of officials not supported by law but we place our confidence in the democratic process of elections to deal with the arbitrary use of legislative powers. These are separate and distinct threats to our freedom and have separate and distinct protections. To say that since the courts do a good job in providing protection in one area against the arbitrary use of power by officials they must also do it in relation to the passage of arbitrary legislation is to misunderstand the democratic process by downgrading the importance of holding a government responsible to the will of the electors.

• • •

[39] In the result, I find that there is no basis to challenge the validity of the legislation which was used to impose the GRIP 92 contract and to extinguish the right to challenge its application through reliance upon the usual common law remedies.

The Saskatchewan Court of Appeal's reasoning in *Bacon* has been followed by other courts. In *PSAC v Canada* (2000), 192 FTR 23 (TD), at issue was the justiciability of a union's complaint about a statute ordering striking workers back to the job. The union argued that the legislation was contrary to the rule of law because it was arbitrary and was passed in bad faith. The court held that this argument disclosed no legal foundation for the lawsuit. In arriving at this decision it made these observations:

Unlike the Parliament at Westminster, the Parliament of Canada is not supreme. It has never been so. The division of powers found in sections 91 and 92 of the *Constitution Act, 1867* (formerly the *British North America Act*) identified certain subjects in respect of which Parliament could not legislate. Federal legislation which touched upon matters reserved to the provinces was struck down. Since the advent of the *Canadian Charter of Rights and Freedoms* (the "Charter"), Parliament has been further constrained in that it cannot legislate in ways which infringe the rights enumerated in the Charter. Legislation which did so has been declared invalid.

... On the basis of the conventional view that Parliament's sovereignty is limited only by the division of powers in the *Constitution Act, 1867* and the enumerated rights in the *Canadian Charter of Rights and Freedoms*, I find that the plaintiff does not have a cause of action arising from breach of the rule of law.

Indeed, even when it is alleged that an ill-intentioned ministry tricked Parliament into enacting legislation, the courts will not probe that statute's promulgation. Consider the following decision.

Turner v Canada
[1992] 3 FC 458 (CA)

MAHONEY JA:

[1] This is an appeal from a decision of the Trial Division ... which struck out the substantive allegations of the statement of claim herein, preserving only those

paragraphs identifying the parties and claiming relief. The learned Trial Judge refused, however, to dismiss the action as against any of the individual defendants: the Prime Minister and three named Ministers of the Crown, and gave the respondent [plaintiff] leave to amend the statement of claim. The appellants say the Trial Judge erred in not dismissing the action entirely as the statement of claim discloses no reasonable cause of action and also in not dismissing it as against the named individuals for want of jurisdiction.

• • •

[3] It is pleaded that the respondent was engaged in a lawsuit with another party in the Yukon Supreme Court when an amendment to the *Yukon Quartz Mining Act* ..., having retroactive effect, deprived him of his defence in the action and led him to an unfavourable settlement. It alleges that the Ministers "through their negligence and outright connivance" caused the enactment of legislation which abridged his rights and injured him and he claims damages therefor.

[4] The fundamental allegations iterated and reiterated throughout the pleading are that Parliament was tortiously misled to enact the retroactive amendment and that the respondent was denied a fair hearing by surreptitious procedures adopted by Parliament. That procedural fairness is not required in a legislative process is well established. ...

[5] Both the *Canadian Bill of Rights* and the *Canadian Charter of Rights and Freedoms* are pleaded. In our opinion, while those may undoubtedly affect the validity and construction of legislation, ... they do not bear on the process of legislating. This action is not framed on the basis that the impugned legislation is invalid or inoperative but as a claim for damages as a result of the tainted process whereby it is said to have been enacted. That brings Parliamentary sovereignty squarely into issue.

[6] The elements of that sovereignty enunciated by Lord Simon in *Pickin v. British Railways Board* ...

[Firstly, this (Parliamentary sovereignty)] involves that ... the courts in this country have no power to declare enacted law to be invalid. ...

A second concomitant of the sovereignty of Parliament is that the Houses of Parliament enjoy certain privileges. These are vouchsafed so that Parliament can fulfil its key functions in our system of democratic government. ...

... Among the privileges of the Houses of Parliament is the exclusive right to determine the regularity of their own internal proceedings. ...

It is well known that in the past there have been dangerous strains between the law courts and Parliament—dangerous because each institution has its own particular role to play in our constitution, and because collision between the two institutions is likely to impair their power to vouchsafe those constitutional rights for which citizens depend on them. So for many years Parliament and the courts have each been astute to respect the sphere of action and the privileges of the other—Parliament, for example, by its *sub judice* rule, the courts by taking care to exclude evidence which might amount to infringement of parliamentary privilege. ...

• • •

[Thirdly, a] further practical consideration is that if there is evidence that Parliament may have been misled into an enactment, Parliament might well—indeed, would be likely to—wish to conduct its own inquiry. It would be unthinkable that two inquiries—one parliamentary and the other forensic—should proceed concurrently, conceivably arriving at different conclusions; and a parliamentary examination of parliamentary procedures and of the actions and understandings of officers of Parliament would seem to be clearly more satisfactory than one conducted in a court of law—quite apart from considerations of Parliamentary privilege.

The second and third of those elements are pertinent here, the first not at all since the validity of the legislation is not questioned.

[7] We are all of a view that an action against Her Majesty based on allegations that Parliament has been induced to enact legislation by the tortious acts and omissions of Ministers of the Crown is not justiciable. The appeal will be allowed with costs, the statement of claim entirely struck out and the action dismissed with costs.

Still, even if Parliament is competent to pass bad (but still constitutionally valid) laws, it is not to be presumed that it means to do so. Parliament may strip away contractual rights, for instance, but to do so it must be emphatic. Consider the Supreme Court of Canada's views in the following case.

Wells v Newfoundland
[1999] 3 SCR 199

MAJOR J:

[1] This appeal deals with the position of the Crown and its senior civil servants who hold tenured appointments subject to good behaviour. Are such office-holders owed compensation in the event that their positions are eliminated by legislation? There is no dispute that Parliament and the provincial legislatures have the authority to structure the public service as they see fit, and to eliminate or alter positions in the process. But can it escape the financial consequences for doing so without explicitly extinguishing the rights they have abrogated? I conclude that they cannot.

• • •

[2] In August 1985, the respondent Andrew Wells, was appointed as a member of the Public Utilities Board ("Board") with the designation Commissioner (Consumer Representative) under the provisions of the *Public Utilities Act*, RSN 1970, c. 322 ("1970 Act"). ...

• • •

[4] The respondent's tenure proved to be a short and turbulent one. On April 6, 1988, the Executive Council of the Government of Newfoundland ordered the Departments of Justice and Transportation and the Treasury Board Secretariat to assess the continuing need for the Board.

• • •

[6] All the foregoing factors resulted in a substantially decreased workload for the Board given its loss of jurisdiction over two areas of authority that had previously accounted for a substantial amount of its work. The assessment recommended a differently constituted Board with fewer Commissioners, and that the respondent's position be replaced by an office of Consumer Advocate in the Department of Consumer Affairs and Communications or the Department of Justice.

[7] In the wake of this review, a new *Public Utilities Act* was tabled. The respondent was informed by the Minister of Justice that the government intended to act on the recommendations of the review and that on "the balance of probabilities" his position would be abolished. On December 18, 1989, the Newfoundland House of Assembly passed Bill 44, which comprehensively restructured the Board, reduced the number of Commissioners from six to three, and abolished the Consumer Representative position. Under its provisions, all existing commissioners were to cease holding office, but remained eligible for re-appointment to limited positions on the new Board.

[8] This Bill was proclaimed into force on February 16, 1990, as the *Public Utilities Act, 1989*, ... and the respondent ceased to hold office on that date. ...

• • •

[37] The appellant Crown asserts that even if it breached the respondent's contract of employment by eliminating his position, it was entitled to do so as an exercise of its unfettered sovereign power. ...

[38] The Crown's argument is that no matter what the terms of the respondent's engagement may have been, the legislature retained the power to eliminate his position.

• • •

[41] ... [T]here is no question that the Government of Newfoundland had the authority to restructure or eliminate the Board. There is a crucial distinction, however, between the Crown legislatively avoiding a contract, and altogether escaping the legal consequences of doing so. While the legislature may have the extraordinary power of passing a law to specifically deny compensation to an aggrieved individual with whom it has broken an agreement, clear and explicit statutory language would be required to extinguish existing rights previously conferred on that party. ...

[42] The respondent's contractual rights relating to his employment as a Commissioner were acquired under the *Public Utilities Act*, and its repeal did not, of itself, strip him of those rights. ... The government was free to pass such a bill and they were equally free to pass a bill which would have explicitly denied the respondent compensation. ... However, since no such Act was passed, the respondent's basic contractual rights to severance pay remain.

• • •

[46] In a nation governed by the rule of law, we assume that the government will honour its obligations unless it explicitly exercises its power not to. In the absence of a clear express intent to abrogate rights and obligations—rights of the highest importance to the individual—those rights remain in force. To argue the opposite is to say that the government is bound only by its whim, not its word. In Canada this is unacceptable, and does not accord with the nation's understanding of the relationship between the state and its citizens.

• • •

[50] The appellant Crown argues that the respondent's contract was frustrated by the passage of the new Act, which made further employment of Wells in his previous position impossible. ...

[51] The obvious objection to this submission is that self-induced frustration does not excuse non-performance. ... The Crown responds that the separation of powers between the legislative and executive branches means that a legislative act which bars the executive from performing pending contractual obligations does not constitute self-induced frustration, as these branches are independent entities.

[52] The doctrine of separation of powers is an essential feature of our constitution. It maintains a separation of powers between the judiciary and the other two branches, legislature and the executive, and to some extent between the legislature and the executive. ... The government cannot, however, rely on this formal separation to avoid the consequences of its own actions. While the legislature retains the power to expressly terminate a contract without compensation, it is disingenuous for the executive to assert that the legislative enactment of its own agenda constitutes a frustrating act beyond its control.

[53] On a practical level, it is recognized that the same individuals control both the executive and the legislative branches of government. As this Court observed

in *Attorney General of Quebec v. Blaikie*, ... "There is thus a considerable degree of integration between the Legislature and the Government. ... [I]t is the Government which, through its majority, does in practice control the operations of the elected branch of the Legislature on a day to day basis." Similarly, in *Reference re Canada Assistance Plan*, ... Sopinka J said:

> ... [T]he true executive power lies in the Cabinet. And since the Cabinet controls the government, there is in practice a degree of overlap among the terms "government," "Cabinet" and "executive." ... In practice, the bulk of the new legislation is initiated by the government.

[54] The separation of powers is not a rigid and absolute structure. The Court should not be blind to the reality of Canadian governance that, except in certain rare cases, the executive frequently and *de facto* controls the legislature. The new *Public Utilities Act* in Newfoundland was a government bill, introduced by a member, as directed by Cabinet Directive C 328-'89. Therefore, the same "directing minds," namely the executive, were responsible for both the respondent's appointment and his termination. Moreover, since a number of positions equivalent to that previously held by the respondent were created under the new Act, the executive could have reappointed him and remedied its breach of contract. This continues to demonstrate the futility of the frustration argument in the circumstances of this case.

[55] The Crown had a contractual obligation to the respondent, which it breached by eliminating his position. As his right to seek damages for that breach was not taken from him by legislation, he is entitled to compensation.

2. The Power to Follow Unfair Procedures

The discussion above underscores that the courts may not cure every ill that afflicts a statute, even in a system where the constitution constrains Parliament's sovereignty. More than that, it is also true that in reviewing the *process* by which Parliament makes its laws, courts are even more reluctant to impose standards on the legislative branch. Certainly, the *Constitution Act, 1867* does specify some requirements for the legislative process: matters are to be decided in both the Senate and the Commons by a majority of votes; the quorum of the Senate is 15 senators, including the Speaker, and of the Commons, 20 members; money bills must originate in the Commons; bills must be in French and English; and all bills require royal assent. (*Constitution Act, 1867*, ss 36, 49, 35, 48, 53, 133, and 55, respectively.)

But so long as these prerequisites are met, courts have no role in querying the procedure Parliament selects in passing its law. Any effort by courts to scrutinize the procedure by which laws are passed by Parliament would quickly trench on parliamentary privilege. The internal procedure immunized from external court scrutiny includes the manner in which Parliament passes acts. In the British parliamentary tradition, it is for "Parliament to lay down the procedures which are to be followed before a Bill can become an Act": see Lord Morris of Borth-y-Gest in *Pickin v British Railways Board*, [1974] AC 765 at 790 (HL), cited with approval in *Martin v Ontario*, [2004] OJ No 2247 at para 21 (QL) (Sup Ct J). These are all matters of parliamentary privilege. In *Mikisew Cree First Nation v Canada (Governor General in Council)*, 2018 SCC 40, the Supreme Court of Canada reaffirmed this position, even where at issue was the duty to consult that is part of Aboriginal rights under s 35 of the *Constitution Act, 1982*, being Schedule B to the *Canada Act 1982* (UK), 1982, c 11. For more on the duty to consult, see Chapter 3. The Indigenous applicants claimed that ministers and Cabinet must meet this duty to consult when formulating legislation to be considered in Parliament. In separate decisions, a majority of the Court rejected the idea that these officials had such a duty. Justice Brown, in reasoning accepted by three other judges and constituting a plurality position, concluded that ministers developing legislation acted in their parliamentary (and not executive) capacity: "the entire law-making process—from initial policy development to and including royal assent—is an exercise of legislative power which is immune from judicial interference." Moreover,

[122] Imposing a duty to consult with respect to legislative policy development would ... be contrary to parliamentary privilege, understood as freedom from interference with "the parliamentary work of a Member of Parliament—*i.e.,* any of the Member's activities that *have a connection* with a proceeding in Parliament" ∴ This is no anachronism or technical nicety. Parliamentary privilege is "the necessary immunity that the law provides for Members of Parliament ... in order for these legislators to do their legislative work, 'including the assembly's work in holding the government to account'" ... Since "holding the government to account" is the *raison d'être* of Parliament ..., parliamentary privilege is therefore essential to allowing Parliament to perform its constitutional functions. As this Court said in *Re Canada Assistance Plan,* at p. 560, "[a] restraint ... in the introduction of legislation is a fetter on the sovereignty of Parliament itself." Parliament therefore has the right to "exercise unfettered freedom in the formulation, tabling, amendment, and passage of legislation" (*Galati v. Canada (Governor General)*, 2015 FC 91 ... at para. 34).

Another three judges agreed with this basic position, for different reasons.

Does this mean that Parliament would be free to act unfairly—perhaps by passing a law without any notice to those implicated by it? The answer is likely "yes." The Supreme Court has implied that "three readings in the Senate and House of Commons" is a procedure due any citizen of Canada by "[l]ong-standing parliamentary tradition": see *Authorson v Canada (AG)*, 2003 SCC 39 at para 37, [2003] 2 SCR 40. However, nothing constitutionalizes this practice. Canadians are not entitled to any sort of due process or procedural fairness in the law-making process.

Consider how the Supreme Court addressed this issue in *Wells v Newfoundland*. Recall that, here, Wells was arguing that legislative changes eliminating the board of which he was a member violated employment rights and entitled him to compensation. Another of his arguments—ultimately successful for the reasons outlined in the extract above—failed:

[57] The thrust of the respondent's submission was that since he lost his job as a result of governmental action, he had a right to fairness in the making of that decision. Procedurally unfair or arbitrary decisions by government lack the force of law and are reviewable by the courts ...

• • •

[59] Both the decision to restructure the Board, and the subsequent decision not to re-appoint the respondent, were *bona fide* decisions. The decision to restructure the Board was deliberated and enacted by the elected legislature of the Province of Newfoundland. This is fatal to the respondent's argument on bad faith, as legislative decision making is not subject to any known duty of fairness. Legislatures are subject to constitutional requirements for valid law-making, but within their constitutional boundaries, they can do as they see fit. The wisdom and value of legislative decisions are subject only to review by the electorate. The judgment in *Reference re Canada Assistance Plan* [(BC), [1991] 2 SCR 525] ... was conclusive on this point in stating that: "the rules governing procedural fairness do not apply to a body exercising purely legislative functions." ...

[60] In *Reference re Amendment of Constitution of Canada,* [[1981] 1 SCR 753] ... it was stated ... :

How Houses of Parliament proceed, how a provincial legislative assembly proceeds is in either case a matter of self-definition, subject to any overriding constitutional or self-imposed statutory or indoor prescription. It is unnecessary here to embark on any historical review of the "court" aspect of Parliament and the immunity of its procedures from judicial review. *Courts come into the picture when legislation is enacted and not before* (unless references are made to them for their opinion on a bill or a proposed enactment). [Emphasis added.]

[61] The respondent's loss resulted from a legitimately enacted "legislative and general" decision, not an "administrative and specific" one ... While the impact on him may be singularly severe, it did not constitute a direct and intentional attack upon his interests. His position is no different in kind than that of an unhappy tax-payer who is out-of-pocket as a result of a newly enacted budget, or an impoverished welfare recipient whose benefits are reduced as a result of a legislative changes in eligibility criteria. This was not a personal matter, it was a legislative policy choice. ...

In *Authorson v Canada*, a group of disabled veterans and their representatives sued the federal government for payment of interest on pension moneys held and managed by the government on their behalf over many years, alleging this to constitute a breach of fiduciary duty. The government conceded that it had owed such a duty and had breached it by failing to pay interest. However, the attorney general defended the claim on the basis that Parliament had passed legislation denying any such claim for moneys owed prior to 1990, effectively expropriating the claim without compensation. The veterans argued that the *Canadian Bill of Rights*, SC 1960, c 44 (an ordinary statute passed by Parliament in 1960 and described by the Supreme Court as "quasi-constitutional" in nature) applied to the expropriating legislation and both obligated Parliament to engage in a fair process before adopting the legislation and, as a matter of substantive law, prohibited expropriation without compensation. The veterans cited in particular the reference to "due process" in s 1(a) of the *Canadian Bill of Rights*:

1. It is hereby recognized and declared that in Canada there have existed and shall continue to exist without discrimination by reason of race, national origin, colour, religion or sex, the following human rights and fundamental freedoms, namely,

(a) the right of the individual to life, liberty, security of the person and enjoyment of property, and the right not to be deprived thereof except by due process of law;

The court rejected this argument, as follows.

Authorson v Canada (AG)
2003 SCC 39, [2003] 2 SCR 40

MAJOR J:

[1] The deceased respondent, Authorson, a disabled veteran of World War II, was the representative of a large class of disabled veterans of Canada's military forces. He died in 2002, but the action continues to be prosecuted by his litigation administrator and guardian.

[2] This litigation raises difficult questions. The government of Canada, through the appellant, the Attorney General of Canada, agrees that throughout the relevant time it acted as a fiduciary for each of the veterans, that the funds owed the veterans and administered by the government were rarely credited with interest, and that a full accounting was never made to the respondent.

[3] It is not in dispute that the respondent is owed interest, and that this omission continued until legislation changing government practice was enacted in 1990. The appellant, while agreeing that the respondent is owed money, argues that Parliament has, by enacting legislation to that effect, made the debt unenforceable.

[4] The respondent submits that the *Canadian Bill of Rights*, SC 1960, c. 44 (reproduced in RSC 1985, App. III) (the "*Bill of Rights*"), ensures him due process in

the expropriation of his property. The appellant's position is that the expropriative legislation was a valid exercise of its legislative power, and that no remedy exists.

• • •

[14] Does the *Bill of Rights* require that Parliament give just compensation to the veterans? The governmental expropriation of property without compensation is discouraged by our common law tradition, but it is allowed when Parliament uses clear and unambiguous language to do so.

[15] The *Department of Veterans Affairs Act*, s. 5.1(4) takes a property claim from a vulnerable group, in disregard of the Crown's fiduciary duty to disabled veterans. However, that taking is within the power of Parliament. The appeal has to be allowed.

• • •

(1) Procedural Rights in Legislative Enactment

[39] As well, see *Wells v. Newfoundland*, [1999] 3 SCR 199, at para. 59:

... [L]egislative decision making is not subject to any known duty of fairness. Legislatures are subject to constitutional requirements for valid law-making, but within their constitutional boundaries, they can do as they see fit. The wisdom and value of legislative decisions are subject only to review by the electorate. The judgment in *Reference re Canada Assistance Plan* ... was conclusive on this point in stating that: "the rules governing procedural fairness do not apply to a body exercising purely legislative functions."

[40] The submission that a court can compel Parliament to change its legislative procedures based on the *Bill of Rights* must fail. The *Bill of Rights* purports to guide the proper interpretation of every "law of Canada," which s. 5 of the *Bill of Rights* defines to mean "an Act of the Parliament of Canada enacted before or after the coming into force of this Act." Court interference with the legislative process is not an interpretation of an already enacted law.

[41] Due process protections cannot interfere with the right of the legislative branch to determine its own procedure. For the *Bill of Rights* to confer such a power would effectively amend the Canadian constitution, which, in the preamble to the *Constitution Act, 1867*, enshrines a constitution similar in principle to that of the United Kingdom. In the United Kingdom, no such pre-legislative procedural rights have existed. From that, it follows that the *Bill of Rights* does not authorize such power.

• • •

V. Conclusion

[62] The respondent and the class of disabled veterans it represents are owed decades of interest on their pension and benefit funds. The Crown does not dispute these findings. But Parliament has chosen for undisclosed reasons to lawfully deny the veterans, to whom the Crown owed a fiduciary duty, these benefits whether legal, equitable or fiduciary. The due process protections of property in the *Bill of Rights* do not grant procedural rights in the process of legislative enactment. They do confer certain rights to notice and an opportunity to make submissions in the adjudication of individual rights and obligations, but no such rights are at issue in this appeal.

[63] While the due process guarantees may have some substantive content not apparent in this appeal, there is no due process right against duly enacted legislation unambiguously expropriating property interests.

3. Ethics in Law-Making

The discussion to this point suggests that no prudential constraints exist on Parliament, other than those found in the Constitution. But a word of caution should be voiced about Parliament's latitude to pass laws as it wills. Parliament may be sovereign, but individual parliamentarians are not. A parliamentarian induced by the prospect of financial gain to vote one way or another in performing his or her law-making functions is subject to sanction in several different ways, including possible criminal charges. Ethics rules also exist, found both in statutory law and in the internal procedural rules governing each house of Parliament. Consider the following discussion.

Michel Bédard, Kristen Douglas & Élise Hurtubise-Loranger, Conflict of Interest at the Federal Level: Legislative Framework

(Ottawa: House of Commons, Library of Parliament, 24 November 2010)

1 Introduction

Conflict of interest rules applicable to ministers, parliamentary secretaries, other public office holders and parliamentarians were once found in various federal statutes such as the *Criminal Code* and the *Parliament of Canada Act*. Over time, beginning in 1973 with then prime minister Pierre Trudeau's guidelines for Cabinet ministers, conflict of interest rules and guidelines have replaced or supplemented these statutory rules.

The federal conflict of interest regime is now governed mainly by the *Conflict of Interest Act*, which is applicable to public office holders such as ministers, and by the parliamentary conflict of interest codes that the Senate and the House of Commons have adopted to govern the conduct of their respective members. Integral to the regime are two independent conflict of interest watchdogs, namely the Conflict of Interest and Ethics Commissioner and the Senate Ethics Officer.

2 Legislative Framework

2.1 Amendments to the Parliament of Canada Act (2004)

In 1985, the government introduced the first *Conflict of Interest and Post-Employment Code for Public Office Holders* (often referred to as the "Prime Minister's Code"), which replaced existing guidelines. This code applied to Cabinet ministers, parliamentary secretaries and other senior public office holders. In 1994, then prime minister Jean Chrétien issued a new Code and created the position of Ethics Counsellor with responsibility for its administration. Because that position was contained within the Department of Industry, it was often criticized for not being independent from the government.

In 2004, amendments to the *Parliament of Canada Act* provided a legal framework for the establishment of a conflict of interest regime for both houses of Parliament. Two independent conflict of interest watchdog positions were created: the Senate Ethics Officer and the Ethics Commissioner. These officers were responsible for the duties and functions assigned to them, respectively, by the Senate and the House of Commons with regard to governing the ethical conduct of members. The 2004 Act also contemplated the adoption by each house of a conflict of interest code pertaining to the conduct of its members.

The Ethics Commissioner, in addition to his or her duties and functions with respect to the members of the House of Commons, replaced the position of the Ethics Counsellor and assumed the functions of that office as it related to public office holders and the *Conflict of Interest and Post-Employment Code for Public Office Holders*.

2.2 The Federal Accountability Act (2006)

The *Federal Accountability Act* (FAA), which received Royal Assent on 12 December 2006, made two fundamental changes to the Canadian conflict of interest regime. First, it enacted the *Conflict of Interest Act*, which enshrined in legislation the *Conflict of Interest and Post-Employment Code for Public Office Holders*. The *Conflict of Interest Act* set out the rules and obligations that apply to Cabinet ministers, parliamentary secretaries and other senior public office holders such as political staff of ministers and most Governor in Council appointees. Second, the FAA amended the *Parliament of Canada Act* to replace the office of the Ethics Commissioner with that of the Conflict of Interest and Ethics Commissioner.

3 Public Office Holders and Members of the House of Commons

3.1 Conflict of Interest and Ethics Commissioner

The Conflict of Interest and Ethics Commissioner has a dual mandate: she or he is responsible both for public office holders under the *Conflict of Interest Act* and for members of the House of Commons under the *Conflict of Interest Code for Members of the House of Commons*.

The Commissioner's mandate in respect of public office holders, as set out in the *Conflict of Interest Act*, includes the following:

- providing confidential advice to the prime minister, including at the request of the prime minister, with respect to the application of the Act to individual public office holders;
- providing confidential advice to individual public office holders with respect to their obligations under the Act;
- examining and reporting on possible contraventions of the Act by public office holders or former public office holders; and
- administering the disclosure regime whereby senior public office holders confidentially disclose their assets and liabilities and other information to the Commissioner and preparing a summary of that information for the public.

The *Conflict of Interest Act* permits any parliamentarian to request, in writing, that the Commissioner investigate the conduct of a present or former office holder if the parliamentarian has a reasonable belief that the person in question has contravened the Act. The Commissioner may also conduct such an examination on her or his own initiative. He or she reports on such investigations to the prime minister, and his or her reports are made public, although particular types of information obtained from the investigations must be kept confidential.

Consistent with the dual mandate, the Conflict of Interest and Ethics Commissioner reports to two House of Commons committees, as follows:

- the Standing Committee on Procedure and House Affairs with respect to duties and functions governed by the *Conflict of Interest Code for Members of the House of Commons*; and

- the Standing Committee on Access to Information, Privacy and Ethics with respect to responsibilities prescribed by the *Conflict of Interest Act*, as well as with respect to the general administration of the Office of the Conflict of Interest and Ethics Commissioner.

As stipulated by the *Parliament of Canada Act*, the Conflict of Interest and Ethics Commissioner also provides confidential policy advice and support to the prime minister in respect of conflict of interest and ethical issues in general.

3.2 The Conflict of Interest Code for Members of the House of Commons

Members of the House of Commons are bound by the *Conflict of Interest Code for Members of the House of Commons*, which is Appendix 1 to the *Standing Orders of the House of Commons*. The Code articulates several purposes, including that of maintaining and enhancing public confidence and trust in the integrity of members, along with a number of principles intended to guide members in reconciling their private interests and public duties.

This Code came into force upon the first sitting of the 38th Parliament on 4 October 2004. It addresses the maintenance of the public registry of all members' public disclosure summaries; the provision of written confidential opinions to members; and the conduct of inquiries into any member's alleged non-compliance with the Code's obligations. The Commissioner reports on her or his inquiries to the House and also reports annually on her or his activities respecting members.

The Code prohibits members from voting or acting in a way that would further their own or others' private interests, and requires that their private interests be disclosed whenever a decision that would affect those interests is under consideration. Members and their families must report to the Commissioner any travel or gifts valued in excess of specified limits. Members, and any corporations owned by them, are prohibited from entering into federal government contracts.

All members are required to file statements with the Commissioner disclosing the assets and liabilities belonging to them and their families. The Office of the Conflict of Interest and Ethics Commissioner then prepares a disclosure summary based on each member's statement and makes these summaries available for public review on the Commissioner's website.

Members of the House of Commons may, at any time, ask the Commissioner to offer a confidential opinion about their obligations under the Code. Also, any member who is of the opinion that another member has not fulfilled her or his obligations under the Code may request that the Commissioner conduct an inquiry into the matter. The Commissioner may also conduct an inquiry on her or his own initiative. In conducting such inquiries, the Commissioner must operate in private and with due dispatch, and at all appropriate stages throughout the inquiry the Commissioner must give the member reasonable opportunity to be present and to make representations. In a report on an inquiry, the Commissioner may recommend sanctions and must offer reasons for the conclusions and recommendations. The Code also requires the Standing Committee on Procedure and House Affairs to undertake a comprehensive review of its provisions and operation every five years.

3.3 The Conflict of Interest Act

The *Conflict of Interest Act* requires that, once they are appointed, public office holders must arrange their private affairs so as to prevent conflicts of interest from arising. With limited exceptions, they must not solicit or accept money or gifts;

assist individuals in their dealings with government in such a way as to compromise their own professional status; take advantage of information obtained because of their positions as insiders; or, after they leave public office, act so as to take improper advantage of having held that office. Since 1994, information relating to the spouses and dependent children of ministers, secretaries of state and parliamentary secretaries has also been considered relevant.

Bound by the Act are approximately 1,100 full-time public office holders, including not only the prime minister, ministers, ministers of state, parliamentary secretaries and ministers' exempt staff, but also full-time Governor in Council appointees, including deputy and associate deputy ministers and heads of agencies, Crown corporations, boards, commissions and tribunals, and 1,900 part-time public office holders.

The *Conflict of Interest Act* makes a distinction between reporting and non-reporting public office holders. Reporting office holders include ministers, parliamentary secretaries, ministerial staff who work on average 15 hours or more a week, part-time Governor in Council appointees who receive an annual salary and benefits, and full-time Governor in Council appointees. The obligations imposed on reporting public office holders are, by and large, more stringent than those imposed on non-reporting public office holders.

The *Conflict of Interest Act* provides that, in order to reduce the risk of conflict of interest, public office holders should use such means as avoidance, a confidential report, a public declaration, divestment, or recusal, depending on the asset or interest in question. Divestment can include making an asset subject to a trust or management agreement. In relation to outside activities, a public office holder must not engage in the practice of a profession; actively manage or operate a business or commercial venture; retain or accept directorships or offices in a financial or commercial corporation; hold office in a union or professional association; or serve as a paid consultant.

The *Conflict of Interest Act* also deals with public office holders after they leave office. Many of the post-employment rules are the same as those in the Prime Minister's Code. One of the most important changes brought about through the FAA was contained in the *Lobbying Act* rather than the *Conflict of Interest Act*. The *Lobbying Act* imposes a five-year ban on lobbying activities for designated public office holders. The Commissioner of Lobbying may, however, exempt individuals, applying any criteria deemed relevant, including being a designated public office holder for only a short time, being employed on an acting or administrative basis only, or being employed as a student. The reasons for any exemptions must be made public.

Under the *Conflict of Interest Act*, the Conflict of Interest and Ethics Commissioner is required to administer the Act and apply its conflict of interest compliance provisions to public office holders. Any information he or she receives is to be kept confidential until and unless a public declaration is made. Arrangements made by public office holders to reduce the risk of a conflict of interest must be approved, in the case of ministers of the Crown, ministers of state and parliamentary secretaries, by the prime minister, in consultation with the Commissioner. In the case of all other public office holders, including the prime minister, approval must be obtained from the Conflict of Interest and Ethics Commissioner. Once arrangements are completed, summaries and public declarations are posted in the public registry. Section 43 sets out the requirement, previously found in section 72.07 of the *Parliament of Canada Act*, that the Commissioner provide confidential advice to the prime minister, as well as to individual public office holders, on the application of the Act.

In a significant change from the previous regime, section 44 of the *Conflict of Interest Act* permits parliamentarians to request, based on a belief on reasonable grounds, that the Commissioner examine a possible contravention of the *Conflict of Interest Act* by any current or former public office holder. The Commissioner may consider information from the public or brought to her or his attention by a member of the Senate or the House of Commons that suggests a public office holder has not complied with the *Conflict of Interest Act*.

Section 45 permits the Commissioner to examine a matter on her or his own initiative when he or she has reason to believe that a current or former public office holder has contravened the *Conflict of Interest Act*. The Commissioner must provide the affected public office holder with a reasonable opportunity to present his or her views before reporting on an examination.

The Commissioner may summon witnesses and compel them to give evidence or to produce documents.

4 Senators

4.1 Senate Ethics Officer

The Senate has, in the Senate Ethics Officer, its own conflict of interest watchdog. This office has been the subject of some debate over the years.

When the establishment of a parliamentary conflict of interest regime was initially considered in the 1990s, thought was given to having a single ethics officer for both houses of Parliament. In 1997, a committee of both houses of Parliament, the Special Joint Committee on a Code of Conduct, recommended the establishment of a single commissioner to administer one code of conduct and conflict of interest regime for members of both the Senate and the House of Commons. Although these recommendations were not implemented at the time, they were tabled by the government in 2002 for reconsideration by both chambers.

The Standing Senate Committee on Rules, Procedures and the Rights of Parliament, which was called upon to look into the matter, objected to the creation of a single commissioner. Asserting the Senate's independence from the House of Commons and the government, as well as its separate constitutional role and function, the Committee requested that the Senate have its own ethics officer.

Echoing these demands, a legislative proposal introduced in 2003 contemplated the establishment of two positions: a Senate Ethics Officer, who would be responsible for the administration of the conflict of interest regime for Senators, and an Ethics Commissioner, who would be responsible for the conflict of interest regimes of members of the House of Commons and public office holders. This legislative proposal, as discussed above, was enacted in 2004.

Despite the creation of a separate ethics officer for each house of Parliament in 2004, the government introduced, in 2006 and 2009, further bills aimed at abolishing the position of the Senate Ethics Officer and implementing a single conflict of interest regime for members of both houses of Parliament. In 2006, the FAA as originally introduced would have abolished the position of Senate Ethics Officer and transferred his or her duties to the yet-to-be-created position of Conflict of Interest and Ethics Commissioner. This portion of the bill was, however, amended by the Senate, and the FAA, as enacted, made no change to the office of the Senate Ethics Officer. In 2009, the government introduced Bill C-30, the *Senate Ethics Act*, with the same purpose. That bill died on the *Order Paper* with the 30 December 2009 prorogation.

The Senate Ethics Officer performs the duties and functions assigned by the *Conflict of Interest Code for Senators*. In short, he or she administers the confidential disclosure regime and the public registry of senators' public disclosure summaries, provides senators with opinions and advice with respect to their obligations under the Code, and may be called upon to inquire into possible breaches of the Code.

4.2 Conflict of Interest Code for Senators

Under the 2004 amendments to the *Parliament of Canada Act*, the Senate was called upon to establish a conflict of interest code for senators, and the report of the Standing Committee on Rules, Procedures and the Rights of Parliament recommending such a code was adopted by the Senate on 18 May 2005.

The *Conflict of Interest Code for Senators* and the *Conflict of Interest Code for Members of the House of Commons* are identical in some regards and similar in many others. One distinctive feature of the *Conflict of Interest Code for Senators* is the role played by the Standing Committee on Conflict of Interest for senators, to which the Senate Ethics Officer confidentially reports after an inquiry and which may be called upon to conduct its own investigation on a matter. Since its adoption, the *Code for Senators* has been amended twice, when the Standing Committee on Conflict of Interest for Senators completed the mandated periodical comprehensive review of its provisions in 2008 and 2012.

5 Conclusion

The Canadian conflict of interest regime has evolved considerably since the promulgation of the first prime ministerial guidelines on conflict of interest in 1973. Conflict of interest rules are now embodied in legislation such as the *Conflict of Interest Act* and in formal orders of both houses of Parliament, namely the *Conflict of Interest Code for Senators* and the *Conflict of Interest Code for Members of the House of Commons*. Moreover, whereas rules were once interpreted and administered by the Ethics Counsellor, who had no independent status and reported directly to the prime minister, two independent officers, the Conflict of Interest and Ethics Commissioner and the Senate Ethics Officer, are now entrusted with the administration of conflict of interest rules and are required to report to Parliament.

The Canadian conflict of interest regime has the capacity to adapt itself to contemporary circumstances. Through committees, the House of Commons in 2007 and the Senate in 2008 and 2012 conducted comprehensive reviews of their respective conflict of interest codes; these reviews have led to numerous amendments to both codes. On that matter, the Senate and the House of Commons espouse the principle that the conflict of interest regime is always a "work in progress" and that adjustments, improvements and refinements will be required over time. Indeed, this continuous search for "best practices" is enshrined in the provisions for periodic review included in the *Conflict of Interest Act* and in both parliamentary codes.

B. PARLIAMENT'S LAW-MAKING PROCEDURE

If Parliament is free to determine its own procedure and pass laws as it pleases within its constitutional zone of jurisdiction, what rules does it, in fact, follow? The law-making process is governed mostly by the rules of procedure of each chamber of Parliament—for example, the standing orders of the House of Commons. Consider the following description of how Parliament makes laws.

House of Commons, House of Commons Procedure and Practice

2nd ed (Ottawa: House of Commons, 2009)

Types of Bills

There are two main categories of bills: public bills and private bills. While public bills deal with matters of national interest (*jus generale publicum*), the purpose of private bills is to grant special powers, benefits or exemptions to a person or persons, including corporations (*jus particulare*).

Public Bills

A public bill may be initiated by a Minister, in which case it is referred to as a "government bill." A private Member may also initiate a public bill, in which case it is called a "private Member's bill."

Government Bills

A government bill is a written legislative initiative submitted to Parliament by the government for approval, and possibly for amendment, before becoming law. Such bills relate to matters of public interest and may include financial provisions. Government bills are normally introduced in the House of Commons, although bills that do not provide for the expenditure of public funds or the levying of new taxes may be introduced in either House.

Private Members' Bills

A private Member's bill is the text of a legislative initiative submitted to Parliament by a Member who is neither a Minister nor a Parliamentary Secretary, for approval, and possibly for amendment, before becoming law. Most but not all bills of this type originate in the House of Commons.

Debate on private Members' bills can take place only during the hour set aside daily for Private Members' Business. Before being taken up for debate by the House, any such bill must have been selected following a random draw, as provided for by the Standing Orders.

Private Bills

The purpose of a private bill is to confer special powers or benefits (in excess of or in conflict with the general law) upon one or more person or group of persons (including corporate entities) or to exempt them from the application of a statute. It may not be introduced by a Minister, and must be founded on a petition signed by the person(s) promoting it. Thus, the distinction between a public bill and a private bill is primarily a function of the purpose of the bill.

While most private bills are introduced in the Senate, they may also be introduced in the House of Commons, although this is now a rare occurrence. Private bills before the House are dealt with as Private Members' Business, since they may only be moved by Members who do not hold ministerial office. Although private bills must pass through the same stages as any other legislative measure, there are preliminary stages that must be completed before they are introduced.

Bills that appear to be both public and private in nature are referred to as hybrid bills. While British parliamentary practice makes allowance for this type of bill,

Canadian parliamentary procedure requires that all bills be designated either as public bills or as private bills. When a single bill incorporates both private and public considerations, it is dealt with as a public bill.

Forms of Bills

The enactment of a statute by Parliament is the final step in a long process that starts with the proposal, preparation and drafting of a bill. The drafting of a bill is a vital stage in this process—one which challenges the decision makers and drafters to take carefully into account certain constraints, since a failure to abide by these may have negative consequences in relation to the eventual interpretation and application of the law and to the proper functioning of the legislative process.

Limits on Legislative Action

The Constitution of Canada sets out a number of rules that limit the legislative powers and activity both of the government and of Parliament. The Canadian legal duality sometimes results in differences in the application and interpretation of a federal statute, depending on whether the part of Canada in which it is being applied is governed by the common law or by civil law.

Bills must be enacted, published and printed simultaneously in French and English. Section 133 of the *Constitution Act, 1867* requires that bills proceed in both languages through the entire legislative process, including first reading. Section 18 of the *Constitution Act, 1982* further requires that both versions of federal statutes be treated as equally authoritative.

Drafting Bills

Government Bills

A decision by the government to transform a policy initiative into a legislative proposal triggers the drafting process. The Department of Justice prepares a draft bill, following instructions given by Cabinet. The Minister of Justice is required to examine every bill introduced by a Minister in order to ascertain that it is consistent with the *Canadian Bill of Rights* and the *Canadian Charter of Rights and Freedoms*.

Once a bill has been drafted in both official languages, it must be approved by Cabinet, after which the Government House Leader customarily reviews it and recommends in favour of or against its introduction in Parliament. Generally, the Government House Leader asks Cabinet to delegate the latter responsibility to him or her.

Private Members' Bills

Members of the House of Commons who are neither Ministers nor Parliamentary Secretaries may introduce bills for consideration under Private Members' Business. Legislative services are made available under the authority of the Speaker of the House to assist them in drafting their bills. Before a bill is introduced in the House, the legislative services of the House of Commons will certify that it is acceptable as to its form and compliance with legislative and parliamentary conventions.

Private Bills

A private bill may not be introduced by a Minister. It must be sponsored by a private Member and founded on a petition which must first have received a favourable report from the Examiner of Petitions or from the Standing Committee on Procedure and House Affairs. While the form of a private bill is similar to that of a public bill, a private bill must have a preamble, which is optional for a public bill. The Standing Orders of the House include certain rules of drafting specific to private bills, as well as rules relating exclusively to bills for Acts of incorporation and to bills amending or repealing existing Acts.

Drafting by a Committee

A committee may be instructed to prepare and bring in a bill or a committee may be appointed for that specific purpose. Motions to this effect may be moved only by a Minister. A committee that has been instructed to prepare a bill shall, in its report, recommend the principles, scope and general provisions of the bill and may, if it deems it appropriate, recommend specific legislative wording. If the House concurs in the committee's report, this will constitute an order of the House to bring in a bill based on the report.

Other Drafting Characteristics

Bills may have other drafting characteristics, depending on the purpose of the proposed legislation.

- New legislation: Bills resulting from policy decisions or, in some cases, to implement treaties, conventions or agreements, to accept recommendations arising out of a report of a Task Force or Royal Commission of Inquiry, to carry out administrative measures, or to deal with emergencies.
- Major revisions of existing Acts: Bills to revise an Act because it contains a sunset clause (providing that it must be revised after a certain period of time) or because of changing economic or social standards or circumstances.
- Amendments to existing Acts: Bills to amend existing Acts. The amendments may be either of a substantive or of a housekeeping nature.
- Statute law amendment bills: Initiatives to eliminate anomalies, inconsistencies, archaisms or errors in existing legislation and to deal with other matters of a non-controversial and uncomplicated nature.
- Ways and means bills: Initiatives based on ways and means motions, the purpose of which is to create a new income tax or other taxes, to continue a tax which is expiring, to increase a tax or to extend the scope of a tax. These bills are governed by specific provisions of the Standing Orders. Only a Minister may introduce a ways and means bill.
- Appropriation bills: Initiatives introduced in the House in response to the adoption of main or supplementary estimates or interim supply. These bills are also governed by specific provisions of the Standing Orders. Only a Minister may introduce an appropriation bill.
- Borrowing authority bills: Initiatives to seek authority to raise money when public revenues are not adequate to cover government expenditures.
- Pro forma bills: A pro forma bill is introduced by the Prime Minister at the beginning of each session. It affirms the right of the House to conduct its proceedings and to legislate, regardless of the reasons stated in the Speech from the Throne for convening the House. The bill is entitled An Act Respecting the Administration of Oaths of Office; it is numbered C-1 but is not usually printed. It is given first reading, but not second reading.
- Draft bills: This expression is used to refer to the draft form of bills that have not yet been introduced in either House. Occasionally, the House

may have the draft of a government bill sent to a committee for examination. As the bill has not yet been given first reading, the committee may examine the proposed legislation without being constrained by the rules of the legislative process, and may recommend changes. The government can then take the committee's report into consideration when finalizing the draft of the bill.

- Omnibus bills: Although this expression is commonly used, there is no precise definition of an omnibus bill. In general, an omnibus bill seeks to amend, repeal or enact several Acts, and is characterized by the fact that it is made up of a number of related but separate initiatives. An omnibus bill has "one basic principle or purpose which ties together all the proposed enactments and thereby renders the Bill intelligible for parliamentary purposes." One of the reasons cited for introducing an omnibus bill is to bring together in a single bill all the legislative amendments arising from a single policy decision in order to facilitate parliamentary debate.

The use of omnibus bills is unique to Canada. The British Parliament does enact bills that are similar in type, but its legislative practice is different, specifically in that there is much tighter control over the length of debate. In the Australian Parliament, the opposite practice seems to be followed (the procedure allows for related bills to be considered together for the purpose of debate and voting).

It is not known exactly when omnibus bills first appeared, but from the introduction of a private bill to confirm two separate railway agreements, it would appear that the practice existed as early as 1888. A number of omnibus bills were subsequently introduced and passed without any procedural objection to their form being raised by Members.

It appears to be entirely proper, in procedural terms, for a bill to amend, repeal or enact more than one Act, provided that the requisite notice is given, that it is accompanied by a royal recommendation (where necessary), and that it follows the form required. However, on the question of whether the Chair can be persuaded to divide a bill simply because it is complex or composite in nature, there are many precedents from which it can be concluded that Canadian practice does not permit this.

Members have often rejected the government's reasons for introducing omnibus bills and have argued that some omnibus bills are not acceptable. Frequently, they have attempted to invoke their "ancient privilege" to vote separately on each proposal which is contained in a complex question. Speakers of the House have nonetheless ruled that their power to divide complex questions could extend only to substantive motions, and not to motions concerned with the progress of bills. In calling for the division of an omnibus bill, Members sometimes argue that the bill embodies more than one principle. Occasionally, Members also contend that the long title of an omnibus bill should refer to every act being amended. The Chair has ruled this unnecessary.

When moved in committee, motions to divide omnibus bills have been ruled out of order. Unless a committee has been otherwise instructed by the House, it may only report the bill with or without amendment. Members have, from time to time, proposed motions of instruction to their committees to divide bills already referred to them.

Committee Chairs have also ruled against motions to submit two reports on one bill in which each addressed specific topics in the bill, thus effectively dividing the bill. On the other hand, committee Chairs have ruled in order motions that a committee seek instruction to divide a bill.

Despite their refusal to divide omnibus bills, Speakers have expressed deep concern for the right of Members to make themselves heard properly, and have accordingly felt the need on occasion to remind the House of the remedies available to Members faced with the dilemma of having to approve several legislative provisions at the same time.

While there has never been an occasion on which the Chair has decided that a bill should be divided on the ground of complexity, there are three cases that are of particular interest. In 1981, during examination of Bill C-54, *An Act to amend the statute law relating to income tax and to provide other authority for raising funds*, Speaker Sauvé ordered that Part I of the bill, relating to borrowing authority, be struck because the necessary notice had not been given. Later in the same session, another amending bill that dealt both with taxation and borrowing authority was introduced (Bill C-93). At the insistence of the opposition, the government withdrew the bill, on May 7, 1982, and subsequently introduced two separate pieces of legislation on May 10, 1982. The division of the omnibus bill resulted from the political process and not from any procedural argument. Finally, on March 2, 1982, in response to a point of order raised the day before, appealing to the Chair to divide Bill C-94, the *Energy Security Act, 1982*, Speaker Sauvé ruled that there were no precedents which would permit her to do so. This led to the famous "bell-ringing" incident, as a consequence of which the government ultimately moved, and the House passed, a motion to divide the bill into eight separate pieces of legislation. Once again, the division of the omnibus bill was brought about by political interaction.

• • •

Structure of Bills

A bill is composed of a number of elements, some of which, such as the title, are essential, while others, such as the preamble, are optional. The following is a description of the various elements of a bill.

Number

When a bill is introduced in the House, it is assigned a number to facilitate filing and reference. During each session of a Parliament, government bills are numbered consecutively from C-2 to C-200, while private Members' bills are numbered consecutively from C-201 to C-1000 throughout the life of a Parliament, since they are not nullified by prorogation. Private bills, which are rarely introduced in the House, are numbered beginning at C-1001. In order to differentiate between bills introduced in the two Houses of Parliament, the number assigned to bills introduced in the Senate begins with an "S" rather than a "C." Government bills originating in the Senate are numbered consecutively from S-1 to S-200, Senators' public bills are numbered consecutively from S-201 to S-1000, and Senators' private bills are numbered beginning at S-1001. Senate bills are neither renumbered nor reprinted when they are sent to the Commons.

Title

The title is an essential element of a bill. A bill may have two titles: a full or long title and an abbreviated or short title. The long title appears both on the bill's cover page, under the number assigned to the bill, and at the top of the first page of the document. It sets out the purpose of the bill, in general terms, and must accurately reflect its content. The short title is used mainly for purposes of citation, and does not necessarily cover all aspects of the bill. The first clause of the bill normally sets out the short title (except in the case of bills amending other Acts, which do not have a short title).

Preamble

Sometimes a bill has a preamble, which sets out its purposes and the reasons for introducing it. The preamble appears between the long title and the enacting clause.

Enacting Clause

The enacting clause is an essential part of the bill. It states the authority under which it is enacted, and consists of a brief paragraph following the long title and preceding the provisions of the bill: "Her Majesty, by and with the advice and consent of the Senate and House of Commons of Canada, enacts as follows:." In the event that there is a preamble, the enacting clause follows it.

Clause

Clauses—particular and separate articles of a bill—are its most fundamental constitutive element. Clauses may be divided into subclauses, and then into paragraphs and even subparagraphs. A bill may (but need not) also be divided into parts, divisions and subdivisions, each containing one or more clauses; however, the numbering of the clauses is continuous from beginning to end. A clause should express a single idea, preferably in a single sentence. A number of related ideas may be set out in subclauses within a single clause.

Interpretation Provisions

A bill will sometimes include (usually among its initial clauses) definitions or rules of interpretation which provide a legal definition of key expressions used in the legislation and indicate how those expressions apply. There is, however, no formal requirement that a bill include interpretation provisions.

Coming-into-force Provisions

A clause may be included in a bill specifying when the bill or certain of its provisions shall come into force. The coming-into-force of legislation may be delayed after Royal Assent, if the bill contains a clause providing for its proclamation on another specific date or on a date to be fixed by Order in Council. Otherwise, the bill will come into force on the day it is assented to.

Schedules

Schedules providing details that are essential to certain provisions of a bill may be appended to it. There are two types of schedules: those that contain material unsuited to insertion in the main body of the bill, such as, for example, tables, diagrams, lists and maps, and those that reproduce agreements falling within the prerogative of the Crown, such as, for example, treaties and conventions.

Explanatory Notes

When the purpose of a bill is to amend an existing Act, the drafters will insert notes to explain the amendments made by the bill. Among other things, these notes reproduce the original text of the provisions affected by the bill. They are not considered to be part of the bill, and they disappear from subsequent reprints.

Summary

The summary is a comprehensive and usually brief recapitulation of the substance of a bill. It offers "a clear, factual, non-partisan summary of the purpose of the bill and its main provisions." The purpose of the summary is to contribute to a better understanding of the contents of the bill, of which it is not a part. For this reason, it appears separately at the beginning of the bill. Once the bill has been passed, it will also appear on a page affixed to the front of printed versions of the resulting Act.

Marginal Notes

Marginal notes are short explanations that appear in the margin of a bill. They are not part of the bill, and are included only as readers' aids or for information purposes.

Underlining and Vertical Lines

In a bill that amends an existing Act, new text is underlined when it consists of long passages, or simply indicated with a vertical line (in the margin beside the new clauses, subclauses or paragraphs). When a bill that has been amended in committee is reprinted, only the additions made since the last printing are highlighted in this manner.

Headings

To assist the reader, legislative drafters insert headings throughout the text. In past practice, such headings have never been considered to be part of the bill and have not therefore been subject to amendment.

Table of Contents

As an aid to readers, legislative drafters sometimes add a table of contents to a bill. It is not, however, considered to be part of the bill.

Royal Recommendation

Bills that involve the expenditure of public funds must be accompanied by a royal recommendation issued by the Governor General and generally (although not necessarily) communicated to the House before a bill is introduced. The royal recommendation must be published in the *Notice Paper* and printed in or annexed to the beginning of the bill. The royal recommendation is not a part of the bill, but appears separately at its beginning. After the bill is given first reading, the text of the royal recommendation is printed in the *Journals*. A royal recommendation may only be obtained by the government, since it is granted by the Governor General on the advice of the Prime Minister and Cabinet.

Stages in the Legislative Process

A bill is carried forward through all the stages of the legislative process "by a long chain of standardized motions" which must be adopted by the House before the bill becomes law. It is these motions, and not the bill, that are the subject of the debates and decisions of the House. The stages to which the motions correspond "constitute a simple and logical process in which each stage transcends the one immediately before it, so that although the basic motions—that the bill be read a first (second or third) time—appear the same, and seem repetitious, they have very different meanings." Moreover, the House does not commit itself conclusively to a bill until the final stage, when it takes a decision on whether or not the bill should receive final passage.

The Standing Orders of the House require that every bill receive three readings, on different days, before being passed. The practice of giving every bill three separate readings derives from an ancient parliamentary practice which originated in the United Kingdom. At that time, when the technology was not yet available to reproduce large numbers of copies at low cost, bills were introduced in handwritten form, one copy at a time. In order for Members to discern the content of the bill, the Clerk read it to them; thus, the idea of "reading" the bill was originally taken literally.

Today, while a bill is no longer read aloud, the readings have remained as formalities. When the Speaker declares that the motion for first reading has passed, a clerk at the Table rises and announces "First reading of this bill," thus signifying that the Order of the House has been obeyed. This scenario is repeated when the House has ordered a second and then a third reading of the bill.

A certification of reading must be affixed to every bill immediately after the motion for each of the three readings is adopted. The Clerk of the House is responsible for certifying each reading, and entering the date of passage at the foot of the bill. A bill remains in the custody of the Clerk throughout the stages of consideration. No substantive alteration to the bill is permitted without the express authority of the House or of a committee, in the form of an amendment. The original bills, certified by the Clerk, form part of the official records of the House.

All bills must pass through the same stages of the legislative process, but they do not necessarily follow exactly the same route. Since the House adopted new rules to make the legislative process more flexible, three avenues have existed for the adoption of legislation (see Figure 16.1):

- After appropriate notice, a Minister or a private Member may introduce a bill, which is given first reading immediately. The bill is then debated generally at the second reading stage, after which it is sent to a committee for clause-by-clause study.
- A Minister may propose a motion that a committee be instructed to prepare a bill. A bill will be presented by the committee and carried through the second reading stage without debate or amendment.
- A Minister may move that a bill be referred to a committee for study before second reading.

Regardless of the avenue taken, the bill will have to be carried through report stage, be read a third time and be sent to the Senate for consideration and passage before receiving Royal Assent.

At the start of a new session, a government bill may, if it is identical to a bill introduced in the preceding session, be reinstated at the stage it had reached at the time of prorogation. This may be accomplished by passing a motion to that effect. Private Members' bills, on the other hand, are not affected by prorogation and do not, therefore, require reinstatement at the beginning of a new session. A separate procedure is set out for the reinstatement of Senate bills.

Figure 16.1   The Three Options of the Legislative Process (Government Bills Originating in the House of Commons)

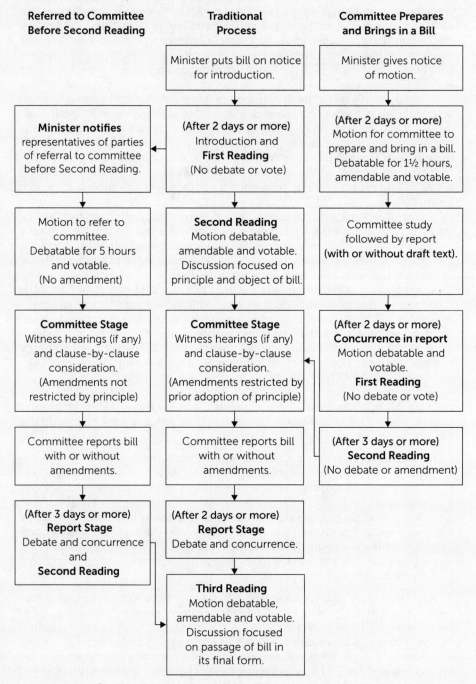

On urgent or extraordinary occasions, if the House so decides, a bill may receive two or three readings on the same day, or be advanced two or more stages in one day. This provision of the Standing Orders applies only to the reading stages. It is up to the House itself, and not to the Chair, to determine whether the matter is sufficiently urgent.

The following are the stages that a bill must pass through before becoming law:

- Notice of motion for leave to introduce and placement on the House of Commons *Order Paper*;
- Preparation of a bill by a committee (where applicable);
- Introduction and first reading;
- Reference to a committee before second reading (where applicable);
- Second reading and reference to a committee;
- Consideration in committee;
- Report stage;
- Third reading (and passage);
- Consideration and passage by the Senate;
- Passage of Senate amendments by the Commons (where applicable);
- Royal Assent; and
- Coming into force.

A bill that is introduced in the Senate must pass through essentially the same stages, except that it is considered first in the Senate and subsequently in the House of Commons. Most bills may be introduced in either House, except for bills which involve spending or relate to taxation, which must be introduced in the House of Commons.

Notice of Motion for Leave to Introduce and Placement on the Order Paper

Forty-eight hours' written notice is required prior to the introduction of any public bill. Once notice has been given for the introduction of a bill, no further notice is required in respect of the bill at the other stages of consideration (with the exception of motions to concur in Senate amendments, and to amend at the report stage). Separate requirements apply in respect of the notice required for private bills.

A private Member or a Minister who intends to introduce a bill in the House of Commons must first give notice to the Clerk of the House before 6:00 p.m. (2:00 p.m. on Friday). The title of the bill to be introduced is then placed on the *Notice Paper*. The day after it appears on the *Notice Paper*, the title of the bill will appear in the *Order Paper* in the order in which the notices were received, together with the titles of other bills awaiting introduction in the House. This is understood to satisfy the 48-hour notice requirement in the Standing Orders. The title of the bill remains on the *Order Paper*, under the rubric "Order of Business," until such time as the private Member or Minister decides to introduce the bill.

There are special rules dealing with the introduction of bills that contemplate the expenditure of public funds and of bills based on ways and means motions. ...

Preparation of a Bill by a Committee

The Standing Orders provide that a motion to appoint or to instruct a committee to prepare a bill may be moved by a Minister.

In order to instruct a committee to prepare and bring in a bill, a Minister must give 48 hours' written notice of the requisite motion. Once the notice period has elapsed, the motion is placed on the *Order Paper* under Government Orders. When it is called by the government, it may be debated for a maximum of 90 minutes, after which the Speaker will interrupt the debate and put all questions necessary to dispose of the motion.

Once a motion to concur in a report of a committee instructed to prepare and bring in a bill is adopted by the House, it becomes an order to bring in the bill. If, at the time the motion for first reading of the bill is proposed, the mover states that the bill is based on the committee report, the motion for second reading will be moved at a later date, without debate or amendment. Consideration of a government bill at the second reading stage may not begin before the third sitting day after first reading. After second reading, the bill will then be subjected to the other ordinary stages for public legislation.

Introduction and First Reading

The first real stage in the legislative process is the introduction and first reading of a bill in the House. The notice period having elapsed, the sponsor of the bill, once ready to do so, notifies the Chair of his or her intention to proceed during Routine Proceedings when the rubric "Introduction of Government Bills" (if the sponsor is a Minister) or "Introduction of Private Members' Bills" is called. Leave to introduce a bill is granted automatically, and the motion is deemed carried, without debate, amendment or question put. A Minister seldom provides any explanation when requesting leave to introduce a bill, but may do so. On the other hand, a private Member normally provides a brief explanation of the bill he or she is introducing in the House.

First reading allows a bill to be formally brought before the House, printed and distributed to all Members. It is at that point that it is assigned a specific bill number. Passage of the motion for first reading involves no commitment on the part of the House beyond agreement that the bill be made generally available for the information of Parliament and the public. No discussion is permitted at this stage. Once leave to introduce the bill has been granted, the Speaker proposes the following motion to the House: "That this bill be read a first time and be printed." The motion is deemed carried, without debate, amendment or question put. The Speaker then asks: "When shall the bill be read a second time?," and answers, "At the next sitting of the House." The question is in fact a formality which enables the bill to be placed on the *Order Paper* under the heading Government Orders or Private Members' Business, as the case may be.

Since Senate bills have already been printed when they are sent to the House of Commons, no request for leave to introduce the bill is required. The motion for first reading is deemed carried without debate, amendment or question put. Senate bills then pass through the same stages as House of Commons bills.

Reference to Committee Before Second Reading

Traditionally, adoption of the motion for second reading amounts to approval by the House of the principle of the bill. This effectively limits the scope of any amendments that may be made during committee study and at report stage. In order to provide more flexibility in the legislative process, the House amended its Standing Orders in 1994, instituting a new procedure that allows Ministers to move that a government bill be referred to committee before second reading. This empowers Members to examine the principle of a bill before second reading, and enables them to propose amendments to alter its scope. The procedure also applies to bills based on ways and means motions.

When the Order of the Day is read for second reading of a government bill, a Minister may, after notifying representatives of the opposition parties, propose a motion that the bill be forthwith referred to a committee before second reading. The Standing Orders are silent as to the manner in which the representatives of the opposition parties are to be notified. The current practice is for the Government House Leader to give such notice during the Thursday Statement, although it is not uncommon for a Minister to inform the House of the government's intention at the time of the introduction and first reading of the bill. The motion to refer forthwith the bill to a committee is not subject to amendment, and debate is limited to five hours. At the end of the five hours, or when no Member rises to speak, the Speaker puts the question. If the motion is adopted, the bill is referred to a standing, special or legislative committee for consideration.

In general, during clause-by-clause consideration of a bill, the committee follows the same rules and procedures as those that apply to the consideration of bills in committee after second reading. It may hear witnesses and receive briefs. However, the scope of the amendments that may be made to the bill is much wider, given that the committee study is not limited by the principle of the bill, the principle not yet having been approved by the House. At the conclusion of its study, the committee reports the bill to the House, with or without amendment. The report stage of the bill may not commence prior to the third sitting day following the presentation of the report.

After the committee has reported the bill to the House, the next stage essentially fuses report stage and second reading. Members may propose amendments, after giving written notice two sitting days prior to the bill being called. When consideration of report stage is concluded, a motion "That the bill (as amended) be concurred in at report stage (with (a) further amendment(s)) and read a second time" or "That the bill be concurred in at report stage and read a second time" is put and forthwith disposed of by the House, without debate or amendment. Once concurred in at report stage and read a second time, the bill is set down for third reading and passage at the next sitting of the House.

Second Reading and Reference to a Committee

Central to the second reading stage is a general debate on the principle of a bill. Although the Standing Orders make no specific reference to this practice, it is deeply rooted in the procedural tradition of the House. Accordingly, debate must focus on the principle of the bill and not on its individual provisions.

Perceptions of the importance of this stage of the legislative process have evolved over the years. Traditionally, it was felt that second reading was the most important stage in the legislative process. In 1968, the Special Committee on Procedure and Organization of the House stated in its report, after examining the stages of the process, that the significance of the second reading stage had been over-emphasized in the past, and that the decisive stage should occur later in a bill's passage, after it had been reported by a committee. In the Committee's view, passage of the motion for second reading simply implied that the House had given preliminary consideration to the bill, without any commitment to its final passage, and had authorized its reference to a committee for detailed scrutiny and possible amendment.

Second reading of a bill and reference to a committee are moved in a single motion which specifies the committee (standing, special, legislative) to which the bill is referred. In most cases, this allows the sponsor of the bill to select the committee to which it is to be referred. The Standing Orders require, in certain cases, that a bill be referred to a Committee of the Whole.

Debate on second reading begins when the Minister or Member, as the case may be, rises when the Order of the Day is read for the second reading of the bill and moves "That Bill (number and title) be now read a second time and referred to the (name of committee) Committee."

The Standing Orders regulate the length of speeches of Members during debate. Only speeches by the Prime Minister and the Leader of the Official Opposition are not subject to time limits. Otherwise, during the initial round of speeches and during the first five hours of debate that follow, Members may speak for no more than 20 minutes, after which, a period not exceeding 10 minutes is made available for questions and comments. If there are no questions or comments, or if the time has not been fully used, another Member may then speak. Questions and comments must be relevant to the Member's speech.

After the initial round of debate and the five hours of debate that follow, any other Member rising to speak has a maximum of 10 minutes, followed by a 5-minute period for questions and comments. The Whip of a party may indicate to the Chair at any time during a debate that one or more of the 20-minute or 10-minute periods of debate allotted to Members of his or her party will be divided in two. Alternatively, Members may themselves advise the Speaker of their intention to divide their time when they are recognized to speak. By custom, every Member who moves a substantive motion is allowed a reply. In current practice, a Member who proposes a motion for second reading of a bill is also permitted a reply. In the case of government bills, a Parliamentary Secretary may exercise that right on behalf of the Minister only with the unanimous consent of the House.

Amendments to the Motion for Reading

A public bill not referred to a committee before second reading may not be amended before being read a second time and referred to a committee. On the other hand, the motion for second reading of a bill may itself be amended, but only three types of amendments may be moved without notice: a three or six months' hoist; a reasoned amendment; and a motion for referral of the subject matter to a committee.

The Hoist Amendment

The hoist is an amendment that may be moved to a motion for the second reading of a bill. Its effect is to prevent a bill from being "now" read a second time, and to postpone the reading for three or six months. If it is adopted, the bill is deemed withdrawn for the remainder of the current session. If it is defeated, the debate has nonetheless been extended as a result and Members enabled to speak a second time.

• • •

The Reasoned Amendment

The reasoned amendment, which may also be moved during debate on a motion for second reading, allows a Member to state the reasons for his or her opposition to second reading of a bill with a relevant proposal replacing the original question. A reasoned amendment is introduced in the form of a motion, and deletes and replaces all of the text of the main motion after the word "That."

• • •

Referral of the Subject Matter of a Bill to a Committee

During debate on the motion for second reading, a Member may propose an amendment to withdraw the bill and to refer its subject matter to a committee for the latter to consider and report to the House. This type of amendment replaces all the words after "That" with a proposal that the bill be not now read a second time, that the order for second reading be discharged, the bill withdrawn from the *Order Paper* and the subject matter referred to a committee.

Certain conditions must be met, however, for this type of amendment to be in order. First, the subject matter of the bill may be referred neither to more than one committee nor to a non-existent body. Second, an amendment that would attach a condition to the adoption of the motion for reading of a bill is out of order. Third, the actual provisions of the bill may not be referred to a committee since this would amount to instructing the committee to consider certain provisions of a bill even before it has been read a second time and referred to a committee.

Unless the amendment specifies a deadline for reporting to the House, the committee to which the subject matter of a bill is referred is free to do so within a time frame of its own choosing.

• • •

Royal Consent

Royal Consent (which should not be confused with Royal Assent or royal recommendation) is derived from British practice, and is among the unwritten rules and customs of the House of Commons of Canada. Any legislation that affects the prerogatives, hereditary revenues, property or interests of the Crown requires Royal Consent, which in Canada originates with the Governor General in his or her capacity as representative of the Sovereign. Consent is necessary when property rights of the Crown are postponed, compromised or abandoned, or for any waiver of a prerogative of the Crown. It was, for example, required for bills in connection with railways on which the Crown had a lien, with property rights of the Crown (in national parks and Indian reserves), with the garnishment, attachment and diversion of pensions and with amendments to the *Financial Administration Act*.

The consent of the Crown is not required where the bill relates to property held by the Crown for its subjects. The consent of the Crown does not, however, signify approval of the substance of the measure; it means only that the Crown agrees to remove an obstacle to the progress of the bill so that the latter may be considered by both Houses, and ultimately submitted for Royal Assent.

Although Royal Consent is often signified when a bill is read for the second time, this may take place at any stage prior to final adoption by the House. It may take the form of a special message, but it is normally transmitted by a Minister who rises in the House and states: "His/Her Excellency the Governor General has been informed of the purport of this bill and has given his/her consent, as far as Her Majesty's prerogatives are affected, to the consideration by Parliament of the bill, that Parliament may do therein as it thinks fit." If consent is not given in advance, the Speaker will refuse to put the question for passage at third reading. If, through inadvertence, a bill requiring Royal Consent were to pass all its stages in the House without receiving consent, it would be necessary to declare the proceedings in relation to the bill null and void.

Consideration in Committee

During consideration in committee, Members examine the clauses of a bill in detail. It is at this stage that they have their first opportunity to propose amendments to its text. It is also at this stage that witnesses may be invited to present their views and to answer Members' questions. A bill is referred to a standing, special or legislative committee for consideration, normally *after* second reading in the House, but sometimes *before* second reading. While any bill based on a supply motion must be referred to a Committee of the Whole, any bill may be referred to a Committee of the Whole by unanimous consent, typically after having passed through more than one stage of the legislative process in a single sitting. The House may also adopt a special order to refer a bill to a Committee of the Whole.

Mandate of the Committee

When a bill is referred to a committee, the order of reference is understood exclusively as a mandate to examine the bill and to report it to the House, with or without amendment. If the bill has already received second reading, the committee is bound by the decision of the House and may not amend it contrary to its principle. This is not the case when the committee considers a bill that has not yet been read the second time.

During consideration of a bill, a committee may receive clarification from the House of its order of reference. Such "instructions" from the House may extend the committee's mandate by giving it additional powers.

A committee may be asked by the House to reconsider a bill which it has already reported. This reference is normally proposed in the form of an amendment to the motion for third reading of the bill. The House may refer a bill back to a committee to have only certain clauses amended or reviewed; it may refer the bill several times, and it may refer it with or without any limitation. In the latter case, the whole bill is open to reconsideration. When a bill is referred with limitations, the committee can consider only the clauses or amendments referred to it.

Role of a Committee on a Bill

The role of the committee is to consider a bill clause-by-clause and, if necessary, word by word, and to approve the text or to modify it.

The committee has the power to modify the provisions of a bill to the extent that when it is reported to the House it may be completely different in substance from the bill referred to the committee. For example, the committee may negative a clause or clauses of a bill (even to the extent that nothing is left of the text of the bill) and report the bill to the House with amendments; the committee may also negative all the clauses of a bill and substitute new clauses, as long as the new clauses respect the rules of admissibility.

• • •

Hearing of Witnesses

A committee to which a bill is referred usually chooses to hold public hearings. Its steering committee (referred to as the subcommittee on agenda and procedure), or the whole committee, if no steering committee has been established, may discuss a timetable for meetings and compile a list of witnesses whom the members wish to invite to appear. A steering committee will usually present its recommendations to the whole committee in the form of a report. The committee may then adopt the report with or without amendments. It may also elect to call upon the services of the research officers of the Library of Parliament, or to retain any other specialist it deems necessary to assist it in its work.

Before proceeding with clause-by-clause examination of the bill, the Chair of the committee calls Clause 1 for debate (or Clause 2, if Clause 1 contains the short title) to permit general discussion of the bill and questioning of witnesses, if any are appearing. Ordinarily the first witness to appear before the committee is either the sponsor of the bill, the Minister responsible for it or the Minister's Parliamentary Secretary. Other witnesses may then be invited to express their views on the bill. Such witnesses may include individuals, experts or representatives of organizations potentially affected by the legislative measure. At this stage, discussion is wide-ranging, and relates both to the general principle and to the details of the bill. Later, upon commencement of clause-by-clause consideration of the bill, the Minister responsible, or the Minister's Parliamentary Secretary, may again address the committee. Departmental officials will also make themselves available during this phase, to provide explanations of complex or technical aspects of the legislative proposal.

On occasion, committees have considered two bills at a single meeting in order to question a Minister and witnesses on both bills at the same time. The bills in question had points in common that made it practical to consider them simultaneously. Notwithstanding these similarities, the bills were examined separately at the clause-by-clause stage. A committee has also simultaneously considered a bill referred to it and the subject matter of another bill.

Clause-by-Clause Consideration

Once the witnesses have been heard, the committee proceeds to clause-by-clause consideration of the bill. It is during this phase of the committee's deliberations that members may propose amendments to the bill.

• • •

Consideration of the Clauses

Each clause of the bill is a distinct question requiring separate consideration. The committee Chair calls each clause successively by number and, after discussion, puts the question on the clause if no amendment is proposed. If an amendment is proposed, the Chair recognizes the mover, who reads the amendment. A new question is then placed under consideration and there is a new debate. When debate has concluded, the Chair first puts the question on the amendment to the clause and then on the clause itself (as amended, if applicable). Once the clause is carried, it may not be discussed further without unanimous consent.

The committee may adopt a motion to divide a clause in order to debate its parts separately or to put the question on the parts separately.

• • •

Adoption of the Bill

Once the committee has concluded its clause-by-clause consideration, the bill in its entirety, with or without amendments, is submitted for the approval of the committee. While the normal practice is for the committee to agree at this point to the question "Shall the bill carry?," opposition to the bill is normally expressed either by voting against all the clauses of the bill before adoption, or by adopting a motion that the bill not be further proceeded with ...).

Leave to Report to the House

After the bill is adopted, the Chair asks the committee for leave to report the bill to the House. The standard formula is as follows: "Shall I report the bill (as amended) to the House?" If the committee agrees, the Chair reports the bill to the House as soon as possible, unless the committee declines to report the bill immediately, in which case, it must do so later.

Reprinting of the Bill

If the number of amendments adopted necessitates it, the committee generally orders that the bill be reprinted for the use of the Members who will have to consult it at report stage.

Report to the House

The committee is bound by its order of reference—the bill—and may only report the bill with or without amendment to the House. Consequently, the committee may not include substantive recommendations in its report ... .

On the other hand, after a bill has been reported, there is nothing to prevent a standing committee, under its permanent mandate in the Standing Orders, from presenting another report in which it sets out substantive recommendations with respect to the subject matter of the bill.

• • •

Presentation of Report

The report of a committee which has completed its examination of a bill is presented to the House by the Chair of the committee, during Routine Proceedings, when the rubric "Presenting Reports from Committees" is called. No debate is permitted at that point.

Report Stage

Once a bill has been examined in committee, it is considered again by the whole House. At this stage, called "report stage," Members may, after giving written notice, propose amendments to the text of the bill as it was reported by the committee. Those motions are then debated.

• • •

Notice of Amendment

In order that a motion to amend a bill may be considered at report stage, notice must be given in writing at least one sitting day prior to the commencement of report stage, if the bill was referred to committee after second reading, and two sitting days before, if the bill was referred to committee before second reading. ...

• • •

Admissibility of Motions in Amendment

It is up to the Speaker to decide what amendments will be considered at report stage. The Speaker rules not on whether the purport of the amendment or its substance is worthy of debate, but rather on whether the amendment is procedurally acceptable within the framework of the rules established for the admissibility of amendments presented at report stage.

At report stage, a bill is examined as a whole and not clause-by-clause as is the case at committee stage.

. . .

Debate

When the Order of the Day for the consideration of a bill at report stage is called, the House first considers any motion in amendment of which notice has been given, and each motion in amendment is open to debate and amendment. However, if no notice of motion(s) in amendment has been given at report stage, no debate is held.

. . .

During debate at this stage, no Member may speak more than once or longer than 10 minutes on any motion (or group of motions) in amendment. The sole exception to this is the 20-minute limit applicable to the first round of speeches on the first motion in amendment at report stage of a bill that has not yet been read the second time. Members' speeches are followed by 10-minute (following the 20-minute speeches discussed above) or 5-minute (after all other speeches) questions and comments periods. Of course, debate at report stage is subject to the general rules of debate, such as the rule of relevance.

. . .

Concurrence at Report Stage

The report stage of a bill that has not yet been read a second time is an integral part of the second reading stage of the bill. At the end of report stage, a motion "That the bill (as amended) be concurred in at report stage (with (a) further amendment(s)), and be read a second time" or "That the bill be concurred in at report stage and read a second time" is moved, the question is put on the motion, and the House disposes of it forthwith, without amendment or debate.

At the end of report stage of a bill that has already been read a second time, the motion for concurrence at report stage is also put forthwith, without amendment or debate. The wording of the concurrence motion will vary, depending on whether the original bill has been amended or not, and depending on the stage at which the amendments were made. If, for example, a bill was not amended in committee or at report stage, the motion is as follows: "That the bill be concurred in at report stage." However, if a bill was amended in committee, but not at report stage, the motion will read as follows: "That the bill, as amended, be concurred in at report stage." When the bill was amended at report stage, but not in committee, the motion is as follows: "That the bill be concurred in at report stage, with an amendment or with amendments." Lastly, if the bill was amended in committee and at report stage, the following motion is made: "That the bill, as amended, be concurred in at report stage, with (a) further amendment(s)."

If no motion in amendment is moved at report stage of a bill that has already been read a second time, no debate may take place and consideration of report stage becomes the simple adoption (or rejection) of the motion for concurrence at report stage, before proceeding to third reading. ...

Third Reading (and Passage)

Third reading is the final stage through which a bill must pass in the House of Commons. It is then that Members must decide whether the bill should be adopted by the House. Although third reading is often regarded as a formality, it is in fact a decisive stage in the legislative process. This is particularly so in the case of a highly controversial bill.

• • •

Debate on third reading commences when the Order of the Day is read for third reading and the Minister or Member, as the case may be, moves: "That the bill be now read a third time and do pass." The rules relating to the length of speeches during debate are the same as those applicable to speeches and to questions and comments at second reading.

Debate at this stage of the legislative process focuses on the final form of the bill. The amendments that are admissible at this stage are similar to those that were admissible at second reading stage. It is in order to propose an amendment for a three- or six-month hoist, as well as a reasoned amendment. However, at third reading stage, reasoned amendments must deal strictly with the bill and may not be contrary to the principle of the bill as adopted at second reading.

• • •

When the motion for third reading has carried, the Clerk of the House certifies that the bill has passed, and records the date of passage at the foot of the bill. The bill is then sent to the Senate for approval. Defeat of a motion for third reading will result in the withdrawal of the bill.

Consideration and Passage by the Senate

Once the House of Commons has passed a bill, it is sent (in the form of a parchment) to the Senate with a message requesting its passage by that House. ... The legislative process through which bills must pass in the Senate is very similar to that in the House of Commons. When the Senate has passed a bill, it so informs the House of Commons by message.

Because most government bills originate in the House of Commons, the Senate is sometimes asked to expedite its consideration of a bill. The Rules of the Senate provide for a procedure known as pre-study, which involves referring the subject matter of a bill that has been introduced in the House of Commons, but has not yet been adopted at first reading in the Senate, to a standing committee of the Senate. In this way, the Senate may consider the bill and form its opinion even before the bill is sent to it. When the bill does arrive, the Senate is accordingly in a position to adopt or to amend it in a very short time. As always, these and other requests to the Senate are dependent on the willing cooperation of the latter. As Speaker Parent, in other circumstances, reminded the House, "The rules of one House cannot be applied to the other, nor can one House compel the other to conduct its work in a specific manner or according to a specific timetable."

Passage of Senate Amendments (if any) by the House of Commons

When the Senate adopts a bill without amendment, a message is sent to the House of Commons to inform it that the bill has been passed, and it normally receives Royal Assent very shortly thereafter, or during the following few days. The bill itself is not sent back to the House, unless it is a supply bill. However, when the Senate amends the bill, it informs the House of the amendments in the message it sends back to the House, along with the bill. The Senate sometimes includes observations or recommendations of the Senate committee that examined the bill in its message to the House. ...

Once they are received, Senate amendments to a bill are brought before the House for consideration. It is not for the Speaker of the House of Commons to rule as to the procedural regularity of proceedings in the Senate and of the amendments it makes to bills. Rather, it is for the House itself to decide whether it accepts or rejects the amendments proposed by the Senate and whether it wishes to inform the latter of the reasons for its decision. A motion for the consideration of Senate amendments requires 24 hours' written notice. In such a motion, the sponsor of a bill may propose that the House concur in, amend or reject the amendments made by the Senate. The motion may simultaneously reject some amendments made by the Senate, and concur in or amend others. The motion must relate exclusively to the Senate amendments, and not to other provisions of the bill not contemplated by the amendments. The House may elect to reject the Senate amendments for a variety of reasons, for instance, because it believes that they contradict the principle of the bill or that they infringe upon the financial initiative of the Crown (and the House of Commons). "Motions Respecting Senate Amendments to Bills" appear on the *Notice Paper* under that heading. Such motions are considered during Government Orders, if the bill in question is a government bill, or during Private Members' Business, if it is a private Member's bill.

The Senate amends bills fairly often, and the House is normally disposed to accept such amendments, since they are usually intended to correct drafting errors or to improve administrative details. ...

When the House agrees to Senate amendments, a message to that effect is sent to the Senate and the bill is returned to it while awaiting Royal Assent. If the House amends or rejects Senate amendments, it so acquaints the Senate by message as well. The Senate may then reconsider its amendments, having regard to the message from the House. It may decide to accept the decision of the House, to reject that decision and insist that its amendments be maintained, or to amend what the House has proposed. Regardless of what the Senate decides, it sends another message to the House to inform it of the decision. Communication between the two Houses continues in this fashion until they ultimately agree on a text. If agreement cannot be reached by exchanging messages, the House in possession of the bill may request that a conference be held.

Conference Between the Houses

When a disagreement arises between the House of Commons and the Senate as to the amendments to be made to a bill, there are two possible ways of proceeding: the disagreement may be communicated in a message (this is normally the first step taken), or a conference may take place. Although this practice has fallen into disuse, a conference may be requested by either of the two Houses in the following cases: to communicate a resolution or an address to which the concurrence of the other House is desired; to discuss the privileges of Parliament; to discuss any matter that warrants the use of this procedure; to require or to communicate statements of facts on which bills have been passed by either House; or to offer reasons for disagreeing to, or insisting on, amendments to a bill.

• • •

Royal Assent

Royal Assent brings all three constituent elements of Parliament together (the Crown, the Senate and the House of Commons). An integral part of the legislative process, it is the stage that a bill must complete before officially becoming an Act of Parliament. A version of the bill identical to that passed by the two Houses is approved by a representative of the Crown and thereby attains "the complement and perfection of a law." This approval may be conveyed in either of two ways: by ceremony or by written declaration. The traditional way is an essentially ceremonial procedure which takes place in the presence of Members and Senators, after the Members have been summoned by the Usher of the Black Rod to go to the Senate to attend the Royal Assent ceremony. Since relevant statutory provisions came into effect in 2002, this formal ceremony is frequently dispensed with and Royal Assent to bills is signified by written declaration.

• • •

Coming into Force

A distinction must be made between the date on which a legislative measure is enacted by Parliament and the date on which it comes into force. The *Interpretation Act* contains provisions governing the coming into force of statutes. A bill becomes law after it has been passed by both Houses in the same form; the resulting statute comes into force either when it receives Royal Assent, if no date of commencement is provided for in the Act, or on another date provided for in the Act. Accordingly, an Act may come into force on one or more dates specified in the Act itself or fixed by an order of the Governor in Council.

CHAPTER EIGHT

THE EXECUTIVE AND ITS FUNCTIONS

I. INTRODUCTION

Notwithstanding the absence of a rigid separation of powers doctrine in Canada, it is still useful to speak about a distinct executive branch of government. The executive branch refers to those institutions in government that are responsible for providing government services and implementing and enforcing laws, whether those laws are formulated by the legislature or, in the case of the common law, by the judiciary.

Following from that broad definition, the executive branch is not a single institution, but rather it consists of a highly varied assortment of institutions and officials ranging from constitutionally recognized positions, such as the Queen, the governor general and lieutenant governors, and the Queen's Privy Council for Canada (in effect, the Cabinet), to the public service and entities that operate at arm's length from the formal government apparatus, but nevertheless perform governmental functions. Examples of the latter include independent boards and tribunals, professional regulatory bodies, and Crown corporations. It is not uncommon for legal commentators to draw a distinction between the "political executive," those elected officials who are responsible for the political direction of government, and the wider constellation of administrative institutions and officials. This chapter uses the term "executive" in a broad sense and interchangeably with the term "administrative."

While the institutional arrangements used for the exercise of executive authority are wide ranging, a reasonably coherent set of legal principles establishing the boundaries of executive powers and the manner by which executive powers are to be exercised has developed. This body of jurisprudence is referred to as administrative law, and is largely (although not exclusively) a creature of the common law. We will provide a brief overview of key administrative law principles in Chapter 11.

At the heart of administrative law is a requirement that government officials exercise their powers in furtherance of public, not private, interests. As we suggested in Chapter 7, a similar expectation underlies the exercise of legislative powers, but in the case of legislators, public preferences are made known, and the creation of public policy is legitimized through democratic processes. However, with some notable exceptions such as municipal councillors, most administrative officials are not elected.

In cases where administrative officials exercise narrow powers that are carefully defined through legislation, the democratic legitimacy of administrative decisions is derived from the close relationship between administrative officials and the legislature. In circumstances where administrative officials exercise broader discretion, there are potentially much greater concerns about whether administrative discretion is being exercised in a manner that is fair to those affected by the decision and in a way that has sufficient regard to the public interest. To a significant degree, the legal rules that have developed in administrative law constrain the exercise of administrative discretion in ways that respect the intentions of the legislative branch and promote outcomes that further the public interest.

This chapter continues in Section II with a brief description of the types of functions performed by executive institutions in Canada. An understanding of the breadth and diversity of these functions is useful because it helps to explain why we have such a diverse set of executive institutions in Canada. In Section III, we identify the royal prerogative and authority delegated by statute as the key sources of executive powers. Section IV describes the constitutional constraints on the statutory delegation of power to the executive, and in particular the limited constraints the Canadian Constitution places on the statutory delegation of legislative and judicial power to executive institutions. Finally, in Section V, we look at a number of executive branch institutions—namely, the Crown, Cabinet, the public service, independent administrative agencies, Crown corporations, enforcement officials, and municipalities—and explore their relationship with the political executive. The focus of Section V will be on the extent to which different institutions can be said to operate independently from the political executive.

II. FUNCTIONS PERFORMED BY EXECUTIVE INSTITUTIONS IN CANADA

As we will see in Section IV below, the Canadian Constitution places very few restrictions on the ability of the legislature to "delegate" authority to executive bodies. "Delegate" in this context means the legislature enacts statutes giving an executive body powers. In our system of government, the political executive (the prime minister or premier and Cabinet) exercise significant control over the legislative agenda. As a result, it should come as no surprise that, in practice, delegated authority has been granted by statute to a variety of executive bodies in virtually every area of public policy. Although there is no accepted typology classifying the various forms of delegated power, it is common for commentators on administrative law to discuss administrative powers in terms of legislative, judicial, and administrative functions.

The characterization of the exercise of delegated authority in terms of function has historic legal significance in that many of the rules respecting the exercise of delegated authority varied depending on the nature of the powers exercised. For example, common law courts developed a set of procedural requirements, referred to as the rules of natural justice (rules that applied to decisions that were characterized as judicial or quasi-judicial, but not to those decisions that were classified as legislative or administrative in nature). Thus, how an administrative power was classified determined to a significant degree the procedures the administrative body had to follow in exercising that power.

Since the Supreme Court of Canada's decision in *Nicholson v Haldimand-Norfolk Regional Police Commissioners*, [1979] 1 SCR 311, the use of these classifications as a basis to determine the availability of procedural rights and remedies has given way to an approach that recognizes that a general duty to be fair is owed by a broader range of administrative decision-makers and is related to matters beyond simply the identity of the decision-maker, such as the type of interest affected and nature of the decision itself. We will consider these procedural rules in more detail in Chapter 11.

A. RULE-MAKING (DELEGATED LEGISLATION)

The rise in the use of executive bodies to perform legislative functions and to create rules of general application parallels the more general rise of administrative bodies. The most pervasive form of administrative rule-making is the regulation-making power that the legislature delegates to the Cabinet, through the "governor in council." However, administrative rule-making is not restricted to this form. Regulation-making power is often delegated to bodies other than Cabinet. For example, municipal by-laws are another prevalent form of delegated legislation, as are rules developed by administrative agencies that are delegated statutory authority to make rules.

The parent statute determines the legal effect of delegated legislation. In the case of regulations and municipal by-laws, these instruments are as potent as legislation in the sense that they give rise to legally enforceable obligations. However, delegated legislation, sometimes referred to as "subordinate legislation," is considered inferior to statutes; a conflict between a statute and delegated legislation is always resolved in favour in the statutory provision. In this context, a conflict is said to arise only in cases of direct conflict—that is, where compliance with both enactments is not possible. No conflict normally arises where delegated legislation, such as a municipal by-law, imposes more onerous regulatory requirements than those enacted by a superior legislative body. See, for example, *114957 Canada Ltée (Spraytech, Société d'arrosage) v Hudson (Town)*, 2001 SCC 40, [2001] 2 SCR 241.

The benefits of resorting to delegated forms of legislation relate chiefly to the relative flexibility of regulations. The availability of time in the legislature to debate and enact legislation is limited, especially when one takes into account the time needed to obtain Cabinet and other approvals before government legislation is introduced. The statutory process is much more cumbersome and time-consuming, especially at the federal level, than the process for making regulations, and regulations are, consequently, preferred in situations that require adjustment of rules over time or detailed consultation with specific stakeholder groups. In many cases, it is impossible for legislators to know in advance the range of circumstances that will require specialized rules. Instead of amending or enlarging statutes in response to unforeseen cases, legislators often prefer to delegate the authority to enact rules to those persons who are charged with the implementation of the statutes, such as the minister (usually acting through Cabinet) or an agency. Delegated rule-making authority also allows for rule creation by those persons with specialized knowledge of the regulatory field, which legislators will generally lack. The result is a system of rule-making that is more flexible, more responsive, and more sensitive to the regulatory context to be addressed.

The expansive use of delegated legislation has led to concerns over the amount of scrutiny by elected officials and the public that regulations receive. The multiple readings of a bill in the legislature and the committee process in practice ensure that there is opportunity for interested groups and opposition politicians to consider the contents of a bill before it passes into law. Cabinet can make regulations, on the other hand, without prior notice or consultation. These concerns were identified in an early consideration of the role of delegated rule-making by a House of Commons Special Committee on Statutory Instruments (Third Report, *Journals*, 22 October 1969) 1411 at 1418:

> The more fundamental of the criticisms can be summarized as follows: the parliamentary tendency to enact statutes in skeleton form, leaving the "details" to be filled in by regulations—such regulations bring often the very matters that are of most importance to the citizen; uncertainty in enabling statutes as to the extent of the area regulations are intended to cover; sweeping or subjective terms used in enabling acts which exclude the judicial control of the regulations made under their authority; lack of public debate, and inadequate consultation of all interested parties before the making of the regulations; lack of precision in the form and content of the regulations; inadequate publicity given to the regulations after they are made; inadequate parliamentary control over the regulations; and the danger that civil servants may be transformed into our masters.

To date, the courts have not generally been willing to extend the administrative law procedural obligations relating to notice and the opportunity to be heard to the executive's rule-making functions. That said, it should be noted that the courts have been more willing to impose procedural obligations in rule-making processes where the legislative outcomes have a particular impact on specific individuals. For example, where land-use by-laws particularly affect the property rights of individual landowners, the courts look past the formal legislative nature of the decision in imposing procedural obligations on municipal councils. See, for example, *Homex Realty and Development v Wyoming*, [1980] 2 SCR 1011.

In practice, regulation-making is usually made reasonably transparent by virtue of government policy and some statutory law. In particular, the *Statutory Instruments Act*, RSC 1985, c S-22 and the *Statutory Instruments Regulations*, CRC, c 1509 set out the basic legal requirements that must be followed in connection with the enactment of subordinate legislation at the federal level, which includes an examination of the instrument to ensure its legality, and the registration and publication of the instrument in the *Canada Gazette*. The enabling legislation may also contain further specific requirements.

The principal policy document governing the federal regulatory process is the *Cabinet Directive on Regulation* (online: <https://www.canada.ca/en/treasury-board-secretariat/services/federal-regulatory-management/guidelines-tools/cabinet-directive-regulation.html>), which came into force on September 1, 2018 and sets out requirements for the analysis and assessment of regulatory proposals and for procedures of notice and consultation. Section 3.0 of the Directive sets out the guiding principles of federal regulatory policy in the following terms:

> It is the duty of the Government of Canada to respect Parliament and the authorities granted by Parliament, as expressed in legislation; and to ensure that regulations result in the greatest overall benefits to current and future generations of Canadians. In fulfilling this duty, departments and agencies are to be guided by four principles:
> 1. **Regulations protect and advance the public interest and support good government:** Regulations are justified by a clear rationale in terms of protecting the health, safety, security, social and economic well-being of Canadians, and the environment.
> 2. **The regulatory process is modern, open, and transparent:** Regulations, and their related activities, are accessible and understandable, and are created, maintained, and reviewed in an open, transparent, and inclusive way that meaningfully engages the public and stakeholders, including Indigenous peoples, early on.
> 3. **Regulatory decision-making is evidence-based:** Proposals and decisions are based on evidence, robust analysis of costs and benefits, and the assessment of risk, while being open to public scrutiny.

4. **Regulations support a fair and competitive economy:** Regulations should aim to support and promote inclusive economic growth, entrepreneurship, and innovation for the benefit of Canadians and businesses. Opportunities for regulatory cooperation and the development of aligned regulations should be considered and implemented wherever possible.

Section 5.0 of the *Cabinet Directive* sets out the general approach to the development of regulations. Departments and agencies responsible for the development of regulations are mandated to determine the approach that should be used to address the relevant subject matter and to engage in appropriate consultation with stakeholders prior to preparing a draft of any proposed regulation. In general, the *Cabinet Directive* requires any draft regulation, along with a Regulatory Impact Analysis Statement, to be pre-published in the *Canada Gazette* for a 30-day notice and comment period before final approval is given. Exemptions from the pre-publication obligation may be granted by Treasury Board or the relevant regulation-making authority if there are no statutory requirements for pre-publication, and exemptions from other regulatory development requirements may be granted by Treasury Board in exceptional circumstances.

Regulatory Impact Analysis Statements are designed to provide an analysis of the benefits and costs of the proposed regulation. They are supposed to consider not only financial implications but to assess impacts on the environment and social and economic impacts on diverse groups of Canadians, using a "gender-based analysis plus" approach that considers multiple and intersecting identity factors that influence the differential impact the proposals may have on different groups of Canadians. The *Cabinet Directive* gives specific direction to departments and agencies to prepare an analysis of any implications the proposed regulation may have for modern treaties or self-government agreements with Indigenous peoples, and to ensure that the government meets its obligations under these treaties and agreements. Likewise, there is an obligation to ensure that Canada is meeting its international obligations in carrying out regulatory activity.

Section 4.0 of the *Cabinet Directive* mandates a "life cycle" approach to regulation that requires attention to be given not only to the development of new regulations but to the implementation, evaluation, and review of existing regulations. The "life cycle" approach pays particular attention to the proliferation of regulations and the coordination of regulatory activity in order to reduce regulatory duplication, promote efficiencies, and generally reduce the burden of regulation where possible. The *Cabinet Directive* also directs departments and agencies to ensure that, where regulatory activities may have the potential to adversely affect established Aboriginal or treaty rights protected by s 35 of the *Constitution Act, 1982*, being Schedule B to the *Canada Act 1982* (UK), 1982, c 11 steps are taken to satisfy the Crown's duty to consult and, where appropriate, accommodate the rights of Aboriginal peoples.

B. COLLECTING AND SPENDING MONEY

The revenue that government collects, primarily though not exclusively through taxation, furnishes government with the resources it needs to maintain the machinery of government and to provide government services. In addition, it is not unusual for governments to use taxation to create incentives or disincentives for certain behaviours. For example, income tax deductions for charitable contributions create an incentive for taxpayers to contribute to charitable causes. Conversely, the so-called "sin" taxes on alcoholic beverages and tobacco products make the consumption of these products more expensive than it would be otherwise, creating a disincentive for their use. Incentives can also take the form of expenditure of revenue by government—for example, through programs providing grants or subsidies to encourage certain kinds of activities.

Section 53 of the *Constitution Act, 1867* (UK), 30 & 31 Vict, c 3, reprinted in RSC 1985, Appendix II, No 5 requires federal legislation imposing taxation or appropriating revenue to originate in the House of Commons. This provision recognizes the fundamental role played by the legislative branch of government in authorizing the imposition of taxation and in supervising the government's expenditure of funds. In addition, s 54 of the *Constitution Act, 1867* provides that a recommendation be provided by the governor general for any bill imposing taxation or appropriating revenue before the bill is adopted by the House of Commons. As noted in Chapter 7, the standing orders of the House of Commons have specific provisions governing ways and means bills (bills that raise taxes) and appropriation bills, one element of which is that only a minister can introduce these types of bills. These arrangements allow the executive branch to exercise control over the government's finances subject to legislative oversight.

In *Re Eurig Estate*, [1998] 2 SCR 565, the Supreme Court of Canada ruled that the principles established by s 53 of the *Constitution Act, 1867* are binding on provincial governments as well as the federal government, even though provincial governments do not have bicameral legislatures. In other words, s 53 does not deal simply with the relationship between the House of Commons and the Senate, but with the relationship between the legislative and executive branches of government. Writing for the majority of the Court, Major J made the following observations:

> [29] To date, s. 53 has been the subject of only limited academic and jurisprudential discussion. It has been suggested that the purpose of s. 53 is to prevent the introduction of taxation legislation in the Senate, and that with the abolition of bicameral legislatures in the provinces it has become redundant: see, e.g., W. H. McConnell in *Commentary on the British North America Act* (1977), at p. 132.
>
> [30] In my view, the rationale underlying s. 53 is somewhat broader. The provision codifies the principle of no taxation without representation, by requiring any bill that imposes a tax to originate with the legislature. My interpretation of s. 53 does not prohibit Parliament or the legislatures from vesting any control over the details and mechanism of taxation in statutory delegates such as the Lieutenant Governor in Council. Rather, it prohibits not only the Senate, but also any other body other than the directly elected legislature, from imposing a tax on its own accord.
>
> [31] In our system of responsible government, the Lieutenant Governor in Council cannot impose a new tax *ab initio* without the authorization of the legislature. As Audette J. succinctly stated in *The King v. National Fish Co.*, [1931] Ex. C.R. 75, at p. 83, "[t]he Governor in Council has no power, *proprio vigore*, to impose taxes unless under authority specifically delegated to it by Statute. The power of taxation is exclusively in Parliament."
>
> [32] The basic purpose of s. 53 is to constitutionalize the principle that taxation powers cannot arise incidentally in delegated legislation. In so doing, it ensures parliamentary control over, and accountability for, taxation. As E. A. Driedger stated in "Money Bills and the Senate" (1968), 3 *Ottawa L. Rev.* 25, at p. 41:

> > Through the centuries, the principle was maintained that taxation required representation and consent. The only body in Canada that meets this test is the Commons. The elected representatives of the people sit in the Commons, and not in the Senate, and, consistently with history and tradition, they may well insist that they alone have the right to decide to the last cent what money is to be granted and what taxes are to be imposed.

While this approach has been criticized (see Peter Hogg, "Can the Taxing Power Be Delegated?" (2002) 16 SCLR (2nd) 305), the *Eurig* principle does not prevent the legislature from delegating the authority to impose taxation, providing it does so in clear and unambiguous language. Writing for the Court in *Ontario English Catholic Teachers' Assn v Ontario (AG)*, 2001 SCC 15, Iacobucci J observed:

> [74] The delegation of the imposition of a tax is constitutional if express and unambiguous language is used in making the delegation. The animating principle is that only the legislature can impose a new tax *ab initio*. But if the legislature expressly and clearly authorizes the imposition of a tax by a delegated body or individual, then the requirements of the principle of "no taxation without representation" will be met. In such a situation, the delegated authority is not being used to impose a completely new tax, but only to impose a tax

that has been approved by the legislature. The democratic principle is thereby preserved in two ways. First, the legislation expressly delegating the imposition of a tax must be approved by the legislature. Second, the government enacting the delegating legislation remains ultimately accountable to the electorate at the next general election.

Although explicit statutory language is required to delegate the imposition of a tax, it is not uncommon for the legislature to delegate authority to the executive to impose and set the amount of user fees or regulatory charges. A user fee is a charge for the use of government services. For the user fee to be valid, there must be a nexus between the amount of the fee and the cost to government of providing the services for which the fee is charged. For example, in *Re Eurig Estate*, [1998] 2 SCR 565 at paras 21-22, the Supreme Court of Canada held that the Ontario probate fees that were challenged were a tax rather than a user fee because there was no relationship between the amount of the fee and the cost to Ontario of providing probate services. Since the relevant enabling legislation only provided the authority to set fees rather than to impose taxes, the fee regulation was invalid.

It is not necessary for the amount of a regulatory charge be linked to the cost to government of administering the regulatory scheme, but there must be a nexus between the charge and the purpose of the regulatory scheme. In *620 Connaught Ltd v Canada (AG)*, 2008 SCC 7 at paras 19-20, the Supreme Court of Canada upheld the validity of liquor licensing charges imposed by regulation on establishments selling alcoholic beverages in Jasper National Park. It did so even though the amount of the licensing charges greatly exceeded the cost of regulating the sale of liquor in the park. The Court concluded that the relevant regulatory scheme was the broader one of regulating the administration and operation of Jasper National Park, and there was a reasonable relationship between the charges imposed on the liquor vendors and that regulatory scheme.

It can sometimes be difficult to draw the distinction between a regulatory charge and a tax. A number of provinces, including Saskatchewan, Alberta, and Ontario, have challenged the constitutional validity of the greenhouse gas emission charges imposed in some provinces by the federal government through regulations enacted under the authority of the *Greenhouse Gas Pollution Pricing Act*, SC 2018, c 12, s 186. The main ground of challenge to the legislation is that the scheme cannot be supported under any federal head of power and that it interferes with valid provincial schemes of regulation of greenhouse gas emissions. Both the Saskatchewan and Ontario Court of Appeal, in majority judgments, dismissed this line of argument on the basis that the federal government has the authority to regulate greenhouse gas emissions under the national concern branch of the "peace, order and good government" power found in s 91 of the *Constitution Act, 1867* (see *Reference re Greenhouse Gas Pollution Pricing Act*, 2019 SKCA 40; *Reference re Greenhouse Gas Pollution Pricing Act*, 2019 ONCA 544). The Alberta Court of Appeal, in a majority judgment, accepted the province's argument that the law could not be upheld on this basis (see *Reference re Greenhouse Gas Pollution Pricing Act*, 2020 ABCA 74). The alternative line of argument in these cases, which is of greater interest for present purposes, was that the charges are a tax and, because they are imposed by regulation rather than directly in the legislation itself, they are contrary to s 53 of the *Constitution Act, 1867*. The Saskatchewan and Ontario courts ruled that the charges were valid regulatory charges rather than taxes, as did the dissenting judge in Alberta, with the majority expressing no opinion on the issue. Nevertheless, a minority in the Saskatchewan Court of Appeal concluded that the charges constituted a form of taxation, and that authority to impose taxation in this form had not been properly delegated by Parliament to the governor in council. These decisions are being appealed to the Supreme Court of Canada.

C. DISPUTE RESOLUTION

It is common for administrative agencies to be created in order to hear and decide specific kinds of disputes—that is, to perform a role most of us would associate with judicial functions. In some cases, administrative tribunals are very similar in their form to courts in that they adjudicate claims between competing parties strictly on the basis of existing law, they cannot initiate proceedings themselves, and they are given similar powers to courts, such as the power to summon witnesses and to award costs. In some cases, distinct tribunals are created to hear appeals by parties dissatisfied with a decision from an administrative decision-maker of first instance.

On the other hand, administrative dispute resolution mechanisms do not always take a form that closely imitates the functioning of courts. Indeed, one justification for the use of administrative dispute resolution over courts is that the formalities associated with court proceedings can be dispensed with, making administrative tribunals more open to public participation. There is also greater flexibility in determining who the decision-makers may be. For example, membership in a tribunal is typically not restricted to lawyers, and often includes experts in the policy area of the tribunal.

In addition, the use of administrative tribunals may afford greater flexibility in the range of considerations that decision-makers may appropriately take into account in making decisions. Courts are restricted to resolving disputes in accordance with the rules of law and equity, but are generally discouraged from engaging in excessive policy-making. Administrative tribunals can, on the other hand, be designed such that tribunal members are statutorily given broad discretion to determine and apply public policy. The Ontario Court of Appeal in *Re Cloverdale Shopping Centre Ltd v Township of Etobicoke*, [1966] 2 OR 439 discussed the nature of the Ontario Municipal Board's adjudicative function in the following terms:

> The function of the Board as well as the function of the Minister is administrative in character. The decision to be made transcends the interests of the immediate parties.
>
> • • •
>
> The Minister or the Board is not deciding a *lis* in the sense that the issue is confined to those for or against the proposal but he or it has to consider the safety, welfare and convenience, *i.e.*, the interests, of the public in the municipalities affected. In doing so the Minister or equally the Board is required to "act judicially" but not beyond the sense that the parties are to be accorded a full and fair hearing and their submissions considered. When this has been accorded to the parties, the decision—an administrative decision—has then to be made. The decision is not a decision upon the objections to the proposal; those objections may be, and frequently are, of validity and importance; they may, however, be overruled upon the larger considerations of administrative policy.
>
> • • •
>
> With no offence intended, it is trite to say that the Board in its general operation as well as in the case at bar pursues "hybrid" functions and it is perhaps because of the varied and important duties conferred upon the Board by numerous statutes that confusion may well arise as to its exact functions in a particular kind of case. Reference need only be made in this regard to the varied duties and functions of the Board in hearing, for example, assessment appeals, applications for annexation of additional territory to a municipality, arbitrations for the award of damages in connection with the compulsory taking of land. In discharging some of these functions the Board throughout the proceedings will be required to act judicially, in others to act administratively and in still others to discharge the "hybrid" functions. ... In the case at bar the evidence and the very reasons of the Board disclose that the Board considered in connection with the application, the matters mentioned in the Act such as the health, safety, convenience or welfare of the inhabitants of the area and the requirements for land uses, communications and public services—*i.e.*, the "standards or principles" as appellants put it, envisioned by the Act. Having so considered such matters and the objections to alteration of the official plan, the Board proceeded to its administrative decision. Save in the limited field which has already been discussed, that administrative decision is not open to review by the Court.

D. BENEFIT OR OBLIGATION DETERMINATION

The most prevalent, and the most diverse, group of administrative decision-makers are those empowered to determine whether a person will be granted a particular public benefit (such as a welfare entitlement or the issuance of a licence), will be subject to a tax or other obliga-tion, or will be assessed a penalty. These activities are typically characterized as purely or truly "administrative" functions, but that has not prevented courts from imposing procedural requirements on the persons making these decisions in appropriate circumstances.

Benefit determinations will sometimes have distributive consequences that require decision-makers to confer a certain benefit, such as a broadcast licence, on some applicants but not on others, raising fairness concerns. In addition, benefit determination may require decision-makers to attach complex sets of conditions to an approval, as is the case with many land-use or environmental approvals.

Obligation determinations may raise slightly different issues than benefit determinations. They are usually initiated by the imposing agency, leaving an affected person to take affirma-tive steps to protect his or her interests, if he or she feels aggrieved. As noted in relation to the dispute resolution functions of administrative decision-makers, in cases where the imposition potentially has a significant impact on the affected person, the scheme may provide an admin-istrative avenue for further consideration, such as a right of appeal to an administrative tribunal or other administrative official.

The desire for fairness in individual cases is often in conflict with the need for administrative efficiency. In many cases, benefit and obligation determinations need to occur on a very large scale given the high number of applications involved. For example, in 2018 the Immigration and Refugee Board disposed of 26,805 refugee protection claims out of a total of 55,383 new cases referred to it, leaving a total of 71,675 claims pending as of the end of the year. The volume of matters that must be addressed by some agencies can result in decisions being taken by persons with little or no direct contact with the affected person and with impor-tant discretionary decisions being made, at least in the first instance, by relatively low-level decision-makers within the agencies.

E. ENFORCEMENT DECISIONS

Another area of delegated authority is those decisions and activities that are required to pro-mote compliance with legal obligations, including criminal and quasi-criminal enforcement proceedings. The executive branches of government use police and prosecutors to investigate and prosecute violations of statutory and regulatory requirements, most commonly through the courts. It is quite common for statutes to confer investigatory powers on other administrative officials for the purposes of a particular scheme and to confer upon them special powers such as the right to conduct searches and interviews and to require the production of documents.

Where reasonable grounds for violations of legal requirements are found by this type of body, the statute may empower the investigator to lay an information in order to initi-ate proceedings before a court pursuant to a statutory offence provision. Alternatively, the scheme may provide that a penalty be imposed directly by the investigating agency or by an administrative tribunal after hearing evidence. For example, s 7.7 of the *Aeronautics* Act, RSC 1985, c A-2, authorizes the federal minister of transportation to assess monetary penalties for contraventions of certain designated provisions of the Act. If the minister issues a notice of contravention, the person notified has the alternative of paying the penalty specified in the notice or seeking a review by the Transportation Appeal Tribunal. This procedure is an alterna-tive to the provisions of the Act making such contraventions a summary conviction offence, and persons who are assessed administrative monetary penalties cannot be prosecuted by way of summary conviction.

F. OVERLAPPING FUNCTIONS

It should perhaps be apparent from these discussions that any one administrative body may carry out a variety of functions. Taking the Canadian Human Rights Commission as an example, the commission engages in rule-making in issuing guidelines, it has investigatory powers in connection with discriminatory practices complaints, and it has decision-making powers, such as the authority to dismiss a complaint, that affect the rights of individuals. Similarly, while some decisions are easily recognizable as being of a legislative or judicial character, many others defy classification in functional terms. As noted, tribunals may be structured in ways that are similar to courts, but may engage in policy creation. Conversely, an ostensibly legislative body, such as a municipal council, may have to exercise some of its powers of decision in accordance with certain procedural requirements because of the nature of the interests affected. The legal requirements that qualify the exercise of delegated power are taken up in Chapter 11.

G. PROVISION OF SERVICES, GOODS, AND FACILITIES

Perhaps the most traditional form of executive activity is the direct provision of services, and to a lesser extent goods and facilities. Services have traditionally included the public safety and security services provided by the armed forces, and by police and fire departments. The executive branch of government has also traditionally assumed responsibility for the provision of transportation infrastructure, such as roads and port facilities, and for the repair and maintenance of those facilities. In addition, the executive branch of government has increasingly taken responsibility for the provision of important social services. This can occur directly, for example, through the operation of public schools and hospitals, or indirectly through the use of public funds to subsidize the provision of medical and pharmaceutical services or the provision of post-secondary education. At various times the executive branch of government has undertaken the provision of other services, such as electricity, air and rail transportation, automobile insurance, and broadcasting and telecommunications services, sometimes as a monopoly and other times in competition with private sector providers of these services. Governments have sometimes chosen to divest themselves, either fully or partially, from these activities and turn them over to the private sector. The executive branch of government also has an important role in the provision of information to members of the public, and increasingly in protecting the privacy of personal information held by public agencies and in some instances by private bodies.

Given the diversity of the services government may provide, it should not be surprising that the types of institutional arrangements that can be made for the provision of these services are equally varied. The traditional structure through which governments have organized their policy development and service delivery functions is through ministries headed by members of Cabinet, and this system continues to play a central role in the operation of the executive branch of government in Canada. At the same time, governments have also chosen to deliver services through using legislation to establish Crown corporations or hospitals and universities that are governed by boards that operate, to some extent at least, at arm's length from government. Finally, governments have increasingly chosen to contract with private sector organizations for the delivery of services, including such things as waste collection and disposal, snow removal, and even child protection and welfare services.

III. SOURCES OF EXECUTIVE POWER

Where does executive power come from? As we have already suggested, all executive power (except the limited authority existing in the *Constitution Act, 1867* or by virtue of constitutional convention) flows from the royal prerogative and statutory delegation.

A. PREROGATIVE POWERS

Prerogative powers are those powers exercisable by the Crown that do *not* arise from a statutory grant of power to the Crown. Prerogative powers are "residual" in the sense that historically the power of the Crown pre-existed that of the legislature and as a result prerogative powers are those traditional powers that have remained with the Crown (and thus the executive branch of government).

In exercising prerogative powers, the Crown is restricted to executive acts. Consequently, the Crown cannot exercise legislative powers pursuant to its prerogative, nor can it exercise judicial powers.

The prerogative powers themselves are not static in the sense that these powers will remain undiminished over time. To the contrary, where the legislature enacts a statute in relation to a matter previously addressed through the exercise of prerogative powers, the statute has the effect of superseding the prerogative power. The ability of the legislature to abolish prerogative powers derives from parliamentary supremacy, the superior position of the legislature in our constitutional system.

At the present time, the powers exercised by way of prerogative include many of the Crown's powers of appointment, and powers relating to foreign affairs, such as declarations of war, the appointment of ambassadors, and the issuing of passports. They also include powers to control the parliamentary agenda, such as the power to prorogue or dissolve Parliament, to the extent these powers have not been limited by legislation.

There has been some legal debate over who in the executive can exercise prerogative powers and whether prerogative powers can be subjected to judicial oversight. These questions are considered in the following excerpt from *Black v Canada (Prime Minister)*, a case involving a decision by the prime minister to recommend against the conferral of a foreign honour on a Canadian citizen, Conrad Black.

Black v Canada (Prime Minister)
(2001), 54 OR (3d) 215 (CA)

LASKIN JA:

[23] The motions judge concluded that the Prime Minister's communication with the Queen was an exercise of the prerogative power to grant honours and conduct foreign affairs. I agree with the motions judge that Prime Minister Chrétien was exercising a prerogative power, although I rest my own conclusion on the honours prerogative alone.

[24] Mr. Black submits that the motions judge erred in his conclusion for four reasons. First, because Mr. Black did not plead that the Prime Minister exercised a Crown prerogative, the motions judge should not have concluded that he did. Second, in Canada the Prime Minister does not have the power to exercise the Crown prerogative, only the Governor General does. Third, the actions of Prime Minister Chrétien pleaded in the statement of claim were not an exercise of the Crown prerogative, either in relation to the granting of honours or the conduct of foreign affairs, but an unsolicited personal intervention in which the Prime Minister gave wrong legal advice. Fourth, in Canada the prerogative power to conduct foreign affairs has been displaced by the *Department of Foreign Affairs and International Trade Act*, RSC 1985 c. E-22.

[25] To put these submissions in context, I will briefly review the nature of the Crown's prerogative power. According to Professor Dicey, the Crown prerogative is "the residue of discretionary or arbitrary authority, which at any given time is left

in the hands of the Crown." Dicey, *Introduction to the Study of the Law of the Constitution* 10th ed. (London: Macmillan, 1959) at p. 424. Dicey's broad definition has been explicitly adopted by the Supreme Court of Canada and the House of Lords. ...

[26] The prerogative is a branch of the common law because decisions of courts determine both its existence and its extent. In short, the prerogative consists of "the powers and privileges accorded by the common law to the Crown." Peter Hogg, *Constitutional Law in Canada* Loose-Leaf Edition (Toronto: Carswell, 1995) at 1.9. See also *Case of Proclamations* (1611), 77 ER 1352 (Eng. KB). The Crown prerogative has descended from England to the Commonwealth. ...

[27] Despite its broad reach, the Crown prerogative can be limited or displaced by statute. See *Parliament of Canada Act*, RSC 1985 c. P-1 s. 4. Once a statute occupies ground formerly occupied by the prerogative, the prerogative goes into abeyance. The Crown may no longer act under the prerogative, but must act under and subject to the conditions imposed by the statute ... In England and Canada, legislation has severely curtailed the scope of the Crown prerogative. Dean Hogg comments that statutory displacement of the prerogative has had the effect of "shrinking the prerogative powers of the Crown down to a very narrow compass" (supra). ... Nonetheless, as I will discuss, the granting of honours has never been displaced by statute in Canada and therefore continues to be a Crown prerogative in this country.

• • •

[31] Mr. Black's second submission is that the Prime Minister cannot exercise the Crown prerogative. He submits that in Canada, only the Governor General can exercise the prerogative. I find no support for this proposition in theory or in practice. Admittedly, the Governor General is the Queen's permanent representative in Canada. ...

[32] Still, nothing in the *Letters Patent* [by which the monarch delegates most of her prerogative powers to the Governor General] or the case law requires that all prerogative powers be exercised exclusively by the Governor General. As members of the Privy Council, the Prime Minister and other Ministers of the Crown may also exercise the Crown prerogative. See Lordon, [P Lordon, QC, *Crown Law* (Toronto: Butterworths, 1991)], at p. 71. The reasons of Wilson J in *Operation Dismantle* affirm that prerogative power may be exercised by cabinet ministers and therefore does not lie exclusively with the Governor General. ... This gradual relocation of the prerogative is consistent with Professor Wade's general view of the Crown prerogative as an "instrument of government." Commentary on Dicey's *Introduction to the Study of the Law of the Constitution* 9th ed. (London: Macmillan, 1950). The conduct of foreign affairs, for example, "is an executive act of government in which neither the Queen nor Parliament has any part."

[33] Counsel for the respondents points out that if Mr. Black were correct, the Prime Minister—whose powers are not enumerated in any statute—would have no legal authority to speak for Canada on foreign affairs. This proposition is, on its face, absurd. I therefore reject Mr. Black's submission that only the Governor General can exercise prerogative powers in Canada. I conclude that the Prime Minister and the Government of Canada can exercise the Crown prerogative as well.

• • •

Second Issue: Is the Prerogative Power Exercised by the Prime Minister Reviewable in the Courts?

[42] This is the main question on this appeal. The motions judge concluded ... that Mr. Black's complaint about the Prime Minister was not justiciable. He wrote:

"It is not within the power of the court to decide whether or not the advice of the PM about the prerogative honour to be conferred or denied upon Black was right or wrong. It is not for the court to give its opinion on the advice tendered by the PM to another country. These are non-justiciable decisions for which the PM is politically accountable to Parliament and the electorate, not the courts."

[43] Mr. Black submits that the motions judge erred in concluding that Prime Minister Chrétien's exercise of the honours prerogative was not reviewable by the court. The amended statement of claim pleads that the Prime Minister gave the Queen wrong legal advice, which detrimentally affected Mr. Black. Mr. Black argues that had the advice been given under a statutory power, it would have been subject to judicial review; it should similarly be subject to judicial review if given under a prerogative power.

[44] I agree with Mr. Black that the source of the power—statute or prerogative— should not determine whether the action complained of is reviewable. However, in my view, the action complained of in this case—giving advice to the Queen or communicating to her Canada's policy on the conferral of an honour on a Canadian citizen—is not justiciable. Even if the advice was wrong or given carelessly or negligently, it is not reviewable in the courts. I therefore agree with the motions judge's conclusion.

[45] Under the law that existed at least into the 1960s, the court's power to judicially review the prerogative was very limited. The court could determine whether a prerogative power existed and, if so, what its scope was, and whether it had been superseded by statute. However, once a court established the existence and scope of a prerogative power, it could not review how that power was exercised. ... The appropriateness or adequacy of the grounds for its exercise, even whether the procedures used were fair, were not reviewable. The courts insisted that the source of the power—the prerogative—precluded judicial scrutiny of its exercise. The underlying rationale for this narrow review of the prerogative was that exercises of prerogative power ordinarily raised questions courts were not qualified or competent to answer.

[46] Even this narrow view of the court's role in reviewing the prerogative power now has to be modified in Canada because of the *Canadian Charter of Rights and Freedoms*. By s. 32(1)(a), the *Charter* applies to Parliament and the Government of Canada in respect of all matters within the authority of Parliament. The Crown prerogative lies within the authority of Parliament. Therefore, if an individual claims that the exercise of a prerogative power violates that individual's *Charter* rights, the court has a duty to decide the claim. See *Operation Dismantle* ... . However, Mr. Black does not assert any *Charter* claim.

[47] Apart from the *Charter*, the expanding scope of judicial review and of Crown liability make it no longer tenable to hold that the exercise of a prerogative power is insulated from judicial review merely because it is a prerogative and not a statutory power. The preferable approach is that adopted by the House of Lords in the *Civil Service Unions* case ... . There, the House of Lords emphasized that the controlling consideration in determining whether the exercise of a prerogative power is judicially reviewable is its subject matter, not its source. If, in the words of Lord Roskill, the subject matter of the prerogative power is "amenable to the judicial process," it is reviewable; if not, it is not reviewable. Lord Roskill provided content to this subject matter test of reviewability by explaining that the exercise of the prerogative will be amenable to the judicial process if it affects the rights of individuals. Again, in his words at p. 417:

... If the executive in pursuance of the statutory power does an act affecting the rights of the citizen, it is beyond question that in principle the manner of the exercise of that power may today be challenged on one or more of the three grounds which I have mentioned earlier in this speech. If the executive instead of acting under a statutory power acts under a prerogative power and in particular a prerogative power delegated to the respondent under article 4 of the Order in Council of 1982, so as to affect the rights of the citizen, I am unable to see, subject to what I shall say later, that there is any logical reason why the fact that the source of the power is the prerogative and not statute should today deprive the citizen of that right of challenge to the manner of its exercise which he would possess were the source of the power statutory. In either case the act in question is the act of the executive.

• • •

[51] Under the test set out by the House of Lords, the exercise of the prerogative will be justiciable, or amenable to the judicial process, if its subject matter affects the rights or legitimate expectations of an individual. Where the rights or legitimate expectations of an individual are affected, the court is both competent and qualified to judicially review the exercise of the prerogative.

[52] Thus, the basic question in this case is whether the Prime Minister's exercise of the honours prerogative affected a right or legitimate expectation enjoyed by Mr. Black and is therefore judicially reviewable. To put this question in context, I will briefly discuss prerogative powers that lie at the opposite ends of the spectrum of judicial reviewability. At one end of the spectrum lie executive decisions to sign a treaty or to declare war. These are matters of "high policy." ... Where matters of high policy are concerned, public policy and public interest considerations far outweigh the rights of individuals or their legitimate expectations. In my view, apart from *Charter* claims, these decisions are not judicially reviewable.

[53] At the other end of the spectrum lie decisions like the refusal of a passport or the exercise of mercy. The power to grant or withhold a passport continues to be a prerogative power. A passport is the property of the Government of Canada, and no person, strictly speaking, has a legal right to one. However, common sense dictates that a refusal to issue a passport for improper reasons or without affording the applicant procedural fairness should be judicially reviewable. This was the position taken by the English Court of Appeal in *R v. Secretary of State for Foreign & Commonwealth Affairs, ex parte Everett*, ... Two passages from that case are worth highlighting. O'Connor LJ wrote at p. 658:

> The judge held that the issue of a passport fell into an entirely different category. That seems common sense. It is a familiar document to all citizens who travel in the world and it would seem obvious to me that the exercise of the prerogative, because there is no doubt that passports are issued under the royal prerogative in the discretion of the Secretary of State, is an area where common sense tells one that, if for some reason a passport is wrongly refused for a bad reason, the court should be able to inquire into it. I would reject the submission made on behalf of the Secretary of State that the judge was wrong to review the case.

And Taylor LJ wrote at p. 660:

> ... At the top of the scale of executive functions under the prerogative are matters of high policy, of which examples were given by their Lordships: making treaties, making law, dissolving Parliament, mobilising the armed forces. Clearly those matters, and no doubt a number of others, are not justiciable. But the grant or refusal of a passport is in a quite different category. It is a matter of administrative decision, affecting the rights of individuals and their freedom of travel. It raises issues which are just as justiciable as, for example, the issues arising in immigration cases.

• • •

[60] The refusal to grant an honour is far removed from the refusal to grant a passport or a pardon, where important individual interests are at stake. Unlike the refusal of a peerage, the refusal of a passport or a pardon has real adverse consequences for the person affected. Here, no important individual interests are at stake. Mr. Black's rights were not affected, however broadly "rights" are construed. No Canadian citizen has a right to an honour.

[61] And no Canadian citizen can have a legitimate expectation of receiving an honour. In Canada the doctrine of legitimate expectations informs the duty of procedural fairness; it gives no substantive rights. ... Here Mr. Black does not assert that he was denied procedural fairness. Indeed, he had no procedural rights.

[62] But even if the doctrine of legitimate expectations could give substantive rights, neither Mr. Black nor any other Canadian citizen can claim a legitimate expectation of receiving an honour. The receipt of an honour lies entirely within the discretion of the conferring body. The conferral of the honour at issue in this case, a British peerage, is a discretionary favour bestowed by the Queen. It engages no liberty, no property, no economic interests. It enjoys no procedural protection. It does not have a sufficient legal component to warrant the court's intervention. Instead, it involves "moral and political considerations which it is not within the province of the courts to assess." See *Operation Dismantle* ... , per Dickson J at p. 465.

[63] In other words, the discretion to confer or refuse to confer an honour is the kind of discretion that is not reviewable by the court. In this case, the court has even less reason to intervene because the decision whether to confer a British peerage on Mr. Black rests not with Prime Minister Chrétien, but with the Queen. At its highest, all the Prime Minister could do was give the Queen advice not to confer a peerage on Mr. Black.

[64] For these reasons, I agree with the motions judge that Prime Minister Chrétien's exercise of the honours prerogative by giving advice to the Queen about granting Mr. Black's peerage is not justiciable and therefore not judicially reviewable.

[65] Once Prime Minister Chrétien's exercise of the honours prerogative is found to be beyond review by the courts, how the Prime Minister exercised the prerogative is also beyond review. Even if the advice was wrong or careless or negligent, even if his motives were questionable, they cannot be challenged by judicial review. To paraphrase Dickson J in *Thorne's Hardware* ... , at p. 112: "It is neither our duty nor our right" to investigate the Prime Minister's motives or his reasons for his advice. Therefore, the declaratory relief and the tort claims asserted by Mr. Black cannot succeed. For these reasons, I would dismiss his appeal.

While the plaintiff lost, do not read *Black* as suggesting *all* prerogative powers are non-justiciable. Be attentive to the Court of Appeal's efforts to distinguish between justiciable and non-justiciable exercises of the prerogative. For an example of prerogative powers that were justiciable, see, for example, *Canada (Prime Minister) v Khadr*, 2010 SCC 3, [2010] 1 SCR 44. For an example of an exercise of prerogative power that was non-justiciable, see the *Guergis* matter extracted below in Section V.B. The boundary between the types of exercise of prerogative power that are justiciable and those that are noted was addressed by the Supreme Court of the United Kingdom in the context of Prime Minister Boris Johnson's advice to the Queen that Parliament be prorogued in a manner that would have significantly restricted the time available to Parliament to debate the United Kingdom's withdrawal from the European Union on a proposed withdrawal date of October 31, 2019 (see *R (on the application of Miller) v The Prime Minister*, [2019] UKSC 41). The Court concluded that the giving of this advice, in these highly unusual circumstances, was reviewable by the courts and the advice itself was unlawful. We will consider the question of justiciability in greater detail in Chapter 11.

B. STATUTORY POWERS

Far and away the vast majority of executive powers originate from a statutory delegation of authority by the legislature. The provisions from the *Canadian Human Rights Act*, RSC 1985, c H-6 excerpted in Section V.D below, are illustrative of the typical form of delegation. Here the statute creates the administrative body, in this case the Canadian Human Rights Commission, and enumerates the specific powers to be exercised by it. The authority of the commission is determined solely by the statutory grant because, as an administrative body, the commission has no inherent powers.

As we will see in Section IV, there are relatively few constitutional constraints on the legislature's authority to delegate powers to administrative bodies. For example, unlike the exercise of prerogative powers, which are restricted to executive functions, there are no functional restrictions on delegated powers. Consequently, it is common for the legislature to delegate even extensive legislative and adjudicative functions to administrative bodies. Legislation establishing institutions that are designed to deliver services, such as Crown corporations and health authorities or universities, typically grants authority in extremely general terms, and the way those services are delivered is often left in large measure to the governing bodies of those organizations.

IV. CONSTITUTIONAL CONSTRAINTS ON THE DELEGATION OF STATUTORY POWER TO THE EXECUTIVE

The principle of parliamentary sovereignty recognizes that the ability of Parliament or a provincial legislature to enact legislation delegating the exercise of authority to some other body, be it Cabinet or an independent administrative body, is qualified only by constitutional considerations. Broadly speaking, these constitutional constraints take three forms. First, Parliament and provincial legislatures may only delegate the authority that they actually possess as a matter of law. Second, they must not irrevocably abdicate their legislative authority, nor may Parliament delegate its legislative authority to a provincial legislature or vice versa. Third, Parliament or provincial legislatures may not withdraw adjudicative authority that falls within the core jurisdiction of the superior courts and confer that judicial power on an executive body such as an administrative tribunal.

The first constraint flows logically from the idea that the Constitution limits the legislature's power so the legislature cannot, in law, delegate power that it does not possess. This is true whether the powers that Parliament or a provincial legislature is purporting to delegate fall into a sphere of authority allocated exclusively to the other, or is a power that neither legislature possesses because it involves interference with rights or freedoms protected by the Constitution.

The second set of constraints deal with situations where Parliament or a provincial legislature has the authority to make laws, and the issue is what limitations, if any, exist on its authority to delegate that law-making authority to another body. This question was considered by the Supreme Court of Canada in *In Re George Edwin Gray*, a case that considered the sweeping delegation of authority to the governor general in council under the *War Measures Act, 1914*, 5 Geo V, c 2.

In Re George Edwin Gray
(1918), 57 SCR 150

[This case concerned the legality of changes to statutory conscription rules that were enacted by Cabinet pursuant to a general delegation of powers. The delegation in question provided that

[t]he Governor-in-Council shall have power to do and authorize such acts and things, and to make from time to time such orders and regulations, as he may by reason of the existence of real or apprehended war, invasion or insurrection, deem necessary or advisable for the security, defence, peace, order and welfare of Canada.

In rejecting the argument that the delegation amounted to an unconstitutional abdication of legislative powers to the executive, the chief justice made the following comments:]

FITZPATRICK CJ: ... The practice of authorizing administrative bodies to make regulations to carry out the object of an Act, instead of setting out all the details in the Act itself, is well known and its legality is unquestioned. But it is said that the power to make such regulations could not constitutionally be granted to such an extent as to enable the express provisions of a statute to be amended or repealed; that under the constitution Parliament alone is to make laws, the Governor in Council to execute them, and the Court to interpret them; that it follows that no one of these fundamental branches of government can constitutionally either delegate or accept the functions of any other branch.

In view of *Rex v. Halliday*, [1917] AC 260, 86 LJKB 1119, I do not think this broad proposition can be maintained. Parliament cannot, indeed, abdicate its functions, but within reasonable limits at any rate it can delegate its powers to the executive government. Such powers must necessarily be subject to determination at any time by Parliament, and needless to say the acts of the executive, under its delegated authority, must fall within the ambit of the legislative pronouncement by which its authority is measured.

It is true that Lord Dunedin, in the case referred to, said:

The British constitution has entrusted to the two Houses of Parliament, subject to the assent of the King, an absolute power untrammelled by any written instrument, obedience to which may be compelled by some judicial body.

That, undoubtedly, is not the case in this country, which has its constitution founded in the Imperial statute, *The BNA Act*, 1867. I cannot, however, find anything in that constitutional Act which, so far as material to the question now under consideration, would impose any limitation on the authority of the Parliament of Canada to which the Imperial Parliament is not subject.

• • •

It seems to me obvious that Parliament intended, as the language used implies, to clothe the executive with the widest powers in time of danger. Taken literally, the language of the section contains unlimited powers. Parliament expressly enacted that, when need arises, the executive may for the common defence make such orders and regulations as they may deem necessary or advisable for the security, peace, order and welfare of Canada. The enlightened men who framed that section, and the members of Parliament who adopted it, were providing for a very great emergency, and they must be understood to have employed words in their natural sense, and to have intended what they have said. There is no doubt, in my opinion, that the regulation in question was passed to provide for the security and welfare of Canada and it is therefore *intra vires* of the statute under which it purports to be made.

• • •

There are obvious objections of a political character to the practice of executive legislation in this country because of local conditions. But these objections should have been urged when the regulations were submitted to Parliament for its approval, or better still when *The War Measures Act* was being discussed. Parliament was the delegating authority, and it was for that body to put any limitations on the power conferred upon the executive. I am not aware that the authority to pass these regulations was questioned by a vote in either house. Our legislators were no doubt impressed in the hour of peril with the conviction that the safety of the country is the supreme law against which no other law can prevail. It is our clear duty to give effect to their patriotic intention.

[Justice Anglin was equally emphatic in his rejection of the argument that the delegation amounted to an abdication:]

· · ·

A complete abdication by Parliament of its legislative functions is something so inconceivable that the constitutionality of an attempt to do anything of the kind need not be considered. Short of such an abdication, any limited delegation would seem to be within the ambit of a legislative jurisdiction certainly as wide as that of which it has been said by incontrovertible authority that it is

as plenary and as ample ... as the Imperial Parliament in the plentitude of its powers possessed and could bestow. [*Hodge v Reg*, 9 App Cas 117 at 133, 53 LJPC 1.]

I am of the opinion that it was within the legislative authority of the Parliament of Canada to delegate to the Governor in Council the power to enact the impugned orders in council. To hold otherwise would be very materially to restrict the legislative powers of Parliament.

It is important to note that neither Fitzpatrick CJ nor Anglin J rejects the existence of a constitutional principle that denies the legislature the power to fully divest itself of its legislative powers. However, in light of the wide scope of the delegation in *Re Gray*, it is difficult to conceive of a delegation, short of one that purports to be of a permanent nature, that would offend this principle. The provinces were also found to possess a similarly wide authority to delegate legislative functions in *Hodge v The Queen* (1883), 9 App Cas 117, quoted in *Re Gray* above.

A related principle that constrains the ability of legislatures to delegate legislative authority requires that neither the federal Parliament nor the provincial legislatures may delegate legislative powers to the other. The basis of this rule is that an inter-delegation would upset the constitutional division of powers contained in ss 91 and 92 of the *Constitution Act, 1867*. In the *Nova Scotia Inter-Delegation* case (*Attorney General of Nova Scotia v Attorney General of Canada*, below), the Supreme Court of Canada was required to consider the constitutionality of a scheme by which provincial powers regarding employment matters would be delegated to the federal Parliament and certain taxation powers would be delegated from Parliament to the Nova Scotia legislature in order to facilitate an unemployment insurance scheme.

Attorney General of Nova Scotia v Attorney General of Canada
[1951] SCR 31

RAND J:

[60] Can either of these legislative bodies, then, confer upon the other or can the latter accept and exercise in such a subsidiary manner legislative power vested in

the former? They are bodies of co-ordinate rank; in constitutional theory, legislative enactment is that of the Sovereign in Parliament and in Legislature, to each of which, as legislative organs of a federal union, has been given exclusive authority over specified matters in a distribution of total legislative subject-matter. Delegation has its source in the necessities of legislation; it has become an essential to completeness and adaptability of much of statutory law; but if one legislature is adequate, by its own action, to enactment, so, surely, is the other; in the proposed bill, there is no suggestion of authorizing Parliament, as delegate, in turn to sub-delegate to agencies of its own, and the practical ground of delegation is absent. But even where the broadest authority is intended, can we seriously imagine the Imperial Parliament, in the implication of the power to delegate, intending to include delegation by and to each other? These bodies were created solely for the purposes of the constitution by which each, in the traditions and conventions of the English Parliamentary system, was to legislate, in accordance with its debate and judgment, on the matters assigned to it and on no other. To imply a power to shift this debate and this judgment of either to the other is to permit the substance of transfer to take place, a dealing with and in jurisdiction utterly foreign to the conception of a federal organization.

[61] So exercising delegated powers would not only be incompatible with the constitutional function with which Nova Scotia is endowed and an affront to constitutional principle and practice, it would violate, also, the interest in the substance of Dominion legislation which both the people and the legislative bodies of the other provinces possess. In a unitary state, that question does not arise; but it seems to be quite evident that such legislative absolutism, except in respects in which, by the terms express or implied of the constituting Act, only one jurisdiction is concerned, is incompatible with federal reality. If a matter affects only one, it would not be a subject for delegation to the other; matters of possible delegation, by that fact, imply a common interest. Dominion legislation in relation to employment in Nova Scotia enacted by the legislature may affect interests outside of Nova Scotia; by delegation Nova Scotia might impose an indirect tax upon citizens of Alberta in respect of matters arising in Nova Scotia; or it might place restrictions on foreign or interprovincial trade affecting Nova Scotia which impinge on interests in Ontario. The incidence of laws of that nature is intended by the constitution to be determined by the deliberations of Parliament and not of any Legislature. In the generality of actual delegation to its own agencies, Parliament, recognizing the need of the legislation, lays down the broad scheme and indicates the principles, purposes and scope of the subsidiary details to be supplied by the delegate: under the mode of enactment now being considered, the real and substantial analysis and weighing of the political considerations which would decide the actual provisions adopted, would be given by persons chosen to represent local interests.

[62] Since neither is a creature nor a subordinate body of the other, the question is not only or chiefly whether one can delegate, but whether the other can accept. Delegation implies subordination and in *Hodge v. The Queen (supra)*, the following observations (at p. 132) appear:

> Within these limits of subjects and area the local legislature is supreme, and has the same authority as the Imperial Parliament, or the parliament of the Dominion, would have had under like circumstances to confide to a municipal institution or body of its own creation authority to make by-laws or resolutions as to subjects specified in the enactment, and with the object of carrying the enactment into operation and effect.

• • •

It was argued at the bar that a legislature committing important regulations to agents or delegates effaces itself. That is not so. It retains its powers intact, and can, whenever it pleases, destroy the agency it has created and set up another, or take the matter directly into his own hands. How far it shall seek the aid of subordinate agencies, and how long it shall continue them, are matters for each legislature, and not for Courts of Law, to decide.

[63] Subordination, as so considered, is constitutional subordination and not that implied in the relation of delegate. Sovereign states can and do confer and accept temporary transfers of jurisdiction under which they enact their own laws within the territory of others; but the exercise of delegation by one for another would be an incongruity; for the enactments of a state are of its own laws, not those of another state.

[64] Subordination implies duty: delegation is not made to be accepted or acted upon at the will of the delegate; it is ancillary to legislation which the appropriate legislature thinks desirable; and a duty to act either by enacting or by exercising a conferred discretion not, at the particular time, to act, rests upon the delegate. No such duty could be imposed upon or accepted by a co-ordinate legislature and the proposed bill does no more than to proffer authority to be exercised by the delegate solely of its own volition and, for its own purposes, as a discretionary privilege. Even in the case of virtually unlimited delegation as under the Poor Act of England, assuming that degree to be open to Canadian legislatures, the delegate is directly amenable to his principal for his execution of the authority.

• • •

[67] The practical consequences of the proposed measure, a matter which the Courts may take into account, entail the danger, through continued exercise of delegated power, of prescriptive claims based on conditions and relations established in reliance on the delegation. Possession here as elsewhere would be nine points of law and disruptive controversy might easily result. The power of revocation might in fact become no more feasible, practically, than amendment of the Act of 1867 of its own volition by the British Parliament.

[68] I would, therefore, dismiss the appeal with costs.

Shortly after deciding the *Nova Scotia Inter-Delegation* case, the Supreme Court of Canada was presented with another inter-delegation scheme, except in this case the delegations were made, not directly from one legislature to another, but from Parliament to a provincially created administrative body. Here the object of the scheme was to confer comprehensive regulatory authority to market potatoes from PEI to the provincial marketing board, which required the federal Parliament to delegate powers relating to the export and interprovincial trade in PEI potatoes to the marketing board, a provincial administrative body. This form of inter-delegation was found to be unobjectionable on the basis that the inter-delegation was to an administrative body, as opposed to the legislature itself: see *PEI Potato Marketing Board v Willis*, [1952] 2 SCR 392. The principal policy basis behind the distinction between invalid legislative inter-delegation and valid administrative inter-delegation relates to the democratic expectations of the legislature, which must be seen to be acting free of allegiances to other bodies, as opposed to those of an administrative body, where the recipient of authority is expected to exercise that power in accordance with the requirements of the delegating body.

The third set of constitutional constraints addresses the question whether there are any limits on the power of a legislative body to confer adjudicative functions on a body other than a court. This issue will be addressed in more detail in Chapter 9, but for present purposes it is sufficient to note that the Canadian Constitution does not contain a general demarcation between judicial functions that can be exercised only by courts and adjudicative authority that can properly be exercised by administrative tribunals. For example, there is no general restriction on the ability of administrative tribunals to address constitutional questions that arise in the course of adjudicating cases that fall properly within their jurisdiction. In *Nova Scotia (Workers' Compensation Board) v Martin; Nova Scotia (Workers' Compensation Board) v Laseur*, 2003 SCC 54, [2003] 2 SCR 504, the Supreme Court of Canada held that, as a general principle, tribunals that have the jurisdiction to address general questions of law also have the jurisdiction to address constitutional questions concerning the validity or applicability of their own enabling legislation.

The Canadian Constitution does, however, prevent Parliament and provincial legislatures from improperly interfering with the jurisdiction of the superior courts as defined by ss 96 to 100 of the *Constitution Act, 1867*. Again, in the absence of a general separation of powers doctrine in Canada, there is no overarching prohibition against administrative tribunals exercising judicial functions. Instead, the prohibition is against bodies that are not constituted in accordance with the requirements of ss 96 to 100—namely, appointed by the governor general, from the ranks of the bar and with security of tenure and security of salaries—exercising the powers of a superior court as contemplated under s 96.

The difficulty has been determining with any exactitude what the powers of a s 96 court are. To answer this question, the Supreme Court of Canada has developed a three-part test, enunciated first in *Re Residential Tenancies Act*, [1981] 1 SCR 714. This test was elaborated in *MacMillan Bloedel Ltd v Simpson*, [1995] 4 SCR 725, where the Supreme Court of Canada majority observed, at para 15: "The superior courts have a core or inherent jurisdiction which is integral to their operations. The jurisdiction which forms this core cannot be removed from the superior courts by either level of government, without amending the Constitution." It is worth noting that this prohibition not only prevents legislatures from interfering with the core jurisdiction of superior courts by removing it and allocating it to an administrative tribunal, it also prevents Parliament and provincial legislatures from removing the core jurisdiction from a superior court and allocating it to another court. For example, in *MacMillan Bloedel Ltd v Simpson* itself, the majority held that it was not open to Parliament to remove the authority of superior courts to address issues of contempt of court committed by young persons and confer that authority exclusively on provincial youth courts.

V. EXECUTIVE INSTITUTIONS AND THEIR RELATIONSHIP TO THE POLITICAL EXECUTIVE

A. THE CROWN

Section 9 of the *Constitution Act, 1867* states: "The Executive Government and Authority of and over Canada is hereby declared to continue and be vested in the Queen." As a formal matter then, the entire authority of the executive branch is vested in the monarchy. Consequently, "the Crown," as a symbol of the monarchy, is a reference to the executive itself.

The Crown is the formal legal entity of government and, like other entities possessing a legal personality, the Crown is the bearer of both legal rights and legal obligations. In this regard, the "Crown" has the capacity to own property, to enter into contracts, and to sue and be sued. In the context of federalism, the Crown is divisible in the sense that the governments of the provinces and the federal government are each themselves distinct legal entities, notwithstanding the identification of each with the same monarch. Consequently, legal obligations attaching to one level of government cannot be attributed to another level of government by virtue of their respective executive powers being rooted in a common monarch. In order to clearly identify which executive body is being referred to in legal and other official documents, it is common to refer to the "Crown in the right of Canada," in the case of the federal government, and the "Crown in the right" of New Brunswick or Alberta, as the case may be, in relation to provincial governments.

The identification of the government with the Crown speaks only to the formal legal status of the executive. As discussed also in Chapter 6, the Queen herself does not exercise authority over matters of public policy in Canada, or for that matter in the United Kingdom. First, by Letters Patent issued by George VI in 1947, the governor general is "to exercise all powers and authorities lawfully belonging to Us [the monarch] in respect of Canada." Consequently, it is commonplace in both the *Constitution Act, 1867* and in many provincial statutes to see references to powers exercised by the "Governor General in Council," or the "Lieutenant General in Council."

However, in a system of responsible government like Canada's, the Crown's representative is not as potent as these provisions imply. As discussed in Chapter 6, the Queen appoints the governor general and lieutenant governors to act as her representatives, although by constitutional convention these appointments are now made on the advice of the prime minister, whose advice the Queen is bound to follow. In turn, the governor general and the lieutenant governors for each province are bound by constitutional convention to exercise their powers with the advice of the Cabinet of their respective government. (This requirement is also alluded to, in part, in the *Constitution Act, 1867* in ss 12 and 65 addressing the powers of the governor general and the lieutenant governor, respectively.)

As discussed further below, "Cabinet" is the collective decision-making committee comprising the prime minister (or premier) and his or her ministers. However, the *Constitution Act, 1867* never actually mentions "Cabinet." Instead, the reference is to the "Queen's Privy Council." Thus, s 13 provides that references to the "Governor General in Council" in the 1867 Act "shall be construed as referring to the Governor General acting by and with the Advice of the Queen's Privy Council for Canada." (An identical provision is found in the federal *Interpretation Act*, guiding interpretation of federal statutes.) Under s 11 of the 1867 Act, the Privy Council is a body to "aid and advise in the Government of Canada."

The Privy Council is not technically the same thing as the federal Cabinet. The governor general swears in privy councillors for life. Cabinet ministers serve in their Cabinet capacity for a much shorter tenure. Furthermore, the governor general often swears in other, "distinguished" Canadians to the Privy Council (including, in the past, the provincial premiers). As a consequence, all Cabinet ministers are privy councillors, but not all (or even a majority) of privy councillors are sitting Cabinet ministers.

Nevertheless, by constitutional convention, only those privy councillors who are also presently in Cabinet are entitled to exercise the powers of the Privy Council. For this reason, where powers in the 1867 Act are exercisable by the "Governor General in Council" or the "Lieutenant Governor in Council," they are in effect exercised by federal and provincial cabinets, respectively.

B. THE PRIME MINISTER AND CABINET

Ministers and the prime minister together comprise the "ministry," a category sometimes also referred to colloquially as the government. The terms "ministry" and "Cabinet" are usually used interchangeably. However, a minister is not automatically a Cabinet member. The question of who obtains a seat at the Cabinet table is a political matter for the prime minister to decide.

While sometimes characterized as "first among equals," the prime minister truly stands above all other members of the ministry. It is the prime minister who presides over Cabinet. He or she has the sole authority to determine who the governor general swears in as a minister, who sits in Cabinet, and what portfolio within Cabinet that person holds. And all ministerial appointments are "at the pleasure" of the prime minister—meaning the prime minister has unfettered authority to compel the removal of ministers.

By constitutional convention, the prime minister also possesses authority to exercise so-called personal prerogatives. For example, the prime minister appears, in practice, to select people to fill some important appointments that (technically) are made by the governor general (such as appointments to the Senate, the Supreme Court of Canada, and the appointment of chief justices). As noted in Chapter 7, it is the prime minister who advises the governor general as to the dissolution of Parliament, effectively giving the prime minister the power to control the timing of elections.

Formally, beyond these powers, the prime minister does not hold a privileged position in the sense that he or she can unilaterally exercise Cabinet powers. As a political matter, however, the prime minister exercises considerable influence over what is done in the name of Cabinet, not least because it is the prime minister who has the exclusive power to decide who sits in Cabinet in the first place and who may stay in Cabinet. Consider the following case, in which a former Cabinet member sued after being dismissed from Cabinet.

Guergis v Novak
2012 ONSC 4579

HACKLAND RSJ:

Overview

[1] The moving parties seek an order striking out the statement of claim in this action, without leave to amend, or, in the alternative, an order for particulars of the conspiracy alleged in this pleading.

[2] The plaintiff is a former Member of Parliament and former minister of state for the status of women. She alleges a conspiracy, as well as certain other tort claims—defamation, misfeasance in public office, intentional infliction of mental suffering and negligence—against the defendants. The alleged conspiracy is described at para. 24 of the statement of claim, as follows:

> The conspiracy was to engage in unlawful acts in order to remove and/or justify the removal of the Plaintiff from her positions as ... the Minister of State for the Status of Women, in a manner deemed by the Defendants to be to their political, personal, and/or financial benefit.

[3] The defendants, moving parties on this motion, are (a) the Right Honourable Stephen Harper, prime minister of Canada; (b) Guy Giorno, the prime minister's chief of staff at the material time; (c) Raymond Novak, the prime minister's principal secretary at the material time; (d) the Honourable Lisa Raitt, minister of labour; (e) Axelle Pellerin, an official on Minister Raitt's staff; (f) the Conservative Party of Canada ("CPC"); (g) Arthur Hamilton, a lawyer with the law firm Cassels Brock & Blackwell LLP ("Cassels Brock"), who was the lawyer for the prime minister and the CPC at the material time; and (h) Shelly Glover, a Conservative Member of Parliament. The defendant Derrick Snowdy takes no part in this motion.

[4] The statement of claim alleges that the Prime Minister's Office received a report of alleged criminal misconduct concerning the plaintiff, originating from the defendant Snowdy. On the advice of Mr. Giorno and Mr. Novak, the prime minister communicated this information in a telephone call to the plaintiff in an attempt to have her resign from cabinet. According to the plaintiff, the object of the conspiracy was "to effect or justify the plaintiff's removal as a member of the caucus of CPC, her removal as the candidate for the CPC in the Electoral District

of Simcoe-Grey, and her removal from her position as Minister of State for the Status of Women."

[5] Further, it is alleged that on April 9, 2010, the same day of the prime minister's telephone call to the plaintiff, the prime minister, with Mr. Giorno and Mr. Novak, sent letters to the commissioner of the RCMP and the conflict of interest and ethics commissioner, repeating the allegations that the plaintiff had been involved in improper, unlawful and/ or criminal conduct. It is alleged that these letters were defamatory of the plaintiff and were written in furtherance of the conspiracy engaged in by the defendants.

• • •

The Issues

[7] The principal submission made by the moving parties on this motion is that the conspiracy and other tort claims advanced in the action are neither justiciable nor subject to judicial process, as such claims relate to the exercise of Crown prerogative or parliamentary privilege. ...

Crown Prerogative

[10] As previously noted, the plaintiff asserts, at para. 24 of her statement of claim, that the object of the conspiracy was to engage in unlawful acts "in order to remove and/or justify the removal" of the plaintiff as a Minister of the Crown. The plaintiff pleads that the prime minister, his chief of staff and his principal secretary were all part of this conspiracy.

[11] The moving parties submit that the power to appoint or dismiss cabinet ministers at pleasure is a Crown prerogative, exercised by the prime minister, that is not justiciable at law. Therefore, the alleged tortious conduct, directed as it is to the removal of a cabinet minister from office, is not justiciable.

[12] The plaintiff's position is that while her expulsion from cabinet would be within the prime minister's prerogative in the normal course, the Crown prerogative does not insulate the Prime Minister's Office from responsibility for tortious conduct in relation to the plaintiff's removal from cabinet. In the plaintiff's submission, the fact that such tortious conduct ultimately led to the resignation of the plaintiff from cabinet—an end which could have been achieved by the prime minister lawfully—does not absolve or protect the prime minister from liability for such tortious conduct, on the basis of Crown prerogative.

[13] The law is well settled that the appointment of ministers and their dismissal is a core aspect of the Crown prerogative exercised by the prime minister. *Black v. Canada (Prime Minister)* (2001), 54 O.R. (3d) 215, [2001] O.J. No. 1853 (C.A.) ("*Black*"), a decision of the Ontario Court of Appeal, deals with the prime minister's prerogative regarding the bestowal of honours. In *Black*, at para. 58, the court approved Lord Roskill's enumeration of specific exercises of the prerogative power "whose subject matters were by their very nature not justiciable":

> So characterized, it is plain and obvious that the Prime Minister's exercise of the honours prerogative is not judicially reviewable. Indeed, in the *Civil Service Unions* case, Lord Roskill listed a number of exercises of the prerogative power whose subject matters were by their very nature not justiciable. Included in the list was the grant of honours. He wrote, in a passage I have already referred to, at p. 418:
>
> > But I do not think that that right of challenge can be unqualified. It must, I think, depend upon the subject matter of the prerogative power which is

exercised. Many examples were given during the argument of prerogative powers which as at present advised I do not think could properly be made the subject of judicial review. Prerogative powers such as those relating to the making of treaties, the defence of the realm, the prerogative of mercy, the grant of honours, the dissolution of Parliament and the appointment of ministers as well as others are not, I think, susceptible to judicial review because their nature and subject matter are such as not to be amenable to the judicial process. The courts are not the place wherein to determine whether a treaty should be concluded or the armed forces disposed in a particular manner or Parliament dissolved on one date rather than another. ...

[14] As noted, the plaintiff contends that because, as pleaded, the minister's removal from office was the product or effect of the prime minister's tortious conduct, the prerogative otherwise applicable does not apply to protect his conduct from judicial scrutiny. In other words, the contention is that the prime minister and his senior advisors can be called into court to explain and justify the prime minister's removal of the plaintiff from the federal cabinet because her removal was part of a conspiracy or motivated by improper, tortious intentions.

[15] I am of the opinion that the plaintiff's contentions are wrong and, if sustained, would render meaningless this important privilege. The prime minister would be required to answer, in court, for the political decisions he makes as to the membership of his cabinet. Crown privilege is an important principle of our legal system and it cannot be displaced or attacked collaterally by way of allegations of tortious conduct. There is no authority that would support the proposition that Crown prerogative is waived or is inapplicable if the otherwise-protected decisions are alleged to be tortious. On the contrary, the result must be that when Crown privilege applies, the court lacks the jurisdiction to review the acts protected by the privilege. In this case, I find that it is plain and obvious that the actions of the prime minister, in relation to the removal of the plaintiff from cabinet, fall within Crown prerogative and this court lacks the jurisdiction to review the tort allegations related to the prime minister's actions. These actions are pleaded to be taken on the advice of the prime minister's two senior advisors, Mr. Giorno, chief of staff, and Mr. Novak, principal secretary, whose conduct in the circumstances alleged must also be protected by Crown prerogative.

The Superior Court's decision in this matter was upheld on appeal. See *Guergis v Novak*, 2013 ONCA 449.

Cabinet is, in the words of Peter Hogg, "in most matters the supreme executive authority": see Peter Hogg, *Constitutional Law of Canada*, 3rd ed (Toronto: Carswell, 1992). It is Cabinet that determines the legislative agenda of the government in Parliament, and it is Cabinet and its ministers that are responsible for the administration of the individual departments of the government.

The separation of the executive branch (and especially Cabinet) from the legislative branch is not, however, absolute. The constitutional convention of "responsible government" lies at the foundation of Canadian governance. Two key elements of responsible government should be noted. First, in a system of responsible government, Cabinet members are drawn from the legislative branch, almost always the House of Commons for the federal Cabinet. Ministers may hold office pending election to the Commons or while a senator, but all ministers are expected to also be members of the legislature.

Second, under the system of responsible government, the ministry is accountable to the legislative branch both collectively and individually. Collective responsibility requires that the ministry maintain the confidence of the Parliament. Confidence votes are discussed in Chapter 7. Individual ministerial responsibility requires that each minister be answerable in Parliament for the activities of his or her department.

In this last respect, in addition to their Cabinet responsibilities, Cabinet ministers have administrative responsibility for departments under their charge, which may often include specific powers to make decisions affecting the rights of individuals. For example, under s 40 of the federal *Extradition Act*, SC 1999, c 18, the federal minister of justice has wide-ranging discretion to make decisions respecting orders of surrender of persons to other jurisdictions to face prosecution for a crime committed in that other state; a discretion that must be exercised "personally"—meaning it cannot be delegated to another department official.

At times, the multiple roles of ministerial officials can give rise to claims of conflict of interest. In *Idziak v Canada (Minister of Justice)*, [1992] 3 SCR 631, it was argued that the minister of justice's involvement in the two-step extradition process raised questions of bias. Before a suspect can be extradited, there is a hearing before a judge in order to determine whether there is a sufficient factual and legal basis to support extradition (that is, that a crime was committed in the jurisdiction seeking extradition), and a further determination made by the minister as to whether the person must be surrendered. The minister of justice, in his or her capacity as the head of the Justice Department, oversees the prosecution in the extradition hearing, and is personally required to make a determination on the order of surrender. The Supreme Court of Canada, in rejecting the claim of bias, emphasizes the distinct nature of the competing ministerial roles:

> It has been seen that the extradition process has two distinct phases. The first, the judicial phase, encompasses the court proceedings which determine whether a factual and legal basis for extradition exists. If that process results in the issuance of a warrant of committal, then the second phase is activated. There, the Minister of Justice exercises his or her discretion in determining whether to issue a warrant of surrender. The first decision-making phase is certainly judicial in its nature and warrants the application of the full panoply of procedural safeguards. By contrast, the second decision-making process is political in its nature. The Minister must weigh the representations of the fugitive against Canada's international treaty obligations.

> • • •

> Parliament chose to give discretionary authority to the Minister of Justice. It is the Minister who must consider the good faith and honour of this country in its relations with other states. It is the Minister who has the expert knowledge of the political ramifications of an extradition decision. In administrative law terms, the Minister's review should be characterized as being at the extreme legislative end of the *continuum* of administrative decision-making.

> The appellant contends that a dual role has been allotted to the Minister of Justice by the *Extradition Act*. The Act requires the Minister to conduct the prosecution of the extradition hearing at the judicial phase and then to act as adjudicator in the ministerial phase. These roles are said to be mutually incompatible and to raise an apprehension of bias on their face. This contention fails to recognize either the clear division that lies between the phases of the extradition process, each of which serves a distinct function, or to take into account the separation of personnel involved in the two phases.

> It is correct that the Minister of Justice has the responsibility to ensure the prosecution of the extradition proceedings and that to do so the Minister must appoint agents to act in the interest of the requesting state. However the decision to issue a warrant of surrender involves completely different considerations from those reached by a court in an extradition hearing. The extradition hearing is clearly judicial in its nature while the actions of the Minister of Justice in considering whether to issue a warrant of surrender are primarily political

in nature. This is certainly not a case of a single official's acting as both judge and prosecutor in the same case. At the judicial phase the fugitive possesses the full panoply of procedural protection available in a court of law. At the ministerial phase, there is no longer a *lis* in existence. The fugitive has by then been judicially committed for extradition. The Act simply grants to the Minister a discretion as to whether to execute the judicially approved extradition by issuing a warrant of surrender.

C. THE PUBLIC SERVICE

The employees of the various ministries of the government, often referred to as civil servants, are also part of the executive branch. Unlike the political members of the executive, the civil servants are politically neutral and as such continue their employment with the government regardless of the political fortunes of the government of the day. The concept of a professional and neutral civil service seeks to draw a notional line between the political responsibilities of the minister in charge of the department and the administrative responsibilities of the civil service. Kenneth Kernaghan, a political scientist, identifies three principles that structure the relationship between the civil service and political officials within the government: (1) ministerial responsibility; (2) political neutrality; and (3) public service anonymity: see Kenneth Kernaghan, *The Future Role of a Professional Non-Partisan Public Service in Ontario* (Panel on the Role of Government, Research Paper Series No 13, 2003).

Ministerial responsibility requires that the presiding minister be held politically accountable for all matters arising within the department, including policy decisions by civil servants. Political neutrality requires that civil servants carry out their responsibilities loyally to the government in power without regard for the civil servant's own political views. Related to this, public servants are (at least in the classic model) restricted in their ability to engage in partisan political activities and cannot express publicly their personal views on policy issues. Public service anonymity, which follows as a consequence of the first two principles, provides that bureaucrats should be held accountable to their political overseers, but are not answerable to Parliament: see Kernaghan, above, at 3-11.

While the principles regarding public service neutrality have been traditionally understood as constitutional conventions, and therefore acting as political but not legal constraints, Professor Lorne Sossin has argued that there exists in Canadian administrative and constitutional law a dense web of legal norms concerning "bureaucratic independence" that "includes, but is not limited to, the protection of the neutrality of the civil service, the protection of the whistle-blowing exception to the duty of loyalty, the protection against improper political interference in administrative decision making, the preservation of the rule of law, and the maintenance of objective guarantees of separation from the political executive, including the merit principle for hiring and promotion [protection against patronage] and security of tenure": see Lorne Sossin, "Speaking Truth to Power? The Search for Bureaucratic Independence in Canada" (2005) 55 UTLJ 1 at 57-58.

As these comments suggest, the loyalty owed by civil servants is not boundless, but requires that civil servants refrain from public criticism of government policies. In *Fraser v PSSRB*, excerpted below, the appellant, who was an employee of Revenue Canada, was discharged after repeatedly criticizing the government's policies regarding switching over to the metric system (the process known as "metrification" took place between 1975 and 1985; it was highly controversial in some quarters). On a review of the original decision, the appellant argued that the duty to refrain from criticism only extends to areas related to the civil servants' direct responsibilities. In upholding the original decision of an adjudicator of the Public Service Staff Relations Board (a tribunal established to consider employment issues in the federal civil service), the Supreme Court commented on the particular nature of public service employment.

Fraser v PSSRB
[1985] 2 SCR 455

DICKSON CJ:

[38] It is true that Mr. Fraser's major criticisms were directed against two poli-cies, the metric conversion program and the Charter. It is also true that his job and the policies of his department did not bear on these two policies. But it does not follow that the Adjudicator erred in law in finding that Mr. Fraser's criticisms were related to his job. A job in the public service has two dimensions, one relating to the employee's tasks and how he or she performs them, the other relating to the perception of a job held by the public. In my opinion, the Adjudicator appreciated these two dimensions. His discussion on this point is in these terms:

> When Mr. Fraser suggested on the Floyd Patterson radio hot-line program on February 5, 1982 that the Prime Minister in the conduct of the nation would prefer to act in a similar manner to the present regime in Poland, he adversely affected his own ability to conduct the affairs of the department in which he worked. For example, a corporate taxpayer who is selected as the subject of an audit by Mr. Fraser who also assigns the auditor to examine his records might well specu-late about the reasons for having been selected and be concerned about the pro-fessionalism of the exercise. Surely a relatively influential official of Revenue Canada who publicly and vehemently accuses his employer, the Government of Canada, and the Prime Minister of autocratic and coercive behaviour is unlikely to instill confidence in a clientele that has a right to expect impartial and judicious treatment. And if a taxpayer's reservations were to be perceived by an auditor as an obstacle to an effective investigation, Revenue Canada officials could then rely on the widest and most far-reaching instruments of search and seizure. In this con-text Mr. Lowe's concern about the public's perception of Revenue Canada merits some attention. A public servant simply cannot be allowed under the rubric of free speech to cultivate distrust of the employer amongst members of the constituency whom he is obliged to serve. I am satisfied that Mr. Fraser cast doubt on his effec-tiveness as a Government employee once he escalated his criticism of Govern-ment policy to a point and in a form that far exceeded the issues of general public interest that he espoused before February 1, 1982. Or, more succinctly, his incipient and persistent campaign in opposition to the incumbent Government conflicted with the continuation of his employment relationship. Once that situation arose he either had to cease his activities or resign from the position he occupied.

[39] This analysis and conclusion, namely that Mr. Fraser's criticisms were job-related, is, in my view, correct in law. I say this because of the importance and necessity of an impartial and effective public service. There is in Canada a sepa-ration of powers among the three branches of government—the legislature, the executive and the judiciary. In broad terms, the role of the judiciary is, of course, to interpret and apply the law; the role of the legislature is to decide upon and enunci-ate policy; the role of the executive is to administer and implement that policy.

[40] The federal public service in Canada is part of the executive branch of Gov-ernment. As such, its fundamental task is to administer and implement policy. In order to do this well, the public service must employ people with certain important characteristics. Knowledge is one, fairness another, integrity a third.

[41] As the Adjudicator indicated, a further characteristic is loyalty. As a general rule, federal public servants should be loyal to their employer, the Government of Canada. The loyalty owed is to the Government of Canada, not the political party in

power at any one time. A public servant need not vote for the governing party. Nor need he or she publicly espouse its policies. And indeed, in some circumstances a public servant may actively and publicly express opposition to the policies of a government. This would be appropriate if, for example, the Government were engaged in illegal acts, or if its policies jeopardized the life, health or safety of the public servant or others, or if the public servant's criticism had no impact on his or her ability to perform effectively the duties of a public servant or on the public perception of that ability. But, having stated these qualifications (and there may be others), it is my view that a public servant must not engage, as the appellant did in the present case, in sustained and highly visible attacks on major Government policies. In conducting himself in this way the appellant, in my view, displayed a lack of loyalty to the Government that was inconsistent with his duties as an employee of the Government.

[42] As the Adjudicator pointed out, there is a powerful reason for this general requirement of loyalty, namely the public interest in both the actual, and apparent, impartiality of the public service. The benefits that flow from this impartiality have been well-described by the MacDonnell Commission. Although the description relates to the political activities of public servants in the United Kingdom, it touches on values shared with the public service in Canada:

> Speaking generally, we think that if restrictions on the political activities of public servants were withdrawn two results would probably follow. The public might cease to believe, as we think they do now with reason believe, in the impartiality of the permanent Civil Service; and Ministers might cease to feel the well-merited confidence which they possess at present in the loyal and faithful support of their official subordinates; indeed they might be led to scrutinise the utterances or writings of such subordinates and to select for positions of confidence only those whose sentiments were known to be in political sympathy with their own.
>
> If this were so, the system of recruitment by open competition would provide but a frail barrier against Ministerial patronage in all but the earlier years of service; the Civil Service would cease to be in fact an impartial, non-political body, capable of loyal service to all Ministers and parties alike; the change would soon affect the public estimation of the Service, and the result would be destructive of what undoubtedly is at present one of the greatest advantages of our administrative system, and one of the most honourable traditions of our public life.
>
> See paragraphs 10-11 of c. 11 of MacDonnell Committee quoted in *Re Ontario Public Service Employees Union and Attorney-General for Ontario* (1980), 31 OR (2d) 321 (CA), at p. 329.

[43] There is in Canada, in my opinion, a similar tradition surrounding our public service. The tradition emphasizes the characteristics of impartiality, neutrality, fairness and integrity. A person entering the public service or one already employed there must know, or at least be deemed to know, that employment in the public service involves acceptance of certain restraints. One of the most important of those restraints is to exercise caution when it comes to making criticisms of the Government.

A related issue to the matter of public service loyalty is the extent to which members of the civil service can engage in partisan political activities. The statutes governing public service employment include restrictions on the kinds of political activities that certain bureaucrats can participate in: see *Public Service Employment Act*, SC 2003, c 22, ss 111-117. These types of statutory restrictions have been the subject of judicial scrutiny, most notably in two Supreme Court of Canada decisions, *Ontario (AG) v OPSEU*, [1987] 2 SCR 2, and *Osborne v Canada (Treasury Board)*, [1991] 2 SCR 69. Both cases acknowledged the existence of a constitutional convention of public service neutrality and affirmed its importance as a principle of executive governance. In the *OPSEU* case, Ontario legislation restricting provincial civil servants' political activities, including activities in federal politics, was upheld as valid provincial legislation, but the legislation was not subject to Charter scrutiny in that case.

In *Osborne*, the question whether such restrictions were consistent with the Charter was considered, and resulted in the federal statutory restrictions being struck down as contrary to the right of free expression. Of particular concern to the Court was that the legislation, which applied to all civil servants, was overinclusive because it failed to make distinctions between the kinds of work the employee may be involved in and his or her level of responsibility within the civil service. The restrictions on political activities now apply only to senior members of the bureaucracy.

D. INDEPENDENT ADMINISTRATIVE AGENCIES

As a matter of express constitutional recognition and constitutional convention, the formal executive bodies are limited to the governor general and lieutenant governors, the federal and provincial Cabinets, and the system of governmental departments and ministries that are overseen by individual ministers, including the civil service. However, as noted above, executive functions are extensively carried out by a variety of bodies that have a measure of independence from the government. This naturally leads to the question of why it is seen as necessary or desirable to establish bodies that are independent from the government to carry out governmental functions. There is no single answer to this question. However, the reasons for establishing administrative bodies will determine the structure and form of the body created.

The legislature may determine that certain decisions are best made on a principled basis and therefore should be insulated from considerations of political expediency. This is often the case where decisions affect the legal rights of many individuals and there is merit in having those rights determined in a consistent manner. In this regard, the government may create a specialized tribunal to adjudicate individual cases free from direct government oversight. Here the role of an administrative body approaches that of the judiciary; although, in the case of administrative tribunals, the scope of cases heard is limited to a defined subject area. As an example, the Immigration and Refugee Board of Canada hears only matters relating to immigration admissibility and refugee claims.

A similar justification underlies the creation of independent agencies to administer government entitlement disputes. Here, one of the parties to the dispute is the government itself, which militates in favour of an independent and impartial decision-maker. In other, often economic, matters, insulation from political forces is seen as desirable to ensure that long-term goals are not compromised by short-term political interests or the undue influence of interest groups. The creation of the Bank of Canada to oversee currency and related macroeconomic issues is a prominent example of such a body. In other cases, there will be a need for a particular kind of expertise that is best undertaken by a specialized body staffed by experts. In this regard, independence may facilitate specialization because of the restricted mandate of an administrative agency, as opposed to a government department. Finally, some public services requiring close cooperation and coordination between different jurisdictions can be delivered by multijurisdictional agencies. One such agency is the Canada–Newfoundland and Labrador Offshore Petroleum Board; another, addressing Canada–United States transboundary water issues, is the International Joint Commission.

Independent administrative bodies appear in a broad range of forms depending on their function. The nomenclature used to identify independent agencies is sometimes confusing in that a variety of terms, such as board, commission, authority, council, tribunal and agency, are used to describe administrative bodies, although the use of different terms does not necessarily signify different functions or structures. An administrative body is the product of the legislative instrument that creates it. In this regard there are few restrictions placed on legislators who want to create an administrative body and delegate powers to it. The provisions establishing the Canadian Human Rights Commission are typical of the statutory provisions used to create an independent administrative body.

Canadian Human Rights Act
RSC 1985, c H-6, ss 26-27

26(1) A commission is hereby established to be known as the Canadian Human Rights Commission, in this Part and Part III referred to as the "Commission," consisting of a Chief Commissioner, a Deputy Chief Commissioner and not less than three or more than six other members, to be appointed by the Governor in Council.

(2) The Chief Commissioner and Deputy Chief Commissioner are full-time members of the Commission and the other members may be appointed as full-time or part-time members of the Commission.

(3) Each full-time member of the Commission may be appointed for a term not exceeding seven years and each part-time member may be appointed for a term not exceeding three years.

(4) Each member of the Commission holds office during good behaviour but may be removed by the Governor in Council on address of the Senate and House of Commons.

(5) A member of the Commission is eligible to be re-appointed in the same or another capacity.

27(1) In addition to its duties under Part III with respect to complaints regarding discriminatory practices, the Commission is generally responsible for the administration of this Part and Parts I and III and

(a) shall develop and conduct information programs to foster public understanding of this Act and of the role and activities of the Commission thereunder and to foster public recognition of the principle described in section 2;

(b) shall undertake or sponsor research programs relating to its duties and functions under this Act and respecting the principle described in section 2;

(c) shall maintain close liaison with similar bodies or authorities in the provinces in order to foster common policies and practices and to avoid conflicts respecting the handling of complaints in cases of overlapping jurisdiction;

(d) shall perform duties and functions to be performed by it pursuant to any agreement entered into under subsection 28(2);

(e) may consider such recommendations, suggestions and requests concerning human rights and freedoms as it receives from any source and, where deemed by the Commission to be appropriate, include in a report referred to in section 61 reference to and comment on any such recommendation, suggestion or request;

(f) shall carry out or cause to be carried out such studies concerning human rights and freedoms as may be referred to it by the Minister of Justice and include in a report referred to in section 61 a report setting out the results of each such study together with such recommendations in relation thereto as it considers appropriate;

(g) may review any regulations, rules, orders, by-laws and other instruments made pursuant to an Act of Parliament and, where deemed by the Commission to be appropriate, include in a report referred to in section 61 reference to and comment on any provision thereof that in its opinion is inconsistent with the principle described in section 2; and

(h) shall, so far as is practical and consistent with the application of Part III, try by persuasion, publicity or any other means that it considers appropriate to discourage and reduce discriminatory practices referred to in sections 5 to 14.1.

(2) The Commission may, on application or on its own initiative, by order, issue a guideline setting out the extent to which and the manner in which, in the opinion of the Commission, any provision of this Act applies in a class of cases described in the guideline.

(3) A guideline issued under subsection (2) is, until it is revoked or modified, binding on the Commission and any member or panel assigned under subsection 49(2) with respect to the resolution of a complaint under Part III regarding a case falling within the description contained in the guideline.

(4) Each guideline issued under subsection (2) shall be published in Part II of the *Canada Gazette*.

The Canadian Human Rights Commission is a creation of the federal Parliament, with the commissioners themselves being appointed by the governor in council (in effect, Cabinet). The independence of the commission is established through the provision of security of tenure to the commissioners who may only be removed upon the address of both Houses (that is, by motions in both the Commons and the Senate). Independence is also established through the assignment of powers under s 27, which can be exercised without political oversight. A further provision of the *Canadian Human Rights Act*, s 61, requires that the commission submit an annual report to Parliament detailing the commission's activities. In this way, the commission has some direct accountability to Parliament.

Section 27 confers on the commission broad powers to carry out its statutory mandate, including the ability to undertake, at its initiative, reviews of regulatory instruments for the purpose of ensuring their adherence to the anti-discriminatory purposes of the Act and to enact binding guidelines regarding the application of the Act. These powers are to be exercised without direct oversight by political officials. The provision of a degree of discretion exercisable by the commission further contributes to the commission's independence because the commission has the authority to develop policies and procedures largely unfettered by senior political officials, including the minister of justice, who is responsible for the Act. The commission has the authority to investigate human rights complaints against the federal government, making independence from the government critical to the legitimacy of the commission.

In addition to creating the commission, the *Canadian Human Rights Act* also creates a further independent body called the Canadian Human Rights Tribunal, which has the responsibility of holding, at the request of the commission, inquiries into human rights complaints filed with the commission. The tribunal is independent from the commission and fulfills a different role in the overall scheme under the Act. Whereas the commission has wide-ranging powers to investigate discriminatory practices and to seek the resolution of human rights complaints— which include as noted above the exercise of policy creation functions and administrative functions—the tribunal acts in a quasi-judicial capacity inquiring into human rights complaints. The commission has the authority to appear before the tribunal, and in doing so it is required to represent the "public interest."

Provincial human rights legislation has created similar independent administrative bodies to those created under the *Canadian Human Rights Act*, although not all provinces use both a commission to investigate complaints and a tribunal to adjudicate complaints forwarded to it by the commission. In British Columbia, for example, the Human Rights Commission was abolished in 2002, and a person who wishes to file a human rights complaint does so directly with the British Columbia Human Rights Tribunal, which has the authority to assist the parties to resolve the complaint or to adjudicate it. See *Human Rights Code*, RSBC 1996, c 210. In 2018, British Columbia enacted legislation to revive the office of the Human Rights Commissioner, though that body is designed to promote human rights and assist complainants rather than to perform an investigative or screening function in relation to complaints: see *Human Rights Code Amendment Act, 2018*, SBC 2018, c 48.

Does this discussion mean that, as a constitutional matter, adjudicative administrative bodies must be independent in a manner that is analogous to the independence of courts? As we will see from the decisions below, the answer is usually "no." Certainly, there are circumstances where independence may be required. For example, s 7 of the Charter bars deprivation of life, liberty, or security of the person in the absence of fundamental justice. Likewise, the *Canadian Bill of Rights*—a 1960 statute of Parliament that purports to trump all inconsistent federal laws—guarantees in s 2(e) that no law may "deprive a person of the right to a fair hearing in accordance with the principles of fundamental justice for the determination of his rights and obligations." The Supreme Court has recognized that where a body exercises power of a sort triggering these provisions, some measure of independence may be required of that organization. Nevertheless, in *Ocean Port Hotel Ltd v British Columbia (General Manager, Liquor Control and Licensing Branch)*, the Supreme Court drew a distinction between administrative tribunals and decision-makers, as emanations of the executive that must take their policy direction from the legislature, and the courts, which are protected by the constitutional principle of judicial independence.

Ocean Port Hotel Ltd v British Columbia (General Manager, Liquor Control and Licensing Branch)
2001 SCC 52, [2001] 2 SCR 781

McLACHLIN CJ (for the court):

[1] This appeal raises a critical but largely unexplored issue of administrative law: the degree of independence required of members sitting on administrative tribunals empowered to impose penalties. As the intervening Attorneys General emphasize, this is an issue that implicates the structures of administrative bodies across the nation.

• • •

[8] Before the Court of Appeal, Ocean Port argued for the first time that the Board lacked sufficient independence to make the ruling and impose the penalty it had, and that as a result the decision must be set aside. It also objected to the order on the grounds that: (1) the Board relied on hearsay, irrelevant evidence and insufficient evidence to support the allegations against Ocean Port, in contravention of the principles of natural justice and its duty of fairness; (2) the Board erred in law in its application of s. 10(3) of the *Evidence Act*, RSBC 1996, c. 124; and (3) the jurisdiction of the General Manager under the Act was limited to matters of compliance and could not ground a decision on an "offence," a power reserved to the courts.

• • •

III. Legislation

[15] [The *Liquor Control Act* states:]

30(1) The Liquor Appeal Board is continued consisting of a chair and other members the Lieutenant Governor in Council may appoint.

(2) The chair and the members of the appeal board

   (a) serve at the pleasure of the Lieutenant Governor in Council, and

   (b) are entitled to

      (i) receive the remuneration set by the Lieutenant Governor in Council, and

      (ii) be paid reasonable expenses incurred in carrying out their duties as members of the appeal board.

• • •

IV. Discussion

[18] This appeal concerns the independence of the Liquor Appeal Board. The Court of Appeal concluded that members of the Board lacked the necessary guarantees of independence required of administrative decision makers imposing penalties. More specifically, it held that the tenure enjoyed by Board members—appointed "at the pleasure" of the executive to serve on a part-time basis—was insufficiently secure to preserve the appearance of their independence. As a consequence, it set aside the Board's decision in the present case.

[19] The appellant, with the support of the intervening Attorneys General, argues that this reasoning disregards a fundamental principle of law: absent a constitutional challenge, a statutory regime prevails over common law principles of natural justice. The *Act* expressly provides for the appointment of Board members at the pleasure of the Lieutenant Governor in Council. The decision of the Court of Appeal, the appellant contends, effectively struck down this validly enacted provision without reference to constitutional principle or authority. In essence, the Court of Appeal elevated a principle of natural justice to constitutional status. In so doing, it committed a clear error of law.

[20] This conclusion, in my view, is inescapable. It is well established that, absent constitutional constraints, the degree of independence required of a particular government decision maker or tribunal is determined by its enabling statute. It is the legislature or Parliament that determines the degree of independence required of tribunal members. The statute must be construed as a whole to determine the degree of independence the legislature intended.

[21] Confronted with silent or ambiguous legislation, courts generally infer that Parliament or the legislature intended the tribunal's process to comport with principles of natural justice ... In such circumstances, administrative tribunals may be bound by the requirement of an independent and impartial decision maker, one of the fundamental principles of natural justice ... Indeed, courts will not lightly assume that legislators intended to enact procedures that run contrary to this principle, although the precise standard of independence required will depend "on all the circumstances, and in particular on the language of the statute under which the agency acts, the nature of the task it performs and the type of decision it is required to make": [citation omitted].

[22] However, like all principles of natural justice, the degree of independence required of tribunal members may be ousted by express statutory language or necessary implication. ... Ultimately, it is Parliament or the legislature that determines the nature of a tribunal's relationship to the executive. It is not open to a court to apply a common law rule in the face of clear statutory direction. Courts engaged in judicial review of administrative decisions must defer to the legislator's intention in assessing the degree of independence required of the tribunal in question.

[23] This principle reflects the fundamental distinction between administrative tribunals and courts. Superior courts, by virtue of their role as courts of inherent

jurisdiction, are constitutionally required to possess objective guarantees of both individual and institutional independence. The same constitutional imperative applies to the provincial courts ... . Historically, the requirement of judicial independence developed to demarcate the fundamental division between the judiciary and the executive. It protected, and continues to protect, the impartiality of judges—both in fact and perception—by insulating them from external influence, most notably the influence of the executive ... .

[24] Administrative tribunals, by contrast, lack this constitutional distinction from the executive. They are, in fact, created precisely for the purpose of implementing government policy. Implementation of that policy may require them to make quasi-judicial decisions. They thus may be seen as spanning the constitutional divide between the executive and judicial branches of government. However, given their primary policy-making function, it is properly the role and responsibility of Parliament and the legislatures to determine the composition and structure required by a tribunal to discharge the responsibilities bestowed upon it. While tribunals may sometimes attract Charter requirements of independence, as a general rule they do not. Thus, the degree of independence required of a particular tribunal is a matter of discerning the intention of Parliament or the legislature and, absent constitutional constraints, this choice must be respected.

[25] In the present case, the legislature of British Columbia spoke directly to the nature of appointments to the Liquor Appeal Board. Pursuant to s. 30(2)(a) of the Act, the chair and members of the Board "serve at the pleasure of the Lieutenant Governor in Council." In practice, members are appointed for a one-year term (pursuant to an Order-in-Council), and serve on a part-time basis. All members but the chair are paid on a per diem basis. The chair establishes panels of one or three members to hear matters before the Board "as the chair considers advisable": s. 30(5).

• • •

[27] In my view, the legislature's intention that Board members should serve at pleasure, as expressed through s. 30(2)(a) of the Act, is unequivocal. As such, it does not permit the argument that the statute is ambiguous and hence should be read as imposing a higher degree of independence to meet the requirements of natural justice, if indeed a higher standard is required. It is easy to imagine more exacting safeguards of independence—longer, fixed-term appointments; full-time appointments; a panel selection process for appointing members to panels instead of the Chair's discretion. However, in each case one must face the question: "Is this what the legislature intended?" Given the legislature's willingness to countenance "at pleasure" appointments with full knowledge of the processes and penalties involved, it is impossible to answer this question in the affirmative. Huddart JA concluded that the tenure enjoyed by Board members was "no better than an appointment at pleasure" (para. 27). However, this is precisely the standard of independence required by the Act. Where the intention of the legislature, as here, is unequivocal, there is no room to import common law doctrines of independence, "however inviting it may be for a Court to do so" [citation omitted].

• • •

[29] Nor is a constitutional guarantee of independence implicated in the present case. The respondent does not argue that the proceedings before the Board engage a right to an independent tribunal under ss. 7 or 11(d) of the *Canadian Charter of Rights and Freedoms*. Instead, it contends that the preamble to the *Constitution Act, 1867* mandates a minimum degree of independence for at least some administrative tribunals. In support, the respondent invokes Lamer CJ's discussion of judicial independence in the *Provincial Court Judges Reference*.

In that case, Lamer CJ, writing for the majority, concluded that "judicial independence is at root an *unwritten* constitutional principle ... recognized and affirmed by the preamble to the *Constitution Act, 1867*" (para. 83 (emphasis in original)). The respondent argues that the same principle binds administrative tribunals exercising adjudicative functions.

[30] With respect, I find no support for this proposition in the Provincial Court Judges Reference. The language and reasoning of the decision are confined to the superior and provincial courts. Lamer CJ addressed the issue of judicial independence; that is, the independence of the courts of law comprising the judicial branch of government. Nowhere in his reasons does he extend his comments to tribunals other than courts of law.

[31] Nor does the rationale for locating a constitutional guarantee of independence in the preamble to the *Constitution Act, 1867* extend, as a matter of principle, to administrative tribunals. Lamer CJ's reasoning rests on the preamble's reference to a constitutional system "similar in Principle to that of the United Kingdom." Applied to the modern Canadian context, this guarantee extends to provincial courts (at para. 106):

> The historical origins of the protection of judicial independence in the United Kingdom, and thus in the Canadian Constitution, can be traced to the *Act of Settlement of 1701*. As we said in *Valente* ..., at p. 693, that Act was the "historical inspiration" for the judicature provisions of the *Constitution Act, 1867*. Admittedly, the Act only extends protection to judges of the English superior courts. However ... judicial independence [has] grown into a principle that now extends to all courts, not just the superior courts of this country.

These comments circumscribe the requirement of independence, as a constitutional imperative emanating from the preamble, to the provincial and superior courts.

[32] Lamer CJ also supported his conclusion with reference to the traditional division between the executive, the legislature and the judiciary. The preservation of this tripartite constitutional structure, he argued, requires a constitutional guarantee of an independent judiciary. The classical division between court and state does not, however, compel the same conclusion in relation to the independence of administrative tribunals. As discussed, such tribunals span the constitutional divide between the judiciary and the executive. While they may possess adjudicative functions, they ultimately operate as part of the executive branch of government, under the mandate of the legislature. They are not courts, and do not occupy the same constitutional role as courts.

[33] The Constitution is an organic instrument, and must be interpreted flexibly to reflect changing circumstances ... Indeed, in the *Provincial Court Judges Reference*, Lamer CJ relied on this principle to extend the tradition of independent superior courts (derived from the constitution of the United Kingdom) to all courts, stating that "our Constitution has evolved over time" (para. 106). However, I can find no basis upon which to extend the constitutional guarantee of judicial independence that animated the *Provincial Court Judges Reference* to the Liquor Appeal Board. The Board is not a court, nor does it approach the constitutional role of the courts. It is first and foremost a licensing body. The suspension complained of was an incident of the Board's licensing function. Licences are granted on condition of compliance with the Act, and can be suspended for non-compliance. The exercise of power here at issue falls squarely within the executive power of the provincial government.

It is not clear that the *Ocean Port* decision settled the matter of the degree of independence required of administrative tribunals as a general proposition because the Supreme Court of Canada's analysis gave close consideration to the actual functions of the administrative body and the intent of the legislature in creating the administrative body. The issue was revisited in *Bell Canada v Canadian Telephone Employees Association*, [2003] 1 SCR 884, where a decision of the Canadian Human Rights Tribunal was challenged on the basis of the lack of independence of the tribunal stemming from the ability of the Canadian Human Rights Commission to issue guidelines (on the facts, actual regulations) that bound the tribunal and the power of the tribunal chair to extend tribunal members' terms in ongoing inquiries. Seizing on the Supreme Court of Canada's statement in *Ocean Port* that administrative tribunals "may be seen as spanning the constitutional divide between executive and judicial branches of government" (para 24), the Supreme Court of Canada in *Bell Canada* went on to consider the precise nature of the tribunal:

[21] ... Some administrative tribunals are closer to the executive end of the spectrum: their primary purpose is to develop, or supervise the implementation of, particular government policies. Such tribunals may require little by way of procedural protections. Other tribunals, however, are closer to the judicial end of the spectrum: their primary purpose is to adjudicate disputes through some form of hearing. Tribunals at this end of the spectrum may possess court-like powers and procedures. These powers may bring with them stringent requirements of procedural fairness, including a higher requirement of independence ... .

[22] To say that tribunals span the divide between the executive and the judicial branches of government is *not* to imply that there are only two types of tribunals—those that are quasi-judicial and require the full panoply of procedural protections, and those that are quasi-executive and require much less. A tribunal may have a number of different functions, one of which is to conduct fair and impartial hearings in a manner similar to that of the courts, and yet another of which is to see that certain government policies are furthered. In ascertaining the content of the requirements of procedural fairness that bind a particular tribunal, consideration must be given to *all* of the functions of that tribunal. It is not adequate to characterize a tribunal as "quasi-judicial" on the basis of one of its functions, while treating another aspect of the legislative scheme creating this tribunal—such as the requirement that the tribunal follow interpretive guidelines that are laid down by a specialized body with expertise in that area of law—as though this second aspect of the legislative scheme were external to the true purpose of the tribunal. All aspects of the tribunal's structure, as laid out in its enabling statute, must be examined, and an attempt must be made to determine precisely what combination of functions the legislature intended that tribunal to serve, and what procedural protections are appropriate for a body that has these particular functions.

[23] The main function of the Canadian Human Rights Tribunal is adjudicative. It conducts formal hearings into complaints that have been referred to it by the Commission. It has many of the powers of a court. It is empowered to find facts, to interpret and apply the law to the facts before it, and to award appropriate remedies. Moreover, its hearings have much the same structure as a formal trial before a court. The parties before the Tribunal lead evidence, call and cross-examine witnesses, and make submissions on how the law should be applied to the facts. The Tribunal is not involved in crafting policy, nor does it undertake its own independent investigations of complaints: the investigative and policy-making functions have deliberately been assigned by the legislature to a different body, the Commission.

In this case, the Supreme Court of Canada held that in light of these functions "the Tribunal, though not bound to the highest standard of independence by the unwritten constitutional principle of adjudicative independence, must act impartially and meet a relatively high standard of independence, both at common law and under s 2(e) of the *Canadian Bill of Rights*" (at para 31).

Part of the challenge to the Canadian Human Rights Tribunal's impartiality arose from the commission's dual role as a creator of guidelines that are binding on the tribunal and as a party that appears before the tribunal.

[40] ... Bell objects that Parliament has placed in one and the same body the function of formulating guidelines, investigating complaints, and acting as prosecutor before the Tribunal. Bell is correct in suggesting that the Commission shares these functions. However, this overlapping of different functions in a single administrative agency is not unusual, and does not on its own give rise to a reasonable apprehension of bias . ... As McLachlin CJ observed in *Ocean Port*, [[2001] 2 SCR 781], at para. 41, "[t]he overlapping of investigative, prosecutorial and adjudicative functions in a single agency is frequently necessary for [an administrative agency] to effectively perform its intended role."

[41] Indeed, it may be that the overlapping of functions in the Commission is the legislature's way of ensuring that both the Commission and the Tribunal are able to perform their intended roles. In *Public Service Alliance*, [[2000] 1 FC 146 (TD)], Evans J noted that although it was unusual for Parliament to have conferred the power to make subordinate legislation on the Commission and not the Governor in Council, Parliament must have contemplated that "the expertise that the Commission will have acquired in the discharge of its statutory responsibilities for human rights research and public education, and for processing complaints up to the point of adjudication" (para. 140) was necessary in the formulation of the guidelines, and was more important than certain other goals. In our view, Evans J's conjecture regarding Parliamentary intent is correct. The Commission is responsible, among other things, for maintaining close liaisons with similar bodies in the provinces, for considering recommendations from public interest groups and any other bodies, and for developing programs of public education (s. 27(1)). These collaborative and educational responsibilities afford it extensive awareness of the needs of the public, and extensive knowledge of developments in anti-discrimination law at the federal and provincial levels. Placing the guideline power in the hands of the Commission may therefore have been Parliament's way of ensuring that the Act would be interpreted in a manner that was sensitive to the needs of the public and to developments across the country, and hence, that it would be interpreted by the Tribunal in the manner that best furthered the aims of the Act as a whole.

[42] This point is related to our earlier discussion of the importance of considering the aims of the Act as a whole, in assessing whether the requirement of impartiality has been met. We noted there that the Act's ultimate aim of identifying and rectifying instances of discrimination would only be furthered if ambiguities in the Act were interpreted in a manner that furthered, rather than frustrated, the identification of discriminatory practices. If, as the Act suggests, this can best be accomplished by giving the Commission the power to make interpretive guidelines that bind the Tribunal, then the overlapping of functions in the Commission plays an important role. It does not result in a lack of impartiality, but rather helps to ensure that the Tribunal applies the Act in the manner that is most likely to fulfill the Act's ultimate purpose.

What the Supreme Court of Canada recognizes in the excerpt above is the desirability in many instances of creating executive entities that are capable of exercising multiple and overlapping functions that respond to the regulatory demands at hand. Often administrative bodies can be created that are better placed than the legislature to address the particular requirements of a regulatory scheme owing to their expertise, flexibility, independence, efficiency, or combination thereof, as the case may be. Litigants continued to argue, however, that the *Ocean Port* decision did not rule out the possibility that *some* administrative tribunals that exercised adjudicative functions analogous to those exercised by provincial courts of civil jurisdiction could be protected by the unwritten constitutional principle of judicial independence. See *McKenzie v Minister of Public Safety and Solicitor General*, 2006 BCSC 1372, appeal dismissed as moot, 2007 BCCA 507. The Saskatchewan Court of Appeal addressed this line of argument in the decision that follows.

Saskatchewan Federation of Labour v Government of Saskatchewan
2013 SKCA 61, [2013] 9 WWR 515

CAMERON JA (for the court):

[1] Following the Saskatchewan general election held on November 7, 2007, which saw a change of government, the Lieutenant Governor in Council made an order-in-council terminating the appointments of the then chairperson and vice-chairpersons of the Saskatchewan Labour Relations Board and appointing a new chairperson.

[2] The order-in-council terminating these appointments was made on the authority of section 20 of *The Interpretation Act, 1995*, S.S. 1995, c. I-11.2. This section empowers the Lieutenant Governor in Council, on a change of government, to bring to an end the term of office of any member of any board, commission, agency, or other appointed body of the Government of Saskatchewan. There is an exception in the case of persons whose appointments are subject to termination by the Legislative Assembly, but the exception does not apply to members of the Labour Relations Board.

[3] Shortly after the order-in-council was made, the Saskatchewan Federation of Labour and two unions, namely the Saskatchewan Joint Board Retail, Wholesale and Department Store Union and the Canadian Union of Public Employees, applied to the Court of Queen's Bench for a declaration declaring the order-in-council void. They contended it was void because the Lieutenant Governor in Council lacked the power to make it, or had made it for an impermissible purpose or improper motive. The Court of Queen's Bench disagreed and dismissed their application.

[4] They then appealed to this Court. It dismissed their appeal on the two-fold ground the Lieutenant Governor in Council (i) was empowered by section 20 of *The Interpretation Act, 1995* to make the impugned order-in-council and (ii) did not abuse that power in making the order for the impermissible purpose or improper motive of influencing the decisions of the Board and undercutting its independence.

[5] Immediately after the dismissal of their appeal, the Saskatchewan Federation of Labour and the Saskatchewan Joint Board Retail, Wholesale and Department Store Union made a second application to the Court of Queen's Bench to have the order-in-council declared void. They were joined on this occasion by the Saskatchewan Government and General Employee's Union. This time they contended the order-in-council was void on the ground section 20 of *The Interpretation Act, 1995* is unconstitutional to the extent it empowers the Lieutenant Governor in Council to terminate the fixed terms of office of the chairperson and vice-chairpersons of the Labour Relations Board.

[6] It is unconstitutional, they said, because it is inconsistent with the "unwritten constitutional principle of judicial independence" secured by the *Constitution Act, 1867.* In their submission this principle, which applies to the Provincial Court in its capacity as an inferior court of civil jurisdiction and protects its judges from arbitrary removal from office, also applies to persons such as the chairperson and vice-chairpersons of the Labour Relations Board and, therefore, protects these persons from like treatment. It does so, according to the submission, because there is no meaningful distinction between the adjudicative function of these two institutions in the realm of the civil law.

• • •

[40] Judicial independence generally means the capacity of the courts to function without actual or apparent interference by anyone, including in particular the legislative and executive branches of government. As this applies to the conditions under which judges serve, the hallmarks or essential conditions of judicial independence are three-fold: (i) security of tenure, (ii) financial stability, and (iii) administrative freedom in relation to the exercise of their judicial duties ... . As explained in *Valente* [*v The Queen*, [1985] 2 SCR 673] at p. 685, these indicia have to do with "a status or relationship to others, particularly to the executive branch of government, that rests on objective conditions or guarantees." Thus, judicial independence has both personal and institutional aspects.

[41] As also explained in *Valente*, at p. 685, judicial independence is intrinsically linked to the concept of impartiality, which is to say with "the state of mind or attitude" of the judge regarding the issues and the parties in a particular case—a state of mind prompting judges to perform their judicial duties without fear or favour from any quarter, as the saying goes, including the legislative and executive branches of government. Indeed, it has been said that judicial independence is the means to the end of impartiality. "Independence is the cornerstone, a necessary prerequisite, for judicial impartiality": Lamer C.J. in *R. v. Lippé*, [[1991] 2 SCR 114 at 139].

[42] All of this, of course, has more to do with nature of judicial independence than the bases upon which it rests and the purposes it serves. The latter were summed up as follows by Major J., who delivered the judgment of the Supreme Court of Canada in *Ell v. Alberta*, 2003 SCC 35, [2003] 1 SCR 857:

> [22] In modern times, it has been recognized that the basis for judicial independence extends far beyond the need for impartiality in individual cases. The judiciary occupies an indispensable role in upholding the integrity of our constitutional structure: see *Provincial Court Judges Reference, supra* [1997 CanLII 317 (SCC) ...], at para. 108. In Canada, like other federal states, courts adjudicate on disputes between the federal and provincial governments, and serve to safeguard the constitutional distribution of powers. Courts also ensure that the power of the state is exercised in accordance with the rule of law and the provisions of our Constitution. In this capacity, courts act as a shield against unwarranted deprivations by the state of the rights and freedoms of individuals. Dickson C.J. described this role in *Beauregard, supra* [[1986] 2 S.C.R. 56]], at p. 70:
>
> > Courts act as protector of the Constitution and the fundamental values embodied in it—rule of law, fundamental justice, equality, preservation of the democratic process, to name perhaps the most important.
>
> This constitutional mandate gives rise to the principle's institutional dimension: the need to maintain the independence of a court or tribunal as a whole from the executive and legislative branches of government.
>
> [23] Accordingly, the judiciary's role as arbiter of disputes and guardian of the Constitution require that it be independent from all other bodies. A separate, but related, basis for independence is the need to uphold public confidence in the administration of justice. Confidence in our system of justice requires a healthy perception of judicial independence to be maintained amongst the citizenry. Without the perception of independence, the judiciary is unable to "claim any legitimacy or command the respect and acceptance that are essential to it": see *Mackin v. New Brunswick (Minister of Finance)*, ... 2002 SCC 13 at para. 38, *per* Gonthier J. The principle requires the judiciary to be independent both in fact and perception.

[43] Viewed in this light, the business of judicial independence may be seen to be of fundamental significance to the relationship between the executive and legislative branches of government, on the one hand, and the judicial branch, on the other. Hence, judicial independence is secured by the Canadian Constitution, most notably by the *Constitution Act, 1867* and the *Constitution Act, 1982*, including the *Canadian Charter of Rights and Freedoms*. In one way or another (though in quite different ways), these components of the Constitution secure the judicial independence of all Canadian courts.

• • •

[47] The question, of course, is whether the unwritten constitutional principle of judicial independence extends to the chairperson and vice-chairpersons of the Labour Relations Board so as to have precluded the Lieutenant Governor in Council from validly terminating their terms of office on the authority of 20 of *The Interpretation Act, 1995*.

[48] The analysis of the question is heavily driven by the decision of the Supreme Court of Canada in *Ocean Port Hotel Ltd. v. British Columbia (General Manager, Liquor Control and Licensing Branch* [2001 SCC 52, [2001] 2 SCR 781].

• • •

[50] The Supreme Court held that there was no basis, either in common law or in constitutional law, to require a greater degree of independence in the Board than that conferred upon the Board by its enabling legislation. In so holding, the Court observed that the degree of independence required of a particular government decision-maker or tribunal is determined by its enabling statute, for as a matter of principle it is for the legislature or Parliament, absent constitutional constraints, to determine the degree of independence of tribunal members. [The court then quoted from paras 23-24 of Chief Justice McLachlin's decision in *Ocean Port*.] ...

[51] These passages plainly contain expressions of principle of general application and, therefore, suggest that in light of the fundamental distinction between courts and administrative tribunals, (including administrative tribunals empowered to make quasi-judicial decisions), the independence of the courts is constitutionally secured, whereas that of administrative tribunals is not—not unless the proceedings before a tribunal engage the rights guaranteed by section 7 or 11(d) of the *Canadian Charter of Rights and Freedoms*. Otherwise, it is for the legislatures or Parliament, as the case may be, to determine the composition, structure, and degree of independence of administrative tribunals.

[52] To be clear about the implications of this in relation to the question before us, I note that the Federation of Labour and two unions did not contend that proceedings before the Labour Relations Board engage the rights guaranteed by sections 7 and 11(d) of the *Charter*. Rather, they rested their argument on the unwritten constitutional principle of judicial independence grounded in the preamble to the *Constitution Act, 1867*. And they argued that this principle extended to members of administrative tribunals responsible for quasi-judicial decision-making of the kind required of the chairperson and vice-chairpersons of the Labour Relations Board.

[53] Their argument strikes me as highly problematic inasmuch as the Supreme Court rejected a similar argument in *Ocean Port*. ... [The court then quoted from paras 29-32 of Chief Justice McLachlin's decision in *Ocean Port*.]

• • •

[56] Given what I regard as the clear import of these passages, I am of the view the argument of the Federation of Labour and the two unions is not only problematic but must fail. In other words, I am of the opinion that, in light of reasons for judgment in *Ocean Port*, the unwritten constitutional principle of judicial

independence grounded in the preamble to the *Constitution Act, 1867* cannot be seen to extend to the Saskatchewan Labour Relations Board, including the chairperson and vice-chairpersons of the Board.

[57] In fairness to the position taken by the Federation of Labour and the two unions, I should say that they contended otherwise, urging upon us a less definitive interpretation of *Ocean Port*. In their submission, *Ocean Port* should not be seen to apply to all manner of administrative tribunals—not in itself and not in light of other decisions of the Supreme Court, including in particular the subsequent decisions of the Court in *Ell v. Alberta, supra* and *Bell Canada v. Canadian Telephone Employees Assn.*, 2003 SCC 36 ... .

[58] As for *Ocean Port* itself, so the submission goes, the decision should be understood in light of the fact the British Columbia Liquor Appeal Board was an administrative tribunal charged with regulating liquor licensing and functioned, as such, at the administrative end of the constitutional divide between the executive and the judicial branches of government, rather than at the judicial end, whereas the Labour Relations Board functions at or near the judicial end. While this is true, meaning that *Ocean Port* is distinguishable in fact from the present case, the body of principle expounded in *Ocean Port* is, in my opinion, of general application and must be applied accordingly in keeping with the doctrine of *stare decisis*. So I cannot accept this submission, which is to say I cannot accept it even though I agree with the Federation of Labour and the two unions that the Labour Relations Board functions near the judicial end of the divide rather than the administrative end.

[59] As for the subsequent decisions of the Supreme Court in *Ell* and *Bell Canada*, the Federation of Labour and the two unions submitted that these decisions and others served to temper the rigour of *Ocean Port* and thus leave it open to the lower courts to extend the reach of the unwritten constitutional principle of judicial independence beyond the courts to a limited class of administrative tribunals, being those whose quasi-judicial adjudicative function places them at the judicial end of the constitutional divide rather than at the administrative end or somewhere in between. The submission was developed along the lines of the reasoning found in *McKenzie v. British Columbia (Minister of Public Safety and Solicitor General)*, 2006 BCSC 1372 ... .

[60] With respect, I cannot subscribe to this submission. In *Ell* the Supreme Court held that the unwritten constitutional principle of judicial independence applies to the office of justice of the peace, given the judicial functions exercised by justices of the peace in enforcing the criminal law within the court system. I see nothing in the reasons for judgment of the Court to support the position advocated by the Federation of Labour and the two unions.

[61] Indeed, their position seems the weaker by reason of *Ell*. I say this because, as noted above in para. 42, the Supreme Court was at pains in *Ell* to more fully explain the basis upon which the constitutional principle of judicial independence rests, and the purposes it serves. Its explanation is grounded in the unique role of courts of law, especially in relation to the indispensible role of the courts in upholding the integrity of our constitutional order as the "guardian of the Constitution." And the explanation serves in full to reinforce the nature of the gulf between courts of law and administrative tribunals, even administrative tribunals whose legislated mandate places them near the judicial end of the constitutional divide between the legislative and executive branches of government, on the one hand, and the judicial branch on the other.

[62] Nor do I see anything in *Bell Canada* to support the position advocated by the Federation of Labour and the two unions. *Bell Canada* had to do with the degree of independence of the Canadian Human Rights Tribunal, given the terms

of the enabling statute and the requirements of the common law principles of natural justice. The Supreme Court was invited to apply the unwritten constitutional principle of judicial independence to the Tribunal. It declined to do so, however, even though the function of the Tribunal was *exclusively adjudicative*, and even though the Tribunal was charged with the duty of adjudicating disputes in the field of *human rights*.

[63] Still, the Federation of Labour and the two unions submitted that the Court declined to do so for the reason it was unnecessary to do otherwise, with the Court having intimated that, had it been necessary to do otherwise, it may well have extended this constitutional principle to the Tribunal. Even if this were so, I am of the view it would not allow for this Court to depart from *Ocean Port* in light of the doctrine of *stare decisis*.

[64] In conclusion, and for essentially the whole of these reasons, I must say I cannot agree with the position taken by the Federation of Labour and the two unions. In other words I am of the opinion *Ocean Port* is dispositive of the question under consideration and, therefore, dispositive of the appeal.

E. CROWN CORPORATIONS

It is not uncommon for administrative bodies to be created that have a legal personality separate from the government. The principal justification for the creation of Crown corporations is that where there is a strong commercial aspect to the government service, it may require that decisions be made free from political influences that may unduly interfere with commercial objectives. Additionally, the commercial nature of some activities may be ill suited to government departmental structures and the related rules respecting financial matters, such as controls on the expenditure of public funds and the management of debt. The use of Crown corporations should also be understood as a distinct form of regulation that arises from direct ownership, as opposed to the imposition of regulatory controls on private entities.

Of course, if Crown corporations were solely concerned with commercial objectives, there would be little incentive to resort to the creation of a Crown corporation, as opposed to a wholly private sector approach. It follows that Crown corporations will have public objectives. In some instances, the Crown corporation may have an express regulatory mandate, as is the case with the Bank of Canada. Alternatively, the Crown corporation may deliver services that are considered to be of public importance; examples include Canada Post, VIA Rail, and the provision of electrical power generation and distribution by provincial Crown corporations. In some cases, the government may decide that the justification for providing a service through a Crown corporation can no longer be maintained, resulting in the elimination or privatization of the Crown corporation, as was the case with Petro-Canada and Air Canada.

The private and public objectives of Crown corporations require the government to balance the operational benefits of independence and the need for accountability. Given the diversity of the size, mandates, and sources of funding of Crown corporations, a "one size fits all" approach to accountability is difficult. The primary vehicle for accountability of federal Crown corporations is the *Financial Administration Act*, RSC 1985, c F-11, which imposes standardized governance and accountability requirements on listed Crown corporations, including approval of annual corporate plans, capital budgets, and in some cases, operating budgets. The government has in many cases the authority of appointment over corporate directors and key corporate officers. The *Financial Administration Act* also provides authority for the government to intervene in the management of a Crown corporation by directing the board of directors to follow a particular course of action where such action is in the public interest. This authority, called a "directive power," is an extraordinary power and requires the appropriate minister to consult with the board of directors of the affected Crown corporation in advance of the issuance of the directive and to table the directive in both Houses once issued. In practice, if an issue is of sufficient significance to the political executive, its control over the appointment and removal of corporate directors and officers typically enables it to exercise a significant measure of influence on corporate decision-making without needing to have recourse to the use of the "directive power." See Philip Bryden & Barry Slutsky, "The Governance of Commercial Crown Corporations: How Much Independence Can We Expect from Corporate Directors?" in Janis Sarra, ed, *Corporate Governance in Global Capital Markets* (Vancouver: University of British Columbia Press, 2003) at 225.

F. ENFORCEMENT BODIES: POLICE AND PROSECUTORS

The executive branch of the government, in addition to being responsible for the implementation of government policy, is required to enforce those policies that have the force of law. In respect of criminal law and provincial quasi-criminal law, the enforcement duties of the executive fall primarily on the police, who are responsible for maintaining order and investigating conduct that is potentially illegal, and to prosecutors, who are responsible for representing the Crown in prosecuting criminal charges. Policing functions are the responsibility of both the provincial and federal governments. Provincial police, including those employed by municipal police forces, have the authority to investigate matters in relation to both provincial laws and federal criminal laws. The federal police force, the Royal Canadian Mounted Police, has the authority to police federal statutes (although provincial policing bodies have primary enforcement responsibility for offences under the *Criminal Code*), to police the federal territories, and in much of Canada, to provide provincial and municipal policing services under contract. Both the federal government and the provinces have prosecutorial power, exercised by their respective attorneys general.

While enforcement agencies in Canada derive their authority from legislation, they hold a unique legal position within the broader executive framework. In common law, police and prosecutors have been distinguished from other civil servants in that, in their enforcement duties, they are not subject to political oversight in the sense that they must exercise their powers without direction from political officials or in furtherance of partisan political activities. On the other hand, police and prosecutors cannot operate without accountability for their actions. The two case excerpts that follow consider the tension between accountability and independence in the context of enforcement.

In the first excerpt, *R v Campbell*, the police engineered a "reverse sting" operation by arranging the sale of narcotics to the accused and then charging him with conspiracy to traffic. A stay of proceedings was sought on the basis that the police had engaged in a serious breach of the law. In response, the Crown argued that any illegal conduct should be subject to Crown immunity from statutory offences. In the course of considering this argument, the Supreme Court of Canada considered the nature of the relationship between the police and the Crown. At the heart of this consideration was the degree to which the RCMP is independent from the political executive.

In the second excerpt, *Krieger v Law Society of Alberta*, the petitioner, Krieger, was a Crown prosecutor who was subject to a complaint to the Law Society, which stemmed from Krieger's conduct during a prosecution. Krieger sought to prevent the Law Society from reviewing the matter on the basis that to do so would interfere with the exercise of prosecutorial discretion. In this case, the independence of Crown prosecutors from political interference lay beneath the petitioner's claim not to be subject to regulatory oversight by the Law Society.

R v Campbell
[1999] 1 SCR 565

BINNIE J:

[27] The Crown's attempt to identify the RCMP with the Crown for immunity purposes misconceives the relationship between the police and the executive government when the police are engaged in law enforcement. A police officer investigating a crime is not acting as a government functionary or as an agent of anybody. He or she occupies a public office initially defined by the common law and subsequently set out in various statutes. In the case of the RCMP, one of the relevant statutes is now the *Royal Canadian Mounted Police Act*, RSC 1985, c. R-10.

[28] Under the authority of that Act, it is true, RCMP officers perform a myriad of functions apart from the investigation of crimes. These include, by way of examples, purely ceremonial duties, the protection of Canadian dignitaries and foreign diplomats and activities associated with crime prevention. Some of these functions bring the RCMP into a closer relationship to the Crown than others. The *Department of the Solicitor General Act*, RSC 1985, c. S-13, provides that the Solicitor General's powers, duties and functions extend to matters relating to the RCMP over which Parliament has jurisdiction, and that have not been assigned to another department. Section 5 of the *Royal Canadian Mounted Police Act* provides for the governance of the RCMP as follows:

> 5(1) The Governor in Council may appoint an officer, to be known as the Commissioner of the Royal Canadian Mounted Police, who, under the direction of the [Solicitor General], has the control and management of the Force and all matters connected therewith.

[29] It is therefore possible that in one or other of its roles the RCMP could be acting in an agency relationship with the Crown. In this appeal, however, we are concerned only with the status of an RCMP officer in the course of a criminal investigation, and in that regard the police are independent of the control of the executive government. The importance of this principle, which itself underpins the rule of law, was recognized by this Court in relation to municipal forces as long ago as *McCleave v. Moncton (City)* (1902), 32 SCR 106 (SCC). That was a civil case, having to do with potential municipal liability for police negligence, but in the course of his judgment Strong CJ cited with approval the following proposition, at pp. 108-09:

> Police officers can in no respect be regarded as agents or officers of the city. Their duties are of a public nature. Their appointment is devolved on cities and towns by the legislature as a convenient mode of exercising a function of government, but this does not render them liable for their unlawful or negligent acts. The detection and arrest of offenders, the preservation of the public peace, the enforcement of the laws, and other similar powers and duties with which police officers and constables are entrusted are derived from the law, and not from the city or town under which they hold their appointment.

[30] At about the same time, the High Court of Australia rejected the notion that a police constable was an agent of the Crown so as to enjoy immunity against a civil action for wrongful arrest. Griffith CJ had this to say in *Enever v. R* (1906), 3 CLR 969 (Australia HC) at p. 977:

> Now, the powers of a constable, *qua* peace officer, whether conferred by common or statute law, are exercised by him by virtue of his office, and cannot be exercised on the responsibility of any person but himself. If he arrests on suspicion of felony,

the suspicion must be his suspicion, and must be reasonable to him. If he arrests in a case in which the arrest may be made on view, the view must be his view, not that of someone else. ... A constable, therefore, when acting as a peace officer, is not exercising a delegated authority, but an original authority, and the general law of agency has no application.

[31] Over 70 years later, Laskin CJ in *Nicholson v. Haldimand-Norfolk (Regional Municipality) Commissioners of Police* (1978), [1979] 1 SCR 311 (SCC) at p. 322, speaking with reference to the status of a probationary police constable, affirmed that "we are dealing with *the holder of a public office*, engaged in duties connected with the maintenance of public order and preservation of the peace, important values in any society" (emphasis added). See also *Ridge v. Baldwin* (1963), [1964] AC 40 (UK HL) at p. 65.

[32] Similar sentiments were expressed by the Judicial Committee of the Privy Council in *Attorney General for New South Wales v. Perpetual Trustee Co.*, [1955] AC 457 (Australia PC), another civil case dealing with the vicarious liability of the Crown, in which Lord Viscount Simonds stated, at pp. 489-90:

> [A constable's] authority is original, not delegated, and is exercised at his own discretion by virtue of his office: he is a ministerial officer exercising statutory rights independently of contract. The essential difference is recognized in the fact that his relationship to the Government is not in ordinary parlance described as that of servant and master.

[33] While for certain purposes the Commissioner of the RCMP reports to the Solicitor General, the Commissioner is not to be considered a servant or agent of the government while engaged in a criminal investigation. The Commissioner is not subject to political direction. Like every other police officer similarly engaged, he is answerable to the law and, no doubt, to his conscience. As Lord Denning put it in relation to the Commissioner of Police in *R v. Metropolitan Police Commissioner*, [1968] 1 All ER 763 (Eng. CA), at p. 769:

> I have no hesitation, however, in holding that, *like every constable in the land, he [the Commissioner of Police] should be, and is, independent of the executive.* He is not subject to the orders of the Secretary of State, save that under the *Police Act 1964* the Secretary of State can call on him to give a report, or to retire in the interests of efficiency. I hold it to be the duty of the Commissioner of Police, as it is of every chief constable, to enforce the law of the land. He must take steps so to post his men that crimes may be detected; and that honest citizens may go about their affairs in peace. He must decide whether or not suspected persons are to be prosecuted; and, if need be, bring the prosecution or see that it is brought; *but in all these things he is not the servant of anyone, save of the law itself.* No Minister of the Crown can tell him that he must, or must not, keep observation on this place or that; or that he must, or must not, prosecute this man or that one. Nor can any police authority tell him so. The responsibility for law enforcement lies on him. He is answerable to the law and to the law alone. [Emphasis added.]

Krieger v Law Society of Alberta
2002 SCC 65, [2002] 3 SCR 372

IACOBUCCI and MAJOR JJ:

[23] Prior to considering the specific questions raised by this appeal, we believe it is useful to discuss the nature and development of the Attorney General's office in

Canada. Although we ultimately conclude that the Law Society retains jurisdiction over the alleged misconduct at the bottom of this dispute, the respondents rightly observed the unique and important role of the Attorney General and his agents as distinct from private lawyers.

[24] The office of Attorney General started in England as early as the thirteenth century as the King's Attorney. In essence, the Attorney General exercised on the King's behalf the prerogative to bring and terminate prosecutions. See J.L.J. Edwards, *The Law Officers of the Crown* (London: Sweet and Maxwell, 1964), at pp. 12-14; Law Reform Commission of Canada, Working Paper 62, *Controlling Criminal Prosecutions: The Attorney General and the Crown Prosecutor* (Ottawa: The Commission, 1990). Although there are great differences between the constitution of the Canadian and English offices of Attorney General, the power to manage prosecutions of individuals for criminal acts has changed little since these early times and between these countries. ...

[25] Although prosecutions were predominantly brought privately in England until 1879, the original power of the Attorney General was and is of initiating, managing and terminating both private and public prosecutions. This power finds its source in the Attorney General's general role as the official legal advisor to the Crown.

[26] In Canada, the office of the Attorney General is one with constitutional dimensions recognized in the *Constitution Act, 1867.* Although the specific duties conventionally exercised by the Attorney General are not enumerated, s. 135 of that Act provides for the extension of the authority and duties of that office as existing prior to Confederation. A similar provision applicable to the Attorney General of Alberta is found in the *Alberta Act*, SC 1905, c. 3 (reprinted in RSC 1985, App. II, No. 20), at s. 16(1). Furthermore, s. 63 of the *Constitution Act, 1867* requires that the cabinets of Quebec and Ontario include in their membership the Attorneys General.

[27] Attorneys General in this country are, of course, charged with duties beyond the management of prosecutions. As in England, they serve as Law Officers to their respective legislatures, and are responsible for providing legal advice to the various government departments. Unlike England, the Attorney General is also the Minister of Justice and is generally responsible for drafting the legislation tabled by the government of the day. The numerous other duties of the provincial and federal Attorneys General are broadly outlined in the various Acts establishing the Departments of Justice in each jurisdiction.

• • •

[29] The gravity of the power to bring, manage and terminate prosecutions, which lies at the heart of the Attorney General's role, has given rise to an expectation that he or she will be in this respect fully independent from the political pressures of the government. In the UK, this concern has resulted in the long tradition that the Attorney General not sit as a member of Cabinet. See Edwards, *supra*, at pp. 174-76. Unlike the UK, Cabinet membership prevails in this country. However, the concern remains the same, and is amplified by the fact that the Attorney General is not only a member of Cabinet but also Minister of Justice, and in that role holds a position with partisan political aspects. Membership in Cabinet makes the principle of independence in prosecutorial functions perhaps even more important in this country than in the UK.

[30] It is a constitutional principle in this country that the Attorney General must act independently of partisan concerns when supervising prosecutorial decisions. Support for this view can be found in Law Reform Commission of Canada, *supra*, at pp. 9-11. See also Binnie J in *R v. Regan*, [2002] 1 SCR 297, at paras. 157-158 (dissenting on another point).

[31] This side of the Attorney General's independence finds further form in the principle that courts will not interfere with his exercise of executive authority, as reflected in the prosecutorial decision-making process. In *R v. Power*, [1994] 1 SCR 601 (SCC), L'Heureux-Dubé J said, at pp. 621-23:

> It is manifest that, as a matter of principle and policy, courts should not interfere with prosecutorial discretion. This appears clearly to stem from the respect of separation of powers and the rule of law. Under the doctrine of separation of powers, criminal law is in the domain of the executive.
>
> Donna C. Morgan in "Controlling Prosecutorial Powers—Judicial Review, Abuse of Process and Section 7 of The Charter" (1986-87), 29 *Crim. LQ* 15, at pp. 20-21, probes the origins of prosecutorial powers:
>
> > Most (prosecutorial powers) derive ... from the royal prerogative, defined by Dicey as the residue of discretionary or arbitrary authority residing in the hands of the Crown at any given time. Prerogative powers are essentially those granted by the common law to the Crown that are not shared by the Crown's subjects. While executive action carried out under their aegis conforms with the rule of law, prerogative powers are subject to the supremacy of Parliament, since they may be curtailed or abolished by statute.
>
> ⋯
>
> In "Prosecutorial Discretion: A Reply to David Vanek" (1987-88), 30 *Crim. LQ* 378, at pp. 378-80, J.A. Ramsay expands on the rationale underlying judicial deference to prosecutorial discretion:
>
> ⋯
>
> > It is fundamental to our system of justice that criminal proceedings be conducted in public before an independent and impartial tribunal. *If the court is to review the prosecutor's exercise of his discretion the court becomes a supervising prosecutor. It ceases to be an independent tribunal.* [Emphasis in original.]

[32] The court's acknowledgment of the Attorney General's independence from judicial review in the sphere of prosecutorial discretion has its strongest source in the fundamental principle of the rule of law under our Constitution. Subject to the abuse of process doctrine, supervising one litigant's decision-making process—rather than the conduct of litigants before the court—is beyond the legitimate reach of the court. In *Hoem v. Law Society (British Columbia)* (1985), 20 CCC (3d) 239 (BC CA), Esson JA, for the court, observed, at p. 254, that:

> The independence of the Attorney-General, in deciding fairly who should be prosecuted, is also a hallmark of a free society. Just as the independence of the bar within its proper sphere must be respected, so must the independence of the Attorney-General.

We agree with these comments. The quasi-judicial function of the Attorney General cannot be subjected to interference from parties who are not as competent to consider the various factors involved in making a decision to prosecute. To subject such decisions to political interference, or to judicial supervision, could erode the integrity of our system of prosecution. Clearly drawn constitutional lines are necessary in areas subject to such grave potential conflict.

In both *R v Campbell* and *Krieger v Law Society of Alberta*, the Supreme Court of Canada is careful not to view the relationship between enforcement authorities and political branches of government in absolute terms. In *Campbell*, the Court's finding of police independence is limited to the police in the exercise of their law enforcement functions. Similarly, in *Krieger*, the Court distinguishes between activities that go directly to the exercise of prosecutorial discretion, which ought not to be reviewable, and activities, such as a prosecutor's tactics and conduct in court, which may properly be the subject of review by professional regulatory bodies like the Law Society.

The dual role of the attorney general in Canada as both a member of Cabinet who has partisan political responsibilities and as an independent quasi-judicial officer who must supervise prosecutions in a manner that is free from partisan considerations has occasionally been the source of controversy. As a general proposition, this controversy is avoided by a practice of insulating the attorney general from the day-to-day exercise of prosecutorial discretion and having prosecutorial decisions made by individual Crown counsel or their supervisors within the relevant prosecution service. Normally, attorneys general confine their oversight role to the issuance of prosecution policy directives rather than becoming involved in individual cases. At the federal level, following the lead of a number of provinces, the separation of the attorney general from the day to day operation of the Public Prosecution Service of Canada is formalized through the *Director of Public Prosecutions Act*, SC 2006, c 9, s 121, which gives overall direction of federal prosecutions to the Director of Public Prosecutions. At the same time, in s 10(1), the Act specifically retains the right of the attorney general to give direction in specific prosecutions provided that direction is made in writing and published in the *Canada Gazette*. See Anne McLellan, *Review of the Roles of the Minister of Justice and Attorney General of Canada* (2019), online (pdf): <https://pm.gc.ca/sites/pm/files/inline-files/Review%20of%20the%20Roles%20of%20the%20Minister%20of%20Justice%20and%20Attorney%20General%20of%20Canada_3.pdf>, at 16-21.

In the context of the prosecution of SNC-Lavalin for alleged breaches of the *Corruption of Foreign Public Officials Act*, SC 1998, c 34 and the fraud provisions of the *Criminal Code*, RSC 1985, c C-46, Prime Minister Justin Trudeau and officials acting on his behalf attempted to persuade then-Attorney General Jody Wilson-Raybould to exercise the authority conferred on her by s 10(1) of the *Director of Public Prosecutions Act* to direct the Director of Public Prosecutions to negotiate a remediation agreement with SNC-Lavalin to address the charges. Allegations were raised that Prime Minister Justin Trudeau breached the federal *Conflict of Interest Act*, SC 2006, c 9, s 2, in doing so, and on August 14, 2019, federal Conflict of Interest and Ethics Commissioner Mario Dion released a report finding that the Prime Minister's conduct violated s 9 of the Act (online: <https://ciec-ccie.parl.gc.ca/en/investigations-enquetes/Pages/TrudeauIIReport-RapportTrudeauII.aspx>)

Section 9 of the *Conflict of Interest Act* prohibits a public office holder from seeking to influence a decision of another person in order to improperly further the private interests of another person. The Commissioner found that the representations to the Attorney General conveyed on behalf of the Prime Minister were intended to influence her decision and that the decision had the potential to have significant impacts on the private financial interests of SNC-Lavalin. They key question for the Commissioner was whether the Prime Minister's efforts "improperly" furthered SNC-Lavalin's interests. Counsel for the Prime Minister argued that the Prime Minister's representations were designed to further national economic interests since a conviction would prevent the company from bidding on federal contracts, which would have significant impacts on the company's employees. Since s 715.32(3) of the *Criminal Code* prohibits prosecutors from taking into account the "national economic interest" in deciding whether or not to enter into a remediation agreement, the Commissioner concluded that the Prime Minister could not successfully advance this type of argument as a way of justifying his representations as being made in furtherance of the public interest. More fundamentally, the Commissioner concluded that the representations were "improper" because they included representations concerning the partisan political consequences of failure to secure a remediation agreement for the company. In concluding that the inclusion of partisan political considerations into representations made to the Attorney General in relation to a prosecution is improper, Commissioner Dion relied (at paras 321-22 of his report) on the reasoning provided by Lord Shawcross to the House of Commons of the United Kingdom in 1951:

> I think the true doctrine is that it is the duty of an Attorney-General, in deciding whether or not to authorize the prosecution, to acquaint himself with all the relevant facts, including, for instance, the effect which the prosecution, successful or unsuccessful as the case may be, would have upon public morale and order, and with any other considerations affecting public policy. In order so to inform himself, he may, although I do not think he is obliged to, consult with any of his colleagues in the Government; and indeed, as Lord Simon once said, he would in some cases be a fool if he did not. On the other hand, the assistance of his colleagues is confined to informing him of particular considerations, which might affect his own decision, and does not consist, and must not consist, in telling him what that decision ought to be. The responsibility for the eventual decision rests with the Attorney-General, and he is not to be put, and is not put, under pressure by his colleagues in the matter. Nor, of course, can the Attorney-General shift his responsibility for making the decision on to the shoulders of his colleagues. If political considerations which, in the broad sense that I have indicated, affect government in the abstract arise, it is the Attorney-General, applying his judicial mind, who has to be the sole judge of those considerations.

> • • •

> In deciding whether to prosecute, Lord Shawcross also stated: "there is only one consideration that is altogether excluded, and that is the repercussion of my decision upon my personal or my party's or the government's political fortunes; that is a consideration which never enters into account."

While Commissioner Dion was conducting his inquiry under the *Conflict of Interest Act*, Prime Minister Justin Trudeau asked former Attorney General of Canada Anne McLellan to assess the current structure in which the roles of the minister of justice and the attorney general of Canada are held by the same person, and to determine whether any changes should be made to this structure. As a result of her review, McLellan drew the following conclusions:

> It is clear to me that there is no system for managing prosecutorial decisions that absolutely protects against the possibility of partisan interference, while providing for public accountability.

> I do not believe that further structural change is required in Canada to protect prosecutorial independence and promote public confidence in the criminal justice system. Legislation, education, protocols, cultural norms, constitutional principles and public transparency all play a role. The *Director of Public Prosecutions Act* provides strong structural protections against political interference. The personal integrity of the Attorney General is also essential; indeed, it is probably the most important element in a system which protects the rule of law.

> The model of having the same person hold the Minister of Justice and Attorney General roles was deliberately chosen at Confederation, and for good reason. Our system benefits from giving one person responsibility for key elements of the justice system. Joinder of the roles creates important synergies. That person gains a perspective over the entire system which could not be achieved if the roles were divided; so too do the lawyers and policy experts who work together in the Department of Justice.

> Removing the Attorney General from Cabinet would also affect the credibility and quality of legal advice they provide. In my view, Cabinet colleagues are more likely to pay attention to the Attorney General's legal advice because they know that the Attorney General, as a member of Cabinet, understands the political context in which they are operating. That advice is also likely to be better informed, and therefore more helpful to Cabinet.

> I believe that any concerns about the joined roles can be addressed through a comprehensive protocol on ministerial consultations on the public interest; an education program for

ministers and others on the role of the Attorney General and related issues; a new oath of office for the Ministry of Justice and Attorney General of Canada which recognizes the unique role of the Attorney General; and changes to the *Department of Justice Act*, the federal prosecutors' manual, and *Open and Accountable Government*, the guide for Cabinet ministers on their roles and responsibilities.

(Anne McLellan, *Review of the Roles of the Minister of Justice and Attorney General of Canada* (2019), online (pdf): <https://pm.gc.ca/sites/pm/files/inline-files/Review%20of%20the%20 Roles%20of%20the%20Minister%20of%20Justice%20and%20Attorney%20General%20of%20 Canada_3.pdf>, at 1-2 (references omitted).)

G. MUNICIPALITIES AND OTHER ELECTED SUBORDINATE BODIES

The predominant model for independent administrative bodies is for the political executive to directly appoint or create a system of appointments for members of administrative bodies. However, in many cases it is desirable that service delivery account for local circumstances and local values. Consequently, there exist in Canada and elsewhere administrative bodies, such as municipalities and school boards, that provide for the direct election of the governing body. Despite the presence of elected officials, and a broad policy-making function, bodies such as municipalities are not a distinct level of government in the sense of being a constitutionally recognized level of government within Canada. Ultimately, like other independent administrative bodies, municipal powers are subject to the regulatory qualifications that superior levels of government place on them, including the radical restructuring or even elimination of municipalities. In *Citizens' Legal Challenge Inc v Ontario (AG)* (1997), 36 OR (3d) 733, 153 DLR (4th) 299 (CA), a decision by the Ontario government to amalgamate a number of municipalities into a single municipal government (the Toronto "megacity") was challenged on the basis that such a radical alteration required the consent of the affected local governments. In rejecting this argument, the Court was unequivocal about the subordinate status of municipal governments, holding in essence that municipalities, as creations of the province, may be altered by the province without constraint. More recently, in *Toronto (City) v Ontario (AG)*, 2018 ONCA 761, the Ontario Court of Appeal granted a stay of a lower court ruling invalidating Ontario legislation, enacted while a municipal election campaign was underway, that changed the number of wards in the city from 47 to 25. The lower court had ruled that the legislation infringed the freedom of expression, protected by s 2(b) of the Charter, of both municipal candidates and municipal electors. In entering the stay, the Court of Appeal ruled that there was a strong likelihood that the attorney general's appeal on the merits would be successful. The Court of Appeal observed that the lower court judge was understandably motivated by the fact that the legislation changed the rules in mid-campaign, which he perceived to be unfair to both the candidates and the voters. In the eyes of the Court of Appeal, however, the issue for the courts was not whether the legislation was unfair but whether it violated the Constitution, and the Court of Appeal concluded that there was a strong likelihood that the lower court erred in concluding that it did. When the appeal was heard on the merits, a majority of the Court of Appeal ruled that the City's challenge to the constitutional validity of the legislation could not succeed. Toronto (City) v Ontario (AG), 2019 ONCA 732. On March 27, 2020, the Supreme Court of Canada granted the City's application for leave to appeal.

Because municipalities are governed by elected officials and because they exercise broad plenary powers, municipalities are unlike most other forms of independent administrative bodies, where officials are appointed by senior levels of government. The legal significance of an administrative body with direct lines of democratic accountability was considered by the Supreme Court of Canada in *Shell Canada Products Ltd v Vancouver (City)*, a case concerning the legal authority of a municipality to refuse to do business with companies that had business ties to South Africa during the apartheid era.

Shell Canada Products Ltd v Vancouver (City)
[1994] 1 SCR 231

[This legal proceeding arose out of an application by Shell Canada Products Ltd to quash resolutions passed by Vancouver City Council that directed staff not to conduct business with Shell Canada as long as Shell continued to do business in South Africa on the basis, *inter alia*, that the resolutions were beyond the power of the municipality to make. The municipality argued that a provision stating that the "Council may provide for the good rule and government of the city" authorized the resolution. The majority, relying on a long-standing rule that municipal authority could only be exercised in relation to activities that fell within municipal purposes, held that the extraterritorial purpose of the resolutions was improper. In a dissenting judgment, McLachlin J (as she then was) considered the question of permissible municipal purposes in light of the democratic nature of municipal government.]

McLACHLIN J: ... Recent commentary suggests an emerging consensus that courts must respect the responsibility of elected municipal bodies to serve the people who elected them and exercise caution to avoid substituting their views of what is best for the citizens for those of municipal councils. Barring clear demonstration that a municipal decision was beyond its powers, courts should not so hold. In cases where powers are not expressly conferred but may be implied, courts must be prepared to adopt the "benevolent construction" which this Court referred to in *Greenbaum* [[1993] 1 SCR 674], and confer the powers by reasonable implication. Whatever rules of construction are applied, they must not be used to usurp the legitimate role of municipal bodies as community representatives.

Such an approach serves a number of purposes which the narrow interventionist approach does not. First, it adheres to the fundamental axiom that courts must accord proper respect to the democratic responsibilities of elected municipal officials and the rights of those who elect them. This is important to the continued healthy functioning of democracy at the municipal level. If municipalities are to be able to respond to the needs and wishes of their citizens, they must be given broad jurisdiction to make local decisions reflecting local values.

Second, a generous approach to municipal powers will aid the efficient functioning of municipal bodies and avoid the costs and uncertainty attendant on excessive litigation. Excessive judicial interference in municipal decision-making can have the unintended and unfortunate result of large amounts of public funds being expended by municipal councils in the attempt to defend the validity of their exercise of statutory powers. The object of judicial review of municipal powers should be to accord municipalities the autonomy to undertake their activities without judicial interference unless clearly warranted.

Thirdly, a generous approach to municipal powers is arguably more in keeping with the true nature of modern municipalities. As McDonald [Ann McDonald, "In the Public Interest: Judicial Review of Local Government" (1983) 9 Queen's LJ 62] asserts (at p. 100), the municipal corporation "has come a long way from its origins in a rural age of simple government demands." She and other commentators (see [Stanley M Makuch, *Canadian Municipal and Planning Law* (Toronto: Carswell, 1983) and Sue Arrowsmith, *Government Procurement and Judicial Review* (Toronto: Carswell, 1988)]) advocate that municipal councils should be free to define for themselves, as much as possible, the scope of their statutory authority. Excessive judicial interference in the decisions of elected municipal councils may, as this case illustrates, have the effect of confining modern municipalities in the straitjackets of tradition. This rationale for a restrained approach to judicial intervention in the decisions of municipal bodies is eloquently set out by McDonald (at pp. 100-101):

> Once elected ... the council is entrusted with responsibility for governing, not just in the interest of those who elected them, but in the interest of the community generally, that is, *in the public interest*. This is a fairly vague and controversial concept, however. It is a generalized judgment of what is best for individuals, *as a part of a community*. From the perspective of particular individuals and interest groups, the public interest may be conceived differently and, as amongst them, views of the public interest will inevitably conflict. A council making its decision on the public interest will identify and weigh a wide variety of competing considerations: the demands of various interested parties, the advice of its experts, data from its own research resources. And it will undoubtedly be influenced by the preferences expressed by the electorate. The decision is ultimately a matter of choice and what a council decides is necessarily its own collective perception of the public interest.
>
> The voters of a community give their elected council members the final judgment in this controversy. Whether the councillors are right or wrong in their judgment depends on the vantage point of the person making this assessment, but in any event, this is the decision they were elected to make. There may, in fact, be no right or wrong in the matter. Persons displeased with a council's decision have "a remedy at the polls." [Footnote omitted.]
>
> It is not the court's function to make these decisions—either directly or indirectly. Primary responsibility for deciding the welfare of the community belongs to the municipal corporation. If the courts take upon themselves the judgment of the rightness or wrongness of council's decisions in these matters, they, as a body having no connection with local inhabitants, usurp the choice which the inhabitants conferred, by democratic process, on the council. If the courts are to interfere in this process, they must have a positive justification for doing so and that justification must relate to their own peculiar nature and function. [Emphasis in original.]

• • •

The question is whether City Council's motives in this case fall outside the area of the City's legitimate concern. The *Vancouver Charter* [SBC 1953, c 55] empowers Council to "provide for the good rule and government of the city": s. 189. My colleague and I agree that this clause permits Vancouver City Council to enact measures for the benefit or welfare of the inhabitants of the City. We part company on what this phrase includes.

My colleague adopts a narrow view of the welfare of the inhabitants of the City. He asserts that the City's Resolutions effect a purpose "without any identifiable benefit to its inhabitants" (p 23 [p 280]) and speaks of "matters external to the interests of the citizens" (p. 21 [p 279]). He appears to define "municipal purposes" essentially in terms of provision of basic services to the inhabitants of the City.

I would cast the proper functions of a municipality in a larger mould. The term "welfare of the citizens," it seems to me, is capable of embracing not only their immediate needs, but also the psychological welfare of the citizens as members of a community who have an interest in expressing their identity as a community. Our language recognizes this: we speak of civic spirit, of city pride. This suggests that City Council may properly take measures related to fostering and maintaining this sense of community identity and pride. Among such measures may be found community expression of disapproval or approval of different types of conduct, wherever it is found. The right of free expression, one of the most fundamental values of our society, may be exercised individually or collectively. Are the citizens of a city to be prevented from expressing through their elected representatives their disapproval of conduct which they feel to be improper? Are they to be forced to do business with a firm whose conduct they see as objectionable, simply because the conduct occurs outside the territorial boundaries of the city? Can the desire of the citizens' elected representatives to express their views on such matters and to withdraw support for the conduct to which they object by refusing to do business with its perpetrators be said to be totally unrelated to the welfare and interests of the citizens of the city? To all these questions I would answer no.

• • •

As discussed earlier, scholars are critical of the frequency with which courts disguise an assessment for reasonableness in the cloak of a review for vires. On one view of my colleague's reasons, they do this very thing. Sopinka J correctly states that the reasonableness of the Resolutions is not in issue, only the power of the City to pass them (p. 15 [p 274]). Yet he goes on to hold that the Resolutions must fall because they are "based on matters external to the interests of the citizens of the municipality" (p. 21 [p 279]). But that is the very question at stake. What *is* external to the interests of the citizens? What conversely, is in their interests? The City councillors, after hearing both sides, took one view—a view which many other municipal councils have taken. My colleague takes another. In my view, it is the Council's judgment which should prevail. To repeat the words of Estey J in *Kuchma v. Tache (Rural Municipality)* [[1945] SCR 234] (at p. 243):

> Upon the question of public interest, courts have recognized that the municipal council, familiar with local conditions, is in the best position of all parties to determine what is or is not in the public interest. ...

In summary on the first issue, I am satisfied that the purposes of City Council in resolving not to do business with Shell were proper and fell within the powers of the City under the *Vancouver Charter.*

In the majority decision in *Shell v Vancouver,* Sopinka J was less willing to see the purposes of municipal government in such broad terms, preferring instead to see municipal purposes as having to relate more directly to matters within the boundaries of the local area. Whereas McLachlin J was inclined to see the municipalities as a distinct form of administrative decision-maker in light of its democratic structure, Sopinka J was more circumspect about deferring to democratic entities, noting (at para 95):

> The suggestion that the only remedy is at the polls is of no value to the minority, who would be left with no remedy, and Council could continue to enlarge its statutory powers as long as it was able to retain its majority support. The public policy in favour of restricting a municipality to its statutory powers exists as much for the minority as for the majority.

Of particular concern in this case was the open-ended nature of the authorizing provision relied on by the City of Vancouver in support of its action, which could be taken to confer an almost limitless authority if not checked by the courts. In a subsequent case, *114957 Canada Ltée (Spraytech, Société d'arrosage) v Hudson (Town),* 2001 SCC 40, [2001] 2 SCR 241, addressing municipal authority, LeBel J (at para 53) sought to draw a line between the kinds of popular concerns that could properly become the subject of municipal legislation:

> It appears to be sound legislative and administrative policy, under such [broadly worded] provisions, to grant local governments a residual authority to deal with the unforeseen or

changing circumstances, and to address emerging or changing issues concerning the welfare of the local community living within their territory. Nevertheless, such a provision cannot be construed as an open and unlimited grant of provincial powers. It is not enough that a particular issue has become a pressing concern in the opinion of a local community. This concern must relate to problems that engage the community as a local entity, not a member of the broader polity. It must be closely related to the immediate interests of the community within the territorial limits defined by the legislature in a matter where local governments may usefully intervene.

The *Spraytech* case also introduced the concept of "subsidiarity" into governance-related legal disputes. Subsidiarity is described by the Supreme Court of Canada as "the proposition that law-making and implementation are often best achieved at a level of government that is not only effective, but also closest to the citizens affected and thus most responsive to their needs, to local distinctiveness, and to population diversity" (para 3). In the *Spraytech* case, the principle was relied upon in support of an expansive approach to the interpretation of municipal powers. There is an implicit empirical assumption with the principle of subsidiarity that local governments are more democratically responsive, although such a claim seems hardly beyond contention, particularly in light of low voter turnout rates in municipal elections.

CHAPTER NINE

THE COURTS AND THE JUDICIARY

We turn now to a detailed discussion of the structure of the Canadian court system and the composition of the judiciary. Section I of this chapter provides an overview of the structure of the Canadian court system, including the constitutional foundation for the judiciary in Canada. Section II describes the process by which judges are appointed to the bench, with a special emphasis on the federal judiciary. Section III examines in detail the concept of judicial independence because it is the most important public law concept with regard to the judiciary. This section focuses on the security of tenure, financial independence, and administrative independence of Canada's judges.

I. STRUCTURE OF THE CANADIAN COURT SYSTEM

A. OVERVIEW OF THE CURRENT CANADIAN COURT SYSTEM

The Canadian court system is complicated because of Canada's constitutional foundations described in Section I.B. This section will help you understand how the courts are organized, and the next section will explain the constitutional basis for this organization.

Department of Justice Canada, Canada's Court System
(Ottawa: Department of Justice, 2017)

How Does Canada's Court System Work?

Courts in Canada help people resolve disputes fairly—whether they are between individuals, or between individuals and the state. At the same time, courts interpret and pronounce law, set standards, and decide questions that affect all aspects of Canadian society.

Canada's **judiciary** is one branch of our system of government, the others being the legislature and the executive. Whereas the judiciary resolves disputes according to law—including disputes about how legislative and executive powers are exercised—the legislature (Parliament) has the power to make, alter and repeal laws. The executive branch (in particular, the prime minister and ministers, the public service, as well as a variety of agencies, boards, and commissions) is responsible for administering and enforcing the laws.

The courts interpret and apply the Constitution, as well as legislation passed by both levels of government. They also develop and apply the common law.

Canada's system of courts is complex. Each province and territory has its own courts, as well as courts that have national jurisdiction. The Supreme Court of Canada presides over the entire system.

The courts' primary task is administering justice—that is, ensuring that disputes are settled and crimes are prosecuted fairly and in accordance with Canada's legal and constitutional structure. The provinces and territories are responsible for providing everything the courts under their jurisdiction need, from building and maintaining the courthouses, to providing staff and resources, such as interpreters, court reporters to prepare transcripts, sheriffs, and registry services, to paying provincial/territorial court judges. The federal government appoints and pays judges for the superior courts in each province, as well as judges at the federal level. It is also responsible for the administration of the Supreme Court of Canada and federally created courts.

Courts are not the only mechanism for settling differences between people. Less formal processes include alternative dispute resolution, private commercial arbitration, and appearing before administrative boards and tribunals. Even for issues that never get to court, court decisions influence people's choices and actions. They provide guidance on what the law is, and how people should conduct themselves to ensure they are in compliance with it.

In the sections that follow we explain the structure of the court system—how the courts are organized and how the various elements connect to one another. ...

How the Courts Are Organized

Each type of court has its own jurisdiction, which means that it has the authority to decide specific types of cases. Canada has four levels of court.

1. Provincial and territorial (lower) courts: These courts handle most cases that come into the system. They are established by provincial and territorial governments.

2. Provincial and territorial superior courts: These are courts of plenary, or complete, jurisdiction established under section 96 of the *Constitution Act, 1867*. They deal with more serious crimes and also hear appeals from provincial and territorial courts. The Federal Court is on the same level, but

is responsible for deciding civil matters assigned to it by statute, such as immigration and patents.

3. Provincial and territorial courts of appeal and the Federal Court of Appeal.
4. The Supreme Court of Canada, which is the final court of appeal for Canada.

Outline of Canada's Court System

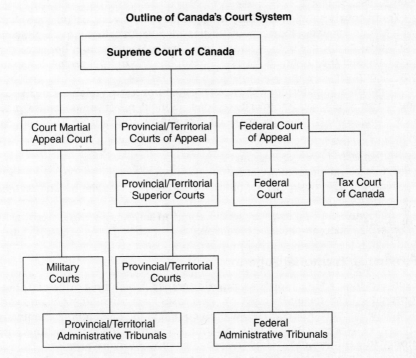

Provincial/Territorial Courts

Each province and territory has a provincial/territorial court and hears cases involving either federal or provincial/territorial laws.

In Nunavut, the Nunavut Court of Justice, which is Canada's only single-level trial court, combines the power of the superior trial court and the territorial court so that the same judge can hear all cases that arise in the territory.

Provincial/territorial courts deal with:

- most criminal offences, except the most serious ones;
- family law matters (e.g., child support, child protection, adoption, but not divorce);
- young persons from 12 to 17 years old in conflict with the law;
- traffic and bylaw violations;
- provincial/territorial regulatory offences;
- claims involving money, up to a certain amount (set by the province or territory in question);
- small claims (civil cases that resolve private disputes involving limited sums of money); and
- all preliminary inquiries (hearings to determine whether there is enough evidence to justify a full trial in serious criminal cases).

Some courts at this level are dedicated to particular types of offences or groups of offenders. One example is the Drug Treatment Court. The object of these courts is to address the needs of non-violent offenders who are charged with criminal offences that were motivated by their addiction. Those who qualify are offered judicial supervision and treatment for their addiction, with the help of community support services.

Youth courts handle cases for young people 12 to 17 years old who are charged with an offence under federal youth justice laws. Youth courts provide protections appropriate to the age of the accused, including protecting his or her privacy. Any court at either the provincial/territorial or superior court level can be designated a youth court.

All provinces and territories have established **Domestic Violence Courts** so that the justice system can improve its response to incidents of spousal abuse, provide better support to victims, and make offenders more accountable. These courts do this by

- decreasing court processing time;
- increasing prosecution rates;
- providing a focal point for programs and services for victims and offenders; and
- allowing police, Crown prosecutors, and, in some cases, the judiciary to specialize in domestic violence matters.

Provincial/Territorial Superior Courts

Each province and territory has **superior courts**, which are courts of "inherent jurisdiction." This means that they can hear cases in any area except when a statute or rule limits that authority. The superior courts try the most serious criminal and civil cases. These include divorce cases and cases that involve large amounts of money (the minimum is set by the province or territory in question). The jurisdiction of superior courts originally came from the first courts in England, whose authority over government actions was based on Magna Carta. Proceedings in superior courts are thus a continuation of a court process that dates right back to the beginnings of the common law system.

The superior courts also act as a court of first appeal for the provincial and territorial courts that the provinces and territories maintain. Although the provinces and territories administer superior courts, the federal government appoints and pays the judges.

Although there are permanent court houses and judicial centres in all of Canada's provinces and territories, Canada's population is scattered widely across huge expanses of land, and it may be difficult for individuals to travel to a court house to have their matter heard. In response, courts often travel "on circuit" to small or isolated areas.

For example, in Nunavut, most of the communities are small and isolated from Iqaluit, the capital, so the court travels to them. The circuit court includes a judge, a clerk, a court reporter, a prosecutor, and at least one defence attorney. Interpreters are hired in the communities when possible, or travel with the circuit court when necessary. The court holds regular sessions in Iqaluit and flies to about 85 percent of all 25 communities in Nunavut, as often as every six weeks or as seldom as every two years, depending on how often it's needed.

Family Courts

In most provinces and territories, the superior court has special divisions, such as the family division. Some superior courts have established specialized family courts to deal with specific family law matters, including divorce and property claims.

Several provinces (Manitoba, New Brunswick, Newfoundland and Labrador, Nova Scotia, Ontario, Prince Edward Island and Saskatchewan) use unified family courts. This allows a single court to deal with all aspects of family law, using specialized superior court judges and services. These courts encourage constructive, non-adversarial techniques to resolve issues, and provide access to support services through community organizations. These services typically include such programs as parent-education sessions, mediation, and counselling.

Provincial/Territorial Courts of Appeal

Each province and territory also has a **court of appeal**. These courts hear appeals from the decisions of the superior courts and the provincial/territorial courts. These can include commercial disputes, property disputes, negligence claims, family disputes, bankruptcies, and corporate reorganizations. Appeals are usually heard by a panel of three judges. The courts of appeal also hear constitutional questions that may be raised in appeals involving individuals, governments, or governmental agencies.

Courts and Other Bodies Under Federal Jurisdiction

The federal court system runs parallel to the provincial and territorial court systems and consists of the Federal Court and the Federal Court of Appeal. The judges of these courts (as well as the Tax Court of Canada, described below) are based in Ottawa, but travel across the country to hear cases. They deal with certain matters specified in federal statutes (laws), such as immigration and refugee law, navigation and shipping, intellectual property, and tax. They can also deal with matters of national defence, security, and international relations.

The Federal Court

The Federal Court is Canada's national trial court. It hears and decides federal legal disputes whose subject matter has been assigned to the Court by Parliament.
These disputes include

- claims against the Government of Canada;
- civil suits between private parties in federally-regulated areas; and
- reviews of the decisions of most federal tribunals.

The Federal Court's jurisdiction includes

- interprovincial and many federal-provincial disputes;
- immigration and refugee matters;
- intellectual property proceedings (e.g., copyright);
- citizenship appeals;
- *Competition Act* cases; and
- cases involving Crown corporations or departments of the Government of Canada.

The federal courts have the power to review decisions, orders, and other administrative actions of most federal boards, commissions, and tribunals. That means most federal government decisions can be challenged in a federal court. With some exceptions, those bodies may refer questions of law, jurisdiction, or practice to one of the federal courts at any stage of a proceeding.

In some areas of law, such as maritime law, the Federal Court shares jurisdiction with the provincial superior courts. It also has concurrent jurisdiction with respect to civil claims against the federal government.

The Federal Court of Appeal

The Federal Court of Appeal hears appeals from the Federal Court and the Tax Court of Canada, and judicial reviews of certain federal tribunals listed in the *Federal Courts Act*. Like provincial and territorial courts of appeal, its decisions can only be appealed to the Supreme Court of Canada. The Court hears most legal matters under federal jurisdiction or that involve the federal government.

It has three basic roles:

1. to ensure that federal law is applied consistently throughout Canada;
2. to conduct judicial reviews of specified federal decision makers, as listed in section 28 of the *Federal Courts Act*; and
3. to provide an avenue of appeal from decisions of the Federal Court and the Tax Court of Canada.

Specialized Federal Courts

The federal government has created specialized courts to deal more effectively with certain areas of the law. These include the Tax Court of Canada and the courts that serve the military justice system: the military courts and the Court Martial Appeal Court of Canada. These courts have been created by statute and can only decide matters that fall within the jurisdiction given to them by those statutes. The Tax Court thus deals with tax matters defined under the *Tax Court of Canada Act* and the Court Martial Appeal Court of Canada hears appeals from courts martial.

The Tax Court of Canada

The Tax Court of Canada is a superior court that determines cases and appeals about matters that arise under federal tax and revenue legislation. The Tax Court of Canada hears disputes between the federal government and taxpayers after the taxpayer has pursued all other avenues provided for by the *Income Tax Act*. The Tax Court is independent of the Canada Revenue Agency and all other government departments.

Military Courts

Military courts, or courts martial, are established under the *National Defence Act* to hear cases involving the Code of Service Discipline. The Code applies to all members of the Canadian Forces as well as civilians who accompany the Forces on active service. It lays out a system of disciplinary offences designed to further the good order and proper functioning of the Canadian Forces.

The Court Martial Appeal Court of Canada hears appeals from military courts. Judges in the Court Martial Appeal Court are selected from the federal courts and other superior courts throughout the country. Like other courts of appeal, a panel of three judges hears cases in the Court Martial Appeal Court.

The Supreme Court of Canada

The Supreme Court of Canada is the final court of appeal from all other Canadian courts. It has jurisdiction over disputes in all areas of the law. These include constitutional law, administrative law, criminal law, and civil law. The Court does not hold trials, but hears appeals from all other Canadian appeal courts.

The Court consists of a Chief Justice and eight other justices. Members of the Court are appointed by the federal government as new vacancies occur. Three judges traditionally come from Ontario, two from Western Canada, and one from the Atlantic provinces. In addition, the *Supreme Court Act* requires that at least three judges must come from Quebec.

The Supreme Court sits in Ottawa for three sessions a year—winter, spring, and fall. Each year the Supreme Court considers an average of between 500 to 600 applications for leave to appeal and hears 65 to 80 appeals.

What Kinds of Cases Does the Supreme Court of Canada Hear?

The Supreme Court of Canada only hears cases that it considers to be of public importance and to have national significance. That could mean a case that raises an important issue of law, or mixed law and fact, or if the matter is, for any other reason, significant enough to be considered by the country's highest court. In limited instances, there may also be an appeal as of right. Judgements of the Supreme Court are listed at <https://www.scc-csc.ca/home-accueil/index-eng.aspx>.

Before a case can reach the Supreme Court of Canada, it must have used up all available appeals at other levels of court. Even then, the court usually must grant permission or "leave" to appeal before it will hear the case. Leave applications are usually made in writing and reviewed by three members of the court. They then grant or deny the request without providing reasons for the decision.

The right to appeal is automatic in certain situations. For instance, no leave is required in criminal cases where a judge on the panel of a court of appeal has disagreed, or dissented, on how the law should be interpreted. It is also not required when a court of appeal has found someone guilty who had been acquitted at the original trial. That person automatically has the right to appeal to the Supreme Court.

The Supreme Court can also be asked by the Governor in Council to hear references. These are important questions of law, such as the constitutionality or interpretation of federal or provincial legislation, on which the Court is asked to give its opinion before an actual legal dispute arises. The federal government may ask the Court to consider questions on any important matter of law or fact, especially about how to interpret the Constitution. The Court may also be asked to interpret federal or provincial/territorial legislation or the powers of Parliament or the legislatures. Provincial and territorial courts of appeal may also be asked to hear references from their respective governments, which are then sometimes appealed to the Supreme Court of Canada.

Administrative Tribunals and Boards

Different kinds of administrative tribunals and boards deal with disputes over the interpretation and application of laws and regulations, such as entitlement to employment insurance or disability benefits, refugee claims, and human rights.

Administrative tribunals are less formal than courts and are not part of the court system. However, they play an essential role in resolving disputes in Canadian society. Decisions of administrative tribunals may be reviewed in court to ensure that tribunals act fairly and according to the law.

Alternative Approaches

There are other approaches that can allow people to settle disputes without having to go to court.

Alternative Dispute Resolution

Alternative Dispute Resolution (ADR) traditionally refers to the wide variety of methods used to resolve conflicts and disputes outside the courtroom. It includes both informal, consensual processes such as negotiation as well as formal rights-based processes such as litigation.

With ADR, people can usually settle their differences in ways that are more informal, less expensive, and often quicker than formal court proceedings. Some parties prefer confidentiality and to have greater control over the selection of individuals who will decide their dispute and the rules that will govern the proceedings. The main ADR processes include:

- **Mediation:** An independent third party is brought in to help the parties negotiate an agreement.
- **Arbitration:** The parties agree to refer the dispute to a third party for judgment.
- **Negotiation:** The parties get together and sort out a problem between themselves.

The parties may also decide to seek the opinion of an expert chosen by both of them.

Agreements reached through mediation and negotiation are consensual, so they generally cannot be appealed. In the case of arbitration, there is a limited ability to appeal that depends on the terms of the arbitration agreement and the applicable legislation.

As with administrative tribunals, the courts and ADR work together. The courts themselves often make use of ADR. For example, some provinces now insist on mediation as part of the litigation process. However, the court system remains the appropriate forum for trying serious or violent crimes, and is also an option when parties to a dispute reject mediation or arbitration.

Sentencing Circles

In sentencing circles, which can be part of the court process but are not separate courts in and of themselves, the court invites interested members of the community to join the judge, prosecutor, defence counsel, police, social service providers, and community elders—along with the offender, the victim, and their families and supporters—to meet in a circle format to discuss:

- the offence;
- the factors that might have contributed to it;
- sentencing options; and
- ways of reintegrating the offender into the community.

Sentencing circles can be a valuable way of getting input and advice from the community to help the judge set an appropriate and effective sentence. Often the circle will suggest a restorative community sentence involving some form of restitution to the victim, community service, and treatment or counselling, and/or a period of custody. It is important to note, however, that the judge is not bound to accept the circle's recommendations.

Sentencing circles have been used in much of the country, mostly at the provincial/territorial court level, in minor criminal cases involving Aboriginal offenders and their victims. Various Supreme Court of Canada decisions have interpreted changes to the *Criminal Code* that instructed courts to consider alternative sentences for all offenders, and to pay particular attention to the circumstances of Aboriginal offenders. The Supreme Court found that sentencing judges must examine the unique factors which may have played a part in bringing a particular Aboriginal offender before the courts, and the types of available sanctions and sentencing procedures (including sentencing circles) which may be appropriate in light of the offender's Aboriginal heritage or identity.

Additional Resources on the Courts

Each court has its own website that contains a wealth of information about the structure and operation of the court as well as biographies of the judges of the courts. Many also have social media accounts. A simple web search of the name of the specific court will produce the link to its homepage. Here are the links to the federally established courts:

- Supreme Court of Canada: <https://www.scc-csc.ca>
- Federal Court of Appeal: <http://www.fca-caf.gc.ca>
- Federal Court of Canada: <http://www.fct-cf.gc.ca>
- Tax Court of Canada: <http://www.tcc-cci.gc.ca>
- Court Martial Appeal Court: <http://www.cmac-cacm.ca>

The Courts Administration Service provides support to the federal courts and is responsible for, among other things, ensuring public access to the courts and their records. Its website is <http://www.cas-satj.gc.ca>.

B. CONSTITUTIONAL FRAMEWORK OF THE JUDICIARY

The starting point in understanding the Canadian court system is the *Constitution Act, 1867* (UK), 30 & 31 Vict, c 3, reprinted in RSC 1985, Appendix II, No 5. As we have noted throughout this book, this instrument creates the basic institutions of the Canadian government and divides power between the federal and provincial levels of government. In relation to the judiciary, it crafts a court system that straddles the federal–provincial division of powers. To this end, s 92(14) of the 1867 Act gives exclusive power to the provincial legislatures with respect to

> [t]he Administration of Justice in the Province, including the Constitution, Maintenance, and Organization of Provincial Courts, both of Civil and of Criminal Jurisdiction, and including Procedure in Civil Matters in those Courts.

And yet s 96 provides that "[t]he Governor General shall appoint the Judges of the Superior, District, and County Courts in each Province ... ." As noted in Chapter 5, the generic name for these s 96 courts is "superior courts" or, more correctly, "provincial superior courts." In addition to being responsible for appointing the judges in these superior courts, the federal government is also responsible for paying their salaries. Section 100 reads: "The Salaries, Allowances, and Pensions of the Judges of the Superior, District, and County Courts ... shall be fixed and provided by the Parliament of Canada."

All told, these provisions mean that the provincial governments create s 96 courts, but it is the federal government that appoints the judges to these "superior" courts and pays their salaries. This peculiar arrangement—courts created by the provinces and judges appointed by the federal government—reflects efforts by the framers of the 1867 Act to maintain federal control over a key source of patronage. See the discussion in Martin Friedland, *A Place*

Apart: Judicial Independence and Accountability in Canada (Ottawa: Canadian Judicial Council, 1995) at 234.

The provincial superior courts are not the only courts of the land. Under the authority given in s 101 of the *Constitution Act, 1867*, the federal government has created the Supreme Court as the "general court of appeal for Canada." It also created the Federal Court, the Federal Court of Appeal, and the Tax Court of Canada. Section 101 reads:

> The Parliament of Canada may, notwithstanding anything in this Act, from Time to Time provide for the Constitution, Maintenance, and Organization of a General Court of Appeal for Canada, and for the Establishment of any additional Courts for the better Administration of the Laws of Canada.

Each of these s 101 courts is created by federal statute. Thus, the Supreme Court is created by the *Supreme Court Act*, RSC 1985, c S-26, the Federal Courts by the *Federal Courts Act*, RSC 1985, c F-7, and the Tax Court by the *Tax Court of Canada Act*, RSC 1985, c T-2. However, in *Reference re Supreme Court Act, ss 5 and 6*, 2014 SCC 21, [2014] 1 SCR 433, the Supreme Court of Canada held that the Constitution now "entrenches" the essential qualities of the Supreme Court; Parliament must now "maintain—and protect—the essence of what enables the Supreme Court to perform its current role." The Supreme Court therefore now has constitutional status.

The provinces, meanwhile, appoint and pay the salaries of the judges of the "provincial" courts—that is, courts that are not superior courts that provinces may choose to create from time to time. These courts have different names in different provinces; in Nova Scotia, New Brunswick, Prince Edward Island, Newfoundland and Labrador, Manitoba, Saskatchewan, Alberta, and British Columbia, these courts are named the "Provincial Court" of their respective province. However, in Ontario they are known as the Ontario Court of Justice and in Quebec as the Court of Quebec.

An obvious question is this: in what circumstances may the provinces create these "provincial" courts that are not s 96 courts? If provinces were free to create non-s 96 courts readily, over time, one might expect that superior courts would disappear, and along with them, the federal judicial selection process. As we have suggested on several occasions before, the Supreme Court of Canada has repeatedly guarded against this possibility, employing s 96 to limit provincial (and now federal) powers to strip jurisdiction from the superior courts. Consider the concerns voiced by the Supreme Court in *Re Residential Tenancies Act*, [1981] 1 SCR 714:

> As Professor Hogg has noted in his work on *Constitutional Law of Canada* (1977), p. 129, there is no general "separation of powers" in the *British North America Act, 1867*. Our Constitution does not separate the legislative, executive, and judicial functions and insist that each branch of government exercise only its own function. Thus it is clear that the Legislature of Ontario may confer non-judicial functions on the courts of Ontario and, subject to s. 96 of the *BNA Act*, which lies at the heart of the present appeal, confer judicial functions on a body which is not a court.
>
> Under s. 92(14) of the *BNA Act* the provincial legislatures have the legislative power in relation to the administration of justice in the province. This is a wide power but subject to subtraction of ss. 96 to 100 in favour of the federal authority. Under s. 96 the Governor General has the sole power to appoint the judges of the Superior, District and County Courts in each province. Under s. 97 the judges who are to be appointed to the Superior, District and County Courts are to be selected from the respective bars of each province. Under s. 100 the Parliament of Canada is obliged to fix and provide for their salaries. Section 92(14) and ss. 96 to 100 represent one of the important compromises of the Fathers of Confederation. It is plain that what was sought to be achieved through this compromise, and the intended effect of s. 96, would be destroyed if a province could pass legislation creating a tribunal, appoint members thereto, and then confer on the tribunal the jurisdiction of the superior courts. What was conceived as a strong constitutional base for national unity,

through a unitary judicial system, would be gravely undermined. Section 96 has thus come to be regarded as limiting provincial competence to make appointments to a tribunal exercising s. 96 judicial powers and therefore as implicitly limiting provincial competence to endow a provincial tribunal with such powers.

Consider also this passage from *Ref re Remuneration of Judges of the Prov Court of PEI*, [1997] 3 SCR 3 at para 88 [*Provincial Judges Reference*]:

> Section 96 seems to do no more than confer the power to appoint judges of the superior, district, and county courts. It is a staffing provision, and is once again a subtraction from the power of the provinces under s. 92(14). However, through a process of judicial interpretation, s. 96 has come to guarantee the core jurisdiction of the courts which come within the scope of that provision. In the past, this development has often been expressed as a logical inference from the express terms of s. 96. Assuming that the goal of s. 96 was the creation of "a unitary judicial system," that goal would have been undermined "if a province could pass legislation creating a tribunal, appoint members thereto, and then confer on the tribunal the jurisdiction of the superior courts": *Re Residential Tenancies Act, 1979*, [1981] 1 SCR 714, at p. 728. However, as I recently confirmed, s. 96 restricts not only the legislative competence of provincial legislatures, but of Parliament as well: *MacMillan Bloedel*, [*infra*]. The rationale for the provision has also shifted, away from the protection of national unity, to the maintenance of the rule of law through the protection of the judicial role.

In *Re Residential Tenancies Act*, the issue there was whether a province was encroaching on the federal government's s 96 power to appoint judges by creating its own quasi-judicial body to adjudicate in an area of jurisdiction that belongs to the superior courts. In response, the Supreme Court established a three-part test for determining whether the provincial grant of power is valid. The first part requires a consideration of whether the powers exercised by the impugned provincial tribunal conformed to those that were under the "exclusive jurisdiction" of a s 96 court at the time of Confederation. Consequently, powers shared with inferior courts at Confederation fall outside the area addressed in this first question and can validly be exercised by a provincial tribunal.

If the powers were found to fall under the exclusive jurisdiction of a s 96 court at Confederation, one must ask whether the power in question is to be exercised in a judicial manner—that is, do the tribunal's proceedings concern a *lis* (a dispute) that is to be determined on solely legal, as opposed to policy, grounds?

Finally, the third part of the test requires a consideration of whether the "institutional setting" itself is fundamentally judicial. Here the inquiry looks at whether the tribunal is ancillary to a broader administrative scheme. Only where a tribunal is found not to be ancillary to an administrative scheme will the tribunal's authority be found to be unconstitutional.

Cases that have modified the test are *McEvoy v New Brunswick (AG)*, [1983] 1 SCR 704; *Sobeys Stores Ltd v Yeomans and Labour Standards Tribunal (NS)*, [1989] 1 SCR 238; *Reference re Young Offenders Act (PEI)*, [1991] 1 SCR 252; and *MacMillan Bloedel Ltd v Simpson*, [1995] 4 SCR 725. These cases establish that the superior courts are a fundamental institution protected by our Constitution through the interpretation of s 96. The provinces cannot enact legislation to encroach on their core jurisdiction, nor may the federal Parliament.

II. JUDICIAL APPOINTMENTS

Given that courts play such a fundamental role in preserving our constitutional order, the natural question this observation raises is: how are people selected to be judges? The manner in which judges are chosen has been an issue of some controversy, especially at the federal level. In this section, we look at the judicial selection process.

A. FEDERAL JUDICIAL APPOINTMENT PROCESS

The process by which the federal government appoints superior court judges varies. Section 96 courts, Federal Court, and Tax Court judges are appointed by the governor in council (effectively, the Cabinet) usually following review of candidates by an advisory committee. Until 2006, no such advisory committees existed for Supreme Court of Canada appointments. Instead, Supreme Court justices had traditionally simply been appointed by the governor in council on the recommendation of the prime minister. As discussed below, after 2006 there was an "ad hoc" process for appointment of Supreme Court justices. By 2015, this process seemed to have collapsed, but it was revived by the Trudeau government in 2016 for its first appointment to the Supreme Court and has continued through 2020.

1. Non–Supreme Court of Canada Appointments

a. Overview

The Office of the Commissioner for Federal Judicial Affairs oversees the federal judicial appointment process for s 96 courts, the Federal Courts, and the Tax Court. Information about the details of the process are available in on the Commissioner's website at <https://www.fja.gc.ca/appointments-nominations/guideCandidates-eng.html>. In order to be eligible for appointment, a candidate must have at least ten years' experience as a lawyer or be a provincial or territorial judge. Candidates complete a very detailed questionnaire, which was added in 2016; list references; and complete a background check authorization form. The advisory committee speaks with the references but does not interview any candidates. Each committee consists of seven members representing the bench, the bar, and the general public; and one ex-officio non-voting member being either the Commissioner for Federal Judicial Affairs Canada, the Executive Director, Judicial Appointments, or their designate. The advisory committees assess each candidate as "highly recommended," "recommended," or "unable to recommend" for appointment. The committees do not rank candidates or create a shortlist for any appointment. Their assessments are forwarded to the minister of justice, who exercises complete discretion in choosing which candidates to recommend to the governor in council for judicial appointment. Statistics on the number of applicants, gender, diversity, language abilities, and the assessment of candidates are available on the Commissioner's website. For example, in 2018-19, the Commissioner received 320 applications. It assessed 182 candidates and evaluated 41 as highly recommended (22.5 percent); 45 as recommended (24.7 percent); and 96 as unable to recommend (52.7 percent) (Office of the Commissioner for Federal Judicial Affairs Canada, "Statistics regarding Judicial Applicants and Appointees, October 28, 2018-October 28, 2019," online: *Government of Canada* <https://www.fja.gc.ca/appointments-nominations/StatisticsCandidate-StatistiquesCandidat-2019-eng.html>.)

Ultimately, appointments must be made by the governor in council as required by s 96 of the *Constitution Act, 1867* or the statutes governing the s 101 courts. The minister of justice makes the recommendation to Cabinet for appointment of a judge. Historically, political patronage played a prominent role in Canadian judicial appointments. The system described above is presented to the public as placing merit and objectivity above repaying political favours. But the government retains a broad discretion in making appointments, and skepticism and criticism persist.

b. Criticisms of the Non-Supreme Court Federal Appointment Process

It was not until the 1960s that any process at all was established to assist the minister of justice in deciding on what recommendations to make to the Cabinet. A variety of changes have been made to the "advisory system" over the years. In 1994, Justice Minister Allan Rock committed to appointing only persons who received a "recommended" or "highly recommended" assessment from the evaluating committee. Such a commitment is not legally binding but could be embarrassing to ignore. In 2007, the Conservative government of Prime Minister Stephen Harper changed this classification process to simply "recommended" and "unable to recommend." It also added a law enforcement representative to the advisory committee. In 2016, the new Liberal government of Prime Minister Justin Trudeau restored the previous system of "highly recommended," "recommended," and "unable to recommend."

There is no requirement in law for the government to follow the recommendations of any advisory committee. (And an argument could be made that an attempt to impose such a legal requirement would be prohibited by s 96, at least for provincial superior court judges.) The federal appointment process is established as a matter of "policy" rather than law. The federal government can change this process and it did so in 2007 when it changed the classification scheme described above and added a member of the law enforcement community to each advisory committee.

There have been many criticisms of this appointment process. One long-running criticism is that the advisory committees' recommendations leave too wide a range of candidates from which the minister selects appointees. Regardless of which party has been in power federally, there have always been complaints that partisan considerations influence the minister's choice of judges. Consider this newspaper report from 2005 (spanning the years that the Liberals were in government in Ottawa):

> More than 60 per cent of the 93 lawyers who received federal judicial appointments in Ontario, Alberta and Saskatchewan since 2000 donated exclusively to the [governing] Liberal party in the three to five years before securing their $220,000-per-annum posts.
>
> Just a handful donated exclusively to the Conservatives or New Democrats during the same period, according to a CanWest News Service analysis of the appointments.
>
> Individual annual donations tended to be small, ranging from $100 to a few thousand dollars, an examination of Elections Canada political donation records reveals as the Gomery inquiry considers allegations that the Liberals handed out federal judgeships as rewards for party loyalists in Quebec.

(Cristin Schmitz, with files from Lisa Tuominen, Peter O'Neil & Graeme Hamilton, "Federal Judges Often Liberal Donors, Survey Finds," *Ottawa Citizen* (6 May 2005) A5.)

A 2010 study by Postmedia News and the *Ottawa Citizen* revealed that the Harper government appointed dozens of judges who donated to the Conservative Party prior to their appointments. Professor Jacob Ziegel's research (referenced below) also showed that a majority of judges appointed as chief justices had Conservative links prior to being appointed to the bench.

Calls for changes to the process have been made by various bar associations, independent public policy organizations, and legal scholars. In a report on the Federal Judicial Appointment Process (October 2005), the Canadian Bar Association states: "Some modifications would strengthen the process to ensure that it is open and transparent, and results in judicial appointments based solely on merit and which are ultimately representative of the diversity of Canadian society."

More recent criticisms have focused on the lack of diversity in judicial appointments. See Rosemary Cairns Way, "Deliberate Disregard: Judicial Appointments Under the Harper Government" (2014) 67 SCLR (2nd) 43, Ottawa Faculty of Law Working Paper No 2014-08, online: *Social Science Research Network* <http://ssrn.com/abstract=2456792>. Statistics relating to the diversity of applicants and appointees are available on the Commissioner's website: see Office of the Commissioner for Federal Judicial Affairs Canada, "Statistics Regarding Judicial Applicants and Appointees, October 28, 2018-October 28, 2019," online: *Government of Canada* <https://www.fja.gc.ca/appointments-nominations/StatisticsCandidate-Statistiques-Candidat-2019-eng.html>.

Other models for appointment are discussed in the Section II.C, "A Range of Models."

2. Supreme Court Appointments

a. Overview of the Issues

The appointment processes described above do not apply to the Supreme Court of Canada. As a direct consequence, calls for changes to the federal appointment process have been especially persistent in relation to appointments to the Supreme Court. This relates to the great influence that the court's decisions may have on public policy, especially in the post-Charter era. It is argued that because the Supreme Court is, in effect, "legislating," it should be more account-able to the public through the appointment process. Some authors have argued that the Court should be "democratized" by requiring public scrutiny of potential appointees. This might include the questioning of potential appointees by a parliamentary committee. Consider the views of Professor Ted Morton, one the strongest critics of the traditional appointment process:

> [W]hen a national court of appeal is given the function of constitutional review, of supervis-ing the laws passed by Parliament, it is no longer simply enforcing laws; it is also making law. In a 21st century democracy, law-making institutions are expected to be accountable and representative, not independent. ...
>
> As for warnings that the public parliamentary hearings would politicize the court, it's a little late in the day for that kind of political prudery. There is already intense behind-the-scenes lobbying for Supreme Court appointments. ...
>
> The current system, rather than preventing the politicization of the appointment process, as its defenders would have us believe, simply drives the politics underground, beyond pub-lic knowledge and public scrutiny. ...
>
> The Constitution belongs to all Canadians. You, the members of Parliament, represent all the Canadian people in all their diversity. You would be well within your democratic man-date and the tradition of parliamentary democracy to adopt reforms that make the Supreme Court, in its Constitution, reflect your own diversity. There is no reason to continue with a system in which a party that receives only 40% of the votes makes 100% of the appointments to our country's highest court.

(Submissions, Standing Committee on Justice, Human Rights, Public Safety and Emergency Preparedness, *Evidence* (1 April 2004).)

Others have argued that the concept of "democratization" is misplaced in relation to the judiciary. Judges should not be "accountable" to any constituency but must be free to decide each case in accordance with their view of the law and their own conscience. While judges may have predilections, their role requires that they allow any personal views to be overcome by the requirements of the particular case they are deciding. Because the vast majority of Supreme Court appointments are made from the appellate courts, appointees already have a "track record." The public has easy access to information on how they have decided cases, how well they write, and how productive they have been.

Further, US-style confirmation hearings have been criticized as political theatre. A critique by Professor Edward Ratushny describes some of their worst features:

> It is obvious that the confirmation requirement of the US Constitution was intended to impose a legislative restraint on the President's power of appointment. It is also obvious that the confirmation process has evolved into a highly politicized exercise. Some hearings have degenerated into grossly political spectacles that have little to do with the professional qualifications of the nominees or their ability to serve as judges.

(Edward Ratushny, "Confirmation Hearings for Supreme Court of Canada Appointments: Not a Good Idea!" in Pierre Thibault et al, eds, *Essays in Honour of Gérald-A Beaudoin: The Chal-lenges of Constitutionalism* (Cowansville, Que: Yvon Blais, 2002) at 411.)

For reasons like these, the Canadian Bar Association, for one, is strongly opposed to a US-style confirmation hearing process:

> [As the CBA has argued in the past,] public confirmation hearings similar to the US by a Parliamentary Committee risked politicizing the process and could deter prospective judges from putting their names forward. A US-type confirmatory process seeks to predetermine how a prospective judge would decide cases. With the advent of the *Charter* and the increase in judicial consideration of socio-political issues, there were increased concerns that political influence could impact on the appointment of judges.
>
> The CBA is strongly opposed to any system which would expose judges to Parliamentary criticism of their judgments, or cross-examination on their beliefs or preferences or judicial opinions, or any measure which would give to Canadians the mistaken impression that the judicial branch answers to the legislative branch.

(Canadian Bar Association, *Supreme Court Appointments Process* (March 2004) at 8.)

In response, supporters of a form of public hearings for nominees in Canada take the view that some of the most controversial hearings in the United States were "aberrations" rather than the norm and that, in any event, we should be able to adopt the concept without all of its worst features. Consider the views of Professor Jacob Ziegel:

> The horror stories the critics have in mind [in relation to the US system] no doubt are the confirmation hearings of Robert H. Bork and Clarence Thomas before the US Senate. However, they overlook the fact that public questioning of candidates is a relatively recent innovation in proceedings by the Senate Judiciary Committee and that there were exceptional features about the Bork and Thomas cases. The more recent nominees that have appeared before the Judiciary Committee have been approved without difficulty and they have not complained about unfair treatment. The nominees have reserved the right not to answer questions concerning their position on future cases that could come before the Supreme Court, and that right is generally conceded. If it was deemed appropriate or necessary in the Canadian context, rules could also be adopted to delimit the scope of a nominee's examination before the parliamentary committee.

(Jacob Ziegel, "Merit Selection and Democratization of Appointments to the Supreme Court of Canada" (June 1999) 5:2 Choices 3 at 10 [Institute for Research on Public Policy].)

In many ways, the cat is out of the bag now because public hearings for Supreme Court nominees—judges who have been named to the Supreme Court by the prime minister but not formally appointed—were held in 2006, 2011, 2012, 2013, 2016, 2017, and 2019 (for the appointments of Rothstein J, Karakatsanis J, Moldaver J, Wagner J, the voided appointment of Nadon J, and the appointments of Rowe J, Martin J, and Kasirer J). After the failed appointment of Nadon J, however, the government reverted to a more insular, closed-door process without any public hearing at all. In 2014 and 2015, Prime Minister Stephen Harper appointed Gascon J, Côté J, and Brown J without any parliamentary involvement and minimal, if any, public backlash. However, after Liberal leader Justin Trudeau was elected in 2015, he reinstated the previous public hearings and made additional changes to the process, which are described here: Office of the Federal Judicial Affairs Canada, "Supreme Court Appointment Process-2019 (Appointment of the Honourable Nicholas Kasirer)," online: *Government of Canada* <https://www.fja.gc.ca/scc-csc/2019/index-eng.html>. The Supreme Court appointment process is likely to continue to be in the spotlight in the coming years due to the scheduled retirements of Justice Rosalie Abella in 2021 and Justice Michael Moldaver in 2022.

The article reproduced below provides a more detailed description of the trials and tribulations of Supreme Court appointment processes between 2004 and 2014.

b. A Short History of the Supreme Court Appointment Process, 2004-2014

Adam M Dodek, "Reforming the Supreme Court Appointment Process, 2004-2014: A 10-Year Democratic Audit"
(2014) 67 SCLR (2nd) 111 (footnotes omitted)

The ten year period between 2004 and the end of 2013 produced more changes to the appointment process for Supreme Court judges than any period since the Court was created in 1875. Reform to the Supreme Court appointment process began when Paul Martin became Prime Minister in December 2002. ... Martin had made reform of the Supreme Court appointment process part of his Democratic Action Plan, both as a candidate to succeed Jean Chrétien as the leader of the Liberal Party in 2002 and then as Prime Minister in 2003. The changes were first implemented with the surprise announcements by Justices Frank Iacobucci and Louise Arbour in the spring of 2004 that they both intended to step down from the court at the end of June.

Prior to 2004, the appointment process was closed, secretive and largely unknown and unknowable to the vast majority of Canadians. More was known about the process for electing a new Pope than about the process for selecting a new Supreme Court justice. While vacancies were publicly known—through the public announcement of a justice's retirement or, cases like Justice Sopinka, by a sudden death—no information was publicly available about the selection process. The lack of transparency caused some to believe that the process was partisan; understandably since lack of information will lead to speculation and speculation about politics naturally leads to pondering about partisanship and patronage. Jacob Ziegel rightly described the process as one "shrouded in vagueness, and unsubstantiated rumour and gossip."

In March 2004, Minister of Justice Irwin Cotler appeared before the House of Commons Standing Committee on Justice and Human Rights examining the Supreme Court appointment process and lifted the shroud that hid the process from public view for so long. Minister Cotler's testimony was both historic and illuminating in shining significant light on the process. In his testimony, Cotler explained that ...

> ... what I would like to do now, in the interests of both transparency and accountability, is to describe to you the consultative process or protocol of consultation that is being used to select members of the Supreme Court. I cannot claim, nor would I, that this consultative process or protocol has always been followed in every particular. I can only undertake to follow it as the protocol by which I will be governed as Minister of Justice. I might add that this is the first time that this protocol or appointments protocol is being released, which I would say is yet another expression of the beneficiary of this parliamentary review.
>
> The first step taken in this appointments process is the identification of prospective candidates. As you are aware, candidates come from the region where the vacancy originated—be it the Atlantic, Ontario, Quebec, the Prairies and the North, and British Columbia regions. This is a matter of convention, except for Quebec, where the Supreme Court Act establishes a requirement that three of the justices must come from Quebec.
>
> The candidates are drawn from judges of the courts of jurisdiction in the region, particularly the courts of appeal, as well as from senior members of the bar

and leading academics in the region. Sometimes, names may be first identified through previous consultations concerning other judicial appointments.

In particular, Mr. Chairman, the identification and assessment of potential candidates is based on a broad range of consultations with various individuals. As Minister of Justice, I consult with the following: the Chief Justice of Canada and perhaps other members of the Supreme Court of Canada, the chief justices of the courts of the relevant region, the attorneys general of the relevant region, at least one senior member of the Canadian Bar Association, and at least one senior member of the law society of the relevant region.

I may also consider input from other interested persons, such as academics and organizations who wish to recommend a candidate for consideration. Anyone is free to recommend candidates, and indeed, some will choose to do so by way of writing to the Minister of Justice, for example.

The second step is assessment of the potential candidates. Here, the predominant consideration is merit. In consultation with the Prime Minister, I use the following criteria, divided into three main categories: professional capacity, personal characteristics, and diversity.

Let me begin with professional capacity. Under the heading of professional capacity are the following considerations, and I will just cite them: highest level of proficiency in the law, superior intellectual ability and analytical and written skills; proven ability to listen and to maintain an open mind while hearing all sides of the argument; decisiveness and soundness of judgment; capacity to manage and share consistently heavy workload in a collaborative context; capacity to manage stress and the pressures of the isolation of the judicial role; strong cooperative interpersonal skills; awareness of social context; bilingual capacity; and specific expertise required for the Supreme Court. Expertise can be identified by the court itself or by others.

As I mentioned, Mr. Chairman, this goes to what might be called the professional capacity. This is the comprehensive set of criteria here. Not every candidate must have each of these criteria. This is the composite set of criteria through which evaluation takes place.

[TRANSLATION] Under the rubric of personal qualities, the following factors are considered: impeccable personal and professional ethics, honesty, integrity and forthrightness; respect and regard for others, patience, courtesy, tact, humility, impartiality and tolerance; personal sense of responsibility, common sense, punctuality and reliability.

The diversity criterion concerns the extent to which the court's composition adequately reflects the diversity of Canadian society.

[ENGLISH] Mr. Chairman, these are the criteria.

In reviewing the candidates, I may also consider jurisprudential profiles prepared by the Department of Justice. These are intended to provide information about the volume of cases written, areas of expertise, the outcome of appeals of the cases, and the degree to which they have been followed in the lower courts.

After the above assessments and consultations, as I've described, are completed, I discuss the candidates with the Prime Minister. There may also have been previous exchanges with the Prime Minister. Indeed, I may be involved in a consultation more than once with a range of persons with whom I've indicated that I engaged in consultations. A preferred candidate is then chosen. The Prime Minister, in turn, recommends a candidate to cabinet and the appointment proceeds by way of an order in council appointment, as per the Constitution.

This concludes the description of the current protocol or appointment process, which I'm sharing with you.

Cotler explained "the old process" at the same time as work was underway within government to reform it and create a new process for appointing Supreme Court judges.

Cotler appeared before the House of Commons Standing Committee on Justice, Human Rights, Public Safety and Emergency Preparedness ("Justice Committee") because earlier that month Prime Minister Paul Martin's Minister of Democratic Reform, the Honourable Jacques Saada, asked that committee for "recommendations on how best to implement prior review of Supreme Court of Canada Justices." The Justice Committee also heard testimony from retired Supreme Court justice L'Heureux-Dubé and from academics. It produced a report that recommended that as an interim process the Minister of Justice appear before the committee to explain both the process followed for filling the vacancies and the qualification of the two nominees. The committee report further recommended a more permanent process involving the creation of an advisory committee composed of MPs from each official party, representation from the provinces, members of the judiciary, the legal profession and lay members which would provide the Minister of Justice with a shortlist of candidates for appointment. Again, the Minister of Justice would appear before the committee to explain both the process and the reasons for appointee's qualifications. Each of the Conservative Party, Bloc Quebecois and NDP filed dissenting opinions to the effect that the recommendations did not go far enough in various respect.

Initially, Prime Minister Martin announced that he intended to give MPs a role in screening the nominees that he selected for the Supreme Court. However, with a federal election intervening and pressure on the government to have the vacancies filled by the end of the summer, the federal government backtracked from its reform plans and put in place an interim process as recommended by the Justice Committee whereby the Prime Minister would select the nominees and the Minister of Justice would appeared before a committee of MPs.

Thus, in August 2004, Minister of Justice Irwin Cotler appeared before an interim Ad Hoc Committee on the Appointment of Supreme Court Judges to explain both the process that led to the Prime Minister's selection of Justices Abella and Charron as well as the basis for selecting them. The committee was composed of seven MPs plus a representative of the Canadian Judicial Council and the Law Society of Upper Canada. The panel questioned Minister Cotler and prepared a report, with dissenting opinions expressed about the process, not the nominees. The Prime Minister then formally appointed Justices Abella and Charron to the Supreme Court.

In 2005, Cotler introduced a "permanent reform" process consisting of four stages. In the first stage, the Minister was to conduct the same sort of consultations and review as in the past with a view to creating a "long-list" of five to eight candidates. In the second stage, an Advisory Committee assesses the candidates and produces a confidential short list of three names "along with a commentary of the strengths and weaknesses of each candidate" to the Minister. The Committee was also to provide the Minister with the complete record of consultations and other material upon which it relied. The Minister could request the Committee to undertake further consultations if the Minister felt they were incomplete. In the third stage, the Prime Minister, with the advice of the Minister of Justice, would select and appoint a candidate from the shortlist. In the fourth stage, the Minister of Justice would appear before a committee to explain both the process and the selection.

The Liberals had the opportunity to put their plan into action when Justice Major announced his retirement in August 2005, effective Christmas Day later that year. Minister of Justice Irwin Cotler consulted with the persons previously identified and created a list of five to eight candidates which he sent to the Advisory Committee that he created. The Advisory Committee was composed of four MPs (one from each of the recognized political parties in the House of Commons), one retired judge nominated by the Canadian Judicial Council, one member nominated by the provincial Attorneys General in the region, one member nominated by the provincial law societies in the region; and "two eminent people of recognized stature in the region," nominated by the Minister of Justice of Canada. Minister Cotler apparently gave the Advisory Committee a mandate letter, "setting out the objectives of the Committee, describing the merit-based criteria, establishing timeframes and providing for a general procedure, particularly in relation to confidentiality." Cotler also apparently met with the Committee before it began its work.

The Advisory Committee shortened the list to three names after reviewing the resumes and publications of the candidates and consulting with third parties (the same persons the Minister had consulted with earlier). The committee submitted its list to Minister of Justice Cotler but the Liberal government fell at the end of November 2005 and after an election in January 2006, the Conservative Party led by Stephen Harper formed the government. The new Harper government chose Justice Rothstein from the shortlist but, in a deviation from the Liberal plan, had the nominee appear, instead of the Minister of Justice, before an ad hoc parliamentary committee.

Justice Rothstein thus became the first nominee ever to appear for a public hearing prior to being appointed to the Supreme Court. He appeared not before a parliamentary committee but before an ad hoc committee of parliamentarians composed of MPs from the political parties in proportion to their representation in the House. Professor Peter Hogg supervised the proceedings, providing introductory comments "on the limits of judicial speech," in order to guide the committee "as to the kinds of questions that could or could not be answered by the nominee." The members of the Committee were free to ask Justice Rothstein any questions, but as per Professor Hogg's admonitions, they were aware that Justice Rothstein had the prerogative to decline to answer questions involving issues that could before him on the Supreme Court.

The three-hour hearing was televised live and was widely considered a tame affair, in part due to Justice Rothstein's amiable personality and self-deprecating style. The committee did not vote on the appointment and did not produce a report although Minister of Justice Vic Toews did invite the MPs to share their views with the Prime Minister who reportedly watched the proceedings on television. The Prime Minister confirmed Justice Rothstein's appointment two days after the hearing.

Two years elapsed before the Harper government would have another chance to fill a vacancy on the high court. In the interim, they did not make any formal policies or issue any plans on how they would approach the appointment process. This became apparent after April 9, 2008 when Justice Michel Bastarache announced that he would be stepping down from the Supreme Court, effective June 30, 2008. More than six weeks later, the Minister of Justice announced the following process to replace Justice Bastarache. First, the Minister of Justice and Attorney General would consult with the Attorneys General of the four Atlantic provinces as well as leading members of the legal community. Members of the public were invited to submit their input through a Department of Justice website. Based on this process, the Minister would prepare a list of unspecified number of qualified candidates which would be reviewed by a selection panel composed of five MPs—including two Members from the Government Caucus and one Member from each of the recognized Opposition Caucuses, as selected by their respective leaders. This body—known for the first time as "the Supreme Court Selection Panel"—was tasked with the responsibility for assessing the candidates and providing an unranked short list of three qualified candidates to the Prime Minister of Canada and the Minister of Justice for their consideration. Finally, the nominee was to appear at a public hearing of an ad hoc parliamentary committee, as did Justice Rothstein.

The Minister of Justice completed his consultations and submitted his list of qualified candidates to the Supreme Court Selection Panel. That body was beset by partisan bickering and on September 5, 2008, the Prime Minister bypassed the panel and announced Justice Cromwell as the nominee for appointment. The Prime Minister stated that an appointment would not be made until Justice Cromwell appeared at a public hearing of an ad hoc parliamentary committee. Two days later, the Prime Minister asked the Governor General to dissolve Parliament triggering an election for October 14, 2008. Soon after Parliament reconvened in November, Canada was beset by a parliamentary crisis and on December 4, 2008, the Governor General prorogued Parliament at the Prime Minister's request. Prime Minister Harper dispensed with the parliamentary hearing and on December 22, 2008, he formally appointed Justice Cromwell to the Supreme Court. Given fractious and fragile parliamentary relations and the wide support for Justice Cromwell, there was minimal criticism of the Prime Minister's dispensing with the process for parliamentary consultation and hearing.

On May 13, 2011, a newly re-elected Conservative government was suddenly faced with two vacancies. Justices Ian Binnie and Louise Charron jointly announced their retirement on what would otherwise have been a sleepy post-election Friday afternoon. The Prime Minister instituted the following process. First, the Minister of Justice and Attorney General would consult with the Attorney General of Ontario as well as leading members of the legal community in order to identify a pool of qualified candidates for appointment to the Supreme Court. Members of the public were invited to submit their input regarding candidates through a Department of Justice website. Based on this process, the Minister of Justice would create a list of unspecified numbers of qualified candidates. Second, this "long list" of qualified candidates would be reviewed by a selection panel composed of five MPs: three government MPs and one from each of the opposition parties, the NDP and the Liberals as selected by the leaders of those parties. The Supreme Court Selection Panel was tasked with assessing the candidates and providing an unranked short list of six qualified candidates to the Prime Minister and the Minister of Justice for their consideration. Third, while it was unstated, it was implied that the Prime Minister and Minister of Justice would only make a selection of a "nominee" from this shortlist. Fourth, the selected "nominees" would appear at a public hearing of ad hoc parliamentary committee to answer questions from MPs as Justice Rothstein had done in 2006.

This process was followed in 2011 for the appointments of Justice Moldaver and Karakatsanis, in 2012 for the appointment of Justice Wagner and in 2013 for the appointment of Justice Nadon. The Office of Federal Judicial Affairs—the body that oversees and administers federal judicial appointments—administers the appointment process, at least respecting the selection panel. It is not clear what role the Office of Federal Judicial Affairs plays in compiling the long-list. In each of those appointments, the hearing took place two days after the Prime Minister's announcement of the nominee. In 2011, Professor Peter Hogg reprised his role as counsel to the parliamentary committee that he had performed in 2006 at the Rothstein hearing. In both 2012 and 2013, former Quebec Court of Appeal Justice Jean-Louis Baudouin exercised this function. The day after each of these hearings, the Prime Minister formally appointed his nominee to the Supreme Court.

In 2013, a court challenge was brought to the appointment of Justice Marc Nadon to the Supreme Court by Toronto lawyer Rocco Galati. The government responded by amending the *Supreme Court Act* to clarify that judges of the Federal Court (like Nadon J) were eligible for appointment to the Supreme Court as one of the three designated "Quebec judges" under the legislation. The government also directed a reference to the Supreme Court to seek its opinion on the eligibility of Nadon J and the constitutionality of the legislation. In a 6:1 decision, the Supreme Court held that under the *Supreme Court Act* a Federal Court judge did *not* qualify for appointment as one of the three Quebec judges and changing that provision of the act would require the unanimous consent of the provinces via constitutional amendment. It voided Nadon J's appointment to the Supreme Court: *Reference re Supreme Court Act, ss 5 and 6*, 2014 SCC 21, [2014] 1 SCR 433.

The government responded in June 2014—several months after the Nadon decision—by appointing Justice Clément Gascon of the Quebec Court of Appeal to the Supreme Court. The government dispensed with the process it had previously used: there was no Supreme Court Selection Panel and no public hearing for Gascon J. The federal government had informally consulted with the Quebec government and members of the legal and judicial community in Quebec.

Between 2004 and 2020, various appointment processes were used. Between 2011 and 2014, the government settled into a process involving a "Supreme Court Selection Panel," consisting of MPs and an ad hoc committee of MPs that questions the "nominee" at a public hearing. Conservative and Liberal governments have swung back and forth in favouring and dispensing with public hearings: they were introduced by the Conservative government of Stephen Harper in 2004 but were then dispensed with by the Harper government in 2008 and from 2014 to 2015. The Liberal government of Justin Trudeau overhauled the appointment process in 2016 and restored the public hearings.

B. PROVINCIAL JUDICIAL APPOINTMENT PROCESS

For provincially/territorially appointed judges, the process of choosing judges varies depending on the province/territory. The basic model is built on an advisory committee composed of a mixture of members from the legal community and laypersons. The committee accepts applications and interviews candidates before submitting a list of recommendations to the provincial attorney general.

By way of illustration, in Ontario, the Judicial Appointments Advisory Committee is described on the organization's website as follows:

> The Legislation requires the composition of the Committee to reflect the diversity of Ontario's population, including gender, geography, racial and cultural minorities. In addition to seven (7) lay members who are appointed by the Attorney General, two (2) judges are appointed by the Chief Justice of the Ontario Court of Justice, one (1) member is appointed by the Ontario Judicial Council and three (3) from the legal community are appointed by The Law Society of Ontario, Ontario Bar Association and the Federation of Ontario Law Associations, respectively. All members serve for a term of three (3) years and may be re-appointed.

The system operates on an application basis:

> Vacancies on the Bench are advertised in the *Ontario Reports* as the need arises. Candidates must submit 14 copies of a prescribed application form. These applications are reviewed by the Committee and a short list is prepared. The Judicial Appointments Advisory Committee meets to select candidates for interviews from the short list.
>
> After reference checks, confidential inquiries and interviews, the Committee sends a ranked list of its recommendations to the Attorney General who is required to make the appointment from that list.

(Government of Ontario, "Judicial Appointments Advisory Committee," online: *Ontario Courts* <http://www.ontariocourts.ca/ocj/jaac/>.)

The criteria for evaluating candidates are analogous to those applicable at the federal level in relation to personal and professional qualities and experience (discussed below). In addition, the following considerations are applied:

Community Awareness

- A commitment to public service.
- Awareness of and an interest in knowing more about the social problems that give rise to cases coming before the courts.
- Sensitivity to changes in social values relating to criminal and family matters.
- Interest in methods of dispute resolution alternatives to formal adjudication and interest in community resources available for participating in the disposition of cases.

Demographics

- The Judiciary of the Ontario Court of Justice should be representative of the population it serves. The Committee is sensitive to the issue of under-representation in the judicial complement of women, Indigenous, visible and ethnic/cultural minorities, LGBTQ2 and persons with disabilities.

(Government of Ontario, "Policies and Process," online: *Ontario Courts* <https://www.ontariocourts .ca/ocj/jaac/policies-and-procedures/policies-and-process/#Community_Awareness>.)

When the Ontario process was adopted, the attorney general at the time, Ian Scott, undertook to make recommendations to the Cabinet based exclusively on a very short list recommended by the advisory committee. That undertaking was respected. Subsequent attorneys general have, generally, followed this practice. As a result, political patronage is seldom identified as a criticism of these appointments.

The other provinces and territories did not immediately emulate the bold step forward taken by Ontario Attorney General Scott, but a variety of similar committees and procedures have evolved. The exception is Nunavut, which has a unified superior and territorial court called the Nunavut Court of Justice. Judges are appointed to that court by the federal government.

Over the past decade, Quebec overhauled its appointment process as a result of a political scandal that led to the establishment of a public inquiry headed by former Supreme Court of Canada Justice Michel Bastarache. As a result of Bastarache J's recommendations, the government of Quebec adopted an appointment system similar to Ontario's.

C. A RANGE OF MODELS

Judicial selection processes vary internationally. It is worth considering three alternative (or sometimes mixed) models. These models are: (1) confirmation hearings; (2) nominating committees; and (3) direct elections. Consider how each of these approaches is employed to varying degrees in the United States.

US Department of Justice, State Court Organization 1998
(NCJ 178932) (Washington, DC: US Department of Justice, 2000)

How judges are selected and their terms of service on the bench differ sharply between the federal and state courts, and the differences among states are often nearly as significant. All federal judges are nominated by the President and serve "during good behavior" once confirmed by the US Senate unless they resign or are impeached and convicted by the US Congress. State court judges are likely to face an election as a part of their selection process and to serve fixed terms, which for [courts of final appeal] justices range between six and 14 years (15 years in the District of Columbia). Only Rhode Island offers appellate judges lifetime appointments, while the judges of the New Hampshire and Massachusetts Supreme Courts serve until age 70.

Judicial selection occurs for three purposes in the state courts: to fill an unexpired term upon the retirement, resignation, or death of an incumbent judge; to select for a full term (often referred to as the initial selection); and at the end of a term. ...

One marker for examining the diverse selection methods adopted by the states is the "Missouri Plan." In 1940 the State of Missouri amended its constitution to establish a statewide nominating committee for appellate judgeships and circuit-level commissions for general jurisdiction trial court judgeships. A judge, representatives of the state bar association, and nonlawyers appointed by the governor make up the commissions. The governor must appoint one of a commission's three nominees to fill a vacancy. The new appointee then faces a retention election in one year's time, running against his or her own record, and then further retention elections at 12-year intervals. Thirty-nine states use some form of judicial nominating commission in judicial selection, which became popular in the 1970s ... , although only 16 combine such a commission with retention elections on the Missouri model.

This description of the US system prompts further observations. First, note the prevalence of electoral models for state court judges. Few Canadian critics would support a system of election for our judges, even those who advocate "democratization" of the judiciary.

One problem is that election campaigns require financing. Who is most likely to contribute to such campaigns? When lawyers make financial contributions to a person who is "running for judge," do they expect favoured treatment in the courtroom if the judge is successful? Even the perception of the judge favouring a "supporter" detracts from the perception of judicial impartiality.

Another problem is that in deciding cases or rendering sentences, the judge may be inclined to court public sentiment rather than to make the "right," but unpopular, decision. This could be especially tempting when the next election is imminent. During a campaign, the judge might also appeal to public sentiment, establishing personal constraints on future decision-making. Both of these problems raise questions of judicial independence, a key concept addressed below.

Second, note the US federal process: executive appointment following Senate confirmation. In the United States, at the federal level, there are district courts, district appellate courts, and the Supreme Court. Federal judges are appointed in accordance with article II, s 2 of the US Constitution, which anticipates the participation of the US Senate in a confirmation process:

[The President] ... shall nominate, and by and with the Advice and Consent of the Senate, shall appoint ... Judges of the Supreme Court, and all other Officers of the United States.

The nomination and confirmation process may be summarized as follows:

Supreme Court justices, court of appeals judges, and district court judges are nominated by the President and confirmed by the United States Senate, as stated in the Constitution. Senators or sometimes members of the House who are of the President's political party often recommend potential nominees. The Senate Judiciary Committee typically conducts confirmation hearings for each nominee.

(Administrative Office of the US Courts, *About Federal Judges*, online: *United States Courts* <https://www.uscourts.gov/judges-judgeships/about-federal-judges>. As noted above, senate confirmation has sometimes been a highly political process.

Third, note how the Missouri model (with or without subsequent "retention" elections) depends on a nomination or shortlisting committee process. The executive appoints a judge from the short list developed by the committee. Other jurisdictions have employed variations on this nomination process. Consider these provisions of the South African Constitution.

178. Judicial Service Commission

1. There is a Judicial Service Commission consisting of—
   a. the Chief Justice, who presides at meetings of the Commission;
   b. the President of the Supreme Court of Appeal;
   c. one Judge President designated by the Judges President;
   d. the Cabinet member responsible for the administration of justice, or an alternate designated by that Cabinet member;
   e. two practising advocates nominated from within the advocates' profession to represent the profession as a whole, and appointed by the President;
   f. two practising attorneys nominated from within the attorneys' profession to represent the profession as a whole, and appointed by the President;
   g. one teacher of law designated by teachers of law at South African universities;
   h. six persons designated by the National Assembly from among its members, at least three of whom must be members of opposition parties represented in the Assembly;
   i. four permanent delegates to the National Council of Provinces designated together by the Council with a supporting vote of at least six provinces;
   j. four persons designated by the President as head of the national executive, after consulting the leaders of all the parties in the National Assembly; and
   k. when considering matters relating to a specific High Court, the Judge President of that Court and the Premier of the province concerned, or an alternate designated by each of them. ...

174. Appointment of judicial officers

1. Any appropriately qualified woman or man who is a fit and proper person may be appointed as a judicial officer. Any person to be appointed to the Constitutional Court must also be a South African citizen.

2. The need for the judiciary to reflect broadly the racial and gender composition of South Africa must be considered when judicial officers are appointed.

3. The President as head of the national executive, after consulting the Judicial Service Commission and the leader of parties represented in the National Assembly, appoints the Chief Justice and the Deputy Chief Justice and, after consulting the Judicial Service Commission, appoints the President and Deputy President of the Supreme Court of Appeal.

4. The other judges of the Constitutional Court are appointed by the President, as head of the national executive, after consulting the Chief Justice and the leaders of parties represented in the National Assembly, in accordance with the following procedure:
   a. The Judicial Service Commission must prepare a list of nominees with three names more than the number of appointments to be made, and submit the list to the President.
   b. The President may make appointments from the list, and must advise the Judicial Service Commission, with reasons, if any of the nominees are unacceptable and any appointment remains to be made.
   c. The Judicial Service Commission must supplement the list with further nominees and the President must make the remaining appointments from the supplemented list.

5. At all times, at least four members of the Constitutional Court must be persons who were judges at the time they were appointed to the Constitutional Court.

6. The President must appoint the judges of all other courts on the advice of the Judicial Service Commission.

7. Other judicial officers must be appointed in terms of an Act of Parliament which must ensure that the appointment, promotion, transfer or dismissal of, or disciplinary steps against, these judicial officers take place without favour or prejudice.

8. Before judicial officers begin to perform their functions, they must take an oath or affirm, in accordance with Schedule 2, that they will uphold and protect the Constitution.

One of the most recent developments in the world of judicial appointments is in Great Britain. There, the Judicial Appointments Commission is established by statute, with mechanisms to ensure its influence. The following is taken from its website: <https://www.judicialappointments .gov.uk/about-us>.

The Judicial Appointments Commission (JAC) is an independent commission that selects candidates for judicial office in courts and tribunals in England and Wales, and for some tribunals whose jurisdiction extends to Scotland or Northern Ireland.

We select candidates for judicial office on merit, through fair and open competition, from the widest range of eligible candidates.

We were set up on 3 April 2006 in order to maintain and strengthen judicial independence by taking responsibility for selecting candidates for judicial office out of the hands of the Lord Chancellor and making the appointments process clearer and more accountable. Our creation was one of the major changes brought about by the *Constitutional Reform Act* (CRA) 2005, which also reformed the office of Lord Chancellor and established the Lord Chief Justice as head of the judiciary of England and Wales.

Under the CRA, Parliament gave us very specific duties in regard to the selection of judges. Our statutory responsibilities are:

- to select candidates solely on merit;
- to select only people of good character; and
- to have regard to the need to encourage diversity in the range of persons available for judicial selection.

• • •

The Commission

In accordance with the CRA, as amended by the Judicial Appointments Regulations 2013 there are fifteen Commissioners, including the Chairman. All are recruited and appointed through open competition with the exception of three judicial members who are selected either by the Judges' Council or the Tribunals' Council. Membership of the Commission is drawn from the judiciary, the legal profession, non-legally qualified judicial officer holders and the public.

The Commission has responsibility for ensuring that the JAC fulfils its role, achieving its aims and objectives, and for promoting the efficient and effective use of staff and other resources. JAC Commissioners work closely with JAC staff, the Chief Executive and Directors.

The judicial appointments for which the JAC makes selections are set out in Schedule 14 to the CRA as amended by the Crime and Courts Act 2013. The JAC does not select judicial office-holders for the UK Supreme Court.

The JAC may be required to select a candidate for immediate appointment under section 87 of the CRA, or to identify candidates for future vacancy requests under section 94. The JAC selects one candidate for each vacancy, providing there are sufficient numbers of selectable candidates available for each vacancy, and recommends that candidate for appointment to the Appropriate Authority. The Appropriate Authority can accept or reject a recommendation, or ask the Commission to reconsider it. If the Appropriate Authority rejects a recommendation or asks for reconsideration he must provide written reasons to the JAC.

The JAC is also involved in the selection of the Lord Chief Justice, Heads of Division and the Lords Justices of Appeal. Under the CRA, the JAC's role is to convene a selection panel, which will be a committee of the Commission. The members are specified in the relevant sections of the CRA, as amended by the Judicial Appointments Regulations 2013 and it is for the panel to determine the selection process and make a recommendation. The provisions in Part 2 of Schedule 13 to the *Crime and Courts Act* relating to diversity considerations will also apply to these roles.

III. JUDICIAL INDEPENDENCE

No discussion of the Canadian court system is complete without an examination of the concept of "judicial independence." Put simply, judicial independence is the notion that judges are at arm's length from the other branches of government. In *British Columbia v Imperial Tobacco Canada Ltd*, 2005 SCC 49 at para 45, [2005] 2 SCR 473, the Supreme Court described judicial independence as follows:

> Judicial independence consists essentially in the freedom "to render decisions based solely on the requirements of the law and justice": *Mackin v. New Brunswick (Minister of Finance)*, [2002] 1 SCR 405, 2002 SCC 13, at para. 37. It requires that the judiciary be left free to act without improper "interference from any other entity" ... i.e. that the executive and legislative branches of government not "impinge on the essential 'authority and function' ... of the court" (*MacKeigan v. Hickman*, [1989] 2 SCR 796, at pp. 827-28).

Judicial independence is not an end in itself. Rather, it serves various other social and political objectives. As Lamer CJ said in the *Provincial Judges Reference*, excerpted below, judicial independence "is a means to secure those goals": [1997] 3 SCR 3 at para 9. See also Beverley McLachlin, "Judicial Accountability" (2008) 1 JPPL 293 at 298.

What are these other objectives? The customary case for judicial independence is based on its necessity to ensure judicial impartiality, which in turn, promotes public confidence in the impartial adjudication of disputes, which secures the legitimacy of the legal system. Together, this confidence and legitimacy helps uphold the rule of law. See generally Adam Dodek, "Judicial Independence as a Public Policy Instrument" in Adam Dodek & Lorne Sossin, eds, *Judicial Independence in Context* (Toronto: Irwin Law, 2010) 295 at 301. As the former Chief Justice of Ontario explained, courts cannot effectively fulfill their role in society without public confidence. Roy McMurtry, *Memoirs and Reflections* (Toronto: Osgoode Society for Legal History, 2013) 487.

The Supreme Court has explained that "impartiality refers to a state of mind or attitude of the tribunal in relations to the issues and the parties in a particular case" whereas independence refers to the "status or relationship to others—particularly to the executive branch of government—that rests on objective conditions or guarantees": see *Valente v The Queen*, [1985] 2 SCR 673 at 685. Independence is necessary, therefore, in order to ensure impartiality.

A. SOURCES AND SCOPE

Although not explicitly mentioned in the constitutional text, judicial independence is a richly constitutional concept. Judicial independence in Canada is an unwritten constitutional principle, arguably our strongest one; it has equal if not stronger force than some of the textual provisions of Canada's Constitution. Adam Dodek, "Judicial Independence as a Public Policy Instrument" in Adam Dodek & Lorne Sossin, eds, *Judicial Independence in Context* (Toronto: Irwin Law, 2010) 295 at 299. While not mentioned explicitly in the constitutional text, judicial independence of some degree is clearly envisioned by certain provisions of the Constitution. Sections 96 to 100 of the *Constitution Act, 1867* provide for the appointment, tenure, and remuneration of federally appointed judges. We have already discussed how courts have interpreted s 96 as not merely indicating who has the power of appointment, but also establishing the superior courts as a fundamental institution protected by our Constitution. The scope of ss 99 and 100 also has been elaborated by judicial interpretation to further protect judicial independence.

Section 99 specifies the tenure of office of superior court judges as follows:

> (1) Subject to subsection two of this section, the Judges of the Superior Courts shall hold office during good behaviour, but shall be removable by the Governor General on Address of the Senate and House of Commons.
>
> (2) A Judge of a Superior Court, whether appointed before or after the coming into force of this section, shall cease to hold office upon attaining the age of seventy-five years. ...

In other words, federally appointed superior court judges are removable only for breach of "good behaviour," until the mandatory retirement age of 75. As we shall see, physical or mental incapacity—that is, the inability to act as a judge—has been interpreted to be a breach of "good behaviour."

Meanwhile, s 100 indicates that the "salaries, allowances and pensions" of superior court judges "shall be fixed and provided by the Parliament of Canada." This provision has been interpreted by the Supreme Court as guaranteeing the "financial security of judges of the superior, district, and county courts": see *Provincial Judges Reference*, [1997] 3 SCR 3 at para 84.

Note, however, that these *Constitution Act, 1867* provisions apply only to superior courts. Does that mean that judicial independence does not exist as a constitutional matter for other courts, such as provincial courts? The answer is "no" for several reasons. Most obviously, s 11(d) of the Charter imposes a requirement for judicial independence in certain circumstances:

> 11. Any person charged with an offence has the right
>> (d) to be presumed innocent until proven guilty according to law in a fair and public hearing by an independent and impartial tribunal.

Because most criminal cases are tried by provincially appointed judges, this Charter provision requires that these courts and the individual judges that are appointed to provincial courts be "independent and impartial." Otherwise, an accused person facing trial before such a court would be entitled to a stay of proceedings for the denial of the Charter right under s 11(d).

The meaning of "an independent and impartial tribunal" in s 11(d) received extensive consideration through the 1980s and early 1990s. In this period, the Supreme Court of Canada developed the concept of "institutional independence," referring to those requirements that must be in place in order for the judiciary to be sufficiently independent of pressures from the other branches of the state in order to meet this standard. Three such requirements were identified by the court: (1) security of tenure; (2) financial security; and (3) administrative control or independence with respect to the management of court business. Each of these three features was subject to elaboration.

Most notably, in the mid-1990s, a political and legal crisis arose with respect to the issue of "financial security" of the provincial court, or non–s 96 judiciary across the country. In a period of severe budgetary constraint, several provincial governments imposed salary freezes or rollbacks on their provincial civil services, and included in these regimes the provincial court judiciary. In several provinces, criminal accused made claims that these unilateral moves by executive governments with respect to judicial salaries violated the parameters of "financial security" of judges, and denied them trials before independent tribunals. A number of such challenges succeeded. A reference case came before the Supreme Court of Canada dealing with the situations in three provinces: Alberta, Manitoba, and Prince Edward Island. The Court majority recognized that the issues in the case could be resolved solely within the context of interpreting and applying s 11(d). Nevertheless, the majority took the opportunity to consider the constitutional status of the judiciary as a whole, and not merely in its criminal law jurisdiction. The Court majority recognized an unwritten principle of judicial independence in the Constitution.

Portions of the majority judgment are reproduced here for their enunciation of the principle of judicial independence in our Constitution. Other portions are included below under Section III.C, related more specifically to financial security. Finally, the dissenting judgment is reproduced in Chapter 11.

Ref re Remuneration of Judges of the Prov Court of PEI; Ref re Independence and Impartiality of Judges of the Prov Court of PEI
[1997] 3 SCR 3

LAMER CJ (L'Heureux-Dubé, Sopinka, Gonthier, Cory, and Iacobucci JJ concurring):

I. Introduction

[1] The four appeals handed down today ... raise a range of issues relating to the independence of provincial courts, but are united by a single issue: whether and how the guarantee of judicial independence in s. 11(d) of the *Canadian Charter of Rights and Freedoms* restricts the manner by and the extent to which provincial governments and legislatures can reduce the salaries of provincial court judges. Moreover, in my respectful opinion, they implicate the broader question of whether the constitutional home of judicial independence lies in the express provisions of the *Constitution Acts, 1867 to 1982*, or exterior to the sections of those documents. I am cognizant of the length of these reasons. Although it would have been possible to issue a set of separate but interrelated judgments, since many of the parties intervened in each other's cases, I find it convenient to deal with these four appeals in one set of reasons. ...

• • •

[9] ... Judicial independence is valued because it serves important societal goals—it is a means to secure those goals.

[10] One of these goals is the maintenance of public confidence in the impartiality of the judiciary, which is essential to the effectiveness of the court system. Independence contributes to the perception that justice will be done in individual cases. Another social goal served by judicial independence is the maintenance of the rule of law, one aspect of which is the constitutional principle that the exercise of all public power must find its ultimate source in a legal rule.

• • •

[82] These appeals were all argued on the basis of s. 11(d), the *Charter*'s guarantee of judicial independence and impartiality. From its express terms, s. 11(d) is a right of limited application—it only applies to persons accused of offences. Despite s. 11(d)'s limited scope, there is no doubt that the appeals can and should be resolved on the basis of that provision. To a large extent, the Court is the prisoner of the case which the parties and interveners have presented to us, and the arguments

that have been raised, and the evidence that we have before us, have largely been directed at s. 11(d). In particular, the two references from PEI are explicitly framed in terms of s. 11(d), and if we are to answer the questions contained therein, we must direct ourselves to that section of the Constitution.

[83] Nevertheless, while the thrust of the submissions was directed at s. 11(d), the respondent Wickman in *Campbell et al.* and the appellants in the PEI references, in their written submissions, the respondent Attorney General of PEI, in its oral submissions, and the intervener Attorney General of Canada, in response to a question from Iacobucci J, addressed the larger question of where the constitutional home of judicial independence lies, to which I now turn. Notwithstanding the presence of s. 11(d) of the *Charter*, and ss. 96-100 of the *Constitution Act, 1867*, I am of the view that judicial independence is at root an unwritten constitutional principle, in the sense that it is exterior to the particular sections of the Constitution Acts. The existence of that principle, whose origins can be traced to the *Act of Settlement of 1701*, is recognized and affirmed by the preamble to the *Constitution Act, 1867*. The specific provisions of the *Constitution Acts, 1867* to *1982*, merely "elaborate that principle in the institutional apparatus which they create or contemplate": *Switzman v. Elbling*, [1957] SCR 285, at p. 306, per Rand J.

[84] I arrive at this conclusion, in part, by considering the tenability of the opposite position—that the Canadian Constitution already contains explicit provisions which are directed at the protection of judicial independence, and that those provisions are exhaustive of the matter. Section 11(d) of the *Charter*, as I have mentioned above, protects the independence of a wide range of courts and tribunals which exercise jurisdiction over offences. Moreover, since well before the enactment of the *Charter*, ss. 96-100 of the *Constitution Act, 1867* separately and in combination, have protected and continue to protect the independence of provincial superior courts: *Cooper* ... , at para. 11; *MacMillan Bloedel Ltd. v. Simpson*, [1995] 4 SCR 725, at para. 10. More specifically, s. 99 guarantees the security of tenure of superior court judges; s. 100 guarantees the financial security of judges of the superior, district, and county courts; and s. 96 has come to guarantee the core jurisdiction of superior, district, and county courts against legislative encroachment, which I also take to be a guarantee of judicial independence.

[85] However, upon closer examination, there are serious limitations to the view that the express provisions of the Constitution comprise an exhaustive and definitive code for the protection of judicial independence. The first and most serious problem is that the range of courts whose independence is protected by the written provisions of the Constitution contains large gaps. Sections 96-100, for example, only protect the independence of judges of the superior, district, and county courts, and even then, not in a uniform or consistent manner. Thus, while ss. 96 and 100 protect the core jurisdiction and the financial security, respectively, of all three types of courts (superior, district, and county), s. 99, on its terms, only protects the security of tenure of superior court judges. Moreover, ss. 96-100 do not apply to provincially appointed inferior courts, otherwise known as provincial courts.

[86] To some extent, the gaps in the scope of protection provided by ss. 96-100 are offset by the application of s. 11(d), which applies to a range of tribunals and courts, including provincial courts. However, by its express terms, s. 11(d) is limited in scope as well—it only extends the envelope of constitutional protection to bodies which exercise jurisdiction over offences. As a result, when those courts exercise civil jurisdiction, their independence would not seem to be guaranteed. The independence of provincial courts adjudicating in family law matters, for example, would not be constitutionally protected. The independence of superior

courts, by contrast, when hearing exactly the same cases, would be constitutionally guaranteed.

[87] The second problem with reading s. 11(d) of the *Charter* and ss. 96-100 of the *Constitution Act, 1867* as an exhaustive code of judicial independence is that some of those provisions, by their terms, do not appear to speak to this objective. Section 100, for example, provides that Parliament shall fix and provide the salaries of superior, district, and county court judges. It is therefore, in an important sense, a subtraction from provincial jurisdiction over the administration of justice under s. 92(14). Moreover, read in the light of the *Act of Settlement of 1701*, it is a partial guarantee of financial security, inasmuch as it vests responsibility for setting judicial remuneration with Parliament, which must act through the public means of legislative enactment, not the executive. However, on its plain language, it only places Parliament under the obligation to provide salaries to the judges covered by that provision, which would in itself not safeguard the judiciary against political interference through economic manipulation. Nevertheless, as I develop in these reasons, with reference to *Beauregard*, s. 100 also requires that Parliament must provide salaries that are adequate, and that changes or freezes to judicial remuneration be made only after recourse to a constitutionally mandated procedure.

[88] A perusal of the language of s. 96 reveals the same difficulty:

> 96. The Governor General shall appoint the Judges of the Superior, District, and County Courts in each Province, except those of the Courts of Probate in Nova Scotia and New Brunswick.

Section 96 seems to do no more than confer the power to appoint judges of the superior, district, and county courts. It is a staffing provision, and is once again a subtraction from the power of the provinces under s. 92(14). However, through a process of judicial interpretation, s. 96 has come to guarantee the core jurisdiction of the courts which come within the scope of that provision. In the past, this development has often been expressed as a logical inference from the express terms of s. 96. Assuming that the goal of s. 96 was the creation of "a unitary judicial system," that goal would have been undermined "if a province could pass legislation creating a tribunal, appoint members thereto, and then confer on the tribunal the jurisdiction of the superior courts": *Re Residential Tenancies Act, 1979*, [1981] 1 SCR 714, at p. 728. However, as I recently confirmed, s. 96 restricts not only the legislative competence of provincial legislatures, but of Parliament as well: *MacMillan Bloedel, supra*. The rationale for the provision has also shifted, away from the protection of national unity, to the maintenance of the rule of law through the protection of the judicial role.

[89] The point which emerges from this brief discussion is that the interpretation of ss. 96 and 100 has come a long way from what those provisions actually say. This jurisprudential evolution undermines the force of the argument that the written text of the Constitution is comprehensive and definitive in its protection of judicial independence. The only way to explain the interpretation of ss. 96 and 100, in fact, is by reference to a deeper set of unwritten understandings which are not found on the face of the document itself.

[90] The proposition that the Canadian Constitution embraces unwritten norms was recently confirmed by this Court in *New Brunswick Broadcasting Co. v. Nova Scotia (Speaker of the House of Assembly)*, [1993] 1 SCR 319. In that case, the Court found it constitutional for the Nova Scotia House of Assembly to refuse the media the right to record and broadcast legislative proceedings. The media advanced a claim based on s. 2(b) of the *Charter*, which protects, inter alia, "freedom of the press and other media of communication." McLachlin J, speaking for a majority of the Court, found that the refusal of the Assembly was an exercise of that Assembly's

unwritten legislative privileges, that the Constitution of Canada constitutionalized those privileges, and that the constitutional status of those privileges therefore precluded the application of the *Charter*.

• • •

[94] In my opinion, the existence of many of the unwritten rules of the Canadian Constitution can be explained by reference to the preamble of the *Constitution Act, 1867*. The relevant paragraph states in full:

> Whereas the Provinces of Canada, Nova Scotia, and New Brunswick have expressed their Desire to be federally united into One Dominion under the Crown of the United Kingdom of Great Britain and Ireland, with a Constitution similar in Principle to that of the United Kingdom:

Although the preamble has been cited by this Court on many occasions, its legal effect has never been fully explained. On the one hand, although the preamble is clearly part of the Constitution, it is equally clear that it "has no enacting force": *Reference re Resolution to Amend the Constitution*, [1981] 1 SCR 753, at p. 805 (joint majority reasons). In other words, strictly speaking, it is not a source of positive law, in contrast to the provisions which follow it.

[95] But the preamble does have important legal effects. Under normal circumstances, preambles can be used to identify the purpose of a statute, and also as an aid to construing ambiguous statutory language: *Driedger on the Construction of Statutes* (3rd ed. 1994), by R. Sullivan, at p. 261. The preamble to the *Constitution Act, 1867* certainly operates in this fashion. However, in my view, it goes even further. In the words of Rand J, the preamble articulates "the political theory which the Act embodies": *Switzman ...* , at p. 306. It recognizes and affirms the basic principles which are the very source of the substantive provisions of the *Constitution Act, 1867*. As I have said above, those provisions merely elaborate those organizing principles in the institutional apparatus they create or contemplate. As such, the preamble is not only a key to construing the express provisions of the *Constitution Act, 1867*, but also invites the use of those organizing principles to fill out gaps in the express terms of the constitutional scheme. It is the means by which the underlying logic of the Act can be given the force of law.

[96] What are the organizing principles of the *Constitution Act, 1867*, as expressed in the preamble? The preamble speaks of the desire of the founding provinces "to be federally united into One Dominion," and thus, addresses the structure of the division of powers. Moreover, by its reference to "a Constitution similar in Principle to that of the United Kingdom," the preamble indicates that the legal and institutional structure of constitutional democracy in Canada should be similar to that of the legal regime out of which the Canadian Constitution emerged. To my mind, both of these aspects of the preamble explain many of the cases in which the Court has, through the normal process of constitutional interpretation, stated some fundamental rules of Canadian constitutional law which are not found in the express terms of the *Constitution Act, 1867*.

• • •

[The court discussed its previous jurisprudence concerning the use of the preamble of the *Constitution Act, 1867* to infer basic rules of Canadian constitutional law.]

[104] These examples—the doctrines of full faith and credit and paramountcy, the remedial innovation of suspended declarations of invalidity, the recognition of the constitutional status of the privileges of provincial legislatures, the vesting of the power to regulate political speech within federal jurisdiction, and the inferral

of implied limits on legislative sovereignty with respect to political speech—illustrate the special legal effect of the preamble. The preamble identifies the organizing principles of the *Constitution Act, 1867*, and invites the courts to turn those principles into the premises of a constitutional argument that culminates in the filling of gaps in the express terms of the constitutional text.

[105] The same approach applies to the protection of judicial independence. In fact, this point was already decided in *Beauregard*, and, unless and until it is reversed, we are governed by that decision today. In that case (at p. 72), a unanimous Court held that the preamble of the *Constitution Act, 1867*, and in particular, its reference to "a Constitution similar in Principle to that of the United Kingdom," was "textual recognition" of the principle of judicial independence. Although in that case, it fell to us to interpret s. 100 of the *Constitution Act, 1867*, the comments I have just reiterated were not limited by reference to that provision, and the courts which it protects.

[106] The historical origins of the protection of judicial independence in the United Kingdom, and thus in the Canadian Constitution, can be traced to the *Act of Settlement of 1701*. As we said in *Valente*[v *The Queen*, [1985] 2 SCR 673], at p. 693, that Act was the "historical inspiration" for the judicature provisions of the *Constitution Act, 1867*. Admittedly, the Act only extends protection to judges of the English superior courts. However, our Constitution has evolved over time. In the same way that our understanding of rights and freedoms has grown, such that they have now been expressly entrenched through the enactment of the *Constitution Act, 1982*, so too has judicial independence grown into a principle that now extends to all courts, not just the superior courts of this country.

[107] I also support this conclusion on the basis of the presence of s. 11(d) of the *Charter*, an express provision which protects the independence of provincial court judges only when those courts exercise jurisdiction in relation to offences. As I said earlier, the express provisions of the Constitution should be understood as elaborations of the underlying, unwritten, and organizing principles found in the preamble to the *Constitution Act, 1867*. Even though s. 11(d) is found in the newer part of our Constitution, the *Charter*, it can be understood in this way, since the Constitution is to be read as a unified whole: *Reference re Bill 30, An Act to amend the Education Act (Ont.)*, [1987] 1 SCR 1148, at p. 1206. An analogy can be drawn between the express reference in the preamble of the *Constitution Act, 1982* to the rule of law and the implicit inclusion of that principle in the *Constitution Act, 1867*: *Reference re Manitoba Language Rights*, ... , at p. 750. Section 11(d), far from indicating that judicial independence is constitutionally enshrined for provincial courts only when those courts exercise jurisdiction over offences, is proof of the existence of a general principle of judicial independence that applies to all courts no matter what kind of cases they hear.

[108] I reinforce this conclusion by reference to the central place that courts hold within the Canadian system of government. In *OPSEU*, ... Beetz J linked limitations on legislative sovereignty over political speech with "the existence of certain political institutions" as part of the "basic structure of our Constitution" (p. 57). However, political institutions are only one part of the basic structure of the Canadian Constitution. As this Court has said before, there are three branches of government—the legislature, the executive, and the judiciary: *Fraser v. Public Service Staff Relations Board*, [1985] 2 SCR 455, at p. 469; *R v. Power*, [1994] 1 SCR 601, at p. 620. Courts, in other words, are equally "definitional to the Canadian understanding of constitutionalism" (*Cooper* ... , at para. 11) as are political institutions. It follows that the same constitutional imperative—the preservation of the basic structure—which led Beetz J to limit the power of legislatures to affect the operation of political institutions,

also extends protection to the judicial institutions of our constitutional system. By implication, the jurisdiction of the provinces over "courts," as that term is used in s. 92(14) of the *Constitution Act, 1867*, contains within it an implied limitation that the independence of those courts cannot be undermined.

[109] In conclusion, the express provisions of the *Constitution Act, 1867* and the *Charter* are not an exhaustive written code for the protection of judicial independence in Canada. Judicial independence is an unwritten norm, recognized and affirmed by the preamble to the *Constitution Act, 1867*. In fact, it is in that preamble, which serves as the grand entrance hall to the castle of the Constitution, that the true source of our commitment to this foundational principle is located.

The Supreme Court returned to this issue in the case of *Ell v Alberta*, 2003 SCC 35, [2003] 1 SCR 857. There the issue related to the application of the principle of judicial independence to the office of justice of the peace. Justice Major wrote:

[3] The principle of judicial independence must be interpreted in light of the public interests it is meant to protect: a strong and independent judiciary capable of upholding the rule of law and our constitutional order, and public confidence in the administration of justice. The reforms in this case reflect a good faith and considered decision of the Legislature that was intended to promote these interests. As a result, the legislation does not undermine the perception of independence in the mind of a reasonable and informed person, and is respectful of the principle of judicial independence.

• • •

[18] Judicial independence has been recognized as "the lifeblood of constitutionalism in democratic societies": see *Beauregard v. Canada*, [1986] 2 SCR 56, at p. 70, per Dickson CJ. It requires objective conditions that ensure the judiciary's freedom to act without interference from any other entity. The principle finds explicit constitutional reference in ss. 96 to 100 of the *Constitution Act, 1867* and s. 11(d) of the *Canadian Charter of Rights and Freedoms*. The application of these provisions is limited: the former to judges of superior courts, and the latter to courts and tribunals that determine the guilt of those charged with criminal offences: see *Reference re Remuneration of Judges of the Provincial Court of Prince Edward Island*, [1997] 3 SCR 3 ("*Provincial Court Judges Reference*"), at para. 84, per Lamer CJ. The respondents do not fall into either of these categories. Nonetheless, as this Court has recognized, the principle of judicial independence extends beyond the limited scope of the above provisions.

• • •

[20] Historically, the principle of judicial independence was confined to the superior courts. As a result of the expansion of judicial duties beyond that realm, it is now accepted that all courts fall within the principle's embrace. See *Provincial Court Judges Reference*, [*supra*], at para. 106:

... [O]ur Constitution has evolved over time. In the same way that our understanding of rights and freedoms has grown, such that they have now been expressly entrenched through the enactment of the *Constitution Act, 1982*, so too has judicial independence grown into a principle that now extends to all courts, not just the superior courts of this country.

The scope of the unwritten principle of independence must be interpreted in accordance with its underlying purposes. In this appeal, its extension to the office held by the respondents depends on whether they exercise judicial functions that relate to the bases upon which the principle is founded.

In the result, the Court held that the justices of the peace were "constitutionally required to be independent in the exercise of their duties."

B. ASSESSING INDEPENDENCE

Before turning to the precise content of the independence requirement, it should be asked how this independence is measured. For the Supreme Court, "[t]he general test for the presence or absence of independence consists in asking whether a reasonable person who is fully informed of all the circumstances would consider that a particular court enjoyed the necessary independent status." *Mackin v New Brunswick (Minister of Finance)*, 2002 SCC 13 at para 38, [2002] 1 SCR 405. Thus, independence includes both a requirement of actual independence, and also conditions sufficient to give rise to a reasonable perception of independence on the part of a reasonable and well-informed person.

In *Canada (Minister of Citizenship and Immigration) v Tobiass*, [1997] 3 SCR 391, the Supreme Court considered whether judicial independence had been impaired by a private meeting between a senior Department of Justice official and the chief justice of the Federal Court in relation to delay in the hearing of certain cases in which the Justice Department was a litigant. The Court wrote:

> [42] This appeal presents three issues. ... The second is whether judicial independence, or the appearance of it, suffered as a result of the meeting between Mr. Thompson and Isaac CJ. The third is whether, if any damage was done to the appearance of judicial independence, the trial judge properly exercised his discretion to enter a stay of proceedings.

• • •

> [67] We conclude that the meeting between Mr. Thompson and Isaac CJ and the subsequent conduct of officials of the Department of Justice did indeed cause damage to the appearance of judicial independence. The question remains as to the extent of that damage and how it should be weighed in considering whether a stay should be granted in these significant and important proceedings.

> [68] The independence of judges has two aspects: an institutional aspect and a personal aspect. As Le Dain J wrote in *Valente v. The Queen*, [1985] 2 SCR 673, at p. 691:

> > ... the word "independent" in s. 11(d) of the *Charter* is to be understood as referring to the status or relationship of judicial independence as well as to the state of mind or attitude of the tribunal in the actual exercise of its judicial function.

> The parties agree that it is the personal aspect of judicial independence—what is sometimes called "impartiality"—that is at issue here. No one alleges, and indeed there is no credible evidence to suggest, that the integrity of the Federal Court as an institution has been compromised.

> [69] Though it is very important that the judiciary should actually remain independent, it is equally important that the judiciary should be seen to be independent. In our view, there is not sufficient evidence to support the conclusion that the Chief Justice and the Associate Chief Justice did not in fact remain independent. However, the evidence does compel us to conclude that the appearance of judicial independence suffered significantly as a result of what happened on March 1, 1996.

> [70] The test for determining whether the appearance of judicial independence has been maintained is an objective one. The question is whether a well-informed and reasonable observer would perceive that judicial independence has been compromised. As Lamer CJ wrote in *R v. Lippé*, [1991] 2 SCR 114, at p. 139, "[t]he overall objective of guaranteeing judicial independence is to ensure a reasonable perception of impartiality."

[71] The essence of judicial independence is freedom from outside interference. Dickson CJ, in *Beauregard v. Canada*, [1986] 2 SCR 56, described the concept in these words, at p. 69:

Historically, the generally accepted core of the principle of judicial independence has been the complete liberty of individual judges to hear and decide the cases that come before them: no outsider—be it government, pressure group, individual or even another judge—should interfere in fact, or attempt to interfere, with the way in which a judge conducts his or her case and makes his or her decision. This core continues to be central to the principle of judicial independence.

[72] What emerges from all of this is a simple test for determining whether the appearance of judicial independence has been maintained: whether a reasonable observer would perceive that the court was able to conduct its business free from the interference of the government and of other judges.

The outcome of this case is discussed below.

C. DIMENSIONS AND CORE CHARACTERISTICS

What does judicial independence require? In the *Provincial Judges Reference*, Lamer CJ also provided a conceptual analysis of judicial independence:

[118] The three core characteristics of judicial independence—security of tenure, financial security, and administrative independence—should be contrasted with what I have termed the two dimensions of judicial independence. In *Valente*, Le Dain J drew a distinction between two dimensions of judicial independence, the individual independence of a judge and the institutional or collective independence of the court or tribunal of which that judge is a member. In other words, while individual independence attaches to individual judges, institutional or collective independence attaches to the court or tribunal as an institutional entity. The two different dimensions of judicial independence are related in the following way (*Valente* ... , at p. 687):

The relationship between these two aspects of judicial independence is that an individual judge may enjoy the essential conditions of judicial independence but if the court or tribunal over which he or she presides is not independent of the other branches of government, in what is essential to its function, he or she cannot be said to be an independent tribunal.

[119] It is necessary to explain the relationship between the three core characteristics and the two dimensions of judicial independence, because Le Dain J did not fully do so in *Valente*. For example, he stated that security of tenure was part of the individual independence of a court or tribunal, whereas administrative independence was identified with institutional or collective independence. However, the core characteristics of judicial independence, and the dimensions of judicial independence, are two very different concepts. The core characteristics of judicial independence are distinct facets of the definition of judicial independence. Security of tenure, financial security, and administrative independence come together to constitute judicial independence. By contrast, the dimensions of judicial independence indicate which entity—the individual judge or the court or tribunal to which he or she belongs—is protected by a particular core characteristic.

[120] The conceptual distinction between the core characteristics and the dimensions of judicial independence suggests that it may be possible for a core characteristic to have both an individual and an institutional or collective dimension. To be sure, sometimes a core characteristic only attaches to a particular dimension of judicial independence; administrative independence, for example, only attaches to the court as an institution (although

sometimes it may be exercised on behalf of a court by its chief judge or justice). However, this need not always be the case. The guarantee of security of tenure, for example, may have a collective or institutional dimension, such that only a body composed of judges may recommend the removal of a judge. However, I need not decide that particular point here.

These three core characteristics of security of tenure, financial security, and administrative independence are discussed in turn below.

1. Security of Tenure

Constitutionally protected security of tenure has both an individual and an institutional dimension. Individual security of tenure means that judges may not be dismissed by the executive before the age of retirement except for misconduct or disability. Thus, a judge may only be removed from office for a reason relating to his or her capacity to perform his or her judicial duties. Arbitrary removal is prohibited: see *Mackin*, 2002 SCC 13 at paras 42 and 43, [2002] 1 SCR 405.

Institutionally, before a judge may be removed for cause, "there must be a judicial inquiry to establish that such cause exists, at which the judge affected must be afforded an opportunity to be heard": see *Re Therrien*, 2001 SCC 35 at para 39, [2001] 2 SCR 3. Superior court judges are removable only by a joint address (in effect, successful motions) of the House of Commons and the Senate, per s 99 of the *Constitution Act, 1867*: see *Ell v Alberta*, 2003 SCC 35 at para 31, [2003] 1 SCR 857.

In the early years after Confederation, only four cases came before Parliament seeking removal, the last of which concluded in 1881. None were successful. In the 1960s, the case of Justice Leo Landreville was referred to a royal commission before coming before Parliament. He ultimately resigned, but his case has been described as a "travesty of justice" and a demonstration of the inadequacy of Parliament as a vehicle for investigating allegations of judicial misconduct: see William Kaplan, *Bad Judgment: The Case of Mr. Justice Leo A. Landreville* (Toronto: University of Toronto Press, 1996).

In 1971, the *Judges Act*, RSC 1985, c J-1 was amended to establish the Canadian Judicial Council (CJC) as the body responsible for investigating complaints about the conduct of federally appointed judges. If the council concludes that removal of a judge is warranted, it makes a report to the minister of justice, who may introduce a motion before Parliament. Authority to recommend removal of a judge from office is found in s 69(3) of the *Judges Act*:

> The Governor in Council may, on the recommendation of the Minister, after receipt of a report described in subsection 65(1) in relation to an inquiry under this section in connection with a person who may be removed from office by the Governor in Council other than on an address of the Senate or House of Commons or on a joint address of the Senate and House of Commons, by order, remove the person from office.

In practice, every judge facing convincing allegations of misconduct has resigned at some stage of the council's proceedings rather than going before Parliament for an ultimate determination.

The description of the CJC complaints process is available on the council's website, online: *Canadian Judicial Council* <https://cjc-ccm.ca/en>.

For an analysis of the role of the council in dealing with judicial misconduct, including five case studies, see Ed Ratushny, "Speaking as Judges: How Far Can They Go?" (2000) 11 NJCL 293.

The reports of formal inquiry committees established by the CJC are available on its website: *Canadian Judicial Council* <https://cjc-ccm.ca/en>. An inquiry committee of the council conducts a formal public hearing into the allegations of misconduct and reports to the full council. The council, in turn, may then make a report to the minister of justice. Consider the 1996 report of the CJC in relation to Bienvenue J.

Report of the Canadian Judicial Council to the Minister of Justice Under Section 63(1) of the Judges Act Concerning the Conduct of Mr. Justice Jean Bienvenue of the Superior Court of Quebec in R v T Théberge

(Ottawa: CJC, October 1996)

The majority of the Canadian Judicial Council, consisting of:

> Chief Justice Lamer (Chief Justice of Canada), Chief Justice Clarke (Nova Scotia), Associate Chief Justice Deslongschamps (Quebec), Associate Chief Justice Dohm (British Columbia), Chief Justice Esson (British Columbia), Chief Justice Fraser (Alberta), Chief Justice Glube (Nova Scotia), Chief Justice Gushue (Newfoundland), Chief Justice Hewak (Manitoba), Mr. Justice Hudson (Yukon Territory), Chief Justice Lemieux (Quebec), Chief Justice LeSage (Ontario), Chief Justice MacPherson (Saskatchewan), Chief Justice McEachern (British Columbia), Chief Justice McMurtry (Ontario), Associate Chief Justice Mercier (Manitoba), Chief Justice Moore (Alberta), Associate Chief Justice Morden (Ontario), Associate Chief Justice Oliphant (Manitoba), Associate Chief Justice Palmeter (Nova Scotia), Chief Justice Scott (Manitoba), and Associate Chief Justice Wachowich (Alberta),

is of the opinion that Mr. Justice Bienvenue has become incapacitated or disabled from the due execution of the office of judge and recommends that he be removed from the office of judge of the Superior Court of Quebec. The majority except Chief Justice McEachern rely on sections 65(2)(b), (c) and (d) of the *Judges Act*; their reasons are attached. In separate concurring reasons, which will follow at a later date, Chief Justice McEachern relies only on section 65(2)(d).

The following members of the Council dissent from this decision:

> Chief Justice Bayda (Saskatchewan), Chief Justice Carruthers (Prince Edward Island), Associate Chief Judge Christie (Tax Court of Canada), Chief Justice Hickman . (Newfoundland), Chief Justice Hoyt (New Brunswick), Chief Justice MacDonald (Prince Edward Island), and Associate Chief Justice Smith (Ontario).

for reasons to follow at a later date.

Antonio Lamer
Chairman
September 20, 1996

Reasons of All Majority Members Except Chief Justice McEachern

We are in substantial agreement with the conclusions stated by the majority of the Inquiry Committee under the heading "Recommendation" in its report dated June 25, 1996, as follows:

> If the judge's meeting with the jury after the verdict [in which he made comments critical of its performance] had been an isolated occurrence, we would merely have expressed our disapproval of this violation of paragraphs 65(2)(b) and (c) of the Act, on the assumption that such an occurrence would not happen again. The judge's remarks about women and his deepseated ideas behind those remarks legitimately cast doubt on his impartiality in the execution of his judicial office. Yet impartiality is the essence of the office of judge. Accordingly, this violation led us to conduct a further analysis to determine whether Mr. Justice Bienvenue had become incapacitated or disabled from the due execution of the office of judge.

That analysis required us to review all the incidents that marked Tracy Théberge's trial or occurred after that trial. We also particularly took account of Mr. Justice Bienvenue's testimony at the inquiry. We find that the judge has shown an aggravating lack of sensitivity to the communities and individuals offended by his remarks or conduct. In addition—the evidence could not be any clearer—Mr. Justice Bienvenue does not intend to change his behaviour in any way.

Because of his conduct during all the incidents that marked Tracy Théberge's trial, Mr. Justice Bienvenue has undermined public confidence in him and strongly contributed to destroying public confidence in the judicial system. In our view, this is the conclusion that would be reached by a reasonable and informed person.

Combining the test used by the Committee of the Canadian Judicial Council in the *Marshall* case and that applied by the Supreme Court to assess judicial impartiality and independence, we believe that if Mr. Justice Bienvenue were to preside over a case, a reasonable and informed person, viewing the matter realistically and practically—and having thought the matter through—would have a reasonable apprehension that the judge would not execute his office with the objectivity, impartiality and independence that the public is entitled to expect from a judge.

We are therefore of the opinion that Mr. Justice Bienvenue has breached the duty of good behaviour under section 99 of the *Constitution Act, 1867* and has become incapacitated or disabled from the due execution of the office of judge for the reasons set out in paragraphs 65(2)(b), (c) and (d) of the *Judges Act*:

- having been guilty of misconduct,
- having failed in the due execution of that office,
- having been placed, by his conduct, in a position incompatible with the due execution of that office,

and we recommend that he be removed from office.

We are, however, of the view that the question whether Mr. Justice Bienvenue breached the duty of good behaviour under s. 99 of the *Constitution Act, 1867*, is one exclusively for consideration by Parliament. We have, therefore, only addressed the provisions of s. 65 of the *Judges Act*.

The totality of the matters dealt with by the Inquiry Committee demonstrably support the majority Committee's conclusion that "Mr. Justice Bienvenue has shown an almost complete lack of sensitivity to the communities and individuals offended by his remarks." Interwoven throughout the evidence is a complete lack of appreciation by Mr. Justice Bienvenue of the duties and responsibilities of a judge.

It is important to note that the majority emphasized that: "In addition—the evidence cannot be any clearer—Mr. Justice Bienvenue does not intend to change his behaviour in any way."

No attempt has been made by Mr. Justice Bienvenue since the delivery of the report of the Inquiry Committee to indicate any intention on his part to, in fact, change his behaviour.

It is essential to the integrity of the administration of justice that the public have confidence in the impartiality of the judiciary. We agree with the majority of the Inquiry Committee that the public can no longer reasonably have such confidence in Mr. Justice Bienvenue.

Concurring Reasons of Chief Justice McEachern

September 27, 1996

I agree with the recommendation of the majority of my colleagues that the Honourable Mr. Justice Bienvenue of the Superior Court of Quebec has become incapacitated or disabled from the due performance of his office of judge but I would limit the basis for this finding to s. 65(2)(d), that is to say by having been placed by his conduct or otherwise in a position incompatible with the due execution of his office.

The standard of proof in this matter is the civil standard of a balance of probabilities. Because of the importance of the issues, the grounds must be powerfully persuasive.

Applying that standard, I am unable to find that Mr. Justice Bienvenue is biased against Jewish persons. His unfortunate and entirely inaccurate comment about the Holocaust in the sentencing proceedings was a highly insensitive, inappropriate and very bad analogy that should not have been used to assist him to describe the nature of the offence with which he was dealing. I note that his apology to the Jewish community satisfied those organizations who reported, after meeting with the judge, that they observed no evidence of anti-Semitism in his attitude.

I depart from the reasons of the majority only because, with all possible deference and respect, I do not wish to base my concurrence on any grounds except the reasonable apprehension he has created, by his words and conduct, that he may permit his strongly held beliefs about the relative qualities of men and women to affect the decisions he may be called upon to decide in the course of his judicial duties.

To put it more bluntly, it is my view that in many cases that arise for decision in the course of the work of a busy court, litigants whose cases are assigned to Mr. Justice Bienvenue, both men and women, may reasonably apprehend, and be fearful, that in some cases he will stereotype women worse than men, and in other cases he will stereotype women better than men.

These simplistic views, when they intrude into legal proceedings, breach the fundamental equality requirements of the Constitution of Canada and the ordinary fairness expectations of litigants in our courts. I wish emphatically to record that there can be no reasonable expectation that judges must all have the same views about all matters. This case, however, crosses the line because Mr. Justice Bienvenue expressed, and later reaffirmed, his idiosyncratic views at a crucial stage in the sentencing proceedings he was conducting and thereby created a reasonable apprehension that his unusual views did play a part in reaching the sentence he imposed.

Moreover, as the evidence shows, Mr. Justice Bienvenue made it clear that he still held firmly to such views at the time of the Inquiry hearings, and he thereby lent support to the reasonable apprehension created by his sentencing remarks that other litigants would risk unfairness in his court.

Because it is unnecessary to go further, I disavow reliance upon any of the other grounds apparently relied upon by the Inquiry Committee, singly or cumulatively, as sufficient grounds for a recommendation for removal even though it appears that Mr. Justice Bienvenue, in the closing days of the trial in question, was conducting himself in a manner other than what is expected of federally appointed judges. It is unnecessary to decide how those other grounds should be classified or what varying degrees of seriousness should be assigned to them.

Reasons of the Minority by Chief Justice Bayda

October 1, 1996

The issue in these proceedings before the Canadian Judicial Council is whether, to use the words of the majority of the Inquiry Committee, "an individual who has been a judge for almost 20 years and whose integrity has not been questioned" did, by his conduct during a three-week murder trial, and by his conduct in speaking to the news media after the trial, demonstrate that he has become incapacitated or disabled from the due execution of his judicial duties and, for that reason, ought to be removed from office.

Sections 65(2)(b), (c) and (d) of the *Judges Act* are the governing provisions:

> 65(2) Where, in the opinion of the Council, the judge in respect of whom an inquiry or investigation has been made has become incapacitated or disabled from the due execution of the office of judge by reason of
>
> • • •
>
> (b) having been guilty of misconduct,
> (c) having failed in the due execution of that office, or
> (d) having been placed, by his conduct or otherwise, in a position incompatible with the due execution of that office,
>
> the Council, in its report to the Minister under subsection (1), may recommend that the judge be removed from office.

They must be read in conjunction with and interpreted in the light of s. 99 of the *Constitution Act*:

> 99. The judges of the superior courts shall hold office during good behaviour but shall be removable by the governor general on address of the Senate and House of Commons.

The proceedings were initiated by a letter from the Minister of Justice of Canada to Council and a letter from the Minister of Justice of Quebec to Council requesting Council to inquire, pursuant to the *Judges Act*, into the conduct of the judge in question, Mr. Justice Bienvenue of the Superior Court of Quebec, during and after the murder trial of Ms. Tracy Théberge.

An Inquiry Committee established in accordance with the *Judges Act*, and comprising three members of Council and two lawyers appointed by the Minister of Justice of Canada, inquired into the judge's conduct. They heard 19 witnesses including the judge, as well as submissions from independent counsel, and the judge's counsel. The Committee considered the matter and prepared a majority and a minority report.

Four members signed the former and one the latter. The reports were filed with the Council. The majority made findings of fact and law and ultimately concluded as follows:

> We are therefore of the opinion that Mr. Justice Jean Bienvenue has breached the duty of good behaviour under section 99 of the *Constitution Act, 1867* and has become incapacitated or disabled from the due execution of the office of judge for the reasons set out in paragraphs 65(2)(b), (c) and (d) of the *Judges Act*:
>
> • having been guilty of misconduct,
> • having failed in the due execution of that office,
> • having been placed, by his conduct, in a position incompatible with the due execution of that office, and we recommend that he be removed from office.

After considering the two reports and further written submissions from both counsel, the Judicial Council reached a decision—not unanimous—to recommend to the Minister that Mr. Justice Bienvenue be removed from office for essentially the reasons given by the majority of the Inquiry Committee. The lack of unanimity has given rise to three reports by Council, one by the majority, excluding Chief Justice McEachern, one by Chief Justice McEachern supporting the majority decision, and this report by the minority. The Council did not hear any oral evidence or any oral submissions. Mr. Justice Bienvenue, although given the opportunity, did not appear before Council.

The majority of the Inquiry Committee made certain findings of primary fact which we accept. We do not, however, accept the Committee's crucial conclusory findings, either of law or fact. The findings of primary fact to which we refer are these:

1. the "Kleenex" remarks to a female juror;
2. certain uncomplimentary remarks about a parking attendant;
3. certain inappropriate comments to a female reporter concerning her attire;
4. remarks to a court official in the judge's private chambers about the jury's competence and about the accused's colour and sexual orientation;
5. meeting of the judge with the jurors after the verdict;
6. remarks by the judge during sentencing concerning women in general (and about men) and separate remarks concerning the victims of the Holocaust;
7. events that occurred after sentencing.

It is the sixth and seventh of these, insofar as they particularly concern women, that were the true focus of the Inquiry Committee and of Council. It is fair to say that the remarks about women were the catalytic force which precipitated the decision to recommend removal.

Had those remarks not been made, the improprieties of conduct reflected in the remainder of the primary facts (1 to 5) taken separately and cumulatively, would not have been a sufficient basis for the decision to recommend removal. They may have given rise to some form of sanction, perhaps even a severe disapproval, but not removal.

It is clear from the Committee's majority report that, while the majority did not brush aside these other improprieties, they were used mainly as a buttress to the conclusion the majority reached regarding the consequences that are to flow from the remarks concerning women in general. It is for these reasons that we will emphasize the aspect of the Committee's report that pertains to the remarks about women—remarks that none of us believes to be true or appropriate for use by a judge.

The judge said this about women in his sentencing remarks:

IT HAS always been said, and correctly so, that when—women—whom I have always considered the noblest beings in creation and the noblest (sic) of the two sexes of the human race—it is said that when women ascend the scale of virtues, they reach higher than men, and I have always believed this. AND it is also said, and this too I believe, that when they decide to degrade themselves, they sink to depths to which even the vilest man could not sink.

ALAS, YOU ARE indeed in the image of these women so famous in history: the Delilahs, the Salome, Charlotte Corday, Mata Hari and how many others who have been a sad part of our history and have debased the profile of women. You are one of them, and you are the clearest living example of them that I have seen.

After the trial was completed the judge repeated some of these remarks several times to various news media. During the hearing before the Inquiry Committee the judge reaffirmed his belief in the truth of these remarks. The judge intimated that the genesis for the belief was his cultural and religious upbringing and the reality that a like belief has been held by many thinkers over the centuries. He made it quite clear that he would not readily be disabused of that belief.

The first point to note is that the misconduct alleged against the judge consists of words spoken by the judge in the context of a judicial proceeding. It is important to keep that context in mind. A judge performing his or her judicial function acts in a very different capacity from a judge who chooses to speak extra-judicially on a certain subject. A judge performing his or her judicial function needs to examine all sides of a particular question, not only the side favoured by one party to the proceeding or the side favoured by a large segment of the population who may have an interest in the proceeding. He or she needs to give full consideration to *individual* interests and should, generally speaking, be more concerned with protecting those individual interests than with pursuing communal goals. The area of communal goals is better left to the legislature whose job it is to enunciate general policy and enact the means to achieve the policy goals, and to the executive branch of government whose job it is to carry into effect such legislative policy.

In the course of examining all sides of a question and giving full consideration to individual interests, a judge is apt to play the role of a devil's advocate, to think out loud and to use language—sometimes appropriate, sometimes inappropriate—that one side or some segment of society may find unacceptable. For example—a judge may feel it necessary in the interests of justice, to tell a litigant that he or she is an "unmitigated liar" or that society will no longer put up with the litigant's "brutal propensities" or "lawless attitude" and so on. Anyone familiar with judicial proceedings will readily recognize this sort of exercise and ought to be very loathe to restrict judges from engaging in it.

Moreover, it is important and sometimes essential that a judge speak his or her mind, giving full reasons for reaching a decision. Not only is this important to litigants it is also important to courts of appeal reviewing the judge's decision. They ought to be in a position of some certainty if they are to rule on whether a judge erred in his or her conclusions and if so where the error occurred. Any restriction that inspires judges to keep their reasons to themselves, generally speaking, should be discouraged, as it does not auger well for the administration of justice. And lastly, in this respect, it is important to keep in mind that remarks made in the course of a judicial proceeding are subject to the scrutiny of a court of appeal and any injustice created by reason of a judge's unacceptable belief is correctable.

It logically follows that from the standpoint of disciplinary consequences which ought to flow from a judge's improper remarks, remarks made during judicial proceedings ought not to be judged as harshly as those made extra-judicially. That, of course, does not mean a judge can with impunity say whatever he or she wants during a judicial proceeding, but it does mean that the boundaries are different for the two contexts. Did the judge cross the boundary in the present case? It is necessary to consider this question from two perspectives: substance and perception.

In our respectful view the belief voiced by the judge reflected a predilection or predisposition, even a bias perhaps, regarding both men and women that is unacceptable to many people in our society and actually repugnant to some, perhaps many. The basic question that needs to be examined is this: What effect, if any, does the "having" of this predilection, predisposition, or bias by a judge, have upon the ability and the capacity of a judge to perform his or her judicial functions?

Every judge knows, and every reasonably informed person not a judge who approaches the issue objectively ought to know, that like every other member of the human species all judges have certain predilections. Judges are not—and society does not want them to be—intellectual eunuchs devoid of any philosophy of life, of society, of government or of law and a judge's world is the same as the public's—a world of realism rather than a world of idealism. The critical question is not: Does the judge have a predilection? Rather the critical question is: Is the judge able and prepared to set the predilection aside and not *put it to work* in the exercise of his or her judicial functions?

Where the misconduct alleged against a judge centres on some unacceptable predilection the judge is said to have, what is the threshold for determining whether the judge is guilty of misconduct, or has failed in the due execution of the office of a judge, or has been placed in a position incompatible with the due execution of this office? The threshold is not whether there is proof the judge in fact *has* that predilection. Nor is the threshold whether the judge is able or intends to shed the predilection. Shedding the predilection or not shedding it is still a question of "having" or "not having" the predilection. The threshold has to go beyond "having." It is whether there is proof the judge has in fact recurringly in the past *put the predilection to work* to the detriment of litigants or in all likelihood intends in the future to recurringly put it to work to the detriment of litigants.

If merely "having" a predilection were sufficient, it is not difficult to envision consequences resembling kafkaesque scenarios, and questions that are downright disturbing. Would judges' past writings, speeches, judgments, etc. be scrutinized to detect evidence of certain kinds of unacceptable predilections? Would the results produce a proliferation of Inquiry Committees looking into the "conduct" of misspoken judges? Would some sort of "thought" police become a reality? Would judgments need to be tailored and crafted with care and precision heretofore not imagined? Does society want its judges to become easier shooting targets for certain disenchanted segments of society? Does the making of judges into easier shooting targets enhance or diminish the administration of justice in the eyes of the reasonably informed members of society? Will judges be prompted to cull from their judicial vocabularies such Shakespearian phrases as "pure as Caesar's wife," and such pedestrian everyday expressions as "christian charity" or "godlike features" which, until now, have simply rolled off one's tongue?

Our form of democratic society envisages a judiciary unfettered in its ability to think and unhobbled in its capacity to hold views that do not accord with those of the mainstream. To be removed from office for merely "having" a predilection or predisposition or bias flies in the face of the legitimacy of that unfettered and unhobbled judiciary.

The next question which needs to be examined is this: What is the proof in the present case of Mr. Justice Bienvenue's "having" the predilection *and* "putting it to work to the detriment of litigants." When he spoke the impugned words in the course of sentencing, he clearly affirmed that he had the predilection. When he spoke to the media in the days after the trial he reiterated the words. This amounted to nothing more than a re-affirmation that he has the predilection. When confronted before the Inquiry Committee he again re-affirmed he has the predilection. He also confirmed that he either would not or could not readily shed it. But as noted, not shedding it does not put the analysis past the "having" stage. The threshold stage is putting the predilection to work to the detriment of litigants.

Is there proof that Mr. Justice Bienvenue put this predilection to work before the Théberge case took place? The answer is *no*. The only evidence in this regard is that upon which the Inquiry Committee found Mr. Justice Bienvenue to be "an individual who has been a judge for almost 20 years and whose integrity has not been questioned." It must be remembered that the terms of reference of the Inquiry Committee did not include an investigation of Mr. Justice Bienvenue's conduct preceding the Théberge case.

Is there proof that Mr. Justice Bienvenue put the predilection to work in the Théberge case to the detriment of Ms. Théberge? Again, in our respectful view, the answer is *no*. The Committee made no finding of fact that would assist in this respect. The only item of evidence that may be interpreted as tending to show that predilection at work is the decision by Mr. Justice Bienvenue to impose a 14-year parole ineligibility on Ms. Théberge's life sentence despite the jury's recommendation of the minimum 10-year period of ineligibility. Whether it is *possible* for that circumstance to be interpreted as the predilection at work is one thing. Whether *in fact* it should be interpreted that way is quite another. There is not the slightest indication that given the viciousness of the killing the judge would not have made an identical ruling had the offender been a male rather than a female. Even if the judge's ruling can be shown to be the predilection at work, this is only one instance of that happening. One instance is hardly evidence of recurrence. Furthermore, the way to correct that one instance is—as has been done—to refer this justiciable matter to the Court of Appeal. That is where the matter rightfully belongs. This one instance is hardly a matter for the Canadian Judicial Council to use as a spearhead for a recommendation consisting of the draconian step of an irrevocable removal of the judge from office.

That leaves for determination the presence of proof of whether Mr. Justice Bienvenue intends in the future to "recurringly put the predilection to work to the detriment of litigants." In our respectful view there is not the slightest evidence of the judge's future intent in respect of putting his predilection to work. There is, as noted earlier, evidence of his inability or disinclination to shed his predilection (perhaps even evidence of his reluctance to express contrition) but, also as noted, all that is evidence of "having" not of "putting the predilection to work"—a distinctly different factor. When the Inquiry Committee found "In addition—the evidence could not be any clearer—Mr. Justice Bienvenue does not intend to change his behaviour in any way," it must have confused "behaviour" with "having." It could not have been referring to "putting the predilection to work" because there was no evidence of his "putting the predilection to work" in the past. And since there was no evidence it makes no sense to talk about "no change" to that "behaviour." The Committee was obviously confusing "having" with "behaviour" or referring to some other kind of behaviour. There is no presumption in law or in the realm of common sense that having a predilection and being disinclined or unable to shed it will automatically mean that the judge will put the predilection to work to the detriment of the litigants either at every opportunity or from time to time. To make the presumption in this case is unfair to Mr. Justice Bienvenue and puts at risk every other judge in the country against whom a like presumption might be made in respect of whatever general predisposition it is the judge may have. The presumption that ought to be made is that the judge, as judges have been doing from time immemorial, will engage his or her professionalism and will set aside such predispositions as often as is required. The presumption should prevail unless there is evidence to the contrary.

In summary it is our respectful view the majority of the Inquiry Committee made two critical interrelated errors.

The first is this: The majority did not make the crucial distinction between "having" a predilection and "putting it to work to the detriment of litigants." This is evident in at least two conclusory findings made by the Committee:

Because of his [having] ideas about both women and men, Mr. Justice Bienvenue's impartiality in the execution of his judicial office has legitimately been called into question.

• • •

Like anyone else, a judge can have a bad day. In this case, the breaches of ethics brought to our attention—the *judge's repeated remarks about women* and the comments he made to the jurors after their verdict—are serious and, as with the other incidents alleged against him, have not been retracted by him. We are therefore not dealing here merely with strong language. (italics added)

The second is this: The majority found that having a predilection and being unable or disinclined to shed it is the same as putting the predilection to work. Alternatively the majority applied a presumption that being unable or disinclined to shed the predilection is automatically followed not by a setting aside of the predilection but by putting the predilection to work to the detriment of litigants.

In our respectful view the majority of this Council repeated those same two errors. In its report it says, "No attempt has been made by Mr. Justice Bienvenue since the delivery of the report of the Inquiry Committee to indicate any intention on his part to, in fact, change his behaviour." (One gets the distinct impression the majority would have been prepared to absolve Mr. Justice Bienvenue had he shown some contrition or expressed penitence.) Although it is not entirely clear, it would appear that when the majority of Council speaks of "behaviour" they mean "having" the predilection concerning women. When they speak of "change" they mean shedding the predilection concerning women. By "behaviour" they do not mean and could not mean "putting the predilection to work" because there is no evidence of the predilection being put to work in the past. The corollary, of course, is that there could be no "change" to "putting the predilection to work."

The foregoing analysis deals primarily with the issue from the perspective of *substance*. From that perspective, the basic question should properly read: What effect, if any, does the "having" of the predilection by a judge, have upon the *actual* ability and the *actual* capacity of a judge to perform his or her judicial function? The answer as we have seen is none.

From the perspective of *perception* the basic question becomes: What effect, if any, does the "having" of the predilection by a judge have upon the *perceived* ability and the *perceived* capacity of a judge to perform his or her judicial function? The majority of the Committee reached this conclusion:

Because of his conduct during all the incidents that marked Tracy Théberge's trial, Mr. Justice Bienvenue has undermined public confidence in him and strongly contributed to destroying public confidence in the judicial system. In our view, this is the conclusion that would be reached by a reasonable and informed person.

Combining the test used by the Committee of the Canadian Judicial Council in the *Marshall* case and that applied by the Supreme Court to assess judicial impartiality and independence, we believe that if Mr. Justice Bienvenue were to preside over a case, a reasonable and informed person, viewing the matter realistically and practically—and having thought the matter through—would have a reasonable apprehension that the judge would not execute his office with the objectivity, impartiality and independence that the public is entitled to expect from a judge.

The majority of Council agreed.

With the greatest of deference to both the majority of the Committee and the majority of Council we strongly disagree that a reasonable and informed person would assess the remarks concerning women in this harsh fashion and would in the end have the complete lack of confidence and the reasonable apprehension described by the majority of the Committee (and agreed with by the majority of the Council) to the point where he or she would vote to remove Mr. Justice Bienvenue from office.

A reasonable and informed person by definition would make the assessment and view all of the issues objectively. That means the person would need to set aside any biases, predilections or predispositions he or she had, and not "put them to work" in making the assessment. A reasonable, informed and objective person would need to consider a series of relevant factors and would likely ask and answer questions such as these:

1. Is having a predilection enough to render a judge incapable, or must there be more? For example, must there be a "putting to work" of the predilection? We have already seen where "having" alone leads. A reasonable, informed, objective person should easily be able to come to the same conclusion.

2. Where did Mr. Justice Bienvenue get these ideas? A reasonable, informed and objective person would know that the ideas reflected in Mr. Justice Bienvenue's words have been around for centuries. One does not need to be a biblical scholar to know that both the Old and New Testaments are replete with thinking not unlike that reflected in Mr. Justice Bienvenue's words. If he was brought up in a Judeo-Christian culture, and he apparently was, it is not difficult to understand why he would think this way.

He, of course, is far from alone in having these outdated beliefs. Some institutions in our society continue to promote this sort of thinking.

A reasonable, informed and objective person will quickly recognize that Mr. Justice Bienvenue is continuing to trade in a variant of the stereotypical view about the essential personalities and characteristics of men and women. The view, once orthodox and mainstream was universally held by leaders and other members of society including our law makers—parliamentarians and judges—and our appointers of judges. It found expression in our many institutions such as our schools and churches, in our many intellectual, social, cultural and sport associations, and, in our laws—both statutory and judge-made. To quickly remind oneself of the type of laws that prevailed, one needs only to read such recent decisions by the Supreme Court of Canada as *R v. Seaboyer*, [1991] 2 SCR 577 and *R v. Butler*, [1992] 1 SCR 452 and some custody cases espousing principles, as for example those embodied in the "tender years doctrine" (see *Talsky v. Talsky*, [1976] 2 SCR 292).

The stereotypical view is the progenitor of what is now considered idiosyncratic thinking and a bias, predisposition or predilection unfavourable to women. A reasonable, informed and objective person who encounters someone in authority who is continuing to trade in the view may be concerned, disappointed, perhaps even surprised. But given the view's recent pervading, universal, long-term reign and its continuing currency in some circles, he or she would hardly be "shocked"—to borrow a term from the *Marshall* test referred to by the Committee.

3. But this is 1996, is it right for judges to have these kinds of outmoded views and beliefs? The answer is no, but the shift from what was orthodox and mainstream to what is now unorthodox and passé is an evolutionary one, not a precipitous one reminiscent of a revolution. It is only in relatively recent times that the evolution has been making progress. Some judges were quick to adjust and adapt. Others have not been so quick. In order to consummate and complete the evolution now well underway should one resort to a "sledge hammer" approach to beat into submission

the remaining judges who still think that way? Or should one opt for a more sophisticated and in the end a more practical approach respecting Mr. Justice Bienvenue and the remaining judges? A reasonable, informed and objective person would have no difficulty in answering the first question in the negative and the second in the affirmative.

4. Is there some way other than removal from office that one could use to ensure that Mr. Justice Bienvenue does not continue to trade in his stereotypical belief (thereby running the risk of putting his predilection to work)? Social context education is clearly a viable avenue and in the end a very real practical approach. There was no evidence before the Committee or before Council that Mr. Justice Bienvenue has been putting his predilection to work during the past twenty years he has been a judge. (As noted his past conduct before the Théberge trial took place was not before the Committee or Council.) With proper and repeated education, there should be very little difficulty ensuring his predilection is not "put to work." Indeed with proper education and time he may even become convinced that his belief is bad, and should that occur one would not need to be concerned about his putting to work the predilection it reflects. A reasonable, informed and objective person would likely conclude that it is much too early to say that he is so irredeemable that one should metaphorically "put him behind bars and throw away the key."

5. Does the fact the words were spoken by Mr. Justice Bienvenue in court and not extra-judicially make a difference? A reasonable, informed and objective person would after reflection conclude that there is a difference, for the reasons outlined earlier. He or she would conclude that any injustice resulting from the words spoken on this one occasion should properly be dealt with by a court of appeal and not by a disciplinary body. Had there been a pattern of such conduct—a recurrence—the matter might need to be viewed in a different light. But there is no evidence of such a pattern.

6. Does the removal of one judge for speaking unacceptable words solve what may be a minor (in terms of numbers) institutional problem? In the decision to remove the judge in these circumstances, is there an element of "judicial cleansing," something in the nature of a "judicial crucifixion" in expiation of past and future "sins of the judiciary," a purported reconciliation of the judiciary with the public? One would hope not but one is not entirely sure.

7. Does removing Mr. Justice Bienvenue for "having" a predilection affecting men and women mean that other judges having other predilections, such as predilections favourable or unfavourable towards abortion, environmental despoiling, big business, the media, governmental bureaucracy, gambling, gun control and so on, ought also to be removed? Would it make any difference if the judge not only held a predilection concerning a subject matter but a bias against the persons involved with the subject matter (e.g. abortionists, pro-lifers, polluters, bureaucrats, gamblers, etc.)? Were the answers to the first and perhaps the second question "yes" the ranks of the judiciary would be depleted quite dramatically. A reasonable, informed and objective person would appreciate the total undesirability of the consequence to society of removal for having such predilections and biases but, more important, would conclude that judges should be presumed to be able and willing to set aside their predilections and biases.

This series of questions is not intended as an exhaustive list. There are other questions that may need to be considered. In the result we are confident that a

reasonable and informed person, viewing and assessing the circumstances objectively would not acquire an apprehension and a lack of confidence of the type
described by the majority of the Committee and the majority of Council.

It is unfortunate that the majority of the Committee treated itself as a court and
the proceedings before it as a court proceeding where there is a *lis inter partes*
rather than as a tribunal with no *lis* before it but whose primary role was a search for
truth (as the Supreme Court of Canada held in *Ruffo v. Conseil de la magistrature*,
[1995] 4 SCR 267).

Had the Committee not overlooked this aspect of its *raison d'être* it would not
have excluded a consideration of the results of a poll Mr. Justice Bienvenue's counsel sought to introduce. We, as members of Council, would very much have liked to
interpret the results of that poll for ourselves rather than have been left in the dark.
The poll may have been a better source of information than the editorial writers for
some of the Quebec press whose views were readily available to all Council members.

The majority of the Committee in its report said this: "Under the Act, this Committee is responsible for assessing the judge's conduct." The Committee seemed to
overlook the fact that s. 65(2) of the *Judges Act* places that responsibility on Council.
As Council members, we would have appreciated any help we could get, including
poll results, to which we could have ascribed whatever weight we thought proper,
in order to make a proper assessment of the state of the public's confidence in the
judiciary and public's apprehension or lack of it, concerning Mr. Justice Bienvenue.

In our respectful view too much emphasis was placed by the majority of both
the Committee and the Council upon what judges think the public's reaction ought
to be rather than upon what the public's reaction actually was. In a matter as serious as the one concerning the removal of a judge, the public whose judges we are,
ought to have more direct say, even at this stage of the proceedings, about what is
their apprehension of bias and their lack of confidence or otherwise in the judiciary.

To this point we have dealt only with the remarks concerning men and women
and have not dealt with any of the other improprieties found by the Committee.
In our respectful view those other improprieties—the buttress for the decision to
remove—when put into the crucible of scrutiny either separately or cumulatively
fare no better than the remarks concerning men and women—the main pillar for
the decision to remove. If the main pillar falls, the buttresses either fall or are considerably diminished in importance from the standpoint of a decision to remove.

The only conduct other than the remarks concerning women and men that
could possibly fall into a category serious enough to consider removing a judge
from office were the remarks concerning Jews and the Holocaust.

It is clear from the evidence considered by the Committee that these remarks,
after due explanation and apology by Mr. Justice Bienvenue, did not raise in the
minds of those most closely affected by them the lack of public confidence in the
judiciary or the apprehension of bias held by the Committee to have been raised
by the other improprieties. Although the remarks were flagrantly insensitive, hurt-
ful, and grossly inappropriate, the Committee did not find any misconduct on the
part of Mr. Justice Bienvenue attributable to the remarks concerning Jews and the
Holocaust. In our respectful view this was a proper finding. By making no reference
to this matter in its report the majority of Council appears to have agreed with the
Committee's finding as well.

In view of the decision reached by the majority of Council it was not necessary
for us, the minority, to consider whether Mr. Justice Bienvenue's conduct, taken as
a whole, during the trial of Ms. Théberge ought to attract some sanction other than
removal from office. And we, of course, make no finding in that respect. We are,
however, prepared to say that, given the primary facts found by the Committee,

we found the conduct of Mr. Justice Bienvenue, taken as a whole, unacceptable, insensitive, and of a type that we do not at all condone.

Before closing we desire to raise three procedural questions that were not put before either the Inquiry Committee or Council. We raise the questions not because we have made any decisions relating to them (we have not) but as suggestions for Council to consider sometime in the future in an effort to improve our disciplinary procedures.

One wonders whether the Inquiry Committee, essentially a fact finding, investigative tribunal, would not have been well advised, given the circumstances of the present case, to canvass the entire federally-appointed judiciary to seek the judiciary's opinion on the relevant questions of the public's lack of confidence and reasonable apprehension and the resultant incapacity or disability of the judge to further perform his judicial functions. As a fact finding body with no *lis* before it, is not the Committee (and ultimately Council) entitled to all the intelligent help it can get on issues like these? The results of the "canvass" would simply have been another "primary fact" available to the Committee and Council to consider. The results would not have been determinative. Rules of evidence governing court procedure should not hold sway where no *lis* is involved. Somehow it does not seem right or advisable for the Committee or Council to arrogate to itself all the wisdom necessary to decide an issue as troubling and as far reaching as the removal of a long-serving federally-appointed judge, particularly where the service is described as "with integrity." Moreover, is there not a similarity in process between a canvass of approximately 950 judges and a vote of 399 members of the House of Commons and the Senate acting under s. 99 of the *Constitution Act*?

The second suggestion pertains to the Committee's power, right, or obligation to recommend removal. There is some doubt whether it has this power, right, or obligation under the Act. If the Committee does have it, perhaps it should not. Council members considering any disciplinary measure as serious as removal should approach the issue with a completely open mind and should not feel straitjacketed by a Committee's recommendation. Perhaps the Committee ought to be what the law says it ought to be, namely, a fact finding, investigative body, leaving it to Council to decide whether any sanctions or further steps should flow from the facts found by the Committee. Perhaps the Committee should be entitled to say: "We think there is nothing here for Council to consider" or "we think there is something here for Council to consider," in much the same way that a judge sitting on a preliminary inquiry finds that there is sufficient evidence for a matter to proceed to trial or that there is no sufficient evidence.

It may well be that Council's position in relation to the Minister of Justice and Parliament should be similar to the position we suggest for the Committee in relation to Council.

The third suggestion relates to the composition of the Inquiry Committee provided for in s. 63(3) of the *Judges Act*. This subsection vests in the Minister of Justice for Canada the power to appoint to the Inquiry Committee "such members, if any, of the bar of a province, as may be designated by the Minister." Apart from the constitutional issue which the presence of such a power raises (considered in the *Gratton* inquiry), there is some question about the propriety—from the standpoint of fairness—of the Minister's having or exercising such a power where the Minister instituted the inquiry pursuant to s. 63(1). It is unusual to say the least for a complainant to have the power to appoint a percentage—in the present case 40%—of the adjudicators or assessors who are required to examine and rule upon certain issues arising out of the complaint while the person complained against has no such similar power.

These three suggestions raise issues that we think ought to be explored further.

Upon learning of the recommendation of the council majority, Bienvenue J resigned as a judge.

The reports of two inquiry committees in 2008 and the consequent reports of the council to the minister of justice provide fertile ground for further exploring the boundaries of security of tenure. Both involved the potential removal of Ontario Superior Court judges and address the same fundamental issue of whether the judge can continue to sit or whether public confidence in the judge and the judiciary requires removal.

The questionable conduct of Justice Theodore Matlow arose out of his involvement as a citizen in a community movement, including a group known as Friends of the Village, to oppose certain commercial development in a Toronto neighbourhood. The following excerpt from the report of the Inquiry Committee reflects some of their concerns about his conduct:

> [152] The Inquiry Committee determines that Justice Matlow's overall conduct in organizing and leading the Friends, his assumption of the role of president, spokesperson and, on occasion, advocate of the Friends, his conduct in seeking to personally be a party and as a result being made a party in the OMB application of First Spadina, his conduct in providing guidance, advice and assistance in the application by some members of the Friends to the Superior Court of Justice, and his conduct in assisting in preparation of the supporting affidavit to which was attached copies of letters from him to the Mayor of the City and the Attorney General of Ontario, constitutes conduct that is highly inappropriate for a judge.

(Inquiry Committee Decisions, Matlow (December 2008), Inquiry Committee Report (28 May 2008).)

This conduct did not arise out of his judicial duties but did not conform to the ethical principles expected to govern judges' behaviour even in their private lives. The five members of the Inquiry Committee unanimously concluded that his removal from the office of judge was warranted.

The conduct of Justice Paul Cosgrove arose out his judicial role in the course of conducting proceedings related to a murder trial. In effect, the judge turned the criminal proceedings into an ill-conceived and distorted investigation into the role of the Crown. The four members of the majority of the Inquiry Committee stated:

> 164. In our opinion, the conduct of the judge referred to in this part in failing to exercise restraint and in abusing the powers of his office is conduct which meets the strict test set out above in Marshall. This conclusion does not rest on the appearance of bias or on the judge's incompetence in failing to control the trial. It rests rather on his words and conduct, in abusing judicial independence and acting beyond the powers of a judge.

(Inquiry Committee Decisions, Cosgrove (March 2009), Inquiry Committee Report (27 November 2008).)

They concluded that the conduct called for a recommendation for his removal from office. The dissenting member was of the view that the judge understood the gravity of his conduct and would avoid such conduct in future. A strong admonition would allow the public to continue to have confidence in him as a judge.

The council had no difficulty in unanimously accepting the advice of the majority of the Inquiry Committee in Cosgrove and unanimously recommended to the minister of justice that he be removed from office. Upon learning of this report, Cosgrove resigned (Inquiry Committee Report Decisions, Cosgrove (March 2009), Report of the CJC to the Minister of Justice).

In contrast, the majority of the council in Matlow rejected the unanimous advice of the Inquiry Committee and recommended to the minister of justice that he not be removed from office. A minority of four chief justices unanimously endorsed the advice of the Inquiry Committee and would have recommended removal (Inquiry Committee Decisions, Matlow (December 2008), Report of the CJC to the Minister of Justice).

One of the most controversial cases that the CJC has dealt with involved allegations that a judge was unfit for judicial office because, among other things, compromising photos of her were posted on a pornographic website. These photos were taken and posted prior to her appointment to the bench. The case thus raises the question of the extent to which alleged misconduct prior to appointment should impact a judge's fitness to continue in office post-appointment. It also raises the question of the extent to which private conduct does or should impact a judge's ability to preside over a courtroom. See Adam Dodek, "Sex on the Internet and Fitness for Judicial Office: Correspondent's Report from Canada" (2010) 13:2 Legal Ethics 215, online: *Social Science Research Network* <http://ssrn.com/abstract=1740578>. This case is known as the "Lori Douglas case" after the Hon Lori Douglas, Associate Chief Justice of the Manitoba Court of Queen's Bench, who was the subject of the inquiry. The case ended abruptly in 2014 with no definitive determination of the issues after Douglas J announced that she would resign in 2015. The CJC decided it was no longer in the public interest to pursue the case against Douglas J. Information about the case is available online: *Canadian Judicial Council* <https://cjc-ccm.ca/en/news/canadian-judicial-council-recommends-justice-robin-camp-be-removed-office>.

In 2017, the CJC recommended that Justice Robin Camp of the Federal Court be removed from office because of remarks that he made as a Provincial Court judge in Alberta while presiding over a sexual assault trial. Justice Camp resigned before he could be removed from office. All 23 members of the CJC agreed that Camp J's comments amounted to judicial misconduct. A minority of four CJC members disagreed with the recommendation for removal. As explained in the CJC Press Release:

> In its Report, Council noted that Canadians expect their judges to know the law and to possess empathy and to recognize and question any past personal attitudes that might prevent them from acting fairly. Judges are expected to demonstrate knowledge of social issues, and awareness of changes in social values, humility, tolerance and respect for others. Those are the very qualities that sustain public confidence in the judiciary. Council decided that the judge's conduct, viewed in its totality and in light of all of its consequences, was so manifestly and profoundly destructive of the concept of impartiality, integrity and independence of the judicial role that the judge was rendered incapable of executing the judicial office.

("Canadian Judicial Council Recommends That Justice Robin Camp Be Removed From Office" (2017) (Press Release), online: *Canadian Judicial Council* <https://cjc-ccm.ca/en/news/canadian-judicial-council-recommends-justice-robin-camp-be-removed-office>.)

2. Financial Security

Financial security relates to the pay judges receive for performing their job. It protects against an "unscrupulous government" that "could utilize its authority to set judges' salaries as a vehicle to influence the course and outcome of adjudication": see *Provincial Judges Reference* at para 145.

The *Provincial Judges Reference* was sparked by a climate in which a number of provincial governments were implementing policies of financial restraint. The remuneration of provincially appointed judges made them a politically vulnerable target because their salaries are high in relation to the average citizen. However, at the time, they were low in relation to federally appointed judges and to the more successful practising lawyers. Some provinces sought to reduce these judicial salaries. One province retroactively repealed its legislation requiring it to accept the recommendations of an advisory committee on judicial salaries. It may be a fair assumption that underlying the Supreme Court's decision in this case was a concern about ongoing and unseemly confrontations between the executive and judicial branches over judicial remuneration.

The Supreme Court addressed the problem in this way.

Ref re Remuneration of Judges of the Prov Court of PEI; Ref re Independence and Impartiality of Judges of the Prov Court of PEI
[1997] 3 SCR 3

LAMER CJ:

[121] What I do propose, however, is that financial security has both an individual and an institutional or collective dimension. *Valente* only talked about the individual dimension of financial security, when it stated that salaries must be established by law and not allow for executive interference in a manner which could "affect the independence of the individual judge" (p. 706). Similarly, in *Généreux*, speaking for a majority of this Court, I applied *Valente* and held that performance-related pay for the conduct of judge advocates and members of a General Court Martial during the Court Martial violated s. 11(d), because it could reasonably lead to the perception that those individuals might alter their conduct during a hearing in order to favour the military establishment.

[122] However, *Valente* did not preclude a finding that, and did not decide whether, financial security has a collective or institutional dimension as well. That is the issue we must address today. But in order to determine whether financial security has a collective or institutional dimension, and if so, what collective or institutional financial security looks like, we must first understand what the institutional independence of the judiciary is. I emphasize this point because, as will become apparent, the conclusion I arrive at regarding the collective or institutional dimension of financial security builds upon traditional understandings of the proper constitutional relationship between the judiciary, the executive, and the legislature.

• • •

[130] ... Independence of the judiciary implies not only that a judge should be free from executive or legislative encroachment and from political pressures and entanglements but also that he should be removed from financial or business entanglement likely to affect or rather to seem to affect him in the exercise of his judicial functions.

[131] Given the importance of the institutional or collective dimension of judicial independence generally, what is the institutional or collective dimension of financial security? To my mind, financial security for the courts as an institution has three components, which all flow from the constitutional imperative that, to the extent possible, the relationship between the judiciary and the other branches of government be depoliticized. As I explain below, in the context of institutional or collective financial security, this imperative demands that the courts both be free and appear to be free from political interference through economic manipulation by the other branches of government, and that they not become entangled in the politics of remuneration from the public purse.

[132] I begin by stating these components in summary fashion.

[133] First, as a general constitutional principle, the salaries of provincial court judges can be reduced, increased, or frozen, either as part of an overall economic measure which affects the salaries of all or some persons who are remunerated from public funds, or as part of a measure which is directed at provincial court judges as a class. However, any changes to or freezes in judicial remuneration require prior recourse to a special process, which is independent, effective, and objective, for determining judicial remuneration, to avoid the possibility of, or the appearance of, political interference through economic manipulation. What judicial

independence requires is an independent body, along the lines of the bodies that exist in many provinces and at the federal level to set or recommend the levels of judicial remuneration. Those bodies are often referred to as commissions, and for the sake of convenience, we will refer to the independent body required by s. 11(d) as a commission as well. Governments are constitutionally bound to go through the commission process. The recommendations of the commission would not be binding on the executive or the legislature. Nevertheless, though those recommendations are non-binding, they should not be set aside lightly, and, if the executive or the legislature chooses to depart from them, it has to justify its decision—if need be, in a court of law. As I explain below, when governments propose to single out judges as a class for a pay reduction, the burden of justification will be heavy.

[134] Second, under no circumstances is it permissible for the judiciary—not only collectively through representative organizations, but also as individuals—to engage in negotiations over remuneration with the executive or representatives of the legislature. Any such negotiations would be fundamentally at odds with judicial independence. As I explain below, salary negotiations are indelibly political, because remuneration from the public purse is an inherently political issue. Moreover, negotiations would undermine the appearance of judicial independence, because the Crown is almost always a party to criminal prosecutions before provincial courts, and because salary negotiations engender a set of expectations about the behaviour of parties to those negotiations which are inimical to judicial independence. When I refer to negotiations, I utilize that term as it is traditionally understood in the labour relations context. Negotiations over remuneration and benefits, in colloquial terms, are a form of "horse-trading." The prohibition on negotiations therefore does not preclude expressions of concern or representations by chief justices and chief judges, and organizations that represent judges, to governments regarding the adequacy of judicial remuneration.

[135] Third, and finally, any reductions to judicial remuneration, including *de facto* reductions through the erosion of judicial salaries by inflation, cannot take those salaries below a basic minimum level of remuneration which is required for the office of a judge. Public confidence in the independence of the judiciary would be undermined if judges were paid at such a low rate that they could be perceived as susceptible to political pressure through economic manipulation, as is witnessed in many countries.

• • •

[166] Although provincial executives and legislatures, as the case may be, are constitutionally permitted to change or freeze judicial remuneration, those decisions have the potential to jeopardize judicial independence. The imperative of protecting the courts from political interference through economic manipulation is served by interposing an independent body—a judicial compensation commission—between the judiciary and the other branches of government. The constitutional function of this body is to depoliticize the process of determining changes or freezes to judicial remuneration. This objective would be achieved by setting that body the specific task of issuing a report on the salaries and benefits of judges to the executive and the legislature, responding to the particular proposals made by the government to increase, reduce, or freeze judges' salaries.

[167] I do not wish to dictate the exact shape and powers of the independent commission here. These questions of detailed institutional design are better left to the executive and the legislature, although it would be helpful if they consulted the provincial judiciary prior to creating these bodies. Moreover, different provinces should be free to choose procedures and arrangements which are suitable to

their needs and particular circumstances. Within the parameters of s. 11(d), there must be scope for local choice, because jurisdiction over provincial courts has been assigned to the provinces by the *Constitution Act, 1867.* This is one reason why we held in *Valente,* supra, at p. 694, that "[t]he standard of judicial independence for purposes of s. 11(d) cannot be a standard of uniform provisions."

• • •

[169] The commissions charged with the responsibility of dealing with the issue of judicial remuneration must meet three general criteria. They must be independent, objective, and effective. I will address these criteria in turn, by reference, where possible, to commissions which already exist in many Canadian provinces to set or recommend the levels of judicial remuneration.

[170] First and foremost, these commissions must be independent. The rationale for independence flows from the constitutional function performed by these commissions—they serve as an institutional sieve, to prevent the setting or freezing of judicial remuneration from being used as a means to exert political pressure through the economic manipulation of the judiciary. It would undermine that goal if the independent commissions were under the control of the executive or the legislature.

[171] There are several different aspects to the independence required of salary commissions. First, the members of these bodies must have some kind of security of tenure. In this context, security of tenure means that the members of commissions should serve for a fixed term, which may vary in length. ... In my opinion, s. 11(d) does not impose any restrictions on the membership of these commissions. Although the independence of these commissions would be better served by ensuring that their membership stood apart from the three branches of government, as is the case in Ontario (*Courts of Justice Act,* Schedule, para. 11), this is not required by the Constitution.

[172] Under ideal circumstances, it would be desirable if appointments to the salary commission were not made by any of the three branches of government, in order to guarantee the independence of its members. However, the members of that body would then have to be appointed by a body which must in turn be independent, and so on. This is clearly not a practical solution, and thus is not required by s. 11(d). As we said in *Valente* ... , at p. 692:

> It would not be feasible ... to apply the most rigorous and elaborate conditions of judicial independence to the constitutional requirement of independence in s. 11(d) of the Charter ... .

What s. 11(d) requires instead is that the appointments not be entirely controlled by any one of the branches of government. The commission should have members appointed by the judiciary, on the one hand, and the legislature and the executive, on the other. The judiciary's nominees may, for example, be chosen either by the provincial judges' association, as is the case in Ontario (*Courts of Justice Act,* Schedule, para. 6), or by the Chief Judge of the Provincial Court in consultation with the provincial judges' association, as in British Columbia (*Provincial Court Act,* s. 7.1(2)). The exact mechanism is for provincial governments to determine. Likewise, the nominees of the executive and the legislature may be chosen by the Lieutenant Governor in Council, although appointments by the Attorney General as in British Columbia (*Provincial Court Act,* s. 7.1(2)), or conceivably by the legislature itself, are entirely permissible.

[173] In addition to being independent, the salary commissions must be objective. They must make recommendations on judges' remuneration by reference to

objective criteria, not political expediencies. The goal is to present "an objective and fair set of recommendations dictated by the public interest" (Canada, Department of Justice, *Report and Recommendations of the 1995 Commission on Judges' Salaries and Benefits* (1996), at p. 7). Although s. 11(d) does not require it, the commission's objectivity can be promoted by ensuring that it is fully informed before deliberating and making its recommendations. This can be best achieved by requiring that the commission receive and consider submissions from the judiciary, the executive, and the legislature. In Ontario, for example, the Provincial Judges' Remuneration Commission is bound to consider submissions from the provincial judges' association and the government (*Courts of Justice Act*, Schedule, para. 20). Moreover, I recommend (but do not require) that the objectivity of the commission be ensured by including in the enabling legislation or regulations a list of relevant factors to guide the commission's deliberations. These factors need not be exhaustive. A list of relevant factors might include, for example, increases in the cost of living, the need to ensure that judges' salaries remain adequate, as well as the need to attract excellent candidates to the judiciary.

[174] Finally, and most importantly, the commission must also be effective. The effectiveness of these bodies must be guaranteed in a number of ways. First, there is a constitutional obligation for governments not to change (either by reducing or increasing) or freeze judicial remuneration until they have received the report of the salary commission. Changes or freezes of this nature secured without going through the commission process are unconstitutional. The commission must convene to consider and report on the proposed change or freeze. Second, in order to guard against the possibility that government inaction might lead to a reduction in judges' real salaries because of inflation, and that inaction could therefore be used as a means of economic manipulation, the commission must convene if a fixed period of time has elapsed since its last report, in order to consider the adequacy of judges' salaries in light of the cost of living and other relevant factors, and issue a recommendation in its report. Although the exact length of the period is for provincial governments to determine, I would suggest a period of three to five years.

[175] Third, the reports of the commission must have a meaningful effect on the determination of judicial salaries. Provinces which have created salary commissions have adopted three different ways of giving such effect to these reports. One is to make a report of the commission binding, so that the government is bound by the commission's decision. Ontario, for example, requires that a report be implemented by the Lieutenant Governor in Council within 60 days, and gives a report of the Provincial Judges' Remuneration Commission statutory force (*Courts of Justice Act*, Schedule, para. 27). Another way of dealing with a report is the negative resolution procedure, whereby the report is laid before the legislature and its recommendations are implemented unless the legislature votes to reject or amend them. This is the model which has been adopted in British Columbia (*Provincial Court Act*, s. 7.1(10)) and Newfoundland (*Provincial Court Act*, 1991, s. 28(7)). The final way of giving effect to a report is the affirmative resolution procedure, whereby a report is laid before but need not be adopted by the legislature. As I shall explain below, until the adoption of Bill 22, this was very similar to the procedure followed in Manitoba (*Provincial Court Act*, s. 11.1(6)).

• • •

[185] By laying down a set of guidelines to assist provincial legislatures in designing judicial compensation commissions, I do not intend to lay down a particular institutional framework in constitutional stone. What s. 11(d) requires is an institutional sieve between the judiciary and the other branches of government.

Commissions are merely a means to that end. In the future, governments may create new institutional arrangements which can serve the same end, but in a different way. As long as those institutions meet the three cardinal requirements of independence, effectiveness, and objectivity, s. 11(d) will be complied with.

In *Provincial Court Judges' Assn of New Brunswick v New Brunswick (Minister of Justice)*, 2005 SCC 44, [2005] 2 SCR 286, the court revisited and somewhat amended the test it established in the 1997 case. In that case, "Provincial Court judges in New Brunswick, Ontario and Quebec, justices of the peace in Alberta and municipal court judges in Quebec sought judicial review of their provincial governments' decisions to reject certain compensation commission recommendations relating to their salaries and benefits" (at para 45).

Provincial Court Judges' Assn of New Brunswick v New Brunswick (Minister of Justice); Ontario Judges' Assn v Ontario (Management Board); Bodner v Alberta; Conférence des juges du Québec v Quebec (AG); Minc v Quebec (AG)
2005 SCC 44, [2005] 2 SCR 286

THE COURT:

[3] ... In the *Reference re Remuneration of Judges of the Provincial Court of Prince Edward Island*, [1997] 3 SCR 3 (*"Reference"*), this Court held that independent commissions were required to improve the process designed to ensure judicial independence but that the commissions' recommendations need not be binding. These commissions were intended to remove the amount of judges' remuneration from the political sphere and to avoid confrontation between governments and the judiciary. The *Reference* has not provided the anticipated solution, and more is needed.

• • •

[21] A commission's report is consultative. The government may turn it into something more. Unless the legislature provides that the report is binding, the government retains the power to depart from the commission's recommendations as long as it justifies its decision with rational reasons. These rational reasons must be included in the government's response to the commission's recommendations.

• • •

[25] The government can reject or vary the commission's recommendations, provided that legitimate reasons are given. Reasons that are complete and that deal with the commission's recommendations in a meaningful way will meet the standard of rationality. Legitimate reasons must be compatible with the common law and the Constitution. The government must deal with the issues at stake in good faith. Bald expressions of rejection or disapproval are inadequate. Instead, the reasons must show that the commission's recommendations have been taken into account and must be based on facts and sound reasoning. They must state in what respect and to what extent they depart from the recommendations, articulating the grounds for rejection or variation. The reasons should reveal a consideration of the judicial office and an intention to deal with it appropriately. They must preclude any suggestion of attempting to manipulate the judiciary. The reasons must reflect the underlying public interest in having a commission process, being the depoliticization of the remuneration process and the need to preserve judicial independence.

The court concluded that the rejection of commission recommendations met the "rationality" test in New Brunswick, Ontario, and Alberta, but not in Quebec.

Chief Justice Lamer's decision in the *Provincial Judges Reference* was the subject of harsh criticism by notable academics, including Professor Peter Hogg. See Peter W Hogg, "The Bad Idea of Unwritten Constitutional Principles: Protecting Judicial Salaries" in Adam Dodek & Lorne Sossin, eds, *Judicial Independence in Context* (Toronto: Irwin Law, 2010) 25. In a rejoinder, Professors Daphne Gilbert and Ed Ratushny take issue with Professor Hogg and argue that such criticism is unfounded and unfair to Lamer CJ. See Daphne Gilbert & Ed Ratushny, "The Lamer Legacy for Judicial Independence" in Adam Dodek & Daniel Jutras, eds, *The Sacred Fire/Le Feu Sacré* (Toronto: LexisNexis, 2009). For somewhat different approaches see Lori Sterling & Sean Hanley, "The Case for Dialogue in the Judicial Remuneration Process" and Lorne Sossin, "Between the Judiciary and the Executive: The Elusive Search for a Credible and Effective Dispute Resolution Mechanism" both in Adam Dodek & Lorne Sossin, eds, *Judicial Independence in Context* (Toronto: Irwin Law, 2010).

3. Administrative Independence

The last component of judicial independence is "administrative independence." Put simply, administrative independence requires that courts themselves have control over the administrative decisions "that bear directly and immediately on the exercise of the judicial function," such as "assignment of judges, sittings of the court, and court lists—as well as the related matters of allocation of court rooms and direction of the administrative staff engaged in carrying out these functions": see *Provincial Judges Reference*, [1997] 3 SCR 3 at para 117. This requirement is met generally in the statutes creating the various courts, which assign to judges themselves these administrative roles. See, for example, *Supreme Court Act*, s 97; *Federal Courts Act*, ss 15 and 16.

Administrative independence was at issue in the *Tobiass* case discussed above. Recall that the Supreme Court was asked to consider whether judicial independence (or at least the perception of that independence) had been impaired by a private meeting between a senior Department of Justice official and the chief justice of the Federal Court. This meeting concerned a delay in the hearing of certain cases in which the Justice Department was a litigant. The Court concluded that at least the appearance of independence was transgressed, for the following reasons.

Canada (Minister of Citizenship and Immigration) v Tobiass
[1997] 3 SCR 391

THE COURT:

[74] First, and as a general rule of conduct, counsel for one party should not discuss a particular case with a judge except with the knowledge and preferably with the participation of counsel for the other parties to the case. ... The meeting between Mr. Thompson and the Chief Justice, at which counsel for the appellants were not present, violated this rule and was clearly inappropriate, and this despite the fact that the occasion for the meeting was a highly legitimate concern about the exceedingly slow progress of the cases.

[75] Second, and again as a general rule, a judge should not accede to the demands of one party without giving counsel for the other parties a chance to present their views. It was therefore clearly wrong, and seriously so, for the Chief Justice to speak to the Associate Chief Justice at the instance of Mr. Thompson. ... [A] chief

justice is responsible for the expeditious progress of cases through his or her court and may under certain circumstances be obligated to take steps to correct tardiness. Yet, the actions of Isaac CJ were more in the nature of a response to a party rather than to a problem. Thus, an action that might have been innocuous and even obligatory under other circumstances acquired an air of impropriety as a result of the events that preceded it. Quite simply, it was inappropriate.

[76] In similar fashion, by responding as he did to the Chief Justice's intervention without the participation of counsel for the appellants, Jerome ACJ acted inappropriately. We believe that there is ample evidence that might lead a reasonable observer to conclude that the Associate Chief Justice was not able to conduct the appellants' cases free from the interference of the federal Department of Justice and of the Chief Justice of his court. Before March 1, 1996, the Associate Chief Justice was content with the pace at which the appellants' cases were advancing through his court. Indeed, even after Mr. Amerasinghe wrote to the Court Administrator to complain about the slow pace of the proceedings, the Associate Chief Justice resolved not to expedite consideration of the preliminary motions. Instead, he insisted on hearing oral argument according to the original, exceedingly dilatory schedule. It was only after the March 1, 1996 meeting between Mr. Thompson and the Chief Justice that Jerome ACJ acquired an appreciation of the Government's position. In his letter of March 1, 1996, the Chief Justice wrote:

> As regards the three cases about which you wrote, the Associate Chief Justice says firstly, that he did not fully appreciate until he read your letter, the urgency of dealing with these matters as expeditiously as the Government would like. However, now that he is aware he will devote one week from 15 May to deal with these cases not only with respect to the preliminary points but also with respect to the merits. Finally, he has authorized me to say that additional cases of this class coming into the Court will be given the highest priority in light of the concerns expressed in your letter. [Emphasis added.]

[77] Subsequent developments confirmed that the Associate Chief Justice had indeed finally received the Government's message. On April 10, 1996, the Associate Chief Justice retreated from his earlier position and announced that he would set aside sufficient time in May to dispose of all the preliminary issues in the appellants' cases. He also indicated that he would bring the cases to a final conclusion by July.

[78] We do not see how a reasonable observer could fail at least to wonder whether the Government, through Mr. Thompson, had succeeded in influencing the Associate Chief Justice to take a position more favourable to the Government's interests than he would otherwise have done. Making this conclusion even more likely is the undertaking of the Chief Justice and the Associate Chief Justice to Mr. Thompson that all reasonable steps would be taken to avoid a reference to the Supreme Court of Canada.

[79] The respondent tries to resist this conclusion by saying that the impetus to efficiency came not from Mr. Thompson and the Government but from the Chief Justice. The Chief Justice, the respondent says, was duty-bound to look into what was, by any objective standard, a serious delay in proceedings in his court. The respondent thus offers the Chief Justice as a kind of *novus actus interveniens* who stands between the Government and the Associate Chief Justice and, by the propriety of his own intentions, severs what would otherwise be an improper link between them.

[80] What the respondent's submission overlooks is that the Chief Justice was not able to exercise his administrative function entirely free from outside

interference. Mr. Thompson approached the Chief Justice and told him that if the Associate Chief Justice did not pick up the pace, the Federal Court would face the embarrassment of having the Government go "over its head" to this Court. The Chief Justice's letter to Mr. Thompson suggests that this "threat" carried some weight with him and with the Associate Chief Justice as well:

> I have discussed your concerns with the Associate Chief Justice and, like me, he is prepared to take all reasonable steps possible to avoid a Reference to the Supreme Court of Canada on these matters.

It is reasonable to suppose that the threat of appeal to a higher authority influenced the Chief Justice and Associate Chief Justice to act in a way that would otherwise have been unpalatable to them. In this we agree entirely with Stone JA [in the Federal Court of Appeal], who found that "an informed person would conclude that this decision, by which the hearing of all preliminary motions and the trials would be compressed into a relatively short time frame, would redound to the disadvantage of the individual respondents [now appellants] and was taken so as 'to avoid' a reference to the Supreme Court" (p. 868). To interfere with the scheduling of cases because of delay is one thing but to pledge to take all reasonable steps to avoid a reference to the Supreme Court of Canada is quite another. It is wrong and improper for a judge to give such an undertaking. What is pertinent is to avoid delays, not to avoid appeals or recourse to higher courts.

[81] However, the respondent is quite right to observe that the delay in the Federal Court—Trial Division was inordinate and arguably inexcusable, and posed a real problem for the Department of Justice and for the Chief Justice. The fact is that in the space of a year, the Associate Chief Justice heard only one day of argument, and that on a preliminary motion. In our view, the Associate Chief Justice's dilatoriness defies explanation. The appellants attempt nevertheless to explain it, saying that the Associate Chief Justice had reason to delay the proceedings until judgment had been given by himself in a case called *Nemsila*, which might have cast some light on citizenship revocation cases generally. The Chief Justice for his part mentioned the *Nemsila* case in his letter of March 1, 1996, though he did not attempt to offer it as a justification for delay in the appellants' cases.

[82] However, even accepting that there was reason to await the rendering of judgment in *Nemsila*, the proper procedure would have been to hear argument on the appellants' motion and, if necessary, to reserve judgment. To call three cases to a halt awaiting the outcome of another case strikes us as a procedure calculated to create unnecessary delay. The appellants also point out that the respondent was not ready to proceed to a hearing on the merits. Apparently the respondent had not finished translating certain witness statements. But no one has suggested that the matter should have been brought to a conclusion on the merits before May 15, 1996, only that some progress should have been made toward resolving the preliminary questions before that date, and to settle the preliminary questions would not have required that all the witness statements should be available. Therefore, the fact that the respondent was not yet ready to proceed to trial cannot excuse the delay in the Associate Chief Justice's consideration of the preliminary questions.

[83] What all this means is that Mr. Thompson went to the Chief Justice with a legitimate grievance. This fact does not excuse what Mr. Thompson did—he assuredly chose an impermissible means of presenting his grievance—but it does cast into very real doubt the sinister interpretation that the appellants have attempted to place on his conduct. Given the vexing delay that the respondent had faced in the Trial Division, it is quite understandable that Mr. Thompson would have wished to

do something about it. We believe that Mr. Thompson's motives were proper. It was his judgment that is questionable. What Mr. Thompson did was not wicked or done in bad faith. It is enough to say that what he did was inappropriate. As senior counsel in the Department of Justice, he arranged to speak privately—without opposing counsel present—to the Chief Justice, concerning cases which were pending. This he should not have done.

• • •

[85] In short, the evidence supports the conclusion that the appearance of judicial independence suffered a serious affront as a result of the March 1, 1996 meeting between Mr. Thompson and Isaac CJ. This affront very seriously compromised the appearance of judicial independence. A reasonable observer apprised of the workings of the Federal Court and of all the circumstances would perceive that the Chief Justice and the Associate Chief Justice were improperly and unduly influenced by a senior officer of the Department of Justice. However, there is no persuasive evidence of bad faith on the part of any of the actors in this drama, nor is there any solid evidence that the independence of the judges in question was actually compromised.

[Despite this finding, the Supreme Court did not uphold the trial judge's decision to order a stay of proceedings, but instead required that the proceedings be conducted by a trial division judge who was not tainted by the improper communications between the Court and the Department of Justice.]

PART III

INTERPLAY BETWEEN THE COURTS AND THE POLITICAL BRANCHES OF GOVERNMENT

CHAPTER TEN

STATUTORY INTERPRETATION

I. INTRODUCTION

In this chapter and the next, we shift from a discussion of the structure and function of Canadian public law institutions to a closer examination of how the legislative, executive, and judicial branches interact with one another. Our focus here is on the relationship between the courts and the other branches of government—the legislature and the executive.

If Parliament or provincial legislatures observe the constitutional limits on their jurisdiction, they must be considered supreme, and the courts should interpret and carry out the rules, purposes, and principles expressed in the legislation they produce. However, if a legislature steps outside of its constitutional limits, courts are authorized by the Constitution and the rule of law to ensure that this legal mistake is corrected. Here, courts do two things. First, they determine the exact nature and scope of the constitutional limits, by interpreting the written Constitution and sometimes by discerning unwritten constitutional principles by which the legislature must abide. In this respect, they perform a constitutionalized interpretation role. Second, they decide whether a given statute has exceeded the constitutional limits determined through interpretation. If it has, they provide a remedy. Normally, the remedy is to declare that the offending legislation is invalid and has no force or effect on either federalism or Charter grounds under the s 52 supremacy clause in the *Constitution Act, 1982*, being Schedule B to the *Canada Act 1982* (UK), 1982, c 11. Parliamentary supremacy is an important element of Canadian public law. Nevertheless, an important threshold exists in Canadian constitutional law—*the point where parliamentary supremacy gives way to constitutional supremacy.*

Apart from this practice of *direct* judicial review, the courts often engage in *indirect* review when they interpret legislation in light of common law constitutional values such as respect for individual autonomy, equality, and private property rights as well as common law concepts such as solicitor—client privilege that may appear in statutes. In such cases, the courts presume that the legislature, in enacting a particular provision, did not intend to violate long-recognized constitutional or other important legal values or authorize its delegates to do so. In these kinds of cases, courts may employ other remedial techniques such as "reading in" or the less intrusive "reading down" of provisions in the offending legislation.

Given these constitutional judicial review functions, it is arguable that Canadian democracy rests on a de facto undemocratic system of judicial supremacy. In other words, instead of a condition of relative equality among the three branches—which mirrors how we might initially understand the doctrine of the separation of powers—one branch holds the lion's share of power, which it uses to constrain the power of the other two branches. Therefore, for some, the power exercised by unelected judges in carrying out their review functions is deeply problematic. Others welcome this check on the majoritarian power of the legislature. Clearly, the separation of powers between the judicial and the legislative branch is critically important to Canadian democracy—and often provokes heated debate.

Somewhat less controversial, but perhaps more complicated, is the relationship between the courts and the executive. Like the legislature, the executive is constrained by the Constitution, and policed by the courts accordingly. Recall also that the executive has only limited legal powers, primarily those delegated to it by the legislature by statute. Courts are charged with ensuring that the executive does not stray beyond the scope of those powers. In this manner, the courts serve as the legislature's loyal partner, preventing the executive from usurping power not accorded to it by the legislative branch. This kind of review is the chief focus of administrative law and functions as an indirect form of judicial review because the remedy of striking down or invalidation is not available as a common law remedy.

Chapter 11 will examine judicial review of both legislative and executive action. Before getting there, in this chapter we focus on the rules of statutory interpretation: the doctrines that direct how courts should interpret the legislative will expressed in statutes and regulations. Section II introduces the everyday problem of interpretation and then explains how interpretation forms a distinct field of legal inquiry involving both dynamic and static approaches.

Section III introduces and provides an overview of the main approach to statutory interpretation in Canada—the "modern approach"—including its components, doctrines, methods, and recurring interpretive problems. Through a small set of exemplary cases, Section IV illustrates the modern approach—both its virtues and imperfections—in action for our consideration, critique, and discussion. Section V revisits the problem of interpretation from an historical perspective and by a brief examination of the criticisms of, and weakness in, the modern approach.

II. APPROACHES TO INTERPRETATION

"I don't know what you mean by 'glory,'" Alice said.

Humpty Dumpty smiled contemptuously. "Of course you don't—till I tell you. I meant 'there's a nice knock-down argument for you!'"

"But 'glory' doesn't mean 'a nice knock-down argument,'" Alice objected.

"When I use a word," Humpty Dumpty said, in rather a scornful tone, "it means just what I choose it to mean—neither more nor less."

"The question is," said Alice, "whether you can make words mean so many different things."

"The question is," said Humpty Dumpty, "which is to be master—that's all."

Alice was too much puzzled to say anything ...

(Lewis Carroll, *The Annotated Alice: The Definitive Edition—Alice's Adventures in Wonderland & Through the Looking-Glass*, introduction and notes by Martin Gardner (New York: WW Norton, 2000) 213.)

A. WHY INTERPRETATION?

We engage in interpretation every day, all the time, in our relations with each other and the world. We make mistakes hearing another's words, and we may need clarification from others. We find ourselves confused by ordinary signs and symbols. We inadvertently and sometimes wilfully misunderstand each other and come to sharp disagreements about the correct meaning or the right answer. We cope with ambiguity but hopefully we try to resolve interpretive disputes peacefully and amicably among ourselves. These interpretation problems multiply in number and scope when we live in an environment that uses a different language or if we are interacting with a specialized or technical discourse. We may also require translators. Indeed, because of the pluralistic nature of Canada's legal system, legal actors like lawyers, judges, and administrative decision-makers may need to be acutely aware how meaning differs in English and French (see e.g. the line of cases concluding that "prescribed by law" and *"un règle de droit"* do not mean exactly the same thing in s 1 of the *Canadian Charter of Rights and Freedoms* Part I of the *Constitution Act, 1982,* being Schedule B to the *Canada Act 1982* (UK), 1982, c 11.). To take another example, the South African Constitution contains the Indigenous concept of *ubuntu,* which does not have a parallel English equivalent, but the concept is translated as a principle of community solidarity or a universal bond connecting all humanity. Lastly, with the revitalization and contemporary recognition of multiple Indigenous legal orders in Canada, the issue of translation will become increasingly important.

All of these ordinary problems become acute in law, given that law is a special form of language. Words we regularly use may take on a different meaning in statutes or in the common law. Words used in statutes may reflect older understandings of, say, "marriage," and legal language may have to catch up with change that has already occurred in society. To that end, it is the special role of counsel to advance interpretation arguments in order to change the law or to suggest that it be kept the same, according to the interests of her or his client.

It is the special role of judges to declare what the "true" legal meaning is. Unlike games—which are, by and large, closed rule-bound systems—clear and definite rule-making in law can easily be frustrated by facts, differing intents, lack of information, and the open texture of language.

If every legal provision was clear and could be understood "naturally," the act of interpretation would take little effort. Even if some doubt existed, a reviewing court could (ideally) quickly and efficiently determine the intent of the legislature behind the statute by relying on a "common sense" understanding to clarify the words or the provision in dispute. Although it is certainly possible to aim for, and sometimes achieve, this result, neither of these conditions is the norm and cases involving matters of legal interpretation—statutory interpretation in particular—make up an enormous amount of the day-to-day caseload of judges at all court levels, both federally and provincially.

This is because words can be vague, even when they appear to have a settled meaning in the dictionary. For instance, what is "reasonable"—a common legal test—is a recurring interpretation problem. The answer largely depends on the context rather than the precise dictionary definition of "reasonableness"—something that will be acutely evident in the discussion of how courts engage in reasonableness review in administrative law. Alternatively, the language that is used may offer opportunities to describe the legal issue generally or more specifically. We could ask ourselves, "What did she do?" Our answer might be that "she moved the knife." Or, it might be, "She stabbed him." Or, it might be, "She killed him." Each of these answers could be empirically true, but only one descriptor will be appropriate for the particular legal context.

To take another example, in a contractual situation, the parties' intent behind the contract may be ambiguous because the words they use to construct the terms may refer to a range of diverse, related things—not all of which they wish to have included in their agreement. When a dispute arises, it becomes clear that a meeting of minds may not have taken place, and it will become the role of the courts to settle the dispute if the parties cannot. In other cases, legal principles and values appear to conflict or even be diametrically opposed to each other—this is a common situation in statutes. Often, statutory language and purposes may contradict each other inadvertently or deliberately. Finally, legal language about rights and duties requires concrete facts in order to know the precise nature of the right or duty at issue. As a result, and to follow English philosopher Thomas Hobbes, not only do "[a]ll Laws, written and unwritten, have need of Interpretation," we also require a fair and impartial authority to resolve these controversies in order to resolve conflicts and reconcile parties in society (*Leviathan*, ed by Richard Tuck (Cambridge: Cambridge University Press, 2002) at 190). How this final authority goes about resolving interpretive disagreements in public law is the subject of this chapter.

1. Interpretation as an Everyday Activity: A Short Exercise About Ambiguity

A large, urban park called Pacific Peace exists on the west side of Vancouver by the water. At all of the entrances to the park, signs have been placed communicating the following municipal by-law: "No vehicles are allowed in this park at any time." Pacific Peace Park contains miles of intersecting paths through an old forest, which was at one time logged. Some of the paths are old logging roads. Other paths are designated for walkers, while still others permit users to ride horses. Because of its historical lineage as Crown land, and because of the commitment to peace that it represents, the park contains many pieces of Indigenous and non-Indigenous art.

1. Before going any further, what is the meaning of "vehicle" that first spontaneously comes to your mind? Write it down.
2. What sorts of vehicles do you think this prohibition intends to cover? Consider this your "common sense" or "ordinary meaning" response.

3. Read the following list and consider which would be clearly caught by the rule, which would clearly not be caught by the rule, and which would fall into a "penumbra" of uncertainty about whether or not they could be classified as a "vehicle":
   a. car,
   b. public bus,
   c. bicycle,
   d. baby carriage,
   e. skateboard,
   f. tank,
   g. hot dog truck, and
   h. motorized wheelchair.

4. You undoubtedly thought "tank" was not only definitely ruled out, but possibly clearly absurd. Imagine, however, that a veterans' association asked the city of Vancouver to install a decommissioned tank in the park to commemorate the 100th anniversary of the First World War. Does this factual twist make "tank" more of a "borderline" case that could potentially fall outside the rule? Why or why not?

5. The city rejected the veterans' request because it considered the tank to be an inappropriate and inconsistent use of park land. Stand in the place of the city, think about the implicit objectives and purposes of the by-law, and provide two reasons why the tank constitutes an inappropriate and inconsistent use of the park space.

6. The veterans' association challenges the city's decision in court. Imagine that you are the judge at first instance who hears the dispute. Your assessment of the facts and arguments leads you to a preliminary view that the veterans' tank project is neither an inappropriate nor an inconsistent use of the park space. Provide two reasons why their request is appropriate and consistent with the by-law.

"Vehicle" may not be such a hard case after all about rule application, but this short exercise aims to show that you have come to law school already possessing interpretive skills such as clarifying words, handling abstract concepts, and discerning the meaning of rules when they are applied to particular fact scenarios. Legal education hones these skills through analytic and analogical reasoning, drafting and writing legal opinions, making and communicating legal arguments, and applying skills to handle (or juggle, as the case may be) more complex abstract concepts and factual matters.

B. THE TWO INTERPRETIVE APPROACHES SHARED BY THE CONSTITUTION, THE COMMON LAW, AND STATUTES

Our domestic legal system can be divided into three distinct areas where interpretive disputes occur: the common law, the Constitution, and statutes. Each area possesses its own approaches to interpretation and, often, its own rules. In the first year of law school, one learns how the common law approaches the interpretation of rules and rights in contract, property, and tort law. These rules have been created by common law courts over the centuries. Students also learn approaches to the interpretation of constitutional rights as well the division of powers relating to federalism. In several chapters, you were introduced to the Canadian "living tree" method of interpretation and learned how much this approach differs from "originalist" approaches to constitutional texts. As you will read below, the living tree approach is a dynamic approach to interpretation, while originalist or textualist methods are static. An approach similar to the living tree doctrine underpins exercises of statutory interpretation, but it operates under a different name and possesses a different set of rules. In Canadian public law, this approach is called the "modern approach" to statutory interpretation.

1. Static Approaches to Interpretation

Static interpretive approaches are animated by the belief that interpretation should be firmly constrained by the original intent legislators had in mind at the time of enactment, both for the Constitution and for statutes. The legal text is understood to be an "artifact of history" that is unresponsive to temporal change. In the American context, the "Framers' intent" method of interpreting the Constitution ascribes meaning to today's text that mirrors what was thought in the 18th century. In statutory interpretation, the equivalent approach is called the "plain," "original," or "literal" meaning approach. In Canada, the "ordinary" meaning represents the starting point for statutory interpretation and, depending on how it is used, can appear more static or more dynamic. This point will be further explained below.

Traditionally, static approaches seemed to offer certainty, objectivity, and determinate answers when interpretive disputes arose. One only had to determine what the original meaning was. You might consider the "right to bear arms" found in the Second Amendment of the United States Constitution as an example: "A well regulated militia being necessary to the security of a free state, the right of the people to keep and bear arms shall not be infringed." How should we interpret the right to bear arms in today's context? Does it mean that an individual has an absolute right to own a firearm whose use is unrelated to any military purpose? According to the Supreme Court of the United States, the answer is "yes." In the 2008 case *District of Columbia v Heller*, 554 US 570 (2008), the US Supreme Court struck down—by a narrow 5:4 majority—portions of the District of Columbia's *Firearms Control Regulations Act of 1975* requiring that all firearms, including rifles and shotguns, should be kept "unloaded and disassembled or bound by a trigger lock." The Court considered these provisions an unconstitutional constraint on the right to bear arms because modern handguns are "arms" for the purposes of the Second Amendment. The District of Columbia, therefore, could not regulate modern guns in the manner it chose. Justice Antonin Scalia, still the most famous proponent of an originalist approach to constitutional interpretation, penned the majority judgment. The dissenting judgment, written by Justice John Paul Stevens, rejected the majority on the basis that the Second Amendment omits any purpose related to the right to use firearms for hunting or personal self-defence. According to Stevens J, if one were really to discern the Founders' intent, it is that the text clearly refers to state militia service only and, therefore, does not include an individual or private right to bear arms. Moreover, the Founding Fathers rejected the idea that the state would not want to regulate civilian use of weapons. Many critics agree with Stevens J that the originalist method of interpretation should have produced the exact opposite result than the one reached in the majority judgment.

While perhaps intuitively appealing, static approaches fail to constrain interpretation in the ways critics want. (See chapters 1 and 2 in William Eskridge, *Dynamic Statutory Interpretation* (Cambridge, Mass: Harvard University Press, 1994).) They cannot provide a firm and conclusive link to original expectations, they lack transparency about interpretive choices (especially if history is "fudged"), and they do not give objective answers. Moreover, they may inappropriately exclude relevant and legitimate post-enactment considerations.

2. Dynamic Approaches to Interpretation

In contrast, dynamic approaches are evolutionary and responsive to change. As William Eskridge maintains, dynamic approaches understand the context in which we interpret legal languages as "elastic" so that the context can broaden and stretch to include historical change, political culture, application to current problems, and multi-faceted arguments. (See "The Dynamics of Statutory Interpretation," in William Eskridge, *Dynamic Statutory Interpretation* (Cambridge, Mass: Harvard University Press, 1994) ch 2.) A static approach assumes that only one correct answer can exist. It is the answer to the question: What was originally intended? Dynamic approaches, on the other hand, engage in a form of pragmatic, practical reasoning that is inherently pluralist in its methods and scope. An interpreter who adopts a dynamic approach knows that "one right answer" may not exist in a particular case and the question becomes "who is best placed to provide the best interpretation?" In some cases, it will be the courts. But, in other cases, a different actor may be recognized as the expert or the authority who can offer the better interpretation. These potential other interpreters include: an adjudicative body such as a human rights tribunal; a labour arbitrator; a minister or a lower-ranking delegate of the minister; and/or a police officer. In statutory interpretation, dynamic approaches include a weakly dynamic form of the "original" meaning approach and the modern "contextual and purposive" approach.

Dynamic approaches account for different interpreters and perspectives over time. The text is understood to be situated in a web of sources about its meaning: general and legal history, precedent, policy, and past and current norms and values. Interpretation is not controlled by the "dead hand of the past" but, rather, is a future-oriented enterprise because texts evolve beyond the original meaning, even while the range of possible interpretations is constrained by some sense of what the original meaning was. This dynamism is particularly acute with statutes. Eskridge conceives of legislation as a political response to a problem or cluster of problems that is translated into legal form containing general, universal, and abstract language.

This legislative process is profoundly imperfect. Statutes may contain ambiguities or are rendered confusing because they overlook or do not anticipate future issues that animate later interpretive problems. Statutes may also be deliberately vague because they represent a weak political compromise, and so unresolved or submerged issues in the statute may reappear as future interpretation disputes in particular legal cases. Statutes may also meet with resistance in social and political culture so that actors in civil society may wish to interpret the text differently in order to avoid or evade statutory obligations. Because of all of these considerations, dynamic interpreters rework statutes into the future. They may engage in strong or weak forms of dynamic interpretation. Weak forms of dynamic interpretation may not depart too far from the original meaning—this can be the case with ordinary meaning. "Sea changes" in social attitudes, however, can wreak havoc with pre-existing statutory regimes. Actors may therefore offer interpretations that actively work *against* original assumptions or even seek to *transform* the meaning in order to avoid having the statute become obsolete—this is a strong form of dynamic interpretation. When a statute is no longer relevant, and interpretation cannot assist, it may wither and die, having bare existence until it is finally repealed. As you now know, creating a new statute takes a lot of time and work.

Multiple interpretive communities compete to put forward their preferred meaning. As mentioned above, administrators in the executive branch, private parties, social movements, interest groups, and judges at all levels could each advance a slightly different interpretation from each other. For this reason, several plausible interpretations may be advanced while a case makes its way through the legal system. Courts may impose their views on what is the best interpretation, but they may also defer to the interpretation given by another actor. Administrative law focuses on the question of when and why courts will defer to interpretations given by actors in the executive branch.

Some of you may be familiar with static and dynamic approaches to interpretation from courses in history, language, literature, philosophy, or religion. While recognizing these analogies, it is important to underscore an essential difference in legal interpretation. Multiple interpretations abound in other disciplines and often happily co-exist. Not in law. Legal institutions presuppose a "final authority," as Hobbes claimed above. Law, and especially statutes, have a "coercive force" that the arts do not (though some religious approaches to interpreting texts could be closer to the methods and effects of legal interpretation). When a case reaches our Supreme Court, the pre-existing multiplicity of meanings will be suppressed, and the institution that has a special interpretive role in society—the judiciary—will validate one interpretation as the most appropriate. The authorized interpretation may be that of a court or another state official, but the majority decision nevertheless "lays down the law." In a common law system, however, interpretive pluralism is kept alive through the practice of concurring and dissenting judgments.

The living tree doctrine is an example of a dynamic approach to interpretation, while original intent is an example of a static approach to interpretation. These approaches are diametrically opposed to each other in their methods and their results. You have already read a number of constitutional cases that employ a dynamic approach to constitutional interpretation. Notable examples include the *Edwards v AG Canada* (the *"Persons"* case), [1930] AC 124, 1 DLR 98 (PC) in Chapter 2; *Halpern v Canada (AG)* (2003), 65 OR (3d) 161 (CA), regarding same-sex marriage, in Chapter 4; *Reference re Secession of Quebec*, [1998] 2 SCR 217 (*Quebec Secession Reference*) in Chapter 5; and the *Reference re Prov Electoral Boundaries (Sask)*, [1991] 2 SCR 158 in Chapter 6.

The tensions between broad and narrow, or dynamic and static, approaches are not unique to constitutional law. Rather, it is better understood as a basic model for any interpretation dispute in law: one side will argue for a broader interpretation that is open to reflect change, while the other side will argue for a narrower interpretation that seeks to keep the original meaning (or an interpretation as close to the original meaning as possible) in place. Interpretive rules and approaches in the common law, the Constitution, and statutory interpretation therefore all reflect this basic argumentative opposition. In terms of cases involving statutes, you may have already encountered static approaches to interpretation in the majority's judgment in *Shell v City of Vancouver*, [1994] 1 SCR 231 in Chapter 8, as well as *BC v Imperial Tobacco*, 2005 SCC 49, [2005] 2 SCR 473 in Chapter 5. Examples of dynamic interpretive approaches to the interpretation of statutes include Rand J's judgment in *Roncarelli v Duplessis*, [1959] SCR 121 in Chapter 5 and the dissenting judgment in *Shell v City of Vancouver*.

III. AN OVERVIEW OF THE MODERN APPROACH TO STATUTORY INTERPRETATION: ITS COMPONENTS AND ITS METHODS

A. THE UBIQUITY OF STATUTES AND THE NEED FOR INTERPRETATION

Thousands of federal and provincial statutes govern virtually every aspect of human activity. Paradoxically, although this legislation is by far the most important source of law in modern democratic states, little attention is paid to statutory interpretation in North American law schools outside Quebec. The theory and methodology of statutory interpretation is a challenging subject, as extensive and complex as the theory and methodology of the common law. Yet the common law is the focus of most standard first-year courses—property, contracts, and torts. Even the so-called public law subjects—constitutional law, criminal law, and tax law—are generally taught through case law, using common law methodology. In most law schools, the knowledge and skills required to master statutory interpretation are addressed perfunctorily as part of an introductory public law course or a research and writing course. Some law schools offer valuable upper-year courses in statutory interpretation or legal drafting.

Neglect of statutory interpretation is problematic because all areas of law are governed in part by legislation. Tort law has the Occupiers Liability Act; contract law has the Consumer Protection Act; and property law has the Personal Property Security Act. Family law, succession law, corporate and commercial law, employment and labour law, intellectual property law, insurance law, environmental law, health law, and professional self-regulation (e.g., doctors, teachers, accountants, and lawyers)—and more—are all grounded in legislation.

Furthermore, the skills required to read legislation and resolve interpretation disputes are necessary for private law documents such as contracts, collective agreements, wills, and trusts.

They are also needed to deal with the Constitution Acts against which ordinary legislation is tested as well as treaties with Indigenous peoples and international agreements. All these texts rely on language to set out legally binding rules and principles. To determine their content, it is necessary to interpret the language of the text.

B. THE MODERN APPROACH TO STATUTORY INTERPRETATION

In 1974, Elmer Driedger, a legislative drafter with the federal Department of Justice, published an influential text entitled *The Construction of Statutes* (Toronto: Butterworths, 1974) in which, after reviewing the evolution of statutory interpretation described above, he reached the following conclusion (at 67):

> Today there is only one principle or approach, namely, the words of an Act are to be read in their entire context, in their grammatical and ordinary sense harmoniously with the scheme of the Act, the object of the Act, and the intention of Parliament.

Driedger's principle or approach has been dubbed "the modern principle" and has been relied on in innumerable decisions by Canadian courts as the preferred approach to interpretation.

The following extract from *Sullivan on the Construction of Statutes* draws attention to the chief features of the modern principle.

Ruth Sullivan, Sullivan on the Construction of Statutes
5th ed (Toronto: Butterworths, 2008) at 1-3

The chief significance of the modern principle is its insistence on the complex, multi-dimensional character of statutory interpretation. The first dimension emphasized is textual meaning. Although texts issue from an author and a particular set of circumstances, once published they are detached from their origin and take on a life of their own—one over which the reader has substantial control. Recent research in psycholinguistics has shown that the way readers understand the words of a text depends on the expectations they bring to their reading. These expectations are rooted in linguistic competence and shared linguistic convention; they are also dependent on the wide-ranging knowledge, beliefs, values and experience that readers have stored in their brain. The content of a reader's memory constitutes the most important context in which a text is read and influences in particular his or her impression of ordinary meaning—what Driedger calls the grammatical and ordinary sense of the words.

A second dimension endorsed by the modern principle is legislative intent. All texts, indeed all utterances, are made for a reason. Authors want to communicate their thoughts and they may further want their readers to adopt different views or adjust their conduct. A cooperative reader tries to discover what the author had in mind. In the case of legislation, the law-maker wants to communicate the law that it intended to enact because that law, as set out in the successive provisions of a statute or regulation, is the means chosen by the law-maker to achieve a set of desired goals. Law-abiding readers (including those who administer or enforce the legislation and those who resolve disputes) try to identify the intended goals of the legislation and the means devised to achieve those goals, so that they can act accordingly. This aspect of interpretation is captured in Driedger's reference to the scheme and object of the Act and the intention of Parliament.

A third dimension of interpretation referred to in the modern principle is compliance with established legal norms. These norms are part of the "entire context" in which the words of an Act must be read. They are also an integral part of legislative intent, as that concept is explained by Driedger. In the second edition he wrote:

> It may be convenient to regard "intention of Parliament" as composed of four elements, namely
>
> - the expressed intention—the intention expressed by the enacted words;
> - the implied intention—the intention that may legitimately be implied from the enacted words;
> - the presumed intention—the intention that the courts will in the absence of an indication to the contrary impute to Parliament; and
> - the declared intention—the intention that Parliament itself has said may be or must be or must not be imputed to it.
>
> [Elmer A Driedger, *The Construction of Statutes*, 2nd ed (Toronto: Butterworths, 1983) at 106. (Bullets added.)]

The modern principle may be criticized for not providing enough guidance about what Parliament intends and, as you will see in the cases that follow, judges have a lot of leeway in selecting which of the four elements they will use to determine legislative intent. The modern principle may also be criticized for encouraging the assumption that statutory interpretation consists of resolving doubt about the meaning of particular words. A significant number of interpretation disputes turn on issues other than the meaning of words. Section III.C below illustrates why this is so.

C. THE RANGE OF ISSUES THAT CAN ARISE IN MODERN STATUTORY INTERPRETATION

Statutory interpretation involves more than disputes about the meaning of the legislative text. Sometimes the meaning is clear, but there is a gap in the legislative scheme, and the question is whether or not a court can do anything about it. Sometimes there is overlap between a clear provision and the common law, and the issue is whether both apply. Many disputes are about the circumstances in which a court should update a statute or decline to apply a legislative rule even though its meaning appears to be clear. In short, determining the meaning of words in a legislative text is an important task of interpreters, a necessary first task, but it is only part of the work of interpretation. (This account of the several types of argument available to interpreters, and the claims associated with each, is based on Ruth Sullivan, "Statutory Interpretation in a Nutshell" (2003) 82 Can Bar Rev 51 at 64-65.)

Table 10.1 lays out the range of issues that typically arise in modern statutory interpretation. It shows how the issues are addressed by interpretive actors such as counsel, administrative decision-makers, and judges, and it provides a short, concrete example of each issue.

The types of argument surveyed above are not mutually exclusive. The issues that arise in applying legislation to a given set of facts can often be framed in more than one way. How an issue is *framed* is rhetorically significant and can often affect the outcome of a case.

Table 10.1   Issues Arising in Statutory Interpretation

Issue	Type of Argument Used to Address the Issue, Description, and Example
Ambiguous, vague, or incomplete text	**Disputed meaning** The interpreter claims that, properly interpreted, the provision in question has a particular preferred meaning. He or she must establish that this preferred meaning is the ordinary meaning, an intended technical meaning, or at least a plausible meaning. If the legislation is bilingual, the interpreter must address both language versions. In *Perrier Group of Canada Inc v Canada*, [1996] 1 FCR 586 (CA), the Court had to decide whether carbonated water sold under the Perrier label was a "beverage" within the meaning of the *Excise Tax Act*, RSC 1985, c E-15. Perrier Group argued that "beverage" meant a manufactured drink, produced by mixing ingredients, and therefore excluded naturally carbonated water. The minister of revenue argued that "beverage" meant any liquid fit for human consumption and therefore included water. The Court preferred the minister's understanding of the term.
Evolving context	**Static versus dynamic interpretation** The interpreter claims that the text should be interpreted as it would have been when the text was first enacted (static interpretation) or interpreted in light of current understanding of language and social conditions (dynamic interpretation). In *Harvard College v Canada (Commissioner of Patents)*, 2002 SCC 76, [2002] 4 SCR 45, the issue was whether the so-called oncomouse was an "invention" within the definition of the *Patent Act*, RSC 1985, c P-4, which included "any new and useful art, process, machine, manufacture or composition of matter." Even though a genetically altered mouse could be thought of as a "composition of matter," the majority preferred a static interpretation. The Court held that Parliament had not contemplated the patenting of higher life forms when it drafted the definition of "invention." Such a "radical departure from the traditional patent regime" could not be achieved through interpretation but, rather, required legislative intervention. See also *Daniels v Canada (Indian Affairs and Northern Development)*, 2016 SCC 12, [2016] 1 SCR 99, where the Supreme Court concluded that the historical, philosophical, and linguistic contexts together established that the term "Indians" in s 91(24) of the *Constitution Act, 1867* encompasses *all* Indigenous peoples, including "non-status Indians" and Métis.
Overinclusive text	**Non-application** The interpreter identifies a reason not to apply a provision to the facts even though, given its ordinary meaning, it would otherwise apply. A provision may be "read down" in this way for any number of reasons—to promote legislative purposes, to avoid absurdity, or to comply with the presumptions of legislative intent. In *Re Vabalis* (1983), 2 DLR (4th) 382 (Ont CA), a married woman applied to change her name from Vabalis to Vabals under Ontario's *Change of Name Act*, RSO 1980, c 6. Section 4(1) of the Act provided as follows:

(Continued on next page.)

Table 10.1   Issues Arising in Statutory Interpretation (Continued)

Issue	Type of Argument Used to Address the Issue, Description, and Example
Overinclusive text (cont.)	A married person applying for a change of surname shall also apply for a change of the surnames of his or her spouse and all unmarried minor children of the husband or of the marriage.
	Since Ms Vabalis had not adopted her husband's name when she married, applying this provision to her would have required her husband, whose surname was different, to change his name to Vabals. The Court held that this requirement was absurd and should be limited to married applicants who have the same surname as the spouse. In effect, the Court narrowed the scope of the provision by reading in words of qualification:
	A married person who applies for a change of surname *and has the same surname as his or her spouse* shall also apply for a change of the surname of his or her spouse.
Underinclusive text	**1. Incorrigible gap in legislative scheme: supplementation with common law rule or remedy**
	The interpreter claims that the legislation as drafted cannot apply to the facts even though, given its purpose, it probably should apply. Whether this omission is deliberate or inadvertent, the court has no jurisdiction to fill a gap in a legislative scheme by "reading in" or otherwise enlarge the scope of legislation. Courts may intervene if the flaw can be characterized as a minor "drafting error."
	In *Beattie v National Frontier Insurance Co* (2003), 68 OR (3d) 60 (CA), a man was seriously injured in an accident and was eventually convicted of dangerous driving. The insurer argued that because of s 30(4) of the Statutory Accident Benefits Schedule (SABS), the claimant's criminal conviction relieved it of the obligation to pay income replacement and various other types of benefits. The Court refused to correct a legislative gap. First, the Court found clear legislative intent in ss 30(1) and (2) of the SABS to permanently exclude benefits if the claimant had committed one of the impugned acts that were listed in these provisions. In contrast, s 30(4) excluded payment of benefits *from the date of an accident to the date of a conviction*. However, s 30(4) was silent about whether or not benefits should be paid *after* a criminal conviction. This made s 30(4) inconsistent with the other, clearer provisions. The result would be the claimant would only lose his entitlement to benefits up to the date of his conviction, but would be entitled to benefits after that date.
	Even though the Court was invited to make s 30(4) consistent with ss 30(1) and (2) by stipulating that a criminal conviction released the insurer from the obligation to pay benefits, the Court refused to do so. The Court agreed that the wording of s 30(4) was probably the result of "faulty drafting that has created a lacuna, or gap, in the legislative scheme" (para 12). There was nothing in the Act or regulations denying a claimant access to benefits once he or she was convicted of an offence.

Issue	Type of Argument Used to Address the Issue, Description, and Example
Underinclusive text (cont.)	The Court accepted the legislation as drafted because the language was clear, and despite the fact that the language failed to achieve the legislative purpose, it was not the Court's role to correct it by engaging in "impermissible judicial redrafting" (para 16). The statute was later amended. **2. Supplementation of a corrigible gap** The interpreter concedes that the legislation as drafted does not apply, but claims that the common law does apply so as to supplement the underinclusive legislation. Supplementation arguments are generally successful when the court relies on its *parens patriae* jurisdiction (common law power to protect people, like children, who are unable to care for themselves) or its inherent jurisdiction to control its own process. In *Beson v Director of Child Welfare (Nfld)*, [1982] 2 SCR 716, the Court acknowledged that although the province's *Adoption of Children Act*, 1972 (Nfld), c 36 created various appeals to the Adoption Appeal Board, it apparently did not provide for an appeal in the circumstances of the case. Justice Wilson wrote: > If the Besons had indeed no right of appeal under the statute ... there is a gap in the legislative scheme which the Newfoundland courts could have filled by an exercise of their *parens patriae* jurisdiction.
Contradictory or incoherent text	**Corrigible mistake** The interpreter claims that the provision in question contains a drafting mistake, which must be corrected before determining whether the provision applies to the facts. He or she must establish what the legislature clearly intended and what the text would have said had it been properly drafted. This problem arises quite often in interpreting bilingual legislation when the two versions say different things. In *Morishita v Richmond (Township of)* (1990), 67 DLR (4th) 609 (BCCA), the Court had to interpret a provision in a municipal by-law that referred to s 4 of the by-law. Since the reference to s 4 was incoherent, while the reference to s 5 made good sense, the Court concluded that the lawmaker had intended to refer to s 5 and it interpreted the by-law accordingly.
Overlapping provisions	**1. No conflict: overlap versus exhaustive code** In the absence of conflict, if two or more provisions apply to the same facts, each is to be applied as written. Although not articulated as such, the courts work with a presumption of overlap. Any law, whether common law or legislation, that could apply is presumed to apply in the absence of evidence to the contrary. With an exhaustive code argument, the interpreter concedes that the overlap between legislative provisions or between legislation and the common law does not create a conflict, but claims that a particular act or provision was meant to apply exhaustively, to the exclusion of other law, whether statutory or common law.

(*Continued on next page.*)

Table 10.1 Issues Arising in Statutory Interpretation (Continued)

Issue	Type of Argument Used to Address the Issue, Description, and Example
Overlapping provisions (cont.)	In *Gendron v Supply & Services Union of the Public Service Alliance of Canada, Local 50057*, [1990] 1 SCR 1298, the issue was whether a union member could bring an action against the union for breaching the common law duty of fair representation. The Court ruled that the duties owed by unions to union members were set out in the *Canada Labour Code* and, on this issue at least, the statute was meant to be an exhaustive code, displacing recourse to the common law.
	2. Conflict: paramountcy rule
	The interpreter claims that a conflict between two provisions or between a provision and the common law exists and that one type of law takes precedence over the other on the basis of some principled reason—for example, legislation prevails over the common law or the specific prevails over the general.
	In *Insurance Corporation of BC v Heerspink*, [1982] 2 SCR 145, Heerspink challenged the statutory right of an insurance company to terminate an insurance contract upon giving 15 days' notice without establishing any cause. BC's *Human Rights Code* provided that persons could not be denied a "service … customarily available to the public … unless a reasonable cause exists for such denial." Reconciling this apparent conflict, Lamer J (as he then was) wrote (at 178):
	When the subject matter of a law is said to be the comprehensive statement of the "human rights" of the people living in the jurisdiction, then there is no doubt in my mind that the people of that jurisdiction have through their legislature clearly indicated that they consider that law, and the values it endeavours to buttress and protect are, save their constitutional laws, more important than all others. Therefore, short of that legislature speaking to the contrary in express and unequivocal language in the Code or in some other enactment, it is intended that the Code supersede all other laws when conflict arises.

D. GUIDES FOR THE TASK OF INTERPRETATION UNDER THE MODERN APPROACH

The judicial task of constructing presumed legislative intention potentially encompasses the entire body of evolving legal norms present in the particular legal context in which an act of official interpretation occurs. These norms are found in the Constitution Acts, in constitutional and quasi-constitutional legislation, and in international law, both customary and conventional. Their primary source, however, is the common law. (This is true even in Quebec. While the *Civil Code of Quebec*, CQLR c CCQ-1991 constitutes the primary source of legal norms for private law matters, public law is derived from common law sources.) Over the centuries, courts have identified certain values that are deserving of legal protection, and these have become the basis for the strict and liberal construction doctrines and the presumptions of legislative intent. These norms are an important part of the context in which legislation is made and read.

Numerous rules exist to guide statutory interpretation, but the *first* thing an interpreter must always do is read the statute and form an impression of the text's meaning.

1. Legal Sources of Interpretation Law That Assist with the Modern Approach to Statutory Interpretation

To guide the modern approach, three main sources of interpretation law exist: interpretation acts, interpretation rules in individual statutes and regulations (and, in Quebec, the *Civil Code*), and, most importantly, the common law. Under the separation of powers doctrine, the role of the legislature is to make law, while the role of the judiciary is to interpret law, test its validity, and apply it to particular facts. However, it is open to a sovereign legislature to issue instructions on how particular legislation, or legislation in general, should be interpreted.

Every Canadian jurisdiction—federal and provincial/territorial—has an Interpretation Act that contains various rules applicable to statutes in general. The federal act, for example, has rules respecting corporations, offences, evidence, the appointment of civil servants, the exercise of administrative powers, reports to Parliament, the coming into force of legislation, the impact of amendment and repeal, how to calculate majorities and time periods, and more. It also contains a list of defined terms that are found throughout the federal statute book, such as "bank," "holiday," "person," "month," and "Her Majesty." These definitions apply unless the context indicates otherwise. Interpretation rules are also found in general acts governing the making of regulations (at the federal level, the *Statutory Instruments Act*, RSC 1985, c S-22) and statute revisions (at the federal level, the *Legislation Revision and Consolidation Act*, RSC 1985, c S-20). Note that the federal Act applies only to federal legislation; the relevant provincial or territorial act governs provincial or territorial legislation.

The Interpretation Act of every Canadian jurisdiction also includes a provision that directs interpreters to give every enactment "such fair, large and liberal construction and interpretation that best ensures the attainment of its objects." This is found in s 12 of the federal Act. These provisions require a preference for an interpretation that promotes the purpose of legislation over one that uses strict construction.

Individual acts and regulations often contain definitions, application provisions, purpose statements, and the like. Definitions tell interpreters how particular words used in the legislation are to be understood. Application sections indicate the scope of the legislation in terms of space (territorial application), time (temporal application), persons affected (e.g., the Crown), and subject matter (some things may be excepted). Preambles and purpose statements, at the beginning of statutes, indicate the reasons for the new legislation—the concerns addressed, the values reflected in the legislation, and the anticipated benefits. Commencement and transitional provisions, at the end of statutes, indicate when the legislation will commence or come into force and how it will apply to situations in progress.

2. Common Law Presumptions Used to Determine Legislative Intent Under the Modern Approach

All legislation is enacted for a purpose—to achieve a particular outcome by imposing new obligations or prohibitions or by creating new rights or privileges. The common law presumptions of legislative intent are formal expressions of evolving common law expectations about how statutes should be read. One of the recurring issues in statutory interpretation is whether the courts should apply the same rules and techniques to all legislation, regardless of each act's subject matter or purpose. Historically, the courts have distinguished between legislation that takes away the freedom or property of an individual or otherwise interferes with his or her rights on the one hand, and legislation designed to cure mischief, or otherwise confer benefits on the other. Legislation that interferes with individual rights or freedoms is considered "penal" and attracts a "strict" construction. Legislation that cures mischief (i.e., social problem or defect in the law) or confers benefits is considered "remedial" and attracts a "liberal" construction.

When legislation is liberally construed, the focus is on achieving the benevolent purpose of the legislation: general principles are applied as fully as their wording permits, while exceptions and qualifications are strictly interpreted. If doubts or ambiguities arise, they are resolved in favour of the person seeking the benefit of the statute.

Provisions like s 12 of the federal *Interpretation Act*, RSC 1985, c I-21 were clearly enacted to eliminate the distinction between penal and remedial legislation by deeming all legislation to be remedial. This was an effort by legislators in the late 19th century to push back against the judicial tendency to deem all legislation to be penal. Courts today are far less likely to invoke strict construction than were courts in the past, but the distinction continues to figure in modern statutory interpretation.

The courts also control legislative initiatives by imputing to the legislature an intention to abide by norms that the courts consider important. These are the so-called presumptions of legislative intent. Table 10.2 contains some of the main presumptions, but the table is not exhaustive. Table 10.3 describes extrinsic aids that courts will employ in attempting to determine legislative intent.

Table 10.2   Common Law Presumptions Used to Determine Legislative Intent

Presumption	Requirement and Reasons for Using
Legislative purpose	The interpreter must always try to determine the purposes of legislation and, insofar as the text permits, adopt an interpretation that promotes or is at least consistent with those purposes. Interpretations that would tend to defeat legislative purpose are considered absurd.
	The vaguer the language of the legislative text, the more discretion is conferred on the tribunal or court that applies it, and the greater is the importance of constructing purposes in an appropriate interpretation.
	Liberal versus strict construction
	Liberal construction
	Liberal construction is given to quasi-constitutional legislation such as human rights codes as well as social welfare or benefit-conferring legislation. Liberal construction of legislation affecting Indigenous peoples means that it must be interpreted in their favour. The purpose of liberal construction is to confer benefits and amplify remedies. Interpretation acts direct that liberal constructions should generally be preferred over strict ones.
	When legislation has been drafted in an overly broad fashion, however, a narrow interpretation will be chosen as the one that best ensures the attainment of the statute's objects.
	Strict construction
	When legislation is strictly construed, the emphasis is on the wording of the text: general terms are read down, conditions of application are fully enforced, and ambiguities are resolved in favour of non-application.
	Strict construction is applied to criminal law, laws that expropriate private property, and exceptions to well-established legal principles. The purpose of strict construction is to protect individuals from incursions on liberty, property, and security and also to protect them from state punishment.
Legislative scheme	The provisions of an act are presumed to work together as parts of a coherent scheme designed to implement the legislature's goals. It is often helpful to look at the titles, headings, and subheadings and at the sequence of marginal or sectional notes to get an indication of the scheme. To determine how a particular provision contributes to the scheme, ask why the provision was included—what does it add to the other provisions, how does it qualify or limit them, what was the underlying rationale? Knowing how a provision contributes to a scheme generally is a good indicator of how it should be interpreted.

Presumption	Requirement and Reasons for Using
Legislative scheme (cont.)	**Mistakes and gaps in the legislative scheme**
	Corrigible mistakes
	Although the legislature is presumed not to make mistakes, the presumption is rebutted by persuasive evidence that the text does not accurately reflect the rule the legislature intended to enact. The courts have jurisdiction to correct such mistakes, unless the mistake amounts to a gap in the legislative scheme.
	Incorrigible gaps
	The courts almost always deny jurisdiction to cure a gap in a legislative scheme or to otherwise cure underinclusive provisions by making them apply to facts outside the ambit of the language of the text. Curing an underinclusive scheme or provision amounts to "reading in," which is generally considered a form of judicial legislation, as opposed to "reading down," which is not.
	Supplementing legislation by reliance on common law or the Civil Code
	Although the courts cannot cure underinclusive legislation by expanding its scope beyond what the text allows, it can rely on supplemental sources of law to complement what the legislative scheme provides. In doing so, it must often address the difficult question of the relationship between statute law and the common law.
Coherence in the statutory scheme	**General compliance with constitutional law and values in order to maximize their reach**
	Legislatures are presumed to intend to enact constitutionally valid law and in particular to comply with any limitations on their jurisdiction set out in the various Constitution Acts. For this reason, an interpretation that renders legislation valid is preferred over one that does not.
	This presumption must not be used to defeat the clear intentions of the legislature. Legislatures sometimes do intend to restrict a Charter right or freedom in order to achieve an important goal, and they are entitled to do so if the restriction can be justified under s 1. This possibility must not be taken away through interpretation.
	Compliance with related legislation in order to provide coherence
	Statutes dealing with the same subject matter must be read together and are presumed to offer a coherent and consistent treatment of the subject. Sometimes such statutes form a single, integrated scheme; sometimes they create distinct but overlapping schemes. Interpretation provisions in one statute are presumed to apply to related statutes.
	Referral to the statute book in order to ensure consistency
	Even if statutes do not relate to the same subject, it is often useful to compare provisions in different enactments that deal with a particular matter—for example, limitation of action provisions or search and seizure provisions. Given that drafters are presumed to be consistent in their use of language and techniques, the similarities and differences among the provisions can form the basis for inferring legislative intent.

(*Continued on next page.*)

Table 10.2   Common Law Presumptions Used to Determine Legislative Intent (Continued)

Presumption	Requirement and Reasons for Using
Coherence in the statutory scheme (cont.)	**Compliance with regulations in order to provide coherence** Regulations must be read in light of their enabling provision and their enabling legislation as a whole. The regulations and enabling legislation are presumed to constitute an integrated scheme. Interpretation provisions in the enabling legislation (such as definitions or application provisions) are presumed to apply to regulations and other instruments made under the enabling legislation. **Compliance with common law in order to ensure consistency** *Incorporation* Provincial legislation (outside Quebec) sometimes incorporates common law concepts or terms; and federal legislation sometimes incorporates common law and civil law concepts or terms. In such cases, resort to common law (or civil law) sources is appropriate to determine the meaning of the concept or term. *Codification and displacement* Legislation may also "codify" common law rules or principles—that is, give statutory form to pre-existing common law. In these cases, too, resort to common law sources may be appropriate. However, sometimes the purpose of the legislation is to modify or displace the common law. Legislation that is intended to displace and preclude further resort to the common law is often labelled "a complete code." With respect to offences the *Criminal Code* is a complete code, but with respect to defences it is not. **Compliance with international law in order to comply with obligations in that legal sphere** It is presumed that legislatures, provincial as well as federal, intend to comply with international law, both customary and conventional. This presumption operates most strongly in the case of implementing legislation—that is, legislation enacted for the purpose of making an international agreement an effective part of domestic law. The presumption has also been applied to help resolve ambiguities in non-implementing legislation, but unincorporated norms from international law must receive less weight from judges. **Compliance with the rule of law as an overarching requirement** The rule of law is an unwritten principle that may have full normative force but is more often used as an interpretive aid. The unwritten principle of the rule of law cannot be used on its own to strike down otherwise valid legislation. To strike down legislation, the principle must be anchored in the written text of the Constitution.
General, against	There are general presumptions against: • extraterritorial application of legislation, • retroactive application of legislation, • interfering with vested rights (both common law and statutory), and • applying legislation to the Crown and its agents.

Presumption	Requirement and Reasons for Using
Specific, against absurdity	It is presumed that the legislature does not intend its legislation to produce absurd consequences. An interpretation that avoids such consequences is preferred over one that does not. The clearer and more precise a text seems to be, the greater the absurdity required to depart from its ordinary meaning. The greater the absurdity that flows from a particular interpretation, the more justified an interpreter is in rejecting it. Examples of absurdities that the legislature intends to avoid include: • irrational distinctions such as treating like things differently or different things the same way; • irrational, contradictory, or anomalous effects; • defeating the purpose of the legislation; • undermining the efficient application of legislation; and • violating important norms of justice or fairness.

Table 10.3   Extrinsic Aids to Statutory Interpretation

Aid	Description
Legislative source	Consists of agreements that the legislation in question is intended to implement or of legislation (whether domestic or foreign) on which the legislation has been modelled in whole or in part.
Legislative history	Consists of material formally brought to the attention of the legislature during the legislative process, including ministerial statements, committee reports, recorded debates, and tabled background material.
Legislative evolution	Consists of the successive amendments and re-enactments a provision has undergone from its initial enactment to the time of application; subsequent evolution is not considered a legitimate aid.
Expert opinion*	Consists of precedent, administrative opinion, and scholarly legal publications, as well as expert testimony.

* The rules governing the admissibility and use of this type of extrinsic material are complex and in a state of flux. In practice, the courts tend to accept whatever material is offered, provided that it is *relevant* to the issue before the court and will not take the other party by surprise. However, appellate courts have not gone out of their way to establish clear principles and guidelines in this area. Courts sometimes decline to look at this material if it contradicts what appears to be the "plain meaning" of the legislative text.

3. General Common Law Presumptions About Specific Meaning in the Text

Apart from legislative directives and the common law presumptions about legislative intent described above, statutory interpretation continues to be firmly rooted in other common law methods. Courts make a number of (idealized) assumptions about the way legislation is drafted, which influence the way the finished product is interpreted. These assumptions are the basis of the so-called rules, maxims, presumptions and canons of statutory interpretation. "Maxim" and "canon" are old words that are traditionally used in the common law—these days we would call them "interpretive principles." These canons/maxims/presumptions guide and shape the reasoning process you need to engage in when you read a legal text like a statute where an interpretation dispute arises. This is why they are part of the "toolkit" of interpretation. They do not provide the legal answer but, rather, they are tools to help us make arguments. For example, we would argue that when there are "strings of words" in a statutory provision, we generally think that all of those words are there for a reason and certain maxims guide us to think of the reasons why all of these words are together in the same place (e.g., the *expressio unius est exclusio alterius* maxim or the presumption that "the legislature doesn't legislate in vain"). To take another example, courts presume that the legislature intends consistent expression. If you wanted to rebut this presumption to argue that the legislation in dispute was incoherent, the burden/onus would be on you or your counsel to displace the presumption of legislative coherence. This is not an easy thing to do!

Strictly speaking, these "rules" are not binding in the way that the rules, for example, of the *Criminal Code* are binding. Rather, they operate as principled guidance. It is important to remember that they ought not to operate on their own, but are subsumed under, and therefore work in tandem with, the modern approach to determining legislative intent. They offer interpreters a checklist of relevant considerations to determine specific meaning in the legislative text, suggesting various lines of inquiry, and ensuring that no possibility has been overlooked. They are relied on by counsel in developing arguments and by judges to justify outcomes in interpretation disputes. A few of the most important rules are discussed in Table 10.4, but you will need to consult a textbook on statutory interpretation to see the whole list. The table also sets out the questions that the interpreter needs to ask himself or herself while reading and the strategies he or she needs to keep in mind in order to make persuasive legal arguments. Table 10.5 describes the fundamental *presumptions* about legislative drafting— that is, presumptions about the forms of expression through which legislative intent is conveyed. These presumptions are essential for the construction of legal arguments in court and in administrative hearings. As in other areas of law, a legal presumption assumes that a fact exists (e.g., that the legislature intended *x*) that has the legal effect of shifting the burden of persuasion (or evidence) to the party disputing the effect or outcome of the presumption. The party who wishes to rebut a presumption will have to adduce concrete and contrary evidence in order to displace it.

At the very end of this chapter, you will find a "Cheat Sheet for the Modern Approach to Statutory Interpretation"—a checklist for the various considerations counsel and judges need to know lie behind the words.

Table 10.4   Rules About Meaning in Statutory Interpretation

Rule	Description	Burdens/Rebuttals
Plain meaning	Plain meaning is a textualist approach that presumes only a single, unambiguous and literal meaning exists. Under this approach, the interpreter assumes that an automatic and independent meaning of the words exists separately from the context and is the same for all readers. Note that this is, in fact, an impossibility. Plain meaning does not permit the introduction of extratextual evidence about legislative intent to rebut. If the words of the text are unambiguous and clear, the court must adhere to them regardless of consequences. Plain meaning is not the same as ordinary meaning. The plain meaning and the modern principle are inconsistent with each other.	Historically, the golden rule acted as the "safety net" for the plain meaning rule. The golden rule permitted courts to depart from the literal meaning of the text in order to avoid absurd consequences. Note that the modern approach replaces the plain meaning and golden rules.
Ordinary meaning	Ordinary meaning is the meaning that *spontaneously comes to the mind* of a competent reader upon reading a legislative text. This is presumed to be the meaning intended by Parliament. The ordinary meaning of a word or phrase is not its dictionary meaning. *You shouldn't primarily rely on the dictionary meaning.* Why? Dictionaries can only indicate a range of the meanings a word is capable of bearing. They can never indicate what a word means in a particular context.	To determine the ordinary meaning of language, courts rely on their own linguistic intuitions. The immediate context consists of the other words in the sentence plus the complex store of knowledge, impressions, assumptions, and values the reader brings to the text. The ordinary meaning (unlike the plain meaning) is the *starting point* for the interpretive analysis that follows. The presumption can be rebutted by evidence suggesting that some other meaning was intended.

(*Continued on next page.*)

Table 10.4   Rules About Meaning in Statutory Interpretation (Continued)

Rule	Description	Burdens/Rebuttals
Technical meaning	It is presumed that legislatures use words in their popular, non-technical sense. However, when legislation deals with a specialized subject and uses language that people governed by the legislation would understand in a specialized way, that specialized understanding is preferred over ordinary usage. Experts in the relevant field through testimony or affidavit evidence can offer evidence of technical meaning. For obvious reasons, the courts do not require expert testimony to establish the legal meaning of a word or expression. Reliance may be placed on, e.g., *Black's Law Dictionary*.	A person who claims that a legislative text has a technical meaning different from its popular, non-technical meaning has the burden of establishing: • the technical meaning of the word or expression, and • that the technical meaning was intended in this context. Legal terms of art are considered technical terms. If a word or expression has both a popular meaning and a legal meaning, the popular meaning is presumed.
Shared meaning	If there is a discrepancy between the versions of a bilingual statute, the meaning that is shared by both versions is presumed to be the intended meaning. If one version of bilingual legislation is broader in scope than the other, the narrower version represents the shared meaning and should prevail unless there is evidence that the legislature intended the broader meaning.	The presumption in favour of the shared meaning can be rebutted by evidence suggesting that some other meaning was intended.
Original meaning	The meaning of the words used in a legislative text is fixed at the time of enactment, but its application to facts over time is not fixed. In static interpretation, the text is applied as it would have been when the legislation was first enacted. In dynamic interpretation, the text is applied in light of circumstances and assumptions existing at the time of application.	Language that is technical, concrete, and specific tends to attract a static interpretation; language that is general or abstract attracts a dynamic interpretation.

Rule	Description	Burdens/Rebuttals
Plausible meaning	If the ordinary meaning of a text is rejected to give effect to the actual or presumed intentions of the legislature, the meaning adopted must be one that the text is capable of bearing.	This rule is sometimes honoured in the breach. For example, in *Paul v The Queen*, [1982] 1 SCR 621, the Court concluded that a criminal prosecution "before the same court *at the same sittings*" should be interpreted to mean a criminal prosecution "before the same judge." Justice Lamer acknowledged that this interpretation disregarded the meaning of the words "at the same sittings," but was nonetheless prepared to adopt this interpretation in order to adapt the provision to the current method of dealing with criminal prosecutions.

Table 10.5 Presumptions About Legislative Drafting in Statutory Interpretation

Presumption	Description	Related Maxim
Straightforward expression	The legislature chooses the clearest, simplest, and most direct way of stating its meaning. You cannot assume that a court will agree with you given that the court is facing a potential interpretive dispute. You will need to argue this point and point to the text.	
Uniform expression	The legislature uses the same words and techniques to express the same meaning and different words and techniques to express different meanings.	• Implied exclusion or *expressio unius est exclusio alterius* ("the express mention of one thing excludes all others") If something is not mentioned in circumstances where one would expect it to be mentioned, it is impliedly excluded. • Associated words or *noscitur a sociis* ("it is known from its associates") The meaning of a word or phrase is affected by the other words or phrases with which it is linked in a sentence.

(*Continued on next page.*)

Table 10.5 Presumptions About Legislative Drafting in Statutory Interpretation (Continued)

Presumption	Description	Related Maxim
No superfluous words	Legislation does not contain any superfluous words. Every word, every feature of the text is there for a reason and plays a meaningful role in the legislative scheme.	• *The legislature does not legislate in vain.* There is no tautology or redundancy in the legislation. • Limited class or *ejusdem generis* ("of the same kind, class, or nature"). When a list of things that all belong to an identifiable class is followed by a more general term, the general term may be read down to include only other things within the identifiable class. For example, in the phrase "ice skating, sledding, skiing, and other sports," "sports" may be read down to include only sports that are played in winter.
Internal coherence	All the provisions of a legislative text fit together logically and work together coherently to achieve the purposes of the legislation.	• *The legislature would have said "x."* A legitimate basis for rejecting a proposed interpretation is to point out that if the legislature had intended the proposed interpretation, it would have framed the legislation in a different way, as it did elsewhere in the act or regulation or elsewhere in the statute book.

IV. THE MODERN APPROACH IN ACTION

The modern principle says that the words of a legislative text must be read: (1) in their *entire context*; (2) in their *grammatical and ordinary* sense (i.e., the starting point); (3) *harmoniously* with the *scheme and objects* of the act; and (4) consistent with the *intention* of the legislature (recall the excerpt from Ruth Sullivan in Section III.B above where Driedger identified four elements of legislative intent). In a so-called "easy" case, textual meaning, legislative intent, and relevant norms all support a single, harmonious interpretation—despite opposing views. Remember also that a reviewing court may disagree with litigants and find that no real interpretive ambiguity actually exists—they usually resort to the "plain meaning" approach to bolster this conclusion. In harder cases, however, these dimensions are vague or obscure or point in different directions. In the hardest cases, the textual meaning seems plain, but cogent evidence of legislative intent (actual or presumed) makes the plain meaning unacceptable. Or, more than one plausible interpretation exists and judges must engage in a difficult determination of which interpretation best "fits" legislative intent, history, and public law values. If the modern principle has a weakness, it is its failure to acknowledge and address the dilemma created by these types of "hard" cases.

Why does this matter? In the hardest cases, we see that legislative intent is a legal fiction that is largely created by reviewing courts: the legislature, not being a real person, cannot have an "intent." It is not "found" or "discovered" by judges (or administrative decision-makers) but, rather, actively constructed by them. This reality may raise separation of powers concerns and fears about judicial arbitrariness in the act of interpretation because what else, other than the legislative history, mandated rules, and common law presumptions, constrains judges when they are constructing interpretations of problematic texts? What prevents a judge from imposing the answer that he or she simply thinks is the best because it is *his* or *her* subjective interpretation of the matter?

When a case has no one right answer—in other words, when multiple valid interpretations exist—what is at stake is a judicial choice concerning a rational, legally defensible outcome on the facts of the case. The institutional question becomes: who is best placed to provide the answer? Is it the reviewing court, the expert labour arbitrator, the minister, or the administrative official? Deference and institutional dialogue remain constant concerns.

This section presents not only the leading case on the modern approach, but a set of cases that ask you to consider how well the modern approach works to determine meaning and to guide judicial discretion in the act of interpretation.

A. THE ORIGINAL CASE

The following is the leading case on statutory interpretation. It sets out the preferred approach of the Supreme Court of Canada and has been cited for this purpose in countless subsequent judgments. In reading the case, notice how the Court characterizes the type of interpretation problem it faces and notice as well the particular principles of statutory interpretation relied on.

While reading, keep in mind the following questions:

1. What is the plain meaning of
   a. s 40(1) of the *Employment Standards Act* (ESA),
   b. s 40(7) of the ESA,
   c. s 40*a* of the ESA,
   d. ss 2(1) and 3 of the *Employment Standards Amendment Act* (ESAA),
   e. s 121(1) of the *Bankruptcy Act,* and
   f. ss 10 and 17 of the *Interpretation Act*?
2. What is the disputed meaning of s 40*a*?
3. According to Iacobucci J, what is the primary intent of the legislators in the ESA? Identify the aids Iacobucci J uses to construct intent.
4. Identify the specific "rules" of interpretation that Iacobucci J applied.
5. How did the "plain meaning" interpretation offend Iacobucci J's sense of justice?
6. What, if anything, did Iacobucci J "read into" s 40*a* of the ESA?

Re Rizzo and Rizzo Shoes Ltd
[1998] 1 SCR 27

[In April 1989 a petition in bankruptcy was filed against Rizzo Shoes Ltd, and the company was ordered into bankruptcy. As a result, Rizzo's employees lost their employment and a trustee assumed control of the corporation's property. The trustee was responsible for liquidating the property and distributing the proceeds among the corporation's debtors. A claim was made on behalf of Rizzo's former employees for termination and severance pay said to be owing under Ontario's *Employment Standards Act*, RSO 1980, c 137 as a result of employment loss. The trustee disallowed the claim on the ground that the bankruptcy of an employer does not constitute a dismissal from employment, and therefore no entitlement to severance, termination, or vacation pay arose under the Act. On appeal, the Ontario Court (General Division) reversed the trustee's decision, but on further appeal, the Ontario Court of Appeal restored it. The employees appealed to the Supreme Court of Canada.]

IACOBUCCI J (for the Court):

[1] This is an appeal by the former employees of a now bankrupt employer from an order disallowing their claims for termination pay (including vacation pay thereon) and severance pay. The case turns on an issue of statutory interpretation. Specifically, the appeal decides whether, under the relevant legislation in effect at the time of the bankruptcy, employees are entitled to claim termination and severance payments where their employment has been terminated by reason of their employer's bankruptcy.

• • •

2. Relevant Statutory Provisions

[6] The relevant versions of the *Bankruptcy Act* (now the *Bankruptcy and Insolvency Act*) and the *Employment Standards Act* for the purposes of this appeal are RSC, 1985, c. B-3 (the "*BA*"), and RSO 1980, c. 137, as amended to April 14, 1989 (the "*ESA*") respectively.

Employment Standards Act, RSO 1980, c. 137, as amended:

40(1) No employer shall terminate the employment of an employee who has been employed for three months or more unless the employee [Note: the court has misquoted the statute and s 40(1) should read "unless the employer" here] gives,

(a) one weeks notice in writing to the employee if his or her period of employment is less than one year;

(b) two weeks notice in writing to the employee if his or her period of employment is one year or more but less than three years;

(c) three weeks notice in writing to the employee if his or her period of employment is three years or more but less than four years;

(d) four weeks notice in writing to the employee if his or her period of employment is four years or more but less than five years;

(e) five weeks notice in writing to the employee if his or her period of employment is five years or more but less than six years;

(f) six weeks notice in writing to the employee if his or her period of employment is six years or more but less than seven years;

(g) seven weeks notice in writing to the employee if his or her period of employment is seven years or more but less than eight years;

(h) eight weeks notice in writing to the employee if his or her period of employment is eight years or more,

and such notice has expired.

• • •

(7) Where the employment of an employee is terminated contrary to this section,

(a) the employer shall pay termination pay in an amount equal to the wages that the employee would have been entitled to receive at his regular rate for a regular non-overtime work week for the period of notice prescribed by subsection (1) or (2), and any wages to which he is entitled;

• • •

40a ...

(1a) Where,

(a) fifty or more employees have their employment terminated by an employer in a period of six months or less and the terminations are caused by the permanent discontinuance of all or part of the business of the employer at an establishment; or

(b) one or more employees have their employment terminated by an employer with a payroll of $2.5 million or more,

the employer shall pay severance pay to each employee whose employment has been terminated and who has been employed by the employer for five or more years.

Employment Standards Amendment Act, 1981, SO 1981, c. 22

2(1) Part XII of the said Act is amended by adding thereto the following section:

• • •

(3) Section 40a of the said Act does not apply to an employer who became a bankrupt or an insolvent person within the meaning of the *Bankruptcy Act* (Canada) and whose assets have been distributed among his creditors or to an employer whose proposal within the meaning of the *Bankruptcy Act* (Canada) has been accepted by his creditors in the period from and including the 1st day of January, 1981, to and including the day immediately before the day this Act receives Royal Assent.

Bankruptcy Act, RSC, 1985, c. B-3

121(1) All debts and liabilities, present or future, to which the bankrupt is subject at the date of the bankruptcy or to which he may become subject before his discharge by reason of any obligation incurred before the date of the bankruptcy shall be deemed to be claims provable in proceedings under this Act.

Interpretation Act, RSO 1990, c. I.11

10. Every Act shall be deemed to be remedial, whether its immediate purport is to direct the doing of anything that the Legislature deems to be for the public good or to prevent or punish the doing of any thing that it deems to be contrary to the public good, and shall accordingly receive such fair, large and liberal construction and interpretation as will best ensure the attainment of the object of the Act according to its true intent, meaning and spirit.

• • •

17. The repeal or amendment of an Act shall be deemed not to be or to involve any declaration as to the previous state of the law.

• • •

4. Issues

[17] This appeal raises one issue: does the termination of employment caused by the bankruptcy of an employer give rise to a claim provable in bankruptcy for termination pay and severance pay in accordance with the provisions of the *ESA*?

5. Analysis

[18] The statutory obligation upon employers to provide both termination pay and severance pay is governed by ss. 40 and 40a of the *ESA*, respectively. The Court of Appeal noted that the plain language of those provisions suggests that

termination pay and severance pay are payable only when the employer terminates the employment. For example, the opening words of s. 40(1) are: "No employer shall terminate the employment of an employee ... ." Similarly, s. 40a(1a) begins with the words, "Where ... fifty or more employees have their employment terminated by an employer ... ." Therefore, the question on which this appeal turns is whether, when bankruptcy occurs, the employment can be said to be terminated "by an employer."

[19] The Court of Appeal answered this question in the negative, holding that, where an employer is petitioned into bankruptcy by a creditor, the employment of its employees is not terminated "by an employer," but rather by operation of law. Thus, the Court of Appeal reasoned that, in the circumstances of the present case, the *ESA* termination pay and severance pay provisions were not applicable and no obligations arose. In answer, the appellants submit that the phrase "terminated by an employer" is best interpreted as reflecting a distinction between involuntary and voluntary termination of employment. It is their position that this language was intended to relieve employers of their obligation to pay termination and severance pay when employees leave their jobs voluntarily. However, the appellants maintain that where an employee's employment is involuntarily terminated by reason of their employer's bankruptcy, this constitutes termination "by an employer" for the purpose of triggering entitlement to termination and severance pay under the *ESA*.

[20] At the heart of this conflict is an issue of statutory interpretation. Consistent with the findings of the Court of Appeal, the plain meaning of the words of the provisions here in question appears to restrict the obligation to pay termination and severance pay to those employers who have actively terminated the employment of their employees. At first blush, bankruptcy does not fit comfortably into this interpretation. However, with respect, I believe this analysis is incomplete.

[21] Although much has been written about the interpretation of legislation (see, e.g., Ruth Sullivan, *Statutory Interpretation* (1997); Ruth Sullivan, *Driedger on the Construction of Statutes* (3rd ed. 1994) (hereinafter *"Construction of Statutes"*); Pierre-André Côté, *The Interpretation of Legislation in Canada* (2nd ed. 1991)), Elmer Driedger in *Construction of Statutes* (2nd ed. 1983) best encapsulates the approach upon which I prefer to rely. He recognizes that statutory interpretation cannot be founded on the wording of the legislation alone. At p. 87 he states:

> Today there is only one principle or approach, namely, the words of an Act are to be read in their entire context and in their grammatical and ordinary sense harmoniously with the scheme of the Act, the object of the Act, and the intention of Parliament.

• • •

[22] I also rely upon s. 10 of the *Interpretation Act*, RSO 1980, c. 219, which provides that every Act "shall be deemed to be remedial" and directs that every Act shall "receive such fair, large and liberal construction and interpretation as will best ensure the attainment of the object of the Act according to its true intent, meaning and spirit."

[23] Although the Court of Appeal looked to the plain meaning of the specific provisions in question in the present case, with respect, I believe that the court did not pay sufficient attention to the scheme of the *ESA*, its object or the intention of the legislature; nor was the context of the words in issue appropriately recognized. I now turn to a discussion of these issues.

[24] In *Machtinger v. HOJ Industries Ltd.*, [1992] 1 SCR 986, at p. 1002, the majority of this Court recognized the importance that our society accords to employment and the fundamental role that it has assumed in the life of the individual. The manner in which employment can be terminated was said to be equally important ...

It was in this context that the majority in *Machtinger* described, at p. 1003, the object of the *ESA* as being the protection of "... the interests of employees by requiring employers to comply with certain minimum standards, including minimum periods of notice of termination." Accordingly, the majority concluded, at p. 1003, that, "... an interpretation of the Act which encourages employers to comply with the minimum requirements of the Act, and so extends its protections to as many employees as possible, is to be favoured over one that does not."

[25] The objects of the termination and severance pay provisions themselves are also broadly premised upon the need to protect employees. Section 40 of the *ESA* requires employers to give their employees reasonable notice of termination based upon length of service. One of the primary purposes of this notice period is to provide employees with an opportunity to take preparatory measures and seek alternative employment. It follows that s. 40(7)(a), which provides for termination pay in lieu of notice when an employer has failed to give the required statutory notice, is intended to "cushion" employees against the adverse effects of economic dislocation likely to follow from the absence of an opportunity to search for alternative employment. ...

[26] Similarly, s. 40a, which provides for severance pay, acts to compensate long-serving employees for their years of service and investment in the employer's business and for the special losses they suffer when their employment terminates. In *R v. TNT Canada Inc.* (1996), 27 OR (3d) 546, Robins JA quoted with approval at pp. 556-57 from the words of D.D. Carter in the course of an employment standards determination in *Re Telegram Publishing Co. v. Zwelling* (1972), 1 LAC (2d) 1 (Ont.), at p. 19, wherein he described the role of severance pay as follows:

> Severance pay recognizes that an employee does make an investment in his employer's business—the extent of this investment being directly related to the length of the employee's service. This investment is the seniority that the employee builds up during his years of service. ... Upon termination of the employment relationship, this investment of years of service is lost, and the employee must start to rebuild seniority at another place of work. The severance pay, based on length of service, is some compensation for this loss of investment.

[27] In my opinion, the consequences or effects which result from the Court of Appeal's interpretation of ss. 40 and 40a of the *ESA* are incompatible with both the object of the Act and with the object of the termination and severance pay provisions themselves. It is a well established principle of statutory interpretation that the legislature does not intend to produce absurd consequences. According to Côté, *supra*, an interpretation can be considered absurd if it leads to ridiculous or frivolous consequences, if it is extremely unreasonable or inequitable, if it is illogical or incoherent, or if it is incompatible with other provisions or with the object of the legislative enactment (at pp. 378-80). Sullivan echoes these comments noting that a label of absurdity can be attached to interpretations which defeat the purpose of a statute or render some aspect of it pointless or futile (Sullivan, *Construction of Statutes, supra*, at p. 88).

[28] The trial judge properly noted that, if the *ESA* termination and severance pay provisions do not apply in circumstances of bankruptcy, those employees "fortunate" enough to have been dismissed the day before a bankruptcy would be entitled to such payments, but those terminated on the day the bankruptcy becomes final would not be so entitled. In my view, the absurdity of this consequence is particularly evident in a unionized workplace where seniority is a factor in determining the order of lay-off. The more senior the employee, the larger the investment he or she has made in the employer and the greater the entitlement to termination

and severance pay. However, it is the more senior personnel who are likely to be employed up until the time of the bankruptcy and who would thereby lose their entitlements to these payments.

[29] If the Court of Appeal's interpretation of the termination and severance pay provisions is correct, it would be acceptable to distinguish between employees merely on the basis of the timing of their dismissal. It seems to me that such a result would arbitrarily deprive some employees of a means to cope with the economic dislocation caused by unemployment. In this way the protections of the *ESA* would be limited rather than extended, thereby defeating the intended working of the legislation. In my opinion, this is an unreasonable result.

[30] In addition to the termination and severance pay provisions, both the appellants and the respondent relied upon various other sections of the *ESA* to advance their arguments regarding the intention of the legislature. In my view, although the majority of these sections offer little interpretive assistance, one transitional provision is particularly instructive. In 1981, s. 2(1) of the *ESAA* introduced s. 40*a*, the severance pay provision, to the *ESA*. Section 2(2) deemed that provision to come into force on January 1, 1981. Section 2(3), the transitional provision in question provided as follows:

> 2. ...
>
> (3) Section 40*a* of the said Act does not apply to an employer who became a bankrupt or an insolvent person within the meaning of the *Bankruptcy Act* (Canada) and whose assets have been distributed among his creditors or to an employer whose proposal within the meaning of the *Bankruptcy Act* (Canada) has been accepted by his creditors in the period from and including the 1st day of January, 1981, to and including the day immediately before the day this Act receives Royal Assent.

[31] The Court of Appeal found that it was neither necessary nor appropriate to determine the intention of the legislature in enacting this provisional subsection. Nevertheless, the court took the position that the intention of the legislature as evidenced by the introductory words of ss. 40 and 40*a* was clear, namely, that termination by reason of a bankruptcy will not trigger the severance and termination pay obligations of the *ESA*. The court held that this intention remained unchanged by the introduction of the transitional provision. With respect, I do not agree with either of these findings. Firstly, in my opinion, the use of legislative history as a tool for determining the intention of the legislature is an entirely appropriate exercise and one which has often been employed by this Court ... Secondly, I believe that the transitional provision indicates that the Legislature intended that termination and severance pay obligations should arise upon an employer's bankruptcy.

[32] In my view, by extending an exemption to employers who became bankrupt and lost control of their assets between the coming into force of the amendment and its receipt of royal assent, s. 2(3) necessarily implies that the severance pay obligation does in fact extend to bankrupt employers. It seems to me that, if this were not the case, no readily apparent purpose would be served by this transitional provision.

[33] I find support for my conclusion in the decision of Saunders J in *Royal Dressed Meats Inc. ...* . Having reviewed s. 2(3) of the *ESAA*, he commented as follows (at p. 89):

> ... any doubt about the intention of the Ontario Legislature has been put to rest, in my opinion, by the transitional provision which introduced severance payments into the E.S.A. ... it seems to me an inescapable inference that the legislature

intended liability for severance payments to arise on a bankruptcy. That intention would, in my opinion, extend to termination payments which are similar in character.

[34] This interpretation is also consistent with statements made by the Minister of Labour at the time he introduced the 1981 amendments to the *ESA*. With regard to the new severance pay provision he stated:

> The circumstances surrounding a closure will govern the applicability of the severance pay legislation in some defined situations. For example, a bankrupt or insolvent firm will still be required to pay severance pay to employees to the extent that assets are available to satisfy their claims.
>
> • • •
>
> ... [T]he proposed severance pay measures will, as I indicated earlier, be retroactive to January 1 of this year. That retroactive provision, however, will not apply in those cases of bankruptcy and insolvency where the assets have already been distributed or where an agreement on a proposal to creditors has already been reached.

(*Legislature of Ontario Debates*, 1st sess., 32nd Parl., June 4, 1981, at pp. 1236-37.)

Moreover, in the legislative debates regarding the proposed amendments the Minister stated:

> For purposes of retroactivity, severance pay will not apply to bankruptcies under the Bankruptcy Act where assets have been distributed. However, once this act receives royal assent, employees in bankruptcy closures will be covered by the severance pay provisions.

(*Legislature of Ontario Debates*, 1st sess., 32nd Parl., June 16, 1981, at p. 1699.)

[35] Although the frailties of Hansard evidence are many, this Court has recognized that it can play a limited role in the interpretation of legislation. Writing for the Court in *R v. Morgentaler*, [1993] 3 SCR 463, at p. 484, Sopinka J stated:

> ... until recently the courts have balked at admitting evidence of legislative debates and speeches. ... The main criticism of such evidence has been that it cannot represent the "intent" of the legislature, an incorporeal body, but that is equally true of other forms of legislative history. Provided that the court remains mindful of the limited reliability and weight of Hansard evidence, it should be admitted as relevant to both the background and the purpose of legislation.

[36] Finally, with regard to the scheme of the legislation, since the *ESA* is a mechanism for providing minimum benefits and standards to protect the interests of employees, it can be characterized as benefits-conferring legislation. As such, according to several decisions of this Court, it ought to be interpreted in a broad and generous manner. Any doubt arising from difficulties of language should be resolved in favour of the claimant (see, e.g., *Abrahams v. Attorney General of Canada*, [1983] 1 SCR 2, at p. 10; *Hills v. Canada (Attorney General)*, [1988] 1 SCR 513, at p. 537). It seems to me that, by limiting its analysis to the plain meaning of ss. 40 and 40a of the *ESA*, the Court of Appeal adopted an overly restrictive approach that is inconsistent with the scheme of the Act.

• • •

[40] As I see the matter, when the express words of ss. 40 and 40a of the *ESA* are examined in their entire context, there is ample support for the conclusion that the words "terminated by the employer" must be interpreted to include termination

resulting from the bankruptcy of the employer. Using the broad and generous approach to interpretation appropriate for benefits-conferring legislation, I believe that these words can reasonably bear that construction ... . I also note that the intention of the Legislature as evidenced in s. 2(3) of the *ESAA*, clearly favours this interpretation. Further, in my opinion, to deny employees the right to claim *ESA* termination and severance pay where their termination has resulted from their employer's bankruptcy, would be inconsistent with the purpose of the termination and severance pay provisions and would undermine the object of the *ESA*, namely, to protect the interests of as many employees as possible.

[41] In my view, the impetus behind the termination of employment has no bearing upon the ability of the dismissed employee to cope with the sudden economic dislocation caused by unemployment. As all dismissed employees are equally in need of the protections provided by the *ESA*, any distinction between employees whose termination resulted from the bankruptcy of their employer and those who have been terminated for some other reason would be arbitrary and inequitable. Further, I believe that such an interpretation would defeat the true meaning, intent and spirit of the *ESA*. Therefore, I conclude that termination as a result of an employer's bankruptcy does give rise to an unsecured claim provable in bankruptcy pursuant to s. 121 of the *BA* for termination and severance pay in accordance with ss. 40 and 40*a* of the *ESA*. Because of this conclusion, I do not find it necessary to address the alternative finding of the trial judge as to the applicability of s. 7(5) of the *ESA*.

[42] I note that subsequent to the Rizzo bankruptcy, the termination and severance pay provisions of the *ESA* underwent another amendment. Sections 74(1) and 75(1) of the *Labour Relations and Employment Statute Law Amendment Act*, 1995, SO 1995, c. 1, amend those provisions so that they now expressly provide that where employment is terminated by operation of law as a result of the bankruptcy of the employer, the employer will be deemed to have terminated the employment. However, s. 17 of the *Interpretation Act* directs that, "[t]he repeal or amendment of an Act shall be deemed not to be or to involve any declaration as to the previous state of the law." As a result, I note that the subsequent change in the legislation has played no role in determining the present appeal.

6. Disposition and Costs

[43] I would allow the appeal and set aside paragraph 1 of the order of the Court of Appeal. In lieu thereof, I would substitute an order declaring that Rizzo's former employees are entitled to make claims for termination pay (including vacation pay due thereon) and severance pay as unsecured creditors. ...

Justice Iacobucci appears to agree with the Ontario Court of Appeal that the language of ss 40 and 40*a* of the *Employment Standards Act* plainly excludes loss of employment caused by bankruptcy. To reach this conclusion, what specific language does he rely on? Do you agree with his assessment of this language?

Notice that determining whether a text is "plain" or "ambiguous" is a linguistic judgment based partly on a subjective assessment. Are judges better equipped than others to make such judgments? Would it be appropriate for courts to rely on other experts such as linguists to assist them in determining whether a text is clear or ambiguous?

In *R v McIntosh*, [1995] 1 SCR 68, Lamer CJ complained that "[t]he Crown is asking this Court to read words into s. 34(2) which are simply not there. In my view, to do so would be tantamount to *amending* s. 34(2), which is a legislative and not a judicial function." In *Rizzo*, Iacobucci J appears to disregard certain words in the text—for example, "by the employer" in s 40*a*. Is this a permissible interpretation?

In addressing this question it is useful to distinguish between "reading down" and "reading in" because these concepts are used in statutory interpretation. "Reading down" refers to accepting an interpretation of a provision that is narrower in scope than the ordinary meaning of the text would support. When a provision is read down, words of limitation or qualification are effectively added to the text, for one of the following reasons:

- the court is giving effect to limitations or qualifications that are implicit in the text or the scheme of the legislation; it is, therefore, giving effect to the legislature's intent;
- the court is refusing to apply the legislation to situations that are outside the mischief the legislation was meant to address; it is, therefore, refusing to exceed the legislature's intent; or
- the court is relying on a presumption of legislative intent.

In each case, the additional words narrow rather than enlarge the scope of the provision and are meant to reflect the legislature's intent.

When a court "reads in", it expands the scope of a legislative provision or fills a gap in a legislative scheme, thus making the legislation apply to facts that it would not otherwise encompass given the limits of the language used in the provision or scheme. One way to read in is to ignore words of qualification or limitation in the act; another is to add words of expansion to the act. Usually, courts refuse to read in, on the ground that it amounts to amendment rather than interpretation. Rightly or wrongly, courts associate enlarging the scope of a text with amendment. In the *Rizzo* case, did Iacobucci J rely on reading in? If yes, does this act of interpretation, in effect, amend the legislation?

B. DYNAMIC AND STATIC APPROACHES IN THE SUPREME COURT ACT REFERENCE

In this section, we will reconsider the *Supreme Court Act Reference,* 2014 SCC 21, [2014] SCR 433 (examined in Chapter 5) by contrasting the approaches used to interpret s 5 by the majority and the dissent. Recall that the federal government appointed Justice Marc Nadon, a supernumerary judge of the Federal Court of Appeal, to the Supreme Court of Canada in October 2013. Section 6 of the *Supreme Court Act*, RSC 1985, c S-26 stipulated that three of the nine judges of the Supreme Court should be appointed "from among the judges of the Court of Appeal or of the Superior Court of the Province of Quebec or from among the advocates of that Province." At the time of his appointment, Nadon J was not a current member of the Barreau du Québec, although he had been a member of the Quebec bar for more than ten years prior to his appointment to the Federal Court. Did he, in order to be a valid appointment, need to be a *current* member of the Quebec bar? The majority answered "yes," which meant that Nadon J's appointment was considered void from the beginning, while the dissent answered "no." We will not look at the second question concerning Parliament's unilateral ability to enact the declaratory legislation that it did.

In order to better consider the two decisions, we will reverse the order and read the dissenting judgment first, followed by the majority's. Ask yourselves the following questions while reading:

1. Which decision uses a more static approach and which one employs a more dynamic approach?
2. Which decision offers the better interpretation and why?

Reference re Supreme Court Act, ss 5 and 6
2014 SCC 21, [2014] 1 SCR 433

MOLDAVER J (dissenting):

I. Introduction

. . .

[110] The issue raised in Question 1 is whether former advocates of the Quebec bar of at least 10 years standing meet the eligibility requirements in the *Supreme Court Act* for appointment to the Quebec seats on this Court. That is a legal issue, not a political one. It is not the function of this Court to comment on the merits of an appointment or the selection process that led to it. Those are political matters that belong to the executive branch of government. They form no part of our mandate.

[111] The answer to Question 1 lies in the correct interpretation of ss. 5 and 6 of the Act. For reasons that follow, I would answer Question 1 in the affirmative. Under ss. 5 and 6 of the Act, both current and past advocates of at least 10 years standing at the Quebec bar are eligible for appointment to this Court. In view of my answer to Question 1, the legislation to which Question 2 refers is redundant. It does nothing more than restate the law as it exists. Accordingly, I find it unnecessary to answer Question 2.

[112] That said, as the majority reasons make clear, a different response to Question 1 brings Question 2 to the forefront and makes it far from redundant. It gives rise to constitutional issues that are profoundly important to this Court and its place in our constitutional democracy.

[113] With that in mind, although I need not address the constitutional issues in view of my response to Question 1, I choose to do so to this extent. The coexistence of two distinct legal systems in Canada—the civil law system in Quebec and the common law system elsewhere—is a unique and defining characteristic of our country. It is critical to both Quebec and Canada as a whole that persons with training in civil law form an integral part of this country's highest court. Indeed, a guarantee to that effect was central to the bargain struck between Parliament and Quebec when the Supreme Court was first created in 1875.

[114] Section 6 of the Act protects Quebec's right to have three seats on this Court. Like the majority, I agree that this guarantee has been constitutionally entrenched, and that the three seats allotted to Quebec are an integral part of this Court's composition. As such, any change in this regard would require the unanimous consent of the Senate, the House of Commons, and the legislative assembly of each province under s. 41(d) in Part V of the *Constitution Act, 1982*.

[115] I stop there, however. I do so because I have difficulty with the notion that an amendment to s. 6 making former Quebec advocates of at least 10 years standing eligible for appointment to the Court would require unanimity, whereas an amendment that affected other features of the Court, including its role as a general court of appeal for Canada and its independence, could be achieved under s. 42(1)(d) of the *Constitution Act, 1982* using the 7-50 formula. Put simply, I am not convinced that any and all changes to the eligibility requirements will necessarily come within "the composition of the Supreme Court of Canada" in s. 41(d).

[116] Be that as it may, the first question before us today raises a much narrower issue. Specifically, we are asked to decide whether Quebec appointees are subject to more stringent eligibility requirements than their common law counterparts.

[117] All members of this Court agree that under s. 5 of the Act, both *current and former* members of a provincial bar of at least 10 years standing, and both *current and former* judges of a provincial superior court, are eligible for appointment to this Court. We part company, however, on whether s. 6 restricts the eligibility criteria, in the case of the three Quebec seats, to only *current* members of the Quebec bar and *current* judges of Quebec's superior courts. My colleagues conclude that it does; I reach the opposite conclusion. In my respectful view, the same eligibility criteria in s. 5 apply to all appointees, including those chosen from Quebec institutions to fill a Quebec seat. The currency requirement is not supported by the text of s. 6, its context, its legislative history, or its underlying object. Nor is such a requirement supported by the scheme of the *Supreme Court Act*. In short, currency has never been a requirement under s. 6 and, in my view, any attempt to impose it must be rejected.

II. Analysis

A. The Text, Context and History of Sections 5 and 6

• • •

[119] Section 5 sets out the threshold eligibility requirements to be appointed a judge of this Court. Section 6 guarantees three Quebec seats on the Court by specifying that, for at least three of the judges, the bar mentioned in s. 5 is the Barreau du Québec and the superior courts mentioned in s. 5 are the Superior Court of Quebec and the Quebec Court of Appeal. Put another way, s. 6 builds on s. 5 by requiring that for three of the seats on this Court, the candidates who meet the criteria of s. 5 must be chosen from three Quebec institutions (the Barreau du Québec, the Quebec Court of Appeal, and the Superior Court of Quebec). Section 6 does not impose any additional requirements.

[120] Although the current French version of s. 5 may be cloudy, the current English version is clear. My colleagues point out, and I agree, that the English version therefore governs the interpretation of s. 5 according to the shared meaning rule of bilingual interpretation. As the words "is or has been" indicate, individuals are eligible for appointment if they are current *or* former members of a provincial bar of at least 10 years standing, or if they are current *or* former judges of a superior court. My colleagues accept this to be the case. However, for the Quebec seats, they say that s. 6 imposes the additional requirement that candidates must be *current* members of the Quebec bar or *current* judges of a superior court.

[121] With respect, I disagree. Sections 5 and 6 are inextricably linked—and that is the key to appreciating that the minimum eligibility requirements of s. 5 apply equally to the Quebec appointees referred to in s. 6. Nowhere is this link more evident than in the wording of ss. 5 and 6 themselves, which I repeat here for ease of reference with key words emphasized:

> 5. [Who may be appointed judges.] Any person may be appointed a judge who is or has been a judge of a superior court of a province or a barrister or advocate of at least ten years standing at the bar of a province.

> 6. [Three judges from Quebec.] At least three of the judges shall be appointed from among the judges of the Court of Appeal or of the Superior Court of the Province of Quebec or from among the advocates of that Province.

> 5. [Conditions de nomination.] Les juges sont choisis parmi les juges, actuels ou anciens, d'une cour supérieure provinciale et parmi les avocats inscrits pendant au moins dix ans au barreau d'une province.

6. [Représentation du Québec.] Au moins trois des juges sont choisis parmi les juges de la Cour d'appel ou de la Cour supérieure de la province de Québec ou parmi les avocats de celle-ci.

[122] First, the words "[a]ny person" in s. 5 are a clear indication that the eligibility requirements set out in that section apply to *all* appointees. Second, the words "the judges" in s. 6 refer explicitly to the description of *the* judges provided in s. 5. Manifestly, one must read s. 5 in order to understand *which* judges s. 6 is referring to and what their eligibility requirements are.

[123] Apart from these textual cues, an absurdity results if s. 6 is *not* read in conjunction with s. 5. Section 6 says nothing about the length of Quebec bar membership required before an individual will be eligible for one of the Quebec seats on this Court. Hence, for the purposes of s. 6, if it is not read in conjunction with s. 5, *any* member of the Quebec bar, including a newly minted member of one day's standing, would be eligible for a Quebec seat on this Court. Faced with this manifest absurdity, the majority acknowledges that the phrase "advocates of that Province" in s. 6 *must* be linked to the 10-year eligibility requirement for members of the bar specified in s. 5.

[124] But that, they say, is where the link ends. It does not extend to the fact that under s. 5, both current and past members of the bar of at least 10 years standing are eligible. With respect, this amounts to cherry-picking. Choosing from s. 5 only those aspects of it that are convenient—and jettisoning those that are not—is a principle of statutory interpretation heretofore unknown.

[125] Given that s. 6 contains an explicit reference to the eligibility criteria set out in s. 5 and that an absurdity would result if s. 6 did not take its meaning from s. 5, the next logical question to ask is: What is it in s. 6 that imposes a currency requirement on Quebec appointees? The answer, in my view, is nothing.

[126] Contrary to the view of the majority, the words "from among" found in s. 6 do not, with respect, impose a currency requirement on Quebec appointees. The words convey no temporal meaning. They take their meaning from the surrounding context and cannot, on their own, support the contention that a person must be a *current* member of the bar or bench to be eligible for a Quebec seat. In short, they do not alter the group to which s. 6 refers—the group described in s. 5.

[127] If Parliament *had* intended to distinguish Quebec appointees from other appointees by requiring that Quebec judges be current judges or current advocates, surely it would have said so in clear terms. It would not have masked this crucial distinction between Quebec candidates and non-Quebec candidates by using words as ambiguous and inconclusive as "from among." The addition of the word "current" before the words "judges" and "advocates" in s. 6 would have been a simple—and obvious—solution.

[128] Not only do the words "from among" not convey any temporal meaning, they support the view that ss. 5 and 6 are inextricably linked. This is apparent when one considers the words of the original 1875 Act (S.C. 1875, c. 11). At the time, ss. 5 and 6 were part of the same sentence—s. 4 of the 1875 Act. That provision set out the eligibility criteria for appointment to the newly created Supreme Court:

4. Her Majesty may appoint, by letters patent, under the Great Seal of Canada, one person, who is, or has been, a Judge of one of the Superior Courts in any of the Provinces forming part of the Dominion of Canada, or who is a Barrister or Advocate of at least ten years' standing at the Bar of any one of the said Provinces, to be Chief Justice of the said Court, and five persons who are, or have been, respectively, Judges of one of the said Superior Courts, or who are Barristers or Advocates of at least ten years' standing at the Bar of one of the said Provinces, to be Puisne

Judges of the said Court, two of whom at least shall be taken *from among* the Judges of the Superior Court or Court of Queen's Bench, or the Barristers or Advocates of the Province of Quebec; and vacancies in any of the said offices shall, from time to time, be filled in like manner. The Chief Justice and Judges of the Supreme Court shall be respectively the Chief Justice and Judges of the Exchequer Court: they shall reside at the City of Ottawa, or within five miles thereof.

4. Sa Majesté pourra nommer, par lettres patentes sous le grand sceau du Canada,—comme juge en chef de cette cour,—une personne étant ou ayant été juge de l'une des cours supérieures dans quelqu'une des provinces formant la Puissance du Canada, ou un avocat ayant pratiqué pendant au moins dix ans au barreau de quelqu'une de ces provinces, et,—comme juges puînés de cette cour,—cinq personnes étant ou ayant été respectivement juges de l'une de ces cours supérieures, ou étant avocats de pas moins de dix ans de pratique au barreau de quelqu'une de ces provinces, dont deux au moins seront pris parmi les juges de la Cour Supérieure ou de la Cour du Banc de la Reine, ou parmi les procureurs ou avocats de la province de Québec; et les vacances survenant dans ces charges seront, au besoin, remplies de la même manière. Le juge en chef et les juges de la Cour Suprême seront respectivement le juge en chef et les juges de la Cour de l'Échiquier. Ils résideront en la cité d'Ottawa, ou dans un rayon de cinq milles de cette cité.

[129] This provision uses the words "from among" in relation to Quebec superior court judges. And yet, the surrounding context, namely, the earlier use of the words "who are, or have been, respectively, Judges," makes it abundantly clear that eligibility for the Quebec seats extended to both current *and* former judges—and nothing has ever changed in that regard. Nowhere in Hansard has it ever been suggested— nor in any subsequent revisions has it ever been proclaimed—that former judges of the Quebec superior courts are not eligible for appointment to this Court. What did change was that in 1886, *former* barristers and advocates of at least 10 years standing became eligible for appointment to this Court, along with current barristers and advocates (R.S.C. 1886, c. 135, s. 4(2)).

[130] And once it is understood that current and former judges of the Quebec superior courts have always been included in the eligibility pool, it is a short step to realize that the 1886 amendments did not reduce the eligible groups for Quebec judges to two—rather, they increased the number of eligible groups in Quebec (and elsewhere in Canada) from three to four. One can scour the Hansard debates of 1875—or at any point in time since then—and find no mention that Parliament intended to narrow the four groups of eligible candidates under s. 5 to only two groups in the case of Quebec. In short, the four group/two group distinction has no foundation in fact or law.

[131] To summarize, the plain wording and legislative history of ss. 5 and 6 support the conclusion that the same eligibility requirements set out in s. 5 apply to Quebec appointees. Furthermore, a consideration of the broader scheme of the *Supreme Court Act*—and specifically, s. 30—does not assist in the interpretation of ss. 5 and 6. I include the following discussion of that section only to explain why it does not favour either interpretation of ss. 5 and 6.

B. Section 30 of the Supreme Court Act

[132] Section 30 of the Act is by and large a historical anomaly. It concerns the appointment of *ad hoc* judges to this Court:

30.(1) [Appointment of *ad hoc* judge.] Where at any time there is not a quorum of the judges available to hold or continue any session of the Court, owing to a vacancy or vacancies, or to the absence through illness or on leave or in the discharge of other duties assigned by statute or order in council, or to the disqualification of a judge or judges, the Chief Justice of Canada, or in the absence of the Chief Justice, the senior puisne judge, may in writing request the attendance at the sittings of the Court, as an *ad hoc* judge, for such period as may be necessary,

(a) of a judge of the Federal Court of Appeal, the Federal Court or the Tax Court of Canada; or

(b) if the judges of the Federal Court of Appeal, the Federal Court or the Tax Court of Canada are absent from Ottawa or for any reason are unable to sit, of a judge of a provincial superior court to be designated in writing by the chief justice, or in the absence of the chief justice, by any acting chief justice or the senior puisne judge of that provincial court on that request being made to that acting chief justice or that senior puisne judge in writing.

(2) [Quebec appeals.] Unless two of the judges available fulfill the requirements of section 6, the *ad hoc* judge for the hearing of an appeal from a judgment rendered in the Province of Quebec shall be a judge of the Court of Appeal or a judge of the Superior Court of that Province designated in accordance with subsection (1).

30.(1) [Nomination d'un juge suppléant.] Dans les cas où, par suite de vacance, d'absence ou d'empêchement attribuable à la maladie, aux congés ou à l'exercice d'autres fonctions assignées par loi ou décret, ou encore de l'inhabilité à siéger d'un ou plusieurs juges, le quorum n'est pas atteint pour tenir ou poursuivre les travaux de la Cour, le juge en chef ou, en son absence, le doyen des juges puînés peut demander par écrit que soit détaché, pour assister aux séances de la Cour à titre de juge suppléant et pendant le temps nécessaire :

(a) soit un juge de la Cour d'appel fédérale, de la Cour fédérale ou de la Cour canadienne de l'impôt;

(b) soit, si les juges de la Cour d'appel fédérale, de la Cour fédérale ou de la Cour canadienne de l'impôt sont absents d'Ottawa ou dans l'incapacité de siéger, un juge d'une cour supérieure provinciale désigné par écrit, sur demande formelle à lui adressée, par le juge en chef ou, en son absence, le juge en chef suppléant ou le doyen des juges puînés de ce tribunal provincial.

(2) [Appels du Québec.] Lorsque au moins deux des juges pouvant siéger ne remplissent pas les conditions fixées à l'article 6, le juge suppléant choisi pour l'audition d'un appel d'un jugement rendu dans la province de Québec doit être un juge de la Cour d'appel ou un juge de la Cour supérieure de cette province, désigné conformément au paragraphe (1).

[133] Because federal court judges from Quebec are not listed in s. 30(2), and thus cannot act as *ad hoc* judges on Quebec appeals when the statutory quorum is not met and two or more Quebec judges on this Court are unavailable, the interveners Rocco Galati and the Constitutional Rights Centre Inc. submit that they should not be eligible for appointment to the *permanent* Quebec seats on this Court. My colleagues rely on this as support of the currency requirement, which has the effect of excluding judges of the federal courts from appointment to the permanent Quebec seats.

[134] For the reasons that follow, I do not accept these submissions. Section 30 does not assist in the interpretation of the eligibility requirements set out in ss. 5 and 6 of the Act. In this regard, I am in essential agreement with the submissions of Dean Sébastien Grammond on behalf of the interveners Robert Décary, Alice Desjardins and Gilles Létourneau.

[135] As indicated, s. 30 is a historical anomaly. In order to explain why Quebec judges on the federal courts are not mentioned in s. 30(2), it is necessary to

trace the legislative history of this provision. The provision was first enacted in 1918 (S.C. 1918, c. 7, s. 1). At the time, there were only six judges on the Court, and the statutory quorum was set at five. As a result, if two or more judges were unavailable for whatever reason, the quorum was not met and cases could not be heard. In 1918, the Court faced a crisis resulting from the absence of several judges. Parliament responded by introducing the concept of *ad hoc* judges into the Act. These *ad hoc* judges would temporarily fulfill the functions of a Supreme Court judge so that the quorum would be met and cases could be heard.

[136] For practical reasons, Parliament wanted an *ad hoc* judge to first be appointed from the Exchequer Court (the predecessor to the federal courts), as that court was also located in Ottawa. At the time, there were only two judges on the Exchequer Court—he "judge" and the "assistant judge" (*An Act to amend the Exchequer Court Act*, S.C. 1912, c. 21, s. 1).

[137] Importantly, the assistant judge at the time was a judge from Quebec. Appointing any judge of the Exchequer Court to sit as an *ad hoc* judge could thus have resulted in the assistant judge—a Quebec judge—being appointed. This created the possibility that, if the loss of quorum on this Court was due to the absence of two common law judges, a majority of civil law judges might hear a common law case.

[138] Parliament sought to avoid this result by specifying that only "the judge" of the Exchequer Court could be appointed an *ad hoc* judge—a term that necessarily excluded the assistant judge. In response to Quebec's displeasure, Parliament accepted that if the loss of quorum was caused by the absence of two or more Quebec judges, and if it was a Quebec case, the *ad hoc* judge would be chosen from that province's superior courts.

[139] In sum, Parliament had in mind two specific goals when it created s. 30— the primary goal of ensuring this Court could continue to exercise its functions, and the secondary goal of ensuring that civil law judges could not form a majority on common law cases. The substance of s. 30 was last considered by Parliament in 1920, when an amendment to the *Exchequer Court Act* allowed any member of the Exchequer Court to be appointed as *ad hoc* judge (S.C. 1920, c. 26, s. 1; R.S.C. 1927, c. 35, s. 5). At that time, it was impossible to include Quebec federal court judges in s. 30(2), as the federal courts did not exist and the Exchequer Court that *did* exist had no reserved Quebec seats.

[140] The majority states that "the repeated failure to include the Quebec appointees to the Federal Court and Federal Court of Appeal among the judges who may serve as *ad hoc* judges of this Court in place of s. 6 judges suggests that the exclusion was deliberate" (para. 67). In fact, the evidence suggests the opposite. Updating the names of the courts mentioned in the provision was done by means of statutory revisions that were organizational in nature and necessarily related only to s. 30(1), as s. 30(2) contained no reference to the Exchequer Court and did not require updating. Given that s. 30 has, for all intents and purposes, become obsolete since the number of judges on this Court was increased to nine, it is hardly surprising that the substance of s. 30 has not been foremost on Parliament's mind.

[141] My colleagues note that s. 30(2) refers to s. 6—"[u]nless two of the judges available fulfil the requirements of section 6"—and from this, they state that the sections are "explicitly linked" (para. 65). That the opening line of s. 30(2) refers to s. 6 does not aid in the interpretation of *what s. 6 means*. Indeed, s. 30 clearly contemplates that only current judges of the named courts can be appointed *ad hoc* judges of this Court for *all* appeals, not just Quebec appeals. This is so notwithstanding that s. 5 allows *both* current and former judges to qualify for the permanent seats. Just as the s. 30(1) requirements for *ad hoc* judges have no effect on the s. 5 eligibility

requirements for *permanent* judges (a point on which all members of this Court agree), s. 30(2) cannot be used in support of a currency requirement in s. 6 for *permanent* judges.

[142] For these reasons, I am of the view that s. 30 is of no assistance in the interpretation of ss. 5 and 6.

[143] No statutory interpretation exercise is complete without considering the legislative objectives underlying the provisions at issue. It is to these objectives that I now turn.

C. The Legislative Objectives

(1) The Purpose of Sections 5 and 6

[144] Section 5, as I have explained, sets out *minimum eligibility criteria* for the pool of potential candidates. The very broad eligibility requirements in s. 5 ensure that the executive branch can choose from among the largest possible pool of candidates who meet the basic eligibility requirements.

[145] The legislative objective underlying s. 6 is different. The objective of s. 6 is, and always has been, to ensure that a specified number of this Court's judges are trained in civil law and represent Quebec. By virtue of the fact that these seats must be filled by candidates appointed from the three Quebec institutions named in s. 6 (the Barreau du Québec, the Quebec Court of Appeal, or the Superior Court of Quebec), the candidates will necessarily have received formal training in the civil law. The combination of this training and affiliation with one of the named Quebec institutions serves to protect Quebec's civil law tradition and inspire Quebec's confidence in this Court. To that extent, I agree with the majority. Respectfully, however, I do not agree that s. 6 was intended to ensure that "Quebec's ... social values are represented on the Court" (para. 18). Parliament made a deliberate choice to include only objective criteria in ss. 5 and 6. Importing social values—140 years later—is unsupported by the text and history of the Act.

[146] As noted, the objective of s. 6 is to protect Quebec's civil law tradition and inspire Quebec's confidence in this Court. Section 6 recognizes the uniqueness of Quebec and its important place in our country, and was key to gaining Quebec's support for the formation of the Supreme Court of Canada. Crucially, however, there is no evidence that this support would have been withheld if the issue of both current and past advocates of the Quebec bar qualifying for appointment, as well as current and past judges of the Quebec superior courts, had been debated at the time. Indeed, as I interpret s. 4 of the 1875 Act, both current *and former* judges *have always been* eligible. To the extent there may have been a question mark about former members of the bar, the 1886 statutory revision made it clear that they too were eligible.

[147] To suggest that Quebec wanted to render ineligible former advocates of at least 10 years standing at the Quebec bar is to rewrite history. There is nothing in the historical debates that suggests any such thing. Indeed, it defies logic and common sense to think that Quebec would have had some reason to oppose the appointment to this Court of Court of Québec judges who had been members of the Quebec bar for at least 10 years on the day of their appointment to that court. Court of Québec judges apply the civil law *on a daily basis*. Why such persons, otherwise eligible for appointment to this Court by virtue of their 10 years standing at the bar, would suddenly become unacceptable to the people of Quebec on the day of their elevation to the bench escapes me. Likewise, though the federal courts did not exist at the time, to suggest that Quebec would have resisted the appointment to this Court of a federal court judge occupying a seat on that court reserved for Quebec

is, in my view, equally untenable. These judges have been trained in the civil law and continue to hear federal law cases involving Quebec that require a working knowledge of the civil law.

[148] My colleagues maintain it is Parliament's choice to "draw lines" that may be "under-inclusive when measured against the [objectives of s 6]" and thus "might not achieve perfection" (paras. 57-58). Parliament, they say, chose certain objective criteria and it is not for this Court to question the wisdom of those criteria. I agree. But, when interpreting a statute to determine what the relevant criteria *are*—i.e. what Parliament intended them to be—absurd results are to be avoided. (See, for example, *Rizzo & Rizzo Shoes Ltd. (Re)*, [1998] 1 S.C.R. 27, at para. 27, and *Morgentaler v. The Queen*, [1976] 1 S.C.R. 616, at p. 676.) In my respectful view, that principle should be applied in interpreting s. 6—and when it is, it necessarily leads to a rejection of the currency requirement.

(2) The Currency Requirement Does Not Further the Legislative Objective of Section 6

[149] In addition to rendering ineligible candidates who might otherwise be worthy appointments to this Court, the currency requirement does nothing to promote the confidence of Quebec in this Court. In Quebec, there are approximately 16,000 *current* members of the Quebec bar with at least 10 years standing. Surely it cannot be suggested that the appointment of any one of these 16,000 advocates would promote the confidence of Quebec in this Court.

[150] This becomes all the more apparent when one realizes that a person can maintain his or her Quebec bar membership by simply paying annual fees and completing a set number of hours of continuing legal education—currently, 30 hours over a two-year period. Notably, there is *no* requirement that this continuing legal education have anything to do with the civil law, nor does it actually have to be completed *in* Quebec. Indeed, a person does not have to live in Quebec, *or actually practice law in Quebec*, in order to maintain his or her bar membership. In sum, a person could have only the most tenuous link to the practice of civil law in Quebec, and yet be a current member of that bar of 10 years standing.

[151] This is the reality—and it illustrates how implausible it is that anyone would view *current* membership at the Quebec bar as the *sine qua non* that assures Quebec's confidence in appointments to this Court. Likewise, it is equally implausible that being a *past* member of the Quebec bar could singlehandedly undermine this confidence.

[152] My colleagues have chosen not to address the scope of the currency requirement under s. 6, i.e. whether one day's renewed membership at the Quebec bar is sufficient to qualify as an advocate or whether something more is needed—six months, two years, five years, or perhaps even a continuous 10-year period immediately preceding the appointment.

[153] In my view, *currency means exactly that*. A former Quebec superior court judge or advocate of 10 years standing at the Quebec bar could rejoin that bar for a day and thereby regain his or her eligibility for appointment to this Court. In my view, this exposes the hollowness of the currency requirement. Surely nothing is accomplished by what is essentially an administrative act. Any interpretation of s. 6 that requires a *former* advocate of at least 10 years standing at the Quebec bar, or a *former* judge of the Quebec Court of Appeal or Superior Court, to rejoin the Quebec bar for a day in order to be eligible for appointment to this Court makes no practical sense. Respectfully, I find it difficult to believe that the people of Quebec would somehow have more confidence in this candidate on Friday than they had on Thursday.

1. According to Moldaver J, why was the currency requirement not supported by the text of s 6, its context, or its legislative history?

2. How were ss 5 and 6 "inextricably linked," and what did that entail for the eligibility criteria in s 5?

3. What was the object of s 6?

Reference re Supreme Court Act, ss 5 and 6
2014 SCC 21, [2014] 1 SCR 433

McLACHLIN CJ and LEBEL, ABELLA, CROMWELL, KARAKATSANIS, and WAGNER JJ:

• • •

IV. Question 1

A. The Issue

• • •

[17] In our view, s. 6 narrows the pool from the four groups of people who are eligible under s. 5 to two groups who are eligible under s. 6. By specifying that three judges shall be selected from among the members of a specific list of institutions, s. 6 requires that persons appointed to the three Quebec seats must, in addition to meeting the general requirements of s. 5, be current members of these institutions.

[18] We come to this conclusion for four main reasons. First, the plain meaning of s. 6 has remained consistent since the original version of that provision was enacted in 1875, and it has always excluded former advocates. Second, this interpretation gives effect to important differences in the wording of ss. 5 and 6. Third, this interpretation of s. 6 advances its dual purpose of ensuring that the Court has civil law expertise and that Quebec's legal traditions and social values are represented on the Court *and* that Quebec's confidence in the Court be maintained. Finally, this interpretation is consistent with the broader scheme of the *Supreme Court Act* for the appointment of *ad hoc* judges.

B. General Principles of Interpretation

[19] The *Supreme Court Act* was enacted in 1875 as an ordinary statute under the authority of s. 101 of the *Constitution Act, 1867* (S.C. 1875, c. 11). However, as we explain below, Parliament's authority to amend the Act is now limited by the Constitution. Sections 5 and 6 of the *Supreme Court Act* reflect an essential feature of the Supreme Court of Canada—its composition—which is constitutionally protected under Part V of the *Constitution Act, 1982*. As such, they must be interpreted in a broad and purposive manner and understood in their proper linguistic, philosophic and historical context: *Hunter v. Southam Inc.*, [1984] 2 S.C.R. 145, at pp. 155-56; *Edwards v. Attorney-General for Canada*, [1930] A.C. 124 (P.C.), at p. 136; *R. v. Big M Drug Mart Ltd.*, [1985] 1 S.C.R. 295, at p. 344.

C. Legislative History of Sections 5 and 6

[20] The eligibility requirements for appointments from Quebec are the result of the historic bargain that gave birth to the Court in 1875. Sections 5 and 6 in the current Act descend from the original eligibility provision found in s. 4 of the 1875 Act. ...

[21] The 1875 Act set out in a single provision the appointment process, the number of judges (one chief justice and five puisne judges), the general eligibility requirements, and the specification that two judges shall come from the bench or bar of Quebec: s. 4. The portion of s. 4 that evolved into ss. 4, 5 and 6 of the current Act stated:

> 4. [Qualification of Chief Justice and Judges, respectively.] Her Majesty may appoint, by letters patent, under the Great Seal of Canada, one person, who is, or has been, a Judge of one of the Superior Courts in any of the Provinces forming part of the Dominion of Canada, or who is a Barrister or Advocate of at least ten years' standing at the Bar of any one of the said Provinces, to be Chief Justice of the said Court, and five persons who are, or have been, respectively, Judges of one of the said Superior Courts, or who are Barristers or Advocates of at least ten years' standing at the Bar of one of the said Provinces, to be Puisne Judges of the said Court, two of whom at least shall be taken from among the Judges of the Superior Court or Court of Queen's Bench, or the Barristers or Advocates of the Province of Quebec;
>
> 4. [Qualités exigées du juge en chef et des juges.] Sa Majesté pourra nommer, par lettres patentes sous le grand sceau du Canada,—comme juge en chef de cette cour,—une personne étant ou ayant été juge de l'une des cours supérieures dans quelqu'une des provinces formant la Puissance du Canada, ou un avocat ayant pratiqué pendant au moins dix ans au barreau de quelqu'une de ces provinces, et,—comme juges puînés de cette cour,—cinq personnes étant ou ayant été respectivement juges de l'une de ces cours supérieures, ou étant avocats de pas moins de dix ans de pratique au barreau de quelqu'une de ces provinces, dont deux au moins seront pris parmi les juges de la Cour Supérieure ou de la Cour du Banc de la Reine, ou parmi les procureurs ou avocats de la province de Québec;

This provision contemplated the appointment of only current lawyers to the Court, both for Quebec and for the rest of the country.

[22] The only substantive change to the eligibility requirements took place in 1886 as part of statutory revisions (R.S.C. 1886, c. 135). Section 4 was divided into several subsections, including ss. 4(2) and 4(3) setting out the general requirements for appointment and, more specifically, the requirements for Quebec appointments. Notably, the language in s. 4(2) (now s. 5) was broadened to encompass any person who "is or has been" ("*sera ou aura été*") a barrister or advocate. Sections 4(2) and 4(3) read:

> 2. [Who may be appointed judge.] Any person may be appointed a judge of the court who is or has been a judge of a superior court of any of the Provinces of Canada, or a barrister or advocate of at least ten years' standing at the bar of any of the said Provinces:
>
> 3. [Judges from bar of Quebec.] Two at least of the judges of the court shall be appointed from among the judges of the Court of Queen's Bench, or of the Superior Court, or the barristers or advocates of the Province of Quebec:
>
> 2. [Qui pourra être nommé juge.] Pourra être nommé juge de la cour quiconque sera ou aura été juge d'une cour supérieure dans quelqu'une des provinces du Canada, ou un avocat ayant pratiqué pendant au moins dix ans au barreau de quelqu'une de ces provinces.
>
> 3. [Juges tirés du barreau de Québec.] Au moins deux des juges de la cour seront pris parmi les juges de la cour du Banc de la Reine ou de la cour Supérieure, ou parmi les avocats de la province de Québec.

[23] We have underlined key aspects of the wording in each official language of the revisions of 1886, which we will discuss below. The 1886 Act contemplated the appointment of current or former lawyers to the Court generally, but it did not change the more restrictive language for the Quebec appointments. The revisions of 1886 stipulated that where the effect of the revised statutes is different from that of the repealed laws, "the provisions contained in [the Revised Statutes] shall prevail": *An Act respecting the Revised Statutes of Canada*, R.S.C. 1886, c. 4, s. 8.

[24] In 1906, ss. 4(2) and 4(3) became ss. 5 and 6, but no substantive changes were made: R.S.C. 1906, c. 139.

[25] In 1927, one judge was added for a total of seven judges on the Court, but the number of Quebec judges remained two: S.C. 1926-27, c. 38, s. 1; R.S.C. 1927, c. 35, ss. 4 and 6. The Court was enlarged again in 1949, when the number of judges of the Court increased to nine and the ratio of Quebec judges was preserved by increasing their number to three: *An Act to amend the Supreme Court Act*, S.C. 1949 (2nd Sess.), c. 37, s. 1.

[26] The current text of ss. 5 and 6 dates to the statutory revisions of 1985. These revisions changed the French wording of ss. 5 and 6, creating an ambiguity that will be discussed below, but did not change the English wording. Parliament did not intend any substantive changes at this time: *Legislation Revision and Consolidation Act*, R.S.C. 1985, c. S-20, s. 6. The 1985 text provides:

> 5. [Who may be appointed judges.] Any person may be appointed a judge who is or has been a judge of a superior court of a province or a barrister or advocate of at least ten years standing at the bar of a province.
>
> 6. [Three judges from Quebec.] At least three of the judges shall be appointed from among the judges of the Court of Appeal or of the Superior Court of the Province of Quebec or from among the advocates of that Province.
>
> 5. [Conditions de nomination.] Les juges sont choisis parmi les juges, actuels ou anciens, d'une cour supérieure provinciale et parmi les avocats inscrits pendant au moins dix ans au barreau d'une province.
>
> 6. [Représentation du Québec.] Au moins trois des juges sont choisis parmi les juges de la Cour d'appel ou de la Cour supérieure de la province de Québec ou parmi les avocats de celle-ci.

[27] In summary, other than the increase from two Quebec judges to three in s. 6, there have been no substantive amendments to ss. 5 and 6 between the 1886 revisions, which explicitly took precedence over the previous version, and the version currently in force.

D. Section 5

[28] To repeat, s. 5 of the Act sets out the eligibility requirements that apply generally to appointments to the Court. The section creates four groups of people who are eligible for appointment: (1) current judges of a superior court of a province, including courts of appeal; (2) former judges of such a court; (3) current barristers or advocates of at least 10 years standing at the bar of a province; and (4) former barristers or advocates of at least 10 years standing. Thus, the section authorizes the appointment to the Court of current *or* former barristers *or* advocates of at least 10 years standing at the bar of a province.

[29] The English version of s. 5 is unambiguous. The specification "is or has been" clearly applies to both judges of a superior court of a province *and* barristers or advocates of at least 10 years standing at the bar of a province. This is confirmed by the provision's legislative history. Under the 1875 Act, appointments were

limited to persons "who are, or have been, respectively, Judges of one of the said Superior Courts, or who are Barristers or Advocates": s. 4. The 1875 Act excluded former advocates from appointment. It permitted the appointment of current or former judges and current, but not former, advocates. As part of statutory revisions of 1886, however, the specification "is or has been" was extended to both judges and advocates, thereby including former advocates as a fourth category of eligible candidates. As we have observed, the changes made under the 1886 statutory revision were intended to have substantive effect.

[30] To the extent that there are ambiguities in the French version of s. 5, they were created by the 1985 revision. Prior to 1985, the wording of the French text ("*est ou a été*") closely mirrored that of the English text ("is or has been"). Between 1886 and 1985, both versions plainly encompassed current as well as former advocates. The English version continues to do so. The French version now requires the selection of judges "*parmi les juges, actuels ou anciens*" or "*parmi les avocats inscrits pendant au moins dix ans.*" It might be suggested that the current wording excludes advocates who are not current members of the bar, because the specification "*actuels ou anciens*" is not applied to them. We reject this argument.

[31] The 1985 change to the French version of s. 5 did not change its meaning. This amendment was part of statutory revisions which were not intended to effect substantive change: s. 6 of the *Legislation Revision and Consolidation Act*; *Sarvanis v. Canada*, 2002 SCC 28, [2002] 1 S.C.R. 921, at para. 13. In short, the meaning of the text of the English and French versions remains the same as before the 1985 revision.

[32] We reach the same conclusion by applying the shared meaning rule of bilingual interpretation, which requires that where the words of one version may raise an ambiguity, one should look to the other official language version to determine whether its meaning is plain and unequivocal: Ruth Sullivan, *Sullivan on the Construction of Statutes* (5th ed. 2008), at pp. 99-116; Pierre-André Côté, in collaboration with Stéphane Beaulac and Mathieu Devinat, *The Interpretation of Legislation in Canada* (4th ed. 2011), at pp. 347-49; *R. v. Daoust*, 2004 SCC 6, [2004] 1 S.C.R. 217, at para. 28. The English version of the text is unambiguous in its inclusion of former advocates for appointment, while the French version is reasonably capable of two interpretations: one which excludes former advocates from appointment, and one which includes them. The meaning common to both versions is only found in the unambiguous English version, which is therefore the meaning we should adopt.

[33] Finally, the inclusion of former advocates of at least 10 years standing at the bar is consistent with the purpose of s. 5, which is to ensure that appointees to the Court have adequate legal experience.

[34] In the result, judges of the Federal Court or Federal Court of Appeal will generally qualify for appointment under s. 5 on the basis that they were formerly barristers or advocates of at least 10 years standing.

E. Section 6

[35] Section 6 specifies that at least three of the nine judges appointed to the Court "shall be appointed from among the judges of the Court of Appeal or of the Superior Court of the Province of Quebec or from among the advocates of that Province" ("*sont choisis parmi les juges de la Cour d'appel ou de la Cour supérieure de la province de Québec ou parmi les avocats de celle-ci*").

[36] The Attorney General of Canada argues that ss. 5 and 6 must be read together as complementary provisions, so that the requirement of at least 10 years standing at the bar applies to appointments from Quebec. Since s. 6 makes no reference to

how many years an appointee must have been at the bar, reading it without s. 5 would lead to the absurd result that a highly inexperienced lawyer would be eligible for appointment to the Court, the Attorney General says.

[37] We agree that ss. 5 and 6 must be read together. We also agree that the requirement of at least 10 years standing at the bar applies to appointments from Quebec. We disagree, however, with the Attorney General's ultimate conclusion that reading these provisions together in a complementary way permits the appointment of *former* advocates of at least 10 years standing to the Quebec seats on the Court. Section 6 does not displace the general requirements under s. 5 that apply to all appointments to the Supreme Court. Rather, it makes additional specifications in respect of the three judges from Quebec. One of these is that they must currently be a member of the Quebec bar.

[38] We reach this conclusion based on the plain meaning and purpose of s. 6, and the surrounding statutory context.

(1) The Plain Meaning of Section 6

[39] The language of s. 5 is general ("[a]ny person may be appointed a judge"), whereas the language of s. 6 is restrictive ("[a]t least three of the judges shall be appointed from among"). As such, s. 6 limits the pool of candidates. It is undisputed that s. 6 does so geographically by requiring that the appointments be made from one of the listed institutions in Quebec. The issue is whether s. 6 also imposes a requirement of current membership in one of the listed institutions.

[40] The Attorney General of Canada argues that the plain meaning of s. 6 does not require current membership in the bar of Quebec. He submits that the phrase "from among" ("*parmi*" in French) does not contain a temporal element and, as a result, s. 6 imports s. 5's temporal specifications ("is or has been").

[41] We do not agree. There is an important change in language between s. 5 and s. 6. Section 5 refers to both present and former membership in the listed institutions by using the words "is or has been" in the English version and "*actuels ou anciens*" in the French version. By contrast, s. 6 refers only to the pool of individuals who are presently members of the bar ("shall be appointed from among" and "*sont choisis parmi*"). The significance of this change is made clear by the plain meaning of the words used: the words "from among the judges" and "*parmi les juges*" do not mean "from among the former judges" and "*parmi les anciens juges*," and the words "from among the advocates" and "*parmi les avocats*" do not mean "from among the former advocates" and "*parmi les anciens avocats*."

[42] It is a principle of interpretation that the mention of one or more things of a particular class excludes, by implication, all other members of the class: Sullivan, at pp. 243-44. By enumerating the particular institutions in Quebec from which appointments shall be made, s. 6 excludes all other institutions. Similarly, by specifying that three judges shall be appointed "from among" the judges and advocates (i.e. members) of the identified institutions, s. 6 impliedly excludes former members of those institutions and imposes a requirement of current membership.

[43] The fact that ss. 5 and 6 originated in a single provision—s. 4 of the 1875 Act—does not undermine our interpretation, because the same textual observations could be made with respect to the original provision. Then, as now, the general requirements for appointment were phrased generally whereas the specification for Quebec judges was expressed more restrictively: "... two of whom at least shall be taken from among the Judges of the Superior Court or Court of Queen's Bench, or the Barristers or Advocates of the Province of Quebec ... ."

[44] Indeed, s. 4 of the 1875 Act adds weight to our conclusion that former advocates are excluded from appointment as Quebec judges. From 1875 until the revisions of 1886, eligibility extended to persons "who are, or have been, respectively, Judges ... or who are Barristers or Advocates." The Quebec requirement was first enacted alongside this general language, which clearly excluded former advocates from appointment. When the general requirements were broadened in 1886, rendering former advocates eligible, the wording of the Quebec requirement did not substantively change. With the exception of the increase from two judges to three in 1949, the wording of the Quebec requirement has remained substantively unchanged since 1875. Absent any express intention to amend the Quebec requirement since its enactment in 1875, we find that s. 6 retains its original meaning and excludes the appointment of former Quebec advocates to the designated Quebec seats. The requirement of current membership in the Quebec bar has been in place—unambiguous and unchanged—since 1875.

[45] In summary, on a plain reading, s. 5 creates four groups of people eligible for appointment: current and former judges of a superior court and current and former barristers or advocates of at least 10 years standing at the bar. But s. 6 imposes a requirement that persons appointed to the three Quebec seats must, in addition to meeting the general requirements of s. 5, be current members of the listed Quebec institutions. Thus, s. 6 narrows eligibility to only two groups for Quebec appointments: current judges of the Court of Appeal or Superior Court of Quebec and current advocates of at least 10 years standing at the bar of Quebec.

(2) The Purpose of Section 6

[46] ... The Attorney General of Canada submits that the purpose of s. 6 is simply to ensure that three members of this Court are trained and experienced in Quebec civil law and that this purpose is satisfied by appointing either current or former Quebec advocates, both of whom would have civil law training and experience.

[47] While the Attorney General of Canada's submissions capture an important purpose of the provision, a review of the legislative history reveals an additional and broader purpose.

[48] Section 6 reflects the historical compromise that led to the creation of the Supreme Court. Just as the protection of minority language, religion and education rights were central considerations in the negotiations leading up to Confederation (*Reference re Secession of Quebec*, [1998] 2 S.C.R. 217 ("*Secession Reference*"), at paras. 79-82), the protection of Quebec through a minimum number of Quebec judges was central to the creation of this Court. A purposive interpretation of s. 6 must be informed by and not undermine that compromise.

[49] The purpose of s. 6 is to ensure not only civil law training and experience on the Court, but also to ensure that Quebec's distinct legal traditions and social values are represented on the Court, thereby enhancing the confidence of the people of Quebec in the Supreme Court as the final arbiter of their rights. Put differently, s. 6 protects both the *functioning* and the *legitimacy* of the Supreme Court as a general court of appeal for Canada. This broader purpose was succinctly described by Professor Russell in terms that are well supported by the historical record:

> ... the antipathy to having the Civil Code of Lower Canada interpreted by judges from an alien legal tradition was not based merely on a concern for legal purity or accuracy. It stemmed more often from the more fundamental premise that Quebec's civil-law system was an essential ingredient of its distinctive culture and therefore it required, as a matter of *right*, judicial custodians imbued with the methods of jurisprudence and social values integral to that culture. [Emphasis in original.]

(Peter H. Russell, *The Supreme Court of Canada as a Bilingual and Bicultural Institution* (1969), at p. 8)

[50] At the time of Confederation, Quebec was reluctant to accede to the creation of a Supreme Court because of its concern that the Court would be incapable of adequately dealing with questions of the Quebec civil law (Ian Bushnell, *The Captive Court: A Study of the Supreme Court of Canada* (1992), at pp. 4-5; Russell, at pp. 8-9). Various Members of Parliament for Quebec expressed concerns about a "Supreme Tribunal of Appeal" that would be

> composed of Judges, the great majority of whom would be unfamiliar with the civil laws of Quebec, which tribunal would be called upon to revise and would have the power to reverse the decisions of all their Quebec Courts ... .

(Debates of the House of Commons, 2nd Sess., 3rd Parl. ("*1875 Debates*"), March 16, 1875, at p. 739, Henri-Thomas Taschereau, M.P. for Montmagny, Quebec)

[51] The bill creating the Supreme Court was passed only after amendments were made responding specifically to Quebec's concerns. Most significantly, the amended bill that became the *Supreme Court Act* provided that two of the six judges "shall be taken from among the Judges of the Superior Court or Court of Queen's Bench, or the Barristers or Advocates of the Province of Quebec": s. 4 of the 1875 Act.

[52] In debating the proposed establishment of the Supreme Court in 1875, members of Parliament on both sides of the House of Commons were conscious of the particular situation of Quebec and the need to ensure civil law expertise on the Court. At second reading, Mr. Taschereau of the governing Liberal Party described Quebec's special interest in the bill:

> This interest arises out of the civil appellate jurisdiction proposed to be given to the Supreme Court, and of the peculiar position of that Province with regard to her institutions and her laws compared with those of the other Provinces. Situated as she is, no Province in the Dominion is so greatly interested as our own in the passage of the Act now under discussion, and which before many days are over, will form a most important chapter in the statute books of the Dominion.

(1875 Debates, March 16, 1875, at p. 738)

[53] Toussaint Antoine Rodolphe Laflamme introduced the provision for a minimum number of Quebec judges. He described the requirement as a matter of right for Quebec: "He understood if this Supreme Court was to regulate and definitely settle all the questions which involved the interests of Lower Canada, that Province was entitled to two of the six Judges" (*1875 Debates*, March 27, 1875, at p. 938). Mr. Laflamme reasoned that with two judges (one third) on the Supreme Court, Quebec "would have more and better safeguards than under the present system," namely appeals to the Privy Council (*ibid.*). Télesphore Fournier, Minister of Justice and principal spokesman for the bill, argued that the two judges would contribute to the civil law knowledge of the bench as a whole: " ... there will be among the Judges on the bench, men perfectly versed in the knowledge of the laws of that section of the Confederation, will be able to give the benefits of their lights to the other Judges sitting with them" (*1875 Debates*, March 16, 1875, at p. 754). David Mills, a supporter of the bill, defended the Quebec minimum against critics who attacked it as "sectionalist." In his view, in light of the "entirely different system of jurisprudence" in Quebec, "it was only reasonable that she should have *security* that a portion of the Court would understand the system of law which it would be called upon to administer" (*1875 Debates*, March 30, 1875, at p. 972 (emphasis added)).

[54] Quebec's confidence in the Court was dependent on the requirement of two (one third) Quebec judges. Jacques-Olivier Bureau, a Senator from Quebec, saw fit to "trust the rights of his compatriots ... to this Supreme Court, as he considered their rights would be quite safe in a court of which two of the judges would have to be taken from the Bench of that Province" (*Debates of the Senate*, 2nd Sess., 3rd Parl., April 5, 1875, at p. 713). The comments of Joseph-Aldéric Ouimet, Liberal-Conservative Member for Laval, also underline that it was a matter of confidence in the Court:

> In Quebec an advocate must have ten years' practice before he can be a Judge. The Judges from the other Provinces might have the finest intelligence and the best talent possible and yet not give such satisfaction to the people of Quebec as their own judiciary.

(*1875 Debates*, March 27, 1875, at p. 940)

[55] Government and opposition members alike saw the two seats (one third) for Quebec judges as a means of ensuring not only the functioning, but also the legitimacy of the Supreme Court as a federal and bijural institution.

[56] Viewed in this light, the purpose of s. 6 is clearly different from the purpose of s. 5. Section 5 establishes a broad pool of eligible candidates; s. 6 is more restrictive. Its exclusion of candidates otherwise eligible under s. 5 was intended by Parliament as a means of attaining the twofold purpose of (i) ensuring civil law expertise and the representation of Quebec's legal traditions and social values on the Court, and (ii) enhancing the confidence of Quebec in the Court. Requiring the appointment of current members of civil law institutions was intended to ensure not only that those judges were qualified to represent Quebec on the Court, but that they were perceived by Quebecers as being so qualified.

[57] It might be argued that excluding former advocates of at least 10 years standing at the Quebec bar does not perfectly advance this twofold purpose because it might exclude from appointment candidates who have civil law expertise and who would in fact bring Quebec's legal traditions and social values to the Court. In other words, it could be argued that our reading of s. 6 is under-inclusive when measured against the provision's objectives.

[58] This argument is not convincing. Parliament could have adopted different criteria to achieve the twofold objectives of s. 6—for instance by requiring a qualitative assessment of a candidate's expertise in Quebec's civil law and legal traditions—but instead it chose to advance the provision's objectives by specifying objective criteria for appointment to one of the Quebec seats on the Court. In the final analysis, lawmakers must draw lines. The criteria chosen by Parliament might not achieve perfection, but they do serve to advance the provision's purpose: see Michael Plaxton and Carissima Mathen, "Purposive Interpretation, Quebec, and the *Supreme Court Act*" (2013), 22 *Const. Forum* 15, at pp. 20-22.

[59] We earlier concluded that a textual interpretation of s. 6 excludes former advocates from appointment to the Court. We come to the same conclusion on purposive grounds. The underlying purpose of the general eligibility provision, s. 5, is to articulate minimum general requirements for the appointment of all Supreme Court judges. In contrast, the underlying purpose of s. 6 is to enshrine the historical compromise that led to the creation of the Court by narrowing the eligibility for the Quebec seats. Its function is to limit the Governor in Council's otherwise broad discretion to appoint judges, in order to ensure expertise in civil law and that Quebec's legal traditions and social values are reflected in the judges on the Supreme Court, and to enhance the confidence of the people of Quebec in the Court.

[60] In reaching this conclusion, we do not overlook or in any way minimize the civil law expertise of judges of the Federal Court and Federal Court of Appeal. For instance, s. 5.4 of the *Federal Courts Act*, R.S.C. 1985, c. F-7, in many ways reflects s. 6 of the *Supreme Court Act* by requiring that a minimum number of judges on each court be drawn from Quebec institutions. The role of Quebec judges on the federal courts is a vital one. Nevertheless, s. 6 makes clear that judges of the federal courts are not, by virtue of being judges of those courts, eligible for appointment to the Quebec seats on this Court. The question is not whether civilist members of the federal courts would make excellent judges of the Supreme Court of Canada, but whether they are eligible for appointment under s. 6 on the basis of being former rather than current advocates of the Province of Quebec. We conclude that they are not.

[61] Some of the submissions before us relied heavily on the context provided by constitutional negotiations following the patriation of the Constitution in 1982, particularly on Quebec's agreement to proposed constitutional reforms that would have explicitly rendered Federal Court and Federal Court of Appeal judges eligible for appointment to one of the Quebec seats on the Court. The Charlottetown Accord went furthest by stipulating that it was entrenching the current *Supreme Court Act* requirement of "nine members, of whom three must have been admitted to the bar of Quebec (civil law bar)" (*Consensus Report on the Constitution: Charlottetown* (1992), at p. 8). This showed, it was argued, that these eligibility requirements were acceptable to Quebec.

[62] We do not find this argument compelling. The Meech Lake and Charlottetown negotiations over the eligibility requirements for the Court took place in the context of wider negotiations over federal–provincial issues, including greater provincial involvement in Supreme Court appointments. In the case of Quebec, the proposed changes would have diminished the significance of s. 6 as the sole safeguard of Quebec's interests on the Supreme Court by requiring the Governor General in Council to make an appointment from a list of names submitted by Quebec. In this context, we should be wary of drawing any inference that there was a consensus interpretation of s. 6 different from the one that we adopt.

(3) Surrounding Statutory Context

[63] The broader scheme of the *Supreme Court Act* reinforces the conclusion reached through a textual and purposive analysis. In addition to addressing who is eligible to be appointed a judge of the Supreme Court of Canada, the Act addresses which judges of other courts are eligible to sit as *ad hoc* judges of the Court. Judges of the federal courts and the Tax Court of Canada, while eligible to sit as *ad hoc* judges generally, are not eligible to sit in Quebec appeals when the quorum of the Court does not include at least two judges appointed under s. 6. In other words, the provisions governing eligibility to sit as an *ad hoc* judge of the Court reflect the same distinction between general eligibility and eligibility for one of the Quebec seats. The point is not that these judges are excluded under s. 6 simply because they are excluded under s. 30(2) of the Act. Rather, the point is that the exclusion under s. 30(2) is part of the overall context that must be taken into account in interpreting ss. 5 and 6 of the Act.

[64] In principle, a quorum of the Court consists of five judges: ss. 25 and 29 of the Act. When there is no quorum, s. 30(1) stipulates that an *ad hoc* judge may be drawn from (a) the Federal Court of Appeal, the Federal Court, or the Tax Court of Canada, or, in their absence, from (b) provincial superior courts. However, under s. 30(2), unless two of the judges available to constitute a quorum fulfil the

requirements for appointment under s. 6—that is, were appointed from the bench or bar of Quebec—an *ad hoc* judge for a Quebec appeal must be drawn from the Court of Appeal or Superior Court of Quebec.

[65] Thus, while judges of the Federal Court, the Federal Court of Appeal and the Tax Court of Canada meet the general eligibility requirements for appointment as an *ad hoc* judge of this Court under s. 30(1), they do not meet the more restrictive eligibility requirements for an *ad hoc* judge replacing a Quebec judge under s. 30(2). Section 30(2) expressly refers to judges who "fulfill the requirements of section 6" and so the two sections are explicitly linked. Moreover, ss. 5 and 6 and ss. 30(1) and 30(2) reflect the same distinction between the general eligibility requirements (s. 5 and s. 30(1)) and the more restrictive eligibility requirements for the Quebec seats on the Court (s. 6 and s. 30(2)).

[66] This exclusion of Federal Court and Federal Court of Appeal judges from appointment as *ad hoc* judges for Quebec lends support to the conclusion that those judges are similarly excluded from appointment to the Court under s. 6.

[67] It was argued that we should give no weight to the wording of s. 30 because it is an obsolete provision that has not been used since the second decade of the 20th century. We do not agree. The statutory history suggests that the exclusion of judges of the federal courts as *ad hoc* judges for Quebec cases was not a mere oversight. In the 1970s after the establishment of the Federal Court, s. 30(1) of the *Supreme Court Act* was revised to refer to the Federal Court (*Federal Court Act*, R.S.C. 1970, c. 10 (2nd Supp.), s. 64). Despite the fact that the very purpose of the revision was to incorporate references to the Federal Court into the Act, as was done in s. 30(1), Parliament did not amend the immediately adjacent provision, s. 30(2). There was similarly no amendment to s. 30(2) when, in 2002, s. 30(1) was amended to refer to the newly separate Federal Court of Appeal and the Tax Court of Canada (S.C. 2002, c. 8, s. 175). While certainly not conclusive, the repeated failure to include the Quebec appointees to the Federal Court and Federal Court of Appeal among the judges who may serve as *ad hoc* judges of this Court in place of s. 6 judges suggests that the exclusion was deliberate. This in turn is consistent with members of those same courts not being eligible for appointment under s. 6.

[68] When s. 30 was first enacted in 1918 (S.C. 1918, c. 7, s. 1), the assistant judge of the Exchequer Court was a judge from Quebec. Appointing him as an *ad hoc* judge to hear an appeal from one of the common law provinces would have meant that a majority of the quorum hearing the appeal would be jurists trained in the civil law. Parliament deemed this undesirable. This legislative history explains why the assistant judge of the Exchequer Court was excluded from serving as an *ad hoc* judge on appeals from common law provinces. But it does not explain why that judge was also excluded from serving as an *ad hoc* judge on appeals from Quebec even though that would have maintained Quebec's representation on appeals from that province. Parliament has, since it first provided for *ad hoc* judges, consistently precluded judges of the federal courts or their predecessor, the Exchequer Court, from sitting on Quebec appeals as *ad hoc* judges of the Supreme Court. If this is an anomaly, it is one that Parliament deliberately created and has consistently maintained.

(4) Conclusion

[69] We therefore conclude that s. 5 establishes general eligibility requirements for a broad pool of persons eligible for appointment to the Supreme Court of Canada. In respect of the three Quebec seats, s. 6 leads to a more restrictive interpretation of the eligibility requirements in order to give effect to the historical compromise aimed at protecting Quebec's legal traditions and social values.

[70] We conclude that a person who was, at any time, an advocate of at least 10 years standing at the Barreau du Québec, may be appointed to the Supreme Court pursuant to s. 5 of the *Supreme Court Act*, but not s. 6. The three appointments under s. 6 require, in addition to the criteria set out in s. 5, current membership of the Barreau du Québec or of the Court of Appeal or Superior Court of Quebec. Therefore, a judge of the Federal Court or Federal Court of Appeal is ineligible for appointment under s. 6 of the Act.

[71] We note in passing that the reference questions do not ask whether a judge of the Federal Court or Federal Court of Appeal who was a former advocate of at least 10 years standing at the Quebec bar could rejoin the Quebec bar for a day in order to be eligible for appointment to this Court under s. 6. We therefore do not decide this issue.

In *Rizzo*, the Court failed to examine the French version of the legislation. In recent years, the Supreme Court has served notice that it expects counsel to consider both language versions of bilingual legislation when arguing interpretation issues before it. The Court now requires parties to include in its factum both the English and the French versions of any legislation that is at issue in the case.

Under the Canadian Constitution, legislation must be enacted in both French and English by Parliament and by the legislatures of Manitoba, New Brunswick, and Quebec. In these jurisdictions, the two language versions of an act or regulation are equally authentic—that is, both are official statements of the law and neither is paramount over the other. In Ontario, the legislature has enacted legislation providing for bilingual enactment and the equal authenticity of both language versions. The legislation of the territories follows the same model.

In principle, the French and English versions of bilingual legislation must say the same thing. In practice, a discrepancy sometimes exists between the versions, which must be resolved. In cases of a discrepancy, a range of possibilities to resolve the problem exists:

- version A is ambiguous while version B lends itself to only one of the possible meanings of version A; version B is the shared meaning;
- both versions are ambiguous, but both lend themselves to a single, particular meaning; this is the shared meaning;
- both versions are clear but say different things; there is no shared meaning; or
- one version is broader in scope than the other; either the narrower version is the shared meaning or the two versions say different things so that there is no shared meaning.

C. THE MODERN APPROACH IN ACTION: TWO CONVENTIONAL CASES

This subsection presents two cases that can be considered typical or conventional examples of interpretive disputes in the Federal Courts. Both involve disagreements among justices of Federal Court and Federal Court of Appeal. Each case makes use of the modern principle as well as several common law presumptions in order to determine the meaning of disputed legislative text. By reading these cases, you will come to understand the kinds of dynamics involved in litigation over meaning. Leave for one of these cases, *Vavilov v Canada (Citizenship and Immigration)*, 2015 FC 960, [2016] 2 FCR 39, was granted, and the Supreme Court of Canada rendered its own interpretation. *Vavilov* is also notable for its renovation of the standard of review and the duty to give reasons in administrative law, matters that are the subject of the case excerpt in Chapter 11.

In the first case, *Heffel Gallery Limited v Canada (AG)*, the Federal Court overturned a decision by the Canadian Cultural Property Export Review Board to delay the issue of an export permit for a painting for six months. Justice Manson found that the Board's interpretation of certain provisions of the *Cultural Property Export and Import Act*, RSC 1985, c C-51 were unreasonable. The Attorney General of Canada appealed the lower court decision to the Federal Court of Appeal. Justice Boivin overturned the Federal Court's decision and upheld the Board's original interpretation as reasonable.

Heffel Gallery Limited v Canada (AG)
2018 FC 605, [2018] 4 FCR 373

MANSON J:

I. Introduction

[1] This is an application for judicial review under section 18.1 of the *Federal Courts Act*, RSC 1985, c F-7, in respect of the decision of the Canadian Cultural Property Export Review Board (the "Board") to delay the issue of an export permit for *Iris bleus, jardin du Petit Gennevilliers*, 1892, oil on canvas, 21¾" × 18¼" by Gustave Caillebotte (the "Painting") for six months, in order to allow an institution or public authority in Canada to make a fair offer to purchase the Painting, in accordance with paragraph 29(5)(a) of the *Cultural Property Export and Import Act*, RSC 1985, c C-51 [*Act*].

II. Background

[2] The Applicant operates a fine-art auction house with offices in Vancouver, Calgary, Toronto, Ottawa and Montreal, under the trade name and style "Heffel Fine Art Auction House."

[3] In November 2016, the Applicant held a public auction, at which it offered the Painting for sale. A commercial gallery based in London, England, purchased the Painting for $678,500 CAD.

[4] The Applicant was required to apply for an export permit in order to send the Painting to London, pursuant to section 40 of the *Act*, because the Painting falls within Group V of the *Canadian Cultural Property Export Control List*, CRC, c 448 [*Control List*].

[5] In determining whether to issue an export permit, a permit officer referred the application to an expert examiner pursuant to subsection 8(3) of the *Act*. The expert examiner was Ms. Michelle Jacques, the Chief Curator of the Art Gallery of Greater Victoria (the "Expert Examiner"). She found that the Painting was of "outstanding significance" and "national importance" and therefore an export permit should not be issued, pursuant to subsections 11(1) and (3) of the *Act*. In accordance with subsection 13(1) of the *Act*, the permit officer advised the Applicant that the permit was denied.

[6] The Applicant then requested that the Board review its application for an export permit, pursuant to subsection 29(1) of the *Act*. An oral hearing was scheduled before a three member panel, including Ms. Katherine Lochnan who had recently been employed with the Art Gallery of Ontario ("AGO"). Both the Applicant and the Expert Examiner made written submissions and then were provided with each other's submissions in order to provide a rebuttal. The Applicant requested the opportunity to cross-examine the Expert Examiner at the oral hearing, but the Board denied this request.

[7] An oral hearing took place before the Board on June 7, 2017. Both the Applicant and the Expert Examiner made submissions.

[8] On July 13, 2017, the Board released its decision. It found that the Painting was of "outstanding significance" and "national importance" as per subsections 29(3) and 11(1) of the *Act*. It also found that a fair offer to purchase the object might be made by an institution or public authority in Canada and therefore it delayed the issuance of an export permit for a period of six months, pursuant to paragraph 29(5)(a) of the *Act*.

[9] On August 10, 2017, the Applicant submitted an application for judicial review of the Board's decision. An amended version of that application was submitted on October 11, 2017.

III. Issues

[10] The issues are:

A. Was the Board's decision unreasonable? In particular:

i. Did the Board adopt an unreasonable interpretation of "national importance" under paragraph 11(1)(b) of the *Act*?
ii. Was the Board's determination that the Painting was of "national importance" unreasonable?

• • •

V. Analysis

A. Was the Board's Decision Unreasonable?

(1) Did the Board Adopt an Unreasonable Interpretation of "National Importance"?

[12] The Applicant submits that the Board's interpretation of "national importance" is inconsistent with the object and purpose of the *Act*. Parliament intended for a high standard to be applied by expert examiners and the Board in order to avoid interfering with personal property rights. However, the Board adopted an overly broad interpretation such that any object that is put on the *Control List* and that meets the threshold of "outstanding significance" would automatically meet the requirement of "national importance." This renders the national importance requirement meaningless and undermines Parliament's intention to only protect objects that are closely connected to our national heritage.

[13] The Respondent submits that the *Act* expressly covers cultural property that is foreign in origin and has no direct connection to Canada, and stricter controls are in place where that property has high market value and has been in Canada for longer than 35 years. In other words, significant value and long-standing presence in Canada indicate that a foreign-origin cultural object is important to our national heritage. Furthermore, the "national importance" criterion is a quantitative assessment that is focused on degrees of quality, significance or rarity, and the Board is entitled to deference when it makes such an assessment.

[14] In my opinion, the Board's interpretation of "national importance" is unreasonable. The fact that Canada is a diverse country with a multitude of cultural traditions and Canadians may wish to study their cultural traditions or the cultural traditions of other Canadians is not sufficient to render an object of national importance where the object or its creator has no connection with Canada. That

interpretation is contrary to the words and scheme of the Act as well as Parliament's intention to restrict the scope of the *Act*.

[15] Subsection 11(1) of the *Act* provides the criteria by which to assess an object that is the subject of an application for an export permit and is included in the *Control List*:

> a) whether that object is of outstanding significance by reason of its close association with Canadian history or national life, its aesthetic qualities, or its value in the study of the arts or sciences; and
> b) whether the object is of such a degree of national importance that its loss to Canada would significantly diminish the national heritage.
> [Emphasis mine]

[16] In determining what constitutes "such a degree of national importance that its loss to Canada would significantly diminish the national heritage," the Board relied on the Department of Canadian Heritage, *Guide to Exporting Cultural Property from Canada,* June 2015 [*Guide*]. It stated:

> Appendix 3 of the [*Guide*] sets out a series of factors supporting national importance that the Review Board may consider in making its determination. These factors include the provenance of the object, the impact of its creator, its origin, its authenticity, its condition, its completeness, its rarity or uniqueness, its representativeness, its documentary or research value, as well as contextual associations that it may have.
>
> [...]
>
> The Review Board is of the view that an object can meet the degree of national importance required by the Act even if the object or the creator has no connection to Canada. Canada is a diverse country with a multitude of cultural traditions. The loss of an object to Canada could significantly diminish the national heritage if that loss would deny a segment of the population exposure to or study of their cultural traditions or the cultural traditions of other Canadians. The [*Guide*] affirms this point in the following terms:
>
> > For the purposes of the Act, national heritage includes cultural property that originated in Canada, or the territory now known as Canada, as well as significant examples of international cultural property that reflects Canada's cultural diversity or that enrich Canadians' understanding of different cultures, civilizations, time periods, and their own place in history and the world.

[17] In other words, the Board held that an object is of national importance even if the object or its creator has no connection to Canada, if the loss of that object to Canada would deny a segment of the population exposure to or study of their cultural traditions or the cultural traditions of other Canadians.

[18] To determine whether this interpretation is reasonable, it is necessary to read the words "national importance" and "national heritage" contextually and in their grammatical and ordinary sense harmoniously with the scheme of the *Act*, the object of the *Act*, and the intention of Parliament (*Rizzo & Rizzo Shoes Ltd (Re)*, [1998] 1 SCR 27 at para 21).

[19] The ordinary meaning of paragraph 11(1)(b) of the *Act* suggests that the object must have a direct connection to Canada. Given a purposive construction, the phrase "whether the object is of such a degree of national importance that its loss to Canada would significantly diminish the national heritage" immediately brings to mind an analysis of whether an object is so important to Canada that its

removal would be a significant loss of a part of Canadian culture. At a minimum, the object must have a significant impact on Canadian culture.

[20] The requirement of a direct connection to Canada is also supported by the dictionary meaning of the words "national" and "heritage." The *Canadian Oxford Dictionary*, 2nd ed, definition of the word "national" includes "of or pertaining to a nation or the nation, especially as a whole" and "peculiar to or characteristic of a particular nation." The definition of the word "heritage" includes "things such as works of art, cultural achievements and folklore that have been passed on from earlier generations" and "a nation's buildings, monuments, countryside, etc., especially when regarded as worthy of preservation." Together, the words "national" and "heritage" require the object to not only be culturally significant, but also for that significance to be particular to Canada and Canadians.

[21] This interpretation accords with the scheme of the *Act*. Most objects in the *Control List* require a direct connection to Canada, such as having been recovered in Canada, made in Canada, made by a person who once resided in Canada, or otherwise having some relation to Canadian history or a Canadian theme or subject. While some objects captured by the *Control List* have no apparent connection with Canada, but merely exceed a specified age and value, those objects are the exceptions, not the norm.

[22] In any event, an object's inclusion in the *Control List* is not determinative of whether or not an export permit should be issued for that object. It triggers a review of the export permit application by an expert examiner or the Board. In other words, those exceptional objects with no apparent connection to Canada are subject to further review under the stricter criteria of "outstanding significance" and "national importance."

[23] Given a purposive construction, the reference to both of "outstanding significance" and "national importance" implies that these two criteria are independent and have distinct considerations. An object may be of outstanding significance due to its aesthetic qualities or its value for study, pursuant to paragraph 11(1)(a) of the *Act*, but those qualities are independent of the necessary criterion that the object is also of national importance and part of Canadian heritage pursuant to paragraph 11(1)(b). An object must be both significant *and* related to national importance and Canadian heritage. To suggest that an object is of national importance only because of its value for study—as was suggested by the Board—would undermine the second criterion and render it meaningless. Courts should avoid adopting an interpretation that would render any portion of a statute meaningless, pointless or redundant (Ruth Sullivan, *Sullivan on the Construction of Statutes*, 6th ed (Markham, Ontario: 2014, LexisNexis Canada) [*Sullivan*] at 211).

[24] Furthermore, Parliament has never adopted the much broader definition of cultural property found in the *Convention for the Protection of Cultural Property in the Event of Armed Conflict*, The Hague, 14 May 1954, Can TS 1999 No 52 [*Convention*]. The *Convention* refers to "cultural property" as objects "of great importance to the cultural heritage of every people." The Act contains provisions related to the *Convention*, but does not incorporate that definition. The distinct contrast between "national heritage" and "cultural heritage of every people" suggests an intent to limit the range of objects captured by the *Act*.

[25] Finally, the legislative history confirms that Parliament intended for the *Act* to have limited application and to focus on objects with a more direct connection with Canadian heritage. The Honourable James Hugh Faulkner, who was Secretary of State at the time the *Act* was introduced, spoke about the loss of "national treasures" and "preserving Canadian heritage." MP Gordon Fairweather spoke about "Canadian nationalism, the Canadian ethic and our

cultural heritage" and the need to prevent the removal of national treasures so that Canadians can discover their shared identity (*House of Commons Debates,* 30th Parl, 1st Sess, Vol III (7 February 1975), Second Reading of Bill C-33 [*Debates*] at 3024-3040).

[26] Equally, Mr. Faulkner stressed the importance of limiting the intrusion into property rights and the freedom of trade. He wished to "emphasize the necessity for limiting control to a minimum," that "a workable system of export control must confine itself to limited, well-defined categories" and only deal with objects "of the first order of importance." He stated that the *Act* should "not attempt to set up too fine a screen which, in addition to creating high administrative costs, would catch objects of minor importance. This would create unnecessary delays in the trade, to the detriment of normal business." (*Debates* at 3024-3040).

[27] The stricter interpretation of the *Act* suggested by Mr. Faulkner accords with the presumed legislative intent to not interfere with property rights, in particular, the freedom of the property owner to use and dispose of property as he or she sees fit, without hindrance or control (*Sullivan* at 503).

[28] There is no question that Canada is a diverse country with a multitude of cultural traditions. I also accept that the Board is entitled to deference when interpreting its home statute and that the Applicant must not only show that its competing interpretation of the *Act* is reasonable, but also that the Board's interpretation was unreasonable (*McLean v British Columbia (Securities Commission),* 2013 SCC 67 at para 41, [2013] 3 SCR 895).

[29] However, to apply the provisions of the *Act* to any object that allows for exposure to or study of the cultural traditions of Canadians, where "cultural traditions" incorporates the multiculturalism of Canada, and therefore the cultural heritage of peoples from around the world, without proper consideration of the express wording of subsection 11(1) of the *Act*, is unreasonably broad.

[30] Such an interpretation could unreasonably capture any work that has outstanding aesthetic qualities or value for study, but no direct connection to Canada or national importance such that its loss would significantly diminish the national heritage. There must be a connection with Canadian heritage that is more direct than the fact that Canada is multicultural and Canadians may wish to study the traditions of any one of the many countries from which their ancestors may have come. Parliament has chosen words that require a direct connection with the cultural heritage that is particular to Canada, to not adopt the broad definition of cultural property found in the *Convention*, and to separate the analysis of aesthetic qualities and value for study from the analysis of national importance. All of this is in accordance with Parliament's stated and presumed intention to restrict the scope of the Act in order to limit the interference with property rights.

[31] I find that the Board's interpretation of paragraph 11(1)(b) of the *Act* did not fall within the range of possible outcomes which were defensible in respect of the facts and the law and therefore it was unreasonable.

(2) Was the Board's Determination That the Painting Was of "National Importance" Unreasonable?

[32] The Respondent submits that the Board reasonably found that the preservation of the Painting in Canada was required to ensure access to the work by Canadians, and that there was an association to an Impressionist work that was currently in the National Gallery of Canada. The Board also referred to the opinions of the Applicant's experts but disagreed with the Applicant on the probative value and weight of that evidence.

[33] The Board gave the following reasons for finding that the loss of the Painting to Canada would significantly diminish the national heritage:

- it was in the inventory of the commercial dealer Ambroise Vollard of Paris, France, who was one of the most important dealers in French contemporary art at the beginning of the 20th century, including the work of French Impressionists;
- Gustave Caillebotte's work has been reassessed over the last 20 years and there is now substantial interest in it;
- the Painting is only the second work of Caillebotte's known to be in Canadian collections. It is a unique work of art and is the only work representative of the series of work depicting flowers and having symbolic significance that were created by the artist late in his life;
- in view of the rarity of works by Caillebotte in Canada and the stature of the artist in French Impressionism, there is no doubt that the Painting will be of considerable interest and importance for research in Canada with respect to French Impressionism; and
- with respect to the Canadian context, one of the greatest masterpieces of the National Gallery of Canada is the painting *Iris,* 1890, by Vincent Van Gogh, which was made just two years before the Painting. It also depicts a blue iris in a garden from a similar perspective to that of the Painting.

[34] The Applicant's experts on this issue were Laurier Lacroix and Carol Lowrey. Dr. Lacroix is professor emeritus of art history and museum studies at the Université du Québec in Montréal. He has devoted most of his professional life to the study of painters from Québec and has undertaken a great deal of research on Canadian artists influenced by the French Impressionist movement. Dr. Lowrey is a Canadian-born art historian and curator based in New York City. She is a graduate of the University of Toronto (MA, MLS) and the City University of New York (PhD) and has written numerous articles, books and exhibition catalogues devoted to aspects of 19th and early 20th century Canadian and American art. She has focused on the tradition of Impressionism as it developed in North America.

[35] Dr. Lacroix submitted in his expert report that:

- the Painting was relatively insignificant;
- the Painting was never exhibited in Canada and it was not reproduced until 1978, long after the period of Canadian Impressionism was over;
- the Painting had no influence on Canadian Impressionist painters;
- the Painting had no influence on the Canadian public nor upon the artistic practices of Canadian artists; and
- there was no reasonable basis to conclude that the export of the Painting from Canada would negatively affect the national heritage in any way.

[36] Dr. Lowrey submitted in her expert report that:

- there was no evidence that the Painting, or Caillebotte's oeuvre in general, inspired the stylistic evolution of any of the artists associated with the Canadian Impressionist tradition;
- there was no evidence that Canadian artists were in contact with Caillebotte;
- the Painting was not exhibited during the years that Impressionism flourished in Canada, having remained abroad until entering a private collection in 1960;
- the Painting has no direct connection to the history of the Canadian Impressionist tradition;
- the export of the Painting would not impact our interpretation of Impressionism as practiced by Canadian artists, nor would it have a deleterious effect on our national heritage.

[37] The Board acknowledged the opinion of these experts, that is, that the Painting has no connection to Canadian Impressionism, that the Painting had no influence on the Canadian public or artistic practices of Canadian artists and that the Painting had no connection to Canadian artists engaged in Impressionism.

[38] These are precisely the types of factors the Board should have considered in its analysis under paragraph 11(1)(b) of the *Act*. The Board unreasonably focused only on the Painting's provenance, rarity, research value and desirability under paragraph 11(1)(a). As outlined above, to analyse only these factors and not the object's connection to Canada renders paragraph 11(1)(b) meaningless and overly broadens the scope of the *Act*, contrary to the intention of Parliament.

[39] There was no reasonable basis for the Board to have concluded that the Painting was of such a degree of national importance that its loss to Canada would significantly diminish the national heritage. The artist and subject matter were not Canadian and the Painting has no connection to the Canadian public or Canadian Impressionism. Essentially, the Board's unreasonable interpretation of paragraph 11(1)(b) of the *Act* caused it to make an unreasonable determination of whether the Painting met the requirements of that provision.

[40] The Board's finding on this issue was unreasonable.

1. Before reading the judgment from the Federal Court of Appeal:

   • consider what is relevant about the Act's legislative history;
   • identify the main interpretive canons that Manson J and/or the other parties (i.e., the Board, Attorney General, Heffel Gallery) relied on; and
   • pinpoint the interpretive error(s) that Heffel Gallery asserts the Board makes, the interpretive error(s) that the Attorney General suggests that Heffel Gallery makes, and the interpretive error(s) that Manson J finds determinative.

Canada (AG) v Heffel Gallery Limited
2019 FCA 82, [2019] 3 FCR 81

BOIVIN JA (Gleason and Rivoalen JJA concurring):

• • •

[22] ... as part of this appeal, this Court heard from 9 museums and galleries across Canada that were granted intervener status, namely: the Musée des Beaux-Arts de Montréal, the Art Gallery of Ontario, the Royal Ontario Museum, the Vancouver Art Gallery, the Remai Modern, The Winnipeg Art Gallery, the Thomas Fisher Rare Book Library at the University of Toronto Libraries, the Musée d'Art contemporain de Montréal and the Beaverbrook Art Gallery.

• • •

V. Analysis

A. The Board's Decision

(1) The Board's Interpretation of "Outstanding Significance" at Paragraph 11(1)(A) of the Act

[24] First, the Board agreed with the expert examiner and the respondent, and determined that the Painting was included in Group V at paragraph 4(*b*) of the Control List (the Act, subsection 29(3)). Specifically, foreign paintings with no direct connection to Canada are controlled through Group V at paragraph 4(*b*).

[25] Having made this determination, the Board then further determined that *Iris bleus* was of "outstanding significance" due to its aesthetic qualities, as expressly set out in paragraph 11(1)(a) of the Act. The Board also emphasized that, apart from *Iris bleus*, there is only one other work of art by Gustave Caillebotte that could be identified in a Canadian collection. The Board further underscored the importance of Gustave Caillebotte's work by referencing the fact that the Metropolitan Museum of Art in New York, "one of the great art museums in the world," is the owner of only one Gustave Caillebotte piece, which was acquired in 2014. Observing that the opportunities to view and study the work of Gustave Caillebotte in Canada remain very limited, the Board was of the view that the Iris bleus further met the criteria of "outstanding significance" for its value in the study of the arts (Board's decision at para. 33):

> ... Given the stature of the artist as one of the leading artists of French Impressionism, the importance of French Impressionism to understanding the history of art and to art practice today (including in Canada), and the fact that the Object is representative of works from late in the artist's career, the Review Board determines that the Object meets the criteria of outstanding significance for its value in the study of the arts.

[26] The Board's reasons also addressed other considerations. For instance, the Board acknowledged in its decision that it was aware that its interpretation under section 11 of the Act would also affect requests for certification under section 32, and that a given interpretation could potentially limit the number of objects eligible for certification (Board's decision at paras. 25 and 30). While these comments were made in the context of the discussion on "outstanding significance" under paragraph 11(1)(a) and are not dispositive of this appeal, it can be inferred that these considerations affected the Board's interpretation of subsection 11(1) in general and its application to the Painting.

(2) The Board's Interpretation of "National Importance" at Paragraph 11(1)(b) of the Act

[27] The final aspect of the Board's analysis was to determine pursuant to paragraph 11(1)(b) whether the Painting was of such a degree of "national importance" that its loss to Canada would significantly diminish the "national heritage." This aspect of the Board's decision regarding paragraph 11(1)(b) was the only one at issue on judicial review before the Federal Court. In this appeal, we are thus solely concerned with the Board's interpretation of paragraph 11(1)(b) of the Act.

[28] In this regard, the seven members of the Board formed the view that a given object can meet the degree of "national importance" even if the object or the creator has no direct connection with Canadian history or Canada. The Board stated the following at paragraph 40:

> The Review Board is of the view that an object can meet the degree of national importance required by the Act even if the object or the creator has no connection to Canada. Canada is a diverse country with a multitude of cultural traditions. The loss of an object to Canada could significantly diminish the national heritage if that loss would deny a segment of the population exposure to or study of their cultural traditions or the cultural traditions of other Canadians. ...

[29] In reaching its conclusion, the Board relied expressly on the *Guide to Exporting Cultural Property from Canada* of the Department of Canadian Heritage which lists a number of factors that the Board can consider in determining

the "national importance" of an object (Published June 2015, online: <https://www
.canada.ca/content/dam/pch/documents/services/movable-cultural-property/
export_permit_application_guide-eng.pdf> at p. 27):

> For the purposes of the Act, national heritage includes cultural property that origi-
> nated in Canada, or the territory now known as Canada, as well as significant
> examples of international cultural property that reflects Canada's cultural diversity
> or that enrich Canadians' understanding of different cultures, civilizations, time
> periods, and their own place in history and the world.

[30] The Board thus concluded, unanimously, that the loss of *Iris bleus* would
significantly diminish the national heritage:

> [46] In view of the provenance of the Object, the condition of the Object, the
> rarity of works of the artist in Canadian collections, the research value of the
> Object, and the fact that the Object is a highly desirable example of Impressionist
> landscape painting, the Review Board determines that the loss of the Object to
> Canada would significantly diminish the national heritage.

[31] Having reached this conclusion, the Board also considered whether an
institution or public authority in Canada might make a fair offer to purchase *Iris
bleus* within six months. Given the outstanding significance of the Painting, the
rarity of Gustave Caillebotte's work in Canada, and the artist's important place in
the French Impressionism movement, the Board determined that there would be
considerable interest in acquiring *Iris bleus*. The Board also noted the expert examiner's evidence that three Canadian curators of European art had indicated that they
would like to see the Painting remain in Canada and that their institutions would
be able to purchase it. As provided for by the Act, the Board therefore established a
delay period of six months during which it would not direct that an export permit
be issued (Board's decision at paras. 50, 51 and 59).

(3) The Reasonableness of the Board's Interpretation of Paragraph 11(1)(b) of the Act

[32] Upon reading the Board's decision with the degree of deference required
on judicial review, I consider that the Board's interpretation of paragraph 11(1)(*b*) of
the Act was reasonable.

[33] It is important to recall that paragraph 11(1)(*b*) requires an assessment of the extent and impact of the loss to Canada if a work is "of such a
degree of national importance that its loss to Canada would significantly diminish the national heritage" [Emphasis added]. The key words in paragraph 11(1)(*b*)—
i.e., "national importance" and "national heritage," are not defined in the Act.
On their face, these elements as worded do not confine the Board to specific
factors in its assessment. Rather, the terms "national importance" and "national
heritage" allow for a broad range of options based on the Board's expertise
(*Schmidt v. Canada (Attorney General)*, 2018 FCA 55 [*Schmidt*]). The provision at
issue also sets forth broad qualifiers—*i.e.*, "of such a degree" and "significantly,"
which further signifies Parliament's intention to confer upon the Board broad
discretion to assess and determine whether or not a given object is of "national
importance." To this end, the Board is composed of members appointed for their
expertise in the specialized context of cultural property, cultural heritage and
cultural institutions.

· · ·

[35] In support of the Board's interpretation, regard may also be given to subsection 4(2) of the Act, which allows the Governor in Council to include in the Control List, "regardless of their places of origin, any objects or classes of objects ... the export of which the Governor in Council deems it necessary to control in order to preserve the national heritage in Canada" [Emphasis added]. I agree with the respondent that objects on the Control List are not *de facto* deemed to form part of the national heritage by the Act. However, they are by virtue of being on the Control List deemed to be necessary to control in order to preserve the national heritage. It follows that objects in each class, including the classes that do not require a Canadian connection, potentially form part of the national heritage. The broad language used in paragraph 11(1)(*b*) confirms such a conclusion.

[36] On this point, the respondent asserts that if the Control List determined "national heritage," there would be no need for the Board's expertise under paragraph 11(1)(*b*). This assertion overlooks the determinative role of the Board in measuring and assessing the impact of losing a given object on the Control List. Indeed, the Board must consider whether the object is of "such a degree of national importance that its loss to Canada would significantly diminish the national heritage." In other words, the degree of importance of the object remains a question for the Board's expert members to assess on a case-by-case basis.

[37] The respondent's contention that the Board conflated the "outstanding significance" (paragraph 11(1)(*a*)) and "national importance" (paragraph 11(1)(*b*)) criteria by "effectively read[ing] out the legislative criteria of 'national importance'" is likewise unfounded (respondent's memorandum of fact and law at para. 64). The "outstanding significance" requirement at paragraph 11(1)(*a*) measures essentially whether an object is significant because of its close association with Canadian history or national life, its aesthetic qualities, or its value in the study of the arts or sciences. By contrast, the "national importance" requirement at paragraph 11(1)(*b*) measures the extent of the effect of the removal of the object from Canada—*i.e.*, the importance of the object to Canada..For example, a painting may meet the "outstanding significance" requirement at paragraph 11(1)(*a*) because of its beauty (aesthetic qualities) but not the "national importance" requirement where, for instance, there are many similar other pieces of art in Canada by the same artist that are in better condition. While certain considerations may overlap with respect to "outstanding significance" and "national importance," I cannot agree with the respondent that this overlap renders paragraph 11(1)(*b*) "mere surplusage" which in turn makes the Board's decision unreasonable (respondent's memorandum of fact and law at para. 63).

[38] Finally, the parties made oral submissions regarding the legislative history of the Act in order to defend (in the case of the appellant) or to attack (in the case of the respondent) the reasonableness of the Board's decision.

[39] Upon reviewing the legislative history of the Act on record, I cannot agree with the respondent that it supports the unreasonableness of the Board's interpretation. The respondent particularly submits that Secretary of State James Hugh Faulkner, who introduced Bill C-33, which became the Act, emphasized during the debate the importance of limiting control and focusing on objects of the "first order of importance" (respondent's memorandum of fact and law at para. 62; *House of Commons Debates*, 30th Legis., 1st sess., Vol. 3, 7 February 1975, p. 3026). This does not however support the respondent's contention that a given object must necessarily have a connection to Canada. This is not the manner in which the Act limits the amount of objects subject to control. Rather, the Act achieves this objective by requiring that: the object must be more than 50 years old and the creator must be deceased; imported objects must have been in Canada for at least 35 years;

the object must be captured by one of the well-defined categories on the Control List; the object must be of "outstanding significance"; and the object must be of "such a degree" of national importance that its loss "significantly decreases" the national heritage. Indeed, objects are excluded from control throughout the entire scheme of the Act. This control is imposed without reference to any requirement that the object have a direct connection with Canada. It was thus reasonable for the Board to determine that an object can meet the degree of "national importance" at paragraph 11(1)(*b*) of the Act even if the said object or its creator have no direct connection to Canada.

(4) Reasonableness of the Board's Determination That Iris Bleus Was of "National Importance"

[40] Having concluded that the Board's interpretation of paragraph 11(1)(*b*) was reasonable, it must further be considered whether the Board's determination that *Iris bleus* meets the "national importance" requirement under paragraph 11(1)(*b*) was likewise reasonable.

[41] From the outset, in reaching the conclusion that the Painting at issue is of "national importance," the Board did not merely rely on the fact enunciated in the *Guide to Exporting Cultural Property from Canada*—i.e., that Canada is a diverse country. The Board was more nuanced than the respondent contends. It discussed "the provenance of the object, the impact of its creator, its origin, its authenticity, its condition, its completeness, its rarity or uniqueness, its representativeness, its documentary or research value, as well as contextual associations that it may have." (Board's decision at para. 38). More specifically, the Board made the following findings rooted in its factual appreciation:

- *Iris bleus* came from the inventory of an important dealer (Ambroise Vollard of Paris, France) who figured amongst the most important dealers of French contemporary art in the 20th century, including the work of French Impressionists (para. 41);
- Interest in the work of Gustave Caillebotte was rediscovered in the mid-1960s and his work has been reassessed over the last 20 years (para. 42);
- *Iris bleus* is only the second work of Gustave Caillebote in Canada. It is a unique work of art and the only work representative of the series depicting flowers and having symbolic significance that were created by the artist late in his life (para. 43);
- Given its rarity, *Iris bleus* will be of considerable interest and importance for research in Canada with respect to French impressionism (para. 44).

[42] The Board also referred to the existence of Vincent Van Gogh's Iris (1890), which is held at the National Gallery of Canada. The respondent alleges that allowing the Board to consider such a factor means that "[t]he Act would have a sweeping application to all manner of cultural objects and would render meaningless the inquiry mandated by [paragraph] 11(1)(b)" (respondent's memorandum of fact and law at para. 80). To accept this contention requires a fragmented reading of the Board's decision which has to be viewed as a whole. Indeed, the consideration of Van Gogh's Iris was but one of a myriad of factors considered by the Board in determining that the loss of the *Iris bleus* would significantly diminish the national heritage.

[43] In doing so, it was open to the Board to discount the parts of the respondent's evidence that were premised on a connection to Canada and to consider more broadly factors mentioned in the *Guide to Exporting Cultural Property from*

Canada. The factors considered by the Board speak to the degree of value and importance of the object as well as its importance in the Canadian context (*i.e.*, the lack of other Gustave Caillebotte paintings in Canada and the presence of similar works by other artists in Canada). As mentioned above, given that no factors are laid out in the legislation, the ones relied upon by the Board in order to identify the impact of *Iris bleus'* departure from Canada were reasonable.

[44] In summary, I am of the view that the Board's decision is reasonable as it falls within a range of possible, acceptable outcomes which are defensible in respect of the facts and the law (*Dunsmuir v. New Brunswick*, 2008 SCC 9, [2008] 1 S.C.R. 190 at para. 47). The Federal Court thus erred in concluding that the Board's interpretation was unreasonable on the basis that it was too broad.

B. The Federal Court Erred in Its Application of the Reasonableness Standard of Review

• • •

[54] First, in engaging in its own statutory interpretation, the Federal Court relied on dictionary definitions to further bolster its textual interpretation that "[t]ogether, the words 'national' and 'heritage' require the object to not only be culturally signifi-cant, but also for that significance to be particular to Canada and Canadians" (Fed-eral Court's reasons at para. 20). This approach led the Federal Court to focus on the ordinary meaning of the words as a complete answer which led it to overlook the "authentic" meaning of the provision (*Schmidt* at paras. 27-28).

[55] The Federal Court also made reference to the *Convention for the Protection of Cultural Property in the Event of an Armed Conflict,* The Hague, 14 May, 1954, Can TS 1990 no. 52 (the Hague Convention) (Federal Court's reasons at para. 24). Yet, neither the appellant nor the respondent relied on international law before the Board and more significantly, Canada acceded to the Hague Convention in 1998—*i.e.*, twenty years after the enactment of the Act and Canada only joined the First and Second Protocols in 2005. It is therefore difficult, in the circumstances, to conclude that the terms Parliament employed in the Act were based on the Hague Convention. To do so in order to support an alternate interpretation is questionable.

[56] The Federal Court repeatedly asserted Parliament's intention in enacting the Act was to avoid interfering with property rights. Relying on Secretary of State Faulkner's interventions during the debates on the Bill, the Federal Court was of the view that a narrower interpretation of subsection 11(1)(*b*) of the Act than the one provided by the Board was warranted (Federal Court's reasons at paras. 12, 26, and 27). In doing so, the Federal Court overlooked other provisions in the Act aimed at establishing a careful balance between property rights and the preservation of cultural heritage for future generations. Indeed, Parliament at the time was well aware of the rights of individual owners of cultural property to participate in a legal international market. This intention is illustrated by the multiple requirements set forth in the Act aimed at limiting the control of cultural objects and therefore limit-ing the impact on property rights. For example, the Board must find that an object is of "outstanding significance" and of "national importance" and be satisfied that a Canadian institution or public authority might make an offer in order to estab-lish a delay period (the Act, subsection 29(5)). The short delay contemplated by the Act allows a cultural institution the opportunity to make a fair offer to purchase the object. If no offer is made during the said period, the Board has no jurisdiction to refuse a permit and the export permit will issue. Hence, the delay is not unlimited and the impact on property rights remains circumscribed.

[57] Finally, the tax incentives provided for at section 32 of the Act, although not necessary to dispose of this appeal, are nonetheless relevant to understanding the overall scheme of the Act; the respondent agrees with this proposition (respondent's memorandum of fact and law at para. 44). Indeed, the tax incentives encourage individuals to donate or sell national cultural property to designated institutions, which, in turn, prevent many Canadian institutions from being "culturally ghettoised" in allowing them to acquire works of art with a view of preserving cultural heritage for future generations. The tax incentives thus play a vital role in the operation of the scheme of the Act as a whole and the Board was alive to it when it rendered its decision (Board's decision at paras. 25, 27, 30 and 52).

VI. Conclusion

[58] For all of the above reasons, I would accordingly allow the appeal, set aside the judgment of the Federal Court dated June 12, 2018 in file T-1235-17 (2018 FC 605), dismiss the application for judicial review and restore the decision of the Board dated July 13, 2017. I would grant costs to the appellant.

1. Note how Boivin JA interprets the scheme and object of the Act in addition to other elements of the modern principle such as legislative history and expert evidence.
2. The Supreme Court of Canada denied Heffel Gallery's request for leave to appeal, thus leaving the Federal Court of Appeal's decision as the final judicial answer. In your legal opinion, does Federal Court or Federal Court of Appeal provide the interpretation that best fits legislative intent and therefore achieves the appropriate balance among public and private interests?
3. Two further developments are worth noting. First, in June 2019 the Government of Canada removed "national importance" as a factor the Board must consider in order to certify cultural property for income tax purposes. Second, in August 2019, with a grant from the federal government the Art Gallery of Ontario purchased *Iris Bleus* for CAD$1 million.

The second case, *Vavilov v Canada (Citizenship and Immigration)*, presents several interpretive disputes, beginning with the original decision-maker (who, as in *Heffel Gallery*, is located in the executive branch) and all the way up to the Supreme Court of Canada. Notably, all parties ostensibly rely on the modern approach to interpret the meaning of the words "employee in Canada of a foreign government" contained in paragraph 3(2)(a) of the *Citizenship Act*, RSC 1985, c C-29 (the Act). The task for this case is to observe and understand how these multiple interpreters came to different legal conclusions and why.

Vavilov v Canada (Citizenship and Immigration)
2015 FC 960, [2016] 2 FCR 39

BELL J:

I. Summary

[1] This is a judicial review of the decision of the Registrar of Citizenship (Registrar) communicated to Alexander Vavilov on August 15, 2014, in which the Registrar revoked Mr. Vavilov's citizenship pursuant to paragraph 3(2)(*a*) of

the *Citizenship Act*, RSC 1985, c C-29. The Registrar based his decision upon the fact that Mr. Vavilov's parents were employees of a foreign government and not lawful Canadian citizens at the time of his birth. ...

• • •

IV. Relevant Provisions

[14] For convenience, ss. 3(1)(a) and 3(2)(a) of the *Citizenship Act* are reproduced below:

Persons who are citizens

 3. (1) Subject to this Act, a person is a citizen if

  (a) the person was born in Canada after February 14, 1977;

  ...

Not applicable to children of foreign diplomats, etc.

 (2) Paragraph (1)(a) does not apply to a person if, at the time of his birth, neither of his parents was a citizen or lawfully admitted to Canada for permanent residence and either of his parents was

  (a) a diplomatic or consular officer or other representative or employee in Canada of a foreign government;

Citoyens

 3. (1) Sous réserve des autres dispositions de la présente loi, a qualité de citoyen toute personne :

  a) née au Canada après le 14 février 1977;

  [...]

Inapplicabilité aux enfants de diplomates étrangers, etc.

 (2) L'alinéa (1)a) ne s'applique pas à la personne dont, au moment de la naissance, les parents n'avaient qualité ni de citoyens ni de résidents permanents et dont le père ou la mère était :

  a) agent diplomatique ou consulaire, représentant à un autre titre ou au service au Canada d'un gouvernement étranger;

V. Analysis

• • •

C. Interpretation of s. 3(2)(a)

[21] Mr. Vavilov's parents were in Canada under assumed identities at the time of his birth. He acknowledges their Canadian passports were obtained by fraud. However, he contends his parents were "lawfully admitted to Canada" and are Canadian citizens because the fraudulently obtained documents were never revoked by the Minister of Citizenship and Immigration. The argument is devoid of any merit and to give it any credence by further analysis would be an affront to all those who attempt to come to this country lawfully and obtain valid Canadian citizenship. Because his parents were not Canadian citizens, if Mr. Vavilov's claim to Canadian citizenship is to succeed, it must be based upon his birth in Canada.

[22] The question to be answered, on the correctness standard, is whether the Registrar erred in finding that individuals living in Canada under an assumed identity and working to establish 'deep cover' operations in order to collect intelligence for a foreign government, are included in the definition of "a diplomatic or consular officer or other representative or employee in Canada of a foreign government" as

contemplated by s. 3(2)(a) of the Citizenship Act. For the reasons that follow, I find the Registrar did not err.

[23] If one reads s. 3(2)(a) in a contextual and purposive manner, taking the plain meaning of the words, it must include representatives and employees in Canada of foreign governments, regardless of diplomatic or consular status. To find otherwise would render the words "other representative or employee in Canada" meaningless. This would be inconsistent with any reasoned approach to statutory interpretation, and offends the rule that Parliament intends each word in a statute to have meaning (See: Ruth Sullivan, *Statutory Interpretation,* 2nd ed., (Irwin Law Inc. 2007, at 184 [*Sullivan*]). This rule flows from the assumption that the legislator avoids tautology.

[24] The question which remains is whether those who establish themselves, at the behest of a foreign government, for the purposes of gathering intelligence for that foreign government constitute "representatives or employees." The fact the section refers to both employees and representatives is telling. My view is re-enforced by the French version which speaks even more broadly about those "représentant à un autre titre ou au service au Canada d'un gouvernement étranger." The wording is clearly meant to cover individuals who are in Canada as agents of a foreign government, whatever their mandate. In this case, the task was to steal identities, obtain fraudulent citizenship and, with the benefit of that citizenship, further the fraud on one of our closest allies—the purpose of the fraud being to obtain intelligence and provide information to the Russian government. Anyone who moves to this country with the explicit goal of establishing a life to further a foreign intelligence operation, be it in this country or any other, is clearly doing so in the service of (French version), or as an employee or representative of, a foreign government.

[25] In my view the Registrar correctly found that this scenario is captured by s. 3(2)(a) of the *Citizenship Act.* To conclude otherwise would lead to the absurd result that children of a foreign diplomat, registered at an embassy, who conducts spy operations, cannot claim Canadian citizenship by birth in Canada but children of those who enter unlawfully for the very same purpose, become Canadian citizens by birth. The proper application of the rules of statutory interpretation should not lead to absurd results (See: Sullivan, above, at 209).

D. Reasonableness

[26] The final issue for determination is whether it was reasonable for the Registrar to conclude that Mr. Vavilov's parents were in Canada as part of their SVR operation for the Russian government. For the reasons that follow, I find that it was.

[27] I find there was sufficient evidence, when considering the arrest and conviction records and use of false identities by Mr. Vavilov's parents, for the Registrar to conclude they were "illegals" working on a deep cover assignment for the SVR, while in Canada. In addition to the public record, the information contained in the internal analyst's report is instructive in that it speaks to the long term pattern one would expect to see from an illegal. This includes pursuing higher education and legitimate employment in a host country, in this case Canada, to establish a "legend" that becomes increasingly documented and plausible. The legend becomes so authentic that it appears to be reality. In the report to the Registrar, which was disclosed to Mr. Vavilov, the analyst states:

> Open-source information indicates that the SVR tasked Mr. Bezrukov with collecting intelligence from U.S. officials on topics related to U.S. foreign policy on a variety of topics related to America's position on Central Asia, Russia, and a variety of national security issues (including the nuclear non-proliferation, the U.S. position

on Iran's nuclear weapons program, and the U.S. foreign policy objectives in Afghanistan).

Considering Mr. Bezrukov's objectives, it is reasonable to believe that his pursuit of undergraduate (i.e.: Bachelor degree at York University in Toronto, Canada) and graduate degrees in the fields of international business and public administration both enhance the strength of his legend.

[28] The record contains no contradictory evidence. It was open to the Registrar to accept this report, which he reasonably did. I am satisfied the Registrar's decision on the facts falls within the range of possible, acceptable outcomes ... .

1. Identify the main interpretive principles Bell J relies on.
2. Whose interests does Bell J's interpretation advance in this case?

Vavilov v Canada (Citizenship and Immigration)
2017 FCA 132

STRATAS JA (Webb JA concurring):

A. Introduction

[1] The appellant appeals from the judgment of the Federal Court (*per* Bell J.): 2015 FC 960. The Federal Court dismissed the appellant's application for judicial review of a decision of the Registrar of Citizenship. The Registrar invoked paragraph 3(2)(a) of the *Citizenship Act*, R.S.C. 1985, c. C-29 and cancelled the appellant's citizenship under subsection 26(3) of the *Citizenship Regulations*, SOR/93-246.

[2] The appellant was born in Canada in 1994. Normally, that would have made him a citizen of Canada: *Citizenship Act*, paragraph 3(1)(a). Until 2010, the appellant assumed he was a Canadian citizen. On July 27, 2010, that assumption was thrown into doubt.

[3] On that day, when the appellant was living with his family in the United States, FBI agents, armed, entered the family home and arrested his parents. Unknown to the appellant, all his life his parents had been acting under assumed names. Unknown to the appellant, his parents were espionage agents for Russia.

[4] This changed everything. The appellant was forced to go to Russia to live in a country to which he had no connection. His surname was changed from Foley to Vavilov. To this day, the appellant considers himself and his brother—also caught up in all of this—to be Canadian.

[5] But the Registrar of Citizenship disagreed. The Registrar found that the appellant is not Canadian and cancelled his citizenship under subsection 26(3) of the *Citizenship Regulations*, SOR/93-246. According to the Registrar, paragraph 3(2)(a) of the *Citizenship Act* applies. Under that paragraph, if neither parent is a citizen or lawfully admitted to Canada for permanent residence and either was "a diplomatic or consular officer or other representative or employee of a foreign government," the child is not a Canadian citizen despite being born in Canada.

[6] According to the Registrar, the appellant's parents were not citizens or permanent residents at the time of his birth. And—in what has been the central issue

here and below—the Registrar found that the appellant's parents were "employees of a foreign government" within the meaning of paragraph 3(2)(a) of the *Citizenship Act*.

[7] The appellant applied for judicial review of the Registrar's decision. The Federal Court dismissed it. The Federal Court reviewed the Registrar's interpretation of "employee of a foreign government" in paragraph 3(2)(a) of the Act for correctness. It agreed with the Registrar. The Federal Court also dismissed a procedural fairness complaint the appellant made.

[8] The appellant appeals to this Court. The appellant reiterates the procedural fairness complaint in this Court. He also submits that both the Federal Court and the Registrar erred in their interpretation of "employee in Canada of a foreign government" in paragraph 3(2)(a) of the *Citizenship Act*.

[9] For the reasons below, I would allow the appeal, set aside the judgment of the Federal Court, allow the application for judicial review, and quash the decision of the Registrar to revoke the appellant's citizenship. Unless another ground for revocation applies—and none has been argued here—the appellant is entitled to Canadian citizenship under paragraph 3(1)(a) of the *Citizenship Act*.

• • •

C. Review of the Substance of the Decision

[19] The appellant says that the Registrar's decision to revoke his citizenship was unreasonable and, thus, must be quashed. He says that his parents were not "employee[s] in Canada of a foreign government" under paragraph 3(2)(a) of the *Citizenship Act*. As a result, paragraph 3(2)(a) does not apply. This leaves paragraph 3(1)(a) of the *Citizenship Act* as the governing provision in his case. As a person born in Canada in 1994, he is entitled to citizenship.

• • •

(2) Analysis

(a) Introduction

[40] Despite the foregoing and even affording the Registrar leeway under the reasonableness standard, I find that the result the Registrar reached on these facts, namely that the appellant's parents were "employee[s] in Canada of a foreign government" in paragraph 3(2)(a) of the Act, is not supportable, defensible or acceptable ... .

[41] It is trite that statutory provisions are to be interpreted in accordance with their text, context and purpose: *Rizzo & Rizzo Shoes Ltd. (Re)*, [1998] 1 S.C.R. 27, 154 D.L.R. (4th) 193; *Bell ExpressVu Limited Partnership v. Rex*, 2002 SCC 42, [2002] 2 S.C.R. 559.

[42] The need to take into account the purpose of statutory provisions is made especially important by section 12 of the *Interpretation Act*, R.S.C. 1985, c. I-21, a section that applies to all, courts and administrative decision-makers alike. It provides that a statutory provision "shall be given such fair, large and liberal construction and interpretation as best ensures the attainment of its objects."

[43] Equally important, as we shall see, is the context of paragraph 3(2)(a) of the *Citizenship Act*: its legislative history, other paragraphs in subsection 3(2) that shed light on it, and the principles of international law surrounding it.

[44] Even on the understanding that the Registrar considered the issue of statutory interpretation and adopted the reasoning contained in the report of an analyst, when the purpose and context of paragraph 3(2)(a) is considered, the Registrar's

interpretation of paragraph 3(2)(a) of the *Citizenship Act* cannot stand. Except for an abbreviated review of legislative history—only textual in nature—the purpose and context of paragraph 3(2)(a) was not considered at all. For example, the analyst's report is striking for its failure to refer to or analyze the other paragraphs of subsection 3(2). Virtually all of the analysis—only textual in nature—fits in a single paragraph in the analyst's report (appeal book, page 30). This sort of cursory and incomplete approach to statutory interpretation in a case like this cannot be acceptable or defensible on the facts and the law: *Dunsmuir*, above at para. 47.

[45] As I shall demonstrate, the purpose of paragraph 3(2)(a) of the Act is to bring Canadian law into accordance with international law and other domestic legislation, including the *Foreign Missions and International Organizations Act*, S.C. 1991, c. 41. The aim was to ensure that paragraph 3(2)(a)—which prohibits the Canadian-born children of employees of foreign governments from obtaining Canadian citizenship—applies only to those employees who benefit from diplomatic privileges and immunities from civil and/or criminal law. Under this interpretation, "employee[s] in Canada of a foreign government" includes only those who enjoy diplomatic privileges and immunities under the *Vienna Convention on Diplomatic Relations*, 500 U.N.T.S. 241.

[46] This purpose makes sense. There is a coherence to it. Citizens of Canada have duties and responsibilities to Canada. They are subject to all Canadian laws. Under this view of the matter, a child born to parents subject to Canadian laws is a person born in Canada for the purposes of Canadian citizenship laws and, thus, under paragraph 3(1)(a), becomes a Canadian citizen upon birth in Canada.

[47] Persons who have diplomatic privileges and immunities do not have duties and responsibilities to Canada and are not subject to all Canadian laws. As such, they and their children are prohibited from acquiring citizenship.

[48] In this regard, I agree with and endorse the following observation of the Federal Court in *Al-Ghamdi v. Canada (Foreign Affairs and International Trade)*, 2007 FC 559, 314 F.T.R. 1 at para. 63:

> It is precisely because of the vast array of privileges accorded to diplomats and their families, which are by their very nature inconsistent with the obligations of citizenship, that a person who enjoys diplomatic status cannot acquire citizenship.

In my view, only those who enjoy diplomatic privileges and immunities fall under the "employee[s] in Canada of a foreign government" exception in paragraph 3(2)(a) of the *Citizenship Act*.

(b) The Administrative Decision in More Detail

[49] The Registrar did not offer any significant reasons herself. However, … we may look to the record in order to discern the reasons. Here, it is reasonable to conclude that the Registrar's reasons are found in the analyst's report the Registrar received.

[50] The analyst's report concluded that for paragraph 3(2)(a) to apply, the foreign employee in Canada need not benefit from privileges and immunities. It reached this conclusion by looking only briefly at an amendment that superficially appeared to narrow the wording of the paragraph:

> The previous iteration of the exception of right to Canadian citizenship to persons born in Canada in the *Canadian Citizenship Act, 1947* is more narrow than the iteration found in subsection 3(2) of the current *Citizenship Act* as the earlier pro-

visions link the terms "representative" and "employee" to an official and/or recognized accreditation or, even more directly, to a diplomatic mission. The way in which subsection 3(2) of the *Citizenship Act* is written, however, differentiates "diplomatic or consular officers" from "representatives to employees of a foreign government."

[51] The analyst looked to the definition of "diplomatic or consular officers" in section 35 of the *Interpretation Act*—"includes an ambassador, envoy, minister, chargé d'affaires, counsellor, secretary, attaché, consul-general, consul, vice-consul, pro-consul, consular agent, acting consul-general, acting consul, acting vice-consul, acting consular agent, high commissioner, permanent delegate, adviser, acting high commissioner, and acting permanent delegate"—and concluded that "employee[s] in Canada of a foreign government" must mean something different.

[52] Textually and logically, this does not necessarily follow. Many persons occupying these offices are "employee[s] in Canada of a foreign government" in the sense that a foreign government employs them. And, as can be seen from the word "includes" in the definition of "diplomatic or consular officers," it is non-exhaustive.

(c) The Federal Court's Reasons

[53] The Federal Court held that "employee[s] in Canada of a foreign government" applied to all such employees, regardless of diplomatic or consular status. It held that to interpret paragraph 3(2)(a) in any other way would leave the section without any meaning.

[54] In my view, this implies that there can be no employees in Canada of a foreign government who have diplomatic or consular status and who are not diplomatic or consular officers. Put another way, the Federal Court has assumed that employees in Canada of a foreign government who have diplomatic privileges and immunities are the same persons as those who have diplomatic or consular status.

[55] This is not the case. There can be employees in Canada of a foreign government who do have privileges and immunities and who are not diplomatic or consular officers: see *Foreign Missions and International Organizations Act*, ss. 3 and 4 and Schedule II, articles 1, 41, 43, 49 and 53.

(d) Further Analysis of the Citizenship Act

[56] In my view, whether or not someone is an employee in Canada of a foreign government is just part of what triggers the operation of paragraph 3(2)(a) of the *Citizenship Act*. The additional element of diplomatic immunity triggers the paragraph. The text is consistent with this interpretation.

[57] Subsection 3(2) mirrors provisions in the *Foreign Missions and International Organizations Act* and the *Vienna Convention on Diplomatic Relations*: see, for example, the similar phrasing of certain terms in article 1 in the *Convention* and subsection 3(2) of the *Citizenship Act*. Together, the *Foreign Missions and International Organizations Act* and the *Vienna Convention on Diplomatic Relations*, among other things, provide for civil and criminal immunity for consular officials who carry out their responsibilities in Canada. The mirroring between these two and subsection 3(2) of the *Citizenship Act* strongly indicates a relationship between the two—i.e., that the presence of diplomatic immunity matters.

[58] According to the *Vienna Convention on Diplomatic Relations*, a consular officer is to protect in the receiving state (here Canada) the interests of the sending

(or foreign) state and its nationals within the limits set out in international law. It defines a consular official as any person entrusted with that capacity and diplomatic agents as members of the diplomatic staff of the mission. Persons not associated with the mission are not considered diplomatic staff and are outside of the Convention and, thus, are outside of the *Foreign Missions and International Organizations Act*. The appellant's parents, who as we shall see, in no way possessed diplomatic immunity, cannot fall under paragraph 3(2)(a) of the *Citizenship Act*.

[59] It is trite that subsection 3(2), including paragraph 3(2)(a), should be interpreted in accordance with relevant principles of customary and conventional international law, here the articles in the *Vienna Convention on Diplomatic Relations* that have been incorporated into Canadian law: *Foreign Missions and International Organizations Act*, s. 3; *R. v. Hape*, 2007 SCC 26, [2007] 2 S.C.R. 292 at paras. 35-39; *B010*, above at para. 47. This is all the more where the provision to be construed has been enacted with a view towards implementing international principles or against the backdrop of those principles: *National Corn Growers Assn. v. Canada (Import Tribunal)*, [1990] 2 S.C.R. 1234 at p. 1371.

[60] The articles of the *Vienna Convention* set out which officials of a foreign government enjoy diplomatic status and civil and criminal immunity. Under those provisions, certain employees of a foreign government can enjoy immunity.

[61] The context of paragraph 3(2)(a) of the *Citizenship Act* must also be examined. It sits within subsection 3(2) and, to some extent, draws meaning from the other paragraphs in the subsection. Key here is a portion of paragraph 3(2)(c). Subsection 3(2) in its entirety reads as follows:

(2) Paragraph (1)(a) does not apply to a person if, at the time of his birth, neither of his parents was a citizen or lawfully admitted to Canada for permanent residence and either of his parents was

    (a) a diplomatic or consular officer or other representative or employee in Canada of a foreign government;

    (b) an employee in the service of a person referred to in paragraph (a); or

    (c) an officer or employee in Canada of a specialized agency of the United Nations or an officer or employee in Canada of any other international organization <u>to whom there are granted, by or under any Act of Parliament, diplomatic privileges and immunities certified by the Minister of Foreign Affairs to be equivalent to those granted to a person or persons referred to in paragraph (a)</u>. [emphasis added]

(2) L'alinéa (1)a) ne s'applique pas à la personne dont, au moment de la naissance, les parents n'avaient qualité ni de citoyens ni de résidents permanents et dont le père ou la mère était :

    a) agent diplomatique ou consulaire, représentant à un autre titre ou au service au Canada d'un gouvernement étranger;

    b) au service d'une personne mentionnée à l'alinéa a);

    c) fonctionnaire ou au service, au Canada, d'une organisation internationale—notamment d'une institution spécialisée des Nations Unies—<u>bénéficiant sous le régime d'une loi fédérale de privilèges et immunités diplomatiques que le ministre des Affaires étrangères certifie être équivalents à ceux dont jouissent les personnes visées à l'alinéa a)</u>. [Non souligné dans l'original.]

[62] The underlined portions suggest that the persons referred to in paragraph 3(2)(*a*) have been granted "diplomatic privileges and immunities." Thus, paragraph 3(2)(*a*) covers only those "employee[s] in Canada of a foreign government" that have "diplomatic privileges and immunities."

[63] Also part of the context surrounding paragraph 3(2)(*a*) of the *Citizenship Act* is its legislative history.

[64] In 1946, any person born in Canada was entitled to Canadian citizenship as of right. No exceptions were made for the children of diplomats or others. See *The Citizenship Act*, S.C. 1946, c. 15.

[65] In 1950, the Act was amended. It provided in subsection 5(2) that if a person were born in Canada and the person's "responsible parent" was

- "an alien" and not a permanent resident, and
- a foreign diplomatic or consular officer or a representative of a foreign government accredited to His Majesty," "an employee of a foreign government attached to or in the service of a foreign diplomatic mission or consulate in Canada" or "an employee in the service" of "a foreign diplomat or consular officer,"

then the person was not entitled to Canadian citizenship by virtue of being born in Canada: *An Act to Amend the Canadian Citizenship Act*, S.C. 1950, c. 29, s. 2.

[66] In 1976, the new *Citizenship Act* came into force and, insofar as the sections in this case are concerned, there has been no change since. The new *Citizenship Act* changed old subsection 5(2) by removing the phrase "an employee of a foreign government" from "attached to or in the service of a foreign diplomatic mission or consulate in Canada" and placed it in new paragraph 3(2)(*a*): *Citizenship Act*, S.C. 1974-75-76, c. 108, ss. 3(2). It also excluded from acquiring Canadian citizenship those children born in Canada to officers or employees of an international organization "to whom there are granted ... diplomatic privileges or immunities certified ... to be equivalent" to "a diplomatic or consular officer or other representative or employee in Canada of a foreign government." This exemption appears as paragraph 3(2)(*c*) in the Act as it stands today.

[67] The analyst drew significance from the separation of "an employee of a foreign government" from "attached to or in the service of a foreign diplomatic mission or consulate in Canada" in the new subsection 3(2). This was incorrect; the Registrar's failure to examine the purpose and context of the provision caused a misunderstanding regarding how the various paragraphs in subsection 3(2) interrelate. If "a foreign diplomatic or consular officer or a representative of a foreign government" already included the idea of an employee of a foreign government who has immunity, the amendments to paragraph 3(2)(*a*) and 3(2)(*b*) merely clarified the legislative intent and eliminated a redundancy. Also of significance is paragraph 3(2)(*c*) that was introduced into the 1976 Act. As we have seen, it sheds further light on the meaning of paragraph 3(2)(*a*): employees falling in paragraph 3(2)(*a*) can only be those enjoying diplomatic privileges and immunities.

[68] A Minister commenting on the 1976 change stated that the government did not want to affect people working for large foreign corporations in the same way as diplomats or those working for international organizations like the United Nations who have immunities: J. Hugh Faulkner, Secretary of State of Canada, February 24, 1976, *Minutes of Proceedings and Evidence of the Standing Committee on Broadcasting, Films and Assistance to the Arts*. This purpose is consistent with the original purpose of the enactment which was to exclude all those, including those employed by foreign governments who have diplomatic immunities, from the benefit of citizenship.

[69] Another important element of context is the customary international law principle, *jus soli*, that is a backdrop to section 3 of the *Citizenship Act*. Under international law, the principle of *jus soli* gives nationality or citizenship to anyone born in the territory of a nation: Professor Ian Brownlie, *Principles of Public International Law*, 5th ed. (Oxford: Clarendon Press, 1998) at pp. 391-393. This is expressed in paragraph 3(1)(a) of the *Citizenship Act*. Paragraph 3(2)(a) derogates from this principle. Since paragraph 3(2)(a) takes away rights that would otherwise benefit from a broad and liberal interpretation, it should be interpreted narrowly: *Brossard v. Quebec*, [1988] 2 S.C.R. 279, 53 D.L.R. (4th) 609 at para. 56. The narrower interpretation is that not all employees of a foreign government fall in paragraph 3(2)(a); only those who have diplomatic immunity fall within it.

[70] In discussing the *jus soli* principle in his text, *Principles of Public International Law*, above, Professor Brownlie confirms that under international law, children born to those in a foreign nation who enjoy diplomatic immunities do not acquire the nationality of the foreign state. This is the principle that, in my view, pervades paragraph 3(2)(a) of the *Citizenship Act*. Professor Brownlie's analysis is at pages 389-390 of his text (the footnotes are reproduced in square brackets):

> A rule which has very considerable authority stipulated that children born to persons having diplomatic immunity shall not be nationals by birth of the state to which the diplomatic agent concerned is accredited. Thirteen governments stated the exception in the preliminaries of the Hague Codification Conference. In a comment [26 A.J. (1929), Spec. Suppl., p. 27] on the relevant article of the Harvard draft on diplomatic privileges and immunities it is stated: "This article is believed to be declaratory of an established rule of international law". The rule receives ample support from the legislation of states [See the *U.N. Legis. Series*, Laws Concerning Nationality (1954) Suppl. Vol. 1959] and expert opinion [Cordova, *Yrbk. ILC* (1953), ii 166 at 176 (Art. III); Guggenheim, i. 317]. The Convention on Certain Questions relating to the Conflict of Nationality Laws of 1930 provides in Article 12: "Rules of law which confer nationality by reason of birth on the territory of a State shall not apply automatically to children born to persons enjoying diplomatic immunities in the country where the birth occurs."
>
> In 1961 the United Nations Conference on Diplomatic Intercourse and Immunities adopted an Optional Protocol concerning Acquisition of Nationality [18 Apr.; 500 U.N.T.S/223 ...], which provided in Article II: "Members of the mission not being nationals of the receiving State and members of their families forming part of their household, shall not, solely by the operation of the law of the receiving State, acquire the nationality of that State" ... . In a few instances legislation [the *Canadian Citizenship Act, 1946*, as amended, s. 5(2) ...] and other prescriptions [...] exclude the *jus soli* in respect of the children of persons exercising official duties on behalf of a foreign government ... .

[71] In the above passage, Professor Brownlie cites Canada's first *Citizenship Act* as embodying the principle that the *jus soli* is excluded in respect of the children of persons exercising official duties on behalf of a foreign government who enjoy immunities. Is it conceivable that since 1946, by virtue of subsequent amendments to the *Citizenship Act*, Canada has departed from this international law principle? I would suggest not. Again, to the extent possible, Canadian legislation should be interpreted as being consistent with international law: see the authorities in paragraph 59, above.

[72] The interpretation of paragraph 3(2)(a) the appellant urges upon us and that which I have set about above is consistent with international law and, in the circumstances, is the only reasonable one that was available to the Registrar.

[73] The respondent submits that "[i]t is the intimate connection with the foreign government in Canada that triggers the provision." The respondent goes even further: under paragraph 3(2)(a), citizenship is to be denied to a child of a foreign national who was in Canada representing the "interests of his or her own government." And it applies to the children of foreign spies. Giving Canadian citizenship to the children of persons of that sort is "inconsistent with the duties and responsibilities of Canadian citizenship." See the respondent's memorandum of fact and law at paras. 72-76.

[74] It seems to me that the respondent is ascribing to paragraph 3(2)(a) a breadth that the text, context and purpose of the paragraph cannot bear. The respondent's interpretation does not explain why the language of subsection 3(2) of the Act borrows many of the same phrases that the *Vienna Convention on Diplomatic Relations* uses in the context of diplomatic immunity. Nor does it explain the legislative history of the subsection. The respondent's suggestion that the provision contemplates that the "interests" of a foreign national must be considered injects a qualitative element into the analysis, the sort of element that Parliament tries to avoid when defining who is a citizen and who is not. (On the need to interpret legislation in certain contexts in a manner that provides bright lines, see, *e.g.*, *Apotex Inc. v. Merck & Co., Inc.*, 2011 FCA 364, 430 N.R. 74 at para. 27.) In my view, much clearer and broader legislative text would be needed in order to persuade me that Parliament intended to exclude from citizenship a child of a foreign national who was in Canada representing the "interests of his or her own government."

(e) Application to the Facts of the Case

[75] The reasons of the Federal Court (at paras. 4-5) set out the facts pertaining to the appellant's parents the Registrar relied upon in applying paragraph 3(2)(a) of the *Citizenship Act* to the appellant and cancelling his Canadian citizenship:

> ... Both parents were charged [in the United States] with one count of conspiracy to act as unregistered agents of a foreign government and two counts of conspiracy to commit money laundering.
>
> The charges related to operations referred to in the United States as the "illegals" program. This constitutes a subversive program whereby foreign nationals, with the assistance of their governments, assume identities and live in the United States while performing "deep cover" foreign intelligence assignments. After undergoing extensive training in their own country, in this case, Russia, these agents work to obscure any ties between themselves and their true identities. They establish seemingly legitimate alternative lives, referred to as "legends," all the while taking direction from the Russian Foreign Intelligence (SVR) service. According to the charging documents, Mr. Vavilov's parents were known to be part of this program since the early 1990s, and were collecting intelligence for the SVR, who paid for their services. On July 8, 2010, Mr. Vavilov's parents pled guilty to the conspiracy charge and were returned to Russia in a spy swap the next day.

[76] Just from these facts alone, one can see that the appellant's parents never enjoyed any immunity from criminal prosecution. They were charged with criminal offences in the United States. Their status was the same in Canada.

[77] The analyst, whose report was relied upon by the Registrar, found the following:

> On the balance of probabilities, it is submitted that [the appellant's parents] were deployed to Canada, a "host country," specifically for the task of stealing the identities of Canadians and building their respective Canadian legends prior to relocating to the United States, the "target country," as Canadians.

[78] While in Canada, the appellant's parents were never enjoying civil or criminal immunity. The analyst found that they did not hold any form or level of diplomatic or consular status. It found that agents of the SVR (the Russian Foreign Intelligence service), which the appellant's parents were, are not afforded diplomatic or consular privileges because such a direct and overt association with Russian authorities would risk jeopardizing their capacity to create convincing and "non-Russian" legends.

[79] On these undisputed facts, and based on the above interpretation of paragraph 3(2)(a) of the *Citizenship Act*—the only reasonable interpretation available and the only one that is consistent with the text, context and purpose of the provision—the revocation of the appellant's citizenship cannot be sustained.

[80] Before concluding, I wish to deal with one reason offered by the Federal Court in upholding the reasonableness of the Registrar's decision. The Federal Court suggested the following (at para. 25):

> In my view the Registrar correctly found that this scenario is captured by s. 3(2)(a) of the *Citizenship Act*. To conclude otherwise would lead to the absurd result that children of a foreign diplomat, registered at an embassy, who conducts spy operations, cannot claim Canadian citizenship by birth in Canada but children of those who enter unlawfully for the very same purpose, become Canadian citizens by birth. The proper application of the rules of statutory interpretation should not lead to absurd results. (See: [Ruth Sullivan, *Statutory Interpretation*, 2nd ed., (Irwin Law Inc. 2007)] at 209).

[81] The absurdity here appears to be based on the Federal Court's own assessment of policy: spies are spies, and the children of spies should not receive Canadian citizenship.

[82] If we delve into our own assessments of policy, it could equally be said, perhaps, that the sins of parents ought not to be visited upon children without clear authorization by law. As well, the evidentiary record is full of evidence about how the appellant knew nothing of his parents' secret life and how much he regards himself as a Canadian.

[83] But, unless made legally relevant by some rule of common law or legislation on the books or a discretion legally bestowed, reviewing courts are not to have regard to such matters. Reviewing courts are restricted to the evidentiary record, the legislation and case law bearing on the problem, judicial understandings of the rule of law and constitutional standards—not freestanding policy divorced from those considerations.

[84] We all have freestanding policy views. But judicial review is about applying legal standards, not our own views of what may or may not be absurd: *Delios v. Canada (Attorney General)*, 2015 FCA 117, 472 N.R. 171 at paras. 38-39. The interpretive principle against absurdity applies to interpretations that run counter to legislative policy or, colloquially, "what the legislator must have intended"—not our own sense of what is right and wrong.

[85] Here, Parliament's legislation, viewed in light of its text, context and purpose, very much dictates the result of this judicial review. It is open to Parliament

to amend this legislation if, after judicial interpretation, it is not implementing the policies it considers appropriate.

. . .

E. Proposed Disposition

[90] The proper stated question and my proposed answer to it are as follows:

Question: Are the words "other representative or employee [in Canada] of a foreign government" found in paragraph 3(2)(a) of the *Citizenship Act* limited to foreign nationals [falling within these words] who [also] benefit from diplomatic privileges and immunities?

Answer: Yes.

[91] Therefore, for the foregoing reasons, I would allow the appeal, set aside the judgment of the Federal Court in file T-1976-14, allow the application for judicial review, and quash the decision of the Registrar to cancel the appellant's citizenship.

GLEASON JA (dissenting):

[92] I have read the reasons of my colleague, Stratas J.A. ... . However, with respect, I disagree with my colleague's analysis of the reasonableness of that decision and therefore would dismiss this appeal and answer the certified question in the negative.

[93] In my view, the breadth of the range of potential reasonable decisions in any given case is a function of the nature of the question before the administrative decision-maker whose decision is being reviewed and is not a function of the nature of the tribunal itself. Thus, the fact that the Registrar is acting under the *Citizenship Act* does not mean that her decision is, by that reason alone, entitled to a lesser degree of deference than the reasonableness standard would normally prescribe. Rather, the range of appreciation for her decision is informed by the nature of the question that was before her due to the teaching of the Supreme Court in *Dunsmuir*, which mandates a unified approach to judicial review of all administrative decisions.

[94] Questions that are poly-centric in nature or that involve the exercise of discretion by a decision-maker will often give rise to more than a single reasonable response and thus a variety of different determinations in respect of these sorts of questions may well be reasonable ... . The decision of the Supreme Court of Canada in *Khosa* [*Canada (Citizenship and Immigration) v Khosa*, 2009 SCC 12, [2009] 1 SCR 339] provides an example of a situation where a discretionary decision of a decision-maker in the immigration context was afforded considerable deference by the Supreme Court of Canada.

[95] Where the question examined by the administrative decision-maker involves statutory interpretation, the text, context and purpose of the provision as well as the reasons (if any) given by the administrative decision-maker will be relevant to discerning the reasonableness of the decision-maker's interpretation of the provision in its constituent statute ... .

[96] If the text of the provision in question rationally admits of more than one interpretation and the context and purpose of the provision do not clearly necessitate adopting one interpretation over the other, I believe that the choice of the administrative decision-maker to adopt one among competing interpretations must be afforded deference. To conclude otherwise is to engage in correctness review as in such circumstances the reviewing court is substituting its views for those of the tribunal on the basis of disagreement as to the correct interpretation

of the provision in question, even though the interpretation of the administrative decision-maker is defensible as a rational textual interpretation that is not necessarily negated by the context or purpose of the provision.

[97] Considerations other than these may also impact the reasonableness of an administrative decision-maker's interpretation. Notably, where that decision-maker declines to follow a well-established line of authority on a point, its decision may well be unreasonable ... .

[98] Turning to the present case, I believe that the text of paragraph 3(2)(a) of the Act admits of at least two rational interpretations: either the term "employee" means what it plainly states and includes all employees of a foreign government who have children in Canada or conversely, as urged by the appellant, the term "employee" includes only those employees of a foreign government who enjoy diplomatic immunity and who have children in Canada. A strong case can be made for the former interpretation as the appellant's interpretation requires the reader to read words into the text of the legislative provision that were abrogated by Parliament in 1976 when it deleted the words "attached to or in the service of a foreign diplomatic mission or consulate in Canada" from the provision covering included "employees." Given the contextual factors framing the provision, I believe it reasonable to interpret this amendment to be substantive and informative, contrary to what is argued by the appellant.

[99] More specifically, I do not find that the context or purpose of the provision necessarily mandates the appellant's interpretation. The comments made by former Secretary of State of Canada J. Hugh Faulkner in 1976 when paragraph 3(2)(c) was adopted are not dispositive as they concern a different provision and, indeed, the difference in wording between paragraphs 3(2)(c) and 3(2)(a) of the Act can reasonably be read to support the interpretation of the Registrar.

[100] Whereas paragraph 3(2)(a) includes no express requirement that covered employees be subject to diplomatic immunity, paragraph 3(2)(c) specifically covers only employees of international organizations who "are granted [...] diplomatic privileges and immunities certified by the Minister of Foreign Affairs to be equivalent to those granted to a person or persons referred to in paragraph (a)." The absence of such a requirement in paragraph (a) makes it possible to interpret that paragraph as including both employees who enjoy and those who do not enjoy diplomatic immunity. The addition of the words "equivalent to those granted to a person or persons referred to in paragraph (a)" at the end of paragraph 3(2)(c) does not necessarily mean that one must conclude that the employees mentioned in paragraph 3(2)(a) of the Act are only those who are entitled to diplomatic immunity as paragraph 3(2)(c) merely creates a parallelism with paragraph (a) and leaves unanswered the question that was before the Registrar in this case, namely, what the term "employee" in paragraph 3(2)(a) of the Act means.

[101] As for issues related to the context and purpose flowing from the *Vienna Convention on Diplomatic Relations*, I likewise believe that this Convention does not necessarily mandate the result urged by the appellant because the Convention and the Canadian domestic legislation that adopts the Convention do not draw a bright line between those who possess diplomatic immunity and those who do not. In fact, by its incorporation of the Convention, the *Foreign Missions and International Organizations Act* extends only partial immunity to entire classes of employees. More specifically, by virtue of Article 37 of the Convention, which is Schedule I to the statute, lower level employees of foreign governments in Canada enjoy certain categories of diplomatic immunity only in respect of acts performed within the course and scope of their duties on behalf of the foreign government. Some employees—"service staff" for example—are thus amendable to civil suit and

to the process of Canadian criminal courts in respect of acts and omissions that fall outside the scope of their employment duties. Article 37 of the Convention, which is Schedule I to the *Foreign Missions and International Organizations Act* provides:

1 The members of the family of a diplomatic agent forming part of his household shall, if they are not nationals of the receiving State, enjoy the privileges and immunities specified in Articles 29 to 36.

2 Members of the administrative and technical staff of the mission, together with members of their families forming part of their respective households, shall, if they are not nationals of or permanently resident in the receiving State, enjoy the privileges and immunities specified in Articles 29 to 35, except that the immunity from civil and administrative jurisdiction of the receiving State specified in paragraph 1 of Article 31 shall not extend to acts performed outside the course of their duties. They shall also enjoy the privileges specified in Article 36, paragraph 1, in respect of articles imported at the time of first installation.

3 Members of the service staff of the mission who are not nationals of or permanently resident in the receiving State shall enjoy immunity in respect of acts performed in the course of their duties, exemption from dues and taxes on the emoluments they receive by reason of their employment and the exemption contained in Article 33.

4 Private servants of members of the mission shall, if they are not nationals of or permanently resident in the receiving State, be exempt from dues and taxes on the emoluments they receive by reason of their employment. In other respects, they may enjoy privileges and immunities only to the extent admitted by the receiving State. However, the receiving State must exercise its jurisdiction over these persons in such a manner as not to interfere unduly with the performance of the functions of the mission.

1 Les membres de la famille de l'agent diplomatique qui font partie de son ménage bénéficient des privilèges et immunités mentionnés dans les articles 29 à 36, pourvu qu'ils ne soient pas ressortissants de l'État accréditaire.

2 Les membres du personnel administratif et technique de la mission, ainsi que les membres de leurs familles qui font partie de leurs ménages respectifs, bénéficient, pourvu qu'ils ne soient pas ressortissants de l'État accréditaire ou n'y aient pas leur résidence permanente, des privilèges et immunités mentionnés dans les articles 29 à 35, sauf que l'immunité de la juridiction civile et administrative de l'État accréditaire mentionnée au paragraphe 1 de l'article 31 ne s'applique pas aux actes accomplis en dehors de l'exercice de leurs fonctions. Ils bénéficieront aussi des privilèges mentionnés au paragraphe 1 de l'article 36 pour ce qui est des objets importés lors de leur première installation.

3 Les membres du personnel de service de la mission qui ne sont pas ressortissants de l'État accréditaire ou n'y ont pas leur résidence permanente bénéficient de l'immunité pour les actes accomplis dans l'exercice de leurs fonctions, et de l'exemption des impôts et taxes sur les salaires qu'ils reçoivent du fait de leurs services, ainsi que de l'exemption prévue à l'article 33.

4 Les domestiques privés des membres de la mission qui ne sont pas ressortissants de l'État accréditaire ou n'y ont pas leur résidence permanente sont exemptés des impôts et taxes sur les salaires qu'ils reçoivent du fait de leurs services. À tous autres égards, ils ne bénéficient des privilèges et immunités que dans la mesure admise par l'État accréditaire. Toutefois, l'État accréditaire doit exercer sa juridiction sur ces personnes de façon à ne pas entraver d'une manière excessive l'accomplissement des fonctions de la mission.

[102] As many employees of foreign governments therefore enjoy only partial immunity in Canada, it is impossible to conclude that such employees' "privileges [...] are by their very nature inconsistent with the obligations of citizenship," as stated at paragraph 63 in the *Al-Ghamdi* case relied on by my colleague.

[103] I therefore believe that it was open to the Registrar to conclude as she did and that it was reasonable to determine that the appellant's parents fall within the scope of paragraph 3(2)(a) of the Act, which disentitles the appellant to Canadian citizenship. I would therefore have dismissed this appeal and answered the certified question in the negative.

1. Identify the main interpretive principles Stratas JA uses and explain how they help him construct a different conclusion than Federal Court reached. Take special note of how Stratas JA uses the presumption of coherence.
2. Why does Gleason JA disagree with Stratas JA? Are her reasons similar to or different from Bell J's reasons?
3. How does this case raise separation of powers concerns?
4. In your legal opinion, who provides the interpretation that best fits legislative intent—Bell J, Stratas JA, or Gleason JA?

The Supreme Court of Canada largely agreed in substance with Stratas JA's interpretive analysis and also concluded that the Registrar of Citizenship made an unreasonable decision. Because no purpose would have been served to remit the matter back for redetermination by the Registrar, the Court applied the *jus soli* principle that persons born in Canada are citizens and declared that Vavilov was a Canadian citizen. When reading this excerpt, think about how much *weight* the Court gives to the citizenship by birth principle as well as consideration of the consequences that the Registrar's interpretation would have had for Vavilov. Lastly, Chapter 11 contains the Court's reformulation of the standard of review and the role of reasons in judicial review of executive actors.

Canada (Minister of Citizenship and Immigration) v Vavilov
2019 SCC 65

WAGNER CJ and MOLDAVER, GASCON, CÔTÉ, BROWN, ROWE, and MARTIN JJ:

• • •

(d) Possible Consequences of the Registrar's Interpretation

[189] When asked why the children of individuals referred to in s. 3(2)(a) would be excluded from acquiring citizenship by birth, another analyst involved in Mr. Vavilov's file (who had also been involved in Mr. Vavilov's brother's file) responded as follows:

> Well, usually the way we use section 3(2)(a) is for—you're right, for diplomats and that they don't—because they are not—they are not obliged ... to the law of Canada and everything, so that's why their children do not obtain citizenship if they were born in Canada while the person was in Canada under that status. But then there is also this other part of the Act that says other representatives or employees of a foreign government in Canada, that may open the door for other person than diplomats and that's how we interpreted in this specific case 3(2)(a) but there is no jurisprudence on that.

(R.R. transcript, at pp. 87-88)

[190] In other words, the officials responsible for these files were aware that s. 3(2)(a) was informed by the principle that individuals subject to the exception are "not obliged ... to the law of Canada." They were also aware that the interpretation they had adopted in the case of the Vavilov brothers was a novel one. Although the Registrar knew this, she failed to provide a rationale for this expanded interpretation.

[191] Additionally, there is no evidence that the Registrar considered the potential consequences of expanding her interpretation of s. 3(2)(a) to include individuals who have not been granted diplomatic privileges and immunities. Citizenship has been described as "the right to have rights": U.S. Supreme Court Chief Justice Earl Warren, as quoted in A. Brouwer, *Statelessness in Canadian Context: A Discussion Paper* (July 2003) (online), at p. 2. The importance of citizenship was recognized in *Benner v. Canada (Secretary of State)*, [1997] 1 S.C.R. 358, in which Iacobucci J., writing for this Court, stated: "I cannot imagine an interest more fundamental to full membership in Canadian society than Canadian citizenship": para. 68. This was reiterated in *Canada (Minister of Citizenship and Immigration) v. Tobiass*, [1997] 3 S.C.R. 391, in which this Court unanimously held that "[f]or some, such as those who might become stateless if deprived of their citizenship, it may be valued as highly as liberty": para. 108.

[192] It perhaps goes without saying that rules concerning citizenship require a high degree of interpretive consistency in order to shield against a perception of arbitrariness and to ensure conformity with Canada's international obligations. We can therefore only assume that the Registrar intended that this new interpretation of s. 3(2)(a) would apply to any other individual whose parent is employed by or represents a foreign government at the time of the individual's birth in Canada but has not been granted diplomatic privileges and immunities. The Registrar's interpretation would not, after all, limit the application of s. 3(2)(a) to the children of spies—its logic would be equally applicable to a number of other scenarios, including that of a child of a non-citizen worker employed by an embassy as a gardener or cook, or of a child of a business traveller who represents a foreign government-owned corporation. Mr. Vavilov had raised the fact that provisions such as s. 3(2)(a) must be given a narrow interpretation because they deny or potentially take away rights—that of citizenship under s. 3(1) in this case—which otherwise benefit from a liberal and broad interpretation: *Brossard (Town) v. Québec (Commission des droits de la personne)*, [1988] 2 S.C.R. 279, at p. 307. Yet there is no indication that the Registrar considered the potential harsh consequences of her interpretation for such a large class of individuals, which included Mr. Vavilov, or the question whether, in light of those possible consequences, Parliament would have intended s. 3(2)(a) to apply in this manner.

[193] Moreover, we would note that despite following a different legal process, the Registrar's decision in this case had the same effect as a revocation of citizenship—a process which has been described by scholars as "a kind of 'political death'"—depriving Mr. Vavilov of his right to vote and the right to enter and remain in Canada: see A. Macklin, "Citizenship Revocation, the Privilege to Have Rights and the Production of the Alien" (2014), 40 *Queen's L.J.* 1, at pp. 7-8. While we question whether the Registrar was empowered to unilaterally alter Canada's position with respect to Mr. Vavilov's citizenship and recognize that the relationship between the cancellation of a citizenship certificate under s. 26 of the *Citizenship Regulations* and the revocation of an individual's citizenship (as set out in s. 10 of the *Citizenship Act*) is not clear, we leave this issue for another day because it was neither raised nor argued by the parties.

D. SOME FURTHER CASES EMPLOYING THE MODERN APPROACH AND SPECIFIC PRESUMPTIONS

Opitz v Wrzesnewskyj, 2012 SCC 55, [2012] 3 SCR 76 (see Chapter 6), is a case that significantly relies on the "associated words" presumption (*noscitur a sociis* or "it is known by its associates") under the modern approach. This common law presumption is invoked when analogous meaning is possible for two or more words linked by "and" or "or," and we must find a common feature among these terms. The principle tells the interpreter that words take their colour from the context. You must therefore consider the words that surround the specific word in question and ask what words are analogous to one another and how they limit and inform each other. Consider this example: If a statute requires that "floors, steps, stairs, passageways, and ramps" must be kept free from obstruction, is a floor that is used for storage included under this rule? Keep in mind that the *noscitur a sociis* principle should be used for specific words, while the *ejusdem generis* or "limited class" rule is used for general words (i.e., where the text sets out a list of specific words followed by a general term, it is usually appropriate to limit the general term to the preceding more specific terms). The central issue in the *Opitz* case is whether the losing candidate, Borys Wrzesnewskyj, could have a court annul the election on the basis that there were "irregularities ... that affected the result of the election" (s 524(1)(b) of the *Canada Elections Act*). When you read this case and encounter s 524(1) of the Act in that excerpt, ask yourself:

1. What do you think the purpose of this provision is?
2. What company does "irregularities" keep? What is the common thread? How is the term restricted in its meaning?
3. What, if any, thresholds does the provision contain that a person who wishes to control an election must meet?
4. Both the majority and dissent invoke the associated words rule and say they are using the modern approach. Which judgment do you find more persuasive?

E. THE CONTEXTUAL AND PURPOSIVE APPROACH WITHIN THE MODERN APPROACH

For many exercises in statutory interpretation, the beginning and end point is the grammatical and ordinary sense of the text. Traditionally, highly dynamic approaches such as the "living tree" approach were reserved for constitutional documents to allow for the evolution of meaning in response to linguistic, political, and social change. Over time, a parallel method of interpreting ordinary legislation evolved, particularly when that legislation was accorded special status. For example, for so-called "quasi-constitutional" texts such as human rights legislation and ordinary legislation relating to Indigenous peoples or affecting their rights, a dynamic, large, liberal, and purposive approach will be the appropriate starting point. This is to ensure that protected rights are given a broad interpretation, while exceptions and defences are given a narrow construction. By way of contrast, penal legislation attracts strict construction because of the potential for serious consequences. Fiscal legislation, on the other hand, used to be interpreted using a strict and literal approach, but it is now subject to the modern principle.

The *Mossop* case below highlights starkly different interpretive approaches to the meaning of the words "family status" in the *Canadian Human Rights Act*, RSC 1985, c H-6. Justice L'Heureux-Dubé is a judge who was well known for applying a robust contextual and purposive methodological approach in order to determine legislative intent under the modern principle. By methodology we mean: How does she go about constructing a persuasive and valid answer to an interpretive dispute? In *Mossop*, she employs principles of interpretation for human rights legislation; Charter values; bilingual text; text and social context; attentiveness to the decision that the Human Rights Tribunal made; and extrinsic aids such as legislative history, reports from parliamentary standing committees, and secondary literature written by academics. Notice how she returns repeatedly to a consideration of the mischief the statute was meant to cure, not only in the past, but in contemporary times.

Contrast her approach to that of Lamer CJ and La Forest J. What are the pros and cons regarding L'Heureux-Dubé J's robust dynamic approach? What are the pros and cons concerning the static approach used in the other two judgments? In your legal opinion, are any of the judgments "activist"?

Canada (AG) v Mossop
[1993] 1 SCR 554

[The following account of the facts and judicial history of this case is taken from the judgment of Lamer CJ, who wrote the majority judgment. In the official report of the case, Lamer CJ's judgment appears first. However, in the version below, the dissenting judgment of L'Heureux-Dubé J is set out after Lamer CJ's introduction. Justice L'Heureux-Dubé fully canvasses the issues raised by the case and offers an accurate account of the principles governing the interpretation of human rights legislation.]

LAMER CJ:

I. Facts

In June 1985, the complainant Brian Mossop was employed in Toronto as a translator for the Department of the Secretary of State. On June 3, 1985, Mossop attended the funeral of the father of the man whom Mossop described as his lover. Mossop testified that the two men have known each other since 1974, and have resided together since 1976 in a jointly owned and maintained home. They share the day-to-day developments in their lives and maintain a sexual relationship. Each has made the other the beneficiary of his will. They are known to their friends and families as lovers.

At the time, Mossop's terms of employment were governed by a collective agreement between the Treasury Board and the Canadian Union of Professional and Technical Employees ("CUPTE"). Article 19.02 of this agreement contained a provision relating to bereavement leave calling for up to four days' leave upon the death of a member of an employee's "immediate family." This term was defined as:

> ... father, mother, brother, sister, spouse (including common-law spouse resident with the employee), child (including child of common-law spouse), or ward of the employee, father-in-law, mother-in-law, and in addition a relative who permanently resides in the employee's household or with whom the employee permanently resides.

In the definition section of the agreement, at art. 2.01(s), it was provided that:

> (s) a "common-law spouse" relationship is said to exist when, for a continuous period of at least one year, an employee has lived with a person of the opposite sex, publicly represented that person to be his/her spouse, and lives and intends to continue to live with that person as if that person were his/her spouse.

The day after the funeral, Mossop applied for bereavement leave pursuant to art. 19.02 of the collective agreement. The application was turned down, and Mossop declined to accept the day of special leave he was offered in its stead.

When his grievance, filed with the approval of and pursued by his union, was rejected on the basis that the denial of his application was in accordance with the collective agreement, Mossop went to the appellant, the Canadian Human Rights Commission. There he laid complaints against his employer, the Department of the Secretary of State (to which was later added the Treasury Board), and his union, CUPTE. The complaints invoked ss. 7(b), 9(1)(c) and 10(b) of the *Canadian Human Rights Act*, RSC, 1985, c. H-6 (formerly SC 1976-77, c. 33, as amended) ("the CHRA").

• • •

II. Relevant Statutory Provisions

Canadian Human Rights Act, RSC, 1985, c. H-6

3(1) For all purposes of this Act, race, national or ethnic origin, colour, religion, age, sex, marital status, family status, disability and conviction for which a pardon has been granted are prohibited grounds of discrimination.

3(1) Pour l'application de la présente loi, les motifs de distinction illicite sont ceux qui sont fondés sur la race, l'origine nationale ou ethnique, la couleur, la religion, l'âge, le sexe, l'état matrimonial, la situation de famille, l'état de personne graciée ou la déficience.

7. It is a discriminatory practice, directly or indirectly,

• • •

(b) in the course of employment, to differentiate adversely in relation to an employee,

on a prohibited ground of discrimination.

9(1) It is a discriminatory practice for an employee organization on a prohibited ground of discrimination

• • •

(c) to limit, segregate, classify or otherwise act in relation to an individual in a way that would deprive the individual of employment opportunities, or limit employment opportunities or otherwise adversely affect the status of the individual, where the individual is a member of the organization or where any of the obligations of the organization pursuant to a collective agreement relate to the individual.

10. It is a discriminatory practice for an employer, employee organization or organization of employers

• • •

(b) to enter into an agreement affecting recruitment, referral, hiring, promotion, training, apprenticeship, transfer or any other matter relating to employment or prospective employment,

that deprives or tends to deprive an individual or class of individuals of any employment opportunities on a prohibited ground of discrimination.

III. Judgments

Canadian Human Rights Tribunal (1989), 10 CHRR D/6064

The Tribunal identified the fundamental question as being whether the denial of bereavement leave in accordance with the collective agreement was based on family status, the prohibited ground of discrimination cited by Mossop. ...

• • •

[The tribunal concluded that the Treasury Board and CUPTE had infringed s 10(b) by entering into a collective agreement that reserved certain benefits to common law couples of the opposite sex, thereby excluding same-sex couples. It wrote:]

> Having determined that persons of the same sex *prima facie* may have the status of a family under the *Act*, and having determined that the family of the complainant is treated differently under the *Act* than other families, including but not limited to families which are very similar in their characteristics to that of the complainant, this Tribunal therefore finds that the collective agreement deprived the complainant of the employment opportunity of bereavement leave on a prohibited ground of discrimination, and that therefore each of the Treasury Board and CUPTE have committed a discriminatory practice under s. 10(b) of the *Act*.

• • •

Federal Court of Appeal, [1991] 1 FC 18

Marceau JA ... held that the Tribunal erred in interpreting the term "family status" in the CHRA as including a homosexual relationship between two individuals. In so concluding, Marceau JA examined the propositions on which the Tribunal based its reasoning and noted that only a legal approach could lead to a proper understanding of the term "family status." In this respect, he stated, at p. 35:

> To these serious difficulties I have with the propositions adopted by the Tribunal, I will add my concern with an approach that simply forgets that the word "family" is not used in isolation in the Act, but rather coupled with the word "status." A status, to me, is primarily a legal concept which refers to the particular position of a person with respect to his or her rights and limitations as a result of his or her being member of some legally recognized and regulated group. I fail to see how any approach other than a legal one could lead to a proper understanding of what is meant by the phrase "family status." Even if we were to accept that two homosexual lovers can constitute "sociologically speaking" a sort of family, it is certainly not one which is now recognized by law as giving its members special rights and obligations.

He added that the *CHRA* was amended in 1983, to express in English what the French version was already saying, "so that the English version must be taken to express the notion underlying the words used in French." He then concluded as follows, at p. 36:

> So, the reasoning of the Tribunal simply does not appear to me acceptable. The Tribunal had no authority to reject the generally understood meaning given to the word "family" and to adopt in its stead, through a consciously *ad hoc* approach, a meaning ill-adapted to the context in which the word appears and obviously not in conformity with what was intended when the word was introduced, as shown by the legislative history of the amendment.

In his analysis of the real issue underlying the complaint, Marceau noted that sexual orientation was the real ground of discrimination involved. ...

[Stone JA concurred in the result.]

L'HEUREUX-DUBÉ J (dissenting): I have had the opportunity of reading the reasons of Chief Justice Lamer and Justice La Forest, and with respect, I cannot agree with them nor with their disposition of this appeal. As the Chief Justice notes, this appeal concerns the interpretation of the term "family status," one of the enumerated grounds of discrimination in s. 3 of the *Canadian Human Rights Act*, RSC, 1985, c. H-6 (formerly SC 1976-77, c. 33 as amended) (the "Act"). ...

• • •

"Family Status" in s. 3 of the Act

1. Interpretation of Human Rights Legislation

It is well established in the jurisprudence of this Court that human rights legislation has a unique quasi-constitutional nature, and that it is to be given a large, purposive and liberal interpretation. [Citations omitted.] This long line of cases mandates that courts interpret human rights legislation in a manner consistent with its overarching goals, recognizing as did my colleague Sopinka J for the majority in *Zurich* ... , at p. 339, that such legislation is often "the final refuge of the disadvantaged and the disenfranchised." In interpreting a statute, *Charter* values must not be ignored. As McIntyre J observed in *RWDSU v. Dolphin Delivery Ltd.*, [1986] 2 SCR 573, at p. 602, referring to *Re Blainey and Ontario Hockey Association* (1986), 26 DLR (4th) 728:

> *Blainey* then affords an illustration of the manner in which *Charter* rights of private individuals may be enforced and protected by the courts, that is, by measuring legislation—government action—against the *Charter*.

In *Hills v. Canada (Attorney General)*, [1988] 1 SCR 513, at p. 558, for the majority, I stressed that "the values embodied in the *Charter* must be given preference over an interpretation which would run contrary to them." ...

The respondent Attorney General of Canada argued that, although the Act should be interpreted as remedial legislation, the ordinary rules of interpretation should apply. Therefore, the Court of Appeal correctly examined the "plain meaning" and textual context of the term, as well as the intention of Parliament. As can be discerned from my opinion in *Thomson Newspapers Ltd. v. Canada (Director of Investigation and Research, Restrictive Trade Practices Commission)*, [1990] 1 SCR 425, at p. 570, I would agree that the rules of interpretation which have guided the courts to this day have not been set aside, and that they continue to play a role in the interpretation of legislation, including constitutional and quasi-constitutional documents. However, I also note Laskin CJ's words in *Miller v. The Queen*, [1977] 2 SCR 680, at p. 690, that the Court had a duty "not to whittle down the protections of the *Canadian Bill of Rights* by a narrow construction of what is a quasi-constitutional document." This observation applies *a fortiori* to human rights legislation, and has continued to be an important caution in the era of the Charter. In *Action Travail des Femmes* ... , Dickson CJ reviewed the jurisprudence on the interpretation of human rights legislation and, at p. 1134, stated the principle as follows:

> Human rights legislation is intended to give rise, amongst other things, to individual rights of vital importance, rights capable of enforcement, in the final analysis, in a court of law. I recognize that in the construction of such legislation the words of the Act must be given their plain meaning, but it is equally important that the rights enunciated be given their full recognition and effect. We should not search for ways and means to minimize those rights and to enfeeble their proper impact. Although it may seem commonplace, it may be wise to remind ourselves of the statutory guidance given by the federal *Interpretation Act* which asserts that statutes are deemed to be remedial and are thus to be given such fair, large and liberal interpretation as will best ensure that their objects are attained.

The Court has repeatedly warned of the dangers of strict or legalistic approaches which would restrict or defeat the purpose of quasi-constitutional documents. For example, in *Tremblay v. Daigle*, [1989] 2 SCR 530, at p. 553, this Court made it clear that the meaning of highly controversial terms "cannot be settled by linguistic fiat." (On avoiding narrow and technical interpretations of *Charter* rights, see also *Law*

Society of Upper Canada v. Skapinker, [1984] 1 SCR 357, at pp. 365-67; *R v. Duarte,* [1990] 1 SCR 30; on avoiding inflexible categorizations, see *Re BC Motor Vehicle Act,* [1985] 2 SCR 486.)

The remarks of Wilson J in *Thomson Newspapers Ltd. v. Canada (Director of Investigation and Research, Restrictive Trade Practices Commission), supra,* at p. 470, are apposite here:

> The principle of statutory construction, *expressio unius,* is ill-suited to meet the needs of *Charter* interpretation. It is inconsistent with the purposive approach to *Charter* interpretation which has been endorsed by the Court and which focuses on the broad purposes for which the rights were designed and not on mechanical rules which have traditionally been employed in interpreting detailed provisions of ordinary statutes in order to discern legislative intent.

Although made in the context of the *Charter,* and while it is clear that there are differences between constitutional and quasi-constitutional documents, these comments apply here since both types of documents require an interpretive approach that is broad and purposive, and identifies the values which the legislation was designed to protect. McIntyre J clearly was of this view when, speaking for a unanimous Court in *Ontario Human Rights Commission v. Simpsons-Sears,* [[1985] 2 SCR 536], at pp. 546-47, he wrote:

> It is not, in my view, a sound approach to say that according to established rules of construction no broader meaning can be given to the Code than the narrowest interpretation of the words employed. The accepted rules of construction are flexible enough to enable the Court to recognize in the construction of a human rights code the special nature and purpose of the enactment (see Lamer J in *Insurance Corporation of British Columbia v. Heerspink,* [1982] 2 SCR 145, at pp. 157-58), and give to it an interpretation which will advance its broad purposes. Legislation of this type is of a special nature, not quite constitutional but certainly more than the ordinary—and it is for the courts to seek out its purpose and give it effect. The Code aims at the removal of discrimination. This is to state the obvious. Its main approach, however, is not to punish the discriminator, but rather to provide relief for the victims of discrimination.

In short, though traditional interpretational tools ought not be ignored, they must be applied in the context of a broad and purposive approach.

2. Purpose of the Act

The purpose of the Act, set out in s. 2 recited earlier, is to ensure that people have an equal opportunity to make for themselves the life that they are able and wish to have without being hindered by discriminatory practices. The social cost of discrimination is insupportably high, and these insidious practices are damaging not only to the individuals who suffer the discrimination, but also to the very fabric of our society. This Court decried the multiple harms caused by discrimination in the context of hate promotion in *R v. Keegstra,* [1990] 3 SCR 697. Dickson CJ remarked, at pp. 746-47, that the consequences of such discriminatory practices "bear heavily in a nation that prides itself on tolerance and the fostering of human dignity through, among other things, respect for the many racial, religious and cultural groups in our society." As McIntyre J confirmed in *Andrews v. Law Society of British Columbia,* [1989] 1 SCR 143, at p. 172, "[d]iscrimination is unacceptable in a democratic society because it epitomizes the worst effects of the denial of equality." The Act, in prohibiting certain forms of discrimination, has the express purpose of promoting the value of equality which lies at the centre of a free and democratic society. Our society is one of rich diversity, and the Act fosters the principle that all members of the community deserve to be treated with dignity, concern, respect and consideration, and are entitled to a community free from discrimination.

• • •

3. Textual Interpretation

It was argued that a correct interpretive approach would warrant that a textual interpretation be determinative, and that the coupling of the terms "family" and "status" in the English text of s. 3 of the Act required the Tribunal to construe "family status" as including only those families who have recognizable status at law. This is the way that the Court of Appeal approached the matter. Leaving aside for the moment the broad and purposive approach which, in my view, should guide the interpretation of human rights legislation, even if one were to take a textual approach to the interpretation of s. 3 of the Act, the result of such an interpretive exercise would not lead to the conclusions of the Court of Appeal, but rather would, in my view, support the Tribunal's findings.

First, the word "status" is capable of bearing several meanings. The *Concise Oxford Dictionary of Current English* (8th ed. 1990) provides the following definition:

> 1. social position, rank, relation to others, relative importance ... . 2. (Law). person's relation to others as fixed by law ... . 3. position of affairs ...

While the term "status" may be used to indicate status at law, it may indicate more factual matters of rank, social position, or relation to others. The use of the term "status" is not sufficient by itself to restrict the notion of "family status" to only those families that are recognized at law. Reference to the French version of the term, "*situation de famille*," is warranted here. *Le Petit Robert* (1990) provides the following definitions of the term "situation":

> 1. Le fait d'être en un lieu; manière dont une chose est disposée, située ou orientée ... . 2. Ensemble des circonstances dans lesquelles une personne se trouve ... . 3. Emploi, post rémunérateur régulier et stable ...

"*Situation*" is not a legal term, is broader than the English term "status," and encompasses a host of meanings. When the meaning of the French term is considered, it is apparent that the scope of "family status" has potential to be very broad. In French, the term "*situation de famille*" would not be used to express a legal notion. "*État matrimonial*" would.

As noted in the Court of Appeal reasons, until 1983, the French text of the Act prohibited discrimination on the basis of "*situation de famille*" while the English text of the Act prohibited discrimination on the basis of "marital status." In 1983 the Act was amended, the French text to include both "*situation de famille*" and "*état matrimonial*," the English text to include both "marital status" and "family status." The amendment did not simply modify the existing terms, but in fact expanded the Act. Had the intention been to narrow the scope of protection, it would have been simple to use one term or the other. In my view the purpose of the amendment could only have been to envelop the two notions. Furthermore, if both terms "*situation de famille*" and "*état matrimonial*," "marital status" and "family status," in the French or in the English texts, were similar, there would have been no need to juxtapose them. One such expression would have been sufficient as the legislator is not presumed to use meaningless words (P.-A. Côté, *The Interpretation of Legislation in Canada* (2nd ed. 1992), at p. 232).

In any event, I have difficulty with the Court of Appeal's proposition that the meaning of "family status" and its French equivalent can be determined through reference to what it found to be the more restrictive English term. First, as I have noted above, the English term is not necessarily more restrictive. Second, even if it could be said that "family status" encompassed only families with legal status, it would be highly inappropriate to interpret the term by relying on the more narrow meaning of the French and English texts. It is an established principle of interpretation in Canada that French and English texts of legislation are deemed to be equally authoritative (*R v. Turpin*, [1989] 1 SCR 1296), and where there is a discrepancy between the two, it is the meaning which furthers the purpose of the legislation which must prevail (*R v. Collins*, [1987] 1 SCR 265; see also P.-A. Côté, *supra*, at pp. 272-79). In this case, given that the purpose of the Act is to prevent discrimination and provide an equal opportunity to make the type of life one wishes, the broader of the two meanings should prevail.

A textual interpretation seems to me to support the conclusion of the Tribunal that "family status" should not be restricted to a narrow legal meaning. Nothing in the textual context indicates that the protection of the Act is to be extended only to certain types of legally validated families. On the contrary, the term "family status" suggests a broader protection that would prohibit discrimination against individuals on the basis of the internal structuring of their families. But, as I said above, a strict textual interpretation is not warranted here. That leaves then the argument concerning legislative intent.

4. Purpose and Intent

The intervener Focus on the Family asserted that the Tribunal should have considered the proceedings in Parliament in an attempt to more accurately discern the intention of Parliament at the time of the legislative enactment. They submitted that the extension of the term "family status" to include same-sex relationships would usurp the legislative function of Parliament, and give the term a meaning never intended by Parliament. This argument implies that the Tribunal exceeded its jurisdiction by interpreting the scope of "family status" as it did.

First, as regards the amendment itself and referring to the evidence before the Tribunal, this intervener argued that legislative debate supports their assertion that the members of the legislature intended the amendment simply to bring the French and English texts into conformity. As Lord Watson observed in *Salomon v. Salomon & Co.*, [1897] AC 22, at p. 38, the "Intention of the Legislature" is a common but very slippery phrase." Legislative intention can be difficult to ascertain, and it is dangerous to rely only on the legislative record in order to infer that intent. While such record may be of some assistance in certain types of cases (for example *Re Anti-Inflation Act*, [1976] 2 SCR 373), legislative intent is derived primarily from the legislation itself ... .

With this caveat, had Parliament intended that the protection for families be restricted to legally recognized families, the amendment to the Act could have made this clear. However, this was not done. Instead, the amendment increased the scope of protection by adding a new ground of discrimination to each text: both "marital status" and "family status" became prohibited grounds. As the terms are juxtaposed, it is reasonable to conclude that "family status" must be something other than "marital status," just as "*situation de famille*" must be something other than "*état matrimonial.*" Since "*état matrimonial*" is closer to a legal notion, "*situation de famille*" or "family status" can only be broader. It was, of course, open to Parliament to define the concept of "family status" within the Act. It did not choose to do so, even in the face of debate about the meaning of the term. Instead, Parliament determined that the task of dealing with any ambiguity in any concepts in the Act should be left to the administrative board charged with the task of implementing the Act. I refer, in this regard, to the comments of the Minister of Justice as reported in the *Minutes of Proceedings and Evidence of the Standing Committee on Justice and Legal Affairs*, Issue No. 114, December 20, 1982, at p. 17: "It will be up to the commission, the tribunals it appoints, and in the final cases, the courts, to ascertain in a given case the meaning to be given to these concepts." When asked why he was reluctant to define these terms within the Act itself, the Minister responded as follows:

> The reason for my reluctance to have such definitions included, Mr. Chairman, is that it is not in accord with the scheme of the bill. *These words are being interpreted by the Canadian Human Rights Commission. We trust them to interpret and issue regulations.*
>
> It is true, of course, that a court can always pronounce on the validity of this; but in most cases, the action of the commission is accepted. Generally speaking, we think that is a better way to proceed. [Emphasis added.]

(*Minutes of Proceedings and Evidence of the Standing Committee on Justice and Legal Affairs*, Issue No. 115, December 21, 1982, at p. 73.)

Though the members of Parliament may perhaps not at that precise moment have envisaged that "family status" would be interpreted by the Tribunal so as to extend to same-sex couples, the decision to leave the term undefined is evidence of clear legislative intent that the meaning of "family status," like the meaning of other undefined concepts in the Act, be left for the Commission and its tribunals to define. In my view, if the legislative record helps here in the search for legislative intent, it rather supports the Tribunal's wide and broad discretion in the interpretation of the provisions of its own Act.

An interpretation of a human rights document, or for that matter any legislation, that may not conform with Parliament's intention can be easily cured by Parliament itself. Because legislation can be amended more readily than a Constitution, legislatures which find the interpretations given by administrative tribunals inconsistent with legislative intent can always amend the legislation, or pass new legislation in order to modify that interpretation. ...

Even if Parliament had in mind a specific idea of the scope of "family status," in the absence of a definition in the Act which embodies this scope, concepts of equality and liberty which appear in human rights documents are not bounded by the precise understanding of those who drafted them. Human rights codes are documents that embody fundamental principles, but which permit the understanding and application of these principles to change over time. These codes leave ample scope for interpretation by those charged with that task. The "living-tree" doctrine, well understood and accepted as a principle of constitutional interpretation, is particularly well suited to human rights legislation. The enumerated grounds of discrimination must be examined in the context of contemporary values, and not in a vacuum. As with other such types of legislation, the meaning of the enumerated grounds in s. 3 of the Act is not "frozen in time" and the scope of each ground may evolve.

• • •

5. The Meaning of "Family Status"

Across the political spectrum, there is broad appreciation of the vital importance of strong, stable families. ...

In her article "'A Family Like Any Other Family': Alternative Methods of Defining Family in Law" (1990-1991), 18 *NYU Rev. L & Soc. Change* 1027, at p. 1029, Kris Franklin notes:

> Families have long been viewed as among the most essential and universal units of society. This sense of the shared experience of family has led to an often unexamined consensus regarding what exactly constitutes a family. Thus, while "(w)e speak of families as though we all knew what family are," we see no need to define the concepts embedded within the term. [Footnotes omitted.]

This "unexamined consensus" leads many to feel that the term "family" in fact has a plain meaning. This belief is reflected in the decision of the Court of Appeal where Marceau JA asks the question, at p. 34, "Is it not to be acknowledged that the basic concept signified by the word has always been a group of individuals with common genes, common blood, common ancestors?" However, the unexamined consensus begins to fall apart when one is required to define the concepts which are embedded in the term "family" in the context of "family status." How are the boundaries of that status to be drawn? Is there a plain meaning for "family status"? Could it not be said that "family status" is an attribute of those who live as if they were a family, in a family relationship, caring for each other?

• • •

The traditional conception of family is not the only conception. The American Home Economics Association (AHEA) defines a family as "two or more persons who share resources, share responsibility for decisions, share values and goals, and have commitments to one another over time" (adopted in 1973, see I. Diamond, *Families, Politics and Public Policy: A Feminist Dialogue on Women and the State* (1983), 1, at p. 8). K.G. Terkelsen in "Toward a Theory of the Family Life Cycle" in E. Carter and M. McGoldrick, eds., *The Family Life Cycle: A Framework for Family Therapy* (1980), 21, at p. 23, defines a family as a:

> small social system made up of individuals related to each other by reason of strong reciprocal affections and loyalties, and comprising a permanent household (or cluster of households) that persists over years and decades.

• • •

... In *Nurses and Families: A Guide to Family Assessment and Intervention* (2nd ed., forthcoming), Wright and Leahey comment as follows (at pp. 3-3 and 3-4):

> Designating a group of people with a term such as "couple," "nuclear family," "single-parent family," specifies attributes of membership but these distinctions of grouping are not more or less "families" by reason of labelling. It is the attributes of affection, strong emotional ties, a sense of belonging and durability of membership that determine family composition. ...

The multiplicity of definitions and approaches to the family illustrates clearly that there is no consensus as to the boundaries of family, and that "family status" may not have a sole meaning, but rather may have varied meanings depending on the context or purpose for which the definition is desired. This same diversity in definition can be seen in a review of Canadian legislation affecting the "family." The law has evolved and continues to evolve to recognize an increasingly broad range of relationships. Different pieces of legislation contain more or less restrictive definitions depending on the benefit or burden of the law to be imposed. These definitions of family vary with legislative purpose, and depend on the context of the legislation. By way of example, one may be part of a family for the purpose of receiving income assistance under welfare legislation, but not for the purpose of income tax legislation.

• • •

The evidence before the Tribunal was that the traditional family form is not the only family form, but co-exists with numerous others. Though there are Canadians whose experience of family does in fact accord with the traditional model, the way many people in Canada currently experience family does not necessarily fit with this model. For example, Harriet Michel, in "The Case for the Black Family" (1987), 4 *Harv. BlackLetter J* 21, gives a substantively different conception of family. She suggests that, in the US black community,

> [b]ecause slavery often denied us the right to live with our biological kin, our definition of family became any group of individuals who collectively come together in order to provide economic and emotional support to the members of the groups.

Similarly, Carol B. Stack, in *All Our Kin: Strategies for Survival in a Black Community* (1974), examined the family networks of the black urban poor. She describes networks of kinship among these groups that are quite different from the traditional understandings of family. These kinship groups include relations based on blood, but extend to include people who would not fit within the traditional model of family. Stack concludes that in studying these families, it is important to look at the way they live, without trying to fit the relationships into the traditional categories. ...

• • •

The above discussion is not intended to provide an authoritative definition of what constitutes the family, but is rather to illustrate that a purposive approach to the term "family status" can result in an interpretation that can vary depending on the specific context. ... The Tribunal did not conclude that there is one definition which will serve for all purposes, but rather determined that the task was to find a reasonable meaning which advanced the rights contained in the Act. Following this approach, it made this assertion, at p. D/6094:

> The Tribunal, giving the term "family status" a reasonable meaning which is neither the narrowest meaning of the term nor a minimizing of rights under the Act, holds that, prima facie, homosexuals in a relationship are not excluded from relying on that prohibited ground of discrimination.

• • •

6. "Family Status" in Context

The Tribunal did not ignore the difficulties involved in finding a practical and reasonable definition which could be applied to determine whether or not "family status" would apply in the matter before them. Given its interpretation of that term as set out in s. 3 of the Act, and accepting that there is no one definition which could serve for all purposes, the Tribunal adopted a functional approach which it describes at p. D/6094:

> As a practical matter, the Tribunal agrees with the complainant that terms should not be confined to their historical roots, but must be tested in today's world, against an understanding of how people are living and how language reflects reality. Dr. Eichler's evidence, as well as that of the complainant, was helpful in making these assessments.

Dr. Eichler's evidence was that it is possible to determine whether or not a family exists for a given purpose by using a functional approach. The functional approach involves an examination of a cluster of variables that may be commonly found in families. These variables might include the existence of a relationship of some standing in terms of time and with the expectation of continuance, self-identification as a family, holding out to the public of the unit as a family, an emotional positive involvement, sexual union, raising and nurturing of children, caregiving to children or adults, shared housework, internal division of life-maintenance tasks, co-residence, joint ownership or joint use of property or goods, joint bank accounts, and naming of other party as beneficiary of a life insurance policy. Dr. Eichler noted that the list is not exhaustive, nor is it determinative. Not all variables are present in any given family, and there is no one variable that is present in all families.

• • •

Utilizing this functional approach, the Tribunal was required to determine whether or not Mr. Mossop and Mr. Popert could properly be considered to come within the scope of "family status." In reaching a determination, the Tribunal noted the importance of remaining focused on the purpose of the Act, and on an understanding of how people are living. It confirmed (at p. D/6094) that:

> Value judgments should play no part in this process, because they may operate to favour a view of the world as it might be preferred over the world as it is. The Tribunal notes the conclusion reached by Hugessen J in *Schaap* that the *Act* does not promote certain types of status over others and that the *Act* is intended to address group stereotypes.

• • •

The Tribunal concluded that the specific relationship before it was one which, on the evidence, could come within the scope of "family status." ...

• • •

The Collective Agreement

• • •

[T]he evidence was that the relationship of these two men had functionally the same characteristics as other relationships for which bereavement leave was deemed appropriate. On the facts and in the context of a bereavement leave benefit, Mr. Mossop and Mr. Popert could clearly be called immediate family. However, as the Tribunal noted, the definition of "immediate family" in the collective agreement had the effect of excluding this couple. In fact, the exclusion rendered invisible the nature of the relationship between Mr. Mossop and Mr. Popert, and treated them as if it did not exist. The Tribunal could only find, as it did, that the collective agreement treats some types of familial relationships differently than others. It summarized its findings as follows, at p. D/6097:

> Having determined that persons of the same sex *prima facie* may have the status of a family under the *Act*, and having determined that the family of the complainant is treated differently [from] other families, including but not limited to families which are very similar in their characteristics to that of the complainant, this Tribunal therefore finds that the collective agreement deprived the complainant of the employment opportunity of bereavement leave on a prohibited ground of discrimination, and that therefore each of the Treasury Board and CUPTE have committed a discriminatory practice under s. 10(b) of the *Act*.

• • •

The Attorney General also argued that the Tribunal erred in finding discrimination on the basis of "family status," rather than based on sexual orientation, a ground not found in s. 3 of the Act. ...

This argument is based on an underlying assumption that the grounds of "family status" and "sexual orientation" are mutually exclusive. However, categories of discrimination often overlap in significant measure. ...

• • •

However, though multiple levels of discrimination may exist, multiple levels of protection may not. There are situations where a person suffers discrimination on more than one ground, but where only one form of discrimination is a prohibited ground. When faced with such situations, one should be cautious not to characterize the discrimination so as to deprive the person of any protection. This was the situation in *Bliss v. Attorney General of Canada*, [1979] 1 SCR 183, where discrimination on the basis of sex was characterized as discrimination on the basis of pregnancy, and therefore left outside the scope of protection. One should not lightly allow a characterization which excludes those from the scope of the Act who should legitimately be included. A narrow and exclusionary approach, in my view, is inconsistent with a broad and purposive interpretation of human rights legislation.

• • •

The Tribunal, acting within its jurisdiction, identified Mr. Mossop's claim as one of discrimination on the basis of "family status." Based on the purpose of the Act, the purpose of the benefit, and all the evidence before it, it was perfectly reasonable for the Tribunal to conclude that the collective agreement violated s. 10(b) of the Act, a conclusion with which the Court has no reason to interfere.

• • •

In the result, I would allow the appeal with costs throughout and reinstate the Tribunal's decision.

LAMER CJ (Sopinka and Iacobucci JJ concurring):

• • •

IV. Issues

• • •

... Did the Federal Court of Appeal err when it held that the term "family status" in the *CHRA* did not include a homosexual relationship between two individuals?

V. Analysis

• • •

The question before the Court in this case is one of statutory interpretation: it is therefore a question of law. ...

• • •

... Accordingly, the issue to be determined, on the facts of this case, is whether there was discrimination on the basis of Mr. Mossop's "family status" under the *CHRA* as it stood at the time the events occurred.

When Mr. Mossop was denied bereavement leave in June 1985, the *CHRA* did not prohibit discrimination on the basis of sexual orientation. In my opinion, this fact is a highly relevant part of the context in which the phrase "family status" in the Act must be interpreted. It is interesting to note in this regard that there was a recommendation by the Canadian Human Rights Commission that sexual orientation be made a prohibited ground of discrimination. Nevertheless, at the time of the 1983 amendments to the *CHRA*, no action was taken to implement this recommendation.

It is thus clear that when Parliament added the phrase "family status" to the English version of the *CHRA* in 1983, it refused at the same time to prohibit discrimination on the basis of sexual orientation in that Act. In my opinion, this fact is determinative. I find it hard to see how Parliament can be deemed to have intended to cover the situation now before the Court in the *CHRA* when we know that it specifically excluded sexual orientation from the list of prohibited grounds of discrimination contained in the Act. In the case at bar, Mr. Mossop's sexual orientation is so closely connected with the grounds which led to the refusal of the benefit that this denial could not be condemned as discrimination on the basis of "family status" without indirectly introducing into the CHRA the prohibition which Parliament specifically decided not to include in the Act, namely the prohibition of discrimination on the basis of sexual orientation.

• • •

While it may be argued that the discrimination here applies to homosexual couples through their familial relationship or in their "family status" and does not apply to the sexual orientation of Mr. Mossop as an individual as such, I am not persuaded by this distinction. I cannot conclude that by omitting sexual orientation from the list of prohibited grounds of discrimination contained in the *CHRA*, Parliament intended to exclude from the scope of that Act only discrimination on the basis of the sexual orientation of individuals. If such an interpretation were to be given to the *CHRA*, the result would be somewhat surprising: while homosexuals who are not couples would receive no protection under the Act, those who are would be protected.

Whatever may be my personal views in that regard, I find that Parliament's clear intent throughout the *CHRA*, before and at the time of the amendment of 1983, was to not extend to anyone protection from discrimination based on sexual orientation.

Absent a *Charter* challenge of its constitutionality, when Parliamentary intent is clear, courts and administrative tribunals are not empowered to do anything else but to apply the law. If there is some ambiguity as to its meaning or scope, then the courts should, using the usual rules of interpretation, seek out the purpose of the legislation and if more than one reasonable interpretation consistent with that purpose is available, that which is more in conformity with the *Charter* should prevail.

But, I repeat, absent a *Charter* challenge, the *Charter* cannot be used as an interpretative tool to defeat the purpose of the legislation or to give the legislation an effect Parliament clearly intended it not to have.

• • •

VI. Conclusion

For these reasons, I would dismiss the appeal.

LA FOREST J (Iacobucci J concurring):

I have read the reasons of the Chief Justice and Justice L'Heureux-Dubé. I share the general approach of the Chief Justice and would dispose of the case in the manner he proposes. I think it advisable, however, to deal more directly with some of the issues raised by my colleague, L'Heureux-Dubé J. I shall, therefore, briefly set forth the main considerations that have led me to the conclusion I have reached.

• • •

2. Family Status

I turn, then, to the meaning to be attributed to the words "family status" under the ordinary rules of statutory interpretation. In determining the intent of Parliament, one must, of course, give to the words used in a statute their usual and ordinary sense having regard to their context and to the purpose of the statute. Here I shall focus particularly on the word "family" because the word "status" must inevitably attach to it. No one denies (and my colleague L'Heureux-Dubé J concedes this) that the dominant conception of family is the traditional family. That, to use the term L'Heureux-Dubé J uses, is the "unexamined consensus." That does not, of course, exhaust the meaning of the term, and we all know that in ordinary parlance it also comprises several derivative meanings that have a real connection with the dominant concept. I recognize, however, that particularly in recent years the word is loosely used to cover other relationships. The appellant here argues that "family status" should cover a relationship dependent on a same-sex living arrangement. While some may refer to such a relationship as a "family," I do not think it has yet reached that status in the ordinary use of language. Still less was it the case when the statute was enacted. In human terms, it is certainly arguable that bereavement leave should be granted to homosexual couples in a long-term relationship in the same way as it applies to heterosexual couples, but that is an issue for Parliament to address. It is not argued here that anything in the context supports the contention that this was the legislative purpose. The appellant's argument ultimately rests on the proposition that human rights statutes should be interpreted "purposefully" so as to favour all disadvantaged groups. I agree that the statute should be interpreted generously with a view to effect its purpose. But this brings us back to the question whether the addition of the words "family status" had as one of its legislative purposes the protection of persons living in the position of the appellant. As noted neither the language relied on nor the other grounds of discrimination listed support this. Nor is there any evidence in the surrounding context that this was the mischief Parliament intended to address, which could afford some credence to the argument that Parliament was using the words "family status" other than in their ordinary sense. As the Chief Justice observes, when one looks at extraneous evidence, there is nothing to show that Parliament intended to cover the situation of a same-sex couple. Indeed, so far as it goes—and I do not attach any significance to it except in the negative way I have just mentioned—this evidence would tend to support the opposite conclusion.

In sum, neither ordinary meaning, context, or purpose indicates a legislative intention to include same-sex couples within "family status." ...

[Cory and McLachlin JJ agreed with La Forest J on certain issues but agreed with L'Heureux-Dubé J on the statutory interpretation issue.]

In *Mossop,* the problem before the Court is the disputed meaning of certain language in s 3 of the *Canadian Human Rights Act.* In your opinion, is the relevant language the word "family" alone or the expression "family status"? Do you think that "family status" in this context is a legal term of art?

Does the word "family" have a plain meaning? If so, should the Court be bound by that meaning in interpreting s 3 of the Act?

Notice the arguments relied on by L'Heureux-Dubé J in the following passage. Do you find them persuasive?

With this caveat, had Parliament intended that the protection for families be restricted to legally recognized families, the amendment to the Act could have made this clear. However, this was not done. Instead, the amendment increased the scope of protection by adding a new ground of discrimination to each text: both "marital status" and "family status" became prohibited grounds. As the terms are juxtaposed, it is reasonable to conclude that "family status" must be something other than "marital status," just as *situation de famille* must be something other than "*état matrimonial.*" Since "*état matrimonial*" is closer to a legal notion, "*situation de famille*" or "family status" can only be broader. It was, of course, open to Parliament to define the concept of "family status" within the Act. It did not choose to do so, even in the face of debate about the meaning of the term. Instead, Parliament determined that the task of dealing with any ambiguity in any concepts in the Act should be left to the administrative board charged with the task of implementing the Act. I refer, in this regard, to the comments of the Minister of Justice as reported in the *Minutes of Proceedings and Evidence of the Standing Committee on Justice and Legal Affairs*, Issue No. 114, December 20, 1982, at p. 17: "It will be up to the commission, the tribunals it appoints, and in the final cases, the courts, to ascertain in a given case the meaning to be given to these concepts." When asked why he was reluctant to define these terms within the Act itself, the Minister responded as follows:

> The reason for my reluctance to have such definitions included, Mr. Chairman, is that it is not in accord with the scheme of the bill. *These words are being interpreted by the Canadian Human Rights Commission. We trust them to interpret and issue regulations.*
>
> It is true, of course, that a court can always pronounce on the validity of this; but in most cases, the action of the commission is accepted. Generally speaking, we think that is a better way to proceed. [Emphasis added.]

(Minutes of Proceedings and Evidence of the Standing Committee on Justice and Legal Affairs, Issue No. 115, December 21, 1982, at p. 73.)

Though the members of Parliament may perhaps not at that precise moment have envisaged that "family status" would be interpreted by the Tribunal so as to extend to same-sex couples, the decision to leave the term undefined is evidence of clear legislative intent that the meaning of "family status," like the meaning of other undefined concepts in the Act, be left for the Commission and its tribunals to define. In my view, if the legislative record helps here in the search for legislative intent, it rather supports the Tribunal's wide and broad discretion in the interpretation of the provisions of its own Act.

An interpretation of a human rights document, or for that matter any legislation, that may not conform with Parliament's intention can be easily cured by Parliament itself. Because legislation can be amended more readily than a Constitution, legislatures which find the interpretations given by administrative tribunals inconsistent with legislative intent can always amend the legislation, or pass new legislation in order to modify that interpretation. ...

Both Lamer CJ and L'Heureux-Dubé J address the question of legislative intent. When Parliament added the words "family status" to the English version of the Act in 1983, according to Lamer CJ, it deliberately declined to extend the Act's protection to sexual orientation, but according to L'Heureux-Dubé J it chose to confer discretion on the Human Rights Tribunal to define "family status" in any way that would advance the purposes of the Act. Which version better captures Parliament's intent? How do you know?

The judgments in *Mossop* illustrate the clash between the textualist and intentionalist approaches to interpretation. Both La Forest J and Lamer CJ insist that courts must give effect to the "plain meaning" of a legislative text, even if it leads to unpalatable results. Justice L'Heureux-Dubé believes that the judicial mandate is to give effect to Parliament's intent, as inferred not only from the language of the text but also from aids such as the evolution of the legislation from common law, to older statutory incarnations, and to its current formulation.

Suppose that Parliament declined to include same-sex couples within "family status" in 1983, and again in 1993 when the *Mossop* case was decided. Would it nonetheless be appropriate for the Court to support the tribunal's interpretation of this expression?

F. THE MODERN APPROACH IN THE MIDST OF A SEA CHANGE IN MEANING?

Given the diverse experiences of interpreters—which give rise to different understandings, impressions, assumptions, and values—is it possible to suppose that ordinary meaning is the same for everyone? Alternatively, what happens to the original meaning over time? The *Agraira* case focuses on "national interest" in the *Immigration Act*, SC 2001, c 27, but it also poses the following question: Did this term undergo a reinterpretation as a result of contemporary socio-political concerns centring on domestic and international terrorism? Because of these serious concerns, the original meaning of the Act experienced considerable stress, and some of the values contained in the Act are in deep tension with this strong focus on Canada's security interests.

Agraira v Canada (Public Safety and Emergency Preparedness)
2013 SCC 36, [2013] 2 SCR 559

LeBEL J (for the Court):

I. Introduction

[1] The appellant, Muhsen Ahmed Ramadan Agraira, a citizen of Libya, has been residing in Canada continuously since 1997, despite having been found to be inadmissible on security grounds in 2002. The finding of inadmissibility was based on the appellant's membership in the Libyan National Salvation Front ("LNSF")—a terrorist organization according to Citizenship and Immigration Canada ("CIC"). The appellant applied in 2002 under s. 34(2) of the *Immigration and Refugee Protection Act*, S.C. 2001, c. 27 ("*IRPA*"), for ministerial relief from the determination of inadmissibility, but his application was denied in 2009. The Minister of Public Safety and Emergency Preparedness ("Minister") concluded that it was not in the national interest to admit individuals who have had sustained contact with known terrorist and/or terrorist-connected organizations. The appellant's application for permanent residence was accordingly denied, and he is now at risk of deportation.

[2] Mr. Agraira appeals to this Court from a decision in which the Federal Court of Appeal dismissed an application for judicial review of the Minister's decision denying relief from the determination of inadmissibility. He contends that the Minister took an overly narrow view of the term "national interest" in s. 34(2) of the *IRPA* by equating it with national security and public safety. ...

• • •

[4] I agree with the Federal Court of Appeal, but for reasons differing in part, that the Minister's decision was reasonable and that the application for judicial review should be dismissed.

II. Background

[5] The appellant left Libya in 1996. He first sought refugee status in Germany on the basis of his connection with the LNSF, but his application was denied. He

entered Canada in 1997, at Toronto, using a fake Italian passport. He applied for Convention Refugee status in this country on the basis of his affiliation with the LNSF. On his personal information form, he described his activities with that organization as follows: as a member of an 11-person cell, he had delivered envelopes to members of other cells, raised funds, and watched the movements of supporters of the regime then in power. As part of his training, he was taught how to engage people in political discourse and how to raise funds.

[6] The appellant was heard by the Convention Refugee Determination Division of the Immigration and Refugee Board. At the hearing, he provided a letter from the LNSF confirming his membership in that organization. On October 24, 1998, he was denied Convention Refugee status on the basis that he lacked credibility.

[7] While his application for refugee status was pending, the appellant married a Canadian woman in a religious ceremony in December 1997. He later married her in a civil ceremony in March 1999. His wife sponsored his application for permanent residence in August 1999.

[8] In May 2002, the appellant was advised by CIC that his application for permanent residence might be refused, because there were grounds to believe that he was or had been a member of an organization that was or had been engaged in terrorism, contrary to s. 19(1)(f)(iii)(B) of the *Immigration Act*, R.S.C. 1985, c. I-2 (*"IA"*), which was then in force.

[9] Later in May 2002, the appellant was interviewed by an immigration officer. In the course of that interview, he confirmed that he had been a member of the LNSF, but claimed that he had previously exaggerated the extent of his involvement in order to bolster his refugee claim. Although he now claimed that he did not know very much about the LNSF, he was able to name its founder and its current leader. Also, after stating that he had attended LNSF meetings in Libya, he said that he had only discussed the group with friends. Finally, he stated that he had had no contact with the LNSF after leaving Libya, but then acknowledged having received newsletters from chapters in the United States since that time. These contradictions led the immigration officer to conclude that the appellant was or had been a member of an organization that engaged in terrorism. He was found to be inadmissible on that basis.

[10] On May 22, 2002, CIC sent the appellant a letter advising him of the possibility of requesting ministerial relief. In July of that year, the appellant applied for that relief. The immigration officer noted, while preparing her report on the interview, that, once again, there were statements in the appellant's application for relief that contradicted earlier statements he had made. For example, the appellant indicated in this application that he had attended meetings of the LNSF at which he had been trained to approach potential members and raise funds. However, in his interview with the immigration officer, the appellant said that he was unaware how the LNSF funded itself or how it recruited members. The officer concluded that the appellant had been and continued to be a member of the LNSF, but that his involvement had been limited to distributing leaflets and enlisting support for the organization. She therefore recommended that he be granted relief.

[11] At the same time (July 2002), the officer prepared a Report on Inadmissibility regarding the appellant under s. 44(1) of the *IRPA*. Her report indicated that he was inadmissible to Canada pursuant to s. 34(1)(f) of the *IRPA* because he was a member of a terrorist organization.

[12] Next, in August 2005, a briefing note for the Minister was prepared by the Canada Border Services Agency ("CBSA"). After having been reviewed by counsel for the appellant, who made no further comment, the note was submitted to the Minister on March 9, 2006. It contained a recommendation that the appellant be

granted relief, as there was "not enough evidence to conclude that Mr. Ramadan Agraira's continued presence in Canada would be detrimental to the national interest" (A.R., vol. I, at p. 9). This recommendation was based on the following considerations:

> Mr. Ramadan Agraira admitted to joining the LNSF but was only a member for approximately two years. There is some information to suggest that he became a member at a time when the organization was not in its most active phase and well after it was involved in an operation to overthrow the Libyan regime. He initially stated that he had participated in a number of activities on behalf of the organization but later indicated that he had exaggerated the extent of his involvement so that he could make a stronger claim to refugee status in Canada. This is supported to some extent by the fact that his attempts to obtain refugee status in Germany and Canada were rejected on the basis of credibility. Mr. Ramadan Agraira denied having been involved in any acts of violence or terrorism and there is no evidence to the contrary. He appears to have been a regular member who did not occupy a position of trust or authority within the LNSF. He does not appear to have been totally committed to the LNSF specifically as he indicated to the immigration officer at CIC Oshawa that he would support anyone who tried to remove the current regime in Libya through non-violent means. [A.R., vol. I, at p. 9]

[13] On January 27, 2009, the Minister rejected the recommendation in the briefing note. The response he gave was as follows:

> After having reviewed and considered the material and evidence submitted in its entirety as well as specifically considering these issues:
>
> - The applicant offered contradictory and inconsistent accounts of his involvement with the Libyan National Salvation Front (LNSF).
> - There is clear evidence that the LNSF is a group that has engaged in terrorism and has used terrorist violence in attempts to overthrow a government.
> - There is evidence that LNSF has been aligned at various times with Libyan Islamic opposition groups that have links to Al-Qaeda.
> - It is difficult to believe that the applicant, who in interviews with officials indicated at one point that he belonged to a "cell" of the LNSF which operated to recruit and raise funds for LNSF, was unaware of the LNSF's previous activity.
>
> It is not in the national interest to admit individuals who have had sustained contact with known terrorist and/or terrorist-connected organizations. Ministerial relief is denied. [A.R., vol. I, at p. 11]

[14] On March 24, 2009, the appellant received notice that his application for permanent residence was denied. He then applied to the Federal Court for judicial review of the Minister's decision regarding relief.

• • •

C. Forms of Ministerial Relief

(1) Sections 25 and 25.1 of the IRPA

[40] Before I turn to the Minister's decision, it will be helpful to explain the two forms of ministerial relief currently available to foreign nationals in Canada who are deemed to be inadmissible. The first form, H&C relief, is provided for in ss. 25 and 25.1 of the *IRPA*:

25.(1) Subject to subsection (1.2), the [MCI] must, on request of a foreign national in Canada who applies for permanent resident status and who is inadmissible or does not meet the requirements of this Act, and may, on request of a foreign national outside Canada who applies for a permanent resident visa, examine the circumstances concerning the foreign national and may grant the foreign national permanent resident status or an exemption from any applicable criteria or obligations of this Act if the [MCI] is of the opinion that it is justified by humanitarian and compassionate considerations relating to the foreign national, taking into account the best interests of a child directly affected.

• • •

25.1(1) The [MCI] may, on the [MCI's] own initiative, examine the circumstances concerning a foreign national who is inadmissible or who does not meet the requirements of this Act and may grant the foreign national permanent resident status or an exemption from any applicable criteria or obligations of this Act if the [MCI] is of the opinion that it is justified by humanitarian and compassionate considerations relating to the foreign national, taking into account the best interests of a child directly affected.

[41] These provisions contemplate the granting of ministerial relief to foreign nationals seeking permanent resident status who are inadmissible or otherwise do not meet the requirements of the *IRPA*. Under them, the MCI may, either upon request or of his own accord, "grant the foreign national permanent resident status or an exemption from any applicable criteria or obligations of" the *IRPA*. However, relief of this nature will only be granted if the MCI "is of the opinion that it is justified by humanitarian and compassionate considerations relating to the foreign national." H&C considerations include such matters as children's rights, needs, and best interests; maintaining connections between family members; and averting the hardship a person would suffer on being sent to a place where he or she has no connections (see *Baker*, at paras. 67 and 72).

(2) Section 34(2) of the IRPA

[42] Section 34(2) of the *IRPA* contemplates a different form of ministerial relief based upon the "national interest." Section 34 reads as follows:

34.(1) [Security] A permanent resident or a foreign national is inadmissible on security grounds for

(a) engaging in an act of espionage or an act of subversion against a democratic government, institution or process as they are understood in Canada;

(b) engaging in or instigating the subversion by force of any government;

(c) engaging in terrorism;

(d) being a danger to the security of Canada;

(e) engaging in acts of violence that would or might endanger the lives or safety of persons in Canada; or

(f) being a member of an organization that there are reasonable grounds to believe engages, has engaged or will engage in acts referred to in paragraph (a), (b) or (c).

(2) [Exception] The matters referred to in subsection (1) do not constitute inadmissibility in respect of a permanent resident or a foreign national who satisfies the Minister that their presence in Canada would not be detrimental to the national interest.

[43] As I mentioned above, the appellant was found to be inadmissible on security grounds for having been, in the words of s. 34(1)(f), "a member of an organization

that there are reasonable grounds to believe engages, has engaged or will engage in acts referred to in paragraph ... (c)," namely acts of terrorism. He sought relief under s. 34(2), which provides that the Minister may make an exception where a person has been found to be inadmissible, on being satisfied that the person's continued "presence in Canada would not be detrimental to the national interest." As the wording of the section ("who satisfies the Minister") implies, the onus is on the person who applies for relief to prove that his or her continued presence in Canada would not be detrimental to the national interest.

[44] In short, s. 34(2) of the *IRPA* establishes a pathway for relief which is conceptually and procedurally distinct from the relief available under s. 25 or s. 25.1. It should be borne in mind that an applicant who fails to satisfy the Minister that his or her continued presence in Canada would not be detrimental to the national interest under s. 34(2) may still bring an application for H&C relief. Whether such an application would be successful is another matter.

• • •

E. Meaning of "National Interest" Under Section 34(2) of the IRPA

[55] The meaning of the term "national interest" in s. 34(2) of the *IRPA* was central to the Minister's exercise of discretion in this case. As is plain from the statute, the Minister exercises this discretion by determining whether he or she is satisfied by the applicant that the applicant's presence in Canada would not be detrimental to the national interest. The meaning of "national interest" in the context of this section is accordingly key, as it defines the standard the Minister must apply to assess the effect of the applicant's presence in Canada in order to exercise his or her discretion.

[56] The Minister, in making his decision with respect to the appellant, did not expressly define the term "national interest." The first attempt at expressly defining it was by Mosley J. in the Federal Court, and he also certified a question concerning this definition for the Federal Court of Appeal's consideration. We are therefore left in the position, on this issue, of having no express decision of an administrative decision maker to review.

[57] This Court has already encountered and addressed this situation, albeit in a different context, in *Alberta (Information and Privacy Commissioner) v. Alberta Teachers' Association*, 2011 SCC 61, [2011] 3 S.C.R. 654. In that case, Rothstein J. held that a decision maker's decision on the merits may imply a particular interpretation of the statutory provision at issue even if the decision maker has not expressed an opinion on that provision's meaning.

[58] The reasoning from *Alberta Teachers' Association* can be applied to the case at bar. It is evident from the Minister's holding that "[i]t is not in the national interest to admit individuals who have had sustained contact with known terrorist and/or terrorist-connected organizations" that the Minister made a determination of the meaning of "national interest." An interpretative decision as to that term is necessarily implied within his ultimate decision on ministerial relief, although this Court is not in a position to determine with finality the actual reasoning of the Minister. In these circumstances, we may "consider the reasons that could be offered for the [Minister's] decision when conducting a reasonableness review" of that decision (*Alberta Teachers' Association*, at para. 54). Accordingly, I now turn to consider what appears to have been the ministerial interpretation of "national interest," based on the Minister's "express reasons" and the Guidelines, which inform the scope and context of those reasons. I will then assess whether this implied interpretation, and the Minister's decision as a whole, were reasonable.

[59] The Minister stated in his reasons that he had "reviewed and considered the material and evidence submitted in its entirety." This material included the following information set out in the CBSA's briefing note, which addressed many of the questions presented in the Guidelines:

1. The extent of the appellant's membership in, and activities on behalf of, the LNSF are in question.

2. At most, the appellant was a "passive member" of the LNSF who carried out "basic functions." He was never involved in violent acts.

3. The appellant joined the LNSF in 1994 to support democracy, freedom of speech, and human rights in Libya. At that time, the organization was, by and large, no longer engaged in violence. In any event, the appellant claimed to have no knowledge of the LNSF's involvement in violence and would not have supported the LNSF had it espoused the use of violence to achieve political change.

4. There is evidence to suggest that the appellant severed all ties with the LNSF when he came to Canada in 1997.

5. Throughout, the appellant's goal has been to support the establishment of a democratic system of government in Libya.

6. The appellant has two children, attended English as a second language classes, and owns his own transport business. (A.R., vol. I, at pp. 5-9)

[60] The Guidelines did not constitute a fixed and rigid code. Rather, they contained a set of factors, which appeared to be relevant and reasonable, for the evaluation of applications for ministerial relief. The Minister did not have to apply them formulaically, but they guided the exercise of his discretion and assisted in framing a fair administrative process for such applications. As a result, the Guidelines can be of assistance to the Court in understanding the Minister's implied interpretation of the "national interest."

[61] Moreover, the Minister placed particular emphasis on matters related to national security and public safety in the reasons he gave for his decision. These included: the appellant's contradictory and inconsistent accounts of his involvement with the LNSF, a group that has engaged in terrorism; the fact that the appellant was most likely aware of the LNSF's previous activity; and the fact that the appellant had had sustained contact with the LNSF.

[62] Taking all the above into account, had the Minister expressly provided a definition of the term "national interest" in support of his decision on the merits, it would have been one which related predominantly to national security and public safety, but did not exclude the other important considerations outlined in the Guidelines or any analogous considerations (see Appendix 1 (the relevant portions of the Guidelines)).

[63] As a result of my comments above on the standard of review, I am of the view that the Minister is entitled to deference as regards this implied interpretation of the term "national interest." As Rothstein J. stated, "[w]here the reviewing court finds that the tribunal has made an implicit decision on a critical issue, the deference due to the tribunal does not disappear" (*Alberta Teachers' Association*, at para. 50).

[64] In my view, the Minister's interpretation of the term "national interest," namely that it is focused on matters related to national security and public safety, but also encompasses the other important considerations outlined in the Guidelines and any analogous considerations, is reasonable. It is reasonable because, to quote the words of Fish J. from *Smith v. Alliance Pipeline Ltd.*, 2011 SCC 7, [2011] 1 S.C.R. 160, it "accords ... with the plain words of the provision, its legislative history,

its evident purpose, and its statutory context" (para. 46). That is to say, the interpretation is consistent with Driedger's modern approach to statutory interpretation:

> Today there is only one principle or approach, namely, the words of an Act are to be read in their entire context and in their grammatical and ordinary sense harmoniously with the scheme of the Act, the object of the Act, and the intention of Parliament.
>
> (*Construction of Statutes* (2nd ed. 1983), at p. 87)

(1) Plain Words of the Provision

[65] There is no dispute between the parties that the term "national interest" refers to matters which are of concern to Canada and to Canadians. There is no doubt that public safety and national security are matters which are of concern to Canada and to Canadians. It is equally clear, however, that more than just public safety and national security are of concern to Canada and to Canadians. For example, the plain meaning of the term "national interest" would also include the preservation of the values that underlie the *Canadian Charter of Rights and Freedoms* and the democratic character of the Canadian federation, and in particular the protection of the equal rights of every person to whom its laws and its Constitution apply. The plain words of the provision therefore favour a broader reading of the term "national interest" than the one suggested by the respondent and by the Federal Court of Appeal, which would limit its meaning to the protection of public safety and national security. The words of the statute are consistent with the Minister's implied interpretation of this term, which relates predominantly to national security and public safety, but does not exclude the other important considerations outlined in the Guidelines or any analogous considerations. The legislative history of the provision is also relevant to an understanding of the range of values and interests underlying the concept of the national interest.

(2) Legislative History of the Provision

[66] The legislative history of s. 34(2) is a long one. In these reasons, I will only discuss the salient points of this history, those which serve to demonstrate that the Minister's implied interpretation of the term "national interest" is consistent with it.

[67] Ministerial relief from a finding of inadmissibility first became available in 1952. Relief was available to persons who were members of or associated with any organization, group or body that was or had been involved in the subversion by force or other means of democratic government, institutions or processes. Those who sought such relief had to satisfy the minister that they had ceased to be members of or associated with the organization, group or body in question *and that their admission "would not be detrimental to the security of Canada"* (*Immigration Act*, R.S.C. 1952, c. 325, s. 5(l)). Parliament made it clear at the time that it intended the focus of an application for ministerial relief to be national security.

[68] In 1977, the provisions of the *Immigration Act* on inadmissibility were revised to read, in part, as follows:

> 19.(1) No person shall be granted admission if he is a member of any of the following classes:
>
> • • •
>
> (e) persons who have engaged in or who there are reasonable grounds to believe will engage in acts of espionage or subversion against democratic government, institutions or processes, as they are understood in Canada, except

persons who, having engaged in such acts, *have satisfied the Minister that their admission would not be detrimental to the national interest*;

(*Immigration Act*, 1976, S.C. 1976-77, c. 52, s. 19(1)(e))

[69] Thus, in 1977, Parliament made a clear decision to change the approach to ministerial relief. The test would no longer focus solely on national security, as access to relief would instead be premised on a broader array of domestic and international considerations constituting the "national interest." Since then, the provisions on ministerial relief in both the *IA* and the *IRPA* have at all times referred to the "national interest."

[70] Parliament was (or at least must be taken to have been) aware of the previous "detrimental to the security of Canada" test when it decided to enact, and later to keep, the "national interest" test for ministerial relief. The fact that, at all material times, the wording of s. 34(2) referred to the applicant's not being detrimental to the "national interest," as opposed to not being detrimental to the "security of Canada," strongly suggests that Parliament did not intend the term "national interest" to relate exclusively to national security and public safety. Had that been the case, Parliament could have returned to the expression "security of Canada" in enacting s. 34(2).

[71] The *IRPA* replaced the *IA* in 2002. As it was enacted in a post-9/11 world, the *IRPA* was clearly in part a response to the threats of the complex and dangerous environment which had been developing internationally. In support of his contention that the interpretation of the term "national interest" should focus on national security and public safety, the respondent quotes the following passage from a Senate Committee report in his factum:

The Committee recognizes that Bill C-11 represents a major overhaul of Canada's immigration and refugee protection legislation, and it will thus likely set the standard for many years to come. The Committee also fully appreciates that the current context in which the Bill is being considered is one of heightened security concerns following the profoundly tragic events of 11 September 2001 in the United States. In this context the Committee realizes that *the Bill must embody a balance that will respect the needs and rights of individuals while simultaneously serving the public interest particularly with respect to security concerns and meeting Canada's international obligations.* [Emphasis added.]

(Standing Senate Committee on Social Affairs, Science and Technology, "Ninth Report," 1st Sess., 37th Parl., October 23, 2001 (online))

[72] This passage certainly highlights the *IRPA*'s role in "serving the public interest ... with respect to security concerns." However, it does not limit the national interest to security concerns. It also highlights the fact that meeting Canada's international obligations (including, presumably, obligations stemming from rules of customary and conventional international human rights law) is an important part of the national interest.

[73] In 2005, the *DPSEPA* formally established both the Department of Public Safety and Emergency Preparedness and the Minister's post. The respondent submits that the creation of this new department and of the CBSA, as well as the transfer of ministerial responsibility for decisions under s. 34(2), formed part of a new national security policy instituted by Parliament in response to the events of September 11, 2001. In particular, he argues that the legislative transfer of the responsibility for making such decisions from the MCI to the Minister, occurring as it did in the broader context of national security and public safety, supports the Federal Court of Appeal's interpretation of the term "national interest."

[74] I am not persuaded that the transfer of ministerial responsibility for s. 34(2) applications serves as a sufficient basis for upholding the Federal Court of Appeal's interpretation of the term "national interest." On its own, this transfer should not be read as changing, nor does it change, the substantive law governing relief applications under s. 34(2). Ministerial responsibilities may be reassigned for a wide variety of reasons. If this argument was valid, it would imply that the meaning of a law might change whenever ministerial responsibilities are reassigned. This would be a new and perplexing principle of interpretation. There is a presumption against the implicit alteration of the law according to which, absent an explicit change in the wording of a provision, it is presumed that Parliament did not intend to amend its meaning. Although the ministerial responsibility for deciding relief applications under s. 34(2) was transferred in 2005, Parliament did not amend the wording of this provision. Therefore, the presumption against implicit alteration applies, and there was no intent to amend the meaning of the term "national interest." As the appellant points out in his factum, this presumption is not rebutted by a mere transfer of ministerial responsibility:

> It does not make sense that every time Parliament decides to change the responsibilities of particular Ministers for administrative purposes, or without indicating that there is a substantive reason for a change, the words of a statute should be given different meanings. A mere transfer in Ministerial responsibility is not sufficient to establish that the change is meant to have a substantive effect on the rights of persons who are affected by legislation administered by the various ministers. The Court of Appeal's interpretation of national interest effectively amends section 34(2). Amending legislation is a legislative function, and falls outside of the judicial function. [para. 76]

[75] In summary, this review demonstrates that the Minister's implied interpretation of the term "national interest"—that it relates predominantly to national security and public safety, but does not exclude the other important considerations outlined in the Guidelines or any analogous considerations—is consistent with the legislative history of the provision.

(3) Purpose of the Provision

[76] The respondent argues that the *IRPA* is concerned with public safety and national security. More specifically, he argues that the purpose of s. 34(1)(c) and (f) is to ensure the safety and security of Canadians, while s. 34(2) provides for relief only for innocent or coerced members of terrorist organizations who would otherwise be inadmissible.

[77] The respondent is correct in saying that the *IRPA* is concerned with national security and public safety. In fact, the Court recognized this in *Medovarski v. Canada (Minister of Citizenship and Immigration)*, 2005 SCC 51, [2005] 2 S.C.R. 539:

> The objectives as expressed in the *IRPA* indicate an intent to prioritize security. ... Viewed collectively, the objectives of the *IRPA* and its provisions concerning permanent residents, communicate a strong desire to treat criminals and security threats less leniently than under the former Act. [para. 10]

[78] That said, the respondent's argument that s. 34(2) is focused exclusively on national security and public safety, and that it provides for relief only for innocent or coerced members of terrorist organizations, fails to give adequate consideration to the other objectives of the *IRPA*. Section 3(1) of the *IRPA* sets out 11 objectives of the Act with respect to immigration. Only two of these are related to public safety

and national security: to protect public health and safety and to maintain the security of Canadian society (s. 3(1)(h)), and to promote international justice and security by fostering respect for human rights and by denying access to Canadian territory to persons who are criminals or security risks (s. 3(1)(i)). The other nine objectives relate to other factors that properly inform the interpretation of the term "national interest" (e.g., "to permit Canada to pursue the maximum social, cultural and economic benefits of immigration" (s. 3(1)(a))). The explicit presence of these other objectives in the *IRPA* strongly suggests that this term is not limited to public safety and national security, but that the Parliament of Canada also intended that it be interpreted in the context of the values of a democratic state. Section 34 is intended to protect Canada, but from the perspective that Canada is a democratic nation committed to protecting the fundamental values of its *Charter* and of its history as a parliamentary democracy.

[79] Accordingly, the Minister's broad implied interpretation of the term "national interest" is also consistent with the purpose of the provision.

(4) Context of the Provision

[80] As the Court noted in *Bell ExpressVu Limited Partnership v. Rex*, 2002 SCC 42, [2002] 2 S.C.R. 559, "[t]he preferred approach [to statutory interpretation] recognizes the important role that context must inevitably play when a court construes the written words of a statute" (para. 27). The context of s. 34(2) provides much guidance for the interpretation of the term "national interest."

[81] First, according to the presumption of consistent expression, when different terms are used in a single piece of legislation, they must be understood to have different meanings. If Parliament has chosen to use different terms, it must have done so intentionally in order to indicate different meanings. The term "national interest" is used in s. 34(2), which suggests that what is to be considered by the Minister under that provision is broader than the considerations of whether the individual is "a danger to the security of Canada" (s. 34(1)(d)) or whether he or she "might endanger the lives or safety of persons in Canada" (s. 34(1)(e)), both of which appear in s. 34(1). If Parliament had intended national security and public safety to be the only considerations under s. 34(2), it could have said so using the type of language found in s. 34(1). It did not do so, however.

[82] In a similar vein, the terms "national security," "danger to the public" and "endanger the safety of any person" each appear several times elsewhere in the *IRPA*. In light of the presumption of consistent expression, "national interest" cannot be synonymous with any of these terms. Rather, the use of the term "national interest" implies that the Minister is to carry out a broader analysis under s. 34(2). Contrary to what the Federal Court of Appeal held in the case at bar, in determining whether a person's continued presence in Canada would not be detrimental to the national interest, the Minister must consider more than just national security and whether the applicant is a danger to the public or to the safety of any person.

[83] Second, if s. 34(2) were concerned solely with the danger an applicant poses to the security of Canada, it would be impossible for a person found to be inadmissible under s. 34(1)(d) ("being a danger to the security of Canada") to obtain relief under s. 34(2). This is an absurd interpretation which must be avoided.

[84] Third, the respondent argues that, because of the possibility of H&C relief under s. 25 of the *IRPA*, the principle of consistent expression dictates that H&C factors should not be relevant to a determination of what is in the national interest under s. 34(2). I agree, but with some qualifications. H&C considerations are more properly considered in the context of a s. 25 application, and s. 34 should not be

transformed into an alternative form of humanitarian review. But s. 34 does not necessarily exclude the consideration of personal factors that might be relevant to this particular form of review. For example, such considerations may have an impact on the assessment of the applicant's personal characteristics for the purpose of determining whether he or she can be viewed as a threat to the security of Canada. Of the considerations in the Guidelines unrelated to national security and public safety which formed part of the Minister's implied interpretation, only very few are H&C factors. The fact that the Minister considered such factors did not render his interpretation of the term "national interest" unreasonable.

[85] Finally, the broader context of s. 34(2) of the *IRPA* also includes the Guidelines. Although not law in the strict sense, and although they are liable to evolve over time as the context changes, thus giving rise to new requirements adapted to different contexts, guidelines are "a useful indicator of what constitutes a reasonable interpretation of the ... section" (*Baker*, at para. 72). The Guidelines were published in 2005, and they applied to applications for ministerial relief under s. 34(2) at the time the Minister reached his decision on the appellant's application. As is evident from the numerous considerations contained in Appendix 1, the Guidelines represent a broad approach to the concept of the "national interest." They do not simply equate the "national interest" with national security and public safety, as the Federal Court of Appeal did. Rather, they suggest that the national interest analysis is broader than that, although its focus may properly be on national security and public safety.

[86] Thus, the Minister's implied interpretation of the term "national interest"— that it relates predominantly to national security and public safety, but does not exclude the other important considerations outlined in the Guidelines or any analogous considerations—is consistent with all these contextual indications of the meaning of this term.

[87] In summary, an analysis based on the principles of statutory interpretation reveals that a broad range of factors may be relevant to the determination of what is in the "national interest," for the purposes of s. 34(2). Even excluding H&C considerations, which are more appropriately considered in the context of a s. 25 application, although the factors the Minister may validly consider are certainly not limitless, there are many of them. Perhaps the best illustration of the wide variety of factors which may validly be considered under s. 34(2) can be seen in the ones set out in the Guidelines (with the exception of the H&C considerations included in the Guidelines). Ultimately, which factors are relevant to the analysis in any given case will depend on the particulars of the application before the Minister ... .

[88] This interpretation is compatible with the interpretation of the term "national interest" the Minister might have given in support of his decision on the appellant's application for relief. It is consistent with that decision. The Minister's implied interpretation of the term related predominantly to national security and public safety, but did not exclude the other important considerations outlined in the Guidelines or any analogous considerations. In light of my discussion of the principles of statutory interpretation, this interpretation was eminently reasonable.

F. Is the Minister's Decision Valid?

[89] Having concluded that the Minister's implied interpretation of the term "national interest" is reasonable, I should also confirm that the decision as a whole is valid. The Minister's reasons were justifiable, transparent and intelligible. Although brief, they made clear the process he had followed in ruling on the appellant's application. He reviewed and considered all the material and evidence before him. Having done so, he placed particular emphasis on: the appellant's contradictory and inconsistent accounts of his involvement with the LNSF, a group that has engaged

in terrorism; the fact that the appellant was most likely aware of the LNSF's previous activity; and the fact that the appellant had had sustained contact with the LNSF. The Minister's reasons revealed that, on the basis of his review of the evidence and other submissions as a whole, and of these factors in particular, he was not satisfied that the appellant's continued presence in Canada would not be detrimental to the national interest. In short, his reasons allow this Court to clearly understand why he made the decision he did.

[90] Furthermore, the Minister's decision falls within a range of possible acceptable outcomes which are defensible in light of the facts and the law. The burden was on the appellant to show that his continued presence in Canada would not be detrimental to the national interest. The Minister declined to provide discretionary relief to the appellant, as he was not satisfied that this burden had been discharged. His conclusion was acceptable in light of the facts which had been submitted to him.

[91] As this Court held in *Suresh*, a court reviewing the reasonableness of a minister's exercise of discretion is not entitled to engage in a new weighing process (para. 37; see also *Lake v. Canada (Minister of Justice)*, 2008 SCC 23, [2008] 1 S.C.R. 761, at para. 39). As the Minister stated in his reasons, he had "reviewed and considered" (i.e. weighed) all the factors set out in the appellant's application which were relevant to determining what was in the "national interest" in light of his reasonable interpretation of that term. He gave particular weight to certain factors pertaining to national security and public safety and emphasized them in his reasons, namely: the appellant's contradictory and inconsistent accounts of his involvement with the LNSF; the fact that the appellant was most likely aware of the LNSF's previous activity; and the fact that the appellant had had sustained contact with the LNSF. Given that the Minister considered and weighed all the relevant factors as he saw fit, it is not open to the Court to set the decision aside on the basis that it is unreasonable.

The *Agraira* decision, for many critics, represents a "counter-reading" of the origins and purposes of the *Immigration and Refugee Protection Act*, SC 2001, c 27 in 20th-century Canadian history. Imagine that you have been asked to write a dissent in this decision. Consider the following issues and construct a hypothetical dissent:

1. the original purposes of the IRPA;
2. the relevance of contemporary circumstances;
3. why courts should or should not defer to ministerial interpretations of enabling legislation; and
4. whether or not courts should "re-weigh" the factors that the minister has considered in his discretionary decision.

V. INTERPRETATION AND CRITICISM OF THE MODERN APPROACH

A. A BRIEF REVIEW OF OLDER APPROACHES TO STATUTORY INTERPRETATION

Before considering some criticisms of the modern approach, it is useful to revisit the traditional approach to statutory interpretation and why it had to be displaced. The traditional common law canonical rules for interpreting legislation were comprised of four main approaches: the plain meaning rule, the golden rule, equitable construction, and presumed intent.

The first is the "plain meaning" rule. It originated in the 16th century. This rule is also called the "natural," "literal," "original," "cardinal," or "grammatical" rule. The presumption on which the rule is based is that words used in legislation are intended to be precise. Plain meaning is therefore firmly attached to the principle of parliamentary supremacy. If the words of the legislation are plain, unambiguous, and precise, the judiciary must construe them in their ordinary and literal sense—as the legislature intended—even if it leads to an absurd or unjust result. The role of the court was limited to analyzing the law as it is, not as it should be, and results in a view of the judge as a mechanical interpreter. In other words, a court would not provide a remedy to the person who seeks judicial relief from the effects of express legislative intent unless it is framed in terms of the Constitution and constitutional rights. The strict nature of the plain meaning rule was emphasized by Lamer CJ in *R v McIntosh*, [1995] 1 SCR 686 at para 34:

> ... [W]here, by the use of clear and unequivocal language capable of only one meaning, anything is enacted by the legislature, it must be enforced however harsh or absurd or contrary to common sense the result may be ... . The fact that a provision gives rise to absurd results is not, in my opinion, sufficient to declare it ambiguous and then embark upon a broad-ranging interpretative analysis.

In complete contrast to the plain meaning rule, the "golden rule" directs judges to adhere to the grammatical and ordinary sense unless doing so results in manifestly absurd results and/ or inconsistency and repugnancy with respect to the legislative scheme or purposes (here reconsider Rand J's judgment in *Roncarelli v Duplessis*, [1959] SCR 121). The plain meaning rule therefore justifies judicial resort to the "golden rule" of statutory construction, but in truth the golden rule is not much different in operation from the plain meaning rule because they both rely on the role of courts to "police" the activities of the other branches of government and their ability to engage in law-making by mediating between the enacted rule and the facts of the case. (Ruth Sullivan, *Sullivan on the Construction of Statutes*, 5th ed (Markham, Ont: Butterworths, 2008) at 4-7.)

Other common law "rules"—like the canons of construction—also helped courts justify intervention in the face of the plain meaning rule in order to supplement the statute's perceived deficiencies. For example, in equitable construction or the "mischief rule," a court's task in interpreting statutes legislation was defined as:

> [T]he office of all the Judges is always to make such construction as shall suppress the mischief [for which the common law did not provide] and advance the remedy [chosen by Parliament to cure the disease of the commonwealth], and to suppress subtle inventions and evasions for continuance of the mischief, *pro privato commodo*, and to add force and life to the cure and remedy, according to the true intent of the makers of the Act, *pro bono publico*. [*Heydon's Case* (1584), 3 Co Rep 7a, 76 ER 637 at 638 (ER)]

The main interpretive goal was to promote statutory purposes by curing any over- or under-inclusions in the implementing provisions and suppressing attempts to avoid the intended impact of the legislation. Clearly, this approach to interpretation was premised on an assumption that judges are active participants in law-making and that—until the Charter—was in deep tension with the principle of parliamentary sovereignty.

Through statutory interpretation, both judges and counsel chose an approach that suited the argumentative path they wished to pursue in the case at bar. Judges could simply "declare" what the plain meaning was, despite sometimes strong indications that the text was more ambiguous than they proclaimed. But, when the apparent meaning of a text produced an unacceptable result, judges were also free to abandon the plain meaning rule. Under the golden rule, the two exceptions were often called "smell tests" because they raised concerns about unconstrained judicial subjectivity: after all, absurdity and repugnancy may be solely in the eye of the beholder. In the British common law system, courts could justify recourse to the golden rule because judges traditionally viewed legislation as an exception to the common law and often an inappropriate incursion. So, in practice, judges used the common law presumptions not so much to construct legislative intent, but to *control* legislative intent, especially when they strongly disagreed with the statute and its purposes. Because the common law presumptions and the older approach have not been entirely eliminated, concerns about recourse to their use are still relevant. But, remember that under the modern principle, these approaches are now integrated.

B. RECONSIDERING THE MODERN APPROACH TO STATUTORY INTERPRETATION

At this point in your legal education, you will have realized how complex interpretation is—and not just in public law. You may have had to abandon your initial assumption that there is only one correct interpretation of the law that must be applied to the facts of each case. You may also be trying to resist the realist conclusion that judges do what they think is right in a particular case and, after they have decided the preferred result, they create the legal argument they need to justify their conclusion. Or, you may be looking at some of the judgments in this chapter for a model of an interpretive approach or style you think provides the best balance between judicial creativity and judicial restraint. You will have already encountered at least one "hard" case that illustrates the burdens the legal system places on judges to come to a principled decision that also provides cogent and persuasive reasons. You have had deeper insights into the role of the judge who is often tasked with not finding the "right" answer, but ensuring a rational, legally defensible outcome on the facts of the case. In doing so, the judge finds himself or herself constrained by statute, precedent, and the common law "rules" of statutory interpretation. How weak or strong those constraints are depends on a complex interaction between the facts, the various legal arguments, and judicial predispositions.

In a seminal article on statutory interpretation, Canadian public law scholar John Willis wryly commented, "If ... the words are ambiguous enough to induce two people to spend good money in backing two opposing views as to their meaning, no man of sense would expect to find the question settled by a reference to such a vast and vague field as 'the rest of the words of the Act' or 'the part of human conduct with which the Act deals'" (J Willis, "Statute Interpretation in a Nutshell" (1938) 16 Can Bar Rev 1 at 4-5). No pithier criticism of the modern approach can be found.

The modern approach is, after all, a guiding principle, not a rule. Although it takes us some distance toward constraining judicial interpretation in a principled way, it does not alleviate the problems of ambiguity, constructing intent, and choosing from potentially multiple plausible interpretations. We assume that Parliament would have intended the meaning that is unambiguous and that it also intends not to create absurd, irrational, arbitrary, and discriminatory results. Sometimes, as in *Mossop*, Parliament may have intended to leave it to the courts or to specialized administrative decision-makers to interpret the provision harmoniously with the broader scheme of human rights legislation or other statutory schemes. As Willis astutely observed, "[A] composite body can hardly have a single intent; it is at most only a harmless, if bombastic, way of referring to the social policy behind the Act" (J Willis, "Statute Interpretation in a Nutshell" (1938) 16 Can Bar Rev 1 at 3). Intention will forever remain a problematic concept.

The chief downside of the modern approach, according to Stéphane Beaulac and Pierre-André Côté, is that its simplicity and certainty is deceptive. It is actually a traditional approach that is modern only when compared with the older rules, and its ability to guide the act of judicial interpretation is not always effective. It seems to truly privilege the intention of Parliament as the central task of the exercise, but then it asks interpreters to consider intent on an equal plane with the ordinary sense, scheme, and objects. These last three are only factors to assist in constructing legislative intent, rather than being goals in themselves. Beaulac and Côté ask whether it is time for courts to acknowledge that they are acting on something more than something that is "already there" in the statute:

> [This] may require courts, especially at the appellate level, to act in a creative manner in order to clarify or supplement legislative provisions, or even to make the necessary adjustments to have them address an unforeseen or changing social reality. We trust that the day will come when the justification of judicial interpretive decisions in this country acknowledges more openly this simple fact, rather than try to obscure it.

(Stéphane Beaulac & Pierre-André Côté, "Driedger's Modern Principle at the Supreme Court of Canada: Interpretation, Justification, Legitimization" (2006) 40 Themis 131 at 172; see also Ruth Sullivan, "Statutory Interpretation in the Supreme Court of Canada" (1998-99) 30 Ottawa L Rev 177.)

Another way of thinking about their point is to acknowledge that, as interpreters, we do not "extract" meaning from text; rather, we put meaning in. How we go about doing that in law is a complex practice.

Perhaps it is best to view the matter pragmatically. Generally, statutory interpretation involves the application of law to facts, balancing the judge's inclination to do justice on the facts against presumptions about what Parliament wanted to be done in the face of such individualized facts, and a concern for not creating precedent that may have a less desirable effect in future cases. Interpretive choices between static and dynamic approaches, or textualism (i.e., the plain meaning rule) and intentionalism (i.e., the modern rule), play out their adversarial battle on this field. With more dynamic approaches, the interpreter will consider a full range of interpretive aids to arrive at an interpretation that conforms to the text and furthers the legislative intent of the provision while producing an outcome that is just and reasonable on the facts of the case under consideration. Resort to other principles of statutory interpretation depends on whether or not a judge agrees that the legislative text is truly ambiguous—at that point, particular common law presumptions or Charter values may also be drawn into the mix in order to construct the meaning.

Interpretation disputes force us to consider the reasons why a court might be willing to accept a line of interpretation argument, and we must consider how the key issues are framed. When engaging in an exercise of statutory interpretation, ask yourself: How should one characterize or frame the legal problem? How would the other party frame the key issue? Might a court rephrase the key question? What is the range of interpretation issues involved? And, how far can a court be persuaded to draw on the policy context to incorporate inferences that qualify or constrain the words used in the statute?

Preparing for the courtroom, further considerations will arise. Counsel will ask himself or herself if the case raises any circumstances where a judge might prefer one presumption to another. Counsel will also ask whether the court is sympathetic to the litigant, the legislation, its purposes, and its goals. Lastly, counsel will ask whether the requested remedy raises any judicial anxieties that may compel judges to resort to a narrow interpretation in order to avoid unwanted consequences. On this point, think about the anxieties that the remedy in *Opitz* raised: annulling an election result that may have had the effect of opening up not only particular election results across the country, but the entire election itself. Alternatively, the connection between the interpretive dispute and the remedy may raise a separation of powers issue where the question becomes whose responsibility it is to correct the problem with the legislation: the courts or Parliament?

The next chapter explores these questions of interpretation and institutional relations further. It also briefly introduces you to an important and evolving area of law concerning judicial review of statutory interpretations made by executive actors: administrative law.

CHEAT SHEET FOR THE MODERN APPROACH TO STATUTORY INTERPRETATION

Today there is only one principle or approach, namely, the words of an Act are to be read in their entire context and in their grammatical and ordinary sense harmoniously with the scheme of the Act, the object of the Act, and the intention of Parliament. (*Rizzo Shoes* at para 21)

The *overall goal* is for the reviewing court to advance a coherent interpretation of an ambiguous provision.

- A court considers three general questions about the statute:

    (1) What is the meaning of the words read alone and understood in the ordinary sense?

    (2) What is the meaning of the words read together with the rest of the Act according to the legislature's intent?

    (3) What is the meaning of the words when read against the reasons for the creation of the statute, the kind of human behaviour it concerns, and the consequences of the proposed interpretations?

- One must also consider the application of the law to the facts, a judge's inclination to "do justice" on the basis of these facts and in the face of presumptions about what the legislature intended, and judicial concerns about creating good and bad precedent.

"Entire context" means:

- Economic, political, and social relations.
- The entire act including its regulations:
    - Its purposes and objects (i.e., purposive interpretation) in order to determine meaning and internal consistency:
        ◦ the purpose of a statute or legislation is the goal of the legislation (e.g., promoting *x* or criminalizing *y*);
        ◦ more than one purpose may exist, so the dominant or most relevant purpose in the circumstances will be selected;
        ◦ a provision in question may assist in fulfilling a statutory purpose, but it may also possess its own secondary purpose that may link up with a primary purpose, thereby providing interpretive assistance for making inferences about purpose(s).
    - Other statutes, regulations, regulatory schemes, and principles.
    - This establishes *horizontal coherence* where statutory contexts are analogous.
    - *Vertical coherence* is achieved through presumptions:
        ◦ the Constitution trumps all;
        ◦ federal legislation prevails over provincial, if they conflict;
        ◦ human rights legislation prevails over general legislation;
        ◦ subordinate legislation must be consistent with the enabling statute; and
        ◦ domestic law should be interpreted consistently with international law.
    - Legislative history:
        ◦ pay attention to changes that are remedial;
        ◦ includes relevant parliamentary history such as briefing notes, alternative drafts of the statute, committee reports, Hansard, ministerial statements, and press releases.

- Relevant judicial precedents and previous interpretations:
  - if no amendment intervenes,
  - attend to date of case, jurisdiction, and court level.
- Relevant interpretations made by administrative decision-makers:
  - courts may defer to specialized knowledge and expertise of administrative decision-makers;
  - courts may defer to ministerial interpretations because to overturn them may invalidate previous decisions or lead to a serious reallocation of resources across the board.
- Policy considerations particular to the subject matter.
- Interpretation acts.
- International law.

Grammatical and ordinary sense incorporates the ordinary meaning rule but subordinates it within the overall approach.

- Courts will depart from the ordinary sense if the text is plausibly unclear or ambiguous.
- Judges often resort to the dictionary as an aid here.
- In bilingual statutes, the court will prefer the version that provides a narrower meaning (often the French version).

Harmoniously with

- the scheme of the act where judges will:
  - ask if the act is benefit-conferring or quasi-constitutional, requiring a broad and generous approach, and where ambiguities will be resolved in favour of the claimant;
  - consider if it is a penal act requiring strict construction and application in favour of the defendant;
  - consider if it is a regulatory statute or municipal law requiring a broad and purposive approach;
  - look to the long title, preamble and purpose sections, definitions, headings and marginal notes for interpretive assistance, bilingual statutes, and schedules because all of these things provide key information on the intended mischief to be remedied and scope of meaning:
    - how provisions and sections are related is a question about the legislative scheme since the scheme may follow a certain logic;
    - schematic elements re-occur across different types of statutes—for example, the definitions section is almost always at the beginning of a statute and there are obvious reasons for this;
    - legislative scheme may require a contextual analysis in order to set more complex features out such as whether a statute sets up a scheme that: shapes how an executive actor (i.e., the decision-maker) can make a decision (i.e., determine whether someone should have refugee status); or sets up a scheme to run a procedure (i.e., like a refugee hearing or an investigatory process); or delegates power to, or impose constraints on, a decision-maker;
    - a court must select the interpretation that best enables that legislative scheme's operation and also helps it meet certain goals—such as coherence, rationality, legality, consistency, etc.;
    - in *Rizzo Shoes,* the interpretation problem involved looking at the statutory scheme the legislature constructed regarding the provision of benefits in the circumstances of loss of employment.

- consider the subject matter of the statute and whether the words bear a particular meaning in relation to that subject matter. For example, should a technical meaning be preferred? Does the legislature intend a broad or narrow scope for the word "family": does it mean only the nuclear family or does it include any grandparents and aunties? Look within the statute!
- inquire into the nature of discretion that is delegated;
- employ the principle that the general word takes its meaning from the preceding specific words with which it is associated by the words "and," "or": *noscitur a sociis*. For example, if a provision makes it an offence to cut, stab, *or* wound, can someone be convicted for punching under this provision?
- employ the principle that a general phrase takes its meaning from the associated preceding specific words or phrases: *ejusdem generis*. For example, "and all kinds of merchandise" really means "and all kinds of merchandise *of the same sort*";
- employ the principle that a general word or phrase takes its meaning from the specific words or phrases that *both follow and precede* it with the effect that the express mention of one thing excludes all others by necessary implication: *espressio unius, exclusio alterius*;
- attend to other common law presumptions about harmonization, non-retroactivity, property rights, Charter values, etc.

Object of the act

- requires a purposive approach to identify the intended goals of the legislation as well as the means designed to achieve those goals.

Intention of Parliament

- requires a purposive approach incorporating the mischief rule ("suppresses the mischief the statute was designed to resolve");
- is consistent with the "fair, large and liberal interpretation that best achieves its objects"; and
- avoids absurdity.

CHAPTER ELEVEN

CONSTRAINTS ON LEGISLATIVE AND ADMINISTRATIVE ACTION

I. INTRODUCTION

This chapter explores the role that the judiciary plays in constraining legislative and administrative or executive action, a theme discussed in passing in Chapters 1 and 8. In a democratic society, governmental actors face a wide range of constraints on their efforts to pursue their understanding of the public good. These constraints may include limits on the support available from political allies; the need to address criticism from political opponents; the scrutiny of the media and affected interest groups; the practical constraints imposed by limited financial resources, personnel, or information needed to pursue an initiative effectively; and sometimes the requirement of cooperation from other levels of government, either domestically or internationally.

For many types of policies or programs, the constraints imposed by the need to comply with the law will be the easiest ones for governmental actors to address. Nevertheless, the availability of law as a constraint on government is important, not only in principle but often as a practical matter. These legal limits are likely to be especially important for individuals and minority interest groups who are unable to achieve their aims in the political or bureaucratic arena.

In Section II of this chapter, we consider the role that judicial review using the Constitution plays in a democratic society. The principle of constitutional supremacy implies a restriction on governmental action that is inconsistent with the Constitution. The Constitution, and particularly the *Canadian Charter of Rights and Freedoms*, Part I of the *Constitution Act, 1982*, being Schedule B to the *Canada Act 1982* (UK), 1982, c 11, is an important tool for controlling unlawful executive or administrative action. As a practical matter, the most common use of the Charter in the courts is to challenge law enforcement activities engaged in by the police. What makes the Constitution distinctive is that it can be used to challenge not only the validity of executive or administrative action, but the validity of legislation as well. One may wish to question how appropriate it is for unelected judges to use their power to interpret and apply the Constitution to thwart the will of the democratically elected representatives of the citizenry. Even if one accepts the legitimacy of judicial review as a general proposition, it is still necessary to explore the appropriate limits of this role, and to consider how judges might attempt to reconcile this aspect of their role with our legal system's general commitment to democratic government.

In Section III, we consider judicial review of administrative decision-making using the common law. In this part we focus on the institutional relationships between courts and different administrative bodies. Judicial review shapes administrative decision-making in three ways— first, by constraining the exercise of power delegated to executive actors by the legislature and, more unusually, by constraining some types of exercise of prerogative authority; second, by influencing the procedures used by governmental bodies in making decisions; and third, by subjecting the substance of the decisions themselves to judicial oversight to ensure compliance with the law. A comprehensive treatment of the complex body of legal doctrines that make up Canadian administrative law is beyond the scope of this introductory text. We will, however, explore the ways in which these three aspects of common law judicial review result in quite different types of institutional relationships between courts and administrative bodies.

II. THE ROLE OF CONSTITUTIONAL JUDICIAL REVIEW IN A DEMOCRATIC SOCIETY

A. THE JUSTIFICATION FOR CONSTITUTIONAL JUDICIAL REVIEW

The passage excerpted below from US Supreme Court Chief Justice Marshall's famous judgment in *Marbury v Madison* offers a principled account of constitutional supremacy and the role the judiciary plays in ensuring that the written Constitution prevails over ordinary legislation. Chief Justice Marshall's argument in support of constitutional supremacy is simple but compelling.

Marbury v Madison
5 US 137 (1803)

MARSHALL CJ: ... The question, whether an act, repugnant to the constitution, can become the law of the land, is a question deeply interesting to the United States; but, happily, not of an intricacy proportioned to its interest. It seems only necessary to recognize certain principles, supposed to have been long and well established, to decide it.

That the people have an original right to establish, for their future government, such principles as, in their opinion, shall most conduce to their own happiness, is the basis on which the whole American fabric has been erected. The exercise of this original right is a very great exertion; nor can it nor ought it to be frequently repeated. The principles, therefore, so established are deemed fundamental. And as the authority, from which they proceed, is supreme, and can seldom act, they are designed to be permanent.

This original and supreme will organizes the government, and assigns to different departments their respective powers. It may either stop here; or establish certain limits not to be transcended by those departments.

The government of the United States is of the latter description. The powers of the legislature are defined and limited; and that those limits may not be mistaken or forgotten, the constitution is written. To what purpose are powers limited, and to what purpose is that limitation committed to writing; if these limits may, at any time, be passed by those intended to be restrained? The distinction between a government with limited and unlimited powers is abolished, if those limits do not confine the persons on whom they are imposed, and if acts prohibited and acts allowed are of equal obligation. It is a proposition too plain to be contested, that the constitution controls any legislative act repugnant to it; or, that the legislature may alter the constitution by an ordinary act.

Between these alternatives there is no middle ground. The constitution is either a superior, paramount law, unchangeable by ordinary means, or it is on a level with ordinary legislative acts, and like other acts, is alterable when the legislature shall please to alter it.

If the former part of the alternative be true, then a legislative act contrary to the constitution is not law: if the latter part be true, then written constitutions are absurd attempts, on the part of the people, to limit a power in its own nature illimitable.

Certainly all those who have framed written constitutions contemplate them as forming the fundamental and paramount law of the nation, and consequently the theory of every such government must be, that an act of the legislature repugnant to the constitution is void.

This theory is essentially attached to a written constitution, and is consequently to be considered by this court as one of the fundamental principles of our society. It is not therefore to be lost sight of in the further consideration of this subject.

If an act of the legislature, repugnant to the constitution, is void, does it, notwithstanding its invalidity, bind the courts and oblige them to give it effect? Or, in other words, though it be not law, does it constitute a rule as operative as if it was a law? This would be to overthrow in fact what was established in theory; and would seem, at first view, an absurdity too gross to be insisted on. It shall, however, receive a more attentive consideration.

It is emphatically the province and duty of the judicial department to say what the law is. Those who apply the rule to particular cases, must of necessity expound and interpret that rule. If two laws conflict with each other, the courts must decide on the operation of each.

So if a law be in opposition to the constitution: if both the law and the constitution apply to a particular case, so that the court must either decide that case conformably to the law, disregarding the constitution; or conformably to the constitution, disregarding the law: the court must determine which of these conflicting rules governs the case. This is of the very essence of judicial duty.

If then the courts are to regard the constitution; and the constitution is superior to any ordinary act of the legislature; the constitution, and not such ordinary act, must govern the case to which they both apply.

Those then who controvert the principle that the constitution is to be considered, in court, as a paramount law, are reduced to the necessity of maintaining that courts must close their eyes on the constitution, and see only the law.

This doctrine would subvert the very foundation of all written constitutions.

It would declare that an act, which, according to the principles and theory of our government, is entirely void, is yet, in practice, completely obligatory.

It would declare, that if the legislature shall do what is expressly forbidden, such act, notwithstanding the express prohibition, is in reality effectual. It would be giving to the legislature a practical and real omnipotence with the same breath which professes to restrict their powers within narrow limits. It is prescribing limits, and declaring that those limits may be passed at pleasure.

That it thus reduces to nothing what we have deemed the greatest improvement on political institutions—a written constitution, would of itself be sufficient, in America where written constitutions have been viewed with so much reverence, for rejecting the construction. But the peculiar expressions of the constitution of the United States furnish additional arguments in favour of its rejection.

The judicial power of the United States is extended to all cases arising under the constitution.

Could it be the intention of those who gave this power, to say that, in using it, the constitution should not be looked into? That a case arising under the constitution should be decided without examining the instrument under which it arises?

This is too extravagant to be maintained.

In some cases then, the constitution must be looked into by the judges. And if they can open it at all, what part of it are they forbidden to read, or to obey?

The historical origins of the principle of constitutional supremacy are different in Canada from those in the United States. As Wilson J explained in her reasons for judgment concurring in the result in *Operation Dismantle v The Queen*, [1985] 1 SCR 441 at 482-83, constitutional supremacy in Canada was originally grounded in s 2 of the *Colonial Laws Validity Act, 1865* (UK), 28 & 29 Vict, c 63, which rendered void and inoperative any act of a colonial legislature that was repugnant to an act of the Imperial Parliament that extended to the colony. Because the *British North America Act* (now the *Constitution Act, 1867* (UK), 30 & 31 Vict, c 3, reprinted in RSC 1985, Appendix II, No 5) was an act of the Imperial Parliament that was binding on the colonial legislatures of Canada and its provinces, federal or provincial legislation that was found to be inconsistent with the *British North America Act* was therefore void for repugnancy with an Imperial statute. The *Statute of Westminster, 1931* (UK), 22 Geo V, c 4 made Canada and its provinces free from Imperial legislation, but s 7 of the Act expressly exempted the *British North America Act* and its amendments from this freedom in order to preserve the principle of constitutional supremacy.

With the patriation of the Canadian Constitution in 1982, the principle of constitutional supremacy was expressly enshrined in s 52(1) of the *Constitution Act, 1982*, being Schedule B to the *Canada Act 1982* (UK), 1982, c 11, which reads: "The Constitution of Canada is the supreme law of Canada, and any law that is inconsistent with the provisions of the Constitution is, to the extent of the inconsistency, of no force or effect."

B. THE LIMITATIONS OF JUDICIAL REVIEW USING THE CONSTITUTION

1. The Issue of Justiciability

Are all actions by the political branches of government "justiciable"—that is, amenable to oversight by the courts? Generally, there are few instances where the government is immune from close judicial review. For instance, in addition to providing the Supreme Court of Canada with an opportunity to explore the principle of constitutional supremacy, the *Operation Dismantle* case also tested the limits of the role that courts play in weighing governmental measures designed to protect national defence against the standards imposed by the Constitution.

Operation Dismantle v The Queen
[1985] 1 SCR 441

DICKSON J (Estey, McIntyre, Chouinard, and Lamer JJ concurring):

[1] This case arises out of the appellants' challenge under s. 7 of the *Canadian Charter of Rights and Freedoms* to the decision of the federal cabinet to permit the testing of the cruise missile by the United States of America in Canadian territory. The issue that must be addressed is whether the appellants' statement of claim should be struck out, before trial, as disclosing no reasonable cause of action. In their statement of claim, the appellants seek: (i) a declaration that the decision to permit the testing of the cruise missile is unconstitutional; (ii) injunctive relief to prohibit the testing; and (iii) damages. Cattanach J of the Federal Court, Trial Division, refused the respondents' motion to strike. The Federal Court of Appeal unanimously allowed the respondents' appeal, struck out the statement of claim and dismissed the appellants' action.

[2] The facts and procedural history of this case are fully set out and discussed in the reasons for judgment of Madame Justice Wilson. I agree with Madame Justice Wilson that the appellants' statement of claim should be struck out and this appeal dismissed. I have reached this conclusion, however, on the basis of reasons which differ somewhat from those of Madame Justice Wilson.

[3] In my opinion, if the appellants are to be entitled to proceed to trial, their statement of claim must disclose facts, which, if taken as true, would show that the action of the Canadian government could cause an infringement of their rights under s. 7 of the Charter. I have concluded that the causal link between the actions of the Canadian government, and the alleged violation of appellants' rights under the Charter is simply too uncertain, speculative and hypothetical to sustain a cause of action. Thus, although decisions of the federal cabinet are reviewable by the courts under the Charter, and the government bears a general duty to act in accordance with the Charter's dictates, no duty is imposed on the Canadian government by s. 7 of the Charter to refrain from permitting the testing of the cruise missile.

• • •

[37] In the present case, the speculative nature of the allegation that the decision to test the cruise missile will lead to an increased threat of nuclear war makes it manifest that no duty is imposed on the Canadian government to refrain from permitting the testing. The government's action simply could not be proven to cause the alleged violation of s. 7 of the Charter and, thus, no duty can arise.

III. Justiciability

[38] The approach which I have taken is not based on the concept of justiciability. I agree in substance with Madame Justice Wilson's discussion of justiciability and her conclusion that the doctrine is founded upon a concern with the appropriate role of the courts as the forum for the resolution of different types of disputes. I have no doubt that disputes of a political or foreign policy nature may be properly cognizable by the courts. My concerns in the present case focus on the impossibility of the Court finding, on the basis of evidence, the connection, alleged by the appellants, between the duty of the government to act in accordance with the *Charter of Rights and Freedoms* and the violation of their rights under s. 7. As stated above, I do not believe the alleged violation—namely, the increased threat of nuclear war—could ever be sufficiently linked as a factual matter to the acknowledged duty of the government to respect s. 7 of the Charter.

• • •

WILSON J (concurring in result only):

• • •

(1) Is the Government's Decision Reviewable?

• • •

(b) Non-Justiciability

[51] Le Dain and Ryan JJ in the Federal Court of Appeal were of the opinion that the issues involved in this case are inherently non-justiciable, either because the question whether testing the cruise missile increases the risk of nuclear war is not susceptible of proof and hence is not triable (per Ryan J) or because answering that question involves factors which are either inaccessible to a court or are of a nature which a court is incapable of evaluating (per Le Dain J). To the extent that this objection to the appellants' case rests on the inherent evidentiary difficulties which would obviously confront any attempt to prove the appellants' allegations of fact, I do not think it can be sustained. It might well be that, if the issue were allowed to go to trial, the appellants would lose simply by reason of their not having been able to establish the factual basis of their claim but that does not seem to me to be a reason for striking the case out at this preliminary stage. It is trite law that on a motion to strike out a statement of claim the plaintiff's allegations of fact are to be taken as having been proved. Accordingly, it is arguable that by dealing with the case as they have done Le Dain and Ryan JJ have, in effect, made a presumption against the appellants which they are not entitled, on a preliminary motion of this kind, to make.

[52] I am not convinced, however, that Le Dain and Ryan JJ were restricting the concept of non-justiciability to difficulties of evidence and proof. Both rely on Lord Radcliffe's judgment in *Chandler v. D.P.P.*, [1964] AC 777, [1962] 3 All ER 142, 46 Cr. App. Rep. 347 (HL), and especially on the following passage at p. 151:

> The disposition and equipment of the forces and the facilities afforded to allied forces for defence purposes constitute a given fact and it cannot be a matter of proof or finding that the decisions of policy on which they rest are or are not in the country's best interests. I may add that I can think of few issues which present themselves in less triable form. It would be ingenuous to suppose that the kind of evidence that the appellants wanted to call could make more than a small contribution to its final solution. The facts which they wished to establish might well be admitted: even so, throughout history men have had to run great risk for themselves and others in the hope of attaining objectives which they prize for all. *The more one looks at it, the plainer it becomes, I think, that the question whether it is in the true interests of this country to acquire, retain or house nuclear armaments depends on an infinity of considerations, military and diplomatic, technical, psychological and moral, and of decisions, tentative or final, which are themselves part assessments of fact and part expectations and hopes.* I do not think that there is anything amiss with a legal ruling that does not make this issue a matter for judge or jury. (Emphasis added)

In my opinion, this passage makes clear that in Lord Radcliffe's view these kinds of issues are to be treated as non-justiciable not simply because of evidentiary difficulties but because they involve moral and political considerations which it is not within the province of the courts to assess. Le Dain J maintains that the difficulty is one of judicial competence rather than anything resembling the American "political questions" doctrine. However, in response to that contention it can be pointed out that, however unsuited courts may be for the task, they are called upon all the time to decide questions of principle and policy. As Melville Weston points out in "Political Questions" (1925), 38 *Harv. L Rev.* 296 at 299:

> The word "justiciable" ... is legitimately capable of denoting almost any question. That is to say, the questions are few which are intrinsically incapable of submission to a tribunal having an established procedure, with an orderly presentation of such evidence as is available, for the purpose of an adjudication from which practical consequences in human conduct are to follow. For example, when nations decline to submit to arbitration or to the compulsory jurisdiction of a proposed international tribunal those questions of honour or interest which they call "nonjusticiable" they are really avoiding that broad sense of the word, but what they mean is a little less clear. Probably they mean only that they will not, or deem they ought not, endure the presentation of evidence on such questions, nor bind their conduct to conform to the proposed adjudications. So far as "non-justiciable" is for them more than an epithet, it expresses a sense of a lack of fitness, and not of any inherent impossibility, of submitting these questions to judicial or quasi-judicial determination.

[53] In the 1950's and early 1960's there was considerable debate in Britain over the question whether restrictive trade practices legislation gave rise to questions which were subject to judicial determination: see Marshall, "Justiciability" in *Oxford Essays in Jurisprudence* (1961), ed. A.G. Guest; Summers, "Justiciability" (1963), 26 *MLR* 530; Stevens, "Justiciability: The Restrictive Practices Court Re-Examined," [1964] *Public Law* 221. I think it is fairly clear that the British restrictive trade practices legislation did not involve the courts in the resolution of issues more imponderable than those facing American courts administering the *Sherman Act.* Indeed, there is significantly less "policy" content in the decisions of the courts in those cases than there is in the decisions of administrative tribunals such as the Canadian Transport Commission or the CRTC. The real issue there, and perhaps also in the case at bar, is not the *ability* of judicial tribunals to make a decision on the questions presented, but the *appropriateness* of the use of the judicial techniques for such purposes.

[54] I cannot accept the proposition that difficulties of evidence or proof absolve the Court from making a certain kind of decision if it can be established on other grounds that it has a duty to do so. I think we should focus our attention on whether the courts *should* or *must* rather than on whether they *can* deal with such matters. We should put difficulties of evidence and proof aside and consider whether as a constitutional matter it is appropriate or obligatory for the courts to decide the issue before us. I will return to this question later.

(c) The Political Questions Doctrine

[55] It is a well established principle of American constitutional law that there are certain kinds of "political questions" that a court ought to refuse to decide. In *Baker v. Carr,* 369 US 186 (1962) at pp. 210-11, Brennan J discussed the nature of the doctrine in the following terms:

> We have said that "[i]n determining whether a question falls within (the political question) category, the appropriateness under our system of government of attributing finality to the action of the political departments and also the lack of satisfactory criteria for a judicial determination are dominant considerations." *Coleman v. Miller,* 307 US 433, 454-455. The nonjusticiability of a political question is primarily

a function of the separation of powers. Much confusion results from the capacity of the "political question" label to obscure the need for case-by-case inquiry. Deciding whether a matter has in any measure been committed by the Constitution to another branch of government, or whether the action of that branch exceeds whatever authority has been committed, is itself a delicate exercise in constitutional interpretation, and is a responsibility of this court as ultimate interpreter of a Constitution.

At p. 217 he said:

It is apparent that several formulations which vary slightly according to the settings in which the questions arise may describe a political question, although each has one or more elements which identify it as essentially a function of the separation of powers. Prominent on the surface of any case held to involve a political question is found a textually demonstrable constitutional commitment of the issue to a coordinate political department; or a lack of judicially discoverable and manageable standards for resolving it; or the impossibility of deciding without an initial policy determination of a kind clearly for nonjudicial discretion; or the impossibility of a court's undertaking independent resolution without expressing lack of the respect due coordinate branches of government; or an unusual need for unquestioning adherence to a political decision already made; or the potentiality of embarrassment from multifarious pronouncements by various departments on one question.

While one or two of the categories of political question referred to by Brennan J raise the issue of judicial or institutional competence already referred to, the underlying theme is the separation of powers in the sense of the proper role of the courts vis-à-vis the other branches of government. In this regard it is perhaps noteworthy that a distinction is drawn in the American case law between matters internal to the United States on the one hand and foreign affairs on the other. In the area of foreign affairs the courts are especially deferential to the executive branch of government: see e.g. *Atlee v. Laird*, 347 F. Supp. 689 (1972) (US Dist. Ct.), at pp. 701ff.

[56] While Brennan J's statement, in my view, accurately sums up the reasoning American courts have used in deciding that specific cases did not present questions which were judicially cognizable, I do not think it is particularly helpful in determining when American courts will find that those factors come into play. In cases from *Marbury v. Madison*, 5 US (1 Cranch) 137 (1803) to *United States v. Nixon*, 418 US 683 (1974), the court has not allowed the "respect due coordinate branches of government" to prevent it from rendering decisions highly embarrassing to those holding executive or legislative office. In *Baker v. Carr* itself, *supra*, Frankfurter J, in dissent, expressed concern that the judiciary could not find manageable standards for the problems presented by the reapportionment of political districts. Indeed, some would say that the enforcement of the desegregation decision in *Brown v. Board of Education of Topeka*, 347 US 483 (1954), gave rise to similar problems of judicial unmanageability. Yet American courts have ventured into these areas undeterred.

• • •

[63] It might be timely at this point to remind ourselves of the question the court is being asked to decide. It is, of course, true that the federal Legislature has exclusive legislative jurisdiction in relation to defence under s. 91(7) of the *Constitution Act, 1867* and that the federal executive has the powers conferred upon it in ss. 9-15 of that Act. Accordingly, if the court were simply being asked to express its opinion on the wisdom of the executive's exercise of its defence powers in this case, the

court would have to decline. It cannot substitute its opinion for that of the executive to whom the decision-making power is given by the Constitution. Because the *effect* of the appellants' action is to challenge the wisdom of the government's defence policy, it is tempting to say that the court should in the same way refuse to involve itself. However, I think this would be to miss the point, to fail to focus on the question which is before us. The question before us is not whether the government's defence policy is sound but whether or not it violates the appellants' rights under s. 7 of the *Charter of Rights and Freedoms*. This is a totally different question. I do not think there can be any doubt that this is a question for the courts. Indeed, s. 24(1) of the Charter, also part of the Constitution, makes it clear that the adjudication of that question is the responsibility of "a court of competent jurisdiction." While the court is entitled to grant such remedy as it "considers appropriate and just in the circumstances," I do not think it is open to it to relinquish its jurisdiction either on the basis that the issue is inherently non-justiciable or that it raises a so-called "political question": see Martin H. Redish, "Abstention, Separation of Powers, and the Limits of the Judicial Function" (1984), 94 *Yale LJ* 71.

[64] I would conclude, therefore, that if we are to look at the Constitution for the answer to the question whether it is appropriate for the courts to "second guess" the executive on matters of defence, we would conclude that it is not appropriate. However, if what we are being asked to do is to decide whether any particular act of the executive violates the rights of the citizens, then it is not only appropriate that we answer the question; it is our obligation under the Charter to do so.

• • •

(3) Could the Facts as Alleged Constitute a Violation of Section 7 of the Charter?

[95] Section 7 of the *Canadian Charter of Rights and Freedoms* provides as follows:

> 7. Everyone has the right to life, liberty and security of the person and the right not to be deprived thereof except in accordance with the principles of fundamental justice.

[96] Whether or not the facts that are alleged in the appellants' statement of claim could constitute a violation of s. 7 is, of course, the question that lies at the heart of this case. If they could not, then the appellants' statement of claim discloses no reasonable cause of action and the appeal must be dismissed. The appellants submit that on its proper construction s. 7 gives rise to two separate and presumably independent rights, namely the right to life, liberty and security of the person, and the right not to be deprived of such life, liberty and security of the person except in accordance with the principles of fundamental justice. In their submission, therefore, a violation of the principles of fundamental justice would only have to be alleged in relation to a claim based on a violation of the second right. As Marceau J points out in his reasons, the French text of s. 7 does not seem to admit of this two-rights interpretation since only one right is specifically mentioned. Moreover, as the respondents point out, the appellants' suggestion does not accord with the interpretation that the courts have placed on the similarly structured provision in s. 1(a) of the *Canadian Bill of Rights*: see e.g. *R v. Miller*, [1977] 2 SCR 680, *per* Ritchie J, at pp. 703-04.

[97] The appellants' submission, however, touches upon a number of important issues regarding the proper interpretation of s. 7. Even if the section gives rise to a

single unequivocal right not to be deprived of life, liberty or security of the person except in accordance with the principles of fundamental justice, there nonetheless remains the question whether fundamental justice is entirely procedural in nature or whether it has a substantive aspect as well. This, in turn, leads to the related question whether there might not be certain deprivations of life, liberty or personal security which could not be justified no matter what procedure was employed to effect them. These are among the most important and difficult questions of interpretation arising under the Charter but I do not think it is necessary to deal with them in this case. It can, in my opinion, be disposed of without reaching these issues.

[98] In my view, even an independent, substantive right to life, liberty and security of the person cannot be absolute. For example, the right to liberty, which I take to be the right to pursue one's goals free of governmental constraint, must accommodate the corresponding rights of others. The concept of "right" as used in the Charter postulate the inter-relation of individuals in society all of whom have the same right. The aphorism that "A hermit has no need of rights" makes the point. The concept of "right" also premises the existence of someone or some group against whom the right may be asserted. As Mortimer J. Adler expressed it in *Six Great Ideas* (1981), at p. 144:

> Living in organized societies under effective government and enforceable laws, as they must in order to survive and prosper, human beings neither have autonomy nor are they entitled to unlimited liberty of action. Autonomy is incompatible with organized society. Unlimited liberty is destructive of it.

[99] The concept of "right" used in the Charter must also, I believe, recognize and take account of the political reality of the modern state. Action by the state or, conversely, inaction by the state will frequently have the effect of decreasing or increasing the risk to the lives or security of its citizens. It may be argued, for example, that the failure of government to limit significantly the speed of traffic on the highways threatens our right to life and security in that it increases the risk of highway accidents. Such conduct, however, would not, in my view, fall within the scope of the right protected by s. 7 of the Charter.

[100] In the same way, the concept of "right" as used in the Charter must take account of the fact that the self-contained political community which comprises the state is faced with at least the possibility, if not the reality, of external threats to both its collective well-being and to the individual well-being of its citizens. In order to protect the community against such threats it may well be necessary for the state to take steps which incidentally increase the risk to the lives or personal security of some or all of the state's citizens. Such steps, it seems to me, cannot have been contemplated by the draftsman of the Charter as giving rise to violations of s. 7. As John Rawls states in *A Theory of Justice* (1971), at p. 213:

> The government's right to maintain public order and security is ... a right which the government must have if it is to carry out its duty of impartially supporting the conditions necessary for everyone's pursuit of his interests and living up to his obligations as he understands them.

[101] The rights under the Charter not being absolute, their content or scope must be discerned quite apart from any limitation sought to be imposed upon them by the government under s. 1. As was pointed out by the Ontario Court of Appeal in *Re Federal Republic of Germany and Rauca* (1983), 41 OR (2d) 225 at 244, 34 CR (3d) 97, 4 CCC (3d) 385, 4 CRR 42, 145 DLR (3d) 638:

> The Charter was not enacted in a vacuum and the rights set out therein must be interpreted rationally having regard to existing law ... .

There is no liberty without law and there is no law without some restriction of liberty: see Dworkin, *Taking Rights Seriously* (1977), p. 267. This paradox caused Roscoe Pound to conclude:

> There is no more ambiguous word in legal and juristic literature than the word right. In its most general sense it means a reasonable expectation involved in civilized life. [See *Jurisprudence*, vol. 4 (1959), p. 56.]

[102] It is not necessary to accept the restrictive interpretation advanced by Pratte J, which would limit s. 7 to protection against arbitrary arrest or detention, in order to agree that the central concern of the section is direct impingement by government upon the life, liberty and personal security of individual citizens. At the very least, it seems to me, there must be a strong presumption that governmental action which concerns the relations of the state with other states, and which is therefore not directed at any member of the immediate political community, was never intended to be caught by s. 7 even although such action may have the incidental effect of increasing the risk of death or injury that individuals generally have to face.

[103] I agree with Le Dain J that the essence of the appellants' case is the claim that permitting the cruise missile to be tested in Canada will increase the risk of nuclear war. But even accepting this allegation of fact as true, which as I have already said I think we must do on a motion to strike, it is my opinion for the reasons given above that this state of affairs could not constitute a breach of s. 7. Moreover, I do not see how one can distinguish in a principled way between this particular risk and any other danger to which the government's action vis-à-vis other states might incidentally subject its citizens. A declaration of war, for example, almost certainly increases the risk to most citizens of death or injury. Acceptance of the appellants' submissions, it seems to me, would mean that any such declaration would also have to be regarded as a violation of s. 7. I cannot think that that could be a proper interpretation of the Charter.

[104] This is not to say that every governmental action that is purportedly taken in furtherance of national defence would be beyond the reach of s. 7. If, for example, testing the cruise missile posed a direct threat to some specific segment of the populace—as, for example, if it were being tested with live warheads—I think that might well raise different considerations. A court might find that that constituted a violation of s. 7 and it might then be up to the government to try to establish that testing the cruise with live warheads was justified under s. 1 of the Charter. Section 1, in my opinion, is the uniquely Canadian mechanism through which the courts are to determine the justiciability of particular issues that come before it. It embodies through its reference to a free and democratic society the essential features of our constitution including the separation of powers, responsible government and the rule of law. It obviates the need for a "political questions" doctrine and permits the court to deal with what might be termed "prudential" considerations in a principled way without renouncing its constitutional and mandated responsibility for judicial review. It is not, however, called into operation here since the facts alleged in the statement of claim, even if they could be shown to be true, could not in my opinion constitute a violation of s. 7.

As we noted in Chapter 8, in 2019 the United Kingdom Supreme Court had to address whether the courts were able to review Prime Minister Boris Johnston's advice to the Queen that Parliament should be prorogued for several weeks leading up to the anticipated withdrawal of the United Kingdom from the European Union, at a time when there was considerable uncertainty about the terms under which withdrawal would take place. Legal challenges to this advice were launched in both England and Scotland. The English Court of Queen's Bench, Divisional Court, concluded that the matter was not justiciable in *R (on the application of Miller) v The Prime Minister,* [2019] EWHC 2381 (QB). The Scottish Court of Session, Inner House, reached the opposite conclusion in *Cherry v Advocate General,* [2019] CSIH 49. On appeal from both decisions, the United Kingdom Supreme Court concluded that the Prime Minister's advice was justiciable for the reasons set out below.

R (on the application of Miller) v The Prime Minister
[2019] UKSC 41

LADY HALE and LORD REED giving the judgment of the Court:

• • •

Is the Question of Whether the Prime Minister's Advice to the Queen Was Lawful Justiciable in a Court of Law?

[28] Counsel for the Prime Minister in the *Miller* proceedings, and the Advocate General as representing the United Kingdom Government in the *Cherry* proceedings, have argued that the court should decline to consider the challenges with which these appeals are concerned, on the basis that they do not raise any legal question on which the courts can properly adjudicate: that is to say, that the matters raised are not justiciable. Instead of the Prime Minister's advice to Her Majesty being reviewable by the courts, they argue that he is accountable only to Parliament. They conclude that the courts should not enter the political arena but should respect the separation of powers.

[29] As we have explained, that argument was rejected by the Inner House in the *Cherry* proceedings, but was accepted by the Divisional Court in the *Miller* proceedings. In the view of the Divisional Court, the Prime Minister's decision that Parliament should be prorogued at the time and for the duration chosen, and his advice to Her Majesty to that effect, were inherently political in nature, and there were no legal standards against which to judge their legitimacy.

[30] Before considering the question of justiciability, there are four points that we should make clear at the outset. First, the power to order the prorogation of Parliament is a prerogative power: that is to say, a power recognised by the common law and exercised by the Crown, in this instance by the sovereign in person, acting on advice, in accordance with modern constitutional practice. It is not suggested in these appeals that Her Majesty was other than obliged by constitutional convention to accept that advice. In the circumstances, we express no view on that matter. That situation does, however, place on the Prime Minister a constitutional responsibility, as the only person with power to do so, to have regard to all relevant interests, including the interests of Parliament.

[31] Secondly, although the courts cannot decide political questions, the fact that a legal dispute concerns the conduct of politicians, or arises from a matter of political controversy, has never been sufficient reason for the courts to refuse to consider

it. As the Divisional Court observed in para 47 of its judgment, almost all important decisions made by the executive have a political hue to them. Nevertheless, the courts have exercised a supervisory jurisdiction over the decisions of the executive for centuries. Many if not most of the constitutional cases in our legal history have been concerned with politics in that sense.

[32] Two examples will suffice to illustrate the point. The 17th century was a period of turmoil over the relationship between the Stuart kings and Parliament, which culminated in civil war. That political controversy did not deter the courts from holding, in the *Case of Proclamations* (1611) 12 Co Rep 74, that an attempt to alter the law of the land by the use of the Crown's prerogative powers was unlawful. The court concluded at p 76 that "the King hath no prerogative, but that which the law of the land allows him," indicating that the limits of prerogative powers were set by law and were determined by the courts. The later 18th century was another troubled period in our political history, when the Government was greatly concerned about seditious publications. That did not deter the courts from holding, in *Entick v Carrington* (1765) 19 State Tr 1029; 2 Wils KB 275, 95 ER 807, that the Secretary of State could not order searches of private property without authority conferred by an Act of Parliament or the common law.

[33] Thirdly, the Prime Minister's accountability to Parliament does not in itself justify the conclusion that the courts have no legitimate role to play. That is so for two reasons. The first is that the effect of prorogation is to prevent the operation of ministerial accountability to Parliament during the period when Parliament stands prorogued. Indeed, if Parliament were to be prorogued with immediate effect, there would be no possibility of the Prime Minister's being held accountable by Parliament until after a new session of Parliament had commenced, by which time the Government's purpose in having Parliament prorogued might have been accomplished. In such circumstances, the most that Parliament could do would amount to closing the stable door after the horse had bolted. The second reason is that the courts have a duty to give effect to the law, irrespective of the minister's political accountability to Parliament. The fact that the minister is politically accountable to Parliament does not mean that he is therefore immune from legal accountability to the courts. As Lord Lloyd of Berwick stated in the *Fire Brigades Union* case (*R v Secretary of State for the Home Department, Ex p Fire Brigades Union* [1995] 2 AC 513, 572-573):

> No court would ever depreciate or call in question ministerial responsibility to Parliament. But as Professor Sir William Wade points out in *Wade and Forsyth, Administrative Law*, 7th ed (1994), p 34, ministerial responsibility is no substitute for judicial review. In *R v Inland Revenue Comrs, Ex p National Federation of Self-Employed and Small Businesses Ltd* [1982] AC 617, 644 Lord Diplock said:
>
> > It is not, in my view, a sufficient answer to say that judicial review of the actions of officers or departments of central government is unnecessary because they are accountable to Parliament for the way in which they carry out their functions. They are accountable to Parliament for what they do so far as regards efficiency and policy, and of that Parliament is the only judge; they are responsible to a court of justice for the lawfulness of what they do, and of that the court is the only judge.

[34] Fourthly, if the issue before the court is justiciable, deciding it will not offend against the separation of powers. As we have just indicated, the court will be performing its proper function under our constitution. Indeed, by ensuring that the

Government does not use the power of prorogation unlawfully with the effect of preventing Parliament from carrying out its proper functions, the court will be giving effect to the separation of powers.

[35] Having made those introductory points, we turn to the question whether the issue raised by these appeals is justiciable. How is that question to be answered? In the case of prerogative powers, it is necessary to distinguish between two different issues. The first is whether a prerogative power exists, and if it does exist, its extent. The second is whether, granted that a prerogative power exists, and that it has been exercised within its limits, the exercise of the power is open to legal challenge on some other basis. The first of these issues undoubtedly lies within the jurisdiction of the courts and is justiciable, as all the parties to these proceedings accept. If authority is required, it can be found in the decision of the House of Lords in the case of *Council of Civil Service Unions v Minister for the Civil Service* [1985] AC 374. The second of these issues, on the other hand, may raise questions of justiciability. The question then is not whether the power exists, or whether a purported exercise of the power was beyond its legal limits, but whether its exercise within its legal limits is challengeable in the courts on the basis of one or more of the recognised grounds of judicial review. In the *Council of Civil Service Unions* case, the House of Lords concluded that the answer to that question would depend on the nature and subject matter of the particular prerogative power being exercised. In that regard, Lord Roskill mentioned at p 418 the dissolution of Parliament as one of a number of powers whose exercise was in his view non-justiciable.

[36] Counsel for the Prime Minister rely on that dictum in the present case, since the dissolution of Parliament under the prerogative, as was possible until the enactment of the *Fixed-term Parliaments Act 2011*, is in their submission analogous to prorogation. They submit that prorogation is in any event another example of what Lord Roskill described as "excluded categories," and refer to later authority which treated questions of "high policy" as forming another such category (*R v Secretary of State for Foreign and Commonwealth Affairs, Ex p Everett* [1989] QB 811, 820). The court has heard careful and detailed submissions on this area of the law, and has been referred to many authorities. It is, however, important to understand that this argument only arises if the issue in these proceedings is properly characterised as one concerning the lawfulness of the exercise of a prerogative power within its lawful limits, rather than as one concerning the lawful limits of the power and whether they have been exceeded. As we have explained, no question of justiciability, whether by reason of subject matter or otherwise, can arise in relation to whether the law recognises the existence of a prerogative power, or in relation to its legal limits. Those are by definition questions of law. Under the separation of powers, it is the function of the courts to determine them.

[37] Before reaching a conclusion as to justiciability, the court therefore has to determine whether the present case requires it to determine where a legal limit lies in relation to the power to prorogue Parliament, and whether the Prime Minister's advice trespassed beyond that limit, or whether the present case concerns the lawfulness of a particular exercise of the power within its legal limits. That question is closely related to the identification of the standard by reference to which the lawfulness of the Prime Minister's advice is to be judged. It is to that matter that we turn next.

By What Standard Is the Lawfulness of the Advice to Be Judged?

[38] In principle, if not always in practice, it is relatively straightforward to determine the limits of a statutory power, since the power is defined by the text of the

statute. Since a prerogative power is not constituted by any document, determining its limits is less straightforward. Nevertheless, every prerogative power has its limits, and it is the function of the court to determine, when necessary, where they lie. Since the power is recognised by the common law, and has to be compatible with common law principles, those principles may illuminate where its boundaries lie. In particular, the boundaries of a prerogative power relating to the operation of Parliament are likely to be illuminated, and indeed determined, by the fundamental principles of our constitutional law.

[39] Although the United Kingdom does not have a single document entitled "The Constitution," it nevertheless possesses a Constitution, established over the course of our history by common law, statutes, conventions and practice. Since it has not been codified, it has developed pragmatically, and remains sufficiently flexible to be capable of further development. Nevertheless, it includes numerous principles of law, which are enforceable by the courts in the same way as other legal principles. In giving them effect, the courts have the responsibility of upholding the values and principles of our constitution and making them effective. It is their particular responsibility to determine the legal limits of the powers conferred on each branch of government, and to decide whether any exercise of power has transgressed those limits. The courts cannot shirk that responsibility merely on the ground that the question raised is political in tone or context.

[40] The legal principles of the constitution are not confined to statutory rules, but include constitutional principles developed by the common law. We have already given two examples of such principles, namely that the law of the land cannot be altered except by or in accordance with an Act of Parliament, and that the Government cannot search private premises without lawful authority. Many more examples could be given. Such principles are not confined to the protection of individual rights, but include principles concerning the conduct of public bodies and the relationships between them. For example, they include the principle that justice must be administered in public (*Scott v Scott* [1913] AC 417), and the principle of the separation of powers between the executive, Parliament and the courts (*Ex p Fire Brigades Union* , pp 567-568). In their application to the exercise of governmental powers, constitutional principles do not apply only to powers conferred by statute, but also extend to prerogative powers. For example, they include the principle that the executive cannot exercise prerogative powers so as to deprive people of their property without the payment of compensation (*Burmah Oil Co Ltd v Lord Advocate* [1965] AC 75).

[41] Two fundamental principles of our constitutional law are relevant to the present case. The first is the principle of Parliamentary sovereignty: that laws enacted by the Crown in Parliament are the supreme form of law in our legal system, with which everyone, including the Government, must comply. However, the effect which the courts have given to Parliamentary sovereignty is not confined to recognising the status of the legislation enacted by the Crown in Parliament as our highest form of law. Time and again, in a series of cases since the 17th century, the courts have protected Parliamentary sovereignty from threats posed to it by the use of prerogative powers, and in doing so have demonstrated that prerogative powers are limited by the principle of Parliamentary sovereignty. To give only a few examples, in the *Case of Proclamations* the court protected Parliamentary sovereignty directly, by holding that prerogative powers could not be used to alter the law of the land. Three centuries later, in the case of *Attorney General v De Keyser's Royal Hotel Ltd* [1920] AC 508, the court prevented the Government of the day from seeking by indirect means to bypass Parliament, in circumventing a statute through the use of the prerogative. More recently, in the *Fire Brigades Union* case, the court again

prevented the Government from rendering a statute nugatory through recourse to the prerogative, and was not deflected by the fact that the Government had failed to bring the statute into effect. As Lord Browne-Wilkinson observed in that case at p 552, "the constitutional history of this country is the history of the prerogative powers of the Crown being made subject to the overriding powers of the democratically elected legislature as the sovereign body."

[42] The sovereignty of Parliament would, however, be undermined as the foundational principle of our constitution if the executive could, through the use of the prerogative, prevent Parliament from exercising its legislative authority for as long as it pleased. That, however, would be the position if there was no legal limit upon the power to prorogue Parliament (subject to a few exceptional circumstances in which, under statute, Parliament can meet while it stands prorogued). An unlimited power of prorogation would therefore be incompatible with the legal principle of Parliamentary sovereignty.

[43] In our view, it is no answer to these points to say, as counsel for the Prime Minister argued, that the court should decline to consider extreme hypothetical examples. The court has to address the argument of counsel for the Prime Minister that there are no circumstances whatsoever in which it would be entitled to review a decision that Parliament should be prorogued (or ministerial advice to that effect). In addressing that argument, it is perfectly appropriate, and necessary, to consider its implications. Nor is it any answer to say that there are practical constraints on the length of time for which Parliament might stand prorogued, since the Government would eventually need to raise money in order to fund public services, and would for that purpose require Parliamentary authority, and would also require annual legislation to maintain a standing army. Those practical constraints offer scant reassurance.

[44] It must therefore follow, as a concomitant of Parliamentary sovereignty, that the power to prorogue cannot be unlimited. Statutory requirements as to sittings of Parliament have indeed been enacted from time to time, for example by the Statute of 1362 (36 Edward III c 10), the Triennial Acts of 1640 and 1664, the Bill of Rights 1688, the Scottish Claim of Right 1689, the *Meeting of Parliament Act 1694*, and most recently the *Northern Ireland (Executive Formation etc) Act 2019*, section 3. Their existence confirms the necessity of a legal limit on the power to prorogue, but they do not address the situation with which the present appeals are concerned.

[45] On the other hand, Parliament does not remain permanently in session, and it is undoubtedly lawful to prorogue Parliament notwithstanding the fact that, so long as it stands prorogued, Parliament cannot enact laws. In modern practice, Parliament is normally prorogued for only a short time. There can be no question of such a prorogation being incompatible with Parliamentary sovereignty: its effect on Parliament's ability to exercise its legislative powers is relatively minor and uncontroversial. How, then, is the limit upon the power to prorogue to be defined, so as to make it compatible with the principle of Parliamentary sovereignty?

[46] The same question arises in relation to a second constitutional principle, that of Parliamentary accountability, described by Lord Carnwath in his judgment in the first *Miller* case as no less fundamental to our constitution than Parliamentary sovereignty (*R (Miller) v Secretary of State for Exiting the European Union* [2017] UKSC 5; [2018] AC 61, para 249). As Lord Bingham of Cornhill said in the case of *Bobb v Manning* [2006] UKPC 22, para 13, "the conduct of government by a Prime Minister and Cabinet collectively responsible and accountable to Parliament lies at the heart of Westminster democracy." Ministers are accountable to Parliament through such mechanisms as their duty to answer Parliamentary questions and to appear before Parliamentary committees, and through Parliamentary scrutiny of

the delegated legislation which ministers make. By these means, the policies of the executive are subjected to consideration by the representatives of the electorate, the executive is required to report, explain and defend its actions, and citizens are protected from the arbitrary exercise of executive power.

[47] The principle of Parliamentary accountability has been invoked time and again throughout the development of our constitutional and administrative law, as a justification for judicial restraint as part of a constitutional separation of powers (see, for example, *R v Secretary of State for the Environment, Ex p Nottinghamshire County Council* [1986] AC 240, 250), and as an explanation for non-justiciability (*Mohammed (Serdar) v Ministry of Defence* [2017] UKSC 1; [2017] AC 649, para 57). It was also an animating principle of some of the statutes mentioned in para 44, as appears from their references to the redress of grievances. As we have mentioned, its importance as a fundamental constitutional principle has also been recognised by the courts.

[48] That principle is not placed in jeopardy if Parliament stands prorogued for the short period which is customary, and as we have explained, Parliament does not in any event expect to be in permanent session. But the longer that Parliament stands prorogued, the greater the risk that responsible government may be replaced by unaccountable government: the antithesis of the democratic model. So the same question arises as in relation to Parliamentary sovereignty: what is the legal limit upon the power to prorogue which makes it compatible with the ability of Parliament to carry out its constitutional functions?

[49] In answering that question, it is of some assistance to consider how the courts have dealt with situations where the exercise of a power conferred by statute, rather than one arising under the prerogative, was liable to affect the operation of a constitutional principle. The approach which they have adopted has concentrated on the effect of the exercise of the power upon the operation of the relevant constitutional principle. Unless the terms of the statute indicate a contrary intention, the courts have set a limit to the lawful exercise of the power by holding that the extent to which the measure impedes or frustrates the operation of the relevant principle must have a reasonable justification. That approach can be seen, for example, in *R (UNISON) v Lord Chancellor* [2017] UKSC 51; [2017] 3 WLR 409, paras 80-82 and 88-89, where earlier authorities were discussed. A prerogative power is, of course, different from a statutory power: since it is not derived from statute, its limitations cannot be derived from a process of statutory interpretation. However, a prerogative power is only effective to the extent that it is recognised by the common law: as was said in the *Case of Proclamations*, "the King hath no prerogative, but that which the law of the land allows him." A prerogative power is therefore limited by statute and the common law, including, in the present context, the constitutional principles with which it would otherwise conflict.

[50] For the purposes of the present case, therefore, the relevant limit upon the power to prorogue can be expressed in this way: that a decision to prorogue Parliament (or to advise the monarch to prorogue Parliament) will be unlawful if the prorogation has the effect of frustrating or preventing, without reasonable justification, the ability of Parliament to carry out its constitutional functions as a legislature and as the body responsible for the supervision of the executive. In such a situation, the court will intervene if the effect is sufficiently serious to justify such an exceptional course.

[51] That standard is one that can be applied in practice. The extent to which prorogation frustrates or prevents Parliament's ability to perform its legislative functions and its supervision of the executive is a question of fact which presents no greater difficulty than many other questions of fact which are routinely decided

by the courts. The court then has to decide whether the Prime Minister's explanation for advising that Parliament should be prorogued is a reasonable justification for a prorogation having those effects. The Prime Minister's wish to end one session of Parliament and to begin another will normally be enough in itself to justify the short period of prorogation which has been normal in modern practice. It could only be in unusual circumstances that any further justification might be necessary. Even in such a case, when considering the justification put forward, the court would have to bear in mind that the decision whether to advise the monarch to prorogue Parliament falls within the area of responsibility of the Prime Minister, and that it may in some circumstances involve a range of considerations, including matters of political judgment. The court would therefore have to consider any justification that might be advanced with sensitivity to the responsibilities and experience of the Prime Minister, and with a corresponding degree of caution. Nevertheless, it is the court's responsibility to determine whether the Prime Minster has remained within the legal limits of the power. If not, the final question will be whether the consequences are sufficiently serious to call for the court's intervention.

Conclusions on Justiciability

[52] Returning, then, to the justiciability of the question of whether the Prime Minister's advice to the Queen was lawful, we are firmly of the opinion that it is justiciable. As we have explained, it is well established, and is accepted by counsel for the Prime Minister, that the courts can rule on the extent of prerogative powers. That is what the court will be doing in this case by applying the legal standard which we have described. That standard is not concerned with the mode of exercise of the prerogative power within its lawful limits. On the contrary, it is a standard which determines the limits of the power, marking the boundary between the prerogative on the one hand and the operation of the constitutional principles of the sovereignty of Parliament and responsible government on the other hand. An issue which can be resolved by the application of that standard is by definition one which concerns the extent of the power to prorogue, and is therefore justiciable.

2. The Issue of Enforcement

Operation Dismantle shows that Canadian courts are generally unwilling to find that government action is insulated from the Charter. However, the conclusion that courts are entitled to determine whether a particular government action that has foreign policy implications infringes a person's constitutionally protected rights does not mean that the courts are indifferent to the respective roles of the executive and the judiciary in fashioning remedies for breaches of constitutional rights where remedial choices could have foreign policy implications. For example, in *Canada (Prime Minister) v Khadr*, 2010 SCC 3, [2010] 1 SCR 44, the Supreme Court of Canada upheld the conclusion of the lower courts that Canadian security intelligence officials breached Khadr's rights under s 7 of the Charter in the course of interrogating him while he was being held by the US military at Guantanamo Bay. Nevertheless, the Court overturned the remedial order imposed by the lower courts that Canada request Khadr's repatriation from Guantanamo Bay. Instead, the Court made a declaration that Khadr's rights had been violated and left it to the government to decide how to address the consequences of this rights violation. The Court did not rule out the possibility that courts could give specific directions to the executive on matters touching on foreign relations in order to vindicate constitutional rights, referring to *United States v Burns*, 2001 SCC 7, [2001] 1 SCR 283, where the Court had required the government to seek assurances that Burns would not face the death penalty before agreeing to his extradition to the United States to face murder charges. In the *Khadr* case, the Court concluded that more specific direction was not appropriate because Khadr was not under the control of Canadian officials, as was the case in *Burns*, and because the Court was not in a position to evaluate the impact of a request that Khadr be repatriated on Canada's foreign relations.

The issue of what types of remedial orders are appropriate to address breaches of constitutional rights is not confined to cases that have foreign policy implications. While Canadian judges accept the proposition that the Constitution is supreme and the corollary that it is their duty to interpret the Constitution and invalidate any legislation that is inconsistent with the Constitution, the practical reality is that courts normally have to rely on the executive and legislative branches of government for the enforcement of their decisions. Canadian courts are usually able to rely on the other branches of government for this support, but it is not inevitable that this will always be the case. In *Doucet-Boudreau v Nova Scotia (Minister of Education)* and *Re Manitoba Language Rights*, the Supreme Court of Canada wrestled with both the principled and practical implications of the choice of appropriate remedies to address the infringement of constitutionally protected minority language rights.

Doucet-Boudreau v Nova Scotia (Minister of Education)
2003 SCC 62, [2003] 3 SCR 3

IACOBUCCI and ARBOUR JJ (McLachlin CJ and Gonthier and Bastarache JJ concurring):

[1] This appeal involves the nature of remedies available under s. 24(1) of the *Canadian Charter of Rights and Freedoms* for the realization of the minority language education rights protected by s. 23 of the Charter. The specific issue is whether a trial judge may, after ordering that a provincial government use its best efforts to build French-language school facilities by given dates, retain jurisdiction to hear reports on the progress of those efforts. The issue of broader and ongoing judicial involvement in the administration of public institutions is not before the Court in this case.

I. Background and Judicial History

[2] The appellants are Francophone parents living in five school districts in Nova Scotia (Kingston/Greenwood, Chéticamp, Île Madame-Arichat (Petit-de-Grat), Argyle, and Clare) and Fédération des parents acadiens de la Nouvelle-Écosse Inc., a non-profit organization that monitors the advancement of educational rights of the Acadian and Francophone minority in Nova Scotia. The Attorney General of Nova Scotia is the respondent, acting on behalf of the Department of Education of Nova Scotia.

[3] Apart from the specific facts of the case, it is most important to note the historical context on which this dispute is centred. As we will discuss below, French-language education in Nova Scotia has not had an enviable record of success. While the situation improved over the rather dismal record of the previous centuries, the twentieth century left much to be achieved. Section 23 of the Charter has been the hope of the French-speaking minority of Nova Scotia to redress the linguistic failings and inequality of history.

[4] It is conceded in this appeal that s. 23 of the Charter entitles the appellant parents to publicly funded French-language educational facilities for their children. For some time, Francophone parents in these five school districts of Nova Scotia

had been urging their provincial government to provide homogeneous French-language schools at the secondary level in addition to the existing primary level facilities. The government of Nova Scotia, for its part, agreed: it did not dispute that the number of students warranted the facilities demanded. The government amended the *Education Act*, SNS 1995-96, c. 1, ss. 11-16, in 1996 to create the Conseil scolaire acadien provincial (the "Conseil"), a province-wide French-language school board, with a view to realizing the Charter's minority language education rights. However, while s. 11(1) empowered the Conseil to deliver and administer all French-language programs, only the Minister, with the approval of the Governor in Council, could construct, furnish and equip schools (see s. 88(1)). Although the government eventually announced the construction of the new French-language school facilities, construction of the promised schools never began. So in 1998, 16 years after the right was entrenched in the Constitution, the appellant parents applied to the Supreme Court of Nova Scotia for an order directing the Province and the Conseil to provide, out of public funds, homogeneous French-language facilities and programs at the secondary school level.

• • •

II. Issues

• • •

[12] The main issue in the appeal is simply this: having found a violation of s. 23 of the Charter and having ordered that the Province make its best efforts to provide homogeneous French-language facilities and programs by particular dates, did the Nova Scotia Supreme Court have the authority to retain jurisdiction to hear reports from the Province on the status of those efforts as part of its remedy under s. 24(1) of the Charter?

[13] Strictly speaking, only the retention of jurisdiction to hear reports, and not the "best efforts" order itself, is at issue in the present appeal. Nonetheless, the best efforts order and the retention of jurisdiction were conceived by the trial judge as two complementary parts of a whole. A full appreciation of the balance and moderation of the trial judge's approach to crafting this remedy requires that the reports respecting the respondents' compliance with the order be viewed and evaluated in the context of the remedy as a whole.

• • •

IV. Analysis

• • •

B. The Retention of Jurisdiction

(1) The Importance of Context: Sections 23 and 24 of the Charter

[23] It is well accepted that the Charter should be given a generous and expansive interpretation and not a narrow, technical, or legalistic one ... . The need for a generous interpretation flows from the principle that the Charter ought to be interpreted purposively. While courts must be careful not to overshoot the actual purposes of the Charter's guarantees, they must avoid a narrow, technical approach to Charter interpretation which could subvert the goal of ensuring that right holders enjoy the full benefit and protection of the Charter. In our view, the approach taken by our colleagues LeBel and Deschamps JJ which appears to contemplate

that special remedies might be available in some circumstances, but not in this case, severely undervalues the importance and the urgency of the language rights in the context facing LeBlanc J.

[24] The requirement of a generous and expansive interpretive approach holds equally true for Charter remedies as for Charter rights (*R v. Gamble*, [1988] 2 SCR 595; *R v. Sarson*, [1996] 2 SCR 223; *R v. 974649 Ontario Inc.*, [2001] 3 SCR 575, 2001 SCC 81 ("Dunedin")). ...

[25] Purposive interpretation means that remedies provisions must be interpreted in a way that provides "a full, effective and meaningful remedy for Charter violations" since "a right, no matter how expansive in theory, is only as meaningful as the remedy provided for its breach" (*Dunedin, supra*, at paras. 19-20). A purposive approach to remedies in a Charter context gives modern vitality to the ancient maxim *ubi jus, ibi remedium*: where there is a right, there must be a remedy. More specifically, a purposive approach to remedies requires at least two things. First, the purpose of the right being protected must be promoted: courts must craft *responsive* remedies. Second, the purpose of the remedies provision must be promoted: courts must craft *effective* remedies.

• • •

[30] To put the matter of judicial remedies in greater context, it is useful to reflect briefly on the role of courts in the enforcement of our laws.

[31] Canada has evolved into a country that is noted and admired for its adherence to the rule of law as a major feature of its democracy. But the rule of law can be shallow without proper mechanisms for its enforcement. In this respect, courts play an essential role since they are the central institutions to deal with legal disputes through the rendering of judgments and decisions. But courts have no physical or economic means to enforce their judgments. Ultimately, courts depend on both the executive and the citizenry to recognize and abide by their judgments.

[32] Fortunately, Canada has had a remarkable history of compliance with court decisions by private parties and by all institutions of government. That history of compliance has become a fundamentally cherished value of our constitutional democracy; we must never take it for granted but always be careful to respect and protect its importance, otherwise the seeds of tyranny can take root.

[33] This tradition of compliance takes on a particular significance in the constitutional law context, where courts must ensure that government behaviour conforms with constitutional norms but in doing so must also be sensitive to the separation of function among the legislative, judicial and executive branches. While our Constitution does not expressly provide for the separation of powers (see *Re Residential Tenancies Act, 1979*, [1981] 1 SCR 714, at p. 728; *Douglas/Kwantlen Faculty Assn. v. Douglas College*, [1990] 3 SCR 570, at p. 601; *Reference re Secession of Quebec*, [1998] 2 SCR 217, at para. 15), the functional separation among the executive, legislative and judicial branches of governance has frequently been noted. (See, for example, *Fraser v. Public Service Staff Relations Board*, [1985] 2 SCR 455, at pp. 469-70.) In *New Brunswick Broadcasting Co. v. Nova Scotia (Speaker of the House of Assembly)*, [1993] 1 SCR 319, McLachlin J (as she then was) stated, at p. 389:

> Our democratic government consists of several branches: the Crown, as represented by the Governor General and the provincial counterparts of that office; the legislative body; the executive; and the courts. It is fundamental to the working of government as a whole that all these parts play their proper role. It is equally fundamental that no one of them overstep its bounds, that each show proper deference for the legitimate sphere of activity of the other.

[34] In other words, in the context of constitutional remedies, courts must be sensitive to their role as judicial arbiters and not fashion remedies which usurp the role of the other branches of governance by taking on tasks to which other persons or bodies are better suited. Concern for the limits of the judicial role is interwoven throughout the law. The development of the doctrines of justiciability, and to a great extent mootness, standing, and ripeness resulted from concerns about the courts overstepping the bounds of the judicial function and their role vis-à-vis other branches of government.

• • •

(b) The Reporting Order Respected the Framework of Our Constitutional Democracy

[70] Our colleagues LeBel and Deschamps JJ appear to consider that the issuance of an injunction against the government under s. 24(1) is constitutionally suspect and represents a departure from a consensus about Charter remedies (see para. 134 of the dissent). With respect, it is clear that a court may issue an injunction under s. 24(1) of the Charter. The power of courts to issue injunctions against the executive is central to s. 24(1) of the Charter which envisions more than declarations of rights. Courts do take actions to ensure that rights are enforced, and not merely declared. Contempt proceedings in the face of defiance of court orders, as well as coercive measures such as garnishments, writs of seizure and sale and the like are all known to courts. In this case, it was open to the trial judge in all the circumstances to choose the injunctive remedy on the terms and conditions that he prescribed.

(c) The Reporting Order Called on the Function and Powers of a Court

• • •

[72] The difficulties of ongoing supervision of parties by the courts have sometimes been advanced as a reason that orders for specific performance and mandatory injunctions should not be awarded. Nonetheless, courts of equity have long accepted and overcome this difficulty of supervision where the situations demanded such remedies (see [RJ Sharpe, *Injunctions and Specific Performance*, 2nd ed (Aurora, Ont: Canada Law Book, 1992) (loose-leaf)], at paras. 1.260-1.380; *Attorney-General v. Birmingham, Tame, and Rea District Drainage Board*, [1910] 1 Ch. 48 (CA), aff'd [1912] AC 788 (HL); *Kennard v. Cory Brothers and Co.*, [1922] 1 Ch. 265, aff'd [1922] 2 Ch. 1 (CA)).

[73] As academic commentators have pointed out, the range of remedial orders available to courts in civil proceedings demonstrates that constitutional remedies involving some degree of ongoing supervision do not represent a radical break with the past practices of courts (see W.A. Bogart, "'Appropriate and Just': Section 24 of the Canadian Charter of Rights and Freedoms and the Question of Judicial Legitimacy" (1986), 10 *Dalhousie LJ* 81, at pp. 92-94; N. Gillespie, "Charter Remedies: The Structural Injunction" (1989-90), 11 *Advocates' Q* 190, at pp. 217-18; Roach, *Constitutional Remedies in Canada* ..., at paras. 13.50-13.80; Sharpe ... , at paras. 1.260-1.490). The change announced by s. 24 of the Charter is that the flexibility inherent in an equitable remedial jurisdiction may be applied to orders addressed to government to vindicate constitutionally entrenched rights.

[74] The order in this case was in no way inconsistent with the judicial function. There was never any suggestion in this case that the court would, for example, improperly take over the detailed management and co-ordination of the construction projects. Hearing evidence and supervising cross-examinations on progress

reports about the construction of schools are not beyond the normal capacities of courts.

· · ·

(5) Conclusion

[87] Section 24(1) of the Charter requires that courts issue effective, responsive remedies that guarantee full and meaningful protection of Charter rights and freedoms. The meaningful protection of Charter rights, and in particular the enforcement of s. 23 rights, may in some cases require the introduction of novel remedies. A superior court may craft any remedy that it considers appropriate and just in the circumstances. In doing so, courts should be mindful of their roles as constitutional arbiters and the limits of their institutional capacities. Reviewing courts, for their part, must show considerable deference to trial judges' choice of remedy, and should refrain from using hindsight to perfect a remedy. A reviewing court should only interfere where the trial judge has committed an error of law or principle.

[88] The remedy crafted by LeBlanc J meaningfully vindicated the rights of the appellant parents by encouraging the Province's prompt construction of school facilities, without drawing the court outside its proper role. The Court of Appeal erred in wrongfully interfering with and striking down the portion of LeBlanc J's order in which he retained jurisdiction to hear progress reports on the status of the Province's efforts in providing school facilities by the required dates.

· · ·

LeBEL and DESCHAMPS JJ (dissenting) (Major and Binnie JJ concurring):

· · ·

II. The Nature of the Issues

· · ·

[94] At the outset, we wish to emphasize that we fully agree with our colleagues in their analysis of the nature and fundamental importance of language rights in the Canadian Constitution, as well as on the need for efficacy and imagination in the development of constitutional remedies. Indeed, we dissent because we believe that constitutional remedies should be designed keeping in mind the canons of good legal drafting, the fundamental importance of procedural fairness, and a proper awareness of the nature of the role of courts in our democratic political regime, a key principle of which remains the separation of powers. This principle protects the independence of courts. It also flexibly delineates the domain of court action, particularly in the relationship of courts not only with legislatures but also with the executive branch of government or public administration.

· · ·

IV. The Appropriate Role of the Judiciary

[105] While superior courts' powers to craft Charter remedies may not be constrained by statutory or common law limits, they are nonetheless bound by rules of fundamental justice, as we have shown above, and by constitutional boundaries, as we shall see below. In the context of constitutional remedies, courts fulfill their proper function by issuing orders precise enough for the parties to know what is expected of them, and by permitting the parties to execute those orders. Such orders are final. A court purporting to retain jurisdiction to oversee the implementation

of a remedy, after a final order has been issued, will likely be acting inappropriately on two levels. First, by attempting to extend the court's jurisdiction beyond its
proper role, it will breach the separation of powers principle. Second, by acting after
exhausting its jurisdiction, it will breach the functus officio doctrine. We will look at
each of these breaches in turn.

1. The Separation of Powers

[106] Courts are called upon to play a fundamental role in the Canadian constitutional regime. When needed, they must be assertive in enforcing constitutional
rights. At times, they have to grant such relief as will be required to safeguard basic
constitutional rights and the rule of law, despite the sensitivity of certain issues or
circumstances and the reverberations of their decisions in their societal environment. Despite—or, perhaps, because of—the critical importance of their functions,
courts should be wary of going beyond the proper scope of the role assigned to
them in the public law of Canada. In essence, this role is to declare what the law
is, contribute to its development and to give claimants such relief in the form of
declarations, interpretation and orders as will be needed to remedy infringements
of constitutional and legal rights by public authorities. Beyond these functions, an
attitude of restraint remains all the more justified, given that, as the majority reasons
acknowledge, Canada has maintained a tradition of compliance by governments
and public servants with judicial interpretations of the law and court orders.

• • •

[111] More specifically, once they have rendered judgment, courts should resist
the temptation to directly oversee or supervise the administration of their orders.
They should generally operate under a presumption that judgments of courts will
be executed with reasonable diligence and good faith. Once they have declared
what the law is, issued their orders and granted such relief as they think is warranted by circumstances and relevant legal rules, courts should take care not to
unnecessarily invade the province of public administration. To do otherwise could
upset the balance that has been struck between our three branches of government.

[112] This is what occurred in the present case. When the trial judge attempted
to oversee the implementation of his order, he not only assumed jurisdiction over a
sphere traditionally outside the province of the judiciary, but also acted beyond the
jurisdiction with which he was legitimately charged as a trial judge. In other words,
he was *functus officio* and breached an important principle which reflects the nature
and function of the judiciary in the Canadian constitutional order, as we shall see now.

2. Functus Officio

• • •

[115] If a court is permitted to continually revisit or reconsider final orders simply
because it has changed its mind or wishes to continue exercising jurisdiction over a
matter, there would never be finality to a proceeding, or, as G. Pépin and Y. Ouellette
have perceptively termed it, the providing of [TRANSLATION] "legal security" for
the parties (*Principes de contentieux administratif* (2nd ed. 1982), at p. 221) ... . The
principle ensures that subject to an appeal, parties are secure in their reliance on the
finality of superior court decisions.

• • •

[117] In addition to this concern with finality, the question of whether a court is
clothed with the requisite authority to act raises concerns related to the separation

of powers, a principle that transcends procedural and common law rules. In our view, if a court intervenes, as here, in matters of administration properly entrusted to the executive, it exceeds its proper sphere and thereby breaches the separation of powers. By crossing the boundary between judicial acts and administrative oversight, it acts illegitimately and without jurisdiction. Such a crossing of the boundary cannot be characterized as relief that is "appropriate and just in the circumstances" within the meaning of s. 24(1) of the Charter.

V. Application of the Relevant Principles to the Present Case

[118] When the above principles are applied to the present facts, it is evident that McIntyre J's admonition in *Mills v. The Queen*, [1986] 1 SCR 863, that s. 24(1) "was not intended to turn the Canadian legal system upside down" is apropos (p. 953). In our view, the trial judge's remedy undermined the proper role of the judiciary within our constitutional order, and unnecessarily upset the balance between the three branches of government. As a result, the trial judge in the present circumstances acted inappropriately, and contrary to s. 24(1).

[119] As we noted above, the trial judge equivocated on the question of whether his purported retention of jurisdiction empowered him to make further orders. Regardless of which position is taken, the separation of powers was still breached. On the one hand, if he did purport to be able to make further orders, based on the evidence presented at the reporting hearings, he was *functus officio*. We find it difficult to imagine how any subsequent order would not have resulted in a change to the original final order. This necessarily falls outside the narrow exceptions provided by *functus officio*, and breaches that rule.

[120] Such a breach would also have resulted in a violation of the separation of powers principle. By purporting to be able to make subsequent orders, the trial judge would have assumed a supervisory role which included administrative functions that properly lie in the sphere of the executive. These functions are beyond the capacities of courts. The judiciary is ill equipped to make polycentric choices or to evaluate the wide-ranging consequences that flow from policy implementation. This Court has recognized that courts possess neither the expertise nor the resources to undertake public administration. In *Eldridge v. British Columbia (Attorney General)*, [1997] 3 SCR 624, at para. 96, it was held that in light of the "myriad options" available to the government to rectify the unconstitutionality of the impugned system, it was "not this Court's role to dictate how this is to be accomplished."

Re Manitoba Language Rights
[1985] 1 SCR 721

THE COURT:

II Manitoba's Language Legislation

[5] Section 23 of the *Manitoba Act, 1870* was the culmination of many years of co-existence and struggle between the English, the French, and the Metis in Red River Colony, the predecessor to the present day province of Manitoba. Though the region was originally claimed by the English Hudson's Bay Company in 1670 under its Royal Charter, for much of its pre-confederation history, Red River Colony was inhabited by anglophones and francophones in roughly equal proportions. On

November 19, 1869 the Hudson's Bay Company issued a deed of surrender to transfer the North-West Territories, which included the Red River Colony, to Canada. The transfer of title took effect on July 15, 1870.

[6] Between November 19, 1869 and July 15, 1870, the provisional government of Red River Colony attempted to unite the various segments of the Red River Colony and drew up a "Bill of Rights" to be used in negotiations with Canada. A Convention of Delegates was elected in January 1870 to prepare the terms upon which Red River Colony would join the Confederation. The convention was made up of equal numbers of anglophones and francophones elected from the various French and English parishes.

[7] The final version of the Bill of Rights which was used by the convention delegates in their negotiations with Ottawa contained these provisions:

> That the English and French languages be common in the Legislature, and in the courts, and that all public documents, as well as all Acts of the Legislature, be published in both languages.

> That the judge of the Superior Court speak the English and French languages.

These clauses were re-drafted by the Crown lawyers in Ottawa and included in a Bill to be introduced in Parliament. The Bill passed through Parliament with no opposition from either side of the House, resulting in s. 23 of the *Manitoba Act, 1870*. In 1871 this Act was entrenched in the *British North America Act, 1871* (renamed *Constitution Act, 1871*, in the *Constitution Act, 1982*, s. 53). The *Manitoba Act, 1870*, is now entrenched in the Constitution of Canada by virtue of s. 52(2)(b) of the *Constitution Act, 1982*.

[8] In 1890 *An Act to Provide that the English Language shall be the Official Language of the Province of Manitoba*, 1890 (Man.), c. 14 (hereafter "the *Official Language Act*") was enacted by the Manitoba Legislature. This Act provides:

> 1) Any statute or law to the contrary notwithstanding, the English language only shall be used in the records and journals of the House of Assembly for the Province of Manitoba, and in any pleadings or process in or issuing from any court in the Province of Manitoba. The Acts of the Legislature of the Province of Manitoba need only be printed and published in the English language.

> 2) This Act shall only apply so far as this Legislature has jurisdiction so to enact, and shall come into force on the day it is assented to.

[9] Upon enactment of the *Official Language Act, 1890*, the province of Manitoba ceased publication of the French version of legislative records, journals and Acts.

• • •

III Legal Challenges to Manitoba's Language Legislation

[10] The *Official Language Act, 1890*, was challenged before the Manitoba courts soon after it was enacted. It was ruled *ultra vires* in 1892 by Judge Prud'homme of the County Court of St. Boniface, who stated: "Je suis donc d'opinion que le c. 14, 53 Vict. est ultra vires de la législature du Manitoba et que la clause 23, de l'Acte de Manitoba, ne peut pas être changée et encore moins abrogée par la législature de cette province": *Pellant v. Hebert*, first published in *Le Manitoba* (a French language newspaper), March 9, 1892, reported in (1981), 12 RGD 242. This ruling was not followed by the legislature or the government of Manitoba. The 1890 Act remained in successive revisions of the Statutes of Manitoba; the government did not resume bilingual publication of legislative records, journals or Acts.

[11] In 1909, the *Official Language Act, 1890* was again challenged in Manitoba courts and again ruled unconstitutional: *Bertrand v. Dussault*, January 30, 1909, Prud'homme Co. Ct. J, County Court of St. Boniface (unreported), reproduced in *Re Forest and Registrar of Court of Appeal of Manitoba* (1977), 77 DLR (3d) 445 at 458-62 (Man. CA). According to Monnin JA in *Re Forest*, supra, at p. 458: "This latter decision, not reported, appears to have been unknown or ignored."

[12] In 1976, a third attack was mounted against the *Official Language Act, 1890* and the Act was ruled unconstitutional: *R v. Forest* (1976), 74 DLR (3d) 704 (Man. Co. Ct.). Nonetheless, the *Official Language Act, 1890* remained on the Manitoba statute books; bilingual enactment, printing and publication of Acts of the Manitoba Legislature was not resumed.

[13] In 1979, the constitutionality of the *Official Language Act, 1890* was tested before this Court. On December 13, 1979, in *Attorney General of Manitoba v. Forest*, [1979] 2 SCR 1032, this Court, in unanimous reasons, held that the provisions of Manitoba's *Official Language Act, 1890* were in conflict with s. 23 of the *Manitoba Act, 1870*, and unconstitutional.

[14] On July 9, 1980, after the decision of this Court in *Forest*, the Legislature of Manitoba enacted *An Act Respecting the Operation of Section 23 of the Manitoba Act in Regard to Statutes*, 1980 (Man.), c. 3 [also CCSM, c S207]. The validity of this Act is the subject of question 4 of this Reference.

[15] In the fourth session (1980) and the fifth session (1980-1981) of the thirty-first legislature of Manitoba, the vast majority of the Acts of the legislature of Manitoba were enacted, printed and published in English only.

[16] Since the first session of the thirty-second legislature of Manitoba (1982), the Acts of the legislature of Manitoba have been enacted, printed and published in both English and French. However, those Acts that only amend Acts that were enacted, printed and published in English only and private Acts have in most instances been enacted in English only.

· · ·

[19] It might also be mentioned that on December 13, 1979, in *Attorney General of Quebec v. Blaikie*, [1979] 2 SCR 1016 (Blaikie No. 1), this Court held that the provisions of *Quebec's Charter of the French Language* (Bill 101), enacted in 1977, were in conflict with s. 133 of the *Constitution Act, 1867.* The Charter purported to provide for the introduction of Bills in the legislature in French only, and for the enactment of statutes in French only. The day after the decision of this court in *Blaikie No. 1*, the Legislature of Quebec re-enacted in both languages all those Quebec statutes that had been enacted in French only. See: *An Act respecting a judgment rendered in the Supreme Court of Canada on 13 December 1979 on the language of the legislature and the courts in Québec*, 1979 (Que.), c. 61.

[20] The implication of this court's holdings in *Blaikie No. 1*, and *Forest*, both *supra*, was that provincial Legislation passed in accordance with the *ultra vires* statutes, i.e., enacted in one language only, was itself in derogation of the constitutionally entrenched language provisions of the *Constitution Act, 1867*, and the *Manitoba Act, 1870*, and therefore invalid. In *Société Asbestos Ltée v. Société nationale de l'amiante*, [1979] CA 342, the Quebec Court of Appeal held, in a judgment also rendered December 13, 1979, that this was indeed the consequence of unilingual enactment and struck down two statutes that had not been enacted in English.

· · ·

B) The Consequences of the Manitoba Legislature's Failure to Enact, Print and Publish in Both Languages

[45] Section 23 of the *Manitoba Act, 1870*, entrenches a mandatory requirement to enact, print, and publish all Acts of the legislature in both official languages (see *Blaikie No. 1, supra*). It establishes a constitutional duty on the Manitoba Legislature with respect to the manner and form of enactment of its legislation. This duty protects the substantive rights of all Manitobans to equal access to the law in either the French or the English language.

[46] Section 23 of the *Manitoba Act, 1870*, is a specific manifestation of the general right of Franco-Manitobans to use their own language. The importance of language rights is grounded in the essential role that language plays in human existence, development and dignity. It is through language that we are able to form concepts; to structure and order the world around us. Language bridges the gap between isolation and community, allowing humans to delineate the rights and duties they hold in respect of one another, and thus to live in society.

[47] The constitutional entrenchment of a duty on the Manitoba legislature to enact, print and publish in both French and English in s. 23 of the *Manitoba Act, 1870*, confers upon the judiciary the responsibility of protecting the correlative language rights of all Manitobans including the Franco-Manitoban minority. The judiciary is the institution charged with the duty of ensuring that the government complies with the Constitution. We must protect those whose constitutional rights have been violated, whomever they may be, and whatever the reasons for the violation.

• • •

[53] Canadian courts have been unanimous in finding that failure to respect mandatory requirements to enact, print and publish statutes and regulations in both official languages leads to inconsistency and thus invalidity: see, *Société Asbestos Ltée v. Société nationale de l'amiante, supra*; *Procureur général du Québec v. Collier*, [1983] CS 366; *Procureur général du Québec v. Brunet*, JE 83-510, reversed on other grounds, JE 84-62 (SC). These cases accord with the general principle that failure to comply with constitutional provisions dealing with the manner and form of the enactment of legislation will result in inconsistency and thus invalidity: see *Bribery Commissioner v. Ranasinghe* ... .

[54] In the present case the unilingual enactments of the Manitoba legislature are inconsistent with s. 23 of the *Manitoba Act, 1870* since the constitutionally required manner and form for their enactment has not been followed. Thus they are invalid and of no force or effect.

C) The Rule of Law

1. The Principle

[55] The difficulty with the fact that the unilingual Acts of the legislature of Manitoba must be declared invalid and of no force or effect is that, without going further, a legal vacuum will be created with consequent legal chaos in the province of Manitoba. The Manitoba Legislature has, since 1890, enacted nearly all of its laws in English only. Thus, to find that the unilingual laws of Manitoba are invalid and of no force or effect would mean that only laws enacted in both French and English before 1890 would continue to be valid, and would still be in force even if the law had purportedly been repealed or amended by a post-1890 unilingual statute; matters that were not regulated by laws enacted before 1890 would

now be unregulated by law, unless a pre-confederation law or the common law provided a rule.

[56] The situation of the various institutions of provincial government would be as follows: the courts, administrative tribunals, public officials, municipal corporations, school boards, professional governing bodies, and all other bodies created by law, to the extent that they derive their existence from or purport to exercise powers conferred by Manitoba laws enacted since 1890 in English only, would be acting without legal authority.

[57] Questions as to the validity of the present composition of the Manitoba legislature might also be raised. Under the *Manitoba Act, 1870*, the Legislative Assembly was to be composed of 24 members (s. 14), and voters were to be male and over 21 (s. 17). By laws enacted after 1890 in English only, the size of the Legislative Assembly was increased to 57 members, and all persons, both women and men, over 18 were granted the right to vote: see *Act to Amend "The Manitoba Election Act,"* 1916 (Man.), c. 36; *Act to Amend "The Election Act,"* 1969 (Man.), 2nd Sess., c. 7; *The Legislative Assembly Act*, RSM, c. L110, s. 4(1). If these laws are invalid and of no force or effect, the present composition of the Manitoba Legislature might be invalid. The invalidity of the post-1890 laws would not touch the existence of the Legislature or its powers since these are matters of federal constitutional law: *Constitution Act, 1867*, ss. 92, 92A, 93, 95; *Manitoba Act, 1870*, s. 2.

[58] Finally, all legal rights, obligations and other effects which have purportedly arisen under all Acts of the Manitoba legislature since 1890 would be open to challenge to the extent that their validity and enforceability depends upon a regime of unconstitutional unilingual laws.

[59] In the present case, declaring the Acts of the legislature of Manitoba invalid and of no force or effect would, without more, undermine the principle of the rule of law. The rule of law, a fundamental principle of our Constitution, must mean at least two things. First, that the law is supreme over officials of the government as well as private individuals, and thereby preclusive of the influence of arbitrary power. Indeed, it is because of the supremacy of law over the government, as established in s. 23 of the *Manitoba Act, 1870*, and s. 52 of the *Constitution Act, 1982*, that this Court must find the unconstitutional laws of Manitoba to be invalid and of no force and effect.

[60] Second, the rule of law requires the creation and maintenance of an actual order of positive laws which preserves and embodies the more general principle of normative order. Law and order are indispensable elements of civilized life. "The Rule of Law in this sense implies ... simply the existence of public order." (W.I. Jennings, *The Law and the Constitution* (5th ed. 1959), at p. 43.) As John Locke once said, "A government without laws is, I suppose, a mystery in politics, inconceivable to human capacity and inconsistent with human society" (quoted by Lord Wilberforce in *Carl Zeiss-Stiftung v. Rayner & Keeler Ltd. (No. 2)*, [1966] 2 All ER 536 (HL), at 577). According to Wade and Phillips, *Constitutional and Administrative Law* (9th ed. 1977), at p. 89:

> ... [T]he rule of law expresses a preference for law and order within a community rather than anarchy, warfare and constant strife. In this sense, the rule of law is a philosophical view of society which in the Western tradition is linked with basic democratic notions.

[61] It is this second aspect of the rule of law that is of concern in the present situation. The conclusion that the Acts of the Legislature of Manitoba are invalid and of no force or effect means that the positive legal order which has purportedly regulated the affairs of the citizens of Manitoba since 1890 will be destroyed

and the rights, obligations and other effects arising under these laws will be invalid and unenforceable. As for the future, since it is reasonable to assume that it will be impossible for the legislature of Manitoba to rectify instantaneously the constitutional defect, the Acts of the Manitoba Legislature will be invalid and of no force or effect until they are translated, re-enacted, printed and published in both languages.

[62] Such results would certainly offend the rule of law. ...

• • •

2. Application of the Principle of the Rule of Law

[67] It is clear from the above that: (i) the law as stated in s. 23 of the *Manitoba Act, 1870*, and s. 52 of the *Constitution Act, 1982*, requires that the unilingual Acts of the Manitoba Legislature be declared to be invalid and of no force or effect, and (ii) without more, such a result would violate the rule of law. The task the court faces is to recognize the unconstitutionality of Manitoba's unilingual laws and the legislature's duty to comply with the "supreme law" of this country, while avoiding a legal vacuum in Manitoba and ensuring the continuity of the rule of law.

• • •

[73] There is no question that it would be impossible for all the Acts of the Manitoba legislature to be translated, re-enacted, printed and published overnight. There will necessarily be a period of time during which it would not be possible for the Manitoba Legislature to comply with its constitutional duty under s. 23 of the *Manitoba Act, 1870*.

[74] The vexing question, however, is what will be the legal situation in the Province of Manitoba for the duration of this period. The difficulties faced by the Province of Manitoba are two-fold: first, all of the rights, obligations and other effects which have arisen under the repealed, spent and current Acts of the Manitoba Legislature will be open to challenge, since the laws under which they purportedly arise are invalid and of no force or effect; and, second, the Province of Manitoba has an invalid and therefore ineffectual legal system until the Legislature is able to translate, re-enact, print and publish its current Acts.

• • •

[83] The only appropriate solution for preserving the rights, obligations and other effects which have arisen under invalid Acts of the Legislature of Manitoba and which are not saved by the *de facto* or other doctrines is to declare that, in order to uphold the rule of law, these rights, obligations and other effects have, and will continue to have, the same force and effect they would have had if they had arisen under valid enactments, for that period of time during which it would be impossible for Manitoba to comply with its constitutional duty under s. 23 of the *Manitoba Act, 1870*. The Province of Manitoba would be faced with chaos and anarchy if the legal rights, obligations and other effects which have been relied upon by the people of Manitoba since 1890 were suddenly open to challenge. The constitutional guarantee of rule of law will not tolerate such chaos and anarchy.

[84] Nor will the constitutional guarantee of rule of law tolerate the province of Manitoba being without a valid and effectual legal system for the present and future. Thus, it will be necessary to deem temporarily valid and effective the unilingual Acts of the Legislature of Manitoba which would be currently in force, were it not for their constitutional defect, for the period of time during which it would be impossible for the Manitoba Legislature to fulfil its constitutional duty. Since this temporary validation will include the legislation under which the Manitoba Legislature is presently constituted, it will be legally able to re-enact, print and publish

its laws in conformity with the dictates of the Constitution once they have been translated.

· · ·

[107] Turning back to the present case, because of the Manitoba legislature's persistent violation of the constitutional dictates of the *Manitoba Act, 1870*, the Province of Manitoba is in a state of emergency: all of the Acts of the Legislature of Manitoba, purportedly repealed, spent and current (with the exception of those recent laws which have been enacted, printed and published in both languages), are and always have been invalid and of no force or effect, and the legislature is unable to immediately re-enact these unilingual laws in both languages. The Constitution will not suffer a province without laws. Thus the Constitution requires that temporary validity and force and effect be given to the current Acts of the Manitoba Legislature from the date of this judgment, and that rights, obligations and other effects which have arisen under these laws and the repealed and spent laws of the province prior to the date of this judgment, which are not saved by the *de facto* or some other doctrine, are deemed temporarily to have been and continue to be effective and beyond challenge. It is only in this way that legal chaos can be avoided and the rule of law preserved.

3. The Issue of Legitimacy

The type of governmental intransigence described in *Re Manitoba Language Rights* is very much the exception in Canada's constitutional history. The more immediate concern for Canadian judges in exercising their mandate to uphold the Constitution is to identify principles that appropriately shape the exercise of this authority. Different aspects of the role played by the courts in reviewing the constitutional validity of legislation typically raise different issues concerning the relationship between democratically elected legislators and unelected judges. When judges are adjudicating constitutional challenges to the validity of legislation based on the division of powers provisions of ss 91-95 of the *Constitution Act, 1867*, the issue is not whether some body of democratically elected legislators has the authority under the Constitution to pass the law that is in dispute, but whether the particular legislative body that has enacted the law has that authority within our federal system of government. The outcomes of particular cases, and even whole lines of authority, may provoke passionate debates between supporters of greater federal authority and those who prefer a more decentralized model of federalism. Nevertheless, it is hard to disagree with the idea that we need an impartial arbiter of federalism disputes, and in our system that role is played by the courts.

The advent of the *Canadian Charter of Rights and Freedoms* in 1982 has changed this aspect of the nature of the judicial role in constitutional adjudication. The Charter requires the courts to give constitutional effect to what Professor Noel Lyon has described as "vague but meaningful generalities"—ideas such as "freedom of thought, belief, opinion, and expression" in s 2(b); "liberty," "security of the person," and "the principles of fundamental justice" in s 7; "equality" in s 15; and "such reasonable limits prescribed by law as can be demonstrably justified in a free and democratic society" in s 1: see N Lyon, "The Teleological Mandate of the Fundamental Freedoms: What to Do with Vague but Meaningful Generalities" (1982) 4 SCLR 57. The concern is that when judges give concrete shape to these and other ideas set out in the Charter and then invalidate laws that do not conform to their interpretation of these requirements, the rule of law may become subtly transformed into the rule of unelected judges.

It is true that on the whole, the Charter—and the courts' interpretation of it—has been largely popular. See, for instance, Joseph F Fletcher & Paul Howe, "Canadian Attitudes Toward the Charter and the Courts in Comparative Perspective" (May 2000) 6:3 Choices 4 [Institute for Research on Public Policy]. Yet because courts now regularly strike down (and reinterpret by "reading in") parliamentary statutes, they have sparked a wave of academic and political critiques that question, and sometimes denounce, their performance.

Most criticisms of constitutional judicial review can be reduced to two core complaints. The first is that under the banner of constitutional supremacy, courts have usurped power that is properly the domain of Parliament and the provincial legislatures. The argument is that the courts have expanded their proper role of interpreting the Constitution—and particularly the Charter—and have thereby unduly shrunk the zone of parliamentary supremacy. The second line of criticism is sparked by the substantive approach taken by the courts to particular rights—rights that may protect unpopular elements of society, such as people convicted of criminal offences, or prompt decisions, such as protection for the LGBTQ+ community, disliked by those holding particular political, social, or religious views. A core question lies at the heart of both these complaints: in making their constitutional decisions, how much deference should courts show elected officials?

In the following passage from the Supreme Court of Canada's majority decision in *Vriend v Alberta*, Iacobucci J uses the analogy of a dialogue to describe the relationship between courts and legislatures under the Charter. The Supreme Court in *Vriend* concluded that the Alberta legislature's failure to include sexual orientation as a prohibited ground of discrimination in the Alberta *Individual Rights Protection Act*, RSA 2000, c A-25.5 violated the appellants' right to equality as protected by s 15 of the Charter and that this action was not justified under s 1. The majority also concluded that the appropriate remedy for this violation was to "read in" sexual orientation as a prohibited ground of discrimination for purposes of the Act.

Vriend v Alberta
[1998] 1 SCR 493

CORY and IACOBUCCI JJ (Lamer CJ and Gonthier, McLachlin, and Bastarache JJ concurring):

[1] In these joint reasons Cory J has dealt with the issues pertaining to standing, the application of the *Canadian Charter of Rights and Freedoms*, and the breach of s. 15(1) of the Charter. Iacobucci J has discussed s. 1 of the Charter, the appropriate remedy, and the disposition.

• • •

IACOBUCCI J:

II. Remedy

A. Introduction: The Relationship Between the Legislatures and the Courts Under the Charter

[129] Having found the exclusion of sexual orientation from the *IRPA* to be an unjustifiable violation of the appellants' equality rights, I now turn to the question of remedy under s. 52 of the *Constitution Act, 1982*. Before discussing the jurisprudence on remedies, I believe it might be helpful to pause to reflect more broadly on the general issue of the relationship between legislatures and the courts in the age of the Charter.

[130] Much was made in argument before us about the inadvisability of the Court interfering with or otherwise meddling in what is regarded as the proper role of the legislature, which in this case was to decide whether or not sexual orientation would be added to Alberta's human rights legislation. Indeed, it seems that hardly a

day goes by without some comment or criticism to the effect that under the Charter courts are wrongfully usurping the role of the legislatures. I believe this allegation misunderstands what took place and what was intended when our country adopted the Charter in 1981-82.

[131] When the Charter was introduced, Canada went, in the words of former Chief Justice Brian Dickson, from a system of Parliamentary supremacy to constitutional supremacy ("Keynote Address," in *The Cambridge Lectures 1985* (1985), at pp. 3-4). Simply put, each Canadian was given individual rights and freedoms which no government or legislature could take away. However, as rights and freedoms are not absolute, governments and legislatures could justify the qualification or infringement of these constitutional rights under s. 1 as I previously discussed. Inevitably disputes over the meaning of the rights and their justification would have to be settled and here the role of the judiciary enters to resolve these disputes. Many countries have assigned the important role of judicial review to their supreme or constitutional courts (for an excellent analysis on these developments see D.M. Beatty, ed., *Human Rights and Judicial Review: A Comparative Perspective* (1994); B. Ackerman, "The Rise of World Constitutionalism" (1997), 83 *Virginia L Rev.* 771).

[132] We should recall that it was the deliberate choice of our provincial and federal legislatures in adopting the Charter to assign an interpretive role to the courts and to command them under s. 52 to declare unconstitutional legislation invalid.

[133] However, giving courts the power and commandment to invalidate legislation where necessary has not eliminated the debate over the "legitimacy" of courts taking such action. As eloquently put by A.M. Bickel in his outstanding work *The Least Dangerous Branch: The Supreme Court at the Bar of Politics* (2nd ed. 1986), "it thwarts the will of representatives of the ... people" (p. 17). So judicial review, it is alleged, is illegitimate because it is anti-democratic in that unelected officials (judges) are overruling elected representatives (legislators) (see e.g. A.A. Peacock, ed., *Rethinking the Constitution: Perspectives on Canadian Constitutional Reform, Interpretation, and Theory* (1996); R. Knopff and F.L. Morton, *Charter Politics* (1992); M. Mandel, *The Charter of Rights and the Legalization of Politics in Canada* (1994), c. 2).

[134] To respond, it should be emphasized again that our Charter's introduction and the consequential remedial role of the courts were choices of the Canadian people through their elected representatives as part of a redefinition of our democracy. Our constitutional design was refashioned to state that henceforth the legislatures and executive must perform their roles in conformity with the newly conferred constitutional rights and freedoms. That the courts were the trustees of these rights insofar as disputes arose concerning their interpretation was a necessary part of this new design.

[135] So courts in their trustee or arbiter role must perforce scrutinize the work of the legislature and executive not in the name of the courts, but in the interests of the new social contract that was democratically chosen. All of this is implied in the power given to the courts under s. 24 of the Charter and s. 52 of the *Constitution Act, 1982*.

[136] Because the courts are independent from the executive and legislature, litigants and citizens generally can rely on the courts to make reasoned and principled decisions according to the dictates of the constitution even though specific decisions may not be universally acclaimed. In carrying out their duties, courts are not to second-guess legislatures and the executives; they are not to make value judgments on what they regard as the proper policy choice; this is for the other branches. Rather, the courts are to uphold the Constitution and have been expressly invited to perform that role by the Constitution itself. But respect by the courts for

the legislature and executive role is as important as ensuring that the other branches respect each others' role and the role of the courts.

[137] This mutual respect is in some ways expressed in the provisions of our constitution as shown by the wording of certain of the constitutional rights themselves. For example, s. 7 of the Charter speaks of no denial of the rights therein except in accordance with the principles of fundamental justice, which include the process of law and legislative action. Section 1 and the jurisprudence under it are also important to ensure respect for legislative action and the collective or societal interests represented by legislation. In addition, as will be discussed below, in fashioning a remedy with regard to a Charter violation, a court must be mindful of the role of the legislature. Moreover, s. 33, the notwithstanding clause, establishes that the final word in our constitutional structure is in fact left to the legislature and not the courts (see P. Hogg and A. Bushell, "The Charter Dialogue Between Courts and Legislatures" (1997), 35 *Osgoode Hall LJ* 75).

[138] As I view the matter, the Charter has given rise to a more dynamic interaction among the branches of governance. This interaction has been aptly described as a "dialogue" by some (see e.g. Hogg and Bushell, *supra*). In reviewing legislative enactments and executive decisions to ensure constitutional validity, the courts speak to the legislative and executive branches. As has been pointed out, most of the legislation held not to pass constitutional muster has been followed by new legislation designed to accomplish similar objectives (see Hogg and Bushell, *supra*, at p. 82). By doing this, the legislature responds to the courts; hence the dialogue among the branches.

[139] To my mind, a great value of judicial review and this dialogue among the branches is that each of the branches is made somewhat accountable to the other. The work of the legislature is reviewed by the courts and the work of the court in its decisions can be reacted to by the legislature in the passing of new legislation (or even overarching laws under s. 33 of the Charter). This dialogue between and accountability of each of the branches have the effect of enhancing the democratic process, not denying it.

[140] There is also another aspect of judicial review that promotes democratic values. Although a court's invalidation of legislation usually involves negating the will of the majority, we must remember that the concept of democracy is broader than the notion of majority rule, fundamental as that may be. In this respect, we would do well to heed the words of Dickson CJ in *Oakes* ... , at p. 136:

> The Court must be guided by the values and principles essential to a free and democratic society which I believe to embody, to name but a few, respect for the inherent dignity of the human person, commitment to social justice and equality, accommodation of a wide variety of beliefs, respect for cultural and group identity, and faith in social and political institutions which enhance the participation of individuals and groups in society.

[141] So, for example, when a court interprets legislation alleged to be a reasonable limitation in a free and democratic society as stated in s. 1 of the Charter, the court must inevitably delineate some of the attributes of a democratic society. Although it is not necessary to articulate the complete list of democratic attributes in these remarks, Dickson CJ's comments remain instructive (see also: *R v. Keegstra*, [1990] 3 SCR 697, *per* Dickson CJ; *B.(R.) v. Children's Aid Society of Metropolitan Toronto* (1994), [1995] 1 SCR 315, *per* La Forest J).

[142] Democratic values and principles under the Charter demand that legislators and the executive take these into account; and if they fail to do so, courts

should stand ready to intervene to protect these democratic values as appropriate. As others have so forcefully stated, judges are not acting undemocratically by intervening when there are indications that a legislative or executive decision was not reached in accordance with the democratic principles mandated by the Charter (see W. Black, "*Vriend*, Rights and Democracy" (1996), 7 *Constitutional Forum* 126; D.M. Beatty, "Law and Politics" (1996), 44 *Am. J Comp. L* 131, at p. 149; M. Jackman, "Protecting Rights and Promoting Democracy: Judicial Review Under Section 1 of the Charter" (1997), 34 *Osgoode Hall LJ* 661).

These comments deserve further elaboration on two points: (1) built-in deference, and (2) the "dialogue" model.

Built-in deference. First, as we have suggested elsewhere, the Canadian Constitution does preserve a huge swath of parliamentary sovereignty. As Iacobucci J puts it in *Vriend*, the "parliamentary safeguards" remain, despite the Court's "reading-in" approach: "Governments are free to modify the amended legislation by passing exceptions and defences which they feel can be justified under s. 1 of the Charter. ... Moreover, the legislators can always turn to s. 33 of the Charter, the override provision, which in my view is the ultimate 'parliamentary safeguard'": see [1998] 1 SCR 493 at para 178.

Section 1 of the Charter provides that the rights contained within it are guaranteed, but then subject "to such reasonable limits prescribed by law as can be demonstrably justified in a free and democratic society." Drawing from this language, the Court has articulated a complex justification test that may excuse a violation of a substantive Charter right, should its conditions be met. See, for example, *R v Oakes*, [1986] 1 SCR 103, and its progeny. In other words, rights in the Charter are not absolute.

Moreover, many of the rights in the Charter (those enshrined in ss 2 and 7-15) may be overridden by the exercise of democratic will. Section 33—the "notwithstanding" provision—allows Parliament to "expressly declare in an Act of Parliament ... that the Act or a provision thereof shall operate notwithstanding" these Charter rights. Section 33 does not require a "super-majority." It may be invoked through the regular enactment process, albeit subject to periodical renewal. It is, in other words, abundantly available to any Parliament or provincial legislature. Thus, s 33 preserves a large measure of parliamentary supremacy, though the political price exacted for explicitly overriding constitutionally protected rights has been sufficiently high that, to date at least, Canadian political leaders rarely have been willing to pay it.

The "dialogue" model. Second, the *Vriend* decision invokes a sort of "dialogue" between courts and legislatures. Retired Supreme Court Justice Bertha Wilson described this "dialogue" in an article entitled "We Didn't Volunteer":

[T]he central feature of the Charter is that all branches of government—the legislatures, the executive and the judiciary—have an equal responsibility to carry out the Charter's mandate, and we should concentrate on their reciprocal roles. If we do this, we see that a sort of "dialogue" is going on. First, the legislatures have to examine any legislation they are contemplating passing in order to ensure that they have discharged their responsibility of Charter compliance. Then, if that legislation, once passed, is called into question, the courts must ask themselves: Did the legislature discharge its responsibility to comply with the Charter when it passed this legislation? If the answer is yes, there is no problem. If the answer is no, then the courts are obliged to strike down the legislation, though in so doing they must identify its vitiating aspects as clearly as possible so that the legislature will be in a position to correct them. The matter then goes back to the legislature for the appropriate remedial action. The courts' assessment of the legislation's constitutionality is not the last word; it is merely one step in the process.

(Bertha Wilson, "We Didn't Volunteer" (April 1999) Policy Options 8 at 10. See also Peter W Hogg & Allison A Bushell, "The Charter Dialogue Between Courts and Legislatures" (1997) 35 Osgoode Hall LJ 75 at 82.)

Other observers dismiss this concept of "dialogue." In an article entitled "Dialogue or Monologue?" Professor Morton argues that the putative dialogue

> is usually a monologue, with judges doing most of the talking and legislatures most of the listening. They suggest that the failure of a government to respond effectively to judicial activism is a matter of personal courage, or the lack thereof, on the part of government leaders. The fault, if there is any, rests with individuals. By contrast, I believe that legislative paralysis is institutional in character—that, in certain circumstances, legislative non-response in the face of judicial activism is the "normal" response. When the issue in play is cross-cutting and divides a government caucus, the political incentive structure invites government leaders to abdicate responsibility to the courts—and this may be even more true in a parliamentary as opposed to a presidential system. If I am correct, the Canadian tradition of responsible government is in for a rough ride in our brave new world of Charter democracy.

(FL Morton, "Dialogue or Monologue?" (April 1999) Policy Options 23 at 26.)

Views such as those expressed by Professor Morton have sparked a spirited defence from some academic writers, and from judges themselves. At the 2004 Conference on the Law and Parliament, then Supreme Court Chief Justice Beverley McLachlin had the following to say.

Remarks of the Right Honourable Beverley McLachlin, PC, Respecting Democratic Roles

(Ottawa: Supreme Court of Canada, 22 November 2004), online: University of Alberta Library <https://ejournals.library.ualberta.ca/index.php/constitutional_forum/article/viewFile/11122/8542>

What is the role of the Courts? At its most basic, it is to decide legal disputes that citizens and the government ask them to decide. In deciding these disputes, the Courts discharge a number of functions essential to democratic governance. First, they define the precise contours of the division of legislative powers between the federal and provincial governments. Second, they rule on legislation alleged to be unconstitutional for violation of the Charter, and in doing so define the scope of constitutional rights and freedoms. Third, the courts exercise *de facto* supervision over the hosts of administrative tribunals created by Parliament and the Legislatures.

The development of the modern regulatory state and the adoption of a constitutional bill of rights in the form of the Charter have increased the importance of these functions. The judicial branch of governance in modern democracies is now more significant and more visible than it was in 19th century British parliamentary democracy. That cannot be denied. But is this unconstitutional? Not, I would suggest, in any meaningful sense of the word. Parliament and the legislatures, in response to the perceived needs of the modern democracy we claim as ours, have created administrative tribunals and entrenched fundamental rights. This has increased the scope of matters on which the courts must adjudicate in discharging their traditional role. But the role remains essentially the same—to answer the legal questions that individuals and governments bring before it.

What then of the accusation that courts have gone beyond their proper role? The charge is made that activist judges—politicians cloaked in judicial robes—have gone beyond impartial judging to advocate for special causes and achieve particular political goals, and that this is undemocratic.

If it is true that judges are acting in this way, then they are indeed going beyond the role allotted to them by the Constitution. The judicial role is to resolve disputes and decide legal questions which others bring before the courts. It is not for judges to set the agendas for social change, or to impose their personal views on society. The role of judges is to support the rule of law, not the rule of judicial whim. Judges are human beings; but they must strive to judge impartially after considering the facts, the law and the submissions of parties on all sides of the question. In our constitutional framework, the role of the politician and the role of the judge are very different. The political role is to initiate the debate and to vote according to judgment on what is best for the country. The judicial role, by contrast is to resolve legal disputes formulated by others, impartially on the basis of the facts and the law.

But is the charge true? Have judges become political actors? Are they encroaching on terrain that is not theirs under our Constitution? In my opinion, the answer is no.

When we deconstruct the charge that the courts are overstepping their boundaries, we find that the claim can be understood in four different ways. First, the claim may be understood as saying that judges should never go against the will of elected representatives. This suggests that the choices of Parliament and legislative assemblies should never be undone by unelected judges. But that, as I have argued, is plainly false under our Constitution. The Legislative and the Executive strive in good faith to discharge their role in a manner that is consistent with our Constitution. They seek to bring forward laws which do not impinge on the Charter, and to implement those laws without infringing fundamental rights. But every now and then, these efforts are called into question, and someone must arbitrate the dispute. Under our Constitution, that "someone" is the judicial branch. As I said earlier, the terms of our *Constitution Acts* call on judges to be the arbiters of constitutional validity, both in terms of division of powers, and in terms of respect for fundamental rights. In performing that duty, judges must inevitably strike down legislation, and go against the will of elected representatives, whenever it fails to meet our constitutional standards.

Second, the charge of judicial activism may be understood as saying that judges are pursuing a particular political agenda, that they are allowing their political views to determine the outcome of cases before them. Very often, on this version, judges are seen as activist when one disagrees with their conclusions. Behind this criticism lies the assumption that the parameters of constitutional adjudication are so indeterminate that judges can bend them at will in the service of their own political objectives.

This version of the charge is also problematic, in my view. It is a serious matter to suggest that any branch of government is deliberately acting in a manner that is inconsistent with its constitutional role. Such a suggestion inevitably breeds cynicism, and undermines public confidence in all of our institutions of governance. It should not be made without convincing evidence of its truth. The evidence that judges in Canada pursue private political agendas is lacking. Judges are conscious of their special but limited role. Their judgments are replete with the need to defer to Parliament and the legislation on complex social issues. Should judges err and impose their personal views instead of the law, they are likely to be overturned on appeal. They may also be subject to internal censure. A visit to any of the thousands of courtrooms in this country—from the local magistrate courts to the Supreme Court of Canada—is unlikely to discover judges acting like politicians. Rather, it will find them discussing the facts of the case and how the law applies to them. This is not some form of role play. It is the morality of their role. An objective review of the thousands of judicial decisions reported each year reveals that judicial concern is focussed not on plans to change society, but on interpreting and applying the law in a way that reflects legislative purpose.

The idea that judges are implementing their own political agenda may emerge from the fact that judges sometimes make decisions that have political implications. But it is wrong to jump from this indisputable fact to the conclusion that judges are therefore assuming the political role. The law is the mechanism by which our society regulates itself. That is the business of politicians. But when the validity and interpretation of the laws is brought before the courts, that is the business of judges. The role of judges may take them into subject matter claimed by politicians. But it does not follow that the judges are acting as politicians; the judicial role remains distinct from the political.

In short, I suggest that the second version of the charge of judicial activism is false. The evidence suggests that constitutional adjudication is not a radically indeterminate activity, and that judges are not hiding behind it to pursue political agendas.

The third version of the charge of judicial activism begins from the opposite assumption. It assumes that law is a totally determinate black and white activity. From there, it proceeds to say that judges should apply the law, not make the law, or rewrite the law. This version of the charge of judicial activism rests on a mistaken perception of the nature of legal decision-making. The law does not apply itself, and the answers to constitutional questions are not obvious or pre-ordained. If they were, we would not need judges. It follows that there is no clear demarcation between applying the law, interpreting the law, and making the law. The Charter is an abstract document, made up of general propositions which must be given concrete application. To give it meaning, and to make it relevant to the lives of Canadians, judges must make choices among competing readings of our constitutional text, choices which can have long term normative consequences. All of this is perfectly consistent with the traditional role of judges in our country.

Let me turn, finally, to the fourth version of the charge of judicial activism. This version suggests that judges are making decisions that should be made by elected representatives, who alone possess the necessary legitimacy for law-making and the institutional competence to weigh all the factors that must be considered in making difficult choices of public policy for Canadians. This is a more subtle claim. Let me simply say that judges are sensitive to this concern, but have little choice in the matter.

Where a legal issue is properly before a court, not deciding is not an option. When a citizen claims that the state has violated his or her constitutional rights, the Courts must referee the dispute. They do so with all necessary deference to legislative and executive expertise in weighing competing demands on the public purse, and competing perspectives on public policy. In deciding difficult social issues, the courts act with deference to the decisions of the legislative branch. Judges recognize that:

> ... in certain types of decisions there may be no obviously correct or obviously wrong solution, but a range of options each with its advantages and disadvantages. Governments act as they think proper within a range of reasonable alternatives, and the [Supreme] Court acknowledged in *M. v. H.* ... that "the role of the legislature demands deference from the courts to those types of policy decisions that the legislature is best placed to make." [*Newfoundland and Labrador Association of Public and Private Employees v Her Majesty The Queen in Right of Newfoundland*, 2004 SCC 66, at para 83.]

There are, however, limits. Deference does not mean simply rubber stamping laws. If a law is unconstitutional, it is the duty of the courts to say so. In the words of my colleague Ian Binnie, in the recent decision of *Newfoundland v. NAPE*:

... Whenever there are boundaries to the legal exercise of state power such boundaries have to be refereed. Canadian courts have undertaken this role in relation to the division of powers between Parliament and the provincial legislatures since Confederation. The boundary between an individual's protected right or freedom and state power must also be refereed. The framers of the Charter identified the courts as the referee. While I recognize that the separation of powers is an important constitutional principle, I believe that the s. 1 test set out in *Oakes* and the rest of our voluminous s. 1 jurisprudence already provides the proper framework in which to consider what the doctrine of separation of powers requires in particular situations, as indeed was the case here. To the extent [that some would] invite a greater level of deference to the will of the legislature, I believe acceptance of such an invitation would simply be inconsistent with the clear words of s. 1 and undermine the delicate balance the Charter was intended to achieve. [2004 SCC 66 at para 116.]

In the end, when we examine what is really being said, the claim fails that judges are overstepping the proper constitutional boundaries of their role.

Let me return to where I began. In our constitutional democracy, each branch of government—legislative, executive and judicial—has an important role to play in Canadian democracy. The role of each branch is different and complementary. The essence of each remains the same through the centuries. The legislative branch's role is to make laws. The executive branch's role is to enforce the law. And the judicial branch's role is to interpret the law and resolve disputes arising from the law. Each branch is a vital part of our democracy. Each branch must discharge its role with integrity and respect for the proper constitutional roles of the other branches. To do less is to diminish our democracy and imperil our future.

The existence of unwritten, but legally enforceable, constitutional principles creates an additional layer of complexity in the debate concerning the appropriate role of the courts in constitutional adjudication. When a court strikes down a law because the court believes that the law unjustifiably infringes rights protected by the Charter, it is fulfilling an obligation that was explicitly assigned to it by the Constitution. As Iacobucci J observed at para 137 of his reasons for judgment in the *Vriend* case, "it was the deliberate choice of our provincial and federal legislatures in adopting the Charter to assign an interpretive role to the courts and to command them under s 52 to declare unconstitutional legislation invalid." When a court invalidates a law because it is inconsistent with an unwritten constitutional principle, it can appear to some observers that the court is unjustifiably creating for itself a mandate to interfere with the democratic process. As the Supreme Court of Canada's decisions in *Quebec Secession Reference* and *Re Manitoba Language Rights* illustrate, recourse to unwritten constitutional principles has sometimes enabled Canadian courts to achieve creative solutions to constitutional dilemmas that are not easily resolved with reference to the text of the Constitution alone. On the other hand, it should be noted that even some members of the Supreme Court of Canada have occasionally expressed the concern that the courts may be exceeding the proper boundaries of their role in constitutional adjudication by making use of unwritten constitutional principles. Consider the following passage from La Forest J's partial dissent in *Ref re Remuneration of Judges of the Prov Court of PEI*.

Ref re Remuneration of Judges of the Prov Court of PEI; Ref re Independence and Impartiality of Judges of the Prov Court of PEI
[1997] 3 SCR 3

LA FOREST J (dissenting):

II. The Effect of the Preamble to the Constitution Act, 1867

[303] I emphasize at the outset that it is not my position that s. 11(d) of the Charter and ss. 96-100 of the *Constitution Act, 1867* comprise an exhaustive code of judicial independence. As I discuss briefly later, additional protection for judicial independence may inhere in other provisions of the Constitution. Nor do I deny that the Constitution embraces unwritten rules, including rules that find expression in the preamble of the *Constitution Act, 1867*; see *New Brunswick Broadcasting Co. v. Nova Scotia (Speaker of the House of Assembly)*, [1993] 1 SCR 319. I hasten to add that these rules really find their origin in specific provisions of the Constitution viewed in light of our constitutional heritage. In other words, what we are concerned with is the meaning to be attached to an expression used in a constitutional provision.

[304] I take issue, however, with the Chief Justice's view that the preamble to the *Constitution Act, 1867* is a source of constitutional limitations on the power of legislatures to interfere with judicial independence. In *New Brunswick Broadcasting, supra*, this Court held that the privileges of the Nova Scotia legislature had constitutional status by virtue of the statement in the preamble expressing the desire to have "a Constitution similar in Principle to that of the United Kingdom." In reaching this conclusion, the Court examined the historical basis for the privileges of the British Parliament. That analysis established that the power of Parliament to exclude strangers was absolute, constitutional and immune from regulation by the courts. The effect of the preamble, the Court held, is to recognize and confirm that this long-standing principle of British constitutional law was continued or established in post-Confederation Canada.

[305] There is no similar historical basis, in contrast, for the idea that Parliament cannot interfere with judicial independence. At the time of Confederation (and indeed to this day), the British Constitution did not contemplate the notion that Parliament was limited in its ability to deal with judges.

• • •

[311] ... By expressing a desire to have a Constitution "similar in Principle to that of the United Kingdom," the framers of the *Constitution Act, 1867* did not give courts the power to strike down legislation violating the principle of judicial independence. The framers did, however, entrench the fundamental components of judicial independence set out in the *Act of Settlement* such that violations could be struck down by the courts. This was accomplished, however, by ss. 99-100 of the *Constitution Act, 1867*, not the preamble.

[312] It might be asserted that the argument presented above is merely a technical quibble. After all, in Canada the Constitution is supreme, not the legislatures. Courts have had the power to invalidate unconstitutional legislation in this country since 1867. If judicial independence was a "constitutional" principle in the broad sense in nineteenth-century Britain, and that principle was continued or established in Canada as a result of the preamble to the *Constitution Act, 1867*, why should Canadian courts resile from enforcing this principle by striking down incompatible legislation?

[313] One answer to this question is the ambit of the *Act of Settlement*. The protection it accorded was limited to superior courts, specifically the central courts of common law; see Lederman, ... , at p. 782. It did not apply to inferior courts. While subsequent legislation did provide limited protection for the independence of the judges of certain statutory courts, such as the county courts, the courts there were not regarded as within the ambit of the "constitutional" protection in the British sense. Generally the independence and impartiality of these courts were ensured to litigants through the superintendence exercised over them by the superior courts by way of prerogative writs and other extraordinary remedies. The overall task of protection sought to be created for inferior courts in the present appeals seems to me to be made of insubstantial cloth, and certainly in no way similar to anything to be found in the United Kingdom.

[314] A more general answer to the question lies in the nature of the power of judicial review. The ability to nullify the laws of democratically elected representatives derives its legitimacy from a super-legislative source: the text of the Constitution. This foundational document (in Canada, a series of documents) expresses the desire of the people to limit the power of legislatures in certain specified ways. Because our Constitution is entrenched, those limitations cannot be changed by recourse to the usual democratic process. They are not cast in stone, however, and can be modified in accordance with a further expression of democratic will: constitutional amendment.

[315] Judicial review, therefore, is politically legitimate only insofar as it involves the interpretation of an authoritative constitutional instrument. In this sense, it is akin to statutory interpretation. In each case, the court's role is to divine the intent or purpose of the text as it has been expressed by the people through the mechanism of the democratic process. Of course, many (but not all) constitutional provisions are cast in broad and abstract language. Courts have the often arduous task of explicating the effect of this language in a myriad of factual circumstances, many of which may not have been contemplated by the framers of the Constitution. While there are inevitable disputes about the manner in which courts should perform this duty, for example by according more or less deference to legislative decisions, there is general agreement that the task itself is legitimate.

[316] This legitimacy is imperiled, however, when courts attempt to limit the power of legislatures without recourse to express textual authority. From time to time, members of this Court have suggested that our Constitution comprehends implied rights that circumscribe legislative competence. On the theory that the efficacy of parliamentary democracy requires free political expression, it has been asserted that the curtailment of such expression is *ultra vires* both provincial legislatures and the federal Parliament: *Switzman v. Elbling*, [1957] SCR 285, at p. 328 (per Abbott J); *OPSEU v. Ontario (Attorney General)*, [1987] 2 SCR 2, at p. 57 (per Beetz J); see also: *Reference re Alberta Statutes*, [1938] SCR 100, at pp. 132-35 (per Duff CJ), and at pp. 145-46 (per Cannon J); *Switzman, supra*, at pp. 306-7 (per Rand J); *OPSEU, supra*, at p. 25 (per Dickson CJ); *Fraser v. Public Service Staff Relations Board*, [1985] 2 SCR 455, at pp. 462-63 (per Dickson CJ); *RWDSU v. Dolphin Delivery Ltd.*, [1986] 2 SCR 573, at p. 584 (per McIntyre J).

[317] This theory, which is not so much an "implied bill of rights," as it has so often been called, but rather a more limited guarantee of those communicative freedoms necessary for the existence of parliamentary democracy, is not without appeal. An argument can be made that, even under a constitutional structure that deems Parliament to be supreme, certain rights, including freedom of political speech, should be enforced by the courts in order to safeguard the democratic accountability of Parliament. Without this limitation of its powers, the argument

runs, Parliament could subvert the very process by which it acquired its legitimacy as a representative, democratic institution ... . It should be noted, however, that the idea that the Constitution contemplates implied protection for democratic rights has been rejected by a number of eminent jurists as being incompatible with the structure and history of the Constitution; see *Attorney General for Canada and Dupond v. Montreal*, [1978] 2 SCR 770, at p. 796 (per Beetz J); Bora Laskin, "An Inquiry into the Diefenbaker Bill of Rights" (1959), 37 *Can. Bar Rev.* 77, at pp. 100-103; Paul C. Weiler, "The Supreme Court and the Law of Canadian Federalism" (1973), 23 *UTLJ* 307, at p. 344; Peter W. Hogg, *Constitutional Law of Canada* (3rd ed. 1992 (loose-leaf)), vol. 2, at pp. 31-12 and 31-13.

[318] Whatever attraction this theory may hold, and I do not wish to be understood as either endorsing or rejecting it, it is clear in my view that it may not be used to justify the notion that the preamble to the *Constitution Act, 1867* contains implicit protection for judicial independence. Although it has been suggested that guarantees of political freedom flow from the preamble, as I have discussed in relation to judicial independence, this position is untenable. The better view is that if these guarantees exist, they are implicit in s. 17 of the *Constitution Act, 1867*, which provides for the establishment of Parliament; see Gibson ... , at p. 498. More important, the justification for implied political freedoms is that they are supportive, and not subversive, of legislative supremacy. That doctrine holds that democratically constituted legislatures, and not the courts, are the ultimate guarantors of civil liberties, including the right to an independent judiciary. Implying protection for judicial independence from the preambular commitment to a British-style constitution, therefore, entirely misapprehends the fundamental nature of that constitution.

[319] This brings us back to the central point: to the extent that courts in Canada have the power to enforce the principle of judicial independence, this power derives from the structure of Canadian, and not British, constitutionalism. Our Constitution expressly contemplates both the power of judicial review (in s. 52 of the *Constitution Act, 1982*) and guarantees of judicial independence (in ss. 96-100 of the *Constitution Act, 1867* and s. 11(d) of the Charter). While these provisions have been interpreted to provide guarantees of independence that are not immediately manifest in their language, this has been accomplished through the usual mechanisms of constitutional interpretation, not through recourse to the preamble. The legitimacy of this interpretive exercise stems from its grounding in an expression of democratic will, not from a dubious theory of an implicit constitutional structure. The express provisions of the Constitution are not, as the Chief Justice contends, "elaborations of the underlying, unwritten, and organizing principles found in the preamble to the *Constitution Act, 1867*" (para. 107). On the contrary, they are the Constitution. To assert otherwise is to subvert the democratic foundation of judicial review.

III. JUDICIAL REVIEW OF ADMINISTRATIVE ACTION

Judicial review of executive action pursuant to "administrative law" principles raises somewhat different questions about institutional relationships than does judicial review of legislative action done with reference to constitutional rules. To be sure, there is some overlap between these questions, at least to the extent that judges will normally want to respect the choice of democratically elected legislatures to allocate decision-making authority to executive institutions. On the other hand, the judicial invalidation of particular administrative acts on non-constitutional grounds often does not preclude the decision-maker from repeating his or her actions, this time in compliance with standards set out in the statute delegating power (as now assessed by the court) or common law procedural fairness (again, as assessed by the court). And, even if the court concludes that there is no fashion in which the actions of the administrative decision-maker could comply with existing statutory authority, it remains open to the legislature to modify the law in ways that validate the same action, if taken subsequent to the change in the law.

For these reasons, constitutional review of legislative action constrains democratically elected legislatures in a way that judicial review of administrative action using ordinary legal principles does not. As a result, non-constitutional review by judges of the actions of administrative officials does not tend to raise the same kinds of questions about the democratic legitimacy of judicial review that arise when judges engage in the constitutional review of legislation.

This does not mean, however, that it is irrelevant to consider the proper institutional relationship between courts and administrative decision-makers. At a superficial level, these relationships stem from the legal rules (typically found in statutes) that define the scope of authority of the administrative decision-maker whose actions are under review. In practice, however, these relationships are influenced significantly by three bodies of common law rules, the first of which deals with the nature and limits of delegated authority, the second of which deals with fair administrative procedure, and the third of which concerns judicial review of the substance of administrative decisions. There are some statutes that set out rules governing administrative procedure, such as the Ontario *Statutory Powers Procedure Act*, RSO 1990, c S.22 and the BC *Administrative Tribunals Act*, SBC 2004, c 45, and other statutory provisions that affect the rules governing judicial review, such as s 18.1 of the *Federal Courts Act*, RSC 1985, c F-7 and ss 58-59 of the BC *Administrative Tribunals Act*. Even where the common law has been modified by statute, however, it establishes the background legal expectations for the nature and scope of delegated authority, fair administrative procedure, and judicial supervision of the legal validity of administrative decisions, and thus is worthy of our consideration.

A. LIMITS ON THE EXERCISE OF DELEGATED AUTHORITY

We have already noted in Chapter 8 that there are relatively few legal constraints on the authority of the legislative branch to delegate authority. Nevertheless, the law does impose significant constraints on the exercise of power by the recipient of delegated authority. The overarching principle that governs the exercise of delegated authority is that it must be exercised within the confines of the delegation itself. Recipients of delegated authority have no inherent authority to act. Their sole source of power (excepting those bodies that exercise prerogative powers or powers under the Constitution) derives from the statutory delegation.

Consequently, any act done outside the boundaries of the statutory grant is without legal authority and unlawful—that is, it is *ultra vires*. The rule that a delegated authority can exercise only those powers that are granted to it is conceptually straightforward and tends to turn on questions of the interpretation of the authorizing legislation. For example, in *Shell Canada Products Ltd v Vancouver (City)*, [1994] 1 SCR 231 (reproduced in Chapter 8), there was no disagreement on the general rule that administrative bodies, in that case municipalities, "must stay within the powers conferred on them by provincial statutes" (per Sopinka J, writing for the majority). However, the majority and the minority disagreed about the proper interpretation of the statutory provision relied on in support of the municipality's decision, with the minority being prepared to take a more expansive approach to the interpretation of the city's statutory powers.

A related rule requires that, in the absence of express or implied authority to subdelegate, the specific delegate to whom the authority is granted must exercise the delegated authority.

This rule is captured in the Latin maxim *delegatus non potest delegare* described by Kerwin J in *Reference re Regulations in Relation to Chemicals*, [1943] SCR 1:

> The statute does not in express terms provide for delegation and the maxim *delegatus non potest delegare* is invoked to support a construction as would deny any implication of such an authority.
>
>> The general principle is stated in Broom's Legal Maxims at page 570, as follows:
>>
>>> This principle is that a delegated authority cannot be re-delegated: *delegata potestas non potest delegari*, that is, one agent cannot lawfully appoint another to perform the duties of his agency. This rule applies wherever the authority involves a trust or discretion in the agent for the exercise of which he is selected, but does not apply where it involves no matter of discretion, and it is immaterial whether the act be done by one person or another, and the original agent remains responsible to the principal.
>
>> The principle thus stated is somewhat qualified by Broom, at page 572, as follows:
>>
>>> Although, however, a deputy cannot, according to the above rule, transfer his entire powers to another, yet a deputy possessing general powers may, in many cases, constitute another person his servant or bailiff, for the purpose of doing some particular act; provided, of course, that such act be within the scope of his own legitimate authority.
>
>> And again:
>>
>>> The rule as to delegated functions must, moreover, be understood with this necessary qualification, that, in the particular case, no power to re-delegate such functions has been given. Such an authority to employ a deputy may be either express or implied by the recognised usage of trade.
>
>> The maxim is most frequently applied in matters pertaining to principal and agent but it is also applied in respect of legislative grants of authority; for example in *Re Behari Lal et al.*, it was held that the power conferred on the Governor General in Council by section 30 of the *Immigration Act* to prohibit the landing of immigrants of a specified class could not be delegated to the Minister of the Interior. Mr. Justice Clement said:
>>
>>> ... In my opinion, nothing short of express words would avail to enable His Excellency in Council to delegate to another or others a power of this nature, the exercise of which is conditioned upon his consideration of its necessity or expediency.
>
>> Again in *Geraghty v. Porter*, it was held that a delegated power of legislation must be exercised strictly in accordance with the powers creating it; and in the absence of express power so to do the authority cannot be delegated to any other person or body.
>
>> The maxim, however, is at most a rule of construction, subject to qualifications, some of which are referred to by Broom.
>
>> In the case of a statute, there, of course, must be a consideration of the language of the whole enactment and of its purposes and objects.

It is important to note, however, that the subdelegation doctrine is qualified by the right to subdelegate where this is expressly or impliedly authorized. Thus, it may be more accurate to speak of a rule against unauthorized subdelegation. For example, one important qualification to the rule against subdelegation, alluded to above, is that matters that are "merely administrative" may lawfully be subdelegated, which is to say that subdelegation is impliedly authorized in these situations. In this context, "merely administrative" matters are those that do not involve the exercise of substantial amounts of discretion. This exception is in keeping with the overall purpose of the rule that recognizes that where the legislature entrusted decision-making powers to a certain official or body, then those powers should be exercised specifically by that delegate. In cases where there is little or no discretion to exercise, it should not matter who the decision-maker is because the outcomes are dictated by the scheme itself. For example, in *Forget v Quebec (AG)*, [1988] 2 SCR 90, the Supreme Court of Canada had to decide whether the power of the Quebec French Language Office to provide for the holding of examinations to determine whether professionals had adequate knowledge of French to satisfy regulatory requirements had been improperly subdelegated to a committee. The Court held that the office had not improperly subdelegated its authority. The office had been granted express statutory authority to establish committees necessary for the attainment of its purposes, and in any event the setting of the examinations involved a purely administrative function.

Other instances where the rule against subdelegation does not apply occur where the right to subdelegate is expressly authorized by statute. Consider, for example, the situations addressed by the *Interpretation Act*, RSC 1985, c I-21, s 24:

> (2) Words directing or empowering a minister of the Crown to do an act or thing, regardless of whether the act or thing is administrative, legislative or judicial, or otherwise applying to that minister as the holder of the office, include
>> (a) a minister acting for that minister or, if the office is vacant, a minister designated to act in the office by or under the authority of an order in council;
>> (b) the successors of that minister in the office;
>> (c) his or their deputy; and
>> (d) notwithstanding paragraph (c), a person appointed to serve, in the department or ministry of state over which the minister presides, in a capacity appropriate to the doing of the act or thing, or to the words so applying.

B. CONTROLLING PROCEDURES: THE DUTY TO BE FAIR

Administrative decision-makers are generally required by the common law to act fairly toward those persons affected by their decisions. In this context, the duty to be fair refers to the *procedures* adopted by the decision-maker, as opposed to imposing a substantive obligation of a *fair outcome*. Historically, the requirements of procedural fairness, at that time referred to as the "rules of natural justice," were found to apply only to decision-makers carrying out a "judicial or quasi-judicial function," a narrowly defined class of administrative decisions that were confined to cases where decision-makers were determining the legal rights of a person, but excluded cases where decision-makers were determining matters of policy, regardless of their effect on individuals.

The difficulty with the traditional rules of natural justice from a policy perspective was that they failed to afford any procedural protections to those affected by decisions found to be of an administrative nature, although it was becoming clearer that these decisions could have significant impacts on individuals. From a legal perspective, the distinction between judicial and quasi-judicial decisions, on the one hand, and administrative decisions, on the other, was hard to maintain because exactly what these terms meant was murky, especially as applied to the complex world of administrative decision-makers with functions that might straddle the categories. For example, some decision-making processes engaged both adjudicatory and policy determination functions. As a consequence of these difficulties, common law courts developed a more flexible approach to the procedural obligations of decision-makers under the rubric of the duty to be fair. In England, the move toward a more flexible approach was firmly adopted in *Ridge v Baldwin*, [1964] AC 40 (HL) and in Canada in *Nicholson v Haldimand-Norfolk Regional Police Commissioners*, [1979] 1 SCR 311.

The essence of the content of the rules of natural justice was captured by these two maxims: *audi alteram partem*—the right of a person to know and answer the case against him or her—and *nemo judex in sua causa*—requiring that a person not be the judge in his or her own cause (i.e., that an administrative decision-maker must not be biased). The extent of their application depended on the particular context. The contours of the duty to be fair are considered in the excerpts that follow.

Baker v Canada (Minister of Citizenship and Immigration)
[1999] 2 SCR 817

[The appellant, who was a citizen of Jamaica, was the subject of a deportation order. Prior to the order being issued, the appellant had lived in Canada for 11 years, but never became a permanent resident. During the time she lived in Canada, she had four children. She also suffered from mental illness, for which she received treatment. The appellant sought an exemption to applying for permanent residency status from outside of Canada on "humanitarian and compassionate" (H & C) considerations, on the grounds that her deportation was not in the best interests of her children, who would suffer in her absence, and that her deportation would negatively affect her mental health. Her application was denied by immigration officials. She was not given official reasons for the denial of her application, but she did receive a copy of notes taken by one of the reviewing immigration officers (Lorenz, whose notes were used by a more senior immigration officer, Caden, who was the decision-maker). These notes disclosed a lack of concern regarding the interests of her children and were insensitive to her mental health issues. The appellant sought to have the H & C decision reviewed by the Court on the grounds that she was denied procedural fairness, including bias, and that the decision itself was unreasonable in that it failed to account for the best interests of her children. On this last point, the appellant argued that the best interests of children were to be a primary consideration under the *Convention on the Rights of the Child*, an international treaty to which Canada was a party (but had not implemented in Canadian domestic law).]

L'HEUREUX-DUBÉ J:

C. Procedural Fairness

[18] The first ground upon which the appellant challenges the decision made by Officer Caden is the allegation that she was not accorded procedural fairness. She suggests that the following procedures are required by the duty of fairness when parents have Canadian children and they make an H & C application: an oral interview before the decision-maker, notice to her children and the other parent of that interview, a right for the children and the other parent to make submissions at that interview, and notice to the other parent of the interview and of that person's right to have counsel present. She also alleges that procedural fairness requires the provision of reasons by the decision-maker, Officer Caden, and that the notes of Officer Lorenz give rise to a reasonable apprehension of bias.

[19] In addressing the fairness issues, I will consider first the principles relevant to the determination of the content of the duty of procedural fairness, and then address Ms. Baker's arguments that she was accorded insufficient participatory rights, that a duty to give reasons existed, and that there was a reasonable apprehension of bias.

[20] Both parties agree that a duty of procedural fairness applies to H & C decisions. The fact that a decision is administrative and affects "the rights, privileges or interests of an individual" is sufficient to trigger the application of the duty of fairness: *Cardinal v. Kent Institution*, [1985] 2 SCR 643 (SCC) at p. 653. Clearly, the determination of whether an applicant will be exempted from the requirements of the Act falls within this category, and it has been long recognized that the duty of fairness applies to H & C decisions: *Sobrie v. Canada (Minister of Employment &*

Immigration) (1987), 3 Imm. LR (2d) 81 (Fed. TD) at p. 88; *Said v. Canada (Minister of Employment & Immigration)* (1992), 6 Admin. LR (2d) 23 (Fed. TD); *Shah v. Canada (Minister of Employment & Immigration)* (1994), 170 NR 238 (Fed. CA).

(1) Factors Affecting the Content of the Duty of Fairness

[21] The existence of a duty of fairness, however, does not determine what requirements will be applicable in a given set of circumstances. As I wrote in *Knight v. Indian Head School Division No. 19*, [1990] 1 SCR 653 (SCC) at p. 682, "the concept of procedural fairness is eminently variable, and its content is to be decided in the specific context of each case." All of the circumstances must be considered in order to determine the content of the duty of procedural fairness: *Knight* at pp. 682-83; *Cardinal, supra*, at p. 654; *Old St. Boniface Residents Assn. Inc. v. Winnipeg (City)*, [1990] 3 SCR 1170 (SCC), *per* Sopinka J.

[22] Although the duty of fairness is flexible and variable, and depends on an appreciation of the context of the particular statute and the rights affected, it is helpful to review the criteria that should be used in determining what procedural rights the duty of fairness requires in a given set of circumstances. I emphasize that underlying all these factors is the notion that the purpose of the participatory rights contained within the duty of procedural fairness is to ensure that administrative decisions are made using a fair and open procedure, appropriate to the decision being made and its statutory, institutional, and social context, with an opportunity for those affected by the decision to put forward their views and evidence fully and have them considered by the decision-maker.

[23] Several factors have been recognized in the jurisprudence as relevant to determining what is required by the common law duty of procedural fairness in a given set of circumstances. One important consideration is the nature of the decision being made and the process followed in making it. In *Knight, supra*, at p. 683, it was held that "the closeness of the administrative process to the judicial process should indicate how much of those governing principles should be imported into the realm of administrative decision making." The more the process provided for, the function of the tribunal, the nature of the decision-making body, and the determinations that must be made to reach a decision resemble judicial decision making, the more likely it is that procedural protections closer to the trial model will be required by the duty of fairness. See also *Old St. Boniface, supra*, at p. 1191; *Russell v. Duke of Norfolk*, [1949] 1 All ER 109 (Eng. CA) at p. 118; *Syndicat des employés de production du Québec & de l'Acadie v. Canada (Human Rights Commission)*, [1989] 2 SCR 879 (SCC) at p. 896, *per* Sopinka J.

[24] A second factor is the nature of the statutory scheme and the "terms of the statute pursuant to which the body operates": *Old St. Boniface, supra*, at p. 1191. The role of the particular decision within the statutory scheme and other surrounding indications in the statute help determine the content of the duty of fairness owed when a particular administrative decision is made. Greater procedural protections, for example, will be required when no appeal procedure is provided within the statute, or when the decision is determinative of the issue and further requests cannot be submitted: see D.J.M. Brown and J.M. Evans, *Judicial Review of Administrative Action in Canada* (loose-leaf), at pp. 7-66 to 7-67.

[25] A third factor in determining the nature and extent of the duty of fairness owed is the importance of the decision to the individual or individuals affected. The more important the decision is to the lives of those affected and the greater its impact on that person or those persons, the more stringent the procedural protections that will be mandated. ...

[26] Fourth, the legitimate expectations of the person challenging the decision may also determine what procedures the duty of fairness requires in given circumstances. Our Court has held that, in Canada, this doctrine is part of the doctrine of fairness or natural justice, and that it does not create substantive rights: *Old St. Boniface, supra,* at p. 1204; *Reference re Canada Assistance Plan (Canada),* [1991] 2 SCR 525 (SCC) at p. 557. As applied in Canada, if a legitimate expectation is found to exist, this will affect the content of the duty of fairness owed to the individual or individuals affected by the decision. If the claimant has a legitimate expectation that a certain procedure will be followed, this procedure will be required by the duty of fairness: *Qi v. Canada (Minister of Citizenship & Immigration)* (1995), 33 Imm. LR (2d) 57 (Fed. TD); *Mercier-Néron v. Canada (Minister of National Health & Welfare)* (1995), 98 FTR 36 (Fed. TD); *Bendahmane v. Canada (Minister of Employment & Immigration),* [1989] 3 FC 16 (Fed. CA). Similarly, if a claimant has a legitimate expectation that a certain result will be reached in his or her case, fairness may require more extensive procedural rights than would otherwise be accorded: D.J. Mullan, *Administrative Law* (3rd ed. 1996), at pp. 214-15; D. Shapiro, "Legitimate Expectation and Its Application to Canadian Immigration Law" (1992), 8 *JL & Soc. Pol'y* 282, at p. 297; *Canada (Attorney General) v. Canada (Human Rights Tribunal)* (1994), 76 FTR 1 (Fed. TD). Nevertheless, the doctrine of legitimate expectations cannot lead to substantive rights outside the procedural domain. This doctrine, as applied in Canada, is based on the principle that the "circumstances" affecting procedural fairness take into account the promises or regular practices of administrative decision-makers, and that it will generally be unfair for them to act in contravention of representations as to procedure, or to backtrack on substantive promises without according significant procedural rights.

[27] Fifth, the analysis of what procedures the duty of fairness requires should also take into account and respect the choices of procedure made by the agency itself, particularly when the statute leaves to the decision-maker the ability to choose its own procedures, or when the agency has an expertise in determining what procedures are appropriate in the circumstances: Brown and Evans, *supra,* at pp. 7-66 to 7-70. While this, of course, is not determinative, important weight must be given to the choice of procedures made by the agency itself and its institutional constraints: *I.W.A. Local 2-69 v. Consolidated Bathurst Packaging Ltd.,* [1990] 1 SCR 282 (SCC), *per* Gonthier J.

[28] I should note that this list of factors is not exhaustive. These principles all help a court determine whether the procedures that were followed respected the duty of fairness. Other factors may also be important, particularly when considering aspects of the duty of fairness unrelated to participatory rights. The values underlying the duty of procedural fairness relate to the principle that the individual or individuals affected should have the opportunity to present their case fully and fairly, and have decisions affecting their rights, interests, or privileges made using a fair, impartial, and open process, appropriate to the statutory, institutional, and social context of the decision.

• • •

(3) Participatory Rights

[30] The next issue is whether, taking into account the other factors related to the determination of the content of the duty of fairness, the failure to accord an oral hearing and give notice to Ms. Baker or her children was inconsistent with the participatory rights required by the duty of fairness in these circumstances. At the heart of this analysis is whether, considering all the circumstances, those whose

interests were affected had a meaningful opportunity to present their case fully and fairly. The procedure in this case consisted of a written application with supporting documentation, which was summarized by the junior officer (Lorenz), with a recommendation being made by that officer. The summary, recommendation, and material was then considered by the senior officer (Caden), who made the decision.

[31] Several of the factors described above enter into the determination of the type of participatory rights the duty of procedural fairness requires in the circumstances. First, an H & C decision is very different from a judicial decision, since it involves the exercise of considerable discretion and requires the consideration of multiple factors. Second, its role is also, within the statutory scheme, as an exception to the general principles of Canadian immigration law. These factors militate in favour of more relaxed requirements under the duty of fairness. On the other hand, there is no appeal procedure, although judicial review may be applied for with leave of the Federal Court—Trial Division. In addition, considering the third factor, this is a decision that in practice has exceptional importance to the lives of those with an interest in its result—the claimant and his or her close family members—and this leads to the content of the duty of fairness being more extensive. Finally, applying the fifth factor described above, the statute accords considerable flexibility to the Minister to decide on the proper procedure, and immigration officers, as a matter of practice, do not conduct interviews in all cases. The institutional practices and choices made by the Minister are significant, though of course not determinative factors to be considered in the analysis. Thus, it can be seen that although some of the factors suggest stricter requirements under the duty of fairness, others suggest more relaxed requirements further from the judicial model.

[32] Balancing these factors, I disagree with the holding of the Federal Court of Appeal in *Shah, supra*, at p. 239, that the duty of fairness owed in these circumstances is simply "minimal." Rather, the circumstances require a full and fair consideration of the issues, and the claimant and others whose important interests are affected by the decision in a fundamental way must have a meaningful opportunity to present the various types of evidence relevant to their case and have it fully and fairly considered.

[33] However, it also cannot be said that an oral hearing is always necessary to ensure a fair hearing and consideration of the issues involved. The flexible nature of the duty of fairness recognizes that meaningful participation can occur in different ways in different situations. The Federal Court has held that procedural fairness does not require an oral hearing in these circumstances: see, for example, *Said, supra*, at p. 30.

[34] I agree that an oral hearing is not a general requirement for H & C decisions. An interview is not essential for the information relevant to an H & C application to be put before an immigration officer, so that the humanitarian and compassionate considerations presented may be considered in their entirety and in a fair manner. In this case, the appellant had the opportunity to put forward, in written form through her lawyer, information about her situation, her children and their emotional dependence on her, and documentation in support of her application from a social worker at the Children's Aid Society and from her psychiatrist. These documents were before the decision-makers, and they contained the information relevant to making this decision. Taking all the factors relevant to determining the content of the duty of fairness into account, the lack of an oral hearing or notice of such a hearing did not, in my opinion, constitute a violation of the requirements of procedural fairness to which Ms. Baker was entitled in the circumstances, particularly given the fact that several of the factors point toward a more relaxed standard. The opportunity, which was accorded, for the appellant or her children to produce

full and complete written documentation in relation to all aspects of her application satisfied the requirements of the participatory rights required by the duty of fairness in this case.

(4) The Provision of Reasons

[35] The appellant also submits that the duty of fairness, in these circumstances, requires that reasons be given by the decision-maker. She argues either that the notes of Officer Lorenz should be considered the reasons for the decision, or that it should be held that the failure of Officer Caden to give written reasons for his decision or a subsequent affidavit explaining them should be taken to be a breach of the principles of fairness.

[36] This issue has been addressed in several cases of judicial review of humanitarian and compassionate applications. The Federal Court of Appeal has held that reasons are unnecessary: *Shah, supra*, at pp. 239-40. It has also been held that the case history notes prepared by a subordinate officer are not to be considered the decision-maker's reasons: see *Tylo v. Canada (Minister of Employment & Immigration)* (1995), 90 FTR 157 (Fed. TD) at pp. 159-60. In *Gheorlan v. Canada (Secretary of State)* (1995), 26 Imm. LR (2d) 170 (Fed. TD), and *Chan v. Canada (Minister of Citizenship & Immigration)* (1994), 87 FTR 62 (Fed. TD), it was held that the notes of the reviewing officer should not be taken to be the reasons for decision, but may help in determining whether a reviewable error exists. In *Marques v. Canada (Minister of Citizenship & Immigration)* (1995), 116 FTR 241 (Fed. TD), an H & C decision was set aside because the decision making officer failed to provide reasons or an affidavit explaining the reasons for his decision.

[37] More generally, the traditional position at common law has been that the duty of fairness does not require, as a general rule, that reasons be provided for administrative decisions: *Northwestern Utilities Ltd. v. Edmonton (City)* (1978), [1979] 1 SCR 684 (SCC); *Supermarchés Jean Labrecque Inc. v. Québec (Tribunal du travail)*, [1987] 2 SCR 219 (SCC) at p. 233; *Public Service Board of New South Wales v. Osmond* (1986), 159 CLR 656 (Australia HC) at pp. 665-66.

[38] Courts and commentators have, however, often emphasized the usefulness of reasons in ensuring fair and transparent decision-making. Though *Northwestern Utilities* dealt with a statutory obligation to give reasons, Estey J held as follows, at p. 706, referring to the desirability of a common law reasons requirement:

> This obligation is a salutary one. It reduces to a considerable degree the chances of arbitrary or capricious decisions, reinforces public confidence in the judgment and fairness of administrative tribunals, and affords parties to administrative proceedings an opportunity to assess the question of appeal. ...

The importance of reasons was recently reemphasized by this Court in *R v. Campbell*, [1997] 3 SCR 3 (SCC) at pp. 109-10.

[39] Reasons, it has been argued, foster better decision making by ensuring that issues and reasoning are well articulated and, therefore, more carefully thought out. The process of writing reasons for decision by itself may be a guarantee of a better decision. Reasons also allow parties to see that the applicable issues have been carefully considered, and are invaluable if a decision is to be appealed, questioned, or considered on judicial review: R.A. Macdonald and D. Lametti, "Reasons for Decision in Administrative Law" (1990), 3 *CJALP* 123, at p. 146; *Williams v. Canada (Minister of Citizenship & Immigration)*, [1997] 2 FC 646 (Fed. CA) at para. 38. Those affected may be more likely to feel they were treated fairly and appropriately if reasons are given: de Smith, Woolf, & Jowell, *Judicial Review of Administrative*

Action (5th ed. 1995), at pp. 459-60. I agree that these are significant benefits of written reasons.

[40] Others have expressed concerns about the desirability of a written reasons requirement at common law. In *Osmond, supra,* Gibbs CJ articulated, at p. 668, the concern that a reasons requirement may lead to an inappropriate burden being imposed on administrative decision-makers, that it may lead to increased cost and delay, and that it "might in some cases induce a lack of candour on the part of the administrative officers concerned." Macdonald and Lametti, *supra,* though they agree that fairness should require the provision of reasons in certain circumstances, caution against a requirement of "archival" reasons associated with court judgments, and note that the special nature of agency decision-making in different contexts should be considered in evaluating reasons requirements. In my view, however, these concerns can be accommodated by ensuring that any reasons require-ment under the duty of fairness leaves sufficient flexibility to decision-makers by accepting various types of written explanations for the decision as sufficient.

• • •

[43] In my opinion, it is now appropriate to recognize that, in certain circum-stances, the duty of procedural fairness will require the provision of a written explanation for a decision. The strong arguments demonstrating the advantages of written reasons suggest that, in cases such as this where the decision has impor-tant significance for the individual, when there is a statutory right of appeal, or in other circumstances, some form of reasons should be required. This requirement has been developing in the common law elsewhere. The circumstances of the case at bar, in my opinion, constitute one of the situations where reasons are necessary. The profound importance of an H & C decision to those affected, as with those at issue in *Orlowski, R v. Civil Service Appeal Board,* and *R v. Secretary of State for the Home Department,* militates in favour of a requirement that reasons be provided. It would be unfair for a person subject to a decision such as this one which is so critical to their future not to be told why the result was reached.

[44] In my view, however, the reasons requirement was fulfilled in this case, since the appellant was provided with the notes of Officer Lorenz. The notes were given to Ms. Baker when her counsel asked for reasons. Because of this, and because there is no other record of the reasons for making the decision, the notes of the subordinate reviewing officer should be taken, by inference, to be the reasons for decision. Accepting documents such as these notes as sufficient reasons is part of the flexibility that is necessary, as emphasized by Macdonald and Lametti, *supra,* when courts evaluate the requirements of the duty of fairness with recognition of the day-to-day realities of administrative agencies and the many ways in which the values underlying the principles of procedural fairness can be assured. It upholds the principle that individuals are entitled to fair procedures and open decision-making, but recognizes that in the administrative context, this transparency may take place in various ways. I conclude that the notes of Officer Lorenz satisfy the requirement for reasons under the duty of procedural fairness in this case, and they will be taken to be the reasons for decision.

(5) Reasonable Apprehension of Bias

[45] Procedural fairness also requires that decisions be made free from a rea-sonable apprehension of bias, by an impartial decision-maker. The respondent argues that Simpson J was correct to find that the notes of Officer Lorenz can-not be considered to give rise to a reasonable apprehension of bias because it was Officer Caden who was the actual decision-maker, who was simply reviewing the

recommendation prepared by his subordinate. In my opinion, the duty to act fairly and therefore in a manner that does not give rise to a reasonable apprehension of bias applies to all immigration officers who play a significant role in the making of decisions, whether they are subordinate reviewing officers, or those who make the final decision. The subordinate officer plays an important part in the process, and if a person with such a central role does not act impartially, the decision itself cannot be said to have been made in an impartial manner. In addition, as discussed in the previous section, the notes of Officer Lorenz constitute the reasons for the decision, and if they give rise to a reasonable apprehension of bias, this taints the decision itself.

[46] The test for reasonable apprehension of bias was set out by de Grandpré J, writing in dissent, in *Committee for Justice & Liberty v. Canada (National Energy Board)* (1976), [1978] 1 SCR 369 (SCC) at p. 394:

> ... the apprehension of bias must be a reasonable one, held by reasonable and right minded persons, applying themselves to the question and obtaining thereon the required information. ... [T]hat test is "what would an informed person, viewing the matter realistically and practically—and having thought the matter through—conclude. Would he think that it is more likely than not that [the decision-maker], whether consciously or unconsciously, would not decide fairly."

This expression of the test has often been endorsed by this Court, most recently in *R v. S. (R.D.)*, [1997] 3 SCR 484 (SCC) at para. 11, *per* Major J; at para. 31, *per* L'Heureux-Dubé and McLachlin JJ; and at para. 111, *per* Cory J.

[47] It has been held that the standards for reasonable apprehension of bias may vary, like other aspects of procedural fairness, depending on the context and the type of function performed by the administrative decision-maker involved: *Newfoundland Telephone Co. v. Newfoundland (Board of Commissioners of Public Utilities)*, [1992] 1 SCR 623 (SCC); *Old St. Boniface, supra*, at p. 1192. The context here is one where immigration officers must regularly make decisions that have great importance to the individuals affected by them, but are also often critical to the interests of Canada as a country. They are individualized, rather than decisions of a general nature. They also require special sensitivity. Canada is a nation made up largely of people whose families migrated here in recent centuries. Our history is one that shows the importance of immigration, and our society shows the benefits of having a diversity of people whose origins are in a multitude of places around the world. Because they necessarily relate to people of diverse backgrounds, from different cultures, races, and continents, immigration decisions demand sensitivity and understanding by those making them. They require a recognition of diversity, an understanding of others, and an openness to difference.

[48] In my opinion, the well-informed member of the community would perceive bias when reading Officer Lorenz's comments. His notes, and the manner in which they are written, do not disclose the existence of an open mind or a weighing of the particular circumstances of the case free from stereotypes. Most unfortunate is the fact that they seem to make a link between Ms. Baker's mental illness, her training as a domestic worker, the fact that she has several children, and the conclusion that she would therefore be a strain on our social welfare system for the rest of her life. In addition, the conclusion drawn was contrary to the psychiatrist's letter, which stated that, with treatment, Ms. Baker could remain well and return to being a productive member of society. Whether they were intended in this manner or not, these statements give the impression that Officer Lorenz may have been drawing conclusions based not on the evidence before him, but on the fact that Ms. Baker

was a single mother with several children, and had been diagnosed with a psychiatric illness. His use of capitals to highlight the number of Ms. Baker's children may also suggest to a reader that this was a reason to deny her status. Reading his comments, I do not believe that a reasonable and well-informed member of the community would conclude that he had approached this case with the impartiality appropriate to a decision made by an immigration officer. It would appear to a reasonable observer that his own frustration with the "system" interfered with his duty to consider impartially whether the appellant's admission should be facilitated owing to humanitarian or compassionate considerations. I conclude that the notes of Officer Lorenz demonstrate a reasonable apprehension of bias.

Note that in para 27 of her reasons for decision in *Baker*, L'Heureux-Dubé J stated that one of the factors to be considered in determining what procedures are required in any particular instance are the procedures chosen by the agency itself. The model for fair administrative procedure is based on the key elements of procedure in the courts: the right to a hearing and the right to an impartial decision-maker. Nevertheless, as the *Baker* case itself illustrates, the model is sufficiently flexible that it can be applied in bureaucratic decision-making settings that bear little resemblance to a civil or criminal trial. One way of thinking about the role that agency choices of procedure play in determining the content of fair administrative procedure is to suggest that courts will, within limits, defer to these procedural choices. The extent to which courts extend deference to procedural choices made by agencies is clearly limited. Not only is the model of fair procedure based on the functioning of courts, but the courts themselves are the ultimate arbiters of fair procedure. Moreover, they make these decisions taking into account a variety of factors, only one of which is the procedural choice made by the agency itself. The idea of deference takes on greater prominence in the next area we will examine, which is judicial review of the substance of administrative decisions.

C. SUBSTANTIVE JUDICIAL REVIEW

Procedural review is about the manner in which decisions are reached (i.e., the process taken). Substantive review is about the substance of the decisions themselves (i.e., the merits of the outcome). The approach that courts should take to reviewing the substantive decisions taken by administrative decision-makers has been the subject of controversy for a considerable period. At various times the Supreme Court of Canada has attempted to provide a comprehensive framework for substantive judicial review, often making significant shifts in previously accepted jurisprudence in the course of doing so. In *Dunsmuir v New Brunswick*, 2008 SCC 9, the Court decided that all administrative decisions should be subject to review using one of two "standards of review." The stricter standard of review is called "correctness," and the more deferential standard of review is called "reasonableness." While the *Dunsmuir* decision was intended to simplify substantive judicial review, courts and commentators continued to be critical of the reliability of the framework as a way of determining which standard of review to employ in different situations and with the limited guidance it provided on how to apply the reasonableness standard properly. The Court attempted to deal with these criticisms in three recent decisions: *Canada (Minister of Citizenship and Immigration) v Vavilov*, 2019 SCC 65, and its companion cases *Bell Canada v Canada (AG)*, 2019 SCC 66, and *Canada Post Corporation v Canadian Union of Postal Workers*, 2019 SCC 67. Before we consider the approach the *Vavilov* decision takes to standards of review, however, it is worthwhile to think more broadly about the reasons for having different standards of review.

When we establish systems that enable parties that are unhappy with particular decisions to seek review of them, we have a natural tendency to differentiate the role of the review body from that of the original decision-maker. It is, of course, possible to establish a system of *de novo* review in which the reviewing body essentially duplicates the process employed by the original decision-maker. Generally, we are reluctant to do this because it seems inefficient and encourages people who are disappointed with a decision to seek review even if there is no reason to believe that the original decision was flawed. Within the judicial system, for example, appeal courts use different procedures from trial courts (they do not normally obtain evidence from oral testimony, for example; whereas it is common for trial courts to do so), and appellate judges use a different standard of review in assessing the findings of trial judges on questions of fact and mixed fact and law than they do in reviewing their decisions on questions of law. Trial judges are considered to be in a better position than appellate judges to make factual determinations and apply the law to the facts because they have first-hand know-ledge of the testimony before them, whereas the judges on appeal must rely on the paper record of the proceedings. This does not mean that the trial judge's findings on questions of fact and mixed fact and law are immune from appellate review, but appeal courts are more reluctant to interfere with the trial judge's conclusions on these types of issues than they are in reviewing the trial judge's decisions concerning questions of law. See *Housen v Nikolaisen*, 2002 SCC 33.

Recall that the facts of *Vavilov* and the decisions of the Federal Court and the Federal Court of Appeal are reproduced in Chapter 10. But beyond answering the specific legal dispute about the *Citizenship Act*, RSC 1985, c C-29 before it, the Supreme Court of Canada went further than the lower courts and sought to clarify and simplify the law governing substantive judicial review by addressing two fundamental questions:

1. How is a reviewing court to determine which of the two standards to review in any particular situation?
2. If the reasonableness standard is being applied, how is the court to approach the assessment of the decision before it?

We will consider each of these questions separately. As you read the passages from the major-ity and minority reasons addressing the choice of applicable standard of review, consider what each set of reasons tells us about the conceptual underpinnings of deference to administra-tive decision-making and the relationship between administrative decision-makers and courts reviewing their decisions.

1. Determining the Applicable Standard of Review

Canada (Minister of Citizenship and Immigration) v Vavilov
2019 SCC 65

WAGNER CJ and MOLDAVER, GASCON, CÔTÉ, BROWN, ROWE, and MARTIN JJ (Abella and Karakatsanis JJ concurring):

II. Determining the Applicable Standard of Review

[16] In the following sections, we set out a revised framework for determining the standard of review a court should apply when the merits of an administrative decision are challenged. It starts with a presumption that reasonableness is the applicable standard whenever a court reviews administrative decisions.

[17] The presumption of reasonableness review can be rebutted in two types of situations. The first is where the legislature has indicated that it intends a different standard or set of standards to apply. This will be the case where the legislature explicitly prescribes the applicable standard of review. It will also be the case where the legislature has provided a statutory appeal mechanism from an administrative decision to a court, thereby signalling the legislature's intent that appellate standards apply when a court reviews the decision. The second situation in which the presumption of reasonableness review will be rebutted is where the rule of law requires that the standard of correctness be applied. This will be the case for certain categories of questions, namely constitutional questions, general questions of law of central importance to the legal system as a whole and questions related to the jurisdictional boundaries between two or more administrative bodies. The general rule of reasonableness review, when coupled with these limited exceptions, offers a comprehensive approach to determining the applicable standard of review. As a result, it is no longer necessary for courts to engage in a "contextual inquiry" (*CHRC* [*Canada (Canadian Human Rights Commission) v Canada (AG)*, 2018 SCC 31, [2018] 2 SCR 230], at paras. 45-47, see also *Dunsmuir*, at paras. 62-64; *McLean* [*McLean v British Columbia (Securities Commission)*, 2013 SCC 67, [2013] 3 SCR 895], at para. 22) in order to identify the appropriate standard.

• • •

A. Presumption That Reasonableness Is the Applicable Standard

[23] Where a court reviews the merits of an administrative decision (i.e., judicial review of an administrative decisions other than a review related to a breach of natural justice and/or the duty of procedural fairness), the standard of review it applies must reflect the legislature's intent with respect to the role of the reviewing court, except where giving effect to that intent is precluded by the rule of law. The starting point for the analysis is a presumption that the legislature intended the standard of review to be reasonableness.

[24] Parliament and the provincial legislatures are constitutionally empowered to create administrative bodies and to endow them with broad statutory powers: *Dunsmuir*, at para. 27. Where a legislature has created an administrative decision maker for the specific purpose of administering a statutory scheme, it must be presumed that the legislature also intended that decision maker to be able to fulfill its mandate and interpret the law as applicable to all issues that come before it. Where a legislature has not explicitly prescribed that a court is to have a role in reviewing the decisions of that decision maker, it can safely be assumed that the legislature intended the administrative decision maker to function with a minimum of judicial interference. However, because judicial review is protected by s. 96 of the *Constitution Act, 1867*, legislatures cannot shield administrative decision making from curial scrutiny entirely: *Dunsmuir*, at para. 31; *Crevier v. Attorney General of Quebec*, [1981] 2 S.C.R. 220, at pp. 236-37; *U.E.S., Local 298 v. Bibeault*, [1988] 2 S.C.R. 1048, at p. 1090. Nevertheless, respect for these institutional design choices made by the legislature requires a reviewing court to adopt a posture of restraint on review.

• • •

B. Derogation from the Presumption of Reasonableness Review on the Basis of Legislative Intent

[33] This Court has described respect for legislative intent as the "polar star" of judicial review: *C.U.P.E. v. Ontario (Minister of Labour)*, 2003 SCC 29, [2003] 1 S.C.R. 539, at para. 149. This description remains apt. The presumption of

reasonableness review discussed above is intended to give effect to the legislature's choice to leave certain matters with administrative decision makers rather than the courts. It follows that this presumption will be rebutted where a legislature has indicated that a different standard should apply. The legislature can do so in two ways. First, it may explicitly prescribe through statute what standard courts should apply when reviewing decisions of a particular administrative decision maker. Second, it may direct that derogation from the presumption of reasonableness review is appropriate by providing for a statutory appeal mechanism from an administrative decision maker to a court, thereby signalling the application of appellate standards.

(1) Legislated Standards of Review

[34] Any framework rooted in legislative intent must, to the extent possible, respect clear statutory language that prescribes the applicable standard of review. This Court has consistently affirmed that legislated standards of review should be given effect: see, e.g., *R. v. Owen*, 2003 SCC 33, [2003] 1 S.C.R. 779, at paras. 31-32; *Khosa [Canada (Citizenship and Immigration) v. Khosa*, 2009 SCC 12, [2009] 1 SCR 339], at paras. 18-19; *British Columbia (Workers' Compensation Board) v. Figliola*, 2011 SCC 52, [2011] 3 S.C.R. 422, at para. 20; *Moore v. British Columbia (Education)*, 2012 SCC 61, [2012] 3 S.C.R. 360, at para. 55; *McCormick v. Fasken Martineau DuMoulin LLP*, 2014 SCC 39, [2014] 2 S.C.R. 108, at para. 16; *British Columbia (Workers' Compensation Appeal Tribunal) v. Fraser Health Authority*, 2016 SCC 25, [2016] 1 S.C.R. 587, at paras. 8 and 29; *British Columbia Human Rights Tribunal v. Schrenk*, 2017 SCC 62, [2017] 2 S.C.R. 795, at para. 28.

[35] It follows that where a legislature has indicated that courts are to apply the standard of correctness in reviewing certain questions, that standard must be applied. In British Columbia, the legislature has established the applicable standard of review for many tribunals by reference to the *Administrative Tribunals Act*, S.B.C. 2004, c. 45: see ss. 58 and 59. For example, it has provided that the standard of review applicable to decisions on questions of statutory interpretation by the B.C. Human Rights Tribunal is to be correctness: *ibid.*, s. 59(1); *Human Rights Code*, R.S.B.C. 1996, c. 210, s. 32. We continue to be of the view that where the legislature has indicated the applicable standard of review, courts are bound to respect that designation, within the limits imposed by the rule of law.

(2) Statutory Appeal Mechanisms

[36] We have reaffirmed that, to the extent possible, the standard of review analysis requires courts to give effect to the legislature's institutional design choices to delegate authority through statute. In our view, this principled position also requires courts to give effect to the legislature's intent, signalled by the presence of a statutory appeal mechanism from an administrative decision to a court, that the court is to perform an appellate function with respect to that decision. Just as a legislature may, within constitutional limits, insulate administrative decisions from judicial interference, it may also choose to establish a regime "which does not exclude the courts but rather makes them part of the enforcement machinery": *Seneca College of Applied Arts and Technology v. Bhadauria*, [1981] 2 S.C.R. 181, at p. 195. Where a legislature has provided that parties may appeal from an administrative decision to a court, either as of right or with leave, it has subjected the administrative regime to appellate oversight and indicated that it expects the court to scrutinize such administrative decisions on an appellate basis. This expressed intention necessarily rebuts the blanket presumption of reasonableness review, which is premised on giving

effect to a legislature's decision to leave certain issues with a body other than a court. This intention should be given effect. As noted by the intervener Attorney General of Quebec in its factum, [TRANSLATION] "[t]he requirement of deference must not sterilize such an appeal mechanism to the point that it changes the nature of the decision-making process the legislature intended to put in place": para. 2.

[37] It should therefore be recognized that, where the legislature has provided for an appeal from an administrative decision to a court, a court hearing such an appeal is to apply appellate standards of review to the decision. This means that the applicable standard is to be determined with reference to the nature of the question and to this Court's jurisprudence on appellate standards of review. Where, for example, a court is hearing an appeal from an administrative decision, it would, in considering questions of law, including questions of statutory interpretation and those concerning the scope of a decision maker's authority, apply the standard of correctness in accordance with *Housen v. Nikolaisen*, 2002 SCC 33, [2002] 2 S.C.R. 235, at para. 8. Where the scope of the statutory appeal includes questions of fact, the appellate standard of review for those questions is palpable and overriding error (as it is for questions of mixed fact and law where the legal principle is not readily extricable): see *Housen*, at paras. 10, 19 and 26-37. Of course, should a legislature intend that a different standard of review apply in a statutory appeal, it is always free to make that intention known by prescribing the applicable standard through statute.

[38] We acknowledge that giving effect to statutory appeal mechanisms in this way departs from the Court's recent jurisprudence. However, after careful consideration, we are of the view that this shift is necessary in order to bring coherence and conceptual balance to the standard of review analysis and is justified by a weighing of the values of certainty and correctness: *Craig* [*Canada v Craig*, 2012 SCC 43, [2012] 2 SCR 489], at para. 27. Our conclusion is based on the following considerations.

[39] First, there has been significant judicial and academic criticism of this Court's recent approach to statutory appeal rights: see, e.g., Y.-M. Morissette, "What is a 'reasonable decision'?" (2018), 31 *C.J.A.L.P.* 225, at p. 244; the Hon. J.T. Robertson, *Administrative Deference: The Canadian Doctrine that Continues to Disappoint* (April 18, 2018) (online), at p. 8; the Hon. D. Stratas, "The Canadian Law of Judicial Review: A Plea for Doctrinal Coherence and Consistency" (2016), 42 *Queen's L.J.* 27, at p. 33; Daly, at pp. 541-42; *Québec (Procureure générale) v. Montréal (Ville)*, 2016 QCCA 2108, 17 Admin. L.R. (6th) 328, at paras. 36-46; *Bell Canada v. 7265921 Canada Ltd.*, 2018 FCA 174, 428 D.L.R. (4th) 311, at paras. 190-92, per Nadon J.A., concurring, and at 66 and 69-72, per Rennie J.A., dissenting; *Garneau Community League v. Edmonton (City)*, 2017 ABCA 374, 60 Alta. L.R. (6th) 1, at paras. 91 and 93-95, per Slatter J.A., concurring; *Nova Scotia (Attorney General) v. S&D Smith Central Supplies Limited*, 2019 NSCA 22, at paras. 250, 255-64 and 274-302, per Beveridge J.A., dissenting; *Atlantic Mining NS Corp. (D.D.V. Gold Limited) v. Oakley*, 2019 NSCA 14, at paras. 9-14. These critiques seize on the inconsistency inherent in a standard of review framework based on legislative intent that otherwise declines to give meaning to an express statutory right of appeal. This criticism observes that legislative choice is not one-dimensional; rather, it pulls in two directions. While a legislative choice to delegate to an administrative decision maker grounds a presumption of reasonableness on the one hand, a legislative choice to enact a statutory right of appeal signals an intention to ascribe an appellate role to reviewing courts on the other hand.

• • •

[41] Second, there is no satisfactory justification for the recent trend in this Court's jurisprudence to give no effect to statutory rights of appeal in the standard of

review analysis absent exceptional wording: see *Tervita Corp. v. Canada (Commissioner of Competition)*, 2015 SCC 3, [2015] 1 S.C.R. 161, at paras. 35-39. Indeed, this approach is itself a departure from earlier jurisprudence: the Hon. J. T. Robertson, "Judicial Deference to Administrative Tribunals: A Guide to 60 Years of Supreme Court Jurisprudence" (2014), 66 *S.C.L.R.* (2d) 1, at pp. 91-93. Under the former "pragmatic and functional" approach to determining the applicable standard of review, the existence of a privative clause or a statutory right of appeal was one of four contextual factors that a court would consider in order to determine the standard that the legislature intended to apply to a particular decision. Although a statutory appeal clause was not determinative, it was understood to be a key factor indicating that the legislature intended that a less deferential standard of review be applied: see, e.g., *Pezim* [*Pezim v British Columbia (Superintendent of Brokers)*, [1994] 2 SCR 557] at pp. 589-92; *British Columbia Telephone Co. v. Shaw Cable Systems (B.C.) Ltd.*, [1995] 2 S.C.R. 739, at paras. 28-31; *Southam* [*Canada (Director of Investigation and Research) v Southam Inc.*, [1997] 1 SCR 748] at paras. 30-32, 46 and 54-55; *Pushpanathan*, at paras. 30-31; *Dr. Q*, at para. 27; *Mattel*, at paras. 26-27; *Law Society of New Brunswick v. Ryan*, 2003 SCC 20, [2003] 1 S.C.R. 247, at paras. 21 and 27-29; *Barrie Public Utilities v. Canadian Cable Television Assn.*, 2003 SCC 28, [2003] 1 S.C.R. 476, at para. 11; *Monsanto Canada Inc. v. Ontario (Superintendent of Financial Services)*, 2004 SCC 54, [2004] 3 S.C.R. 152, at para. 7.

[42] The Court did indeed sometimes find that, even in a statutory appeal, a deferential standard of review was warranted for the legal findings of a decision maker that lay at the heart of the decision maker's expertise: see, e.g., *Pezim*. In other instances, however, the Court concluded that the existence of a statutory appeal mechanism and the fact that the decision maker did not have greater expertise than a court on the issue being considered indicated that correctness was the appropriate standard, including on matters involving the interpretation of the administrative decision maker's home statute: see, e.g., *Mattel*, at paras. 26-33; *Barrie Public Utilities*, at paras. 9-19; *Monsanto*, at paras. 6-16.

[43] Yet as, in *Dunsmuir*, *Alberta Teachers* [*Alberta (Information and Privacy Commissioner) v Alberta Teachers' Association*, 2011 SCC 61, [2011] 3 SCR 654], *Edmonton East* [*Edmonton (City) v Edmonton East (Capilano) Shopping Centres Ltd.*, 2016 SCC 47, [2016] 2 SCR 293] and subsequent cases, the standard of review analysis was simplified and shifted from a contextual analysis to an approach more focused on categories, statutory appeal mechanisms ceased to play a role in the analysis. Although this simplification of the standard of review analysis may have been a laudable change, it did not justify ceasing to give *any* effect to statutory appeal mechanisms. *Dunsmuir* itself provides little guidance on the rationale for this change. The majority in *Dunsmuir* was silent on the role of a statutory right of appeal in determining the standard of review, and did not refer to the prior treatment of statutory rights of appeal under the pragmatic and functional approach.

[44] More generally, there is no convincing reason to presume that legislatures mean something entirely different when they use the word "appeal" in an administrative law statute than they do in, for example, a criminal or commercial law context. Accepting that the word "appeal" refers to the same type of procedure in all these contexts also accords with the presumption of consistent expression, according to which the legislature is presumed to use language such that the same words have the same meaning both within a statute and across statutes: R. Sullivan, *Sullivan on the Construction of Statutes* (6th ed. 2014), at p. 217. Accepting that the legislature intends an appellate standard of review to be applied when it uses the word "appeal" also helps to explain why many statutes provide for *both* appeal and judicial review mechanisms in different contexts, thereby indicating two roles for

reviewing courts: see, e.g., *Federal Courts Act*, R.S.C. 1985, c. F-7, ss. 27 and 28. This offers further support for giving effect to statutory rights of appeal. Our colleagues' suggestion that our position in this regard "hinges" on what they call a "textualist argument" (at para. 246) is inaccurate.

[45] That there is no principled rationale for ignoring statutory appeal mechanisms becomes obvious when the broader context of those mechanisms is considered. The existence of a limited right of appeal, such as a right of appeal on questions of law or a right of appeal with leave of a court, does not preclude a court from considering other aspects of a decision in a judicial review proceeding. However, if the same standards of review applied regardless of whether a question was covered by the appeal provision, and regardless of whether an individual subject to an administrative decision was granted leave to appeal or applied for judicial review, the appeal provision would be completely redundant—contrary to the well-established principle that the legislature does not speak in vain: *Attorney General of Quebec v. Carrières Ste-Thérèse Ltée*, [1985] 1 S.C.R. 831, at p. 838.

[46] Finally, and most crucially, the appeals now before the Court have allowed for a comprehensive and considered examination of the standard of review analysis with the goal of remedying the conceptual and practical difficulties that have made this area of the law challenging for litigants and courts alike. To achieve this goal, the revised framework must, for at least two reasons, give effect to statutory appeal mechanisms. The first reason is conceptual. In the past, this Court has looked past an appeal clause primarily when the decision maker possessed greater relative expertise—what it called the "specialization of duties" principle in *Pezim*, at p. 591. But, as discussed above, the presumption of reasonableness review is no longer premised upon notions of relative expertise. Instead, it is now based on respect for the legislature's institutional design choice, according to which the authority to make a decision is vested in an administrative decision maker rather than in a court. It would be inconsistent with this conceptual basis for the presumption of reasonableness review to disregard clear indications that the legislature has intentionally chosen a more involved role for the courts. Just as recognizing a presumption of reasonableness review on all questions respects a legislature's choice to leave some matters first and foremost to an administrative decision maker, departing from that blanket presumption in the context of a statutory appeal respects the legislature's choice of a more involved role for the courts in supervising administrative decision making.

• • •

C. The Applicable Standard Is Correctness Where Required by the Rule of Law

[53] In our view, respect for the rule of law requires courts to apply the standard of correctness for certain types of legal questions: constitutional questions, general questions of law of central importance to the legal system as a whole and questions regarding the jurisdictional boundaries between two or more administrative bodies. The application of the correctness standard for such questions respects the unique role of the judiciary in interpreting the Constitution and ensures that courts are able to provide the last word on questions for which the rule of law requires consistency and for which a final and determinate answer is necessary: *Dunsmuir*, at para. 58.

[54] When applying the correctness standard, the reviewing court may choose either to uphold the administrative decision maker's determination or to substitute its own view: *Dunsmuir*, at para. 50. While it should take the administrative decision

maker's reasoning into account—and indeed, it may find that reasoning persuasive and adopt it—the reviewing court is ultimately empowered to come to its own conclusions on the question.

(1) Constitutional Questions

[55] Questions regarding the division of powers between Parliament and the provinces, the relationship between the legislature and the other branches of the state, the scope of Aboriginal and treaty rights under s. 35 of the *Constitution Act, 1982*, and other constitutional matters require a final and determinate answer from the courts. Therefore, the standard of correctness must continue to be applied in reviewing such questions: *Dunsmuir*, para. 58; *Westcoast Energy Inc. v. Canada (National Energy Board)*, [1998] 1 S.C.R. 322.

[56] The Constitution—both written and unwritten—dictates the limits of all state action. Legislatures and administrative decision makers are bound by the Constitution and must comply with it. A legislature cannot alter the scope of its own constitutional powers through statute. Nor can it alter the constitutional limits of executive power by delegating authority to an administrative body. In other words, although a legislature may choose what powers it delegates to an administrative body, it cannot delegate powers that it does not constitutionally have. The constitutional authority to act must have determinate, defined and consistent limits, which necessitates the application of the correctness standard.

· · ·

(2) General Questions of Law of Central Importance to the Legal System as a Whole

[58] In *Dunsmuir*, a majority of the Court held that, in addition to constitutional questions, general questions of law which are "both of central importance to the legal system as a whole and outside the adjudicator's specialized area of expertise" will require the application of the correctness standard: para. 60, citing *Toronto (City) v. C.U.P.E., Local 79*, 2003 SCC 63, [2003] 3 S.C.R. 77, at para. 62, per LeBel J., concurring. We remain of the view that the rule of law requires courts to have the final word with regard to general questions of law that are "of central importance to the legal system as a whole." However, a return to first principles reveals that it is not necessary to evaluate the decision maker's specialized expertise in order to determine whether the correctness standard must be applied in cases involving such questions. ... [T]he consideration of expertise is folded into the new starting point adopted in these reasons, namely the presumption of reasonableness review.

[59] As the majority of the Court recognized in *Dunsmuir*, the key underlying rationale for this category of questions is the reality that certain general questions of law "require uniform and consistent answers" as a result of "their impact on the administration of justice as a whole": *Dunsmuir*, para. 60. In these cases, correctness review is necessary to resolve general questions of law that are of "fundamental importance and broad applicability," with significant legal consequences for the justice system as a whole or for other institutions of government: see *Toronto (City)*, at para. 70; *Alberta (Information and Privacy Commissioner) v. University of Calgary*, 2016 SCC 53, [2016] 2 S.C.R. 555, at para. 20; *Canadian National Railway* [*Canadian National Railway Co v Canada (AG)*, 2014 SCC 40, [2014] 2 SCR 135], at para. 60; *Chagnon v. Syndicat de la fonction publique et parapublique du Québec*,

2018 SCC 39, [2018] 2 S.C.R. 687, at para. 17; *Saguenay [Mouvement laïque québécois v Saguenay (City)*, 2015 SCC 16, [2015] 2 SCR 3], at para. 51; *Canada (Canadian Human Rights Commission) v. Canada (Attorney General)*, 2011 SCC 53, [2011] 3 S.C.R. 471 ("*Mowat*"), at para. 22; *Commission scolaire de Laval v. Syndicat de l'enseignement de la région de Laval*, 2016 SCC 8, [2016] 1 S.C.R. 29, at para. 38. For example, the question in *University of Calgary* could not be resolved by applying the reasonableness standard, because the decision would have had legal implications for a wide variety of other statutes and because the uniform protection of solicitor-client privilege—at issue in that case—is necessary for the proper functioning of the justice system: *University of Calgary*, at paras. 19-26. As this shows, the resolution of general questions of law "of central importance to the legal system as a whole" has implications beyond the decision at hand, hence the need for "uniform and consistent answers."

[60] This Court's jurisprudence continues to provide important guidance regarding what constitutes a general question of law of central importance to the legal system as a whole. For example, the following general questions of law have been held to be of central importance to the legal system as a whole: when an administrative proceeding will be barred by the doctrines of *res judicata* and abuse of process (*Toronto (City)*, at para. 15); the scope of the state's duty of religious neutrality (*Saguenay*, at para. 49); the appropriateness of limits on solicitor-client privilege (*University of Calgary*, at para. 20); and the scope of parliamentary privilege (*Chagnon*, at para. 17). We caution, however, that this jurisprudence must be read carefully, given that expertise is no longer a consideration in identifying such questions: see, e.g., *CHRC*, at para. 43.

. . .

(3) Questions Regarding the Jurisdictional Boundaries Between Two or More Administrative Bodies

[63] Finally, the rule of law requires that the correctness standard be applied in order to resolve questions regarding the jurisdictional boundaries between two or more administrative bodies: *Dunsmuir*, para. 61. One such question arose in *Regina Police Assn. Inc. v. Regina (City) Board of Police Commissioners*, 2000 SCC 14, [2000] 1 S.C.R. 360, in which the issue was the jurisdiction of a labour arbitrator to consider matters of police discipline and dismissal that were otherwise subject to a comprehensive legislative regime. Similarly, in *Quebec (Commission des droits de la personne et des droits de la jeunesse) v. Quebec (Attorney General)*, 2004 SCC 39, [2004] 2 S.C.R. 185, the Court considered a jurisdictional dispute between a labour arbitrator and the Quebec Human Rights Tribunal.

[64] Administrative decisions are rarely contested on this basis. Where they are, however, the rule of law requires courts to intervene where one administrative body has interpreted the scope of its authority in a manner that is incompatible with the jurisdiction of another. The rationale for this category of questions is simple: the rule of law cannot tolerate conflicting orders and proceedings where they result in a true operational conflict between two administrative bodies, pulling a party in two different and incompatible directions: see *British Columbia Telephone Co.*, at para. 80, per McLachlin J. (as she then was), concurring. Members of the public must know where to turn in order to resolve a dispute. As with general questions of law of central importance to the legal system as a whole, the application of the correctness standard in these cases safeguards predictability, finality and certainty in the law of administrative decision making.

. . .

E. Other Circumstances Requiring a Derogation from the Presumption of Reasonableness Review

[69] In these reasons, we have identified five situations in which a derogation from the presumption of reasonableness review is warranted either on the basis of legislative intent (i.e., legislated standards of review and statutory appeal mechanisms) or because correctness review is required by the rule of law (i.e., constitutional questions, general questions of law of central importance to the legal system as a whole, and questions regarding jurisdictional boundaries between administrative bodies). This framework is the product of careful consideration undertaken following extensive submissions and based on a thorough review of the relevant jurisprudence. We are of the view, at this time, that these reasons address all of the situations in which a reviewing court should derogate from the presumption of reasonableness review. As previously indicated, courts should no longer engage in a contextual inquiry to determine the standard of review or to rebut the presumption of reasonableness review. Letting go of this contextual approach will, we hope, "get the parties away from arguing about the tests and back to arguing about the substantive merits of their case": *Alberta Teachers*, at para. 36, quoting *Dunsmuir*, at para. 145, per Binnie J., concurring.

[70] However, we would not definitively foreclose the possibility that another category could be recognized as requiring a derogation from the presumption of reasonableness review in a future case. But our reluctance to pronounce that the list of exceptions to the application of a reasonableness standard is closed should not be understood as inviting the routine establishment of new categories requiring correctness review. Rather, it is a recognition that it would be unrealistic to declare that we have contemplated every possible set of circumstances in which legislative intent or the rule of law will require a derogation from the presumption of reasonableness review. That being said, the recognition of any new basis for correctness review would be exceptional and would need to be consistent with the framework and the overarching principles set out in these reasons. In other words, any new category warranting a derogation from the presumption of reasonableness review on the basis of legislative intent would require a signal of legislative intent as strong and compelling as those identified in these reasons (i.e., a legislated standard of review or a statutory appeal mechanism). Similarly, the recognition of a new category of questions requiring correctness review that is based on the rule of law would be justified only where failure to apply correctness review would undermine the rule of law and jeopardize the proper functioning of the justice system in a manner analogous to the three situations described in these reasons.

· · ·

ABELLA and KARAKATSANIS, JJ

[230] The majority's framework rests on a flawed and incomplete conceptual account of judicial review, one that unjustifiably ignores the specialized expertise of administrative decision-makers. Although the majority uses language endorsing a "presumption of reasonableness review," this presumption now rests on a totally new understanding of legislative intent and the rule of law. By prohibiting any consideration of well-established foundations for deference, such as "expertise ... institutional experience ... proximity and responsiveness to stakeholders ... prompt[ness], flexib[ility], and efficien[cy]; and ... access to justice," the majority reads out the foundations of the modern understanding of legislative intent in administrative law.

[231] In particular, such an approach ignores the possibility that specialization and other advantages are embedded into the legislative choice to delegate particular

subject matters to administrative decision-makers. Giving proper effect to the legislature's choice to "delegate authority" to an administrative decision-maker requires understanding the *advantages* that the decision-maker may enjoy in exercising its mandate (*Dunsmuir*, at para. 49). As Iacobucci J. observed in *Southam*:

> Presumably if Parliament entrusts a certain matter to a tribunal and not (initially at least) to the courts, *it is because the tribunal enjoys some advantage that judges do not.* For that reason alone, review of the decision of a tribunal should often be on a standard more deferential than correctness. [Emphasis added; para. 55.]

[232] Chief among those advantages are the institutional expertise and specialization inherent to administering a particular mandate on a daily basis. Those appointed to administrative tribunals are often chosen precisely because their backgrounds and experience align with their mandate (Van Harten et al. [G Van Harten et al., *Administrative Law: Cases, Text, and Materials*, 7th ed (Toronto: Emond, 2015)], at p. 15; Régimbald [G Régimbald, *Canadian Administrative Law*, 2nd ed (Toronto: LexisNexis, 2015)], at p. 463). Some administrative schemes explicitly require a degree of expertise from new members as a condition of appointment (*Edmonton East*, at para. 33; *Dr. Q v. College of Physicians and Surgeons of British Columbia*, 2003 SCC 19, [2003] 1 S.C.R. 226, at para. 29; Régimbald, at p. 462). As institutions, administrative bodies also benefit from specialization as they develop "habitual familiarity with the legislative scheme they administer" (*Edmonton East*, at para. 33) and "grappl[e] with issues on a repeated basis" (*Parry Sound (District) Social Services Administration Board v. O.P.S.E.U., Local 324*, 2003 SCC 42, [2003] 2 S.C.R. 157, at para. 53). Specialization and expertise are further enhanced by continuing education and through meetings of the membership of an administrative body to discuss policies and best practices (Finn Makela, "Acquired Expertise of Administrative Tribunals and the Standard of Judicial Review: The Case of Grievance Arbitrators and Human Rights Law" (2013), 17 *C.L.E.L.J.* 345, at p. 349). In addition, the blended membership of some tribunals fosters special institutional competence in resolving "polycentric" disputes (*Pushpanathan*, at para. 36; *Dr. Q* at paras. 29-30; *Pezim*, at pp. 591-92 and 596).

[233] All this equips administrative decision-makers to tackle questions of law arising from their mandates. In interpreting their enabling statutes, for example, administrative actors may have a particularly astute appreciation for the on-the-ground consequences of particular legal interpretations; of statutory context; of the purposes that a provision or legislative scheme are meant to serve; and of specialized terminology used in their administrative setting. Coupled with this Court's acknowledgment that legislative provisions often admit of multiple reasonable interpretations, the advantages stemming from specialization and expertise provide a robust foundation for deference to administrative decision-makers on legal questions within their mandate (*C.U.P.E.*, at p. 236; *McLean*, at para. 37). As Professor H.W. Arthurs said:

> There is no reason to believe that a judge who reads a particular regulatory statute once in his life, perhaps in worst-case circumstances, can read it with greater fidelity to legislative purpose than an administrator who is sworn to uphold that purpose, who strives to do so daily, and is well-aware of the effect upon the purpose of the various alternate interpretations. There is no reason to believe that a legally-trained judge is better qualified to determine the existence or sufficiency or appropriateness of evidence on a given point than a trained economist or engineer, an arbitrator selected by the parties, or simply an experienced tribunal member who decides such cases day in and day out. There is no reason to believe that a judge whose entire professional life has been spent dealing with disputes one by

one should possess an aptitude for issues which arise often because an administrative system dealing with cases in volume has been designed to strike an appropriate balance between efficiency and effective rights of participation.
("Protection against Judicial Review" (1983), 43 *R. du B.* 277, at p. 289)

• • •

[236] Although the majority's approach extolls respect for the legislature's "institutional design choices," it accords no weight to the institutional advantages of
specialization and expertise that administrative decision-makers possess in resolving questions of law. In so doing, the majority disregards the historically accepted
reason *why* the legislature intended to delegate authority to an administrative actor.

[237] Nor are we persuaded by the majority's claim that "if administrative decision makers are understood to possess specialized expertise on all questions that
come before them, the concept of expertise ceases to assist a reviewing court in
attempting to distinguish questions for which applying the reasonableness standard is appropriate from those for which it is not." Here, the majority sets up a false
choice: expertise must either be assessed on a case-by-case basis or play no role at
all in a theory of judicial review.

[238] We disagree. While not every decision-maker necessarily has expertise on
every issue raised in an administrative proceeding, reviewing courts do not engage
in an individualized, case-by-case assessment of specialization and expertise. The
theory of deference is based not only on the legislative choice to delegate decisions,
but also on institutional expertise and on "the reality that ... those working day to day
in the implementation of frequently complex administrative schemes have or will
develop a considerable degree of expertise or field sensitivity to the imperatives and
nuances of the legislative regime" (*Khosa*, at para. 25; see also *Nor-Man Regional
Health Authority Inc. v. Manitoba Association of Health Care Professionals*, 2011
SCC 59, [2011] 3 S.C.R. 616, at para. 53; *Edmonton East*, at para. 33).

[239] The exclusion of expertise, specialization and other institutional advantages from the majority's standard of review framework is not merely a theoretical
concern. The removal of the current "conceptual basis" for deference opens the
gates to expanded correctness review. The majority's "presumption" of deference
will yield all too easily to justifications for a correctness-oriented framework.

[240] In the majority's framework, deference gives way whenever the "rule
of law" demands it. The majority's approach to the rule of law, however, flows
from a court-centric conception of the rule of law rooted in Dicey's 19th century
philosophy.

[241] The rule of law is not the rule of courts. A pluralist conception of the rule
of law recognizes that courts are not the exclusive guardians of law, and that others in the justice arena have shared responsibility for its development, including
administrative decision-makers. *Dunsmuir* embraced this more inclusive view of
the rule of law by acknowledging that the "court-centric conception of the rule of
law" had to be "reined in by acknowledging that the courts do not have a monopoly on deciding all questions of law" (para. 30). As discussed in *Dunsmuir*, the rule
of law is understood as meaning that administrative decision-makers make legal
determinations within their mandate, and not that only judges decide questions
of law with an unrestricted license to substitute their opinions for those of administrative actors through correctness review (see McLachlin, *Administrative Tribunals and the Courts: An Evolutionary Relationship*; The Hon. Thomas A. Cromwell,
"What I Think I've Learned About Administrative Law" (2017), 30 *C.J.A.L.P.* 307, at
p. 308; *Wilson v. Atomic Energy of Canada Ltd.*, 2016 SCC 29, [2016] 1 S.C.R. 770,
at para. 31, per Abella J.).

[242] Moreover, central to any definition of the rule of law is access to a fair and efficient dispute resolution process, capable of dispensing timely justice (*Hryniak v. Mauldin*, 2014 SCC 7, [2014] 1 S.C.R. 87, at para. 1). This is an important objective for all litigants, from the sophisticated consumers of administrative justice, to, most significantly, the particularly vulnerable ones (Angus Grant and Lorne Sossin, "Fairness in Context: Achieving Fairness Through Access to Administrative Justice," in Colleen M. Flood and Lorne Sossin, eds., *Administrative Law in Context* (3rd ed. 2018), 341, at p. 342). For this reason, access to justice is at the heart of the legislative choice to establish a robust system of administrative law (Grant and Sossin, at pp. 342 and 369-70; Van Harten, et al., at p. 17; Régimbald, at pp. 2-3; McLachlin, *Administrative Tribunals and the Courts: An Evolutionary Relationship*). As Morissette J.A. has observed:

> ... the aims of administrative law ... generally gravitate towards promoting access to justice. The means contemplated are costless or inexpensive, simple and expeditious procedures, expertise of the decision-makers, coherence of reasons, consistency of results and finality of decisions.
> (Yves-Marie Morissette, "What is a 'reasonable decision'?" (2018), 31 *C.J.A.L.P.* 225, at p. 236)

[243] These goals are compromised when a narrow conception of the "rule of law" is invoked to impose judicial hegemony over administrative decision-makers. Doing so perverts the purpose of establishing a parallel system of administrative justice, and adds unnecessary expense and complexity for the public.

[244] The majority even calls for a reformulation of the "questions of central importance" category from *Dunsmuir* and permits courts to substitute their opinions for administrative decision-makers on "questions of central importance to the legal system as a whole," even if those questions fall squarely within the mandate and expertise of the administrative decision-maker. As noted in *Canadian Human Rights Commission*, correctness review was permitted only for questions "of central importance to the legal system *and* outside the specialized expertise of the adjudicator" (para. 28 (emphasis in original)). Broadening this category from its original characterization unduly expands the issues available for judicial substitution. Issues of discrimination, labour rights, and economic regulation of the securities markets (among many others) theoretically raise questions of vital importance for Canada and its legal system. But by ignoring administrative decision-makers' expertise on these matters, this category will inevitably provide more "room ... for both mistakes and manipulation" (Andrew Green, "Can There Be Too Much Context in Administrative Law? Setting the Standard of Review in Canadian Administrative Law" (2014), 47 *U.B.C. L. Rev.* 443, at p. 483). We would leave *Dunsmuir*'s description of this category undisturbed.

[245] We also disagree with the majority's reformulation of "legislative intent" to include, for the first time, an invitation for courts to apply correctness review to legal questions whenever an administrative scheme includes a right of appeal. We do not see how appeal rights represent a "different institutional structure" that requires a more searching form of review. The mere fact that a statute contemplates a reviewing role for a court says nothing about the *degree of deference* required in the review process. Rights of appeal reflect different choices by different legislatures to permit review for different reasons, on issues of fact, law, mixed fact and law, and discretion, among others. Providing parties with a right of appeal can serve several purposes entirely unrelated to the standard of review, including outlining: where the appeal will take place (sometimes, at a different reviewing court than in

the routes provided for judicial review); who is eligible to take part; when materials must be filed; how materials must be presented; the reviewing court's powers on appeal; any leave requirements; and the grounds on which the parties may appeal (among other things). By providing this type of structure and guidance, statutory appeal provisions may allow legislatures to promote efficiency and access to justice, in a way that exclusive reliance on the judicial review procedure would not have.

[246] In reality, the majority's position on statutory appeal rights, although couched in language about "giv[ing] effect to the legislature's institutional design choices," hinges almost entirely on a textualist argument: the presence of the word "appeal" indicates a legislative intent that courts apply the same standards of review found in civil appellate jurisprudence.

[247] The majority's reliance on the "presumption of consistent expression" in relation to the single word "appeal" is misplaced and disregards long-accepted institutional distinctions between how courts and administrative decision-makers function. The language in each setting is different; the mandates are different; the policy bases are different. The idea that *Housen v. Nikolaisen*, 2002 SCC 33, [2002] 2 S.C.R. 235, must be inflexibly applied to every right of "appeal" within a statute—with no regard for the broader purposes of the statutory scheme or the practical implications of greater judicial involvement within it—is entirely unsupported by our jurisprudence.

[248] In addition, the majority's claim that legislatures "d[o] not speak in vain" is irreconcilable with its treatment of privative clauses, which play no role in its standard of review framework. If, as the majority claims, Parliament's decision to provide appeal routes must influence the standard of review analysis, there is no principled reason why Parliament's decision via privative clauses to *prohibit* appeals should not be given comparable effect.

[249] In any event, legislatures in this country have known for at least 25 years since *Pezim* that this Court has not treated statutory rights of appeal as a determinative reflection of legislative intent regarding the standard of review (*Pezim*, at p. 590). Against this reality, the continued use by legislatures of the term "appeal" cannot be imbued with the intent that the majority retroactively ascribes to it; doing so is inconsistent with the principle that legislatures are presumed to enact legislation in compliance with existing common law rules (Ruth Sullivan, *Statutory Interpretation* (3rd ed. 2016), at p. 315).

• • •

[251] The result reached by the majority means that hundreds of administrative decision-makers subject to different kinds of statutory rights of appeal—some in highly specialized fields, such as broadcasting, securities regulation and international trade—will now be subject to an irrebuttable presumption of correctness review. This has the potential to cause a stampede of litigation. Reviewing courts will have license to freely revisit legal questions on matters squarely within the expertise of administrative decision-makers, even if they are of no broader consequence outside of their administrative regimes. Even if specialized decision-makers provide reasonable interpretations of highly technical statutes with which they work daily, even if they provide internally consistent interpretations responsive to the parties' submissions and consistent with the text, context and purpose of the governing scheme, the administrative body's past practices and decisions, the common law, prior judicial rulings and international law, those interpretations can still be set aside by a reviewing court that simply takes a different view of the relevant statute. This risks undermining the integrity of administrative proceedings whenever there is a statutory right of appeal, rendering them little more than

rehearsals for a judicial appeal—the inverse of the legislative intent to establish a specialized regime and entrust certain legal and policy questions to non-judicial actors.

[252] Ironically, the majority's approach will be a roadblock to its promise of simplicity. Elevating appeal clauses to indicators of correctness review creates a two-tier system of administrative law: one tier that defers to the expertise of administrative decision-makers where there is no appeal clause; and another tier where such clauses permit judges to substitute their own views of the legal issues at the core of those decision-makers' mandates. Within the second tier, the application of appellate law principles will inevitably create confusion by encouraging segmentation in judicial review (*Mouvement laïque*, at para. 173, per Abella J., concurring in part; see also Paul Daly, "Struggling Towards Coherence in Canadian Administrative Law? Recent Cases on Standard of Review and Reasonableness" (2016), 62 *McGill L.J.* 527, at pp. 542-43; The Hon. Joseph T. Robertson, "Identifying the Review Standard: Administrative Deference in a Nutshell" (2017), 68 *U.N.B.L.J.* 145, at p. 162). Courts will be left with the task of identifying palpable and overriding errors for factual questions, extricating legal issues from questions of mixed fact and law, reviewing questions of law *de novo*, and potentially having to apply judicial review and appellate standards interchangeably if an applicant challenges in one proceeding multiple aspects of an administrative decision, some falling within an appeal clause and others not. It is an invitation to complexity and a barrier to access to justice.

[253] The majority's reasons "roll back the *Dunsmuir* clock to an era where some courts asserted a level of skill and knowledge in administrative matters which further experience showed they did not possess" (*Khosa*, at para. 26). The reasons elevate statutory rights of appeal to a determinative factor based on a formalistic approach that ignores the legislature's intention to leave certain legal and policy questions to specialized administrative decision-makers. This unravelling of Canada's carefully developed, deferential approach to administrative law returns us to the "black letter law" approach found in *Anisminic* and cases like *Metropolitan Life* whereby specialized decision-makers were subject to the pre-eminent determinations of a judge. Rather than building on *Dunsmuir*, which recognized that specialization is fundamentally intertwined with the legislative choice to delegate particular subject matters to administrative decision-makers, the majority's reasons banish expertise from the standard of review analysis entirely, opening the door to a host of new correctness categories which remain open to further expansion. The majority's approach not only erodes the presumption of deference; it erodes confidence in the existence—and desirability—of the "shared enterprises in the administrative state" of "[l]aw-making and legal interpretation" between courts and administrative decision-makers (Stack [KM Stack, "Overcoming Dicey in Administrative Law" (2018), 68 *UTLJ* 293], at p. 310).

2. Applying the Reasonableness Standard

The second area in which the Court sought to provide guidance in *Vavilov* was with respect to the approach courts should employ in *applying* the reasonableness standard of review. Recall that the *Vavilov* case involved a decision of the Canadian Registrar of Citizenship to cancel the certificate of citizenship of Alexander Vavilov. Vavilov was born in Canada, and would normally enjoy a presumption of Canadian citizenship, but it was revealed some time after his birth that, while they were living in Canada, his parents had been Russian spies. The Registrar's decision turned on her interpretation of section 3(2)(a) of the *Citizenship*

Act. The Federal Court of Appeal quashed this decision, and the Minister of Citizenship and Immigration appealed to the Supreme Court of Canada. In Chapter 10, we reviewed the alternative approaches to the interpretation of this provision. The Supreme Court of Canada concluded that the Registrar's decision should be reviewed using the reasonableness standard. The material below sets out the Court's direction on how reasonableness review should be conducted, and summarizes its reasons for concluding that the Registrar's decision was unreasonable.

Canada (Minister of Citizenship and Immigration) v Vavilov
2019 SCC 65

WAGNER CJ and MOLDAVER, GASCON, CÔTÉ, BROWN, ROWE, and MARTIN JJ (Abella and Karakatsanis JJ concurring):

III. Performing Reasonableness Review

[73] This Court's administrative law jurisprudence has historically focused on the analytical framework used to determine the applicable standard of review, while providing relatively little guidance on how to conduct reasonableness review in practice.

[74] In this section of our reasons, we endeavour to provide that guidance. The approach we set out is one that focuses on justification, offers methodological consistency and reinforces the principle "that reasoned decision-making is the lynchpin of institutional legitimacy": *amici curiae* factum, at para. 12.

• • •

E. A Reasonable Decision Is One That Is Both Based on an Internally Coherent Reasoning and Justified in Light of the Legal and Factual Constraints That Bear on the Decision

[99] A reviewing court must develop an understanding of the decision maker's reasoning process in order to determine whether the decision as a whole is reasonable. To make this determination, the reviewing court asks whether the decision bears the hallmarks of reasonableness—justification, transparency and intelligibility—and whether it is justified in relation to the relevant factual and legal constraints that bear on the decision: *Dunsmuir*, at paras. 47 and 74; *Catalyst* [*Catalyst Paper Corp v North Cowichan (District)*, 2012 SCC 2, [2012] 1 SCR 5], at para. 13.]

[100] The burden is on the party challenging the decision to show that it is unreasonable. Before a decision can be set aside on this basis, the reviewing court must be satisfied that there are sufficiently serious shortcomings in the decision such that it cannot be said to exhibit the requisite degree of justification, intelligibility and transparency. Any alleged flaws or shortcomings must be more than merely superficial or peripheral to the merits of the decision. It would be improper for a reviewing court to overturn an administrative decision simply because its reasoning exhibits a minor misstep. Instead, the court must be satisfied that any shortcomings or flaws relied on by the party challenging the decision are sufficiently central or significant to render the decision unreasonable.

[101] What makes a decision unreasonable? We find it conceptually useful here to consider two types of fundamental flaws. The first is a failure of rationality internal to the reasoning process. The second arises when a decision is in some respect untenable in light of the relevant factual and legal constraints that bear on it. There is however, no need for reviewing courts to categorize failures of reasonableness as belonging to one type or the other. Rather, we use these descriptions simply as a convenient way to discuss the types of issues that may show a decision to be unreasonable.

(1) A Reasonable Decision Is Based on an Internally Coherent Reasoning

[102] To be reasonable, a decision must be based on reasoning that is both rational and logical. It follows that a failure in this respect may lead a reviewing court to conclude that a decision must be set aside. Reasonableness review is not a "line-by-line treasure hunt for error": *Irving Pulp & Paper* [*Communications, Energy and Paperworkers Union of Canada, Local 30 v Irving Pulp & Paper, Ltd*, 2013 SCC 34, [2013] 2 SCR 458], at para. 54, citing *Newfoundland Nurses* [*Newfoundland and Labrador Nurses' Union v Newfoundland and Labrador (Treasury Board)*, 2011 SCC 62, [2011] 3 SCR 708], at para. 14. However, the reviewing court must be able to trace the decision maker's reasoning without encountering any fatal flaws in its overarching logic, and it must be satisfied that "there is [a] line of analysis within the given reasons that could reasonably lead the tribunal from the evidence before it to the conclusion at which it arrived": *Ryan*, at para. 55; *Southam*, at para. 56. Reasons that "simply repeat statutory language, summarize arguments made, and then state a peremptory conclusion" will rarely assist a reviewing court in understanding the rationale underlying a decision and "are no substitute for statements of fact, analysis, inference and judgment": R. A. Macdonald and D. Lametti, "Reasons for Decision in Administrative Law" (1990), 3 *C.J.A.L.P.* 123, at p. 139; see also *Gonzalez v. Canada (Minister of Citizenship and Immigration)*, 2014 FC 750, 27 Imm. L.R. (4th) 151, at paras. 57-59.

[103] While ... formal reasons should be read in light of the record and with due sensitivity to the administrative regime in which they were given, a decision will be unreasonable if the reasons for it, read holistically, fail to reveal a rational chain of analysis or if they reveal that the decision was based on an irrational chain of analysis: see *Wright v. Nova Scotia (Human Rights Commission)*, 2017 NSSC 11, 23 Admin. L.R. (6th) 110; *Southam*, at para. 56. A decision will also be unreasonable where the conclusion reached cannot follow from the analysis undertaken (see *Sangmo v. Canada (Citizenship and Immigration)*, 2016 FC 17, at para. 21) or if the reasons read in conjunction with the record do not make it possible to understand the decision maker's reasoning on a critical point (see *Blas v. Canada (Citizenship and Immigration)*, 2014 FC 629, 26 Imm. L.R. (4th) 92, at paras. 54-66; *Reid v. Criminal Injuries Compensation Board*, 2015 ONSC 6578; *Lloyd v. Canada (Attorney General)*, 2016 FCA 115, 2016 D.T.C. 5051; *Taman v. Canada (Attorney General)*, 2017 FCA 1, [2017] 3 F.C.R. 520, at para. 47).

[104] Similarly, the internal rationality of a decision may be called into question if the reasons exhibit clear logical fallacies, such as circular reasoning, false dilemmas, unfounded generalizations or an absurd premise. This is not an invitation to hold administrative decision makers to the formalistic constraints and standards of academic logicians. However, a reviewing court must ultimately be satisfied that the decision maker's reasoning "adds up."

(2) A Reasonable Decision Is Justified in Light of the Legal and Factual Constraints That Bear on the Decision

[105] In addition to the need for internally coherent reasoning, a decision, to be reasonable, must be justified in relation to the constellation of law and facts that are relevant to the decision: *Dunsmuir*, at para. 47; *Catalyst*, at para. 13; *Nor-Man Regional Health Authority*, at para. 6. Elements of the legal and factual contexts of a decision operate as constraints on the decision maker in the exercise of its delegated powers.

[106] It is unnecessary to catalogue all of the legal or factual considerations that could constrain an administrative decision maker in a particular case. However, in the sections that follow, we discuss a number of elements that will generally be relevant in evaluating whether a given decision is reasonable, namely the governing statutory scheme; other relevant statutory or common law; the principles of statutory interpretation; the evidence before the decision maker and facts of which the decision maker may take notice; the submissions of the parties; the past practices and decisions of the administrative body; and the potential impact of the decision on the individual to whom it applies. These elements are not a checklist for conducting reasonableness review, and they may vary in significance depending on the context. They are offered merely to highlight some elements of the surrounding context that can cause a reviewing court to lose confidence in the outcome reached.

[107] A reviewing court may find that a decision is unreasonable when examined against these contextual considerations. These elements necessarily interact with one another: for example, a reasonable penalty for professional misconduct in a given case must be justified *both* with respect to the types of penalties prescribed by the relevant legislation and with respect to the nature of the underlying misconduct.

(a) Governing Statutory Scheme

[108] Because administrative decision makers receive their powers by statute, the governing statutory scheme is likely to be the most salient aspect of the legal context relevant to a particular decision. That administrative decision makers play a role, along with courts, in elaborating the precise content of the administrative schemes they administer should not be taken to mean that administrative decision makers are permitted to disregard or rewrite the law as enacted by Parliament and the provincial legislatures. Thus, for example, while an administrative body may have considerable discretion in making a particular decision, that decision must ultimately comply "with the rationale and purview of the statutory scheme under which it is adopted": *Catalyst*, at paras. 15 and 25-28; see also *Green [Green v Law Society of Manitoba*, 2017 SCC 20, [2017] 1 SCR 360], at para. 44. As Rand J. noted in *Roncarelli v. Duplessis*, [1959] S.C.R. 121, at p. 140, "there is no such thing as absolute and untrammelled 'discretion,'" and any exercise of discretion must accord with the purposes for which it was given: see also *Congrégation des témoins de Jéhovah de St-Jérôme-Lafontaine [Congrégation des témoins de Jéhovah de St-Jérôme-Lafontaine v Lafontaine (Village)*, 2004 SCC 48, [2004] 2 SCR 650], at para. 7; *Montréal (City) v. Montreal Port Authority*, 2010 SCC 14, [2010] 1 S.C.R. 427, at paras. 32-33; *Nor-Man Regional Health Authority*, at para. 6. Likewise, a decision must comport with any more specific constraints imposed by the governing legislative scheme, such as the statutory definitions, principles or formulas that prescribe the exercise of a discretion: see *Montréal (City)*, at paras. 33 and 40-41; *Canada (Attorney General) v. Almon Equipment Limited*, 2010 FCA 193, [2011] 4 F.C.R. 203, at paras. 38-40. The statutory scheme also informs the acceptable approaches to decision

making: for example, where a decision maker is given wide discretion, it would be unreasonable for it to fetter that discretion: see *Delta Air Lines* [*Delta Air Lines Inc v Lukács*, 2018 SCC 2, [2018] 1 SCR 6], at para. 18].

[109] As stated above, a proper application of the reasonableness standard is capable of allaying the concern that an administrative decision maker might interpret the scope of its own authority beyond what the legislature intended. As a result, there is no need to maintain a category of "truly" jurisdictional questions that are subject to correctness review. Although a decision maker's interpretation of its statutory grant of authority is generally entitled to deference, the decision maker must nonetheless properly justify that interpretation. Reasonableness review does not allow administrative decision makers to arrogate powers to themselves that they were never intended to have, and an administrative body cannot exercise authority which was not delegated to it. Contrary to our colleagues' concern (at para. 285), this does not reintroduce the concept of "jurisdictional error" into judicial review, but merely identifies one of the obvious and necessary constraints imposed on administrative decision makers.

[110] Whether an interpretation is justified will depend on the context, including the language chosen by the legislature in describing the limits and contours of the decision maker's authority. If a legislature wishes to precisely circumscribe an administrative decision maker's power in some respect, it can do so by using precise and narrow language and delineating the power in detail, thereby tightly constraining the decision maker's ability to interpret the provision. Conversely, where the legislature chooses to use broad, open-ended or highly qualitative language— for example, "in the public interest"—it clearly contemplates that the decision maker is to have greater flexibility in interpreting the meaning of such language. Other language will fall in the middle of this spectrum. All of this is to say that certain questions relating to the scope of a decision maker's authority may support more than one interpretation, while other questions may support only one, depending upon the text by which the statutory grant of authority is made. What matters is whether, in the eyes of the reviewing court, the decision maker has properly justified its interpretation of the statute in light of the surrounding context. It will, of course, be impossible for an administrative decision maker to justify a decision that strays beyond the limits set by the statutory language it is interpreting.

(b) Other Statutory or Common Law

[111] It is evident that both statutory and common law will impose constraints on how and what an administrative decision maker can lawfully decide: see *Dunsmuir*, at paras. 47 and 74. For example, an administrative decision maker interpreting the scope of its regulation-making authority in order to exercise that authority cannot adopt an interpretation that is inconsistent with applicable common law principles regarding the nature of statutory powers: see *Katz Group Canada Inc. v. Ontario (Health and Long-Term Care)*, 2013 SCC 64, [2013] 3 S.C.R. 810, at paras. 45-48. Neither can a body instructed by legislation to determine what tax rate is applicable in accordance with an existing tax system ignore that system and base its determination on a "fictitious" system it has arbitrarily created: *Montréal (City)*, at para. 40. Where a relationship is governed by private law, it would be unreasonable for a decision maker to ignore that law in adjudicating parties' rights within that relationship: *Dunsmuir*, at para. 74. Similarly, where the governing statute specifies a standard that is well known in law and in the jurisprudence, a reasonable decision will generally be one that is consistent with the established understanding of that standard: see, e.g., the discussion of "reasonable grounds to suspect" in *Canada*

(Minister of Transport, Infrastructure and Communities) v. Farwaha, 2014 FCA 56, [2015] 2 F.C.R. 1006, at paras. 93-98.

[112] Any precedents on the issue before the administrative decision maker or on a similar issue will act as a constraint on what the decision maker can reasonably decide. An administrative body's decision may be unreasonable on the basis that the body failed to explain or justify a departure from a binding precedent in which the same provision had been interpreted. Where, for example, there is a relevant case in which a court considered a statutory provision, it would be unreasonable for an administrative decision maker to interpret or apply the provision without regard to that precedent. The decision maker would have to be able to explain why a different interpretation is preferable by, for example, explaining why the court's interpretation does not work in the administrative context: M. Biddulph, "Rethinking the Ramification of Reasonableness Review: *Stare Decisis* and Reasonableness Review on Questions of Law" (2018), 56 *Alta. L.R.* 119, at p. 146. There may be circumstances in which it is quite simply unreasonable for an administrative decision maker to fail to apply or interpret a statutory provision in accordance with a binding precedent. For instance, where an immigration tribunal is required to determine whether an applicant's act would constitute a criminal offence under Canadian law (see, e.g., *Immigration and Refugee Protection Act*, S.C. 2001, c. 27, ss. 35-37), it would clearly not be reasonable for the tribunal to adopt an interpretation of a criminal law provision that is inconsistent with how Canadian criminal courts have interpreted it.

[113] That being said, administrative decision makers will not necessarily be required to apply equitable and common law principles in the same manner as courts in order for their decisions to be reasonable. For example, it may be reasonable for a decision maker to adapt a common law or equitable doctrine to its administrative context: see *Nor-Man Regional Health Authority*, at paras. 5-6, 44-45, 52, 54 and 60. Conversely, a decision maker that rigidly applies a common law doctrine without adapting it to the relevant administrative context may be acting unreasonably: see *Delta Air Lines*, at paras. 16-17 and 30. In short, whether an administrative decision maker has acted reasonably in adapting a legal or equitable doctrine involves a highly context-specific determination.

[114] We would also note that in some administrative decision making contexts, international law will operate as an important constraint on an administrative decision maker. It is well established that legislation is presumed to operate in conformity with Canada's international obligations, and the legislature is "presumed to comply with ... the values and principles of customary and conventional international law": *R. v. Hape*, 2007 SCC 26, [2007] 2 S.C.R. 292, at para. 53; *R. v. Appulonappa*, 2015 SCC 59, [2015] 3 S.C.R. 754, at para. 40. Since *Baker*, it has also been clear that international treaties and conventions, even where they have not been implemented domestically by statute, can help to inform whether a decision was a reasonable exercise of administrative power: *Baker*, at paras. 69-71.

(c) Principles of Statutory Interpretation

[115] Matters of statutory interpretation are not treated uniquely and, as with other questions of law, may be evaluated on a reasonableness standard. Although the general approach to reasonableness review described above applies in such cases, we recognize that it is necessary to provide additional guidance to reviewing courts on this point. This is because reviewing courts are accustomed to resolving questions of statutory interpretation in a context in which the issue is before them at first instance or on appeal, and where they are expected to perform their own independent analysis and come to their own conclusions.

[116] Reasonableness review functions differently. Where reasonableness is the applicable standard on a question of statutory interpretation, the reviewing court does not undertake a *de novo* analysis of the question or "ask itself what the correct decision would have been": *Ryan*, at para. 50. Instead, just as it does when applying the reasonableness standard in reviewing questions of fact, discretion or policy, the court must examine the administrative decision as a whole, including the reasons provided by the decision maker and the outcome that was reached.

[117] A court interpreting a statutory provision does so by applying the "modern principle" of statutory interpretation, that is, that the words of a statute must be read "in their entire context and in their grammatical and ordinary sense harmoniously with the scheme of the Act, the object of the Act, and the intention of Parliament": *Rizzo & Rizzo Shoes Ltd. (Re)*, [1998] 1 S.C.R. 27, at para. 21, and *Bell ExpressVu Limited Partnership v. Rex*, 2002 SCC 42, [2002] 2 S.C.R. 559, at para. 26, both quoting E. Driedger, *Construction of Statutes* (2nd ed. 1983), at p. 87. Parliament and the provincial legislatures have also provided guidance by way of statutory rules that explicitly govern the interpretation of statutes and regulations: see, e.g., *Interpretation Act*, R.S.C. 1985, c. I-21.

[118] This Court has adopted the "modern principle" as the proper approach to statutory interpretation, because legislative intent can be understood only by reading the language chosen by the legislature in light of the purpose of the provision and the entire relevant context: Sullivan, at pp. 7-8. Those who draft and enact statutes expect that questions about their meaning will be resolved by an analysis that has regard to the text, context and purpose, regardless of whether the entity tasked with interpreting the law is a court or an administrative decision maker. An approach to reasonableness review that respects legislative intent must therefore assume that those who interpret the law—whether courts or administrative decision makers—will do so in a manner consistent with this principle of interpretation.

[119] Administrative decision makers are not required to engage in a formalistic statutory interpretation exercise in every case. As discussed above, formal reasons for a decision will not always be necessary and may, where required, take different forms. And even where the interpretive exercise conducted by the administrative decision maker is set out in written reasons, it may look quite different from that of a court. The specialized expertise and experience of administrative decision makers may sometimes lead them to rely, in interpreting a provision, on considerations that a court would not have thought to employ but that actually enrich and elevate the interpretive exercise.

[120] But whatever form the interpretive exercise takes, the merits of an administrative decision maker's interpretation of a statutory provision must be consistent with the text, context and purpose of the provision. In this sense, the usual principles of statutory interpretation apply equally when an administrative decision maker interprets a provision. Where, for example, the words used are "precise and unequivocal," their ordinary meaning will usually play a more significant role in the interpretive exercise: *Canada Trustco Mortgage Co. v. Canada*, 2005 SCC 54, [2005] 2 S.C.R. 601, at para. 10. Where the meaning of a statutory provision is disputed in administrative proceedings, the decision maker must demonstrate in its reasons that it was alive to these essential elements.

[121] The administrative decision maker's task is to interpret the contested provision in a manner consistent with the text, context and purpose, applying its particular insight into the statutory scheme at issue. It cannot adopt an interpretation it knows to be inferior—albeit plausible—merely because the interpretation in question appears to be available and is expedient. The decision maker's responsibility is to discern meaning and legislative intent, not to "reverse-engineer" a desired outcome.

[122] It can happen that an administrative decision maker, in interpreting a statutory provision, fails entirely to consider a pertinent aspect of its text, context or purpose. Where such an omission is a minor aspect of the interpretive context, it is not likely to undermine the decision as a whole. It is well established that decision makers are not required "to explicitly address all possible shades of meaning" of a given provision: *Construction Labour Relations v. Driver Iron Inc.*, 2012 SCC 65, [2012] 3 S.C.R. 405, at para. 3. Just like judges, administrative decision makers may find it unnecessary to dwell on each and every signal of statutory intent in their reasons. In many cases, it may be necessary to touch upon only the most salient aspects of the text, context or purpose. If, however, it is clear that the administrative decision maker may well, had it considered a key element of a statutory provision's text, context or purpose, have arrived at a different result, its failure to consider that element would be indefensible, and unreasonable in the circumstances. Like other aspects of reasonableness review, omissions are not stand-alone grounds for judicial intervention: the key question is whether the omitted aspect of the analysis causes the reviewing court to lose confidence in the outcome reached by the decision maker.

[123] There may be other cases in which the administrative decision maker has not explicitly considered the meaning of a relevant provision in its reasons, but the reviewing court is able to discern the interpretation adopted by the decision maker from the record and determine whether that interpretation is reasonable.

[124] Finally, even though the task of a court conducting a reasonableness review is *not* to perform a *de novo* analysis or to determine the "correct" interpretation of a disputed provision, it may sometimes become clear in the course of reviewing a decision that the interplay of text, context and purpose leaves room for a single reasonable interpretation of the statutory provision, or aspect of the statutory provision, that is at issue: *Dunsmuir*, at paras. 72-76. One case in which this conclusion was reached was *Nova Tube Inc./Nova Steel Inc. v. Conares Metal Supply Ltd.*, 2019 FCA 52., in which Laskin J.A., after analyzing the reasoning of the administrative decision maker (at paras. 26-61), held that the decision maker's interpretation had been unreasonable, and, furthermore, that the factors he had considered in his analysis weighed so overwhelmingly in favour of the opposite interpretation that that was the only reasonable interpretation of the provision: para. 61. As discussed below, it would serve no useful purpose in such a case to remit the interpretative question to the original decision maker. Even so, a court should generally pause before definitively pronouncing upon the interpretation of a provision entrusted to an administrative decision maker.

(d) Evidence Before the Decision Maker

[125] It is trite law that the decision maker may assess and evaluate the evidence before it and that, absent exceptional circumstances, a reviewing court will not interfere with its factual findings. The reviewing court must refrain from "reweighing and reassessing the evidence considered by the decision maker": *CHRC*, at para. 55; see also *Khosa*, at para. 64; *Dr. Q*, at paras. 41-42. Indeed, many of the same reasons that support an appellate court's deferring to a lower court's factual findings, including the need for judicial efficiency, the importance of preserving certainty and public confidence, and the relatively advantageous position of the first instance decision maker, apply equally in the context of judicial review: see *Housen*, at paras. 15-18; *Dr. Q*, at para. 38; *Dunsmuir*, at para. 53.

[126] That being said, a reasonable decision is one that is justified in light of the facts: *Dunsmuir*, para. 47. The decision maker must take the evidentiary record and the general factual matrix that bears on its decision into account, and its decision

must be reasonable in light of them: see *Southam*, at para. 56. The reasonableness of a decision may be jeopardized where the decision maker has fundamentally misapprehended or failed to account for the evidence before it. In *Baker*, for example, the decision maker had relied on irrelevant stereotypes and failed to consider relevant evidence, which led to a conclusion that there was a reasonable apprehension of bias: para. 48. Moreover, the decision maker's approach would *also* have supported a finding that the decision was unreasonable on the basis that the decision maker showed that his conclusions were not based on the evidence that was actually before him: para. 48.

(e) Submissions of the Parties

[127] The principles of justification and transparency require that an administrative decision maker's reasons meaningfully account for the central issues and concerns raised by the parties. The principle that the individual or individuals affected by a decision should have the opportunity to present their case fully and fairly underlies the duty of procedural fairness and is rooted in the right to be heard: *Baker*, at para. 28. The concept of responsive reasons is inherently bound up with this principle, because reasons are the primary mechanism by which decision makers demonstrate that they have actually *listened* to the parties.

[128] Reviewing courts cannot expect administrative decision makers to "respond to every argument or line of possible analysis" (*Newfoundland Nurses*, at para. 25), or to "make an explicit finding on each constituent element, however subordinate, leading to its final conclusion" (para 16). To impose such expectations would have a paralyzing effect on the proper functioning of administrative bodies and would needlessly compromise important values such as efficiency and access to justice. However, a decision maker's failure to meaningfully grapple with key issues or central arguments raised by the parties may call into question whether the decision maker was actually alert and sensitive to the matter before it. In addition to assuring parties that their concerns have been heard, the process of drafting reasons with care and attention can alert the decision maker to inadvertent gaps and other flaws in its reasoning: *Baker*, at para. 39.

(f) Past Practices and Past Decisions

[129] Administrative decision makers are not bound by their previous decisions in the same sense that courts are bound by *stare decisis*. As this Court noted in *Domtar* [*Domtar Inc v Quebec (Commission d'appel en matière de lésions professionnelles)*, [1993] 2 SCR 756], "a lack of unanimity is the price to pay for the decision-making freedom and independence" given to administrative decision makers, and the mere fact that some conflict exists among an administrative body's decisions does not threaten the rule of law: p. 800. Nevertheless, administrative decision makers and reviewing courts alike must be concerned with the general consistency of administrative decisions. Those affected by administrative decisions are entitled to expect that like cases will generally be treated alike and that outcomes will not depend merely on the identity of the individual decision maker—expectations that do not evaporate simply because the parties are not before a judge.

[130] Fortunately, administrative bodies generally have a range of resources at their disposal to address these types of concerns. Access to past reasons and summaries of past reasons enables multiple individual decision makers within a single organization (such as administrative tribunal members) to learn from each other's work, and contributes to a harmonized decision-making culture. Institutions also

routinely rely on standards, policy directives and internal legal opinions to encourage greater uniformity and guide the work of frontline decision makers. This Court has also held that plenary meetings of a tribunal's members can be an effective tool to "foster coherence" and "avoid ... conflicting results": *IWA v. Consolidated-Bathurst Packaging Ltd.*, [1990] 1 S.C.R. 282, at pp. 324-28. Where disagreement arises within an administrative body about how to appropriately resolve a given issue, that institution may also develop strategies to address that divergence internally and on its own initiative. Of course, consistency can also be encouraged through less formal methods, such as the development of training materials, checklists and templates for the purpose of streamlining and strengthening institutional best practices, provided that these methods do not operate to fetter decision making.

[131] Whether a particular decision is consistent with the administrative body's past decisions is also a constraint that the reviewing court should consider when determining whether an administrative decision is reasonable. Where a decision maker *does* depart from longstanding practices or established internal authority, it bears the justificatory burden of explaining that departure in its reasons. If the decision maker does not satisfy this burden, the decision will be unreasonable. In this sense, the legitimate expectations of the parties help to determine both whether reasons are required and what those reasons must explain: *Baker*, at para. 26. We repeat that this does not mean administrative decision makers are bound by internal precedent in the same manner as courts. Rather, it means that a decision that departs from longstanding practices or established internal decisions will be reasonable if that departure is justified, thereby reducing the risk of arbitrariness, which would undermine public confidence in administrative decision makers and in the justice system as a whole.

[132] ... [I]t has been argued that correctness review would be required where there is "persistent discord" on questions on law in an administrative body's decisions. While we are not of the view that such a correctness category is required, we would note that reviewing courts have a role to play in managing the risk of persistently discordant or contradictory legal interpretations within an administrative body's decisions. When evidence of internal disagreement on legal issues has been put before a reviewing court, the court may find it appropriate to telegraph the existence of an issue in its reasons and encourage the use of internal administrative structures to resolve the disagreement. And if internal disagreement continues, it may become increasingly difficult for the administrative body to justify decisions that serve only to preserve the discord.

(g) Impact of the Decision on the Affected Individual

[133] It is well established that individuals are entitled to greater procedural protection when the decision in question involves the potential for significant personal impact or harm: *Baker*, at para. 25. However, this principle also has implications for how a court conducts reasonableness review. Central to the necessity of adequate justification is the perspective of the individual or party over whom authority is being exercised. Where the impact of a decision on an individual's rights and interests is severe, the reasons provided to that individual must reflect the stakes. The principle of responsive justification means that if a decision has particularly harsh consequences for the affected individual, the decision maker must explain why its decision best reflects the legislature's intention. This includes decisions with consequences that threaten an individual's life, liberty, dignity or livelihood.

[134] Moreover, concerns regarding arbitrariness will generally be more acute in cases where the consequences of the decision for the affected party are particularly

severe or harsh, and a failure to grapple with such consequences may well be unreasonable. For example, this Court has held that the Immigration Appeal Division should, when exercising its equitable jurisdiction to stay a removal order under the *Immigration and Refugee Protection Act*, consider the potential foreign hardship a deported person would face: *Chieu v. Canada (Minister of Citizenship and Immigration)*, 2002 SCC 3, [2002] 1 S.C.R. 84.

[135] Many administrative decision makers are entrusted with an extraordinary degree of power over the lives of ordinary people, including the most vulnerable among us. The corollary to that power is a heightened responsibility on the part of administrative decision makers to ensure that their reasons demonstrate that they have considered the consequences of a decision and that those consequences are justified in light of the facts and law.

• • •

(2) Review for Reasonableness

[171] The principal issue before this Court is whether it was reasonable for the Registrar to find that Mr. Vavilov's parents had been "other representative[s] or employee[s] in Canada of a foreign government" within the meaning of s. 3(2)(a) of the *Citizenship Act*.

[172] In our view, it was not. The Registrar failed to justify her interpretation of s. 3(2)(a) of the *Citizenship Act* in light of the constraints imposed by the text of s. 3 of the *Citizenship Act* considered as a whole, by other legislation and international treaties that inform the purpose of s. 3, by the jurisprudence on the interpretation of s. 3(2)(a), and by the potential consequences of her interpretation. Each of these elements—viewed individually and cumulatively—strongly supports the conclusion that s. 3(2)(a) was not intended to apply to children of foreign government representatives or employees who have not been granted diplomatic privileges and immunities. Though Mr. Vavilov raised many of these considerations in his submissions in response to the procedural fairness letter (A.R., vol. IV, at pp. 448-52), the Registrar failed to address those submissions in her reasons and did not, to justify her interpretation of s. 3(2)(a), do more than conduct a cursory review of the legislative history and conclude that her interpretation was not explicitly precluded by the text of s. 3(2)(a).

[173] Our review of the Registrar's decision leads us to conclude that it was unreasonable for her to find that the phrase "diplomatic or consular officer or other representative or employee in Canada of a foreign government" applies to individuals who have not been granted diplomatic privileges and immunities in Canada. It is undisputed that Mr. Vavilov's parents had not been granted such privileges and immunities. No purpose would therefore be served by remitting this matter to the Registrar.

• • •

D. Conclusion

[194] Multiple legal and factual constraints may bear on a given administrative decision, and these constraints may interact with one another. In some cases, a failure to justify the decision against any one relevant constraint may be sufficient to cause the reviewing court to lose confidence in the reasonableness of the decision. Section 3 of the *Citizenship Act* considered as a whole, other legislation and international treaties that inform the purpose of s. 3, the jurisprudence cited in the analyst's report, and the potential consequences of the Registrar's decision point

overwhelmingly to the conclusion that Parliament did not intend s. 3(2)(a) to apply to children of individuals who have not been granted diplomatic privileges and immunities. The Registrar's failure to justify her decision with respect to these constraints renders her interpretation unreasonable, and we would therefore uphold the Federal Court of Appeal's decision to quash the Registrar's decision.

[195] As noted above, we would exercise our discretion not to remit the matter to the Registrar for redetermination. Crucial to our decision is the fact that Mr. Vavilov explicitly raised all of these issues before the Registrar and that the Registrar had an opportunity to consider them but failed to do so. She offered no justification for the interpretation she adopted except for a superficial reading of the provision in question and a comment on part of its legislative history. On the other hand, there is overwhelming support—including in the parliamentary debate, established principles of international law, an established line of jurisprudence and the text of the provision itself—for the conclusion that Parliament did not intend s. 3(2)(a) of the *Citizenship Act* to apply to children of individuals who have not been granted diplomatic privileges and immunities. That being said, we would stress that it is not our intention to offer a definitive interpretation of s. 3(2)(a) in all respects, nor to foreclose the possibility that multiple reasonable interpretations of other aspects might be available to administrative decision makers. In short, we do not suggest that there is necessarily "one reasonable interpretation" of the provision as a whole. But we agree with the majority of the Court of Appeal that it was *not* reasonable for the Registrar to interpret s. 3(2)(a) as applying to children of individuals who have not been granted diplomatic privileges and immunities at the time of the children's birth.